NUCLEAR HEURISTICS:
SELECTED WRITINGS OF
ALBERT AND ROBERTA WOHLSTETTER

Robert Zarate

Henry Sokolski

Editors

January 2009

*****

Published by Books Express Publishing
Books Express, 2011
ISBN 978-1-780395-17-3

Books Express publications are available from all good retail and online booksellers. For
publishing proposals and direct ordering please contact us at: info@books-express.com

CONTENTS

PREFACE

Three years ago, I received a phone call and then a visit at my home from a University of Chicago graduate student eager to learn about Albert and Roberta Wohlstetter. Robert Zarate interviewed me for nearly 2 hours. It was clear from the questions that he asked me that his interest in the Wohlstetters' work was more than casual.

After Robert's initial visit, he called me again several times to clarify and pursue additional questions. I recommended other experts who had worked with or studied under the Wohlstetters for him to interview. Harry Rowen, my former Defense Department boss, was one. Andrew Marshall, at the Pentagon's Office of Net Assessment, was another. Both had worked closely with Albert and Roberta at RAND. Later, Harry and I contacted Joan Wohlstetter, Albert and Roberta's daughter, and persuaded her to make her parents' private papers at the Hoover Institution's archives available to Robert. These papers are now open to the public, and some of them are included in this edited volume. Robert's visits to Washington multiplied as he interviewed more of Albert's former protégés, as well as his critics.

In 2006, I asked Robert if he would be willing to help out at my nonprofit research organization, the Nonproliferation Policy Education Center (NPEC). He immediately agreed and assumed responsibility for completing research that had already been begun by Paul Lettow on the meaning of "nuclear energy for peaceful purposes" in the Nuclear Nonproliferation Treaty. Although Robert was planning to write a comprehensive biography of Albert Wohlstetter, I encouraged him instead to publish short pieces on the Wohlstetters. His success here led to the next suggestion: an edited volume of Albert and Roberta's key writings relating to nuclear proliferation and national security affairs, with commentaries by the Wohlstetters' colleagues and students. I worked with him to develop a grant proposal.

The result is this volume, which is designed not as a eulogy or a *Festschrift*, but as a testament to the continuing relevance of the work of Albert and Roberta Wohlstetter in the fields of nuclear and security policy analysis. Albert and Roberta wrote hundreds of articles and studies on U.S. policy on the Balkans, as well as the Persian Gulf; strategic command and control; intelligence and warning; NATO nuclear planning; U.S.-Russian arms control; strategic and theater missile defenses; the economics and military dangers of civilian nuclear energy; nuclear safeguards and nuclear nonproliferation; and military nuclear strategy and methods of policy analysis and design. Their contributions to and influence in these areas of policy were considerable. As a result, it simply is not possible to include in a single volume all of the studies and writings that one would need in order to cover the full extent of their work.

Still, publishing selections of their most important writings is worthwhile. Increased concern about the spread of nuclear weapons in the Far and Middle East, the controversy surrounding civilian nuclear cooperation with India, the global revival of nuclear power and debate over its economics and security implications, the controversies surrounding how the Nuclear Nonproliferation Treaty's obligations and rights are being cynically read by Iran and other states—all of these issues have prompted Washington pundits and national security analysts to cite the Wohlstetters' work. The same can also be said of the security concerns recently raised by Islamic fundamentalism, the continued instability of the Balkans, the questions surrounding NATO's future and America's alliances in the Far East, the relevance of nuclear deterrence after the Cold War, and the emergence of ballistic missile defense as a key ingredient in strategic forces and alliance relations.

This volume can hardly cover all the insights that the Wohlstetters' work might shed on these topics. Instead, it is designed to make some of the most significant of Albert and Roberta's writings—many of which were previously unpublished—much more accessible. Using this volume's references and its companion website, *Albert Wohlstetter Dot Com* (*www.albertwohlstetter.com*), readers will be able to view some of the most interesting of the Wohlstetters' archived analyses. Finally, Robert Zarate's introductory essay and the subsequent commentaries, which have been written by some of Albert and Roberta's closest colleagues and students, should help to introduce the Wohlstetters' works not only to current policymakers and security planners, but to students who may later assume these roles.

HENRY SOKOLSKI
Executive Director
NPEC

ACKNOWLEDGMENTS

The Nonproliferation Policy Education Center (NPEC) began work on this, the 11th of its Strategic Studies Institute (SSI) edited volumes, early in 2007, when the Hoover Institution's Archives at Stanford, California, made portions of the Albert and Roberta Wohlstetter Papers first available. Many of this volume's key themes were influenced by 3 years of research and interviews on the Wohlstetters that James Johnson and Robert Zarate had conducted beginning in 2003.

Among those to whom thanks are due, Joan Wohlstetter—who made access to the Wohlstetter Papers possible and gave freely of her time, recollections and opinions—is clearly first and foremost. Also, heartfelt thanks are owed to Harry Rowen, Alain Enthoven, Richard Perle, Steve Lukasik and Andy Marshall, who contributed commentaries to this edited volume; to the many colleagues, students and critics of the Wohlstetters who offered comments and constructive criticism on the edited volume; to NPEC's Tamara Mitchell and NPEC alumnus Ali Naqvi, who provided invaluable day-to-day administrative assistance; and to Ms. Linda Bernard and the staff of the Hoover Institution's Archives, who care for the Wohlstetter Papers.

Finally, without the help of the staff at SSI, especially the hard work of Ms. Marianne Cowling and Ms. Rita Rummel, and Ms. Kathleen Gildersleeve, of the Army War College Library, this book would not have been possible.

ROBERT ZARATE
Research Fellow
NPEC

HENRY SOKOLSKI
Executive Director
NPEC

INTRODUCTION

ALBERT AND ROBERTA WOHLSTETTER ON NUCLEAR-AGE STRATEGY

Robert Zarate

Given the quality of what has been recently written about Albert James Wohlstetter (1913-1997) and Roberta Mary Morgan Wohlstetter (1912-2007), it would appear that these late strategists have exerted immeasurably more influence on the history of the nuclear age than on historians. Nonetheless, Albert and Roberta — for the sake of brevity, this essay shall sometimes refer to the Wohlstetters by their first names — emerged as two of America's most consequential, innovative, and controversial thinkers of strategy during the latter half of the last century.

They were controversial, in no small part, because their subjects of inquiry — questions of strategy, foreign and defense policy, and morality in the nuclear age — often lent themselves to deep disagreement. However, by engaging these questions, their research aimed above all at rejecting fatalism, at refuting "the belief that the holocaust will be on us unless by some desperate act we achieve some improbable immediate drastic change in the world order."[1] In their view, such fatalism underpinned not only Utopian responses to the nuclear age's dangers (e.g., "One World or None" calls for total disarmament, dissolution of national sovereignty, and world government), but also Dystopian responses (e.g., preventive nuclear war). As Albert explained in 1963:

> We are in the dark about the future of science and technology, still more about the long-term future of military and political developments in the world arena. We should be extremely skeptical, therefore, if sweeping predictions on any subject come tied to a prescription, an exhortation for urgent and sweeping action. We have all heard the apocalyptic pairs of alternatives: "Destroy the Russians or they'll destroy us"; or "Disarm or face world annihilation." These are counsels of desperation, fear of the dark. They abandon not only patience, but intelligence.[2]

1

As a remedy to nuclear-age fatalism and apocalyptic thinking, the Wohlstetters sought to identify and, when needed, to invent and design prudent, pragmatic alternatives to limit and manage nuclear risks—for example, to decrease nuclear war's likelihood by finding ways of improving the U.S. nuclear deterrent's survivability, controllability, and therefore credibility in the face of changing dangers. Nevertheless, some viewed their research agenda very differently. "He believes in learning how to fight with nuclear weapons," Paul Warnke, President Carter's Arms Control and Disarmament Agency director, said bluntly (if not also reductively) of Albert's work on nuclear deterrence in 1987. He continued, "I've never met a general or an admiral who really agrees with that."[3]

Albert was also controversial because, in contrast to Roberta's decidedly more subdued yet nonetheless formidable approach to debate, he engaged in policy disputes, not in a partisan or ideological manner, but rather with an analytical tenacity and intellectual ferocity that gained many admirers as well as detractors. As the venerable military historian, Sir Michael Howard, would later recall of Albert's work on exposing arms race myths, "Wohlstetter tore to pieces the thesis of the arms control lobby, that the weapons policy of the Soviet Union was dictated simply by the perception of U.S. threat, rather than by their own very different agenda." But Sir Michael would hasten to add: "His exposure of muddled, if not wishful thinking, on this issue did a great deal of good, but in his pursuit of [intellectual] adversaries, Wohlstetter showed himself at his most Calvinistic: there was at times a distinct whiff of burning in the air."[4]

Yet that which made the Wohlstetters controversial also helped to make them innovative. They belonged to a small circle of policy-oriented researchers—a group that included Andrew W. Marshall, Herman Kahn, William W. Kaufmann and others—that established the intellectual foundations on which the field of strategic policy analysis now stands. In particular, Albert, Roberta, and their immediate colleagues forever transformed how those who would later work on national security issues would think and talk by introducing concepts like "signal-to-noise ratio" in intelligence collection and analysis; the operational distinction between "first-strike" and "second-strike" capability in nuclear deterrence; "Fail-Safe" operations for nuclear-armed bomber aircraft; and the basing of intercontinental ballistic missiles in "hardened" underground silos. "To abbreviate drastically, Albert Wohlstetter all but invented a distinctly military approach to the military problems, or prudently presumed problems, of the security and utility of nuclear forces," wrote Colin S. Gray, a former adviser to the Reagan Administration. "Wohlstetter's work is on a plane of importance that is exceedingly thinly populated with convincing rivals."[5]

And what made the Wohlstetters controversial and innovative also helped to make them consequential. Although they never officially served as government policymakers during their careers in strategy, they were nevertheless able — through the clarity of their thinking, the rigor of their research, and the persistence of their personalities — to shape the views and aid the decisions of those in government both during and after the Cold War.[6] In turn, both Democratic and Republican Administrations recognized them for their many policy-relevant contributions. In February 1965, Albert received the Medal of Distinguished Service from Secretary of Defense Robert McNamara, becoming the first ever non-Pentagon employee to receive the Department of Defense's (DoD) highest honor. In January 1977, he received that honor again, this time from Secretary of Defense Donald Rumsfeld. And in November 1985, both Albert and Roberta were awarded Medals of Freedom, America's highest civilian honor, by President Ronald Reagan. As political scientist Richard Rosecrance, who served on the State Department's Policy Planning Council during the Johnson Administration, would write in 1991, "Probably no civilian strategic analyst has had more influence in the nuclear age than Albert Wohlstetter."[7]

Contemporary Controversies and Continuing Relevance.

In the early years of the new century, there is renewed interest in the Wohlstetters. One reason why is that although Albert died 4 years before Al Qaeda's September 11, 2001 (9/11), surprise attacks and America's subsequent struggle against violent extremism, several of his former students emerged as figures of consequence during the presidency of George W. Bush. (It is worth observing, though, that formal and informal students of the Wohlstetters have served as policymakers in every Administration since the start of President Kennedy's.)

Paul Wolfowitz, whose dissertation committee Albert had chaired in the University of Chicago's political science department, served as Deputy Secretary of Defense during Bush's first term, and now chairs the Secretary of State's International Security Advisory Board. Richard Perle, whom Wohlstetter had informally mentored since Perle's high school days, chaired from 2001 to 2003 the Defense Policy Board, a high-level panel of outside advisers to the Pentagon. And Zalmay Khalilzad, who also earned his Ph.D. at the University of Chicago under Wohlstetter's tutelage, served as the U.S. Ambassador to post-Ba'athist Iraq and, in his current capacity as America's envoy to the United Nations, is the highest-ranking Muslim in the Executive Branch. Broadly labeled by some as "neoconservatives," Wolfowitz, Perle, and Khalilzad would join Vice President Dick Cheney, Secretary of State Colin Powell, Secretary of Defense Donald Rumsfeld, Director of Central Intelligence George Tenet, National Security Advisor Condoleezza Rice, and others in being associated with President Bush's controversial arguments for war against Ba'athist Iraq.[8]

Another reason behind the renewed interest in the Wohlstetters is the growing awareness of how their Cold War and post-Cold War writings still speak to key challenges that America and its allies are facing in the 21st century. With respect to Roberta's works, one obvious example is *Pearl Harbor: Warning and Decision* (1962), her Bancroft Prize-winning study of the failures of American intelligence and imagination that had preceded Imperial Japan's surprise attack on December 7, 1941 — a study that has found new relevance in the tragic wake of Al Qaeda's 9/11 surprise attacks. In her meticulous analysis of the events and decisions prior to Pearl Harbor, Roberta found that the United States had failed to foresee the attack "not for want of the relevant materials, but because of a plethora of irrelevant ones."[9] Decisionmakers and intelligence analysts — the latter of whom were, at the time, decentralized and dispersed among America's military services — all had failed to distinguish the small, faint signals warning of disaster in Hawaii from the larger, louder mass of background noise suggesting anything but. Only *in retrospect* did these warning signals become so obvious and so discernible. "Signals that are characterized today as absolutely unequivocal warnings of surprise air attack on Pearl Harbor become, on analysis in the context of December 1941, not merely ambiguous but occasionally inconsistent with such an attack," she wrote.[10] "Indeed, at the time there was a good deal of evidence available to support all the wrong interpretations of last-minute signals, and the interpretations appeared wrong only after the event."[11]

This perennial problem of intelligence collection and analysis — of identifying and pulling actionable warning signals

4

from the vast morass of irrelevant background noise — has come to be known within intelligence circles as the "signals-to-noise ratio" problem or, more simply, "the Roberta Wohlstetter Problem."[12] The U.S. intelligence failures that preceded the attacks of 9/11 renewed public awareness of this problem, so it was therefore no surprise that Roberta's *Pearl Harbor* study was prominently cited by *The 9/11 Commission Report*.[13]

Another example of the Wohlstetters' continuing relevance is *The Buddha Smiles: Absent-Minded Peaceful Aid and the Indian Bomb* (1976), Roberta's incisive study of how U.S. and Canadian civil nuclear assistance to India during the 1950s and 1960s had unwittingly furthered New Delhi's secret construction and ultimate detonation in May 1974 of a nuclear explosive device, sometimes referred to as India's "Smiling Buddha" bomb.[14] The Indians had obtained plutonium for their bomb by using a reactor that Canada had built for them to use (in the words of their bilateral nuclear cooperation agreement) "for peaceful purposes only," as well as heavy water to moderate the Canadian-origin reactor that the United States had given to them (according to the terms of their bilateral agreement) only "for peaceful purposes."[15] Indian government officials subsequently explained away "Smiling Buddha" by claiming that the bomb's purpose had been "peaceful," and that their construction and detonation of this "peaceful" nuclear explosive device had therefore not violated *their* understanding of the respective terms of the Indo-American and Indo-Canadian nuclear cooperation agreements. To Roberta, this episode plainly illustrated the need for the Executive and Legislative Branches either to obtain unequivocal terms and bilateral understandings regarding not only what is prohibited in any agreement for nuclear cooperation, but also what consequences shall follow in the event of a violation — or else to decline an agreement altogether. Such insights from *The Buddha Smiles* are worth revisiting and taking seriously today, especially with Washington having concluded a new nuclear cooperation agreement with New Delhi that would carve out an exception in U.S. and international law in order to lift the decades-long prohibition against nuclear exports to India that arose after Smiling Buddha's detonation.

In contrast to Roberta's works, many of Albert's writings have remained dispersed and often difficult for all but the most determined and resourceful to find. As a result, those interested in learning more about this late strategist — a group that includes

5

not only government decisionmakers and policy analysts, but also journalists, scholars, and students—have not been able to read his works first-hand. Rather, they have had to turn to books and articles that offer second-hand (and, in some cases, even third-hand) accounts of his writings. Such accounts, however, have generally been incomplete, and sometimes have misunderstood or even consciously misrepresented Albert's arguments.

In particular, when recent books and articles on "neoconservativism" in the 21st century have discussed Albert (who never identified himself as a "neoconservative," nor was ever labeled one by the secondary literature before 2001 or 2002[16]), the authors of these accounts typically have neither read carefully nor analyzed closely his works. Instead, they have tended merely to cite passages from his writings out of textual and historical context in larger efforts to lionize or demonize today's "neoconservatives." In turn, these books and articles, and those who read them, frequently are drawing distorted and ahistorical conclusions about Wohlstetter and his work.

"Is it too much to ask," wrote Sir Michael Howard (a military historian who describes himself as a critic of Albert's), for someone "to bring together [the Wohlstetters'] widely scattered articles and publish them in a solid lasting form" as part of "the indispensable nucleus of a strategic studies library when all else has been swept away?"[17] The present volume aims to help answer that call by providing readers not only with first-hand access to some of Albert and Roberta's key published and previously unpublished writings on strategy, but also with a fuller understanding of their historical contributions and continuing relevance to U.S. national security policy.

The remainder of this introductory essay offers the basis for such an understanding by examining six key themes in Albert's career in strategy, with attention to Roberta's impact on Albert's work and thought. These themes correspond with this edited volume's six chapters of selected Wohlstetter writings on nuclear-age strategy and policy.

I. ANALYSIS AND DESIGN OF STRATEGIC POLICY

Albert Wohlstetter first entered the world of strategy in 1951, when at the age of 37 he began working at the RAND Corporation, a defense-oriented research organization based in Santa Monica, California. So new and so singular a place was RAND that the

U.S. press would have to coin new terms—neologisms like *think factory* and the more familiar *think tank*—just to describe more succinctly, if not accurately, what this organization was.[18]

RAND—the name is a contraction of the phrase *research and development*—was very much a product of the political, economic, military, and technological "cold war" competition between the West and the Soviet Union that began as World War II was ending. Recognizing the crucial roles that science and technology had played in the Allied victory over the Axis, the U.S. Army Air Forces (USAAF) in October 1945 formed Project RAND, the think tank's institutional predecessor, as an experimental organization to retain wartime scientific and technological expertise. Written at a time when the American military services were struggling to comprehend how the atomic bomb might affect the future character of war and peace, Project RAND's mandate was framed to encompass "study and research on the broad subject of intercontinental warfare, other than surface, with the objective of recommending to the Army Air Forces preferred techniques and instrumentalities for this purpose."[19] This broad mandate enabled a well-funded, cutting-edge, and extremely flexible research agenda that helped to attract some of America's brightest minds in economics, physics, engineering, mathematics, and the social sciences. Although RAND would gain institutional independence from the USAAF's successor, the U.S. Air Force (USAF), after incorporating itself as a private not-for-profit entity in 1948, the USAF would remain RAND's main client for many years to come.[20]

During the 1950s, Albert's research on America's nuclear forces would help to establish the RAND Corporation's reputation as *the* center of U.S. strategic thought. His own journey to RAND would be a circuitous one, however. Given his undergraduate and graduate education in mathematical logic, and his later work in manufacturing as well as prefabricated housing, it may seem perhaps incongruous—even surprising—that he would spend his remaining 46 years immersed in questions of nuclear-age strategy and morality. Yet Wohlstetter would import lessons and insights from earlier disparate experiences into his defense-oriented research at RAND, and thereby shape his own unique approach to the analysis and design of strategic policy.

Road to RAND.[21]

Born in New York City on December 19, 1913, Albert was the youngest of Philip and Nellie Friedman Wohlstetter's four children. Although Philip would die when Albert was 4, a close-knit and cultured extended family — and the efforts of Albert's eldest brother, who forsook university studies to work full-time — would help widowed Nellie to care for her children.[22]

Raised in Manhattan's Washington Heights neighborhood, Wohlstetter attended DeWitt Clinton High School, where he showed an early and strong interest in mathematics, Latin, and modern dance. In 1930, as the Great Depression was descending upon America, 16-year-old Albert entered the City College of New York. As an undergraduate, he concentrated his studies on mathematical logic, and was particularly stimulated by the writings of Charles Sanders Peirce (1839-1914), a philosopher of science whom he would describe in later years as "probably the greatest American philosopher" and "a major influence" on his own work in nuclear-age strategy.[23] On the side, Albert would participate in campus activities like the college's R.O.T.C.[24]

After graduating from City College, Wohlstetter earned a fellowship to Columbia Law School. There, he met a master's degree student in psychology (whom he would marry in 1939) named Roberta Mary Morgan,[25] the daughter of Edmund Morris Morgan, Jr., a distinguished Harvard Law School professor who would later help to modernize the Uniform Code of Military Justice. Although Albert would leave law school after only a year, he would remain at Columbia to pursue a Ph.D., studying mathematical logic and the philosophy of science, and working with some of the era's great logicians, such as Columbia's Ernest Nagel and Harvard's Willard Van Orman Quine.[26] While in graduate school, Wohlstetter would take on odd jobs to help support himself, and would even work for a time as art historian Meyer Shapiro's assistant.

After earning his M.A. in 1937, Albert received several fellowships to finish his doctorate — including one from the Social Science Research Council to introduce modern mathematical methods into economics, a prestigious fellowship that in turn enabled him to intern for a time at the National Bureau for Economic Research. However, when the United States entered World War II, he halted his studies to work initially for the War Production Board's planning committee as an economic consultant, and later for the Atlas Aircraft Products Company as a factory and quality control manager at a plant manufacturing power-generating equipment for Allied forces.

After the war, Wohlstetter declined to complete his doctorate and instead moved with his wife, Roberta, to southern California. Except for a year spent in Washington, DC, where he served as the National Housing Administration's Director of Programs (his one and only official government position), Albert would spend the rest of the decade managing research and development at the General Panel Corporation of California. General Panel would attempt—but in the end fail—to help meet the postwar housing shortage by mass-producing the "Packaged House," a modular prefabricated housing system designed by émigré architects Walter Gropius and Konrad Wachsmann.[27]

In February 1951, as General Panel was folding, Albert was already contemplating a change in career, and even considering a return not only to more academically oriented research, but also to the East Coast. However, Roberta—who had been working part-time in the RAND Corporation's social sciences division since late 1948 while at the same time raising her and Albert's daughter, Joan—was intent on remaining on the West Coast. Toward that end, she set up a meeting for Albert with Charles Hitch, the head of the think tank's economic division. A Missouri-born Rhodes Scholar, Hitch had served in the Office of Strategic Services during World War II before coming to RAND. Upon meeting, the two immediately clicked, and Hitch hired Wohlstetter on at RAND as a part-time consultant.

Wohlstetter's Approach: Key Features.[28]

During the 1950s, Albert would lead a series of highly classified studies at the RAND Corporation that revolutionized how the United States based and operated its strategic nuclear forces. These studies (which the next section of this essay examines in some detail) would also stand out as exemplary applications of his unique methodology, a collaborative and interdisciplinary approach to the analysis and design of strategic policy. (Although Albert would write only a handful essays on methodology, his most accessible work on this subject is probably "Theory and Opposed-Systems Design" (1968), a version of which is included in this edited volume.[29])

First, Albert's approach sought to identify, frame, and answer questions directly relevant to the decisions facing government policymakers. Such decisions encompassed not only choices among "means to accomplish ends that stand a good chance of being opposed by other governments," but also choices among the ends themselves.[30]

In Wohlstetter's view, the ends of government policy could run into opposition in a number of ways. Such opposition, of course, could take the form of a conflict of aims *between or among* several governments. "The ends of any government," he observed, "are multiple and only partially incompatible with those of other governments—even very hostile ones—and of course such conflicts may be resolved without fighting." However, he added: "A peaceful resolution may depend in part on the risks involved in combat."[31]

Such opposition could also take the form of a partial conflict of aims *within* one government. He elaborated:

> While we may talk about national purpose in the singular, the first thing to observe about our aims is that we have many of them. They are connected; some depend on others; many conflict. Obviously two aims may conflict when each represents the interests of a different group. But even ends which the nation as a whole can be said to share oppose other accepted national ends.[32]

Albert thus highlighted the crucial importance of including "a careful critique of constraints and objectives" in any analysis of strategic policy, with particular attention to the cost-effectiveness of availalble choices to meet these objectives. He explained,

> A government's ends cannot be accepted as the final deliverances of authority or intuition. They are subject to revision as the result of an analysis that frequently displays incompatibilities with other ends of that government, or that indicates means so costly that the game is not worth the candle.[33]

Second, Wohlstetter's analytical approach used theoretical models, empirically-driven research, and interdisciplinary collaboration to wade through the complexity and uncertainty surrounding these problems of policy, and arrive systematically at some partial order among preferences and choices of means and ends.

Lessons from his pre-RAND experiences profoundly shaped this approach. On the one hand, Albert's education in mathematical logic and the philosophy of science had given him an appreciation of the uses — and the limits — of quantitative and qualitative theoretical models in capturing and explaining real-world interactions and phenomena. On the other hand, his professional experiences in wartime and peacetime manufacturing had taught him the importance of moving away from the abstract and grappling with the concrete. Indeed, he repeatedly stressed the critical importance in his analyses of "grubby, highly specific empirical work on technologies, operations, costs, and potential interactions among states, factors that are plainly relevant for decisions of the governments of these states — or for citizens evaluating these decisions."[34] Drawing inspiration from the work of the philosopher of science Charles Sanders Peirce, Albert thus sought to use theoretical models and empirically-driven research in a heuristic manner: deductive theoretical models spurred further empirically-driven research, the findings of which helped inductively to refine and improve the deductive theoretical models, and so on, in a method of successive analytical approximation.

In addition, Wohlstetter's professional experiences impressed upon him the need to collaborate with and draw upon the insights and creativity of experts in other relevant fields. Indeed, he expressed pride in how his approach "required the cooperation of several disciplines and, in particular, a kind of close working together of natural science and social science disciplines which remains very unusual, if it exists at all, in universities."[35]

Third, Albert's approach aimed not only to weigh and consider the received range of possible choices, but also to invent and design new alternatives. He explained:

> A central part of the inquiry must look at the current and impending state of the art and at feasible and useful changes. In the past two decades in which such inquiries have grown up, nuclear, electronic, propulsion, and transport technology have changed massively. The problem is not just to predict such changes, however. Since this is a work of design, it must explore how — in the light of interdependencies with military, political, and economic events — the changes may usefully be bent.[36]

Indeed, he would remark in later years that invention and design figured heavily in his most successful analyses of strategic policy.

Fourth, Wohlstetter stressed the importance of being explicit about the limits of one's analytical approach, including the uncertainties surrounding the study. Yet he also noted that certain kinds of uncertainty could be leveraged to make the inquiry, inferences, and conclusions of the analysis more robust and persuasive. He elaborated:

> In comparing alternative systems with one programmed, one cannot eliminate uncertainty, but one can assume that they will be resolved favorably from the standpoint of a dubious programmed system. One cannot avoid theoretical simplification, but one can design a model to favor the programmed or other losing systems and to give them the benefit of the doubt. Then if the comparison shows that, even with all the favors bestowed by the model's assumption, the system programmed or otherwise likely to be chosen is vastly inferior to an alternative, this offers substantial ground for choice. Moreover, it should not be surprising that bureaucrats exhibit enough inertia to make such *a fortiori* analyses possible and very useful, as some opposed-systems analyses have been.[37]

In sum, Wohlstetter saw his approach as applying, in an essentially Peircean manner, the method of scientific investigation to the analysis and design of strategic policy. Moreover, he would argue that his approach stood in stark contrast to the practices of certain distinguished scientists, who would premise their arguments regarding the proper direction of nuclear-age strategy and policy less on the method of scientific investigation and much more on appeals to their own scientific authority.[38]

That said, Wohlstetter emphasized that his particular approach to analysis and design neither exhausted the possibilities, nor could substitute for a capacity for fruitful inquiry. "There are no methods certain of result in a complex field of research," he cautioned. "None is proof against a dim awareness of interesting problems or incompetence in formulating manageable and significant questions."[39]

II. NUCLEAR DETERRENCE

At the RAND Corporation in the 1950s, Albert Wohlstetter would lead a series of highly classified studies on U.S. nuclear forces that would evince his unique approach to the analysis and design of strategic policy, and establish his reputation within government circles as one of America's premier strategists. However, it was not until after the January 1959 publication of "The Delicate Balance of Terror"[40] in *Foreign Affairs*—an essay on the stringent conceptual and technical requirements for nuclear deterrence that military historian Marc Trachtenberg would later describe as "probably the single most important article in the history of American strategic thought"[41]—that Albert would be recognized as one of America's preeminent and controversial public intellectuals of defense. Together, Wohlstetter's RAND studies and the *Foreign Affairs* article would challenge what decisionmakers, military planners, and policy analysts had assumed about nuclear war and peace, and forever change how they would think and talk about nuclear strategy and operational policy.

The Base Study.

In May 1951 Charles Hitch, the head of RAND's economics division, asked Wohlstetter whether he would be interested in researching a problem that the USAF had posed to the think tank: *How should the USAF's Strategic Air Command (SAC) base itself overseas?* Initially, Albert saw this as a run-of-the-mill logistics problem, but after thinking things through over a weekend, he began to appreciate better how SAC's basing choices for its force of medium-range, nuclear-armed, manned bombers raised interesting questions and could have important implications.[42] Wohlstetter thus accepted Hitch's invitation and began a research project that would later come to be known as the "Base Study."[43]

As the 1940s gave way to the 1950s, the political, economic, and military competition between the Western allies and the Soviet Union had intensified. Although Soviet intentions remained unclear, its behavior had appeared at times ominous. After World War II, Soviet-supported Communists had seized power in Poland and Czechoslovakia. In 1948, the Union of Soviet Socialist Republics (USSR) had blockaded West Berlin. In August 1949, the Soviets had exploded their first atomic bomb. In 1950, the USSR not only had signed a defense treaty with the People's Republic of China, but also had backed Kim Il Sung's Stalinist regime after North Korea invaded South Korea and thereby set in motion the Korean War.[44]

Against this background, SAC's bombers, when armed with atomic gravity bombs, constituted at the time America's main military hedge against the prospect of "Central War" — that is, of a Soviet conventional military invasion of Western Europe, the nations of which lacked the political and military means to defend themselves. In time of war or crisis, SAC's *programmed system* of basing for 1956 to 1961 envisioned relocating the bombers from approximately 30 bases in the continental United States (CONUS) to roughly 70 overseas installations. Half of these installations would be large, expensive "primary bases" from which SAC's bombers would launch their offensive operations, and the other half, refueling bases, but in general, all of them would be geographically closer to the USSR than was CONUS. Moreover, this programmed basing system was viewed favorably by SAC, the USAF, and DoD, as well as by the Congress. Indeed, just for fiscal year 1952, the Congress had already appropriated $3.5 billion (roughly equivalent to as much as $30 billion in 2008 dollars) to construct domestic and overseas bases in accordance with the programmed system.[45]

With a team that would feature economists Fred Hoffman and Henry Rowen, and aeronautical engineer Robert Lutz, Wohlstetter set out to understand the relevant economic, operational, logistical, technological, political, and military contexts in which to compare SAC's programmed system of basing to possible alternatives. Working in interdisciplinary consultation with USAF airmen, as well as with engineers, physicists, economists, intelligence analysts, geographers, and other experts, the Wohlstetter team came to identify four critical factors for evaluating base selection: the distances of a given base (1) to predetermined targets in the USSR, (2) to favorable entry points into Soviet territory, (3) to supply sources in the CONUS, and (4) to Soviet offensive airbases. In turn, they examined how variations in these factors, when applied to the SAC bomber force planned for 1956 to 1961, would *jointly* affect:

- the costs of extending the bomber force's round-trip radius;
- the Soviet military's employment of active defenses, as well as the number of SAC bombers which Soviet fighters could intercept and destroy;

- the logistical and operational costs for SAC's bomber force; and,
- the vulnerability of primary operating bases and bombers on the ground to attack by the Soviet's small but growing stockpile of atomic gravity bombs.

Wohlstetter and company's Top Secret March 1953 staff report, *The Selection of Strategic Air Bases* (R-244-S), concluded that the *preferred system* of basing was one of a new — and much less expensive — design that would rely primarily on bases within the continental United States in both peace and war, and supplement that system mainly with austere overseas refueling bases and, to a lesser extent, aerial refueling.[46] Although this alternative system was not optimal for all criteria, it was a clear, across-the-board improvement over the programmed system. When compared to alternatives, it excelled in extending the bomber force's round-trip radius more cheaply; enabling bombers to bypass Soviet defenses and interceptors and reach enemy targets more effectively; decreasing logistical and operational costs; and increasing the quality and time interval of tactical warning, as well as lowering the vulnerability of bases and bombers on the ground to attack by the Soviet Union's growing stockpile of aircraft-delivered atomic bombs.

Many in DoD, the USAF, and SAC initially and even reflexively resisted R-244-S's conclusions. In response, Wohlstetter and colleagues embarked on a briefing campaign of several months to persuade policymakers and military planners of the validity of their findings. In April 1954, they completed the Base Study's Top Secret, 400-page final report, *Selection and Use of Strategic Air Bases* (R-266), which not only detailed their findings, but also recommended new measures and operations to increase tactical warning of Soviet attack, and to better protect bomber aircraft, nuclear weapons, and personnel within each base from the various effects of nuclear explosions.[47] By that time, however, Wohlstetter and company's campaign had already shown results. By late 1953, the USAF had accepted R-244-S's main conclusion, and had begun plans to relocate SAC's primary bases to the continental United States and to implement other key recommendations.[48] In light of this success, the final text of R-266 was changed to describe SAC's originally programmed system of basing as the *formerly programmed system*.

Although the Base Study had implications for nuclear deterrence's stability, it is important to recognize that the study itself did not initially set out to focus on that issue. Rather, the effect of SAC's choices for basing and operations on the survivability, controllability, and credibility of the U.S. nuclear deterrent became evident only as the Wohlstetter team developed and refined their study. Their follow-on Vulnerability Study, however, would examine the issue of nuclear deterrence explicitly.

The Vulnerability Study.

In September 1953, around the time Wohlstetter and company embarked in earnest on their follow-on study, the military-technological context had already begun to change dramatically. Both the United States and the USSR were increasing their stockpiles of atomic bombs, starting to introduce long-range bombers and more indiscriminately destructive hydrogen bombs, and working to develop intercontinental ballistic missiles (ICBMs). Although Soviet ICBMs were likely to be extremely inaccurate, a February 1954 paper by Wohlstetter and Hoffman projected that if ICBMs were coupled with hydrogen bombs, then the hydrogen bomb's powerful blast effects and very large "lethal radius" could help to compensate for such inaccuracies, and enable even errant, imprecisely-delivered ICBMs to destroy intended military targets that were "soft" (e.g., airfields and aircraft, as well as unhardened buildings and structures) with ease and little warning.[49] The Vulnerability Study thus would seek to understand how these and other technological changes would affect the stability of deterrence.

Prior to this study, U.S. military planners had assumed that if the Soviets were to attack, their nuclear strikes—in a continuation of World War II and Korean War strategic bombing doctrine — would be aimed at American economic and industrial targets, as well as cities, and would be so large and so direct as to generate considerable strategic and tactical warning. Even historian-strategist Bernard Brodie had shared this counter-city targeting assumption. In his essays in the edited volume, *The Absolute Weapon* (1946), he had called the urban city the "made-to-order target" for nuclear weapons, and concluded that "the ability to fight back after an atomic bomb attack will depend on *the degree to which the armed forces have made themselves independent of the urban communities and their industries for supply and support."* Brodie did not think that U.S. strategic nuclear forces would be the primary targets of nuclear weapons.[50]

Working again with Hoffman and Rowen, Wohlstetter examined not only these assumed "U.S.-preferred" Soviet methods of attack, but also other attack methods that he would later describe as *lesser excluded cases*.[51] In particular, he considered the possibility of Soviet preclusive *first strikes* with nuclear weapons: that is, nuclear Pearl Harbor-style attacks in which small numbers of enemy forces would try to fly at low altitudes, circumnavigate America's radar-warning networks, and use nuclear weapons to attack, not industrial targets or cities, but rather U.S. strategic nuclear forces themselves—with the explicit aim of precluding any substantial American retaliation or *second strikes*. (Albert and his colleagues coined the now taken-for-granted terms, *first strike* and *second strike*.)

In September 1956, the Wohlstetter team completed the Vulnerability Study's Top Secret staff report, titled *Protecting U.S. Power to Strike Back in the 1950s and 1960s* (R-290).[52] R-290 found that, even given the then-current range of low-to-medium intelligence estimates of existing and future Soviet military capabilities, U.S. nuclear forces could be highly vulnerable to attacks, especially Soviet attempts at a preclusive nuclear first strike, because of four central weaknesses:

1. inadequate strategic and tactical warning before Soviet bomber attacks, and almost no warning before Soviet ICBM attacks;

2. painfully slow and uncoordinated responses to any warning because SAC required hours—sometimes many days—to assemble flight crews, aircraft, and munitions for combat or evacuation;

3. ineffective active and passive defenses because forces, personnel, and command centers were too locally concentrated, and because facilities (e.g., existing aircraft shelters and depots storing nuclear arms) could not structurally resist even an errant atom bomb's blast effects, let alone a hydrogen bomb's; and,

4. a degraded or negated "second-strike" capability because Soviet first strikes could destroy or disable many SAC bombers on the ground, could disrupt post-attack communications and retaliation coordination, and could easily level planned above-ground ICBM launchers.

R-290's findings were startling and provocative, but Albert and colleagues were careful to attach explicit and crucial qualifications. They wrote:

> The attacks described here, and many others studied, clearly indicated the present vulnerability of our strike force. *They do not, of course, imply that a Russian attack is imminent. Nor do we think it is.* That is a matter of Soviet intention rather than Soviet capability, and such intent would be affected in the first instance by Soviet knowledge of our vulnerability and in the second place by the comparative gains and risks of alternatives to central war.[53]

Conventional wisdom in the United States held that by simply possessing nuclear weapons, a government necessarily acquired an ironclad deterrent. The Wohlstetter team took aim at the conventional wisdom by arguing that mere possession of what the historian-strategist Bernard Brodie had once famously called "the absolute weapon" was not sufficient. Their worry was that if the weaknesses of America's strategic nuclear forces remained unaddressed, and if the USSR perceived these vulnerabilities, then in a time of extreme crisis the Soviets might come to view an attempt at a preclusive first strike as a not wholly unreasonable risk. As they explained in R-290:

> Deterrence is hardly attained by simply creating some uncertainty in the enemy's attack plans, that is, by making it somewhat of a gamble. The question is, *how much* of a gamble? and what are his alternatives? On the basis of past experience, we would be taking a very large gamble if we assumed that under no circumstances would the enemy take risks. If this were so, the matter would be easy and, for us, substantially costless.[54]

In short, although a nuclear Pearl Harbor was far from inevitable, in a time of acute crisis U.S. carelessness and complacency could conceivably invite such an attack.

However, Wohlstetter and company stressed that, in efforts to address these serious vulnerabilities, simply numerically increasing the size of U.S. strategic nuclear forces would provide neither an affordable nor an effective solution. "National defense programs do not now give adequate consideration to the problem of protecting the strategic force as distinct from the problem of force size,"[55] they argued. "The criterion for matching the Russians plane for plane, or exceeding them is, in the strict sense, irrelevant to the problem of deterrence."[56] Rather, Albert and his compatriots maintained that the problem of establishing a deterrent that was survivable, controllable, and therefore more credible in the face of changing dangers required U.S. strategic nuclear forces to be *not only* capable of riding out and operating coherently after an actual preemptive attack against them; *but also* completely controllable in times of peace, crisis, and war — and especially in the face of ambiguous warning — so as to avoid unauthorized operations, accidents, and war by mistake.

In turn, such controllability in the face of ambiguous warning required that strategic nuclear forces be able to cope with the operational dangers that attended *false alarm*, the belief that there is a nuclear attack underway when there actually is not, which could commit America to war accidentally; and *false reassurance*, the belief that there is not an imminent nuclear attack when there actually is, which could facilitate an enemy's preclusive first strike.

Wohlstetter and colleagues held that if U.S. strategic nuclear forces could meet these requirements for a survivable, controllable, and credible deterrent, then this would increase the likelihood that the Soviets would tend to view the choice of a preclusive first strike as the riskiest of alternatives *even if* Moscow should somehow stumble into potentially calamitous circumstances.[57] To meet these ends, they identified over 50 operational measures to limit and manage the many risks facing U.S. strategic nuclear forces.[58] In particular, they recommended that the United States should:

- *Extend* the continental radar net's perimeter; *relocate and disperse* bases deep within it; and *install* a "bomb-alarm system" to warn immediately all SAC bases and America's Continental Air Defense forces of an enemy's nuclear warhead detonation anywhere within the basing system.
- *Establish* better alert procedures; *increase* SAC's flight crew and aircraft readiness for evacuation or combat; and *implement* "Fail-Safe," a set of protective actions in which combat-ready SAC bombers would evacuate and disperse in response to ambiguous warning, fly along

predetermined routes, and return to base after arriving at predesignated locations, unless given an explicit order to continue on and attack enemy targets.

- *Shelter* personnel, bombers, fuel, and nuclear bombs in facilities more structurally resistant to atomic and hydrogen bomb blast effects; *locally disperse and protect* these facilities within bases to take better advantage of ICBM inaccuracies; and *shield* planned ICBM launchers in hardened underground silos to make active and passive defenses more effective.

- *Secure* backup civilian and military airfields in the continental United States; and *develop* robust, survivable command, control, and communications systems to protect post-attack communication and coordination with surviving forces.

Although the Vulnerability Study's findings ran into some initial institutional resistance within the U.S. Government, the earlier Base Study's successes made policymakers and military planners much less inclined to dismiss the Wohlstetter team's conclusions.[59] Indeed, many of R-290's recommendations were eventually adopted—though some recommendations, such as Fail-Safe,[60] took much longer than others for SAC, the USAF, and the Defense Department to accept and implement.

Moreover, Wohlstetter and company's Vulnerability Study inspired or helped to inspire others to develop technological innovations that would later have dramatic, and even revolutionary, impact. To take one example, the conventional wisdom prior to R-290 was that structures could be designed to resist—at most—peak overpressures of 30 or 40 pounds per square inch (p.s.i.). Working with Paul Weidlinger, a Hungarian-born engineer whom Albert had met in the 1940s at the National Housing Administration, the Wohlstetter team disproved the conventional wisdom: Weidlinger designed an underground missile silo, the concrete and steel structure of which could resist peak overpressures of as much as 200 p.s.i. In addition, he showed that it was possible to design structures of even greater blast resistance.[61]

To take another example, in the late 1950s RAND political scientist Fred C. Iklé, psychiatrist Gerald Aronson, and statistician Albert Madansky developed the concept of what would later come to be known as Permissive Action Links (PALs), with the aim of preventing the accidental or unauthorized use of nuclear weapons. In brief, PALs require not only the installation of coded safety locks on nuclear weapons and missiles, but also the positive assent of two people to carry out and execute sensitive nuclear operations.[62] PALs remain widely used by the United States to this day.

Yet another important example is the work of a brilliant RAND engineer named Paul Baran. Wohlstetter's R-290 report had helped draw attention to the Defense Department's severe command, control, and communications weaknesses: for instance, in the 1950s SAC communicated using extremely vulnerable civil telephone lines that could be easily disrupted by a nuclear-armed adversary in time of war. To remedy this problem, Baran in the early 1960s came up with the concepts of "distributed networking" and "hot-potato routing" (the latter is commonly known today as "packet-switched networking"), with a view toward creating more robust, secure, and survivable systems for command, control, and communications. Baran's concepts would prove essential to later efforts by the Advanced Research Projects Agency and other organizations that would eventually lead to the creation of the Internet.[63]

The Delicate Balance: Deterrence as a Matter of Comparing Alternative Risks.[64]

Drawing conceptual insights from his classified and empirically-driven RAND studies, Albert Wohlstetter published the article, "The Delicate Balance of Terror," in the January 1959 issue of *Foreign Affairs* that publicly took aim at the conventional wisdom surrounding nuclear deterrence. His targets were twofold: (1) the widespread belief in what his article described as *automatic deterrence*, the view that an always-reliable deterrent is an inevitable consequence of a government's mere possession of nuclear weapons;[65] and (2) the belief in what was popularly known as *minimum deterrence*, a more sophisticated version of automatic deterrence conceding that nuclear forces require the capability to survive the sort of attack they are meant to deter, but maintaining that such capability is easily achieved with only a few technologically crude and indiscriminately destructive nuclear weapons.[66] The article noted that these views were held by many members of America and Europe's foreign policy elite: "In England by Sir Winston Churchill, P. M. S. Blackett, Sir John Slessor, Admiral Buzzard, and many others; in France by such figures as Raymond Aron, General Gallois, and General Gazin;

21

in this country by the titular heads of both parties, as well as almost all writers on military and foreign affairs, by both Henry Kissinger and his critic, James E. King, and by George Kennan, as well as Mr. [Dean] Acheson."[67]

Wohlstetter countered that a survivable, controllable, and therefore credible deterrent against nuclear attack is neither automatically nor easily achieved. "[M]uch of the contemporary Western confidence on the ease of retaliation is achieved by ignoring the full range of sensible enemy plans," he wrote.[68] Automatic deterrers had assumed nuclear attacks against the West that would target cities and civilians, not nuclear-armed military forces themselves; thus, their image of a nuclear attack was that of a nuclear-age extension of World War II strategic bombing campaigns or a repeat of Hiroshima and Nagasaki, not a nuclear Pearl Harbor. Minimum deterrers conceded that an opponent's nuclear attack might target strategic nuclear forces, but failed to appreciate how deeply-rooted systemic weaknesses and operational difficulties in the face of a preclusive nuclear first strike could severely complicate attempts at retaliation.[69]

The fundamental conceptual point of "The Delicate Balance" was that the credible deterrence of a preemptive nuclear attack hinges on the would-be attacker's *comparison of alternative risks* — that is, what specific circumstances a potential aggressor faces, what alternatives to attack it perceives, and how it compares the risks of attack to the risks of perceived alternatives in those circumstances. "The balance is not automatic," Wohlstetter explained. "It should be clear that it is not fruitful to talk about the likelihood of general war without specifying the range of alternatives that are pressing on the aggressor and the strategic postures of both the aggressor and the defender."[70] His crucial insight was that, even despite the horrors of nuclear weapons, the prospect of catastrophic circumstances could make the seemingly sturdy nuclear-age "balance of terror" fragile, and thus make a normally unthinkable course of action (e.g., nuclear preemption) potentially thinkable.

To increase the likelihood of adversaries always viewing a nuclear attack — in particular, a preclusive first strike — as the riskiest of choices requires a nuclear-armed government to acquire and communicate to would-be aggressors the acquisition of what Wohlstetter stringently defined as *second-strike capability*. Such capability demands much more than possession of nuclear arms. It also requires the establishment of a *system* of strategic nuclear forces—a system composed not only of nuclear warheads and delivery vehicles, but also of personnel; command, control, and communications; reconnaissance and radar warning; supporting physical and operational infrastructure; and active and passive defenses. This system would have to be capable of clearing the following six operational hurdles:[71]

1. The system of strategic nuclear forces must operate safely and stably in peacetime and, in particular, overcome problems associated with false alarms, accidents, and unauthorized operations.

2. It must be able to survive and operate coherently after a preclusive first strike—that is, after a preemptive nuclear attack attempting to degrade, disable, or destroy it.

3. It must be able clearly to identify the aggressor, and to receive orders to retaliate from the political leaders after an attack.

4. Delivery vehicles must be able to reach targets on the aggressor's territory.

5. Delivery vehicles must be able to survive attempts to intercept them by the aggressor's active defense.

6. And delivery vehicles must be able to deliver nuclear warheads with accuracy appropriate to the warhead's explosive yield in order to overwhelm the aggressor's passive defenses (e.g., structural hardening, geographical dispersal, and deep underground emplacement of facilities) and destroy intended targets.

Moreover, such second-strike capability needed to be maintained in relation to—and in competition with—the potential aggressor's own changing offensive and defensive military capabilities.

Finally, Albert stressed that even if a government could credibly deter a preclusive nuclear first strike, that did not mean it could also therefore credibly deter limited nuclear or less-than-nuclear aggression in all circumstances. (Albert and Roberta's work on Cuba during and after the Cuban Missile Crisis would examine this issue further.[72]) In other words, a survivable, controllable, and credible deterrent against nuclear preemption could not substitute for a holistic approach to national security, including efforts to improve conventional non-nuclear military capabilities.

The essay's argument was controversial. "Wohlstetter puts much emphasis on the circumstances in which nuclear aggression would be, in his view, both rational and sane," wrote P. M. S.

Blackett (whose views "The Delicate Balance" had criticized) in 1962. "Wohlstetter's argument suggests to me that he has neither thought very deeply or imaginatively about the consequences of the nuclear war, nor has he ever imagined himself in the position of taking the action which he seems to think it sane for the Soviets to take."[73]

However, Wohlstetter—who had derived his arguments from nearly a decade's worth of highly classified research on U.S. strategic nuclear forces at the RAND Corporation—worried about the extent to which government decisionmakers would always act in an objectively "sane" or "rational" manner. Drawing on his wife Roberta's work on Pearl Harbor, he came to view Imperial Japan's December 1941 surprise strike as highly instructive. On the one hand, Tokyo, when faced with the prospect of eventual but almost certain defeat, had reasoned that a daring surprise attack on what it had *correctly perceived* to be vulnerable American naval forces in Hawaii was the less risky choice. As Admiral Osami Nagano, Chief of Japan's Naval General Staff, had explained in 1941:

> The current relations between Japan and the United States might be compared to an illness in which a decision was necessary on whether to perform an operation. Avoiding surgery would [threaten] a gradual wasting away of the patient. Great danger would attend the operation, but it could not be said that surgery offered no hope of saving the patient's life.[74]

On the other hand, U.S. and allied leaders had tragically failed to appreciate the alternative risks that were pressing down on Japan and making arguably insane strategic gambles seem less-and-less unreasonable. In a footnote to "The Delicate Balance," Wohlstetter recalls how:

> . . . in an interview with the press on December 3, 1941, Air Chief Marshal Sir Robert Brooke-Popham, Commander-in-Chief, Far East, for the British forces stated, "There are clear indications that Japan does not know which way to turn. Tojo is scratching his head." As Japan did not have a definite policy to follow, irrevocably, step-by-step, said Sir Robert, "there is a reassuring state of uncertainty in Japan."[75]

Although Albert did not believe the Soviets were imminently bent on a nuclear Pearl Harbor, he could not exclude the possibility that, given the Cold War's vicissitudes, Moscow might someday blunder into a calamitous situation, and find itself contemplating a preemptive nuclear attack.[76] As he elaborated during a private high-level dinner seminar at the Council on Foreign Relations in March 1960:

> The point is that deterrence should not be viewed as an absolute. It is a matter of *comparative risks*. Under some circumstances an aggressor might be faced with several unpleasant alternatives, and we want to guarantee that the most unpleasant always appears to be the risk of making a direct attack on the United States. There are, moreover, many foreseeable contingencies which will put a great strain on the deterrent. For example, the Russians may be faced with a catastrophic defeat in a peripheral war. Or they may fear allied intervention and support for a revolt spreading in the satellites or in Russia. Or, possibly, even more dangerous, we may have suffered some catastrophic defeat on the periphery, and they may doubt that we will accept such a loss.[77]

Thus, in his view, a clear and evident second-strike capability would increase the likelihood that the USSR and other future nuclear-armed adversaries would view, under almost any and all circumstances, a preclusive first strike as the riskiest of available alternatives.

In *Pearl Harbor: Warning and Decision* (1962), a Bancroft Prize-winning book which was published in the same year as the Cuban Missile Crisis, Roberta would describe major practical lessons that had emerged from her study of Imperial Japan's December 1941 surprise attack:

> We cannot *count* on strategic warning. We *might* get it, and we might be able to take useful preparatory actions that would be impossible without it. We certainly ought to plan to exploit such a possibility should it occur. However, since we cannot rely on strategic warning, our defenses, if we are to have confidence in them, must be designed to function without it. If we accept the fact that the signal picture for impending attacks is almost

sure to be ambiguous, we shall prearrange actions that are right and feasible in response to ambiguous signals, including signs of an attack that might be false. We must be capable of reacting repeatedly to false alarms without committing ourselves or the enemy to wage thermonuclear war.[78]

In an application of his wife's insights, Albert's work in nuclear deterrence had sought to identify the sort of posture, operations, and technologies that would enable America's strategic nuclear forces not only to function stably in peacetime, but also to ride out and survive a nuclear-armed adversary's attempt to preclusively degrade, disable, or destroy them—and by so doing, help the United States deter safely and credibly a nuclear-age Pearl Harbor-style attack against it. In "The Delicate Balance," however, he stressed that maintaining such capability in the face of changing nuclear dangers would not be easy. It would require "sustained intelligent effort, attainable only by continuing hard choice."[79]

In later years, some authors and journalists would erroneously associate Wohlstetter with "bomber gap" arguments, and even Senator John F. Kennedy's "missile gap" arguments. However, through outreach like *General Comments on Senator Kennedy's National Security Speeches* (circa 1960),[80] a memorandum to JFK's presidential campaign, Wohlstetter would try to clarify how his work on nuclear deterrence had not only explicitly rejected "bomber gap" and "missile gap" claims, but also refuted arguments for brute numerical increases in U.S. nuclear weapons and delivery vehicles as a feasible, economic, or sensible way of preserving second-strike capability.

"The Delicate Balance of Terror" would be the first of many Wohlstetter writings to publicly challenge developing doctrines of automatic and minimum deterrence, as well as policies derived from these doctrines. In the early 1960s, one such policy would be a contentious U.S. proposal to share nuclear weapons with America's allies in Europe.

III. NUCLEAR PROLIFERATION

Albert Wohlstetter's pioneering research on nuclear deterrence in the 1950s helped to establish his reputation as one of America's premier and most controversial strategists. In the following decades, his efforts to stem nuclear proliferation—efforts which drew insights directly from his RAND studies on the requirements for a survivable, controllable, and credible U.S. nuclear deterrent—would serve to enhance that reputation. During the early 1960s, he would work to debunk an American proposal for a so-called "nuclear sharing" arrangement with the North Atlantic Treaty Organization (NATO) and to promote instead nonproliferation within NATO by convincing the United States to make stronger, clearer, and more believable its promise to protect Western European allies from any potential Soviet nuclear and non-nuclear military aggression. Moreover, in the late 1960s and early 1970s, he and Roberta would conduct a sustained examination of civil nuclear energy's military potential, as well as of the degree to which national and international approaches to nonproliferation were effectively constraining such potential. The Wohlstetters' analyses would help not only to reframe nuclear nonproliferation debates going forward, but also to change U.S. nuclear energy and export policy.

Alliance Commitments.

After France's February 1960 test of an atomic bomb, U.S. policymakers faced again the same sorts of worries that Britain's October 1952 test had raised: *How would the addition of a new nuclear-armed government affect relations within NATO, especially the cohesion among allies? Would other Western European governments move to acquire their independent nuclear arsenals?* Such worries led some in the outgoing Eisenhower Administration to propose that Washington establish with Western Europe a nuclear-armed Multilateral Force (MLF), an expansive "nuclear sharing" arrangement in which not just the United States, but all NATO members themselves would multilaterally command and control naval vessels manned by multinational crews and armed with American-supplied nuclear *Polaris* sea-launched ballistic missiles (SLBMs).[81] The hope was that the proposed MLF would satisfy NATO members who were agitating for greater roles in Western Europe's nuclear defense, and thereby arrest the impulse for more governments to get nuclear weapons. The proposed MLF, it was hoped, would also strengthen the sinews of the alliance.

Wohlstetter, however, opposed not only the acquisition of new nuclear arsenals by individual NATO governments, but also the Multilateral Force nuclear-sharing proposal itself. As an outside adviser to the Kennedy Administration, he would help to persuade key decisionmakers to reject both. In particular, he would serve as DoD's informal representative to the Committee on U.S. Political, Economic, and Military Policy in Europe, an advisory body chaired by former Secretary of State Dean Acheson, and charged by the Kennedy Administration to reexamine transatlantic relations between America and Western Europe. Albert would play a key role in helping Acheson to author draft policy guidance for the White House's National Security Council (NSC) that would aim to promote nuclear nonproliferation in Western Europe through increased political, economic, and military interdependence among the United States and its allies, as well as through improvements in NATO's conventional defense capabilities for resisting less-than-nuclear aggression.[82] This draft guidance would form the basis for the Kennedy NSC's National Security Action Memorandum (NSAM) 40.[83] Wohlstetter's article "Nuclear Sharing: NATO and the N+1 Problem" — published in the April 1961 issue of *Foreign Affairs* (at roughly the same time NSAM 40 was approved) — provides insights into the sort of arguments he made to the Acheson Committee.[84]

To justify the French *force de frappe*, proponents had made use of doctrines of automatic and minimum deterrence. For example, General Pierre Gallois, an adviser to French President Charles de Gaulle, had asserted in *Stratégie de l'âge nucléaire* (1960) that the destructiveness of nuclear weapons created uncertainty for potential aggressors that *necessarily* "increases the risk, counsels discretion, and consequently strengthens the strategy of dissuasion."[85] At the time, Gallois believed that the spread of nuclear weapons to additional states would have a pacifying effect: "As atomic armament grows more widespread and other nations besides America and Great Britain gain possession of it, either in their own right or under a 'double check,' the notion of dissuasion will also become more common, each nation practicing it according to its means."[86] Gallois added: "It will not be long before we may have to give up war altogether."[87]

In "Nuclear Sharing," however, Wohlstetter countered, first, that the independent nuclear arsenals of France — and of other allies that might follow the French example — would face, in times of acute crisis, severe difficulties in deterring safely and believably a Soviet preclusive nuclear first strike. Here, he was very much informed by his earlier RAND Corporation research on strategic nuclear forces, which had revealed how hard it could be for the United States to establish a survivable, controllable, and therefore credible second-strike capability in the face of changing dangers. In his view, the independent nuclear forces of American's allies would likely face an even harder time.

Moreover, Albert was deeply critical of how France's raw desire for greater prestige had played a decisive role in its acquisition of a nuclear-armed *force de frappe*. He believed that de Gaulle's decision would be a costly mistake with little real payoff. In "The Delicate Balance of Terror," he had argued that "[m]ere membership in the nuclear club might carry with it prestige, as the applicants and nominees expect, but it will be rather expensive and in time it will be clear that it does not necessarily confer any of the expected privileges enjoyed by the two charter members."[88] In "Nuclear Sharing," he elaborated this point:

> The burden of deterring a general war as distinct from limited wars is still likely to be on the United States and therefore, so far as our allies are concerned, on the alliance. . . . The problem of deterring a major power requires a continuing effort because the requirements for deterrence will change with the counter-measures taken by the major power. Therefore, the costs can never be computed with certainty; one can be sure only that the initiation fee is merely a down payment on the expense of membership in the nuclear club.[89]

Second, Wohlstetter worried about the effects that the spread of independent nuclear arsenals or the Multilateral Force would have on the Western alliance's cohesion and decisiveness. On the one hand, independent arsenals not only were undermining the U.S. nuclear "umbrella" guarantee in behalf of Europe's security, but also were unraveling the interdependence between the United States and some of its allies. (France would leave NATO in the mid-1960s.) On the other hand, the proposed MLF would multiply and dangerously complicate the allied decisionmaking process: *In the event of a nuclear attack against one or more NATO members, which governments would have the power to decide when to use the MLF's jointly-controlled nuclear weapons? Which governments, if any, would have the right to veto such use? Just the U.S.? All participating NATO members? What would the process for making decisions be? Simple majority? Consensus?* The answers to these critical questions were far from clear.

Moreover, Albert was concerned that both independent nuclear arsenals and the MLF would erode *from within* America's promise to protect Western Europe from nuclear and non-nuclear Soviet military aggression. He wrote:

> [O]ne of the most serious troubles with moves towards NATO or national nuclear strike forces is that they might weaken the American guarantee in the future. If either a national or a joint deterrent can really deter the Soviet Union, it is hard to justify an American commitment for this purpose. If European nuclear forces should present merely a façade of deterrence, they might convince the American Congress even if they do not convince the Russians.[90]

Third, and finally, Wohlstetter feared that the emergence of new independent nuclear arsenals or the Multilateral Force would set precedents encouraging ever more states, both allied and hostile, to acquire nuclear weapons. In his view, American policy needed to account not just for the "Nth" problem country — that is, the immediate would-be nuclear proliferator. It needed also to account for what he termed the "N+1 problem" — that is, the precedent for or against further proliferation which other governments would draw from U.S. policy toward the last prospective "Nth" nuclear power.

Thus Wohlstetter argued that if the United States strengthened its commitment to defend NATO allies from all forms of nuclear and non-nuclear military aggression, then this would serve to reassure allies of their security and interdependence with America, and promote nuclear nonproliferation within Western Europe. To that end, he urged Washington to retain sole launch authority over U.S. nuclear weapons; to emphasize an American "umbrella" strategy in behalf of Europe to deter Soviet preclusive nuclear attacks against both the United States and individual NATO allies; and to work with NATO members to develop more believable conventional military options to meet limited-nuclear and less-than-nuclear provocations. He explained:

> The alliance is viable, because neither our allies nor the United States in the long run can survive without it. This is the reason for deliberately entangling our forces and their dependents in the lot of Europe. We identify

our short-term fate with Europe's because we think our
long-term fate cannot be extricated from theirs. . . . In
fact, the principal implication of my argument is that the
much used notion of interdependence has to be taken
seriously.[91]

Following Wohlstetter's arguments, the United States would
work to reassure non-nuclear-armed NATO allies through
increased American security commitments to Europe, and to
convince them not to build independent nuclear strike forces.
Consequently, Albert's arguments against proliferation within the
Western alliance would earn considerable fame (and infamy) in
Europe. In a 1962 memorandum to the Department of State, Henry
Kissinger (who at the time was serving as an outside adviser to the
Kennedy Administration) would report the response of French
generals in Paris when he had questioned why they believed their
small and unprotected force would be capable of retaliating after
a Soviet first strike: "The generals replied that I seemed infected
by the pernicious Wohlstetter doctrine."[92]

Although Albert also had helped to convince the Kennedy
Administration to bury the Multilateral Force for a time, the
proposal would die a slow death. Indeed, the proposal would
resurface periodically during the Johnson Administration, and
at times severely encumber negotiations between the United
States and the USSR within the Eighteen-Nation Disarmament
Committee, the multilateral forum from which the *Treaty on the
Nonproliferation of Nuclear Weapons* (Nuclear Nonproliferation
Treaty or NPT) would later emerge.[93]

Civil Nuclear Energy's Military Potential.

During the late 1960s and early 1970s, as Albert split time
between his professorship at the University of Chicago (a position
which political scientist Hans Morgenthau had encouraged
and helped him to get[94]) and his work as an outside adviser to
government, he and Roberta embarked on research to understand
better civil nuclear energy's military potential and economic
viability.[95] In late 1975, the Wohlstetters—along with their
colleagues at Pan Heuristics, a consulting company that Albert
and Roberta had helped to form—would complete the study
Moving Toward Life in a Nuclear Armed Crowd? for the U.S. Arms
Control and Disarmament Agency (ACDA).[96]

Styled as a "primer for policy," *Moving Toward Life in a Nuclear Armed Crowd?* was written during a time when the U.S. nuclear industry and many within government were aggressively pushing for the domestic use and foreign export of spent-fuel reprocessing and other plutonium-related nuclear fuel-making technologies. Building on Albert's earlier work on nuclear deterrence and nuclear nonproliferation, their study argued that the prevailing interpretation of the *Treaty on the Nonproliferation of Nuclear Weapons* was dangerously permissive, enabling and even encouraging non-nuclear-weapon states to claim legitimacy as they acquired nuclear fuel-making technologies, accumulated fissile material (principally high enriched uranium and separated plutonium), and came within months — or even days — of building nuclear explosive devices. Moreover, although the NPT requires non-nuclear-weapon signatories to allow the International Atomic Energy Agency (IAEA) to safeguard and inspect their nuclear materials involved in peaceful nuclear energy, the Wohlstetter team worried that IAEA safeguards would not be broad enough, intrusive enough, and transparent enough to provide *timely warning* of a military diversion — that is, to sound a clear and unambiguous alarm in the case of a state's misuse of civil nuclear energy for nuclear weapons or unknown purposes sufficiently early so that other governments could respond effectively before that state acquired a nuclear weapon.

From this, Albert and company identified three main paths — besides the outright purchase, theft, or gift of weapons-usable nuclear material — by which would-be proliferators could obtain material for their first nuclear explosive device. First, nations outside of the Nuclear Nonproliferation Treaty could pursue, covertly or overtly, military programs to get weapons-usable nuclear material. (As Roberta would detail in *The Buddha Smiles: Absent-Minded Peaceful Aid and the Indian Bomb*, India did this by taking advantage of unwitting Canadian and American nuclear assistance.[97]) Second, NPT signatories could cheat the treaty by concealing from the IAEA weapons-related nuclear activities and then withdrawing from the treaty after illegitimately obtaining fissile material. Third, NPT signatories could declare all civil nuclear activities with military potential to the IAEA, accumulate weapons-usable nuclear material in plain sight and with an air of legitimacy, and then later withdraw from the NPT to build nuclear weapons.

This last path particularly disturbed the Wohlstetter team, for it raised the risks of what they dubbed a *Damoclean overhang* of non-nuclear-armed NPT states, for which:

> the critical time required to make a nuclear explosive has been diminishing and will continue to diminish without any necessary violation of clear, agreed rules — without any 'diversion' [of nuclear material declared for civil purposes] to secret military programs needed — and therefore without any prospect of being curbed by safeguards which have been elaborated for the purpose of verifying whether the mutually agreed rules have or have not been broken.[98]

In their view, the growth of such latent or virtual nuclear-weapon states posed *the* fundamental challenge to nuclear nonproliferation. "The real problem of proliferation," they wrote,

> is not that there are numerous countries "champing at the bit" to get nuclear weapons, but rather that all the non-nuclear countries, without making any conscious decision to build nuclear weapons, are drifting upwards to higher categories of competence. This means that any transient incentive, in the ebb and flow of world politics, which inclines a country to build nuclear weapons at some point in the future, will be just that much easier to act upon.[99]

That said, the Wohlstetters and their colleagues rejected fatalism regarding the spread of nuclear weapons. Such fatalism sometimes found expression in phrases like "nuclear proliferation is inevitable," a statement which mechanistically envisions the further spread of weapons-usable nuclear fuel-making and fissile materials, and appears to imply that little, if anything, can be done politically, economically, or otherwise even to slow, let alone reverse, the rate of this spread. "A fatalism which holds that nothing can be done today may be an unconscious cover for a desire to do nothing, to continue as before," they countered.[100] "While it is very likely that there will be *some* further spread, how much and how rapidly is not a matter of fate, but a subject for policy."[101]

Indeed, the Wohlstetter team stressed that the world's movement toward a nuclear-armed crowd is not inevitable. "Although there is a real chance that many countries will take the additional step and acquire nuclear weapons, it is not certain," they argued. "There exist contradictory forces which may substantially moderate the rate of acquisition of nuclear weapons."[102] The steps by which nations decide to acquire nuclear weapons are "more complex than the exponential physical and biological steps which have suggested the standard metaphors of proliferation," they continued. "They are not automatic, but depend on a complex set of political, military, and economic conditions."[103]

To balance better the aims of national security, nonproliferation, and energy security policies, they put forward a number of prudent alternatives for limiting nuclear proliferation and managing its risks when it did occur. In particular, their study urged the United States:

- to strengthen its security commitment to and interdependence with non-nuclear-armed allies, including those outside of the NATO alliance system, and assure them of their safety in the face of changing proliferation dangers so as to obviate any movement toward getting their own nuclear weapons;

- to interpret the NPT less permissively and more pragmatically, using the extent to which the IAEA can *effectively safeguard* a given type of nuclear material or civil nuclear activity as a key metric for determining whether or not Article IV of the Treaty's "inalienable right" to "nuclear energy for peaceful purposes … in conformity with Articles I and II" actually protects the material/activity in the first place;[104]

- to evaluate transparently the economic viability and military dangers of nuclear energy and nuclear fuel-making;

- to limit government energy subsidies and loan guarantees not only to the nuclear industry, but also to other energy industries, so as to enable all energy alternatives — nuclear, fossil fuels, natural gas, cleaner coal, and renewables — to compete on a neutral, market-driven playing field;

- to establish stringent domestic and international controls on the export and use of fissile material and fuel-making technologies; and

- to work both with the IAEA and with other governments to revise and adequately fund the Agency's safeguards system so that it could have a better chance of providing timely warning of a state's close approach to nuclear weapons capability.

With this and later studies,[105] Wohlstetter and colleagues worked with the Arms Control and Disarmament Agency's director Fred C. Iklé, the Nuclear Regulatory Commission's Victor Gilinsky, and others, to forge a consensus in Washington regarding the dubious economic rationales for, and the military dangers of, hitherto encouraged weapons-relevant nuclear activities — in particular, the use and export of plutonium-based fuel and fuel-making technologies.

Partial yet nontrivial changes to America's energy and export policies followed. In October 1976, President Ford decided to defer America's commercial use and export of plutonium-related fuel and fuel-making capabilities, and to call for an international moratorium on the export of plutonium reprocessing and uranium enrichment technologies.[106] (Ford's deferral decision effectively killed earlier proposals to export nuclear fuel-making technologies to the government of Shah Mohammad Reza Pahlavi in Iran.[107]) In April 1977, President Carter made Ford's deferral indefinite.[108] And in 1978, the Congress passed the *Nuclear Nonproliferation Act* (P.L. 95-242), which among other things established stricter guidelines for U.S nuclear cooperation with and nuclear exports to other governments.[109] As Atomic Industrial Forum president Carl Walske — who, as the nuclear industry's chief representative, had vehemently opposed such changes to U.S. policy — would grudgingly concede:

> The most significant single event [in the current call for change], in my view, was the appearance in December 1975 of Albert Wohlstetter's study for the U.S. Arms Control and Disarmament Agency entitled, *Moving Toward Life in a Nuclear Armed Crowd?*[110]

Significant revisions to international nonproliferation controls would not follow, however. Although nuclear proliferation would often take a backseat to the larger struggle between the West and the Soviet bloc, proliferation problems would come to dominate U.S. foreign policy after the Cold War's end, especially in the early years of the 21st century.

IV. ARMS RACE MYTHS VS. STRATEGIC COMPETITION'S REALITY

In the late 1960s, as Albert Wohlstetter expanded the scope of his nonproliferation research, he also became increasingly involved in heated policy debates over whether the United States should qualitatively improve the capabilities of its strategic nuclear forces.

Many proponents of arms control opposed qualitative improvements. They premised their arguments on automatic deterrence and minimum deterrence, doctrines holding that a government could easily and reliably deter a wide range of aggression against it merely by possessing a few technologically crude nuclear weapons which, in the event of an attack, would be used against an aggressor's cities and civilian populations. Moreover, arms controllers typically believed that worst-case analyses were leading the United States to pursue qualitative nuclear improvements that would go far beyond a mere "minimum deterrent" nuclear posture. In their view, such innovations were activating an action-reaction dynamic that was forcing the USSR — which many arms controllers believed wanted only a "minimum deterrent" — to engage in a nuclear arms race with the United States, one that was spiraling out of control, exacerbating bilateral tensions, and increasing the likelihood of war.

In contrast, Wohlstetter (along with other like-minded strategists) supported military-technological innovation. A longtime skeptic of automatic and minimum deterrence, he held that a government's mere possession of nuclear weapons did not guarantee a survivable, controllable, and credible deterrent against a nuclear first strike; rather, the requirements for a system of nuclear forces capable of providing such a deterrent were far more stringent. Moreover, he countered that an action-reaction dynamic was not inexorably governing strategic competition in general, nor Soviet nuclear-weapons development and procurement decisions in particular; and that qualitative improvements would not invariably lead to spiraling arms races and increased tension, let alone to a greater likelihood of war. Indeed, Albert believed that some technological innovations would tend to encourage stability.

These largely opposing views would clash publicly in 1969, when the Senate deliberated over whether to approve the initial deployment of the Safeguard antiballistic missile (ABM) defense system.[111] In the mid-1970s, the aftermath of the ABM debate would inspire Wohlstetter to study systematically the history of the U.S. and USSR's strategic competition in nuclear arms. That study's conclusions would lead him to criticize the arm controllers' claims of inevitable worst-casing, of immutable action-reaction dynamics, and of consequent spiraling arms races as muddled myths that were driving a Luddite approach to arms control. The Wohlstetters and their colleagues would articulate as a better alternative an approach to arms control derived from what they considered to be a more nuanced understanding of strategic competition.

The 1969 ABM Debate.

A revised version of the Johnson Administration's Sentinel ABM program, the Nixon Administration's Safeguard program envisioned using nuclear-tipped missile interceptors to defend U.S. land-based strategic forces as well as the nation's political and military leaders against attacks by Soviet nuclear-armed ICBMs and SLBMs. It also sought to protect population centers against either the accidental or unauthorized launch of an adversary's ICBM or SLBM, or a deliberate but numerically small missile attack by nascent nuclear-armed governments like the People's Republic of China. Safeguard was therefore called a "thin" ABM system because it was intended to defend mainly military and leadership targets and provide only limited protection to civilians—a sharp contrast to the more ambitious "thick" ABM systems that would try to defend most or all of America's civilian population from very large missile attacks. In the early 1960s, the Soviet Union had already begun developing the so-called A-35, a comparable "thin" ABM system using nuclear-tipped Galosh missile interceptors, with the aim of protecting political-military leaders in Moscow from attack.

In the Senate, prominent Safeguard opponents included Stuart Symington (D-MO) and Edward Kennedy (D-MA), as well as Senate Foreign Relations Committee chair J. William Fulbright (D-AR). Outside anti-ABM experts included Jerome Wiesner and George Rathjens, both of the Massachusetts Institute of Technology; former State Department legal adviser Abram Chayes of Harvard Law School; and Wolfgang Panofsky of the Stanford Linear Accelerator Center. Some of these experts would form advocacy groups to assist the anti-ABM senators.

Prominent Safeguard supporters included Senate Armed Services Committee chair John Stennis (D-MS) and Senate Subcommittee on National Security and International Operations chair Henry "Scoop" Jackson (D-WA), as well as the Pentagon's Director of Defense Research and Engineering, Johnny Foster. Outside pro-ABM experts included Albert Wohlstetter, now a professor at the University of Chicago; former Secretary of State Dean Acheson; and former Deputy Secretary of Defense Paul Nitze. These three would join together to form the Committee to Maintain a Prudent Defense Policy, a group that would seek to provide pro-ABM senators with analytic support. (Paul Wolfowitz and Peter Wilson, both of whom were at the time doctoral candidates at the University of Chicago, and Richard Perle, a graduate student at Princeton, would help to staff this group.)

During Senate hearings on the ABM, opponents raised three main objections. First, they asserted that anticipated Soviet strategic nuclear forces would not be capable of knocking out America's land-based second-strike capability, therefore obviating one of Safeguard's stated purposes. In particular, George Rathjens submitted to the Congress an analysis calculating that any attempts at a preclusive nuclear first strike by the Soviets would destroy, at the most, three-quarters of America's land-based *Minuteman* ICBMs.[112] Moreover, Jerome Wiesner charged that ABM proponents were using worst-case scenarios to strengthen their argument. "We always underestimate our own capabilities and overestimate those of the other fellow," Wiesner later claimed in an essay on the ABM.[113]

Second, they argued that qualitative improvements — not only active defense systems like the ABM, but also efforts to develop multiple independently targetable reentry vehicle (MIRV) systems and to improve the delivery accuracy of ICBMs and other nuclear-armed delivery vehicles — would necessarily spark spiraling and therefore destabilizing arms races. To halt what they saw as the action-reaction dynamic governing the strategic competition between the United States and USSR, they called for arms control agreements that would quantitatively cap American and Soviet strategic nuclear forces, and prohibit qualitative improvements to military nuclear technologies.

Third, anti-ABM experts claimed that the United States, at any rate, had cheaper and more effective ways than the ABM to protect its second-strike capability. For example, Rathjens held that a brute increase in the numbers of American ICBMs would be a better alternative than Safeguard. Senator Fulbright even suggested that a "launch-on-warning" nuclear posture would render the ABM unnecessary and provide what he described as "the greatest deterrence." The Senator explained:

> It would seem to me that assurance, the knowledge that these ICBMs, even part of them, would be released immediately without any fiddling around about it, even without asking the computer what to do, it would be the greatest deterrence in the world.[114]

Indeed, as ABM opponent Ralph Lapp would reiterate in *The New York Times*: "As Senator Fulbright pointed out, empty holes [of the ICBMs that would be launched on warning of an attack] may be our most powerful deterrent weapon."[115]

At an April 1969 hearing of the Senate Armed Services Committee, Wohlstetter issued a forceful rejoinder to these Safeguard opponents. First, he challenged claims that anticipated Soviet strategic nuclear forces would be wholly incapable of launching a nuclear first strike to preclude substantially an American second strike by U.S. land-based ICBMs. In particular, Albert criticized Rathjens' analysis, charging that he had found significant methodological errors and distortions of intelligence estimates when he had tried to replicate Rathjens' calculations.[116]

(After the hearing, Wohlstetter and Rathjens' increasingly acerbic exchanges would spill onto the opinion pages of *The New York Times* and other forums. In July 1971, a special committee appointed by the Operations Research Society of America's president would release a detailed peer review of the Wohlstetter-Rathjens debate. This peer review — the idea for which was adamantly opposed by Rathjens, Wiesner *et al.* — would come out in favor of Wohlstetter's analysis as well as of his criticisms of the anti-ABM opponents.[117] In particular, the peer review would conclude that the analyses of the anti-ABM experts "were often inappropriate, misleading, or factually in error."[118] The Society's findings would do little to quell Wohlstetter and Rathjens' increasingly bitter dispute, however.)

Second, Wohlstetter countered claims that Safeguard would necessarily start a spiraling race in nuclear arms or arms spending. "Indeed, despite the stereotype," he said of the U.S. spending on nuclear arms during the 1960s, "there has been no quantitative arms race in the strategic offense and defense budget, no 'ever-

39

accelerating increase,' nor, in fact, any long-term increase at all."[119] (As this essay details below, the Wohlstetters and their colleagues would conduct a study in the 1970s detailing this point.)

Third, Albert argued that Safeguard would be a cheaper and less destabilizing way than brute numerical increases of America's nuclear arsenal to protect land-based U.S. second-strike capability against Soviet strategic nuclear forces — forces which were likely to add more accurate ICBMs with modest MIRVed warhead capability. He elaborated:

> There is an important difference between making qualitative adjustments to technical change and expanding the number of vehicles or megatons or dollars spent. The difference has been ignored in a debate on ABM that seems at the same time impassioned and very abstract, quite removed from the concrete political, economic, and military realities of nuclear offense and defense and their actual history.[120]

He continued:

> For example, one alternative to protecting *Minuteman* [land-based ICBMs] is to buy more *Minutemen* without protection. But adding new vehicles is costly and more destabilizing than an active defense of these hard points, since it increases the capacity to strike first. A one-sided self-denial of new technology can lead simply to multiplying our missiles and budgets, or to a decrease in safety, or to both.[121]

Indeed, in the Base and Vulnerability Studies that Wohlstetter had led at the RAND Corporation during the 1950s, qualitative technological improvements had figured heavily in efforts to protect U.S. second-strike capability without having to resort to destabilizing quantitative increases in the nuclear arsenal. In particular, his research team had leveraged the breakthrough designs of a brilliant engineer named Paul Weidlinger to show that it was indeed possible to shelter and passively defend ICBMs and command-and-control facilities by building complex underground structures that were orders of magnitude more resistant to the blast effects of nuclear explosions than most engineers had ever thought possible.[122] In Albert's view, active defense programs like the ABM fell into a long line of useful and stabilizing qualitative improvements to the capabilities of U.S. strategic nuclear forces.

On a related note, Wohlstetter was deeply critical of statements by Senator Fulbright and others promoting "launch-on-warning" as an actual operational policy. Albert found "launch-on-warning" to be deeply dangerous and politically irresponsible:

> The revival today, by several distinguished senators and some able physicists opposing ABM, of the suggestion that, rather than defend ICBM's, we should launch them at Russian cities simply on the basis of radar represents a long step backward. If we were willing to do this, we would dispense with silos or *Poseidon* submarines or any other mode of protecting our missiles. And we would increase the nightmare possibility of nuclear war by mistake.[123]

The fierce debate between the pro- and anti-ABM crowds would continue into the summer of '69. In August, the Senate would end up approving the initial deployment of Safeguard, with Vice President Spiro Agnew casting the deciding vote to break the Senate's 50-to-50 split. However, 3 years later, at the end of the first round of the Strategic Arms Limitation Talks (SALT), the Nixon Administration would conclude with the Soviets an agreement severely limiting deployments of ballistic missile defense.[124] The ABM Treaty of May 1972 initially allowed the United States and USSR each to field two ABM sites, but was later modified in July 1974 to allow each country only one site.

The United States worked to finish its Safeguard site in North Dakota, but Congress voted to shut it down in late 1975.[125] In contrast, the Soviets would continue to field the A-35 ABM system near Moscow that they had first begun installing in the early 1960s. (Today, the Russian Federation now fields the A-135, an updated version of the A-35 that relies on missile interceptors tipped with non-nuclear explosives, while at the same time opposing U.S. and European Union efforts to build a "thin" ABM system to defend against ballistic missile threats from Iran and other rogue states.)

Strategic Nuclear Competition: Rivalry, But No Race.

As the 1960s gave way to the 1970s, controversies over the wisdom of incorporating technological innovations in U.S. strategic nuclear forces intensified. One key issue was whether the United States should try to improve the accuracy with which nuclear-armed delivery vehicles could be delivered to their intended military targets, even if the purpose was to decrease the possibility of harm to civilian noncombatants.

Echoing their earlier arguments against the ABM, advocates of arms control charged that such technological innovations would inevitably spark new arms races. They held that the United States, which was wrongly alarmed by worst-case analyses, was pursuing technological military innovations that, in turn, were activating the action-reaction dynamic that governs military competition, and inexorably leads to spiraling arms races characterized by increased defense spending, larger and more destructive nuclear arsenals, and a greater likelihood of war. Again, arms controllers called for new treaties that would limit qualitative technological improvements to strategic nuclear forces.

It was in this context that Albert and Roberta Wohlstetter, along with colleagues at their Pan Heuristics consulting company, set out to study the history of how the United States and USSR had competed in strategic nuclear arms. Their research aimed to determine the extent to which the American-Soviet strategic nuclear rivalry actually had conformed to the concept of a spiraling arms race.

The Wohlstetters and their colleagues began by observing that arms control advocates often had not carefully and precisely defined what they meant by the concept, *arms race*. They found that while *arms race* resonated with powerful emotional and pejorative connotations, the term typically had only vague, and sometimes confusing, denotations. In "Is There a Strategic Arms Race?" part one of his controversial two-part essay in *Foreign Policy* (1974), Albert expanded on this point:

> When we talk of "arms" are we referring to the total budget spent on strategic forces? The number of strategic vehicles or launchers? The number of weapons? The total explosive energy that could be released by all the strategic weapons? The aggregate destructive area of these weapons? Or are we concerned with qualitative change — that is, alterations in unit performance characteristics — the speed of an aircraft or missile, its accuracy, the blast resistance of its silo, the concealability of its launch point, the scale and sharpness of optical photos or other sensing devices, the controllability of a weapon

and its resistance to accidental or unauthorized use? When we talk of a "race" what do we imply about the rate at which the race is run, about the ostensible goal of the contest, about how the "race" is generated, about the nature of the interaction among strategic adversaries?[126]

With the concept of arms races, arms controllers had sought to lay bare the action-reaction dynamic that underlay the strategic nuclear competition between the United States and USSR. Albert, however, was deeply skeptical of the notion behind this dynamic. He wrote:

> The very phrase "action-reaction" has an aura of mechanical inevitability. Like Newton's Third Law: For Every Action There Is An Equal and Opposite Reaction. Only here, since the mechanism is explosive, it seems the law is supposed to read: For Every Action There Is An Opposing Greater-Than-Equal Reaction.[127]

Wohlstetter and company acknowledged the concept of spiraling arms races had correctly demonstrated that one government's military decisions may have a partial impact on the decisions of another. However, they believed that spiraling arms races grossly overstated the extent to which an action-reaction dynamic singly and inexorably drove how governments competed militarily. He explained:

> To build a national defense is to recognize serious differences, potentially incompatible goals of possible adversaries. Military forces then are at least partially competitive: What one side does, whether to defend itself or to initiate attack or to threaten attack or response, may be at the partial expense of another side. (Weapons are not by nature altogether friendly.) This means in turn that *some* connection is only to be expected between what one side does and the kind and probable size of a potential opponent's force.
>
> Arms race doctrines plainly want to say much more than these simple truths. They suggest that the competition results from exaggerated fears and estimates of opposing threats, and therefore is not merely, or even mainly,

instrumental to the partially opposed objectives of each side. The competition takes on an explosive life of its own that may frustrate the objectives of both. Explosive in two senses: (a) it leads to "accelerating" (or "exponential" or "spiraling" or "uncontrolled" or "unlimited" or "unbridled" or "infinite") increases in budgets and force sizes; (b) it leads inevitably to war, or at any rate makes war much more likely.[128]

Having attempted to make clearer the conceptual confusions surrounding spiraling arms racing, Wohlstetter and colleagues sought to see whether the history of the U.S.-USSR strategic nuclear competition up to that point in time actually had resembled such an arms race. Their study proceeded in three main parts.

First, they reviewed available American intelligence forecasts to evaluate the extent to which, in fact, the United States had regularly overestimated Soviet strategic nuclear deployments with "worst-case" analyses, as arms race proponents had frequently charged. To begin with, they noted that while U.S. intelligence had overestimated the rapidity with which the USSR would deploy long-range ICBMs in the late 1950s, it had underestimated, at the same time, the number of deployed Soviet intermediate range and medium range ballistic missile (IR/MRBMs) launchers. Moreover, after carefully examining annual intelligence predictions and estimates submitted by the Secretary of Defense to the Congress between 1962 to 1972, Wohlstetter and company arrived at surprising and counterintuitive findings. Within this population of before-the-fact intelligence predictions and after-the-fact observed estimates of Soviet nuclear deployments, the U.S. had *under*estimated repeatedly and systematically over a 10-year period how much the USSR would annually add to its strategic nuclear forces.[129]

Second, the Wohlstetter team looked carefully at the history of budgets for U.S. strategic nuclear forces to determine the rate at which spending on these forces had increased. Again, they arrived at startling and counterintuitive findings. U.S. annual spending on strategic offensive forces, in fact, had decreased from the mid-1950s until the early 1970s. In particular, spending in the 1950s was more than four times spending in 1976 in terms of constant dollars, and the budget for U.S. strategic nuclear forces had declined in an almost exponential manner since 1961.[130]

Third, Wohlstetter and colleagues examined whether qualitative improvements had actually led to more indiscriminate and destabilizing forces. They found that, even though both the United States and Soviets had pursued technological innovations during the 1960s, American trends pointed decidedly downward, not only for spending on U.S. strategic nuclear forces, but also for key qualitative indicators — for example, the stockpile's total explosive energy yield, the number of strategic offense and defense warheads, and the arsenal's equivalent megatonnage.[131]

Taken together, these findings sharply contradicted the sort of invariable enemy overestimation and worst-casing, the unchecked growth in strategic nuclear arms and spending, and the ever-increasing arsenal destructiveness that arms race theorists had claimed was occurring on the U.S. side. This led the Wohlstetter team to caution that arms racing did not provide an insightful model of how the U.S. and USSR actually had competed strategically in the nuclear age. Arms racing was, at best, an emotionally-charged but muddled and inaccurate metaphor.

What disturbed the Wohlstetters perhaps most of all, however, was how many arms control proponents had used (and were still using) the concept of arms racing to advocate for a U.S. nuclear posture based on doctrines of automatic deterrence, minimum deterrence, or the then-emerging doctrine of mutual assured destruction (MAD): that is, for a nuclear posture which, in essence, would assure, in the event of any attack by nuclear-armed adversaries, that the United States would escalate to massive nuclear retaliation against cities and civilian populations. The underlying hope of many such arms control proponents was that if the United States and USSR kept numerically small, technologically crude, and explosively indiscriminate nuclear arsenals aimed only at civilian noncombatants, the sheer horror of this posture would not only make all forms of nuclear war less probable, but also make movement toward total nuclear disarmament — and perhaps toward the dissolution of national sovereignty, world government, and perpetual peace — more likely.

In contrast, Albert and Roberta fiercely opposed such "countervalue" doctrines of nuclear deterrence that targeted cities and civilian noncombatants instead of military forces. Although they deeply doubted the likelihood and verifiability of total nuclear disarmament, they saw themselves as sharing the arms controllers' goal of making nuclear war less likely. But they maintained that the arms control establishment's preferred nuclear posture—a "minimum deterrent" posture which priviledged a sort of indiscriminate destructiveness against civilians that U.S. decisionmakers might not be willing to carry out, even in the most extreme of circumstances—was unstable, immoral, and unlikely to deter plausible forms of aggression. In his article, "Racing Forward? Or Ambling Back?" (1976), Albert elaborated on this point:

> Perverse current dogmas center most of all on an attempt to stop or slow technologies of discrimination and control. However, the remarkable improvements in accuracy and control in prospect will permit non-nuclear weapons to replace nuclear ones in a wide range of contingencies. Moreover, such improvements will permit new forms of mobility for strategic forces, making it easier for deterrent forces to survive. More important, they will also increase the range of choice to include more discriminate, less brutal, less suicidal responses to attack—responses that are more believable. And only a politically believable response will deter.[132]

In other words, the Wohlstetters held that credible deterrence need not rely on a choice between indiscriminate, massively destructive, and therefore implausible forms of nuclear retaliation, or no response at all. Rather, a principal aim of responsible nuclear-age strategic competition should be to increase the range of credible (and especially non-nuclear) responses available to decisionmakers, especially against limited-nuclear and less-than-nuclear aggression, and by so doing actually strengthen U.S. deterrence. Albert explained:

> Some technologies reduce the range of political choice; some increase it. If our concern about technology getting beyond political control is genuine rather than rhetorical, then we should actively encourage the development of techniques that increase the possibilities of political control. There will be a continuing need for the exercise of thought to make strategic forces secure and discriminatingly responsive to our aims, and to do this as economically as we can.[133]

Although the Wohlstetters were skeptical of many of the arms controllers' canonical dogmas, this did not mean that they saw arms control agreements as having no utility. Rather, they viewed such agreements as being useful within clear limits. "Agreements with adversaries can play a useful role, but they cannot replace national choice," Albert pointed out in "Racing Forward? Or Ambling Back?" But he added: "Neither the agreements nor the national choices are aided by the sort of hysteria implicit in theories of a strategic race always on the point of exploding."[134]

In the early 1980s, Albert and Roberta would draft an essay titled "On Arms Control: What We Should Look for in an Arms Agreement" which provides insight into what they viewed to be—and not to be—viable approaches for arms control agreements. (This previously unpublished essay is included in the present volume.) And in the mid-1980s, Albert and his Pan Heuristics colleague, Brian Chow, would coauthor a detailed technical proposal for an arms control agreement to establish self-defense zones in space.[135] (This volume also includes a condensed summary of this proposed agreement as published in the *Wall Street Journal*.)

The Study's Aftermath.

The Wohlstetters' study on the nature of the U.S.-USSR strategic competition exerted influence and elicited controversy in the mid-to-late 1970s. Most notably, their study would form part of the larger context for the so-called "Team B" experiment in competitive intelligence analysis. First suggested by members of the Ford Administration's Presidential Foreign Intelligence Advisory Board (PFIAB) in August 1975, this experiment was officially begun by Director of Central Intelligence (DCI) George H. W. Bush and President Ford's National Security Advisor Brent Scowcroft in June 1976.

A now-declassified December 1976 memorandum provides a summary of the "Team B" exercise from the White House's point of view.[136] The experiment would begin with two groups, an "A" team composed of members of the Intelligence Community that would prepare "the 1976 estimate of Soviet forces for intercontinental attack . . . in accordance with established Community practices," and a "B" team composed of "experts inside or outside of government" that would prepare an alternate assessment.[137] Both teams would be provided with the same body of intelligence information, and each would work to arrive at independent conclusions about three specific topics: namely,

47

"[1] Soviet ICBM accuracy, [2] Soviet low altitude air defense capability, and [3] Soviet strategic policy objectives."[138] Both teams would have access to each other's final products and be allowed to write comments on each other's assessments. Finally, the National Security Advisor, in consultation with the DCI and PFIAB, would review and critique the highly classified results.

In December 1976, Team B completed its Top Secret final report, *Intelligence Community Experiment in Competitive Analysis: Soviet Strategic Objectives: An Alternative View*.[139] Two months earlier, however, information about the exercise had already been leaked to the *Boston Globe* and *Washington Star*. The resulting news stories had set off a politicized firestorm within Washington that prevented dispassionate public discussion of the intelligence experiment's pluses and minuses. Although the highest levels of the Ford Administration had authorized the Team B exercise, critics insistently viewed this experiment in competitive intelligence analysis as nothing more than a direct assault on the Nixon and Ford Administrations' policy of *détente* with the Soviet Union.

Wohlstetter had declined an invitation to join Team B.[140] Nonetheless, a number of journalists and opinion-makers would mistakenly assert that he had worked on the intelligence experiment. In response to a January 4, 1977, op-ed by Joseph Kraft in the *Washington Post*, Albert wrote a letter to the editor to correct the record: "I had no part in the team that recently took an independent look at past and present national intelligence estimates. Nor have I seen their report."[141]

These controversies notwithstanding, Albert and Roberta's study on arms racing helped to reframe Washington's understanding of the U.S.-USSR strategic competition. Indeed, key government decisionmakers would publicly refute the "mirror-imaging" assessments of Soviet nuclear spending and procurement that had led some arms controllers to claim that while the USSR wanted only to field a "minimum deterrent," U.S. actions were activating an action-reaction dynamic that was forcing the Soviets to build more weapons and sparking an unnecessary nuclear arms race.[142] On that point, President Carter's Secretary of Defense Harold Brown would famously observe before a joint meeting of the Senate and House budget committees in 1979: "Soviet spending has shown no response to U.S. restraint—when we build, they build; when we cut, they build."[143]

V. TOWARDS DISCRIMINATE DETERRENCE

In 1962, Thomas Schelling and Morton Halperin published (with research assistance from Donald Brennan) *Strategy and Arms Control*, a book that famously identified what they took to be the three core objectives of all arms control agreements: to reduce "[1] the likelihood of war, [2] its scope and violence if it occurs, and [3] the political and economic costs of being prepared for it."[144] Albert and Roberta Wohlstetter saw themselves as sharing these very same goals, but they diverged from the conventional wisdom of most arms controllers in that they believed the United States (and the USSR) could often achieve these objectives more reliably and effectively by means of independent technological innovation.

In the 1970s and 1980s, Albert would work to demonstrate the stabilizing potential of technological innovation. In particular, he would join a small circle of analysts who identified for U.S. decisionmakers new alternatives for responding to — and thus for deterring — a wide spectrum of possible enemy aggression *without* resorting to the sort of massive nuclear retaliation against cities and civilian populations prescribed by MAD and other doctrines of automatic and minimum deterrence. By promoting the development of technologies and systems that stressed precision, control, and information, Wohlstetter would help the United States to reject MAD-inspired threats against noncombatants, and instead to field a new generation of more discriminate and less destructive non-nuclear capabilities that, in turn, would substantially reduce America's reliance on nuclear weapons.

Birth of MAD: A New Doctrine of Deterrence by Massive Retaliation.

The doctrine of mutual assured destruction first emerged in the late 1960s. Like earlier doctrines of automatic and minimum deterrence, MAD held that a government could deter stably and reliably a wide range of nuclear and non-nuclear aggression simply by threatening to escalate any conflict with massive retaliatory attacks targeting the aggressor's cities and populations. Because MAD required a government to field only a "minimum deterrent" second-strike capability consisting of technologically crude and indiscriminately destructive nuclear weapons aimed at civilians, the doctrine counseled against technological innovation. The reason was that when two governments adopted "minimum deterrent" nuclear postures, MAD doctrine holds that the necessary outcome will be a stable, mutual deterrence. Arms controllers—especially arms race theorists who sought to limit qualitative technological improvements to America's strategic nuclear forces—thus gravitated toward MAD.

In a curious twist, however, it was Donald Brennan, an arms controller at Herman Kahn's Hudson Institute, who first coined the phrase "mutual assured destruction" in the mid-to-late 1960s. Brennan meant MAD as a tongue-in-cheek way of mocking arms controllers who had advocated escalatory threats of massive nuclear retaliation as a means not only of deterring a wide range of nuclear and non-nuclear aggression, but also of achieving deep cuts in nuclear arms. Nonetheless, many such arms controllers ended up embracing the phrase and the concept.

MAD alludes to a concept that was birthed during Secretary of Defense Robert McNamara's tenure. Upon arriving at the Pentagon, Secretary McNamara and his team of analysts—a group which included Charles Hitch, William W. Kaufmann, Alain Enthoven and other alumni of the RAND Corporation—set out to rein in what they saw as the budgetary excesses of the military services. To constrain military spending on nuclear weapons and delivery vehicles, they had introduced by late 1963 the metric of *assured destruction* capability. (Although assured destruction capability is traditionally referred to by the acronym AD, this essay shall refer to it as ADCAP.) Enthoven, a protégé of Albert Wohlstetter who had served initially as McNamara's Deputy Assistant Secretary of Defense for Systems Analysis, explained the concept behind ADCAP in a 1977 essay:

> [T]he size and composition of our strategic retaliatory forces would be determined by the "assured destruction mission." Under this policy, we would buy amounts and kinds of forces sufficient to be sure, even under very pessimistic assumptions, that they could survive a deliberate Soviet attack [aimed directly against them] well enough to strike back and destroy 20 to 25 percent of their population.[145]

With the ADCAP metric, the McNamara Pentagon had sought to provide an argument for limiting the procurement of second-strike nuclear forces among the military services. However, ADCAP was not meant to imply that, in time of war, the United

States would actually target the Soviet civilian population with massive nuclear retaliation. In *How Much is Enough?* (1971), Enthoven and K. Wayne Smith underscored this point:

> The assured destruction test did not, of course, indicate *how* these forces would actually be used in a nuclear war. United States strategic offensive forces have been designed with the additional system characteristics— accuracy, endurance, and good command and control— needed to perform missions other than assured destruction, such as limited and controlled retaliation.[146]

Indeed, when President Kennedy entered into office in 1961, his Administration sought to break away from the Eisenhower Administration's "New Look," a declaratory nuclear policy that sought to deter a broad range of Soviet aggression (including even minor provocations in Western Europe) through threats to escalate any conflict to higher levels of violence with massive nuclear retaliation. Instead, the Kennedy Administration decided to stress a more proportional "flexible response" approach to defense, to that end renouncing "countervalue" or "countercity" targeting of civilians with nuclear weapons. During his 1962 State of the Union address, for instance, President Kennedy declared:

> ... our strength may be tested at many levels. We intend to have at all times the capacity to resist non-nuclear or limited attacks—as a complement to our nuclear capacity, not as a substitute. We have rejected any all-or-nothing posture which would leave no choice but inglorious retreat or unlimited retaliation.[147]

Moreover, at a commencement speech before the University of Michigan on July 9, 1962, Secretary McNamara delivered his famous "Ann Arbor speech" in which he made public the U.S. Government's explicit renunciation of countervalue targeting:

> The U.S. has come to the conclusion that to the extent feasible, basic military strategy in a possible general nuclear war should be approached in much the same way that more conventional military operations have been regarded in the past. That is to say, principal military objectives, in the event of a nuclear war stemming from a major attack on the Alliance, should be the destruction of military forces, not of his civilian population.[148]

51

In the mid-to-late 1960s, however, McNamara began issuing statements that consciously but less-than-accurately conflated assured destruction capability with U.S. targeting policy. Such conflation encouraged advocates of automatic/minimum deterrence to construe ADCAP to be not merely a metric to cap the size and composition of the U.S. nuclear arsenal, but also to constitute actual declaratory policy regarding whom—namely, civilian noncombatants—the United States would target nuclear forces. Arms controller Donald Brennan referred to holders of such views as "MADvocates," and Wohlstetter would join him in denouncing their preferred MAD-inspired threats of massive nuclear retaliation as disproportionate, out of control, and not credible. Moreover, Albert's own work on promoting technologies of precision, control, and information would later help to create non-MAD response options to a broad range of potential nuclear and non-nuclear military provocations.

The Long Range Research and Development Planning Program.[149]

In the early-to-mid 1970s, Wohlstetter participated in a highly classified DoD study that would help to clarify the potentially revolutionary implications that new technologies could have for war and peace in the nuclear age. This study would not only help the United States over time to reject doctrines of automatic and minimum deterrence and MAD-inspired threats of massive nuclear retaliation, but also lay the seeds for America's own "revolution in military affairs."

Initiated by Stephen J. Lukasik, director of the Pentagon's Advanced Research and Projects Agency (ARPA), and Fred Wikner, an informal representative of the Defense Nuclear Agency (DNA), this study was known as the Long Range Research and Development Planning Program or LRRDPP. Because Lukasik and Wikner had intended to keep the study initially low-key, they consciously chose a name for the study that would be clunky, and the acronym for which would not be easy to pronounce.

The LRRDPP sought to examine military applications for emerging technologies: for example, new methods of autonomous-terminal homing to deliver munitions more precisely, planned global positioning system satellites, and anticipated improvements in micro-computing and information-processing. The goal was to lay out how America's military services could leverage these technologies to provide U.S. decisionmakers with new alternatives—that is, choices that would not rely on indiscriminate massive nuclear retaliation—for responding to limited-nuclear and less-than-nuclear aggression.

To work on the study, Lukasik and Wikner brought together technologically innovative industrial contractors with Albert Wohlstetter, Joseph Braddock, Don Hicks, Dom Paolucci, Jack Rosengren, and other analysts who had strong knowledge of the subject of nuclear-age strategy and intimate familiarity with the military services. Lukasik—in the commentary that he contributes to the present edited volume—summarizes how the LRRDPP worked and some of Wohlstetter's contributions:

> The program was organized into three panels supported by four industrial contractors to contribute expertise and advanced concepts in ground, air, and naval warfare, conventional and nuclear munitions, reconnaissance, command and control, and system integration. Albert chaired the strategic alternatives panel, Don Hicks the advanced technology panel, and Jack Rosengren the munitions panel. Senior-level executives from OSD [Office of the Secretary of Defense] and the Services participated in panel sessions. The team members were selected for their in-depth knowledge as well as their skill in working as a multidisciplinary group, combining history, strategy, technology, military operations, and systems. In addition to Albert's broad skills, his ability to synthesize the essence of a problem and its solution and to communicate it to senior executives and political leaders was invaluable.

A number of factors motivated the LRRDPP. For one, both Wikner (who had served as General Creighton Abrams's scientific advisor at Military Assistance Command, Vietnam, and helped to push into the field very early forms of precision-guided munitions) and Lukasik believed that future technological innovations could change the nature of strategy and warfare—just as the advent of nuclear weapons had. For another, contemporaneous Soviet writings on the concept of revolutions in military affairs (RMAs)—in particular, Colonel General Nikolaĭ Andreevich Lomov's 1972 edited volume *Scientific-Technical Progress and the Revolution in Military Affairs (A Soviet View)*[150]—had encouraged high-level strategic thinkers within the U.S. Government to challenge conventional thinking on the transformative potential of military innovation.

In addition, the LRRDPP's summary report of February 1975 would cite two additional crucial developments. The strategic nuclear forces of both the United States and the USSR had apparently acquired survivable, controllable, and therefore credible second-strike capability; and in part because of this, the Executive Branch had called for a reassessment of the World War II-era "strategic bombing" metrics that were still being used to measure the effectiveness of nuclear and conventional strategic attacks—namely, "the number of targets destroyed" and "the percentage of the targets at risk that have been destroyed by the attack."[151]

Citing the potential feasibility of "weapons with near zero miss distance," the LRRDPP strategists proposed what Wohlstetter had termed the *dual-criterion* (or, alternatively, the *dual-criteria*) to replace the persisting World War II-era targeting metrics. Under the dual-criterion, the U.S. military would aim: "(1) to achieve the desired damage expectancy on an intended target or target system with high confidence, while simultaneously (2) not damaging particular regions or population areas, again with high confidence."[152] To meet the dual-criterion's much more stringent targeting requirements, the strategists identified promising weapon system concepts which, by capitalizing on foreseeable improvements in the accuracy of warhead delivery and other technologies, could accomplish their missions using extremely low-yield nuclear and even non-nuclear explosives. Such weapon-system concepts included remotely-piloted vehicles, precision-delivered ballistic missiles, deep-earth penetrators, shallow-earth penetrators, and advanced precision-guided munitions.[153] Improvements in a warhead's delivery accuracy can make greater reliance on non-nuclear explosives possible. When it comes to increasing the probability of destroying a hardened point target (e.g., a missile silo), a ten-fold improvement in the accuracy of a warhead's delivery vehicle is roughly equivalent to a thousand-fold increase in the warhead's indiscriminate explosive yield. This, in part, is why Wohlstetter saw revolutions in precision, control and information as potentially trumping the so-called nuclear revolution.

The LRRDPP strategists then used a number of possible conflict scenarios—contingencies like less-than-nuclear Soviet aggression against non-NATO nations peripheral to the USSR, and Soviet attacks against individual NATO member states—to think through the sort of strategic contexts and operations in which the United States might use these technologically-driven military capabilities to deter and, if necessary, halt such aggression. In particular, they identified two strategies for employing these capabilities:

- *Coercive response.* A "declaratory or implied policy which threatened attack against limited numbers of selected targets in the USSR," the objective of which "would be to help initiate negotiations or to support ongoing negotiations involved with halting the war"; and
- *Stemming the aggression.* A deterrent response policy which would use the military forces of "the threatened country, along with prompt assistance by U.S. forces, [for] actually halting the aggression."[154]

To be sure, the LRRDPP strategists were aware of the positive and potentially negative implications of more precise, less destructive military capabilities. The summary report acknowledges that such capabilities could raise potential "politico-military issues," such as crisis stability, military escalation and the nuclear threshold, and the possibility of heightened arms competition.[155] The strategists cautioned: "The capability to destroy military targets with little collateral damage could be of high utility under some circumstances; but always, there is the other side of the coin, that the very existence of the capability may make conflict more probable."[156]

Yet the LRRDPP strategists also saw the opportunities that military capabilities using non-nuclear technologies of discrimination, control, and information could afford by enabling America to rely substantially less on threats of massive nuclear retaliation, to respond decisively to provocations short of all-out nuclear war, and, by so doing, to deter such aggression all the more credibly.

Revolutions in Technologies of Precision, Control, and Information.

The LRRDPP study profoundly influenced Wohlstetter's thinking. Long opposed to automatic deterrence, minimum deterrence, and other doctrines of massive nuclear retaliation, he had sought as early as the late 1950s to identify for decisionmakers new alternatives to meet limited-nuclear and less-than-nuclear forms of aggression.[157] Indeed, in a conference speech titled

Strength, Interest, and New Technologies delivered in September 1967 and sponsored by the Institute for Strategic Studies (now the International Institute for Strategic Studies), he had displayed remarkable prescience regarding the transformative potential of emerging technologies, suggesting that revolutions in precision, control, and information could very well trump the nuclear revolution and the fatalism that had flowed from it.[158] America's technological means had not yet caught up with Wohlstetter's strategic ends, however.[159] The Long Range Research and Development Planning Program would help to change that.

The education and expertise gained from Lukasik and Wikner's LRRDPP study would considerably inform Wohlstetter's own heated criticisms of MAD-inspired nuclear deterrence and targeting doctrines.[160] The LRRDPP experience would also shape the later work of President Reagan's Commission on Integrated Long-Term Strategy, a high-level panel that outgoing Undersecretary of Defense for Policy Fred C. Iklé and Wohlstetter chaired in the mid-to-late 1980s. (The other members of the Commission were Anne L. Armstrong, Zbigniew Brzezinski, William P. Clark, W. Graham Claytor, Jr., Andrew J. Goodpaster, James L. Holloway III, Samuel P. Huntington, Henry A. Kissinger, Joshua Lederberg, Bernard A. Schriever, and John W. Vessey.) With its final report, the Commission offered a new doctrine of *discriminate deterrence* to meet the future security environment's changing dangers, with the aim of increasing American and allied ability "to bring force to bear effectively, with discrimination and in time, to thwart any of a wide range of plausible aggressions against their major common interest — and *in that way to deter* such aggression."[161]

In the decades following the LRRDPP, the United States developed and acquired, though in stops and starts, many of the technologically-driven military capabilities that the study's strategists had identified.[162] In turn, these non-nuclear technologies of precision, control, and information — the development of which many arms controllers had fiercely opposed in the 1970s and 1980s on the grounds that they would spark spiraling arms races — would substantially reduce America's reliance on indiscriminately destructive nuclear weapons, and thereby help to make all-out nuclear war less likely.

VI. LIMITING AND MANAGING NEW RISKS

In the late 1980s, especially after the fall of the Berlin Wall, the dramatic Soviet decline was leading some to foresee a pacific post-Cold War world. However, Albert Wohlstetter, now a Medal of Freedom-winning strategist[163] in his mid-70s, was already thinking about the next set of strategic challenges. "Does [the Cold War's potential end] mean there are no latent long term dangers demanding prudence?" he asked himself in the conclusion of a June 1989 outline for his memoir. "[T]he political and economic futures of the heavily armed Communist states and of the increasingly lethally armed Third World countries are, to say the least, rather cloudy," he observed apprehensively, adding:

> Even if, implausibly, the Second and Third Worlds change rapidly to the market economies of the First World, nice though this would be, we are likely to discover once again that, contrary to Cobden and the Manchester School, trade and investment — good things though they are — are not all that pacifying. Trading partners have found a good many reasons to go to war. We haven't seen the end of fanaticism, mortal national and racial rivalries, and expansionist ambitions. It is conceivable that all the variously sized lions and lambs will lie down together, that there will be the kind of moral revolution that many hoped for at the end of World War II when they thought it, in any case, the only alternative to nuclear destruction. But, as Jacob Viner [a University of Chicago economist] wrote at the time, "It is a long, long time between moral revolutions." We should not count on it.[164]

In the years following, Wohlstetter's apprehensions would prove well-founded as the end of the Cold War — a global competitive order that his work in strategy had helped in some ways to sustain and in other ways to end — gave way to growing international disorder.

Seventeen months before the USSR's December 1991 dissolution ended the Cold War, Saddam Hussein's Ba'athist Iraqi military invaded Kuwait — producing a Persian Gulf conflict contingency that Wohlstetter and his colleagues had presciently warned of as early as 1980.[165] In the early 1990s, Slobodan Milosevic's pan-Serbian ambitions ignited long-suppressed ethnic rivalries, and then genocide, in the Balkans. In the mid-1990s, deep racial rivalries would also lead to genocide in Rwanda. And in the late 1990s, after Osama bin Laden had issued a *fatwa* urging attacks on American citizens, his Al Qaeda organization carried out deadly bombings against U.S. embassies in Kenya and

Tanzania — in retrospect, harbingers of the violent extremism and suicidal fanaticism that were yet to come.

Moreover, the United States would discover just how lethally armed the former Third World and the Communist holdouts were becoming. In the aftermath of the Gulf War, the American-led coalition uncovered a Ba'athist Iraqi nuclear program far closer to producing a nuclear weapon than either the Western intelligence services or the International Atomic Energy Agency (IAEA) had ever anticipated. And at mid-decade, after North Korea had refused to grant the IAEA access to suspected nuclear weapons-relevant facilities, Washington began long negotiations with Pyongyang for an "Agreed Framework," a "grand bargain" that sought to prevent the North Koreans from acquiring fissile material for a nuclear explosive device.

Wohlstetter remained intellectually active during the post-Cold War period until his death in 1997. As a member of the Defense Policy Board, he supported U.S. efforts to liberate Kuwait from Ba'athist Iraq during the Gulf War. After the war, he lambasted Presidents George H. W. Bush and Bill Clinton for what he saw as their failures to respond meaningfully to Ba'athist aggression against Iraqi Shi'a and Kurdish populations, as well as to Saddam's other violations of the United Nations Security Council resolutions that had established the stringent conditions for the Gulf War's cessation.[166]

In the mid-1990s, Albert, now an octogenarian, focused much of his attention on the Balkans, publishing numerous op-eds (especially on the opinion page of the *Wall Street Journal*, edited by his long-time friend and colleague, Bob Bartley) and articles that sharply rebuked Western leaders for their indifference and indecisiveness towards Slobodan Milosevic's pan-Serbian expansionism, and agitated for greater Western involvement on behalf of Bosnian Muslims and other victims of Milosevic's aggression.[167] Of note, he and former British Prime Minister Margaret Thatcher coauthored "What the West Must Do in Bosnia," an open letter to President Clinton published in the *Wall Street Journal* in September 1993, and signed by more than 100 people from across the globe and the political spectrum — people like Morton Abramowitz, Zbigniew Brzezinski, Osama El Baz, Henry Louis Gates, Jr., Zuhair Humadi, Marshal Freeman Harris, Pierre Hassner, Zalmay Khalilzad, Prince Sadruddin Aga Khan, Teddy Kollek, Laith Kubba, Czeslaw Milosz, Paul Nitze, Richard Perle, Karl Popper, Eugene Rostow, Henry Rowen, George Shultz, George Soros, Susan Sontag, Elie Wiesel, Leon Wieseltier,

58

and Paul Wolfowitz.[168] (The text of this letter is reprinted in this volume.)

And in response to what he considered to be the shortcomings of the Agreed Framework between the United States and North Korea, Wohlstetter called on Washington to admit that the global spread of nuclear fuel-making is significantly driving the problem of proliferation and to face "squarely the challenge of persuading our major allies, not to say our potential adversaries [such as Pyongyang], to abandon the sale or use of plutonium fuel" and other weapons-usable nuclear materials.[169]

*****

Although Albert Wohlstetter died in Los Angeles on January 13, 1997, and Roberta, in New York City on January 6, 2007, their work in strategy remains all too relevant and timely.

In the early years of the 21st century, the United States and its allies are now struggling with many of the problems of nuclear-age policy that the Wohlstetters themselves had anticipated and grappled with throughout their long careers in strategy—problems like the dangers posed by the spread of nuclear bombs, fuel-making technologies, and fissile materials to new states and nonstate actors; the difficulties of enforcing ambiguously interpreted international law and nuclear nonproliferation rules; the uncertain economics surrounding energy security and alternatives for power production; and the proper role of deterrence and military force in an increasingly lethally-armed and disorderly world. Their writings on nuclear-age strategy and policy thus can help decisionmakers and policy analysts (as well as those who aspire to these positions) to clarify their thinking on these most urgent matters.

When Albert spoke of his approach to the analysis and design of strategic policy, he often liked to describe it as "coming down at right angles to an orthodoxy."[170] Indeed, Wohlstetter's approach did not fit well the conventional dichotomy of hawk and dove. He was a strategist who had originally established his reputation for his path-breaking work on nuclear deterrence, a traditionally hawkish concept; yet he had added to that reputation not only by supporting nuclear nonproliferation, an often dovish concern, but also by consistently urging the U.S. Government to block the spread of nuclear weapons, weapons-relevant nuclear technologies, and weapons-usable nuclear material to America's allies and adversaries alike. He was a strategist who, like the doves, was horrified by the brute destructiveness of nuclear weapons and nuclear war, yet hawkishly saw U.S. innovation in military technologies of precision, control, and information as a way of markedly limiting the potential of weapons for indiscriminate killing, thereby strengthening deterrence and making nuclear war less likely in the first place.

Indeed, when President Reagan awarded Medals of Freedom to the Wohlstetters in November 1985, he summarized their work in the following way:

> Albert has always argued that in the nuclear age technological advances can, if properly understood and applied, make things better; but his point, and Roberta's, has been a deeper one than that. He has shown us that we have to create choices and, then, exercise them. The Wohlstetters have created choices for our society where others saw none. They've taught us that there is an escape from fatalism.[171]

In the 21st century, the writings of Albert and Roberta Wohlstetter on strategy can challenge today's and tomorrow's decisionmakers to "escape from fatalism," and come "down at right angles" to stagnant orthodoxies; to move beyond the sort of partisan dichotomies that have come to dominate and even cloud thinking on limiting and managing nuclear risks and to search for, discover, and even invent new policy choices that help America to avoid the nuclear age's worst dangers, and in Albert's own words, "slowly and piecemeal, [to] build a more orderly and safer world."[172]

To these ends, this edited volume provides readers not only with the present essay on the Wohlstetters' key historical contributions, but also with many of Albert and Roberta's most enduring and relevant writings, some of which have never before been published. This volume's six chapters correlate directly with the six themes set forth in the present introductory essay — namely, (1) Analysis and Design of Strategic Policy, (2) Nuclear Deterrence, (3) Nuclear Proliferation, (4) Arms Race Myths vs. Strategic Competition's Reality, (5) Towards Discriminate Deterrence, and (6) Limiting and Managing New Risks. (However, the editors of this volume have remained mindful of James Digby and J. J. Martin's wise caveat that, given Albert and Roberta's "continuity of concepts across many diverse types of military problems," it therefore "may be inconsistent with the nature of [the Wohlstetters'] work to summarize their contributions in terms of discrete categories."[173]) Moreover, each chapter begins with a short commentary by a former colleague or student of Albert and Roberta—Henry S. Rowen, Alain Enthoven, Henry Sokolski, Richard Perle, Stephen J. Lukasik, and Andrew W. Marshall, respectively—before offering the selected Wohlstetter writings themselves.

To conclude, at least two larger themes emerge from a close reading and careful appreciation of the Wohlstetters' work in strategy. First, as a palliative to the fatalism that sometimes besets the nuclear age and gives rise to the extreme responses of the Utopian or the Dystopian, we must learn to tolerate the fact of uncertainty. Indeed, in the conclusion to her magisterial 1962 study of one of America's worst military disasters, Roberta soberly observed, "If the study of Pearl Harbor has anything to offer for the future, it is this: We have to accept the fact of uncertainty and learn to live with it. No magic, in code or otherwise, will provide certainty. Our plans must work without it."[174]

Second, as the United States struggles not only to limit and manage the nuclear risks and changing dangers it faces in this new century, but also to "slowly and piecemeal, build a more orderly and safer world," we must weigh and consider carefully Albert's sober words on the need for facing up to hard choices and sustaining intelligent effort as expressed in *No Highway to High Purpose* (1960):

> The great issues of war and peace deserve to be treated candidly and objectively, without wishfulness or hysteria. . . . [They] are tall orders. They cannot be filled quickly, or finally, or by means of some semiautomatic gadget, or in one heroic burst of energy. Nor will the answer come to us in a dream. . . . Our problem is more like staying thin after thirty—and training for some long steep, rocky climbs. If, as we are told, America is no longer a youth, we may yet hope to exploit the advantages of maturity: strength, endurance, judgment, responsibility, freedom from the extremes of optimism and pessimism—and steadiness of purpose.[175]

ENDNOTES - Zarate

1. Arthur Herzog, *The War-Peace Establishment*, New York: Harper & Row, 1965, p. 66.

2. Albert Wohlstetter, "Technology, Prediction, and Disorder," *Vanderbilt Law Review*, Vol. 17, No. 1, December 1963, pp. 11-12.

3. Quoted in John J. Fialka's profile of Albert Wohlstetter, "Veteran 'Lone Ranger' Strategist Packs Firepower with Cold-Eyed Outlook on Soviet Nuclear Policy," *Wall Street Journal*, July 15, 1987, p. 56.

4. Michael Howard, "Brodie, Wohlstetter, and American Nuclear Strategy," *Survival*, Vol. 34, No. 2, Summer 1992, p. 113. The military historian Sir Michael Howard (b. 1922) should not be confused with the British conservative politician Michael Howard (b. 1941).

5. Colin S. Gray, "The Holistic Strategist," *Global Affairs*, Vol. 7, No. 1, Winter 1992, pp. 174-175, 172-173.

6. Although Albert did not serve in an official capacity in the U.S. Government, he served in many instances as an adviser. For example, he served in 1958 as deputy science adviser of the U.S. delegation to the Surprise Attack Conference in Geneva, Switzerland; during the Cuban Missile Crisis, he and Roberta served on the Quarantine Committee; in 1961 as the Department of Defense's informal representative to the Kennedy Administration's Committee on U.S. Political, Economic and Military Policy in Europe; from 1970 onward as a member of the Chief of Naval Operations Executive Panel; from 1985 to 1992 as a member of the Presidential Foreign Intelligence Advisory Board; and from 1986 to 1992 as a member of the Defense Policy Board. In addition, Albert and Roberta helped to organize numerous seminars and forums within which senior policymakers, military planners, and strategists from the United States, Europe, and East Asia could meet and exchange views. These included: the California Seminar on Arms Control and Foreign Policy (also known as California Seminar on International Security and Foreign Policy), formed with assistance from James F. Digby; the European-American Workshop (later the European American Institute for Security Research or EAI), which they formed and perpetuated with the help of Digby, Uwe Nerlich of West Germany, Pierre Hassner of France, and many others; the Security Conference on Asia and Pacific (SECAP), formed with the assistance of Kiichi

Saeki of Japan; and the New Alternatives Workshop, which built upon themes first examined by the Long Range Research and Development Planning Program (LRRDPP), which section V of this introduction discusses.

7. Richard Rosecrance, "Albert Wohlstetter," in John Baylis and John Garnett, eds., *Makers of Nuclear Strategy*, London, UK: Pinter Publishers, 1991, p. 57.

8. Some authors and journalists have erroneously claimed that when Ahmed Chalabi attended the University of Chicago, he had studied under Albert Wohlstetter in the political science department. According to University records, Chalabi, who had pursued a doctorate in mathematics at the University of Chicago, never took any courses from Wohlstetter. See "Letters: Department of Corrections," *The University of Chicago Magazine*, Vol. 95, No. 6, August 2003, available from *magazine.uchicago.edu/0308/issue/letters.shtml*; and "Letters: Department of Corrections," *The University of Chicago Magazine*, Vol. 95, No. 6, August 2003, available from *magazine.uchicago.edu/0310/issue/letters-dept.shtml*. Indeed, Wohlstetter and Chalabi apparently did not first meet until the early 1990s, around the time of the Persian Gulf War, long after both had left the University of Chicago.

9. Roberta Wohlstetter, *Pearl Harbor: Warning and Decision*, Stanford, CA: Stanford University Press, 1962, p. 387.

10. *Ibid.*, pp. 387-388.

11. *Ibid.*, p. 392.

12. For example, see "This is the Tempest Long Foretold, editorial, *The Daily Telegraph*, September 12, 2001, p. 19.

13. See *The 9/11 Commission Report,* final report of the National Commission on Terrorist Attacks Upon the United States, Washington, DC: U.S. Government Printing Office, July 22, 2004, esp. p. 339, available from *www.gpoaccess.gov/911/index.html*. See also James Johnson and Robert Zarate, "Slow Pearl Harbors: Some Foreign Policy Disasters are a Long Time in the Making," *The Weekly Standard*, Vol. 11, No. 14, December 19, 2005, pp. 14-15, available from *www.weeklystandard.com/Content/Public/Articles/000/000/006/476fjivj.asp*; and Zarate, "First Lady of

Intelligence: Roberta Wohlstetter, 1912-2007," *The Weekly Standard,* Vol. 12, No. 18, January 22, 2007, pp. 16-17, available from *www. weeklystandard.com/Content/Protected/Articles/000/000/013/171kcloi. asp.*

14. Roberta Wohlstetter, *The Buddha Smiles: Absent-Minded Peaceful Aid and the Indian Bomb,* PH-78-04-370-23, final report prepared for the U.S. Energy Research and Development Administration in partial fulfillment of E (49-1)-3747, Los Angeles, CA: Pan Heuristics, November 15, 1976, revised November 1977, available from *www.npec-web.org/essays/19771100-RW-BuddhaSmiles-Revised.pdf,* courtesy Joan Wohlstetter. See also Roberta Wohlstetter, *India's Nuclear Energy Program and U.S. Policies Today,* final report prepared for the Defense Nuclear Agency, in partial fulfillment of DNA-79-C-0067, Marina del Rey, CA: Pan Heuristics, revised February 1980, courtesy Gregory S. Jones.

15. *Agreement on the Canada-India Colombo Plan Atomic Reactor Project,* New Delhi, India, April 28, 1956, available from *www.nci. org/06nci/04/Canada-India%20CIRUS%20agreement.htm;* and *U.S.-India CIRUS Agreement,* March 16, 1956, available from *www.nci. org/06nci/04/US-India%20CIRUS%20agreement.htm.*

16. It is worth observing that, prior to 2002 or 2003, no major book on neoconservativism had identified Albert Wohlstetter as a "neoconservative": e.g., Peter Steinfels, *Neoconservatives: The Men Who Are Changing America's Politics,* New York: Simon and Schuster, 1979; John Ehrman, *The Rise of Neoconservativism: Intellectuals and Foreign Affairs, 1945-1994,* New Haven, CT: Yale University Press, 1995; Mark Gerson, *The Neoconservative Vision: From the Cold War to the Culture Wars,* Lanham, MD: Madison Books, 1996; and Shadia Drury, *Leo Strauss and the American Right,* New York: St. Martin's Press, 1997. Nor had any major essay or news article on neoconservativism identified Wohlstetter as a "neoconservative": e.g., Joshua Epstein, "The New Conservatives: Intellectuals in Retreat," *Dissent,* Vol. 20, No. 2, Spring 1973, pp. 151-162; Michael Harrington, "The Welfare State and Its Neoconservative Critics," *Dissent,* Vol. 20, No. 4, Fall 1973, pp. 435-454; Bernard Weinraub, "Reagan's Brain Trust: Font of Varied Ideas," *The New York Times,* December 1, 1980; Bernard Weinraub, "Neoconservatives Today, They Explain All Their Yesterdays,"

The New York Times, December 28, 1980; David Shribman, "Neoconservatives and Reagan: Uneasy Coalition," *The New York Times*, September 28, 1981; David Shribman, "Group Goes From Exile to Influence," *The New York Times*, November 23, 1981; and Brent Staples, "Undemocratic Vistas: The Sinister Vogue of Leo Strauss," *The New York Times*, November 28, 1994.

17. Howard, "Brodie, Wohlstetter, and American Nuclear Strategy," p. 108.

18. See C. L. Sulzberger, "A New Kind of Policy Adviser," *The New York Times*, April 25, 1955, p. 22; "Valuable Batch of Brains: An Odd Little Company Called RAND Plays Big Role in U.S. Defense," *Life*, Vol. 46, No. 19, May 11, 1959, pp. 101-107; and Sol Stern, "Who Thinks in a Think Tank," *The New York Times*, April 16, 1967, pp. 28, 110-111, 117-120.

19. Quoted by Bruce Smith, *The RAND Corporation: Case Study of a Non-Profit Research Organization*, Cambridge, MA: Harvard University Press, 1966, p. 47.

20. For more on the RAND Corporation's history, see Smith, *The RAND Corporation*, and Andrew May, *Strategic Thought at RAND*, unpublished draft manuscript, 2003. Dr. May's manuscript is based on his 1998 dissertation.

21. In this discussion of Albert and Roberta Wohlstetter's lives before RAND, I draw from research and interviews that Chicago-based independent historian James Johnson and I had conducted, as well as from the following transcripts of interviews with Albert Wohlstetter: James F. Digby and Joan Goldhamer, *An Interview with Albert Wohlstetter: The Development of Strategic Thinking at RAND, 1948-1963: A Mathematical Logician's View*, unpublished, Los Angeles, CA, July 5, 1985, courtesy James F. Digby; Martin Collins and Joseph Tatarewicz, *Smithsonian Interview with Prof. Albert Wohlstetter*, unpublished, Los Angeles, CA, July 29, 1987, final edit, September 9, 1991, courtesy Joan Wohlstetter; and Collins, Tatarewicz, and Gustave Shubert, *RAND Corporation History: Session Four* [for the Smithsonian Videohistory Program]; *Interview with Bruno Augenstein, Edward Barlow, Burton Klein, Robert Specht, Hans Speier, and Albert Wohlstetter*, Santa Monica, CA, January 27, 1989; and Allen Greb and Digby, *An Interview with Albert Wohlstetter: The Strategist Reflects on the Past and Future*

of Nuclear Policies, unpublished, August 2, 1990, revised July 10, 1991, in the Wohlstetter Papers, Interviews, Box 95, Folders 5-7. In addition, Stephen Prowse's 1991 biographical sketches of Albert and Roberta helped with establishing the correct chronology and dates. See Prowse, "Albert Wohlstetter: A Biographical Sketch" and "Roberta Wohlstetter: A Biographical Sketch," in Andrew W. Marshall, J. J. Martin, and Henry S. Rowen, eds., *On Not Confusing Ourselves: Essays on National Security Strategy in Honor of Albert and Roberta Wohlstetter*, Boulder, CO: Westview Press, 1991, pp. 317-320 and 321-322.

22. Albert's three older siblings were William (1902-1967), Helene (1906-1974), and Charles (1910-1995). Charles became a highly successful businessman, establishing in 1961 Continental Telephone (Contel), an independent telephone company that would be acquired by GTE in the 1990s. See John Holusha, "Charles Wohlstetter, 85, Founder of Contel, Dies," obituaries, *The New York Times*, May 25, 1995, p. B16. Helene would end up working at Contel, but would be tragically murdered in the mid-1970s during a disgruntled former Contel employee's shooting rampage. See "Obituaries," *The New York Times*, August 5, 1974, p. 26.

23. See Digby and Goldhamer, *An Interview with Albert Wohlstetter: The Development of Strategic Thinking at RAND, 1948-1963: A Mathematical Logician's View*, p. 3. Albert often cited the importance of two Peircean writings, among others: Charles S. Peirce, "The Fixation of Belief," *Popular Science Monthly*, Vol. 12, November 1877, pp. 1-15; and "How to Make Our Ideas Clear," *Popular Science Monthly*, Vol. 12, January 1878, pp. 286-302. These writings are available in Nathan Houser and Christian J. W. Kloesel, eds., *The Essential Peirce: Selected Philosophical Writings, Vol. 1: 1867-1893*, Bloomington, IN: Indiana University Press, 1992, pp. 109-123, 124-141.

24. See "City College R.O.T.C. Names 81 Officers," *The New York Times*, May 7, 1933, p. 22.

25. Roberta Mary Morgan Wohlstetter was born in Duluth, MN, on August 22, 1912. She earned a Bachelor of Arts degree from Vassar College in 1933, a Master of Arts degree in psychology from Columbia University in 1936, and a Master of Art's degree

in literature from Radcliffe College in 1937. After marrying Albert Wohlstetter in 1939, she taught at Barnard College in the early 1940s and at Howard University in the mid-1940s before joining the RAND Corporation as a consultant in 1947.

26. Willard Van Orman Quine mentions the Wohlstetters several times in his memoir. See Quine, *The Time of My Life: An Autobiography*, Cambridge, MA: MIT Press, 2000, pp. 147, 184, 198, 217.

27. For more on the history of General Panel's "Packaged House," as well as on the roles that Albert Wohlstetter and his brother Charles played in the company, see Gilbert Herbert, *The Dream of the Factory-Made House: Walter Gropius and Konrad Wachsmann*, Cambridge, MA: MIT Press, 1984.

28. In the following discussion of Albert Wohlstetter's methodology, I benefited greatly from many hours of discussion on this subject with former businessman and Chicago-based independent historian James Johnson. As an undergraduate at the University of Chicago in the late 1960s and early 1970s, Mr. Johnson had studied under Wohlstetter and worked for him on projects relating to the use of the method of scientific investigation versus the appeal to scientific authority in debates over public policy.

29. See Albert Wohlstetter, *Theory and Opposed-System Design*, D(L)-16001-1, Santa Monica, CA: RAND Corporation, August 1967, revised January 1968, available from *www.rand.org/about/ history/wohlstetter/DL16001.1/DL16001.1.html*. This was later published in slightly revised form as Wohlstetter, "Theory and Opposed-System Design," *Journal of Conflict Resolution*, Vol. 12, No. 3, September 1968, pp. 302-331. See also Wohlstetter, *No Highway to High Purpose*, P-2084-RC, Santa Monica, CA: RAND Corporation, June 1960, available from *www.rand.org/about/history/ wohlstetter/P2084/P2084.html*, later published in slightly abridged form as "A Purpose Hammered Out of Reflection and Choice," *Life*, Vol. 48, No. 24, June 20, 1960, pp. 115, 126-134; "Analysis and Design of Conflict Systems," in E. S. Quade, ed., *Analysis for Military Decisions*, Chicago, IL: Rand McNally & Co., 1964, pp. 103-148, available from *www.rand.org/pubs/reports/2007/R387.pdf*; and "National Decisions Concerning Defense," in J. Banbury and

J. Maitland, eds., *Proceedings of the Second International Conference on Operations Research* (*in Aix-En-Provence, France, 1960*), London, UK: English Universities Press, February 1961, pp. 517-522.

30. Wohlstetter, "Theory and Opposed-System Design," p. 304.

31. *Ibid.*

32. Wohlstetter, *No Highway to High Purpose.*

33. Wohlstetter, "Theory and Opposed-Systems Design," p. 312.

34. *Ibid.*, p. 303.

35. *Ibid.*

36. *Ibid.*, p. 309.

37. *Ibid.*, p. 316.

38. On this topic, see Albert Wohlstetter, "Scientists, Seers, and Strategy," *Foreign Affairs*, Vol. 41, No. 3, April 1963, pp. 466-478. See also Wohlstetter, *Scientists, Seers, and Strategy*, unpublished book-length manuscript, circa 1963, courtesy Joan Wohlstetter.

39. Wohlstetter, "Theory and Opposed-Systems Design," pp. 303-304.

40. See Albert Wohlstetter, "The Delicate Balance of Terror," *Foreign Affairs*, Vol. 37, No. 2, January 1959, pp. 211-234. For the extended version of the essay, see Wohlstetter, *The Delicate Balance of Terror*, unabridged version, P-1472, Santa Monica, CA: RAND Corporation, November 6, 1958, revised December 1958, available from *www.rand.org/about/history/wohlstetter/P1472/P1472.html*.

41. Marc Trachtenberg, *History and Strategy*, Princeton, NJ: Princeton University Press, 1991, p. 20.

42. As Wohlstetter recalled decades later:

[W]hat attracted me to [the problem] was that there

were forces working in opposing directions. There were some forces that would make you want to be up close, so that you could have close access to targets, be able to act quickly, get in many sorties, use shorter range weapons and so on. And on the other hand, there were some things that made you want to be [further] back because if you were close to him, why, there was just a good chance he would also be close to you, so he would be getting in a lot of whacks. . . . But then you could see that this meant you would need a larger aircraft or you would have to refuel a lot of times, and so on. And it struck me that in the *abstract* there was no way of resolving this. . . . [T]here was no way of knowing how these opposing considerations would work out in the net effect without looking at the geography.

See Digby and Goldhamer, *An Interview with Albert Wohlstetter: The Development of Strategic Thinking at RAND, 1948-1963: A Mathematical Logician's View*, pp. 35-36.

43. For a case study of the Base Study, see E. S. Quade, "The Selection and Use of Strategic Air Bases: A Case History," in Quade, ed., *Analysis for Military Decisions*, pp. 24-64. See also Memorandum from Colonel D. O. Monteith (USAF) to Colonel Watson, *A Brief Resume of RAND Report R-266, "Selection and Use of Strategic Air Bases*, Chairman of the Joint Chiefs of Staff (CJCS) reference no. 381, April 8, 1955, TOP SECRET, declassified on November 2, 1978, DDRS No. CK3100452915.

44. Here I wish to acknowledge Fred Hoffman and Harry Rowen, both longtime Wohlstetter colleagues, who had stressed to me many times the importance of understanding the politico-military historical context in which the Base Study had begun, and the need to explain the Base and Vulnerability Studies in a way that avoided historical anachronism.

45. See Quade, ed., *Analysis for Military Decisions*, p. 24. Using a "back-of-the-envelope" calculation, I crudely estimate that $3.5 billion in FY 1952 dollars is approximately equivalent to as much as $28.5 billion to $30.2 billion in FY 2007 dollars.

46. Albert J. Wohlstetter, Fred S. Hoffman, Robert J. Lutz, and Henry S. Rowen, *The Selection of Strategic Air Bases*, R-244-S,

special staff report, Santa Monica, CA: RAND Corporation, March 1, 1953, TOP SECRET, declassified on July 1, 1963, available from *www.albertwohlstetter.com/writings/19530301-AW-EtAl-R244S.pdf.*

47. Albert J. Wohlstetter, Fred S. Hoffman, Henry S. Rowen, and Robert J. Lutz, *The Selection and Use of Strategic Air Bases*, R-266, final report, Santa Monica, CA: RAND Corporation, April 1954, TOP SECRET, declassified circa 1961, available from *www. rand.org/pubs/reports/R0266/.*

48. From mid-to-late 1953, the Ad Hoc Committee of the U.S. Air Force's Air Staff evaluated the Base Study, and then presented its favorable evaluation to the USAF's Air Force Council, which then debated the Study in Wohlstetter's presence. In late 1953, the Air Force Council decided to endorse key elements of the Base Study's *preferred system*, and this decision was approved by Air Force Chief of Staff General Thomas D. White and Secretary of the Air Force Harold Talbott. See Quade, ed., *Analysis for Military Decisions*, pp. 62-63; Collins and Tatarewicz, *Smithsonian Interview with Prof. Albert Wohlstetter*, pp. 15-17; and Fred Kaplan, *The Wizards of Armageddon*, New York: Simon and Schuster, 1983, pp. 97-110—esp. 105-106, as well as related endnotes on p. 402, one of which cites General Robert Burns, "Decision on AFC 22/4b: Vulnerability of the Strategic Striking Complex," November 2, 1953, in Library of Congress, *Nathan Twining Papers*, Box 103, Air Force Council Chief Staff Decisions, Vol. I, Tab 22/4b.

49. See Albert J. Wohlstetter and Fred S. Hoffman, *Defending a Strategic Force After 1960: With Notes on the Need by Both Sides for Accurate Bomb Delivery, Particularly for the Big Bombs*, D-2270, Santa Monica, CA: RAND Corporation, February 1, 1954, available from *www.albertwohlstetter.com/writings/19540201-AW-FH-D2270.pdf* An implication of this finding, however, was that even modest improvements to warhead delivery accuracies could enable huge reductions in explosive yield.

50. Bernard Brodie "Implications for Military Policy," in Brodie, ed., *The Absolute Weapons*, New York, NY: Harcourt, Brace & Co., 1946, pp. 99, 88.

51. For example, see Albert Wohlstetter, "'Lesser' Excluded Cases," opinion, *The New York Times*, February 14, 1979, p. A25.

52. Albert J. Wohlstetter, Fred S. Hoffman, and Henry S. Rowen, *Protecting U.S. Power to Strike Back in the 1950s and 1960s*, R-290, staff report, Santa Monica, CA: RAND Corporation, September 1, 1956, TOP SECRET, declassified circa 1960s, available from *www.albertwohlstetter.com/writings/19560901-AW-EtAl-R290.pdf*

53. *Ibid.*, pp. 40-41, emphasis added.

54. *Ibid.*, p. 6.

55. *Ibid.*, pp. 2-3.

56. *Ibid.*, p. 5.

57. In R-290, the Wohlstetter team wrote: "We would like this course of Soviet action [i.e., a preclusive nuclear first strike] to be a worse alternative to almost any other they might contemplate — including, for example, the acceptance of defeat in some limited or peripheral war." *Ibid.*, p. 41.

58. For the full description of R-290's recommendations, see Wohlstetter *et al.*, *Protecting U.S. Power to Strike Back in the 1950s and 1960s*, pp. 43-94.

59. Memorandum from Colonel Jack W. Hayes (USAF), Joint Strategic Plans Group, to the Chairman of the Joint Chiefs of Staff, *NSC Briefing on the Vulnerability of SAC*, JCS 2250, July 31, 1956, TOP SECRET, declassified on November 16, 1978, DDRS No. CK3100434873; and Memorandum, *Program Objectives Related to SAC Operational Capability*, AFOPD-PL-SS/Col Sutterlin/mfm/5503, November 17, 1956, TOP SECRET, declassified on January 30, 1980, DNSA No. 01323.

60. For more on the events that led to SAC's adoption of Fail-Safe in Spring 1958, see Albert Wohlstetter, "SAC Test 1957 of Alert Bomber Response — Only Fail-Unsafe," April 29, 1985, Wohlstetter Papers, Notes, Box 102, Folder 6, TAB H. See also Memorandum CSAFM-72-58 from the USAF Chief of Staff to the Joint Chiefs of Staff, *Launching of the Strategic Air Command Alert Force*, JCS 1899/398, March 10, 1958, TOP SECRET, declassified circa 1981, DDRS No. CK3100437133; "Launching of SAC Alert Forces ('Fail Safe')," in Memorandum, *Discussion at the 361st Meeting of the National Security Council, Thursday, April 3, 1958*,

April 4, 1958, TOP SECRET, declassified on July 18, 1989, DDRS No. CK3100278691, pp. 7-8; Note by the Secretariat of the Joint Chiefs of Staff on *Decision on Report by the Joint Strategic Plans Committee (In Collaboration with the Joint Intelligence Committee) on 'Positive Control' Presentation to NSC, JCS 1899/402*, with report attached, May 13, 1958, TOP SECRET, declassified on July 18, 1979, DDRS No. CK3100169750; and Benjamin Welles, "U.S. Bombers in Spain Poised to Take to Air in 15 Minutes: Specially Trained Crews Kept on Alert for Orders from Main Omaha Base—Each Jet Has Assigned Target," *The New York Times*, September 6, 1958, p. 2.

61. See Wohlstetter, Hoffman, and Rowen, *Protecting U.S. Power to Strike Back in the 1950s and 1960s*, pp. 76-77.

62. See Fred C. Iklé, Gerald J. Aronson, and Albert Madansky, *On the Risk of an Accidental or Unauthorized Nuclear Detonation*, RM-2251, Santa Monica, CA: RAND Corporation, October 15, 1958, esp. pp. 100-101 and 154, available from *www.rand.org/pubs/research_memoranda/RM2251/*.

63. Background on Baran's work on survivable and distributed communication networks is available from *rand.org/about/history/baran.html*. See also Virginia Campbell, "How RAND Invented the Postwar World," *Invention & Technology*, Summer 2004, esp. pp. 57-58, available from *www.rand.org/about/history/Rand.IT.Summer04.pdf*.

64. Citations in this section refer not to the abridged *Foreign Affairs* version of the article, but rather to the extended version: Wohlstetter, *The Delicate Balance of Terror*, unabridged.

65. To Wohlstetter, a prototypical *automatic deterrer* was Nobel prize-winning physicist Patrick Maynard Stuart Blackett, who had written: "If it is in fact true, as most current opinion holds, that strategic air power has abolished global war, then an urgent problem for the West is to assess how little effort must be put into it to keep global war abolished." See Blackett, *Atomic Weapons and East-West Relations*, Cambridge, UK: Cambridge University Press, 1956, p. 32. Quoted by Wohlstetter, *The Delicate Balance of Terror*, unabridged.

66. In Wohlstetter's view, General Pierre Gallois of France, who had claimed that "a small number of bombs and a small number of carriers suffice for a threatened power to protect itself against atomic destruction," represented well the school of *minimum deterrence*. See Gallois, "A French General Analyzes Nuclear-Age Strategy," *Réalités*, November 1958, p. 71. Quoted by Wohlstetter, *The Delicate Balance of Terror*, unabridged. See also *1970 Without Arms Control*, Special Committee Report, Washington, DC: National Planning Association, 1958, and P. H. Backus, "Finite Deterrence, Controlled Retaliation," *U.S. Naval Institute Proceedings*, Vol. 84, No. 3, March, 1959, both of which advocate for an essentially "minimum deterrent" approach.

67. Wohlstetter, *The Delicate Balance of Terror*, unabridged.

68. *Ibid.*

69. During a private, high-level dinner at the Council on Foreign Relations in New York City in 1960, Wohlstetter elaborated further on the distinction between automatic deterrers and minimum deterrers:

> Attitudes vary towards the problem of avoiding deliberate attack and towards the problem of avoiding accidental war. This variation, too, qualifies the apparently general agreement on the importance of reducing the likelihood of central war. Those who have held the theory of the automatic balance of terror worry about the accident problem, but not the problem of deliberate attack. Holders of the theory of minimum deterrence think it important to deter deliberate attack, but underestimate its difficulty, because they neglect the accident problem. . . .

Quoted by William C. Staley, Jr., Rapporteur, *Study Group Reports: Strategy and Foreign Policy*, First Meeting, unpublished, Council on Foreign Relations, New York, NY, March 16, 1960, p. 14. Meeting attendees included: James A. Perkins, Wohlstetter, Staley, Frank Altschul, Robert Amory, Jr., Major General C. H. Bonesteel, III (Army), Melvin Conant, Russell H. Fifield, George S. Franklin, Jr., Caryl P. Haskins, William W. Kaufmann, Major General Glen Martin, Oskar Morgenstern, Philip E. Mosely, Garrison Norton, Philip W. Quigg, Dean Rusk, Joseph E. Slater, and Henry M. Wriston.

70. Wohlstetter, *The Delicate Balance of Terror*, unabridged.

71. In a May 1959 internal RAND report, Albert Wohlstetter and Henry Rowen wrote that it is important to view efforts to deter a preclusive nuclear first strike through the "broad" concept of a system of strategic nuclear forces composed of many elements:

> [Deterrence] will require the ability to maintain under conditions of attack a functioning system of elements, including besides the mobile or hardened delivery vehicles with the capacity to reach and penetrate the active and passive enemy defenses, the preservation of centers of responsible decision and control, and a network permitting a protected flow of information to and from these decision centers. The Air Force, which pioneered the weapons systems idea, needs to emphasize a still broader systems concept. With the widespread multiplication and dispersal of weapons, positive signals are essential to avoid war by accident or miscalculation. To deter a deliberate attack, the system of control must be able to survive the attack which we aim to deter. . . . [We need] a broadened systems concept emphasizing the ability to keep a network of elements alive and in communication for the duration of the enemy's and our own attacks — for days, not hours or minutes.

See Wohlstetter and Rowen, "Objectives of the United States Military Posture," RM-2373, Santa Monica, CA: RAND Corporation, May 1, 1959, available from *www.rand.org/about/history/wohlstetter/RM2373/RM2373.html*.

72. For example, see Albert and Roberta Wohlstetter, *Notes on the Cuban Crisis: On the Importance of Overseas Bases in the 1960's, Offense-Defense Semantics, Keeping Open Possible Aid to Cuban Resistance*, D(L)-10647-ISA, Santa Monica, CA: RAND Corporation, October 28, 1962, available from *www.rand.org/about/history/wohlstetter/DL10647/DL10647.html*; *Studies for a Post-Communist Cuba*, D(L)-11060-ISA, Santa Monica, CA: RAND Corporation, February 25, 1963, available from *www.rand.org/about/history/wohlstetter/DL11060/DL11060.html*; *On Dealing with Castro's Cuba, Part I*, D-17906-ISA, Santa Monica, CA: RAND Corporation, January 16, 1965, available from *www.rand.org/about/*

history/wohlstetter/D17906/D17906.html; and *Controlling the Risks in Cuba*, Adelphi Papers No. 17, London, UK: Institute for Strategic Studies, April 1965. See also Roberta Wohlstetter, "Cuba and Pearl Harbor: Hindsight and Foresight," *Foreign Affairs*, Vol. 43, No. 4, July 1965, pp. 691-707.

73. P.M.S. Blackett, *Studies of War: Nuclear and Conventional*, Edinburgh, UK: Oliver and Boyd, Ltd., 1962, pp. 131, 136.

74. See Robert J. C. Butow, *Tojo and the Coming of the War*, Princeton, NJ: Princeton University Press, 1961, p. 255. Quoted by Rosecrance, "Albert Wohlstetter," p. 61.

75. See O'Dowd Gallagher, *Action in the East*, Garden City, NY: Doubleday, 1942, p. 94. Quoted by Wohlstetter, *The Delicate Balance of Terror*, unabridged, fn. 6.

76. Elsewhere in "The Delicate Balance of Terror," Wohlstetter again elaborates:

> The most important thing to say perhaps is that it doesn't make much sense to talk about whether general war is likely or not unless we specify a good deal else about the range of circumstances in which the choice of surprise attack might present itself. . . . Deterrence is a matter of comparative risks. How much the Soviets will risk in surprise attack will depend *in part* on the vulnerability of our future posture. . . . [T]he risks of not striking might at some juncture appear very great to the Soviets, involving, for example, disastrous defeat in peripheral war, loss of key satellites with danger of revolt spreading — possibly to Russia itself — or fear of an attack by ourselves. Then, striking first, by surprise, would be the sensible choice for them, and from their point of view the smaller risk.

Wohlstetter, *The Delicate Balance of Terror* (unabridged), emphasis added.

77. Quoted by Staley, *Study Group Reports: Strategy and Foreign Policy*, p. 16, emphasis added.

78. Roberta Wohlstetter, *Pearl Harbor: Warning and Decision*, Stanford, CA: Stanford University Press, 1962, pp. 400-401.

79. Wohlstetter, *The Delicate Balance of Terror* (unabridged).

80. Albert Wohlstetter, "Some General Comments on Senator [John F.] Kennedy's National Security Speeches," circa 1960, Wohlstetter Papers, Writings, Box 148, Folder 10.

81. See *The North Atlantic Nations: Tasks for the 1960s*, a report to the Secretary of State, August 1, 1960, SECRET, declassified on January 9, 1986, DDRS No. CK3100227683. Known as "the Bowie Report," the study was authored by Robert A. Bowie, who served as Director of the Department of State's Policy Planning Staff from 1953 to 1957.

82. See *A Review of North Atlantic Problems for the Future*, the Committee on U.S. Political, Economic and Military Policy in Europe's Policy Guidance to the National Security Council, March 1961, SECRET, declassified on December 30, 1996, DNSA No. NH01131, esp. pp. 7-11.

83. See *Comparison of "A Review of North Atlantic Problems for the Future" with Existing National Security Council Policy*, National Security Council memorandum, March 28, 1961, SECRET, declassified on May 20, 1994, DDRS No. CK3100055224; and *Policy Directive Regarding NATO and the Atlantic Nations*, National Security [Action] Memorandum No. 40, April 24, 1961, CONFIDENTIAL, declassified on May 4, 1977, DNSA No. BC02034.

84. Albert Wohlstetter, "Nuclear Sharing: NATO and the N+1 Country," *Foreign Affairs*, Vol. 39, No. 3, April 1961, pp. 355-387

85. Pierre Gallois, *The Balance of Terror: Strategy for the Nuclear Age*, trans. Richard Howard, Boston, MA: Houghton Mifflin, 1961, p. 130. Originally published as Gallois, *Stratégie de l'âge Nucléaire*, Paris, France: Calmann-Lévy, 1960.

86. *Ibid.*, p. 109.

87. *Ibid.*, p. 57. By the 1980s, however, General Gallois would reverse some of his minimum deterrence views. See Gallois and John Train, "When a Nuclear Strike is Thinkable," *Wall Street Journal*, March 22, 1984, p. 30.

88. Wohlstetter, *The Delicate Balance of Terror*.

89. Wohlstetter, "Nuclear Sharing: NATO and the N+1 Country," p. 363.

90. *Ibid.*, p. 385.

91. *Ibid.*, pp. 385-386.

92. See Henry A. Kissinger, *Memorandum of Conversation in Paris on February 5, 1962*, Department of State, February 9, 1962, CONFIDENTIAL, declassified on March 2, 1997, DDRS No. CK3100108824, p. 2.

93. For one version of the U.S. Government's history of these negotiations, see U.S. Arms Control and Disarmament Agency, *International Negotiations on the Treaty on the Nonproliferation of Nuclear Weapons*, Washington, DC: U.S. Government Printing Office, 1969. In 1967, as the negotiations for what would eventually become the NPT were coming to an end, Richard T. Cooper of the *Chicago Sun-Times* profiled Wohlstetter's views on proliferation. Wrote Cooper: "A carefully drafted treaty banning the spread of nuclear weapons can be moderately useful for maintaining world order, but no treaty can by itself eliminate the problem, Albert Wohlstetter, an expert on nuclear weapons problems, cautioned." See Cooper, "A Treaty—How Useful?" *Chicago Sun-Times*, February 19, 1967, pp. 1-2.

94. Hans J. Morgenthau was a noted "realist" scholar of international relations, and professor of political science at the University of Chicago. Private correspondence detailing Morgenthau's role in helping Albert Wohlstetter to get an appointment to the University of Chicago is available in the Morgenthau Papers at the Library of Congress.

95. For example, see Albert Wohlstetter, *Strength, Interest, and New Technologies*, opening address before *The Implications of Military Technology in the 1970s*, the Institute for Strategic Studies' ninth annual conference, Elsinore, Denmark, September 28 to October 1, 1967, D(L)-16624-PR, Santa Monica, CA: RAND Corporation, January 24, 1968, available from *www.rand.org/about/*

history/wohlstetter/DL16624/DL16624.html. The address was also published as Wohlstetter, *Strength, Interest and New Technologies*, in *The Implications of Military Technology in the 1970s*, Adelphi Papers No. 46, London, UK: Institute for Strategic Studies, March 1968. See also Wohlstetter, "Perspective on Nuclear Energy," Speech Before the University of Chicago's Twenty-Fifth Anniversary Observance of the First Controlled Self-Sustaining Nuclear Reaction, December 2, 1967, in *Bulletin of the Atomic Scientists*, Vol. 24, No. 4, April 1968, pp. 2-5.

96. See Albert Wohlstetter *et al.*, *Moving Toward Life in a Nuclear Armed Crowd?* ACDA Report No. PH-76-04-389-14, December 4, 1975, revised April 22, 1976. This 1975 ACDA report was published in revised form 4 years later as *Swords from Plowshares: The Military Potential of Civilian Nuclear Energy*, Chicago, IL: University of Chicago Press, 1979. His coauthors were Thomas A. Brown, Gregory S. Jones, David McGarvey, Henry S. Rowen, Vince Taylor, and Roberta Wohlstetter.

97. Roberta Wohlstetter examined how American policies unwittingly assisted Indian efforts to build a nuclear explosive in *The Buddha Smiles: Absent-Minded Peaceful Aid and the Indian Bomb*. For an abridged version of this report, see Roberta Wohlstetter, "The Buddha Smiles: U.S. Peaceful Aid and the Indian Bomb," in Albert Wohlstetter, Victor Gilinsky *et al.*, eds., *Nuclear Policies: Fuel without the Bomb*, Cambridge, MA: Ballinger Publishing, 1979, pp. 57-72.

98. Wohlstetter *et al.*, *Swords from Plowshares*, pp. 24-25.

99. *Ibid*, p. 45.

100. *Ibid*, p. 15.

101. *Ibid*, p. 14, emphasis added.

102. *Ibid.*, p. 127.

103. *Ibid.*, p. 14.

104. See Albert and Roberta Wohlstetter, Gregory S. Jones, and Henry S. Rowen, *Towards a New Consensus on Nuclear Technology*, Vol. 1 of 2, report prepared for the Arms Control Disarmament

Agency in fulfillment of AC7NC106, PH-78-04-832-33, Los Angeles, CA: Pan Heuristics, July 6, 1979, available from *www.npec-web.org/ Essays/19790706-TowardsANewConsensus-Vol01.pdf*; and Arthur Steiner, "Article IV and the 'Straightforward Bargain,'" PAN Paper 78-832-08, in Wohlstetter *et al.*, *Towards a New Consensus on Nuclear Technology*, Vol. 2: *Supporting Papers*, ACDA Report No. PH-78-04-832-33, Marina del Rey, CA: Pan Heuristics, July 6, 1979, available from *www.npec-web.org/Essays/19790706-Steiner-ArticleIV-StraightforwardBargain.pdf*. For a more recent analysis of the relationship between IAEA safeguarding effectiveness and legal interpretations of the Nuclear Nonproliferation Treaty, see Robert Zarate, "The NPT, IAEA Safeguards, and Peaceful Nuclear Energy: An 'Inalienable Right,' But Precisely To What?" in Henry Sokolski, ed., *Falling Behind: International Scrutiny of the Peaceful Atom*, Carlisle, PA: Strategic Studies Institute, 2008, pp. 221-290, available from *www.strategicstudiesinstitute.army.mil/pubs/display. cfm?PubID=841*.

105. For example, see Albert Wohlstetter, "Spreading the Bomb Without Quite Breaking the Rules," *Foreign Policy*, No. 25, Winter 1976-1977, pp. 88-96, 145-179; Wohlstetter, Thomas Brown, Gregory Jones, David McGarvey, Henry S. Rowen, Vincent Taylor, and Roberta Wohlstetter, "The Military Potential of Civilian Nuclear Energy," *Minerva*, Vol. 15, Nos. 3-4, Autumn-Winter 1977, pp. 387-538; Albert Wohlstetter, Victor Gilinsky, Robert Gillette, and Roberta Wohlstetter, eds., *Nuclear Policies: Fuel without the Bomb*, Cambridge, MA: Ballinger, 1978; Wohlstetter *et al.*, *Nuclear Alternatives and Proliferation Risks*, DOE EN-77-C-01-2643, Los Angeles, CA: Pan Heuristics, July 27, 1978; Wohlstetter *et al.*, *Towards a New Consensus on Nuclear Technology*; and Wohlstetter and Henry S. Rowen, *U.S. Non-Proliferation Strategy Reformulated*, Report Prepared for the National Security Council and DOE, August 29, 1979.

106. President Gerald Ford, "Statement of the President on Nuclear Policy," Office of the White House Press Secretary, October 28, 1976.

107. See Henry Sokolski, "The *Washington Post* Bombs Nuclear History," *The Weekly Standard*, March 28, 2005, available from *www. weeklystandard.com/Content/Public/Articles/000/000/005/417gusvl. asp*.

108. President Jimmy Carter, "Statement of the President on Nuclear Power Policy," Office of the White House Press Secretary, April 7, 1977.

109. U.S. Congress, *The Nuclear Non-Proliferation Act of 1978*, Public Law 95-242.

110. Carl Walske, "Nuclear Power and Nuclear Proliferation," Speech Delivered to the *International Conference on Nuclear Power and the Public – A European-American Dialogue*, Geneva, Switzerland, September 27, 1977.

111. For key hearings on the ABM before the Senate Committee on Armed Services held on April 22 and 23, 1969, see *Authorization for Military Procurement, Research and Development, Fiscal Year 1970*, and *Reserve Strength*, hearings before the U.S. Senate's Committee on Armed Services, 1st session, part 2 of 2, Washington, DC: U.S. Government Printing Office, 1969, pp. 1109-1456a.

112. As Dr. George Rathjens stated before the Senate Armed Services Committee:

> Yet even if the Soviet SS-9 missile force were to grow as rapidly as the Defense Department's most worrisome projections, even if the Soviet Union were to develop and employ MIRV's with those missiles and even if they achieved accuracies as good as we apparently expect with our MIRV forces (according to figures released in late 1967 by former Deputy Secretary of Defense [Paul] Nitze), a quarter of our MINUTEMAN force could be expected to survive a Soviet preemptive SS-9 attack. That quarter would alone be more than enough to inflict unacceptable damage on the U.S.S.R.

See Rathjens, "Statement before Senate Committee on Armed Services," excerpt April 23, 1968, in *Programming-Budgeting: Defense Analysis: Two Examples*, reprint by the U.S. Senate's Subcommittee on National Security and International Operations, Committee on Government Operations, of testimony before the U.S. Senate's Committee on Armed Services, Washington, DC: U.S. Government Printing Office, September 10, 1969, p. 2.

113. Jerome Wiesner, in Wiesner, George McGovern, Donald Brennan, and Leon Johnson, *Anti-Ballistic Missile: Yes or No?* New York: Hill and Wang, 1969, pp. 13-14.

114. Quoted by Meg Greenfield, "The Ragged Non-Debate on the ABM," opinion, *Washington Post*, p. A22.

115. According to ABM opponent Ralph E. Lapp, Senator Symington had also broached the possible utility of launch-on-warning:

> Senator Stuart Symington of Missouri, a former Secretary of the Air Force, raised the issue of U.S. policy in the event that radar revealed a massive first strike aimed at Minuteman bases. Would the Minutemen be fired before Soviet warheads began digging into the U.S. soil? If so, Soviet missiles would be hitting empty holes. (As Senator Fulbright pointed out, empty holes may be our most powerful deterrent weapon.)

See Lapp, "A Biography of the ABM: From Nike to Safeguard," *The New York Times*, May 4, 1969, p. SM 129.

116. Albert Wohlstetter, "The Case for Strategic Force Defense," in Johan Jørgen Holst and William Schneider, Jr., eds., *Why ABM? Policy Issues in the Missile Defense Controversy*, New York: Pergamon Press, 1969, pp. 119-142.

117. See "Appendix III: Treatment of Operations-Research Questions in the 1969 Debate," *Operations Research: The Journal of the Operations Research Society of America*, Vol. 19, No. 5, September 1971, pp. 1175-1237.

118. See *ibid.*, p. 1176. On December 22, 1969, George Rathjens, Steven Weinberg, and Jerome Wiesner sent a letter to Thomas Caywood, president of the Operations Research Society of American (ORSA), questioning "both the wisdom of an inquiry and the standing and capacity of the Operations Research Society of America to carry it out." See "Appendix IV: Correspondence and Comments," in *ibid.*, pp. 1250-1251.

119. During the Senate committee hearing, Albert Wohlstetter asserted:

> The budget for strategic offense and defense forces in fiscal 1962 was 11.3 billion dollars. The proposed fiscal 1970 budget, as of June, comes to about 8 billion dollars. Adjusted for price changes, the 1962 figure was well over fifty per cent higher than that for 1970, perhaps even as much as two-thirds higher.

See Wohlstetter, "The Case for Strategic Force Defense," p. 120.

120. *Ibid.*, p. 122.

121. *Ibid.*, italics added.

122. Wohlstetter *et al.*, *Protecting U.S. Power to Strike Back in the 1950s and 1960s*, pp. 76-77.

123. Wohlstetter, "The Case for Strategic Force Defense," p. 123, italics added.

124. *Treaty between the United States of America and the Union of Soviet Socialist Republics on the Limitation of Anti-Ballistic Missile Systems,* May 26, 1972, entered into force on October 3, 1972.

125. For example, see John W. Finney, "Safeguard ABM System to Shut Down," *The New York Times*, November 25, 1975, pp. 1 and 74.

126. Albert Wohlstetter, "Is There a Strategic Arms Race?" *Foreign Policy*, No. 15, Summer 1974, p. 3. This essay was part one in Wohlstetter's two-part series on the strategic competition in *Foreign Policy*. For part two, see Wohlstetter, "Rivals, But No 'Race'," *Foreign Policy*, No. 16, Fall 1974, pp. 48-81. Subsequent reports expanded this two-part series to include the data from which Wohlstetter made his key inferences: See Wohlstetter, *Legends of the Strategic Arms Race*, USSI Report 75-1, Washington, DC: United States Strategic Institute, September 1974, p. 5, available from *www.albertwohlstetter.com*; and Wohlstetter, Thomas Brown, Gregory Jones, David McGarvey, Robert Raab, Arthur Steiner, Roberta Wohlstetter, and Zivia Wurtele, *The Strategic Competition: Perceptions and Response*, final report for the Director of Defense

Research and Engineering (Net Technical Assessment), DAHC 15-73-C-0137, Los Angeles, CA: Pan Heuristics, January 14, 1975. Wohlstetter's two-part essay generated considerable comment and criticism in *Foreign Policy*. Comments in general agreement included: Paul H. Nitze, "Comments," *Foreign Policy*, No. 16, Fall 1974, pp. 82-83; and Johan Jørgen Holst, "What is Really Going On?" *Foreign Policy*, No. 19, Summer 1975, pp. 155-163. Moderately critical responses included: Joseph Alsop, "Comments," *Foreign Policy*, No. 16, Fall 1974, pp. 83-88. Extremely critical responses included: Morton H. Halperin and Jeremy J. Stone, "Comments," *Foreign Policy*, No. 16, Fall 1974, pp. 88-92; Paul C. Warnke, "Apes on a Treadmill," *Foreign Policy*, No. 18, Spring 1975, pp. 12-29; and Michael L. Nacht, "The Delicate Balance of Error," *Foreign Policy*, No. 19, Summer 1975, pp. 163-177. Wohlstetter responded to these comments and criticisms in "Optimal Ways to Confuse Ourselves," *Foreign Policy*, No. 20, Fall 1975, pp. 170-198. A considerably expanded version of this essay is available as: Albert Wohlstetter, Thomas Brown, Gregory Jones, David McGarvey, Robert Raab, Arthur Steiner, Roberta Wohlstetter and Zivia Wurtele, *Methods That Obscure and Methods That Clarify the Strategic Competition*, DAHC 15-73-C-0074, Los Angeles, CA: Pan Heuristics, June 30, 1975, available from *www.albertwohlstetter.com*.

127. Wohlstetter, "Is There a Strategic Arms Race?" p. 10.

128. *Ibid.*, p. 4.

129. *Ibid.*, pp. 10-18.

130. Wohlstetter, "Rivals, But No 'Race'," p. 66.

131. *Ibid.*, pp. 71-79.

132. Albert Wohlstetter, "Racing Forward? Or Ambling Back?" *Survey*, Vol. 22. Nos. 3/4, Summer 1976, p. 216.

133. *Ibid.*

134. *Ibid.* In a 1987 profile of Albert Wohlstetter in the *Wall Street Journal*, John J. Fialka wrote:

In Mr. Wohlstetter's world, arms-control enthusiasts are looked upon with the same deep suspicion he reserves for generals and admirals who measure success by simply adding up megatonnage. He regards the political hoopla surrounding arms-control talks as "a very dangerous game" because it heightens people's hopes for easy solutions. . . . The kinds of agreements that might be enforced, he believes, are those that give each side the freedom to innovate defenses.

See Fialka, "Veteran 'Lone Ranger' Strategist Packs Firepower with Cold-Eyed Outlook on Soviet Nuclear Policy," p. 56.

135. Albert Wohlstetter and Brian G. Chow, "Arms Control That Could Work," opinion, *Wall Street Journal*, July 17, 1985, p. 28; and *Self-Defense Zones in Space*, study for Integrated Long-Term Defense Strategy in partial fulfillment of MDA903-84-C-0325, Marina del Rey, CA: Pan Heuristics, July 1986, available from *www.albertwohlstetter.com*.

136. See *Report on the Origin, Procedures, and Status of the Experiment in Competitive Analysis on National Intelligence Issues*, memorandum, White House, December 13, 1976, SECRET, declassified on October 17, 1996, DDRS No. CK3100092315. The name of this memo's author has been removed.

137. *Ibid.*, p. 2.

138. *Ibid.*, p. 3.

139. *Intelligence Community Experiment in Competitive Analysis: Soviet Strategic Objectives An Alternative View*, Report of Team "B," December 1976, TOP SECRET, declassified on December 16, 1992, DNSA No. SE00501. The "B" team's leader was Dr. Richard Pipes; its associate members were Dr. William Van Cleave, Lieutenant General Daniel Graham, U.S. Army (Ret.), Dr. Thomas Wolfe of the RAND Corporation, and General John Vogt, U.S. Air Force (Ret.); advisory panel members were Amb. Foy Kohler, Paul Nitze, Amb. Seymour Weiss, Maj. General Jasper Welch, U.S. Air Force, and Dr. Paul Wolfowitz, then a member of the U.S. Arms Control and Disarmament Agency.

140. See "The Book by Albert Wohlstetter," in Albert and Roberta Wohlstetter, *Proposal to the Ford Foundation*, unpublished, June 30, 1989, p. 13, courtesy of Joan Wohlstetter. Although he

began writing this memoir, he never completed it. Drafts of the first chapter are available at the Wohlstetter Papers, housed at the Hoover Institution's archives.

141. Albert Wohlstetter, Letter to the Editor, *Washington Post*, January 15, 1977, p. A18.

142. For a critique of "mirror-imaging," see Andrew W. Marshall, *Bureaucratic Behavior and the Strategic Arms Competition*, Santa Monica, CA: Southern California Seminar on Arms Control and Foreign Policy, 1971, esp. pp. 3-6.

143. At a Senate Appropriations Subcommittee hearing that same year, Secretary of Defense Brown made a similar statement: "The Soviets have really been quite single-minded. They increased their defense expenditures as we increased ours. And they increased their defense expenditures as we decreased ours." See Secretary of Defense Harold Brown, testimony, January 31, 1979, in *Department of Defense Appropriations for Fiscal Year 1980*, hearings before a Subcommittee on Appropriations, U.S. Senate, 96th Congress, 1st session, Washington, DC: U.S. Government Printing Office, 1979, p. 278

144. Thomas C. Schelling and Morton H. Halperin (with research assistance by Donald Brennan), *Strategy and Arms Control*, New York: Twentieth Century Fund, 1961, p. 2. Schelling, Halperin, and Brennan continue:

> The essential feature of arms control is the recognition of the common interest, of the possibility of reciprocation and cooperation even between potential enemies with respect to their military establishments. Whether the most promising areas of arms control involve reductions of certain kinds of military force, increases in certain kinds of military force, qualitative changes in weaponry, different modes of deployment, or arrangements super-imposed on existing military systems, *we prefer to treat as an open question* (emphasis added).

145. Alain C. Enthoven, "1963 Nuclear Strategy Revisited," in Harold P. Ford and Francis X. Winters, S.J., eds., *Ethics and Nuclear Strategy?* Maryknoll, NY: Orbis Books, 1977, pp. 76-77. See also Charles Fairbanks, "MAD and U.S. Strategy," in Henry Sokolski,

ed., *Getting MAD: Nuclear Mutual Assured Destruction, Its Origins and Practice*, Carlisle, PA: Strategic Studies Institute, November 2004, pp. 137-147.

146. Alain C. Enthoven and K. Wayne Smith, *How Much Is Enough? Shaping the Defense Program, 1961-1969*, New York: Harper & Row, 1971, p. 195, italics added. As Enthoven later wrote, the assured destruction metric:

> . . . was a criterion for adequacy of our deterrent; *it was not a declaration of how the forces would actually be used in case of war.* Since the amount of forces we needed to achieve the assured destruction mission were not very sensitive to the size of the Soviet offensive forces, this policy appeared to put a ceiling on U.S. offensive force requirements [emphasis in original].

See Enthoven, "1963 Nuclear Strategy Revisited," pp. 76-77.

147. President John F. Kennedy, "State of the Union Address," January 11, 1962.

148. Quoted by William W. Kaufmann, *The McNamara Strategy*, New York: Harper & Row, 1971, p. 116.

149. As I researched the history of the Long Range Research and Development Planning Program, I learned a great deal from conversations with Dr. Stephen Lukasik, the former Advanced Research Projects Agency director who had co-initiated the study in the early 1970s. I also gained considerable historical background from the following paper: Andrew May and Bartlett Bulkley, *The Pre-History of the Revolution in Military Affairs*, unclassified draft report for Hicks & Associates' Strategic Assessment Center, McLean, VA: SAIC, February 2004, available from *www. albertwohlstetter.com/writings/SovietRMA*.

150. Colonel General N. A. Lomov, ed., *Scientific-Technical Progress and the Revolution in Military Affairs (A Soviet View)*, translated and published under the auspices of the U.S. Air Force, Washington, DC: U.S. Government Printing Office, 1973. available from *www.albertwohlstetter.com/writings/SovietRMA*.

151. D. A. Paolucci, *Summary Report of the Long Range Research and Development Planning Program*, Draft, February 7, 1975, TOP SECRET, declassified on December 31, 1983, pp. 6-7, available from *www.albertwohlstetter.com/writings/LRRDPP*. Copy of report courtesy of Andrew May.

152. *Ibid.*, p. 7.

153. *Ibid.*, pp. 29-42.

154. *Ibid.*, pp. 21-28.

155. *Ibid.*, pp. 17-20.

156. *Ibid.*, pp. 23-24.

157. Albert Wohlstetter and Henry S. Rowen, "Objectives of the United States Military Posture."

158. See Wohlstetter, *Strength, Interest, and New Technologies.*

159. For example, see Albert Wohlstetter and Henry S. Rowen, "Objectives of the United States Military Posture"; Wohlstetter, "Arms Debate: Letter in Response to 'The Megadeath Intellectuals,'" *New York Review of Books*, Vol. 1, No. 9, December 26, 1963; and "Sin and Games in America," in Martin Shubik, *ed.*, *Game Theory and Related Approaches to Social Behavior*, New York: John Wiley & Sons, Inc., 1964, pp. 209-225.

160. For example, see Albert Wohlstetter *et al.*, "The Debate on Military Policy: How Much is Enough? How Mad is MAD?" in Fred Warner Neal and Mary Kersey Harvey, *eds.*, *Pacem in Terris III*, Vol. 2 of 4, Washington, DC: Center for the Study of Democratic Institutions, 1974, pp. 37-43; Wohlstetter, "Threats and Promises of Peace: Europe and America in the New Era," *Orbis*, Vol. 17, No. 4, Winter 1974, pp. 1107-1144; "Varying Response with Circumstance in Europe," in Johan Jørgen Holst and Uwe Nerlich, *eds.*, *Beyond Nuclear Deterrence: New Aims, New Arms*, New York: Crane Russak, 1977, pp. 225-238; "Bishops, Statesmen, and Other Strategists on the Bombing of Innocents," *Commentary*, Vol. 75, No. 6, June 1983, pp. 15-35; "Between an Unfree World and None: Increasing Our Choices," *Foreign Affairs*, Vol. 63, No. 5, Summer 1985, pp. 962-994.

161. *Discriminate Deterrence*, report of the Commission on Integrated Long-Term Strategy, Washington, DC: U.S. Government Printing Office, January 1988, p. 64, emphasis added, available from *www.albertwohlstetter.com/writings/Disciminate Deterrence*. For a critical review, see, e.g., Paul Kennedy, "Not So Grand Strategy," *New York Review of Books*, Vol. 35, No. 8. May 12, 1988, pp. 5-8. For Albert's reaction to such critical reviews, see Wohlstetter, "Overseas Reactions to *Discriminate Deterrence*," *Atlantic Community Quarterly*, Vol. 26, No. 3, Fall-Winter 1988, pp. 234-269.

162. See Andrew May and Bartlett Bulkley, *The Pre-History of the Revolution in Military Affairs*.

163. On November 5, 1985, President Reagan awarded the Medal of Freedom to Albert and Roberta Wohlstetter, as well as to Paul H. Nitze.

164. "The Book by Albert Wohlstetter," in Albert and Roberta Wohlstetter, *Proposal to the Ford Foundation*, unpublished, June 30, 1989, p. 17, courtesy of Joan Wohlstetter. He began, but never completed, this memoir. See also Wohlstetter, *The Cumulative Information Revolution and the Future Role of Discriminate Military Force in U.S. Strategy*, proposal to the Smith Richardson Foundation, revised June 12, 1991, courtesy Joan Wohlstetter.

165. Published writings by Albert Wohlstetter on the topic of Persian Gulf contingencies in the late 1970s and early 1980s include Wohlstetter, "'Lesser' Excluded Cases," opinion, *The New York Times*, February 14, 1979, p. A25; "Half Wars and Half Policies in the Persian Gulf," in W. Scott Thompson, ed., *National Security in the 1980s: From Weakness to Strength*, Washington, DC: Institute of Contemporary Studies, 1980; "Meeting the Threat in the Persian Gulf," *Survey*, Vol. 25, No. 2, Spring 1980, pp. 128-188; "*Les États-Unis et la Sécurité du Golfe*," *Politique Étrangére*, Vol. 46, No. 1, March 1981, pp. 75-88. For unpublished writings by Albert on Persian Gulf contingencies, some of which were commissioned by the U.S. Government, see Wohlstetter, *Interests and Power in the Persian Gulf*, Vol. 1: *Overview*, PH-80-4-113700-42C, draft final report prepared for the Director of Net Assessment (Office of Secretary of Defense), the Assistant Secretary of Defense (Program Analysis and Evaluation), and the Assistant Secretary of Defense (International Security Affairs), in partial fulfillment of DNA 001-

78-C-0353 , Marina del Rey, CA: Pan Heuristics, March 31, 1980, courtesy Joan Wohlstetter; *Protecting Persian Gulf Oil: U.S. and Alliance Military Policy*, in *Report on Persian Gulf Oil and Western Security*, Vol. III, Final Report prepared for the U.S. Department of Energy, Contract No. HN-LV-79-2, PH80-11-LV7902-60C, Marina del Rey, CA: Pan Heuristics, November 4, 1980, courtesy Gregory S. Jones; and *Interests and Power in the Persian Gulf: Executive Summary*, draft, Marina del Rey, CA: Pan Heuristics, February 1981, courtesy Gregory S. Jones; and *Interests and Power in the Persian Gulf: An Overview*, Marina del Rey, CA: Pan Heuristics, February 1981, courtesy Gregory S. Jones.

166. See Albert Wohlstetter, "Iraq: Dictatorship Is the Problem," opinion, *Washington Post*, April 24, 1991; Wohlstetter and Fred S. Hoffman, "The Bitter End," *The New Republic*, Vol. 204, No. 17, April 29, 1991, pp. 20-24; Wohlstetter, "Wide Open Secret Coup," *The National Review*, Vol. 44, No. 5, March 16, 1992, pp. 34-36; "Help Iraqi Dissidents Oust Saddam," opinion, *Wall Street Journal*, August 25, 1992; and "High Time," *National Review*, Vol. 45, No. 3, February 15, 1993, pp. 30-33.

167. See Albert Wohlstetter, "The Balkan Quagmire: Why We're in It—Still," opinion, *Wall Street Journal*, July 1, 1993, p. A14; "The Balkan Quagmire II: The Way Out," opinion, *Wall Street Journal*, July 2, 1993; "Genocide by Embargo," opinion, *Wall Street Journal*, May 9, 1994, p. A14; "Arms, Not Words, for Bosnia," opinion, *Wall Street Journal*, May 12, 1994, p. A14; "Notes to Clinton on Bosnia," opinion, *Wall Street Journal*, June 10, 1994, p. A10; "Too Many Flip-Flops," opinion, *Washington Post*, June 26, 1994; "Embargo the Aggressors, Not the Victims," opinion, *Wall Street Journal*, June 28, 1994, p. A18; "Creating a Greater Serbia: Clinton's Final Sell-Out of Bosnia," *The New Republic*, Vol. 211, No. 5, August 1, 1994, pp. 22-27; "Bosnia: Air Power, Not Peacekeepers," opinion, *Wall Street Journal*, December 9, 1994, p. A16; "Inferior U.N. or Superior Coalition Force?" opinion, *Wall Street Journal*, May 3, 1995, p. A14; "Beyond the Cold War: Foreign Policy in the 21st Century; Alternatives to Negotiating Genocide" (with Gregory S. Jones), opinion, *Wall Street Journal*, May 3, 1995, p. A14; "Chirac's Challenge on Bosnia," opinion, *Wall Street Journal*, July 20, 1995, p. A12; "Relentless Diplomacy and Mass Murder," opinion, *Wall Street Journal*, September 5, 1995, p. A14; "NATO: Precise Power, Incoherent Goals," opinion, *Wall Street Journal*, October 19, 1995, p. A22; "Magic Tricks Can't Disguise

This About Bosnia," opinion, *Wall Street Journal*, November 15, 1995, p. A20; "Since Bosnia Has Been Reduced to This...," opinion, *Wall Street Journal*, December 12, 1995, p. A20; "The Cold War is Over and Over and. . . ," opinion, *Wall Street Journal*, October 1, 1996, p. A22; "A Photo-op Foreign Policy," opinion, *Wall Street Journal*, October 23, 1996, p. A22; and "Boris Yeltsin as Abraham Lincoln," in Stjepan G. Meštrovic, ed., *The Conceit of Innocence: Losing the Conscience of the West in the War Against Bosnia*, College Station, TX: Texas A&M University Press, 1997, pp. 200-207.

168. See Albert Wohlstetter and Margaret Thatcher, "What the West Must Do in Bosnia," an open letter to President William J. Clinton, opinion, *Wall Street Journal*, September 2, 1993, p. A12.

169. See Albert Wohlstetter and Gregory Jones, "'Breakthrough' in North Korea?" opinion, *The Wall Street Journal*, November 4, 1994, p. A12.

170. Quoted by Fialka, "Veteran 'Lone Ranger' Strategist Packs Firepower with Cold-Eyed Outlook on Soviet Nuclear Policy," p. 56.

171. President Ronald Reagan, "Remarks at the Presentation Ceremony for the Presidential Medal of Freedom," East Room, White House, Washington, DC, November 5, 1985, available from *www.reagan.utexas.edu/archives/speeches/1985/110785a.htm*.

172. Quoted by Herzog, p. 68.

173. James Digby and J. J. Martin, "On Not Confusing Ourselves: Contributions of the Wohlstetters to U.S. Strategic Thought," in Marshall, Martin, and Rowen, *On Not Confusing Ourselves: Essays on National Security Strategy in Honor of Albert and Roberta Wohlstetter*, quotes from pp. 5 and 3.

174. Roberta Wohlstetter, *Pearl Harbor: Warning and Decision*, p. 401.

175. Albert Wohlstetter, *No Highway to High Purpose*, emphasis added.

I. ANALYSIS AND DESIGN OF STRATEGIC POLICY

Commentary: *How He Worked*

Henry S. Rowen

Albert Wohlstetter (whom for brevity's sake I shall refer to simply as AW) made large contributions to U.S. national security thinking and actions from the 1950s into the 1990s — and arguably beyond — through his ideas, his research findings and those of his associates, and the activities of those he mentored. This chapter focuses on his style of work, the unusual and inventive ways in which he addressed problems of policy, and how he applied his talents to some of the most urgent and difficult issues of the nuclear era.

We know how things turned out in what came to be known as the Cold War, although disputes endure on the correctness of various decisions. (One is reminded of Zhou Enlai's answer to the question about the French Revolution: "Too soon to tell.") The challenges posed at the time were novel and of the utmost seriousness. Enormously destructive weapons had suddenly appeared, first nuclear fission ones, then even more powerful thermonuclear bombs. Key effects of these weapons were poorly known for some time, especially radioactive fallout. Although it was not a big surprise to the Manhattan Project scientists, the first Soviet atomic bomb test of August 29, 1949, was a political shock. The United States and the Union of Soviet Socialist Republics (USSR) were also developing novel delivery systems, notably long-range ballistic missiles, which when mated with nuclear warheads posed unique dangers and new uncertainties. Our security establishment was slow to understand adequately the military significance of these technological innovations. According to Tom Schelling: "I think it took the United States at least 2 decades to learn how to think about nuclear weapons policy after 1945."[1] The phrase "at least" is warranted; arguably, we still aren't quite there.

Throughout his career in strategy, AW worked to improve thinking about the role and consequences of nuclear weapons. One finding from AW's work, soon acted upon, was the need for better protection and control of nuclear forces. The U.S. Air Force had asked him and his associates to examine the large overseas base-building program for our strategic bomber force. Their investigation had consequences not only for that program, but also for the basing and operations of the strategic bomber force at home — and for our missile forces that were to come, and for much more.

AW came to wide attention to those interested in foreign policy, especially in nuclear weapons issues, with the publication of his article, "The Delicate Balance of Terror" (1959), in *Foreign Affairs*. There, he challenged the prevailing assumption that nuclear war was impossible, or had a vanishingly small likelihood, laying out reasons why the nuclear balance was precarious and why the requirements for deterring such a war were stringent. He soon came to be described as an eminent strategist or, more dubiously in some quarters, as a "defense intellectual."[2]

AW went on to become a critic of widely held views about the "arms race" with the Soviet Union in general, and the "nuclear arms race" in particular, writing in the mid-1970s that the facts of nuclear arms competition did not fit much of the rhetoric about nuclear arms racing. This led to a vigorous disputation in print. From AW's perspective, the issues were not that dangerous "gaps" existed between American and Russian nuclear offensive forces (as American politicians often had claimed in the 1950s), or that there was an arms race spiraling out control in the 1960s or 1970s, but that relevant facts were being ignored and the wrong questions were being asked.

Efforts to understand nuclear weapons and their destructiveness led AW to try to break the pattern that had dominated air power from its inception, namely, the indiscriminate "strategic bombing" that had caused vast destruction to civilians during World War II. Over many decades, he worked to promote technologies of precision and control that would make it more possible to hit military targets without killing innocent bystanders. He saw that advances in technologies of sensing and computation could produce vast improvements in the accuracy with which munitions could be delivered. This capability began to be used near the end of the Vietnam War and was widely displayed during the Kosovo operation against Serbia and the two Gulf wars. It has transformed air operations. Hard as it might be for some people to believe, the concept of destroying military targets while sparing civilians is now at the core of American air power doctrine. The "Delicate Balance" aside, perhaps this was his most important intellectual and practical security contribution.

Throughout AW's career, a major concern of him and his team was the future of Europe, a region seen as the main stake in the great power competition. This meant that decisions about nuclear forces, both long range and short, needed to be viewed with the implications for Europe in mind. At the same time, he also pushed our political and military leaders to give more weight to the flanks of NATO and pay much more attention to "out of area" contingencies—or what he called "lesser excluded cases." The 1991 Gulf War and the conflict over Bosnia and Kosovo later in the decade dramatically demonstrated the critical importance of these sorts of contingencies.

Another interest from an early date was the spread of the nuclear bomb to more countries. It was known from near the beginning of the nuclear era that the line between civilian and military uses of atomic energy was thin, but this fact was often obscured—and still is—in our policy actions. An egregious case was the Eisenhower Administration's *Atoms for Peace* program. By actively disseminating civilian nuclear applications, the program was engaged in (as the title of AW's 1976 *Foreign Policy* article would later put it) "Spreading the Bomb without Quite Breaking the Rules." The U.S. government continues to behave in a wildly inconsistent way on this topic.

These and other accomplishments came from a high intelligence used in ways that were at least unusual, and in combination arguably unique. Below, I consider key aspects of AW's style of work.

I. WORKING ON A PROBLEM, REFRAMING OBJECTIVES

It is especially important, and sometimes very difficult, to get objectives right in a policy analysis. A competent analyst who works on such a situation will try to identify available alternatives, to assess their respective costs and benefits in light of given objectives, and recommend a course of action. This is necessary, but it is often where intellectual activity stops.

It is not enough to assume a merely one-sided conflict with a potential adversary. Albert Wohlstetter sometimes used the term *opposed systems* to characterize the sort of competitive— and interactive—situation in which one actor (for instance, a government, a military organization or even a nonstate group) may try to do things that at least partially frustrate some key objectives and activities of others—and vice versa. The policy problem, objectives, and alternatives can look quite different when the game, so to speak, is seriously two-sided (or three- or four-sided), that is, when the frustrating activities are reciprocal, and each actor is both frustrating others while being frustrated in return.[3]

Characteristically, AW not only addressed the policy problem as it was initially posed. He also undertook a more comprehensive inquiry to consider a fuller range of alternatives available to all relevant actors, to evaluate not only the means of policy but also the ends.[4] Sometimes this would lead him to reframe the problem in a more fundamental way and to invent new options. More value, sometimes a great deal more, can be added to the analysis if the problem is redefined in a way that stays true to the spirit of the original question, but also brings to light more crucial yet underappreciated objectives and new ways of achieving them.

Basing and Operating SAC's Bomber Force in a Competitive Environment.

A crucial issue in the immediate aftermath of World War II was what to do about nuclear weapons. Their novelty and extraordinary destructiveness made this both urgent and difficult. By August 1949 the Soviet Union had the atomic bomb. The hydrogen bomb was in the offing, and ballistic missiles were being developed. The Red Army was in the middle of Europe. In 1950 North Korea had attacked the South with Soviet support and later that year China had intervened militarily.

The United States was making jet bombers in large numbers. From 1951, the United States built over 2,000 B-47s, a medium-range bomber with a roundtrip operating radius of 2,100 miles, while the longer-range B-52 bomber, which did not depend on overseas bases, was being developed. Aerial refueling as a means of extending the range of medium-range bombers without using overseas bases was also being developed.

The problem originally posed to the RAND Corporation by the U.S. Air Force's assistant for bases was to look at the far-flung, rapidly expanding system of bases of the Strategic Air Command (SAC) that were being built in the United Kingdom (UK), Morocco, Alaska, and elsewhere, to enable our medium-range bombers in wartime to reach the Soviet Union, return, and repeatedly go back. However, AW and his team quickly realized a critical yet underappreciated aspect of this problem: these planned bases could also be reached by Soviet bombers, a potential vulnerability made critically serious now that the USSR had the atomic bomb.

After much study and analysis, AW's team recommended stopping the elaborate program to build bases overseas and strictly limiting their use (specifically, any overseas bases surviving an enemy attack) to austere refueling points for SAC's medium-range bomber aircraft.[5] By the end of 1955, the U.S. Air Force had accepted and begun implementing this recommendation.

Protecting Our Power to Strike Back Became a Crucial Objective.

Attention then turned to the situation of our force at home. It was assumed to be safe, but an investigation into the possibility of a Soviet sneak attack on the small number of continental bases on which the strategic force was located made that assumption look untenable. AW and his team completed an initial report on this issue.[6] As Philip Taubman would write in *Secret Empire: Eisenhower, the CIA, and the Hidden Story of America's Space Espionage* (2003): "The report, published on April 15, 1953, stunned Gardner [Special Assistant to the Secretary of the Air Force] and other officials in Washington. . . . The lightly defended SAC bases . . . were ideal targets for atomic attack." Taubman would add: "The import was clear and breathtaking: For the first time in its history, the United States was vulnerable to a crippling attack from overseas, and would find it difficult, if not impossible, to retaliate after being struck."[7]

Over the next 3 years, AW and his team worked to understand the issues raised by SAC's potential vulnerabilities on the continental United States, and to identify — and also invent and design — ways to mitigate these vulnerabilities. This work had a large and rapid impact on U.S. decisions regarding nuclear forces.

A key idea emerging was that *relative* risk could dominate decisions in certain situations rather than the widely assumed perception of *absolute* risk. To put it another way, in extreme circumstances it could actually look less risky for decisionmakers to use nuclear weapons than not to use them. This argument was novel — and contested — but from it came the idea of protecting our power to strike back *after* a nuclear attack in order to affect the way a potential nuclear aggressor would view the relative risks of a first strike. This concept soon became an essential aspect of the U.S. military posture.[8]

More broadly, AW argued that the requirements for establishing a credible and safe nuclear deterrent were stringent and not automatic. There were several reasons for this. One was the possibility of operational accidents (compare the August 28, 2007, loading of nuclear-armed missiles on a U.S. Air Force bomber by mistake and its subsequent flight of several thousand miles) or misjudgements higher in the chain of command.

A second reason was that whatever U.S. decisionmakers might believe about nuclear weapons and their use, Soviet decisionmakers might have a different set of beliefs. In fact, the doctrine of nuclear warfighting to win a major conflict had a strong hold there (the Strategic Arms Limitation Talks, known also as SALT, notwithstanding) until well into the 1980s, long after U.S. authorities had come to realize nuclear warfighting's futility as a war-winning strategy.[9]

The third stemmed from the perceived vulnerability of Western Europe. Although the U.S. might be able to deter a Soviet preclusive attack against its nuclear-armed strategic forces, it was far from clear that such deterrence would necessarily extend to other forms of potential Soviet aggression. The Red Army was in Europe's center and was judged to be stronger than NATO's forces.[10] Our putative atomic superiority—no longer monopoly— was widely seen in American officialdom as the chief guarantor of Europe's security. But what did this mean? The answer given by Eisenhower's Secretary of State John Foster Dulles in 1954 was that the United States would respond to military provocation "at places and with means of our own choosing." He also said, "Local defense must be reinforced by the further deterrent of massive retaliatory power." This idea, which came to be known as the doctrine of "massive retaliation," implied using nuclear weapons first, yet it was also widely held in the United States, including by high officials, that nuclear weapons were unusable because of the vast devastation that would result. These conflicting views posed a difficulty that long persisted.[11]

In the late 1950s, a then little-known professor at Harvard, Henry Kissinger, argued that it might be possible to fight a limited nuclear war in Europe, limited in the sense that it would not escalate to attacks on U.S. or Soviet territory.[12] This argument did not have much appeal in Europe, the putative war zone, nor as it turned out in Washington. AW addressed this topic in "The Delicate Balance of Terror" (the relevant passage of which deserves quoting here because, in later disputes over the nuclear "arms race," he was sometimes charged with believing in limited nuclear war as a policy goal):

Whether or not nuclear weapons favor the West in limited war, there still remains the question of whether such limitations could be made stable. . . . It remains to be seen whether there are any equilibrium points between the use of conventional and all-out weapons. In fact the emphasis on the gradualness of the graduated deterrents may be misplaced. The important thing would be to find some discontinuities if these steps are not to lead too smoothly to general war. Nuclear limited war, simply because of the extreme swiftness and unpredictability of its moves, the necessity of delegating authority to local commanders, and the possibility of sharp and sudden desperate reversals of fortune, would put the greatest strain on the deterrent to all-out thermonuclear war.

AW's skepticism about limited nuclear war *as a policy* was consistent with the crucial aim of *controlling such forces* to prevent inadvertent use by us, and to deal with first use of nuclear weapons by the Soviet Union, or later China, or any other nation with them. His answer to the Eisenhower/Dulles doctrine of "first use" by us was that the West needed to enable NATO to defend Europe with conventional forces. (However, AW did not clearly articulate a "no-first use" policy, and was later chastised for this.) The discriminate use of force, especially through a distinction between military forces to be attacked and civilian noncombatants to be avoided, became a consistent theme in his work from the late 1950s onward.

II. PAYING CLOSE ATTENTION TO THE DATA

An important aspect of Albert Wohlstetter's style is shown in the name he chose for the research organization that he created: *Pan Heuristics*, or learning about all things. The excessively ambitious "pan" part of the name was mitigated by "heuristics," an informal approach to solving problems in the spirit of being roughly right rather than being precisely wrong. The idea of "pan heuristics" speaks to AW's strong commitment to gathering and understanding as much data relevant to a policy problem as he could.

Among people who became well known as strategists, AW was probably unique in having industrial experience. During

99

World War II, he worked in quality control and management at a factory manufacturing power-generation equipment for Allied field communications, and after the war, in prefabricated housing design and mass-production. This trained him to pay careful attention to operations and technical data.

In a November 1968 letter to the distinguished British military historian Michael Howard, AW had the following to say about his work style in the aforementioned Base Study and Vulnerability Study:

> For two years, before issuing a summary report and exposing the results to the scrutiny of experienced officers in the Air Staff, SAC and other relevant field commands, and for three years before issuing the final report, we looked systematically and in great detail at the problem of bringing bombs, bombers, bomber crews and tanker aircraft together with equipment in combat-ready condition and getting bombers to targets and back along routes that minimized their exposure to defenses. That included problems of equipment reliability, radar warning, communications and control, and above all logistics. We examined the joint effects of these many factors on "the costs of extending bomber radius; on how the enemy may deploy his defenses, and the numbers of our bombers lost to enemy fighters; on logistics costs; and on base vulnerability and our probable loss of bombers on the ground." We did not begin with any theory about the vulnerability of SAC. The second-strike theory of deterrence grew out of this empirical study; we didn't start with it.

> If the study said nothing that was new, it would hardly have received such attention. If it had been unsound, it could not have survived the extraordinarily widespread and detailed scrutiny it was given by the responsible military men whose work—and lives—it affected.[13]

This background helps to show why AW was skeptical about the significance of claimed "bomber gaps" (assertions of American vulnerability in the mid-1950s made on the grounds that the United States allegedly had fallen behind the USSR in the numbers of bombers) or "missile gaps" (a similar assertion made, among others, by presidential candidate Senator John F. Kennedy concerning intercontinental ballistic missiles).

AW's view was that such "gap" claims — which turned out to be false — missed the point: that it was not the "bean count" of such weapons in peacetime that mattered most, but what the balance of capabilities would look like after one side or the other had struck first. In short, one needed to consider not just raw numbers, but also the potential interactions of the two sides. This required, in part, doing as best one could to look at relevant data, recognizing that not all of it was accessible.

Learning from Many Disciplines: RAND in the 1950s.

AW felt a need to learn the basics about many fields relevant to the topics on which he was working — and he had the talent and determination to do so. The RAND Corporation of the 1950s and 1960s was an ideal environment for doing this. It had a broad mandate to explore topics that fit under the heading of national security, thanks to the wisdom of the U.S. Air Force. RAND's first president, Frank Collbohm, and his management team assembled talents in many fields: e.g., mathematics, physics, engineering, and the social sciences. RAND people did pioneering work on satellite reconnaissance, telecommunications, civil defense, game theory, applications of cost-benefit analysis, finance, and history. Two future Nobel laureates in economics, William Sharpe and Harry Markowitz, were members of the RAND staff when they did the work for which they were later honored. Many excellent scientists, physical and social, and mathematicians came as visitors for varying periods.[14]

From this extraordinarily favorable research environment, AW gained access to a wealth of talent in many fields — talent that for the most part was willing to work across disciplines on large, complex questions. As Andrew Marshall (who made important contributions to strategic thinking at RAND, and who has served for many years as the Director of the Pentagon's Office of Net Assessment) would later remark: "While the group of real strategists at RAND probably never numbered more than about 25 people, the overall quality, in sheer intelligence and intellectual breadth, is simply astonishing."[15]

From Roberta Wohlstetter, who worked as a historian in RAND's social sciences division, AW got help on many matters, including those related to organizational and psychological

101

aspects of behavior. It is impossible for someone outside of the family to know how much of what AW accomplished was due to her direct or indirect help. Roberta herself was an accomplished scholar whose Bancroft Prize-winning *Pearl Harbor: Warning and Decision* (1962) will long be cited as perhaps the best book ever written on military intelligence. Her 1976 study, *The Buddha Smiles: Absent-Minded Peaceful Aid and the Indian Bomb*, showed how India had exploited civil nuclear cooperation from the United States and Canada to make its bomb. (There was a flair for book and article titles in that family.) Among her many talents was that of analyzing the character and motivations of leaders. The husband-wife team also had several joint publications on Cuba, for instance.

On the occasion of awarding the Presidential Medal of Freedom to the Wohlstetters, President Reagan spoke of Roberta's intimate personal and professional partnership with AW:

> I daresay that she has frankly enjoyed posing the same penetrating questions to her husband that she has to the intellectual and political leaders of the country. And that is certainly one explanation for the clarity and persua- siveness of his own voluminous words on strategy, poli- tics, and world affairs.[16]

Experts Needed, but Not as Seers.

AW learned much from specialists in many fields. He saw large decisions affecting war and the conduct of operations as depending not only on political insights, but also on inputs from such experts. But he was wary of specialists who opined with an air of authority on topics outside of their expertise when they had not seriously worked on these topics.

Indeed, there were a number of physicists who knew about the confined topic of nuclear weapons and their effects, but who did not hesitate to pronounce on matters related to strategic nuclear force operations without having carefully studied these operations, and without any particular claims of knowledge as to the aims and strategy of Soviet leaders. He described such experts, especially those who distilled nuclear-age policy choices to decisions between living in "One World or None," as feeling:

charged with a prodigious mission and a great moral urgency. Spurred by an apocalyptic vision of world annihilation, they urge a drastic transformation in the conduct of world affairs in the immediate future. They have been passionately sure that the choices are stark and clear: annihilation on the one hand or a paradise on earth.[17]

He continued:

This vision of the responsibility of the scientists, "a greater responsibility than is pressing on any other body of men," puts him in a very different role from the scientist as technologist or the scientist dealing by tentative and empirical methods with broader questions or cardinal choices. It is fortified … by the related notion of the scientist as specially endowed — a seer or prophet.[18]

He also pointed to the rapid switch in views on fundamentals by some distinguished scientists. Advocates of building active defenses and fallout shelters against nuclear attack soon saw these things as fueling the arms race. Of course, he saw nothing wrong in principle with people changing their views. (He might have quoted, but did not, Lord Keynes: "When the facts change I change my views; what do you do, Sir"?) But these changes raised questions about their foresight, sometimes right and sometimes wrong. As a group, these scientists were not seers.

The scientist and novelist Sir Charles Percy Snow addressed the difficulty of communications between specialists in the physical sciences and the humanities in his Godkin Lecture, "The Two Cultures."[19] (Sir Charles could have included the social sciences as well.) Snow had claimed that the cardinal choices can be fully understood only by scientists, even though in "legal form" these choices are made by non-scientists exposed to advice of only a few experts.

AW was critical of Snow's account of how Britain's wartime leaders made decisions, countering that the reality was a good deal more complex, filled with more salient participants than Snow had allowed. More important, AW maintained that although civilian political leaders might lack expertise, they could be made to understand what was at stake in such cardinal choices.

III. BEYOND ANALYSIS TO DESIGN AND INVENTION

Only in a limited sense is the pubic interest served by finding the best among *established* choices. It is sometimes better to invent or design new ones. This does not come naturally to many people who are otherwise highly competent. It requires a certain mindset, akin to that of an inventor or an architect. AW had such a mentality.

Controlling Forces: Failing Safe.

Few — if any — topics since we have had nuclear weapons have been more important than the rules for launching them. In their 1956 study, *Protecting U.S. Power to Strike Back in the 1950's and 1960's* (R-290), AW and his colleagues recognized that ambiguous warning signals raised two risks for the Strategic Air Command: *false alarm*, which could lead to accidental or unauthorized uses of nuclear weapons, and *false assurance*, which could leave U.S. strategic forces vulnerable in the event of an actual attack.

To deal with these related risks, AW's team invented and then recommended a "Fail-Safe" operating procedure (later called "Positive Control") by which SAC, when confronted with ambiguous warning of a potential attack, would evacuate and protectively scramble its nuclear-armed bomber aircraft without actually committing them to combat — and without risking war by mistake. R-290 explained:

> By a fail-safe procedure we mean one in which the bombers will return to base after reaching a pre-designated point en route — unless they receive an order to continue. (Without a fail-safe procedure, this initial decision comes close to being the final decision; without recall it *is* the final decision.)[20]

The alternative to "Fail-Safe" was known as "Recall," in which combat-ready bombers would not only take off based on (possibly mistaken) warning, but also make their way to pre-designated targets. The only way to stop such bombers from attacking their targets would be, as this procedure's name suggests, to recall them with explicit communication. But "Recall" was fraught with dangers. AW would later recollect having said in a briefing to the Strategic Air Command, "There aren't any good ways of starting World War III, but that would surely be one of the worst."[21]

In Autumn 1957, SAC conducted a test called FRESH APPROACH, which simulated the recall of the alert force by radio (i.e., using a "fail un-safe" procedure). The after-action report was sobering:

> . . . of the ten airborne alert aircraft, one experienced HF [high frequency radio frequency] failure and one failed to monitor HF frequencies as briefed. The eight remaining aircraft . . . did not receive the test message on HF. All ten aircraft received UHF contact from the 9th Bombardment Wing command post, [but] Mountain Home tower and McChord tower were not received. All UHF messages received from the 9th Bombardment Wing were *after the aircraft had struck the target* and were inbound to the local area [emphasis added].[22]

SAC instituted Fail-Safe by the Spring of 1958.

It is worth noting that when the movie *Fail Safe* (1964) needed drama, it found it by showing the opposite of "Positive Control," the possible consequence of having a "fail-dangerous" recall procedure—the procedure in place before the change in 1958 designed and recommended by the AW team. This topic, like several others dealt with by AW and team, has current salience. For example, have India and Pakistan introduced equivalent fail-safe procedures in their nuclear forces?[23]

Challenge of Protecting Missiles, as well as Command, Control, and Communications.

By the mid-1950s it was becoming evident that any place in the United States could soon be reached by intercontinental ballistic missiles, then under development in both the Soviet Union and the United States. They could arrive with little warning and with no possibility then of interception. The main response of SAC to this danger was to keep some aircraft on a high state of alert, ready for quick takeoff or even aloft, in a crisis. These solutions had their problems because early warning was uncertain and keeping bombers aloft for long periods was costly. But a much more difficult question was how to base our own ICBMs. The first generation of ICBMs, *Atlas* and *Titan* missiles, were large, fragile, exposed (think of the space vehicles at the Kennedy Space Center), and vulnerable to nuclear weapons detonated even some miles away.

AW and his team sought to invent and design new ways to make U.S. strategic forces safe from missile attack. As part of their investigation into fixing the vulnerability of bombers on their bases in the United States, thought had been given to blast-resistant shelters. The first generation of enemy ICBMs was expected to be inaccurate, which meant that blast shelters, in principle, might provide adequate protection against expected blast effects. However, the prevailing view of civil engineering experts was discouraging: only 30-40 pounds per square inch (p.s.i.) of resistance to peak overpressure (that is, to the blast effects of a nuclear explosion) was thought to be feasible, a level short of adequacy, and even this would be costly.

This perceived shortfall led AW to inquire more deeply into what was known about the blast effects of nuclear weapons and the technology of blast-resistant structures. He got Paul Weidlinger, a brilliant structural engineer whom he had met in the 1940s, interested in this topic. Weidlinger soon came up with a design that could withstand peak overpressures an order of magnitude greater than most had thought possible. It turned out that while these improved blast-resistant structures could not be cost-effectively applied to aircraft or the first generation of large and liquid-fueled missiles, they could be applied to the much smaller and tougher *Minuteman* missiles by basing them underground in what later became known as "silos."[24]

Weidlinger then came up with designs for underground silo structures that could withstand overpressures approaching 1,000 p.s.i., and later extended blast resistance to even higher levels. After the skepticism of the extant authorities on this topic was overcome, Weidlinger's design approach became the solution. It was not expected to last forever because missiles would become more and more accurate, but it was good solution for many decades (and indeed is still in use).

To take another important example, a major invention came out of a question that AW had asked of a RAND engineer named Paul Baran: "What would happen if the key switching centers of AT&T were destroyed?" Baran's answer: The total collapse of our national communications system.

Inquiries to remedy this problem led Baran in 1964 to invent the concepts of "hot-potato routing" (decentralized and distributed communications systems) and segmenting data into "message blocks" (today, packet-switching networks), two concepts that could be used to design a more robust, survivable command, control, and communications system less prone to disruption and degradation. Baran's concepts provided the impetus for major advances in telecommunications — and contributed to what would become the Internet.

Persistent Efforts in Persuasion: Communicating the Analysis and Design's Results.

It was not AW's style to write a report or an article and simply put it in the mail. If the project was worth doing, it was worth a marketing effort. He took great pains to learn about the views and positions of the decisionmakers involved, and to design arguments that would be most effective. This meant spending a lot of time on the road, especially in Washington, but also at the Strategic Air Command's headquarters in Omaha, NATO headquarters, and elsewhere. To AW, these were not simply "briefings." For one thing, they were usually not brief; for another, these were two-way exchanges, for the presenters themselves learned much from such sessions.

AW's writings were closely reasoned, sometimes eloquent, complete with salient data. But they were not quick and easy reads. Nor was he a person of few words. Training in mathematical logic produced precision in expression, but sometimes a denseness that needed parsing. Here, too, Roberta must have been a big help.

IV. DISPUTATIONS

The Ballistic Missile Defense Dispute.

Albert Wohlstetter's works often evoked vigorous responses — some highly positive, some constructive, some hugely critical, and some scurrilous.[25] Consider the case of the proposed active defense against ballistic missiles (BMD) in behalf of which AW became an advocate. He had a belief that technically it could be made to work in certain situations. He certainly found the "arms race" arguments of many of the opponents of BMD objectionable. Why, in principle, should one object to being able to defend oneself against attack?

In 1969, the Senate Armed Services Committee held a debate on the pros and cons of the *Safeguard* ballistic missile defense system. The purpose of *Safeguard* was to protect *Minuteman* missiles from nuclear attack, and the debate centered on how well such a defense might perform. AW, Paul Nitze, John Foster, and others gave detailed arguments as to why it was a good idea, and their opponents, such as George Rathjens and Jerome Wiesner, as to why it was not.

What turned out to be remarkable about this exchange was not so much its content, but the fact that the Operation Research Society of America (ORSA), at AW's request, did a study of the professionalism of his opponents' contributions. Three faculty members from the Massachusetts Institute of Technology (MIT) who had testified at the Senate hearings, including MIT's president, objected to the standing and capacity of ORSA to conduct such an investigation. ORSA went ahead anyway. It found faults on both sides of the debate, but singled out for criticism the testimony of the opponents, including those from MIT. In striking contrast, the report found "no significant defects" in AW's testimony, and cited one paper that he had submitted to the Senate Armed Services Committee as "a model for the professional and constructive conduct of a debate over important and technical issues."[26]

AW won this debate on points, but was he right? At the time, AW's desire to establish the correctness of the principle that defending oneself is good seems to have overcome his usually sound technical and economic sense. As observed above, one might object to a specific program on grounds of inadequate cost-effectiveness. Here, ballistic missile defenses have struggled against technologically competent attackers in which the offense can adopt countermeasures (e.g., multiple independently tar-getable reentry vehicles, decoys) to negate them. The United States has had active defense programs under development for 50 years and has deployed some systems (one Safeguard site in North Dakota, soon demolished) without achieving notable confidence that the substantial expenditures have been worthwhile. We are still trying, now with the goal of defending against less technically advanced missiles from Iran or North Korea.

The Arms Race Dispute.

AW set off a fierce debate by questioning the existence of a spiraling nuclear "arms race" in two articles published in the mid-1970s.[27] Here is a small sample of the views to which AW responded: from John Newhouse, "America's forces apparently served as both model and catalyst for the Russians"; from journalist Leslie Gelb, "The common practice, as I think we all know, has been to exaggerate and over dramatize"; from Jerome

108

Wiesner, president of MIT and former science adviser to President Kennedy, the arms race makes "an ever-increasing likelihood of war so disastrous that civilization, if not man himself, will be eradicated"; from nuclear physicist Herbert York, who had served on the Manhattan Project and as the first director of the Livermore National Laboratory, we should "slow down the rate of weapons innovation, and hence reduce the frequency of introduction of ever more complex and threatening weapons"; from chemists George Kistiakowsky, a leading Manhattan Project participant, and MIT's George Rathjens, "any understanding that slowed the rate of development and change of strategic systems would have an effect in the right direction." In short, the dangers perceived by the "arms race theorists" (as AW called them) were not merely — or only — the waste of resources in adding to the nuclear stockpile, but catastrophe.

AW asked exactly what was going on in the putative "arms race." He began by dissecting the term:

> When we talk of "arms" are we referring to the total budget spent on strategic forces? The number of strategic vehicles or launchers? The number of weapons? The total explosive energy that could be released by all strategic weapons? The aggregate destructive area of these weapons? Or are we concerned about qualitative change — that is alterations in unit performance characteristics — the speed of an aircraft or missile, its accuracy, the blast resistance of its silo, the concealability of its launch point, the scale and sharpness of optical photos or other sensitive devices, the controllability of a weapon and its resistance to accidental or unauthorized use? When we talk of a "race" what do we imply about the rate at which the race is run, about the ostensible goal of the contest, about how the "race" is generated, about the nature of the interaction among strategic adversaries?[28]

Whatever arms racing was about, AW objected to the use of such words as "explosive," "spiraling," or "uncontrolled" to characterize the U.S.-USSR strategic "competition" (his preferred word) in nuclear arms.

To illustrate his point, AW compared forecasts over time, and also with reality as we gradually came to understand it, of Soviet ICBMs, submarine-launched missiles, and bombers. He found indicators on the American side mostly to have peaked in the late

1950s and early 1960s, and then to have declined to the early 1970s. Given increases in these categories on the Soviet side during those years of U.S. decline, he asserted that we were not "racing" them. Moreover, he maintained that some of the technical advances had helped to stabilize the nuclear balance: the hardening of silos, permissive action links, technology that enabled warheads — and so missiles — to be smaller, hence mobile, hence safer from attack (under the sea or, in the Soviet case, mobile on land); and increases in accuracy, along with smaller missiles, that reduced potential collateral damage to civilians. Advances in technology that made for a more stable relationship were good.

AW agreed that for the United States to have more aircraft or missiles simply because the Soviets were making more of them, or were assumed to have this intention, was a bad idea. However, he argued that his opponents ignored crucial aspects of the strategic competition by assuming that a simple action-reaction process was at work, or that the Soviet Union was aiming for a small "minimum deterrent" force. Most fundamentally, he disagreed that nuclear war was impossible simply because many extremely destructive weapons existed, and worried that the nuclear postures proposed by his opponents would foreclose the possibility of limiting the scope of the conflict if war should break out.

These articles garnered support and criticism. One criticism was that he had chosen dates to favor his argument.[29] Among the critics, a phrase that caught on was supplied by the title of former arms control agency official Paul Warnke's rejoinder: "Apes on a Treadmill." It evoked the image of mindless building of nuclear forces by both sides, something that could happen only if leaders were mistakenly led to believe that they could gain an advantage over nuclear-armed opponents.

This view led to the doctrine of Mutual Assured Destruction (dubbed "MAD" by Donald Brennan), that since only a few nuclear weapons delivered on a city could produce vast damage, why, then, buy more than the number needed to assure *that* result? Arthur Steiner, a colleague of AW, identified it with two propositions: (1) Don't attack weapons; aim at people; and (2) Don't defend against the adversary's weapons.[30] Motivations for proposition (1) might be, *don't attack his weapons because that would be destabilizing and would lead to an arms race*; or alternatively, *don't attack weapons because it can't be done successfully*. Motivations for proposition (2) might be, *don't defend because it's a bad idea*; or alternatively, *don't defend because although it might be desirable it isn't feasible*. A large problem left inadequately addressed by MAD, and often ignored by AW's critics, was how to defend Europe, which was believed to be vulnerable to Warsaw Pact conventional attack. Our policy was to use nuclear weapons first there if such an attack was succeeding. In contrast, AW held that "most of those who rely on tactical nuclear weapons as a substitute for disparities in conventional forces have in general presupposed a cooperative Soviet attacker, one who did not use atomic weapons himself."[31] Moreover, he added:

> . . . nuclear limited war, simply because of the extreme swiftness and unpredictability of its moves, the necessity of delegating authority to local commanders, and the possibility of sharp and sudden desperate reversals of fortune, would put the greatest strain on the deterrent to all-out thermonuclear war. For this reason I believe that it would be appropriate to emphasize the importance of expanding a conventional capability realistically and, in particular, research and development in non-nuclear modes of warfare.[32]

This last sentence foreshadowed his long and successful campaign to improve greatly the effectiveness of conventional airpower.

Civil vs. Military Uses of Nuclear Energy: Revealing a Distinction without Much Difference.

It should not surprise that a logician would be skilled at parsing distinctions. One was the purported distinction between civilian and military uses of atomic energy. This was a highly misleading distinction as dealt with politically. It is at the heart of the international proliferation problem. Although the influential Acheson-Lilienthal Report of 1946 on the potential and the dangers of nuclear technology was initially optimistic about the possibility of making civilian nuclear fuel hard to use in bombs, its authors quickly saw the dangers and proposed that all nuclear enterprises be run by an international authority.[33] The Eisenhower Administration blurred the distinction between civil and military uses of nuclear energy with *Atoms for Peace*, a program which accelerated the distribution of weapons-relevant civil nuclear technology and know-how widely throughout the world.

The economic benefits have turned out to be modest so far, but *Atoms for Peace* advanced the ability of many countries to make the bomb on short notice by training people in nuclear science and technology and giving them experience in handling fissionable materials. Nuclear electric power, the main civilian application, requires fissile material as a fuel, or yields it as a by-product of the reaction process, or both. For various reasons having to do with politics, both domestic and foreign, most of the countries able to make the bomb on short notice — by now a large number — have chosen not to do so. But as the cases of India (written about perceptively by Roberta), Pakistan, North Korea and (prospectively) Iran show, civilian applications can be used to advance military ones. With *Atoms for Peace*, the U.S. Government and others tried to make a distinction where there was not much of a difference. His aforementioned 1976 article on "Spreading the Bomb without Quite Breaking the Rules" described efforts by policymakers to make such unrealistic distinctions.

The Nuclear Nonproliferation Treaty (NPT), signed in 1968, incorporates the manifest tensions, not to say confusions, on this topic. It says that nuclear explosives will not be transferred (Articles I and II), that safeguards will be accepted (Article III), that all countries have an inalienable right to nuclear energy for peaceful purposes in accordance with Articles I and II (Article IV, paragraph 1), that nuclear technologies be shared (Article IV, paragraph 2), and that all parties work towards nuclear disarmament (Article VI). Article IV opened the door to acquiring weapons-related capacities, and three countries are known to have gone through it and violated their safeguards agreements: Iraq in the period leading up to the first Gulf War, North Korea, and Iran. Several that made the bomb had not signed the NPT: India, Pakistan, Israel, and South Africa (which signed the NPT after it had dismantled its bomb program).

When AW and his associates examined the problems posed by civil nuclear energy's military potential in the 1970s, those problems were not as evident as they are today. This work highlighted matters that have become of great public concern in the past decade. Inconsistencies abound. For instance, AW and his associates noted that a major mission of the International Atomic Energy Agency was to market nuclear energy around the world, notably to developing countries. To this day, the IAEA still refers to itself, with no apparent sense of irony, as the "Atoms for Peace Agency."

It cannot be said that the behavior of governments has greatly improved in this arena.

The Need to Use Power Discriminately: The Moral Dimension.

A theme that emerged in AW's work from an early point was how to use military power more effectively against military forces and avoid unintended harm to civilians.[34] There were both utilitarian and moral arguments for this. With nuclear weapons, this was a challenge and, to some people, an oxymoron in the sense that any use of nuclear weapons, no matter how limited in scope, might quickly escalate and produce a holocaust. The predominant view was that *anything* that would mitigate the destructiveness of nuclear weapons would suggest that they could be rationally used.

The question of objectives was addressed by the American Catholic Bishops' *Pastoral Letter on War and Peace* in 1983.[35] AW commented on this letter in "Bishops, Statesmen, and Other Strategists on the Bombing of Innocents" (1983), a magisterial review of central issues of nuclear strategy. He wrote:

> By revising many times in public their pastoral letter on war and peace, American Catholic bishops have dramatized the moral issues which statesmen, using empty threats to end the world, neglect or evade. For the bishops stand in a long moral tradition which condemns the threat to destroy innocents as well as their actual destruction. They try but do not escape reliance on threatening bystanders. . . . The letter offers a unique opportunity to examine the moral, political, and military issues together, and to show that . . . threatening to bomb innocents is not part of the nature of things. Nor has it been, as is now widely claimed, an essential of deterrence from the beginning. Nor is it the inevitable result of "modern technology."[36]

He continued:

> The bishops have been sending a message to strategists in Western foreign-policy establishments — and to strategists in the Western anti-nuclear counter-establishments.

It seems unequivocal: "Under no circumstances may nuclear weapons or other instruments of mass slaughter be used for the purpose of destroying population centers or other predominantly civilian targets." Though that only restates an exemplary part of Vatican II two decades earlier, it is far from commonplace. Nonetheless it should be obvious to Catholics and non-Catholics alike. Informed realists in foreign-policy establishments as well as pacifists should oppose aiming to kill bystanders with nuclear or conventional weapons: indiscriminate Western threats paralyze the West, not the East. We have urgent political and military as well as moral grounds for improving our ability to answer an attack on Western military forces with less unintended killing, not to mention deliberate mass slaughter.[37]

AW then criticized the bishops for adopting the position that it was acceptable for us to have these weapons but never to use them.

Having observed long ago that not even Genghis Khan avoided combatants in order to focus solely on destroying noncombatants, I was grateful, on a first look at this issue in the evolving pastoral letter, to find the bishops on the side of the angels. Unfortunately, a closer reading suggested that they were also on the other side. For, while they sometimes say that we should not threaten to destroy civilians, they say too that we may continue to maintain nuclear weapons — and so implicitly threaten their use as a deterrent — while moving toward permanent verifiable nuclear and general disarmament; *yet we may not meanwhile plan to be able to fight a nuclear war even in response to a nuclear attack* [emphasis original].

Before that distant millennial day when all the world disarms totally, verifiably, and irrevocably — at least in nuclear weapons — if we should not intend to attack noncombatants, as the letter says, what alternative is there to deter nuclear attack or coercion? Plainly only to be able to aim at the combatants attacking us, or at their equipment, facilities, or direct sources of combat supply. That, however, is what is meant by planning to be able to fight a nuclear war — which the letter rejects.[38]

Responses were abundant and mixed. It evoked praise by such prominent people as Samuel Huntington, Aaron Wildavsky, and Brent Scowcroft (on occasion an AW target). Among the critics was the political scientist, Bruce Russett, who had been an adviser to the bishops and who wrote that AW had distorted the bishops' position, and that the final version of their letter had dropped mention of non-use under all circumstances. Russett added he wished that AW had "acknowledged the desirability of a *no-first use* posture" (emphasis added) as being consistent with the views expressed in the article.

V. RADICALLY REDUCING UNINTENDED HARM TO CIVILIANS

AW examined the history of strategic bombing, an undertaking of great imprecision such that if the target were in cities most bombs would miss it and hit civilians. This inevitable inaccuracy during World War II had led to a policy of deliberately targeting civilians, with the result that enormous destruction was done, e.g., Tokyo, Hamburg, and Dresden. Obviously, the destruction would be enormously greater with nuclear weapons aimed at civilians. AW thought planning based on MAD targeting was wrong on both utilitarian and moral grounds.

The alternative path that AW first suggested was a combination of making much lower-yield nuclear bombs and delivering them with greater accuracy against solely military targets. He observed that the thermonuclear process (as distinguished from the fission one), contrary to the initial impression that it would only enable bomb yields to be horrendously large, would actually permit bombs with much smaller weights and yields to be made.

This combination never found enough support to be carried out seriously, but a crucial extension of AW's idea did, one that he worked on for many years. It was that advances in computing and sensors might make it possible to destroy discrete targets with non-nuclear weapons. As it turned out, several technologies made this possible, as demonstrated in the First Gulf War (recall the image of a cruise missile going down a boulevard in Baghdad and turning to hit the defense ministry). Highly precise weapons were then used against Serbia in 1999 and Iraq again in 2003. Of course, the right targets had to be designated. We could now precisely hit the wrong place, as in the bombing of the al Firdos air raid shelter in Baghdad in 1991, or of the Chinese embassy in Belgrade in 1999.

Striking evidence of official acceptance of AW's ideas on discriminate deterrence came in a Defense Department briefing on March 5, 2003, 2 weeks before the invasion of Iraq, about our "military practices and procedures to minimize casualties to non-combatants during military operations."[39] Such a public statement about attack criteria in a war about to occur was extraordinary; its substance was the opposite of the bombing goal against Germany and Japan in World War II. This was the message:

> For each military target, the potential for collateral damage is reviewed and a decision made regarding:
> - Targets likely to result in noncombatant casualties
> - Targets likely to result in damage to noncombatant structures;
> - Targets that affect protected sites;
> - Targets that serve both a military and civilian purpose; and
> - Targets in close proximity to known human shields.[40]

The briefing added that the U.S. military would seek to reduce collateral damage by using smaller weapons, shifting aim points or the time attack to periods of low occupancy, as well as by dispersing of leaflets and of radio broadcasts telling people to stay away from some places. That said, the Pentagon briefing also conceded the inevitability of unintended casualties caused by technical malfunctions, human error, and the fog of war.

No doubt, there were cynics about this announcement, but the ensuing air campaign showed that it was largely carried out according to these principles. AW's long campaign to move the United States away from indiscriminate and uncontrollable military technologies had shown results.

"Never Eat an Unworthy Calorie" and Other Passions.

A recent book describes Albert Wohlstetter as "flamboyant and eccentric."[41] Rather, he had standards, such as great attentiveness to food and wine. Here, his tendency towards excellence was defended with the statement, "Never eat an unworthy calorie."

His passion toward work and life was a quality to be emulated.

Flamboyant he was not. But he did stand out in a crowd, especially in later years when he had a beard and mustache. He and Roberta did much entertaining at home. As for going out, they were more likely to be found watching a jazz ensemble than visiting a nightclub. But they worked too hard to have much time for such entertainments.

They cared about literature and the arts, music, architecture, dance (their daughter Joan became a dancer—and mathematical analyst). Many of their friends, especially in New York City, Los Angeles, and Chicago, were scholars and people in the arts such as the great art historian Meyer Shapiro and the mathematical logician Willard Van Orman Quine. At RAND their friends included, among many others, sociologist Herbert Goldhamer, demographer Fred Iklé, economist Andrew Marshall, physicist Herman Kahn, economist Charles Hitch, and engineer James Digby. In Chicago one met or heard about economists Harry Johnson, Gary Becker, Milton Friedman; the sociologist Edward Shils; law professor Edward Levi (who became Attorney General in the Ford Administration); Nobel Prize-winning novelist Saul Bellow; and the remarkable polymath and social scientist (who had been at RAND) Nathan Leites.

The objects of AW's work and life were large passions, and although he tried to be fair to intellectual opponents, he didn't always succeed. Wrong-headed people could be seen as fools, and he didn't suffer fools easily. But excellence, in the end, trumped and he certainly respected it.

ENDNOTES - Rowen

1. Thomas C. Schelling, "Global Warming: Intellectual History and Strategic Choices," Remarks at the Fourth Annual Hans Landsberg Memorial Lecture, Resources for the Future, Washington, DC; December 6, 2006, available from *www.rff.org/ rff/Events/upload/25573_1.pdf*.

2. Without doubt, the most bizarre tagging of AW was to identify him with the views of the political philosopher Leo Strauss, a fellow professor at the University of Chicago. AW must have known Strauss, but in my many years of association with AW, I cannot recall his name being mentioned once—in contrast to those of the Chicago luminaries noted above.

3. Among the many misconceptions about AW's work is that it involved game theory. It did not formally. Game theory, which was being developed at RAND in the 1950s, deals with opposing choices, but it was too underdeveloped and abstract to deal with the kinds of concrete operational problems that AW and his team had sought to address. It provided metaphors — not useful models of interactions.

4. For more on Albert Wohlstetter's methodology, see Wohlstetter, *Theory and Opposed-System Design*, D(L)-16001-1, Santa Monica, CA: RAND Corporation, August 1967, revised January 1968, available from *www.rand.org/about/history/ wohlstetter/DL16001.1/DL16001.1.html*. AW's essay was later published as "Theory and Opposed-System Design," *Journal of Conflict Resolution*, Vol. 12, No. 3, September 1968, pp. 302-331. A version of that essay is included in this edited volume.

5. See Albert J. Wohlstetter, Fred S. Hoffman, Robert J. Lutz, and Henry S. Rowen, *The Selection of Strategic Air Bases*, R-244-S, special staff report, Santa Monica, CA: RAND Corporation, March 1, 1953, TOP SECRET, declassified on July 1, 1963, available from *www.albertwohlstetter.com/writings/19530301-AW-EtAl-R244S.pdf*; and Wohlstetter, Hoffman, Lutz, and Rowen, *The Selection and Use of Strategic Air Bases*, R-266, final report, Santa Monica, CA: RAND Corporation, April 1954, TOP SECRET, declassified circa 1961, available from *www.rand.org/pubs/reports/R0266/*.

6. See Albert Wohlstetter, Fred S. Hoffman, Robert J. Lutz, and Henry S. Rowen, *Vulnerability of U.S. Strategic Air Power to a Surprise Enemy Attack in 1956*, SM-15, Santa Monica, CA: RAND Corporation, April 15, 1953.

7. Philip Taubman, *Secret Empire: Eisenhower, the CIA, and the Hidden Story of America's Space Espionage*, New York, NY: Simon and Schuster, 2003, p. 12.

8. Despite the rapid acceptance of the need for a protected retaliatory power, the belief in using ballistic missile "launch-on-warning" responses to an attack long persisted among some high military authorities. It was a dangerous belief that entailed fast and irrevocable decisions when information was likely to be sparse and possibly wrong.

9. On this point, see Vojtech Mastny and Malcolm Byrne, eds., *A Cardboard Castle? An Inside History of the Warsaw Pact, 1955-1991*, Budapest, Hungary: Central European University Press, 2005.

10. In the early 1960s, work done under the direction of two of AW's former associates, the author of this chapter, and more systematically by Alain Enthoven in the Pentagon's Office of Systems Analysis, countered the view of Warsaw Pact conventional superiority in Europe. Eventually, this counterview became more widely accepted — notably after the rise of *Solidarity* in Poland — although preserving the traditional argument of Soviet superiority was seen by the U.S. Army as necessary for budgetary reasons.

11. One effort to deal with this contradiction was offered by Tom Schelling in a paper titled "The Threat that Leaves Something to Chance." (This paper was published as a chapter in Schelling, *The Strategy of Conflict*, Cambridge, MA: Harvard University Press, 1960, pp. 187–203.) Here, the view was that it was not rational to use nuclear weapons against an adversary that had them, but uncertainty as to what would happen if there were actually a war would induce caution all around. It was not a wholly comforting theory despite its plausibility.

12. See Henry A. Kissinger, *Nuclear Weapons and Foreign Policy*, New York, NY: Harper & Row, 1957.

13. Albert Wohlstetter, "On the Genesis of Nuclear Strategy: Letter to Michael Howard," unpublished, November 6, 1968, revised circa April 1986 with additional material and annotations by James Digby and Arthur Steiner and a prefatory note by Michael Howard, Wohlstetter Papers, Writings, Box 187, Folder 22. The annotated version of this letter is available in this edited volume.

14. The great mathematician, John von Neumann, was the stimulus for the name of an early computer at RAND, the *Johnniac*. Two economists of distinction who visited for some time were Thomas Schelling and Kenneth Arrow, each of whom later received the Nobel Prize in economics. Herbert Simon (another Nobel laureate in economics) had a long working association with RAND's Allen Newell, doing work on human problem solving.

15. Andrew May, "What Made RAND Work?" unpublished note based on discussions with Andrew Marshall, November 2006.

16. President Ronald Reagan, "Remarks at the Presentation Ceremony for the Presidential Medal of Freedom to Albert and Roberta Wohlstetter," East Room, White House, Washington, DC, November 7, 1985, available from *www.reagan.utexas.edu/archives/speeches/1985/110785a.htm*.

17. Albert Wohlstetter, "Scientists, Seers and Strategy," *Foreign Affairs*, Vol. 41, No. 3, April 1963, p. 471.

18. *Ibid.*

19. C. P. Snow, *Science and Government: The Godkin Lectures at Harvard, 1960*, Cambridge, MA: Harvard University Press, 1961.

20. Albert J. Wohlstetter, Fred S. Hoffman, and Henry S. Rowen, *Protecting U.S. Power to Strike Back in the 1950s and 1960s*, R-290, staff report, Santa Monica, CA: RAND Corporation, September 1, 1956, TOP SECRET, declassified circa 1960s, available from *www.albertwohlstetter.com/writings/19560901-AW-EtAl-R290.pdf*

21. On this topic, see Albert Wohlstetter, "SAC Test 1957 of Alert Bomber Response—Only 'Fail Unsafe'," April 29, 1985, Wohlstetter Papers, Notes, Box 102, Folder 6, Tab H, p. 3.

22. *Ibid.*, p. 4.

23. There has been public discussion of a very important but different topic: Have the Indians and Pakistanis installed Permissive Action Link (PALs) on their nuclear bombs—in effect, combination locks? For more on PALs, see Fred C. Iklé, Gerald J. Aronson, and Albert Madansky, *On the Risk of an Accidental or Unauthorized Nuclear Detonation*, RM-2251, Santa Monica, CA: RAND Corporation, October 15, 1958, esp. pp. 100-101 and 154, available from *www.rand.org/pubs/research_memoranda/RM2251/*.

24. Before what levels of protection were determined to be technically feasible at what cost, AW and Fred Hoffman did a set of "break even" analyses on what such protection would be worth in terms of survival of missiles. It was more than enough to fit reality.

25. For a recently published criticism, see Richard Rhodes, *Arsenals of Folly: The Making of the Nuclear Arms Race*, New York, NY: Alfred A. Knopf, 2007.

26. See "Appendix III: Treatment of Operations-Research Questions in the 1969 Debate," *Operations Research: The Journal of the Operations Research Society of America*, Vol. 19, No. 5, September 1971, pp. 1175-1237. Quoted phrases appear on p. 1217.

27. Albert Wohlstetter, "Is There a Strategic Arms Race?" *Foreign Policy*, No. 15, Summer 1974, pp. 3-20; and Wohlstetter, "Rivals, But No 'Race'," *Foreign Policy*, No. 16, Fall 1974, pp. 48-81.

28. Wohlstetter, "Is There a Strategic Arms Race?" p. 3.

29. Michael L. Nacht, "The Delicate Balance of Error," *Foreign Policy*, No. 19, Summer 1975, pp. 163-77.

30. Henry S. Rowen, "Introduction," in Henry Sokolski, ed., *Getting MAD: Nuclear Mutual Assure Destruction, Its Origins and Practice*, Carlisle, PA: Strategic Studies Institute, November 2004, p. 3, available from *www.npec-web.org/Books. asp?BookID=2116845428*.

31. Albert Wohlstetter, *The Delicate Balance of Terror* (unabridged version), P-1472, Santa Monica, CA: RAND Corporation, November 6, 1958, Revised December 1958, p. 17, available from *www.rand.org/about/history/wohlstetter/P1472/P1472.html*.

32. Wohlstetter, *The Delicate Balance of Terror*, p. 18.

33. Henry Sokolski has called my attention to a press release issued about a week after the report was released saying that "it would be unwise to rely on denaturing to insure an interval of as much as a year." See Press Release No. 235 [on the Secretary of State's Committee on Atomic Energy's *Report on the International*

Control of Atomic Energy, Washington, DC: U.S. Government Printing Office, March 16, 1946], U.S. Department of State, April 9, 1946.

34. An important vehicle for addressing this and other security issues was *Discriminate Deterrence*, final report of the Commission on an Integrated Long Term Strategy, Washington, DC: U.S. Government Printing Office, January 1988, *www.albertwohlstetter. com/writings/Descriminate Deterrence*. Co-chaired by AW and Fred Iklé, the Commission was made up of a distinguished set of members appointed jointly by the Secretary of Defense and the President's National Security Advisor.

35. National Conference of Catholic Bishops, *The Challenge of Peace: God's Promise and Our Response*, a pastoral letter on war and peace, Washington, DC: Office of Publication Services of the U.S. Catholic Conference, May 3, 1983.

36. Albert Wohlstetter, "Bishops, Statesmen, and Other Strategists on the Bombing of Innocents," *Commentary*, Vol. 75, No. 6, June 1983, p. 15.

37. *Ibid*.

38. *Ibid,* p. 16.

39. "Background Briefing on Targeting," news transcript, U.S. Department of Defense, March 5, 2003, available from *www. defenselink.mil/transcripts/transcript.aspx?transcriptid=2007*.

40. See "Targeting and Collateral Damage," presentation slides, Central Command, U.S. Department of Defense, March 5, 2003, slide 4, available from *www.defenselink.mil/news/Briefing Slide.aspx?Briefing SlideID=90*.

41. Jay Winik, *On the Brink: The Dramatic, Behind-the-Scenes Saga of the Reagan Era and the Men and Women Who Won the Cold War*, New York, NY: Simon and Shuster, 1996, p. 50. Quoted by Rhodes, *Arsenals of Folly*, p. 111.

Theory and Opposed-Systems Design (1968)

Albert Wohlstetter

D(L)-16001-1, Santa Monica, CA: RAND Corporation, August 1967, revised January 1968, available from *www.rand.org/about/history/wohlstetter/DL16001.1/ DL16001.1.html*. Courtesy of the Wohlstetter Estate.

I. Madness in Methodology?

When, after nearly a decade of study and work in the field, I left mathematical logic and the logic of science, I made a resolution not to write papers on the methodology or logic of social science—for fear I would never learn any social science. It was all too easy at the time to publish applications of Boolean algebra or the calculus of relations or the like that could just conceivably be relevant to some future empirical study, in, say, economics. But I had the uneasy feeling that in offering guides for new approaches to social science, I might never approach very closely myself. And I did want to learn something of the facts of life and the substantive issues whose powerful interest had dragged me away from the more chaste attractions of logic. I also had an uncomfortable suspicion that the devastating remark of the great French mathematician, Henri Poincaré, about sociology ("The most methods, and the least results") might only too accurately describe the way one might dally in the approach to any social science in order to avoid actually going in and getting lost in a very dense jungle. Maps, brochures, the purchase of compasses, machetes, bush jackets, and rakish tropical helmets can be used as a substitute for a hot and sweaty journey. In short, I sympathize with Johan Galtung's misgivings about theories about theory in a theory-poor field. (And with the feeling expressed by Burton Marshall since I first wrote these lines: reading the behavioralist literature in international relations seems a bit like sitting through an overture that never ends.[1] But I find that traditionalist critiques of behavioral essays on methodology, with rare exceptions like Marshall's own laconic contributions, have their own *longeurs*.)

Nonetheless, I find myself on the point of talking about an approach, and supposedly a distinctive approach, to the study of international relations—a notoriously impenetrable jungle. One customary way to begin such a discussion is to tick off all the other approaches, the wrong ones, and to end up with a shiny, colored brochure describing the right one—that sole hope for social science, your own. That is not the plan of this paper (though flesh being what it is, it might, of course, turn out that way).

The sort of study that has mainly engaged me for the last sixteen years has been pragmatic in purpose. Yet it seems to me that, from time to time, it has displayed traits of the relations among nations that are interesting and even important for theory. It has at any rate involved the extensive use of theory. That is to say, it has used mathematical models in "essentially general" form, models that refer to potential operations among states or other elements in the international system in a way that cannot be reduced merely to elementary statements about individual objects or to a finite conjunction of such singular statements.[2] It has also involved a great deal of grubby, highly specific empirical work on technologies, operations, costs, and potential interactions among states, factors that are plainly relevant for decisions of the governments of these states—or for citizens evaluating these decisions. It has required the cooperation of several disciplines and, in particular, a kind of close working together of natural science and social science disciplines which remains very unusual, if it exists at all, in universities. Hence, "a new approach."

On the other hand, it is quite clear to me that this line of attack hardly exhausts the approaches to the investigation of the relations among states or even the good approaches. And its novelties do not mean a total discontinuity with other ways of looking at the subject. I believe, in fact, that for all the obvious differences in its quantitative form from the classical or traditional writings in the field, with a bit of stretching of both, the approach I shall call "opposed-systems design" can be accommodated within the classical tradition quite as easily as within the more recent behavioral studies. It has indeed dealt with some matters at the heart of traditional international relations theory—namely, power relations among states—in a particularly operational and concrete way. Much behavioral theory does not. It differs from classical theory in subject as well as method.

Declaring yourself neutral in the war between the classicists and the behavioralists is probably about as safe as claiming neutrality between General Cao Ky and the Buddhists in Vietnam, and as little convincing to either side. Nonetheless, it is true that I have a high regard for a good many traditional studies of international relations—so far, for rather more of them perhaps than for the new studies. At the same time, I believe that some numerical relations are essential in understanding the changing relations among states; that they are frequently implicit in at least rudimentary form in the classical works and could stand more rigorous statement, imaginative extension, and systematic confirmation or disconfirmation by evidence. And I suspect that the specific quantitative methods that engage behavioralists today include some of those that might suggest fruitful theory. The current practices of traditional and behavioral studies do not exclude each other, nor do they together — or even in combination with the approach I shall describe — exhaust the possibilities. It is very easy to find miserable examples of any method, including, I would stress, the one I shall describe. There are no methods certain of result in a complex field of research. None is proof against a dim awareness of interesting problems or incompetence in formulating manageable and significant questions. The truth is that international studies are a hard line of work. The useful inquiries in international affairs that contrast in method, in good part, seem to me to complement each other, but to focus on different questions.

My purpose in this paper will be to describe the sort of study I have been concerned with, and then to try to locate it very briefly with respect to other studies in the field, some traditional and some (to use once again the current jargon) behavioral. The precision with which I can locate the method of opposed-systems design is limited by the fact that, while I have been actively concerned for quite a few years in the field of international affairs, I can claim no encyclopedic understanding of the literature. In any case the comparisons, as I have already suggested, are not invidious but orienting.

II. Opposed Systems

A. QUESTIONS FOR DECISION-MAKERS

I shall use the phrase "opposed-systems design" to name a kind of study that attempts to discern and answer questions affecting policy — specifically affecting a choice of ends and of means to accomplish ends that stand a good chance of being opposed by other governments. The ends of any government are multiple and only partially incompatible with those of other governments — even very hostile ones — and of course such conflicts may be resolved without fighting. A peaceful resolution may depend in part on the risks involved in combat. In any case the conflict of aims raises the possibility of combat: and a major part of these studies is concerned therefore with the likelihood and the likely outcomes of such combat. In fact, they grew out of operational research as it had been practiced in World War II.

The positive reasons for my choice of this label will be made clear in what follows. On the negative side, "opposed-systems design" replaces several synonyms—some of my own devising—which have not quite succeeded in fending off casual misunderstanding. One workable synonym might appear to be "strategic studies"; but the phrase is at best ambiguous and at worst a militantly indiscriminate epithet used by antagonists of any study of potential military conflict. The most familiar serious candidate is E. L. Paxson's "systems analysis" and, in fact, this has the largest currency; there is now, for example, an able Assistant Secretary of Defense for Systems Analysis. But the word "system" is everybody's possession. It is used rather differently by engineers in "systems engineering," by theorists of international relations, and in particular by Mr. Kaplan in his "systems theory," and, rather mysteriously, by the general semanticists in their "general systems theory." As a short name for a complex of interdependent elements, the word "system" seems nearly indispensable, but not specific enough. Yet it is used without qualification to designate very different kinds of complexes of interdependent elements. I have tried in the past to discriminate the sort of study Paxson had in mind from many of these others by talking of "conflict-systems design," but that has the difficulty of suggesting that the goal of study is to generate conflict. "Conflict-worthy systems," modeled on "sea-worthy," is a more accurate term but even more awkward. Perhaps "opposed-systems design" is closing in on it. Potential opposition at any rate is an essential.

In both England and the United States during World War II, as is well known, a considerable and very fruitful effort was devoted to operational research, to the systematic analysis of alternative ways of accomplishing various proximate objectives. These analyses aided decisions on how to deploy and operate radars and coordinate them with interceptors in the Battle of Britain, how to pattern the movements of destroyers searching for submarines in the Bay of Biscay, how to determine the optimum altitudes for penetration and bomb delivery in the European theater, and a host of other matters. Studies of similar scope and intent continue today and are applied to aid or implement the decisions not only of national organizations but also of alliance and international (including interadversary) organizations. Among the latter studies are analyses of the instruments and sampling inspection procedures for an underground test ban or to prevent the diversion of material or equipment from peaceful to nonpeaceful uses in nuclear reactors operated under international agreements.

Present as well as past operational research had to do with how best to operate with given organizations and specified equipment in order to achieve various near-term goals. The operations studied have been essentially tactical. After World War II, however, broader analyses to aid decisions were made, dealing with a longer run in which a wider range of alternatives could be made available. New equipment could be designed, developed, and purchased, organizations could be expanded or contracted, and more numerous uncertainties were likely to affect the environment in which they operated and the goals they worked to achieve. Such cardinal choices, to borrow a term from C. P. Snow, might be illustrated by the decision on how to allocate resources for a strategic force that would not be operational until some years hence and that one might expect to constitute a major part of the operational force for the better part of the following decade. How much should one spend on increasing the size of this force and how much on protecting it and making it more subject to control? This specific choice was a vital one in developing a second-strike capability and in clarifying the objective of deterrence. Another question presently much debated, especially in connection with the decision on ballistic missile defense, concerns resource allocation between offense and active and passive defense. In an international environment that includes five countries that have made nuclear explosions and over one hundred and thirty that have not, still another cardinal issue today concerns the choice of military stance, formal or informal alliance commitments, and practicable international treaty arrangements among adversaries that may best reduce the expectation of nuclear war and the damage it would do. Such larger studies contrast with operational research mainly in degree, in the number of factors considered, and in the time perspective. In fact, they normally incorporate many operational research studies as components. They may be said to consider the larger "strategic" alternatives as distinct from the smaller "tactical" choices made in operational research,

127

provided "strategy" is understood broadly enough to include a choice of ends as well as means.

All such studies, whether in the large or in the small, concern alternative systems involving both items of equipment and organizations of men using them. In this respect they are like the systems engineering studies of large complex systems in the public utility field, such as telephony, transportation, or postal systems. But in a public utility like the Bell Telephone system or the Japanese Super Hikari express train system, the principal obstacles to be overcome are natural ones: difficult terrain, storms, earthquakes, atmospheric disturbances, etc., with direct human opposition, such as sabotage, forming only a minor concern. In the field of arms and arms control both the peacetime and wartime decisions that will affect the safety and power relations among states must all be taken with potential man-made obstacles in mind; their success in good part depends on other decisions that may be taken by an at least partially hostile government.

B. THEORETICAL MODELS

In elaborating an analysis of the capabilities in the 1950s of either of the two major nuclear powers for striking back after nuclear attack on its strategic force, or in analyzing the feasibility and cost in the 1970s for one of the two major powers to limit potential damage by using active defenses against an initial ballistic missile attack, mathematical models embodying a theory of these interactions are necessary. Sometimes large-scale computer models are required. Sometimes a small analytic model will catch essential features of the subject matter. A study of the protection of strategic forces in the early 1950s[3] used differential equation models capable of analytic solution on a slide rule, as well as Monte Carlo computer models for some component studies. Optimal solutions found by partial differentiation required fixing in advance the values of a great many variables (numbers of targets struck, the number of vehicles forming a "cell" to saturate defenses, the number of warheads, the number of kilograms per warhead, the overpressure resistance of elements on bases and their dispersal in space, deployment and delay times in the active defenses, approach and penetration routes and altitude profiles, and peacetime costs that varied for alternative readiness choices among others). Though some simple analytic models have been useful, their realism and utility have depended on their being associated with a painstaking empirical examination of variations much too complex to be represented by a well-behaved analytic function or a smooth curve. For example, the losses to be expected by aircraft penetrating distant defenses and many other costs that vary with distance are seldom essentially continuous or linear or monotonic-increasing. They may not even be steadily nondecreasing. Nor are they derivable from common experience.

It is worth observing that, contrary to current legend, opposed-systems analyses have made little or no use of game theory, and while they normally require many map exercises, they have not been heavily dependent on formal games or experimental simulation. I would guess that games and game theory have played a much smaller role in serious studies whose main aim is to aid specific decisions on opposed systems than they do in the more general academic behavioral literature on international conflict appearing in such magazines as the *Journal of Conflict Resolution.*

In the more successful studies, mathematical models of potential military interaction have played a rather pragmatic role, but they are essential. On the other hand, so is a great deal of elementary arithmetic; and much study of data derived from state-of-the-arts studies, theoretical analyses of equipment design, tests of existing equipment and components of future equipment, peacetime operations and logistics; and also political data permitting at least rough judgments of such contingencies as the loss of various overseas base areas. (Political catastrophes such as the loss of bases may affect aircraft and tanker requirements quite as much as technological factors like specific fuel consumption.) Since the choices to be affected extend years into the future, the alternatives compared and studied empirically may include not simply the received or existing alternatives but also invented ones. The invention of operations, organizations, or equipment has, in fact, been crucial in the studies that have worked out best.

C. The Time Span Covered

These theories and the policies they serve deal with a future that is long compared to the models and choices in traditional operational research, which aims at proximate goals for forces substantially fixed in size and composition. On the other hand, their scope in time has been modest by comparison with that of attempts to construct theories of international strategy, as in

129

Schelling, or systems theories, as in Kaplan, or theories of the balance of power like Deutsch and Singer's highly general semi-quantitative construct; or many of the more traditional, less explicitly quantitative theories. The sort of opposed-systems design of which I speak studies technologies, operations, political interactions, and economic costs stretching perhaps for as much as a decade and a half into the future, and designs alternative systems to operate within that period, which has seemed to be about as far in advance as the technological and political context can be foreseen or parameterized with enough constraints to yield conclusions. In fact, though hope and salesmanship may spring eternal for eternal final solutions to our troubles, the best practice is quite self-conscious about the finiteness of the life of measures proposed, and will estimate their end. Thus, at the beginning of the 1950s, it was possible to design a system of deterrence for the rest of the decade in the United States, which used tactical warning to permit alert response as an essential part of a complex set of arrangements. But by the time the system was designed and some of its elements adopted in principle, while it had seven years or so to run, it was also foreseen by the designers that travel times for attacking vehicles in the early 1960s would be so sharply reduced that warning and alert measures, while still useful, would no longer have a decisive importance. They would not, at any rate, be adequate. Measures that did not depend on warning and fast response, such as shelter for strategic vehicles or a mode of operation which kept vehicles on the move, would be an essential both for survival under attack and for reducing the likelihood of a fast and irrevocable response to a false alarm. At the start of 1954, a second study which designed a deterrent system for the 1960s suggested the methods of hardening that were later adopted, but explicitly anticipated that the adequacy of such measures would not outlast the 1960s, when guidance technology could be expected to reduce the inaccuracy exploited by protective construction.[4] (The first sketch of the study was entitled "Defending a Strategic Force After 1960" and had a subsection entitled "After After 1960" which dealt with technological changes likely in the 1970s.[5]) In both studies, estimates of the length of time at the end of which the design measures would no longer suffice turned out to be quite accurate. It is interesting to observe that ambitious smaller powers developing nuclear forces have chugged along, ten years out of phase, just in time to develop first- and second-generation forces capable of meeting the past but not the contemporaneous threat.

The perspective of ten or fifteen years or so may not be an essential permanent feature of such opposed-systems design and analysis. But neither is it accidental. It has been connected with the fact that some of the major technological changes take that long to come into effect, once they are visible. It has taken about that long for some of the potentially decisive changes in the state of the art to go from the stage of well confirmed principle through research, development, engineering, and procurement to operation on a considerable scale. After that they are likely to remain in operation for some time. In the summer of 1953, for example, Bruno Augenstein and (a while later) the Gardner Committee perceived the implications of high-yield, relatively small, light fusion payloads for transforming the performance of the intercontinental ballistic missile program then under desultory development for over a half a dozen years. However, even the crash program that resulted, and many billions of dollars, could not advance the time to a date earlier than the 1960s, at which ballistic missiles would make up the bulk of the force of the two major powers. It was possible in 1951 and 1952 to recognize that vehicles travelling at ballistic speeds *might* appear in the force in the sixties decade; and by 1953 to recognize they *would* be; and in both cases to take such impending changes into account in designing systems of deterrence. Years before forces are in operation, it is possible to analyze their interactions with some success, and frequently also to recognize the time limits in which the analysis is valid. It is not solely, of course, a matter of the technological state of the art. Some of the conditions of the analysis will also concern the rate of change at which political arrangements may take place. So at the start of the 1950s, with base rights in two dozen or more countries, one could safely assume that while some rights would be withdrawn, not all nor, in fact, most of these rights would be lost by the end of the decade. One could, moreover, test alternative base systems for how they would fare under a variety of reasonably likely contingencies; but, beyond a decade, the variety of possibilities multiplies very fast.

I would not exclude the possibility of dealing with longer-run futures. Indeed, some sorts of gross technological and political change may be visible in outline decades off and yet require so long an incubation period that they need some actions now to bring them into being or to prevent some desirable futures from being foreclosed. Even designs for Bell Telephone must sometimes be planned on a time scale involving decades. Changes in urban development and population concentrations are extremely slow, and some of the time constants in urban and regional design need also to be quite long. It is apparent that some major features of the international environment will change only over a period of decades, and, while attempts at increasing safety must be open to the wide variety of contingencies implied by such a scale, some gross limitations on this variety may be decipherable. There are a number of attempts now current to look at such long-run futures, or proposals to do so (Bertrand de Jouvenel's *Futuribles;* the Commission for the Year 2000 of the American Academy of Arts and Sciences; the Hudson Institute Project on the Year 2000; the Institute for 21st Century Studies at Ball State University in Muncie, Indiana; Olaf Helmer's projected Institute for the Future; and many others) and such activity may yield useful guides for designing systems for very long-term changes in international affairs. However, for the time, the empirical success of such studies of the long-run future lies in the future; we may hope in a shorter-run future.

The upshot of the foregoing is that, at best, the theories developed so far in opposed-systems design cover a self-consciously restricted interval of time in which the critical, potential, dynamic interactions are mainly contained within the span of less than a decade and a half, sometimes considerably less.

D. Means

What I have said already makes clear that an opposed-systems design deals with a complex variety of means and conditions including various technologies, modes of operation, organizations, and economic and political factors. Most important, such factors have to be dealt with simultaneously, since there is a great deal of feedback. Take the critical role of technology, for example. If you look at economic treatises you will find statements like "We assume as given the maximum amount of output x, which can be produced from any given set of inputs ($v_1 \ldots v_n$). This catalogue of possibilities is the production function and may be written $x = \Psi (v_1 \ldots v_n)$".

For an opposed-systems design a procedure of taking the technical coefficients as fixed or as undetermined parameters will not do. A central part of the inquiry must look at the current and impending state of the art and at feasible and useful changes. In the past two decades in which such inquiries have grown up, nuclear, electronic, propulsion, and transport technology have changed massively. The problem is not just to predict such changes, however. Since this is a work of design, it must explore how — in the light of interdependencies with military, political, and economic events — the changes may usefully be bent.

Technology with its enormous changes presents not only essential problems for the analysis, but also some of the major distinctive opportunities for such an analysis. For, along with the uncertainties, a system with a large technological component, like the highly organized warning, command, control, communication, and reaction systems of aircraft and missiles, inevitably displays many regularities and predictabilities, and the changed relationships brought about by order-of-magnitude increases in a critical technical variable will also be accessible to theoretical analysis. (Thus changes of three orders of magnitude in the explosive yield of a given volume and weight of payload, and by an order of magnitude in the speed of vehicles, or by an order of magnitude in delivery accuracy, can be expected to have decisive and analyzable effects on the economic and operational variables.)

Analyses of opposed systems have worked out best where the technical component has been large and where, as a result, the problem of predicting the outcome of operational interactions has been more manageable. (Yet not without its surprises: some of the greatest successes have come where large changes in the technical components impend, but the ramified consequences of these changes are obvious only after an analysis of considerable sophistication.) Analyses have worked least well where the systems analyzed have been determined by minutely varied local characteristics, such as terrain, morale, training, etc., with no gross technical components dominating the result. Operational analyses of the interaction of ground forces are seldom convincing for this reason, except where there are many obvious disproportions between the components of strength of opposing sides. The formal models they employ — usually some simple differential equations of a type introduced by F. W. Lanchester near the start of World War I[6] — have not often provided very persuasive or useful representations of these highly variable, locally determined phenomena. In their simplest form, Lanchester's equations state that the rate of change or dissipation in a military force is proportional to the absolute size of the opposing military force. The constant of proportionality in this negative term represents the rate of destruction that can be brought about by a unit of the opposing military force.

$$\frac{dX}{dt} = -k_y Y$$

$$\frac{dY}{dt} = -k_x X$$

Partly, perhaps, because these equations have a simple analytic solution, a vast literature has grown up elaborating them and applying them to a very wide variety of cases.[7]

There are some actual cases which approximate these equations. In this respect there is quite as much to say for them as for Richardson's formally similar equations, now rather popular for representing arms races. In fact, some rather better fits have been found for the Lanchester equations.[8] But they do not represent a universal law governing all combat. And Lanchester himself was aware of situations in which they did not apply at all. They have not been much help in predicting the outcomes of classical war between large armies.

Judging the outcome of potential classical combat is a problem not simply for analysts, of course, but for decision-makers, too. The Israelis, for example, feel themselves menaced in a world in which their hostile neighbors outnumber them by a factor of twenty-five. They regard their own superiority in morale, training, education, and technical skill as making up for some of this numerical difference in population and even in the number of tanks and other equipment, but have made clear that there are some changes in Arab military equipment and even some political changes that they will not tolerate. They believe that such changes would presage a successful Arab attack. But how does one estimate the outcome of such complex interactions in which so many of the variables that influence the result are hard to measure?

Just before the Suez campaign of 1956, Czech and Russian arms arrangements with Egypt drastically increased Egyptian superiority in tanks and jet aircraft to a ratio of four to one. According to General Dayan, "In artillery, naval vessels and infantry weapons, the Israel picture was no better. It was not only the disparity in quantity but also the superiority in quality which decisively upset the arms scales."[9] A maxim attributed to Napoleon is that the moral is to the material as four is to one. It is, however, difficult to establish a unit of moral, and it is therefore rather hard to know how to trade it against jet aircraft and tanks. In any case, the Israelis decided not to wait until the increase in Egyptian armaments had become operationally effective. Again in 1967, on the basis of published figures,[10] it appears that the Egyptians had about 430 combat aircraft, not counting jet trainers, and the Israelis had about 200, not counting their 60 Magister Fouga trainers. There were large discrepancies in other arms, and if one counted in the Iraqi, Syrian, and Jordanian air forces (these countries had all joined Nasser in the week preceding the outbreak), the odds looked again to be close to four to one. Such gross order-of-battle figures are hard to interpret. And in 1967 it is clear that the Israelis and the Egyptians interpreted them differently. Intuition had to serve. But it did not serve the two sides equally.

Intuition plays a role in all theorizing, too, but in a successful systems analysis the theory can do a good deal to support and sharpen and sometimes correct intuition. The Israelis have recently, along with the Swedes and some other of the smaller powers, done a good deal to develop systems analysis and opposed-systems design. But it appears so far that their analytic successes, like those of the NATO countries, have been not as much in large-scale ground war as in very small unit interaction and in the more technologically determined areas, such as those involving aircraft. Air war was Lanchester's starting point a half-century ago, even though he applied it more broadly. So far I know of no convincing opposed-systems analysis in the large (i.e., strategy) of warfare between large armies.

The growing importance of technology and the gross changes in performance effected by new states of the art assure an increasing range of application for the sorts of theory used in opposed-systems design. It is a paradox that we can do better in analyzing the potential outcomes of some sorts of conflict that have never occurred than we can do with conflicts of the sort that have been endemic for ages. This does not mean, of course, that the new sorts of conflicts would not have their surprises. It remains true that anticipating the course and result of a war between armies of men with variable intensities of political motivation and skill on terrain whose multiple surface deformations strongly influence outcomes of separate local engagements over a period of weeks, months, or even years is extraordinarily hard—except possibly for cases where an opponent grossly outclasses the other in all relevant respects. And, by comparison, one can with relative ease predict the consequence of 50 or 100 fusion-tipped intermediate range ballistic missiles with known accuracies and yields exploding on ten or so aircraft bases containing vehicles without benefit of tactical warning or blast protection. A relatively few measurable variables determine the outcome. This "easy" analysis, however, is not trivial. It has substantial contemporary relevance, for example, to an estimate of the second-strike capability of the first-generation French nuclear force based on some ten points in south and southwestern France. Against a small force of Russian rockets used appropriately, it has no significant probability of survival. Slightly more complicated analyses of their second-generation force yield similar results. Neither the Mirage IV bomber force nor the hardened missile force in Haute Provence which will succeed it could survive an attack from the more advanced contemporary forces whose threat they are supposed to deter. Such an analysis would be reinforced by considerations of the problem of protecting centers of command and the flow of information to and from them; and of the cumulative obstacles that can be interposed inside the territory of a major antagonist. Uncertainties qualify all empirical analyses, but in these cases they are much reduced, so gross are the determinants of the cumulative interactions. Rather more complex but quite reliable analyses can be made of the third-generation French force. These analyses of the military performance do not say all there is to say about the *force de frappe,* or the broader questions of incentives and drawbacks to the spread of nuclear weapons, but they say some things of great importance.[11]

Finally, though the regularities introduced by technology have played an important and even a critical role in opposed-systems design, such analyses nonetheless are not purely technological, though some technologists are in the habit of saying so. There are essential interactions and feedbacks, as I have already said, with operational, economic, and political events.

E. ENDS

One of the disabilities of the phrase "strategic studies" as a description or title of the opposed-systems analyses that have grown up since World War II is that at least some of the dictionary definitions of "strategy" limit the word to the study of alternative means to attain fixed ends. These wide-ranging studies, looking ahead for many years, differ from operational research by taking as a salient objective the clarification and revision of the objectives maximized.[12] This point is worth stressing not simply because of the possible misleading associations with the word "strategy," but because of some current semi-comic misunderstandings on the subject. Unlike operational research on tactics, opposed-systems design of major alternatives tends where it is successful to involve a careful critique of constraints and objectives. A government's ends cannot be accepted as the final deliverances of authority or intuition. They are subject to revision as the result of an analysis that frequently displays incompatibilities with other ends of that government, or that indicates means so costly that the game is not worth the candle. Moreover, even when an opposed-systems design does not set out to revise objectives, it is quite likely to end up that way.[13]

The tentative character of the objectives examined in an opposed-systems design and the importance of questioning ends as well as means are not merely minor qualifications in a general practice of finding the best means to fixed, unquestionable ends. They are major points of difference from operational research, stressed from the start by the principal practitioners of opposed-systems design. The need to take objectives only on trial is imposed, in the case of actual research on broad policy issues extending over years, by the very breadth of the inquiry. There is no authoritative or intuitive set of goals perfectly compatible with each other and with content enough to furnish guidance. In fact, there is always a multiplicity of goals in partial conflict. Political circumstances and technologies alter, making the old goals partially irrelevant and sometimes offering opportunities to satisfy several desired objectives simultaneously that had been previously incompatible, or vice versa. The well-defined preference function establishing at least a weak ordering among all possible alternatives, which is a convenient assumption in much of economic theory, is never realized in fact even for individuals, much less for nations. "All possible alternatives" are not in general definable and not all of the possibilities we might specify are strictly speaking "connected," subject to a weak order: there are some complex pairs of alternatives we don't know how to compare, how to establish one member of the pair as no worse than the other. While there are, of course, some *partial* orders among our preferences, frequently we learn how to compare them only in the process of an analysis.[14]

Of course, a government agency seeking aid in its decisions may have quite firm ideas to start with as to what it wants to accomplish by a specific decision and may hope for succor only in the choice of means. Nonetheless, precisely because governments have limited resources and more than one objective, there is always the possibility that the initial objective will be bought at too great a sacrifice of other goals. And, from the standpoint of the sponsoring agency itself, one critical advantage of objective research on policy is that it can aid decision to avoid irrational sacrifice of important goals by pointing to the need for revising ends. Moreover, in governments such as that of the United States, questioning goals need not be terribly dangerous to the questioner; there are always enough factions espousing varied ends to provide some safety in dealing with a short-sighted or dogmatic leadership.

One may ask, however, whether there are not limits in the method of opposed-systems analysis which prevent the questioning of some objectives. Isn't it tied to the "power structure"[15] — whatever mist that hazy phrase designates? If the conclusion of a systems analysis were to propose the overthrow by force of a government sponsoring it, it would be rather unreasonable to suppose that the sponsor would be overjoyed: "Yes, indeed, the analysis has not met my original objectives, but it has hit on something more important: my violent overthrow." Or, "It has met my original objectives, and even better, it involves my violent overthrow." But few foreign-policy objectives of government in the United States seem to be so fundamentally at odds with the realities that they require overthrow of our government for their accomplishment; and if they are, this is hardly a limitation characteristic of the method of analysis. Let me expand on this a little.

So far we have talked about governments and nations. Most of the problems normally considered in international relations have to do with the relations among states. This is, to be sure, somewhat artificial — an approximation useful for some purposes, like the treatment of stars as point-masses in astronomy. However, the internal structure of states may critically affect conflict or cooperation among states, the start or ending of wars, and many other matters. Specific peace terms may look less tolerable to the ruling faction than continuing to fight; concluding the war may then require dealing with a faction previously not in control. Dealings with governments to end World Wars I and II provide several examples. An analytic understanding of alternatives in civil wars is of interest, therefore, to the international theorist as well as to the decision-maker.[16]

I refer to the decision-maker both in and out of the government. There is no reason why a revolutionary might not find it handy to use the tools of opposed-systems design himself. Mao, Giap,

Guevara, and many others have worked out theories of how best to overthrow some sorts of government, complete with suggestions as to the technical equipment for conducting guerrilla war as well as the political devices that seem to have worked out best. A careful reading of their manuals suggests they might use a more tentative and systematic self-correcting mode of theorizing themselves, and there is nothing in the character of opposed-systems design that gives capitalist governments a patent which cannot be infringed. Though revolutionaries normally require rather rigid adherence to their programs, it should be observed, of course, that the ends of revolutionaries are multiple and often turn out to be in conflict, too, and therefore cannot safely be regarded as final. A good opposed-systems design to bring about a revolution would not be too rigidly tied to the unanalyzed goals of the revolutionary power structure.

F. UNCERTAINTIES, SIMPLIFICATIONS, AND THE ROLE OF INEQUALITIES

Statements about new approaches tend to be both pro-grammatic and excessively hopeful. I believe there have been some successes in the analysis and design of opposed systems. But I have tried to suggest, as I have gone along, some of their limits. In fact, very large uncertainties affect both the ends and the means dealt with in an opposed-systems analysis; and the models used, while solving some problems, introduce others. Inevitably they simplify, and therefore introduce error. Simplification is a problem for all theory. I can say just a little about both the uncertainties and about how opposed-systems design has dealt with them and with the biases of theoretical simplification.[17]

First, on the uncertainties. The long period between the gestation of a technology and its birth, operational life, and death has a double aspect, so far as uncertainty is concerned. It means that the system as originally conceived will have to face a great many eventualities that were unlikely to have been foreseen at the time of conception. On the other hand, it confers some element of stability and predictability that can be used in an analysis.

The B-36 took some seventeen years from the idea of it to the time at which it was phased out of the strategic force. It was conceived shortly after the fall of France as insurance against the contingency that Britain might fall, too. Its proponents thought of it as a way of reaching Germany with high explosives from bases at intercontinental distances, if no bases nearby were available. It was at the beginning a propeller plane, designed to operate

139

against defenses consisting of guns and propeller-driven fighter planes. Its designers did not consider the opposition of surface-to-air missiles or jets and knew nothing of the Manhattan Project which was shortly to develop nuclear explosives. In fact, they learned of the Manhattan Project only when most of us did, with the explosion at Hiroshima. By the time the B-36 was phased into the force, after many vicissitudes, it had four jet engines as well as six propeller engines. It was expected to carry a nuclear payload over quite different routes to quite different targets against a different enemy with markedly different active defenses, and an offense that might make even bases at intercontinental distances unsafe.[18] The history of tactical fighter planes seems even more regularly to display disparities between initial conception and actual operating conditions. This can be illustrated by the story of the P-47 Thunderbolt and the P-51 Mustang in World War II.[19]

Such large and ineradicable uncertainties present problems in plenty for analysts, but even more for dogmatists. And large bureaucracies teem with dogmatists. Of necessity most of the bureaucracy will be engaged in the complexities of day-to-day decision of the sort that keeps a bureaucracy afloat. Intelligence tends to be expended in the short run, while frequently very large changes are gathering and — to the persistent eye — are already visible just beyond the short run. The familiar trait of inertia that characterizes large and complex organizations confers an especially great marginal productivity on realistic analysis of the basic changes impending and their significance. New technologies involving dramatic order-of-magnitude improvements take a considerable time to become operational realities; this fact limits the range of uncertainty, making it possible to look ahead. The characteristics of decision-making in large organizations frequently insure that, without a systematic effort at analyzing the distant consequences of coming changes, programs will be obsolete by the time they come into effect. Inventive and realistic systems design has been useful not so much because it is intrinsically so good as because the alternative of routine decision is so bad.

The strategy for dealing with uncertainty is related also to the method of treating the biases introduced by theoretical simplification. The equations of the physical sciences typically simplify: they hold only under ideal conditions. However, in contrast to the empirical associations found in most quantitative social science inquiries, inequalities or differences between predicted and actual values can frequently be explained (by the physical scientist) as due to deviations of the experiment from the ideal conditions assumed in theory. Differences or inequalities, as distinct from equations, have played another role, but a crucial one, in opposed-systems analyses. This role has to do with the prominence of arguments of an *a fortiori* sort, running "even if . . .; then more so, since in fact...." In comparing alternative systems with one programmed, one cannot eliminate uncertainty, but one can assume that they will be resolved favorably from the standpoint of a dubious programmed system. One cannot avoid theoretical simplification, but one can design a model to favor the programmed or other losing systems and to give them the benefit of the doubt. Then if the comparison shows that, even with all the favors bestowed by the model's assumption, the system programmed or otherwise likely to be chosen is vastly inferior to an alternative, this offers substantial ground for choice. Moreover, it should not be surprising that bureaucrats exhibit enough inertia to make such *a fortiori* analyses possible and very useful, as some opposed-systems analyses have been.

III. Links to Other Theories in International Relations

A. THEORIES OF DECISION IN INTERNATIONAL AFFAIRS

Opposed-systems designs have looked at the choices available for government decision-makers where such decisions are interdependent with decisions of other governments. This concern connects them in an obvious way with theories of decision-making in international politics of the sort associated with Richard Snyder, H. W. Bruck, B. Sapin, and J. A. Robinson. However, not just these scholars but most theorists of international relations are, in one way or another, concerned with the foreign-policy decisions of governments, or the decisions of international organizations. A good many such theorists, including many of the behavioralists, take decision processes and decision-makers as their main subject matter: for example, they study how decision-makers behave in crisis. Indeed, Rosecrance and Mueller, in a sympathetic and knowledgeable but critical review of academic quantitative studies of the last decade (those using factor analysis, content analysis, international simulation, and the measurement of communication flows) make the point that these studies cannot be dismissed as they are by the classicists because they sometimes use rather indirect measures, since the "truly relevant information" for both the classical and the newer studies would be data on the processes of government planning and decision and is "scarcely ever available until long after the event."[20] Rosecrance and Mueller assume, in other words, that the proper subject matter for study is the decisions themselves — that theory should be mainly, so to speak, meta-decisional. It seems doubtful that as much of the focus of inquiry in the traditional literature has been meta-decisional. On the other hand, an opposed-systems design will deal with the factors that affect and are the subject of decision rather than only or mainly the decision process and the decision-maker. It will deal with such matters as the deployment of radars, the amount of warning available along various routes against various attacks and how this might be changed, or with the number of tons per day that can be lifted to support a blockaded population, like Berlin's, or with the number of kilograms of fissile material that might be diverted from peaceful uses in a nuclear power plant designed to generate electricity, given specified inspection arrangements under an international atomic energy authority. It will be concerned with analyzing and designing methods of control and response in crises. Crises in fact are likely to be taken as a test of deterrent systems. It will also look at patterns of behavior of various decision-makers, including inert and other irrational forms of behavior. But unlike most of the social-psychological studies with which I am familiar, an opposed-systems design would be likely to concentrate on the substantive consequences of the various alternative decisions that might be taken, and how these consequences might satisfy or disappoint the multiple ends of the governments concerned.

B. POTENTIAL WARS

Opposed-systems analyses have focused on how our national, alliance or interadversary choices might affect the likelihood and likely outcomes of various sorts of combat. This focus is clearly related to a main, historic way of looking at relations among states at least since Hobbes and Rousseau, who viewed the anarchy of sovereign independent nations as a state of war — actual fighting or perpetual anticipation and preparation for it. In the United States the powerful tradition of realism in international theory has, of course, shown a large concern with military power relations among states. But in one way or another almost all approaches to international affairs must cover this ground *en route*.

Realist geopolitical theories of the balance of power have been useful in calling our attention to the interests and aims of nation-states and the way such interests might be realized or bounded by their relative military strengths. Not only the theoretical essays, but some of the theoretically-oriented realist historical works — such as Tang Tsou's monumental study of the *American Failure in China, 1945-51* — have been persuasive and illuminating. But realist theories are often content to dichotomize interests into "vital" and "nonvital." For some purposes such gross distinctions may be serviceable. The functionalists in international law use this rough division to suggest areas which states will not entrust to international adjudication and those they might.[21] Postal service and cultural exchange seem clearly not vital. However, for purposes of weighing actions that might lead to war, such a simple dichotomy is hardly enough. In this connection, as often as not, a "vital" interest is simply defined as one that a nation would fight for. This definition has crowned many a tautology in which, for example, some respected foreign-policy expert warns Congress that it would be a mistake to suppose that China would not fight if it felt its vital interests were at stake; or perhaps reassures Congress that China will not fight unless its vital interests are at stake — two pieces of wisdom derivable by definition rather than by long experience as a China hand. A great many aims of a nation-state may be incompatible with aims strongly held by other nations or coalitions of nations, and actions in furthering such aims may risk war. But just how much they risk war and how much war itself would put at risk can vary from the insignificant to the catastrophic. Much more explicit and systematic treatment of goals and interests, and the costs of fulfilling them, is needed for purposes of policy decision, and is needed in an opposed-system analysis to aid decision.

Balance-of-power theories have come in for a flood of criticism, much of it centering on the term "balance."[22] While the many ambiguities in the notion of equilibrium used in such theories are worth pointing out, I do not think that they are very hard to clarify and correct. A concept of equilibrium and the associated notions of stability and instability have been useful in social as well as biological and physical science. Handled with care, they can be fruitful in theories of international relations. The notion of "power" itself, which in these contexts has had considerably less critical scrutiny, is something else again. Even when it is conceived as military strength, rather than in the broader and vaguer terms of any capability to "affect" the behavior of others, it bristles with alternative meanings, and sometimes seems bereft of all. These lacks sharply limit the uses to which the traditional theories of the power relations among states can be put.

Among traditional theorists even acute critics of balance-of-power theories implicitly take power as if it were measurable by a simple arithmetic quantity. In this respect they are like the objects of their critique. Case studies of the balance of power have frequently described quite concretely the military forces arrayed on opposing sides: the numbers of army divisions, tanks, aircraft, ships of various types, and so on; and also the broad geophysical setting: oceans, land masses, ranges of mountains, and so on. However, such specifics are inputs, not outputs of "power," which, even though it may be tacitly assumed to be a single quantity, is undefined. These inputs offer only impressionistic grounds for judging the outcome of any concrete conflict. But in international affairs we are interested in the possible outcomes of a great many conceivable interactions among nations. These vary from subversion and guerrilla actions, through classic naval or ground engagements in the homeland of major antagonists or in some distant theater of war, to the results of nuclear exchanges under a variety of circumstances of outbreak. A country with few classical military forces and no nuclear capability might be able to manipulate covert force effectively. The delivery range and destructive radius of weapons and the problems of supporting operations logistically vary for different circumstances and kinds of conflict, and at various times. No single, one-dimensional quantity will characterize the range of capabilities usually intended when we talk of military "power." Strength, in short, is a vector with many components. It takes a good many numbers to describe the outcomes that interest us. And systematic analysis may be needed to project even one.

Just as we can be reasonably sure that postal services don't engage "vital" interests of sovereign nations in conflict, so some questions about the relations of force between nation-states are gross enough to be settled on the basis of the impressions about air and naval power and oceans and continental land masses. But a good many others cannot, though they are susceptible to subtler and more systematic analysis.

On military power relations among states, the behavioral studies and the quantitative approaches that are usually contrasted with traditional theories of international relations do not seem to me to be a decided advance. On power relationships the empirical work has been slight; the theory has been too general to be both meaningful and true. Perhaps the slightness is due to a kind of shunning of the subject. For, as I have suggested, though behavioralists may contrast their approach with the traditionalists mainly in terms of method, there seem to be differences in subject matter as well. With a few exceptions, the empirical quantitative work with which I am familiar has been concerned with international organization and integration, and where it has been concerned with conflict, the social-psychological analyses have dealt with subjects like national and international images that might create tension, or decision processes in crisis, or the tendencies of individual decision-makers to distrust the governments of other countries or to see them as threatening. I know of little work, however, on the actual military potentialities of the various states in relation to others and how these might affect the threats as well as how the threats are perceived.

As for theory, let me take by way of illustration the question of how military strength varies with distance. I have treated this at length elsewhere[23] and here can indicate only schematically the results. Nonetheless, this example may serve to display some of the characteristic continuities and differences among (1) traditional theories, (2) the rather general "behavioral" theories, and (3) opposed-systems analyses of power relations among states.

(1) In traditional theories of international relations, some references to distance or proximity and their effects are implicit. Sometimes they appear in describing the possibility of conflict itself. The abundance of Rousseau's idyllic state of nature had something to do with the fact that enough space separated men to enable them to satisfy their desires without seriously clashing with each other. And in the much less idyllic condition of anarchy among the states in Europe, Rousseau's vivid description of their unstable configuration is made in terms of their close juxtaposition, touching "each other at so many points that no one of them can move without giving a deadly jar to all the rest." A casual survey of classic writings on the anarchy of independent states turns up a multiplicity of references to problems of equilibrium of unconnected sovereigns "in the same neighborhood."[24] The power to do harm has limits in range, and so space would seem to provide not only more room for satisfying goals without jostling but also a cushion of safety. Of course, "neighborhood" is a qualitative term, and it is apparent that vicinities are elastic and have stretched in several dimensions with time and improvements in communication, transport, and optimal weapons range. The qualitative condition assumes only that states are close enough to have reason for conflict and means to fight each other. However, not infrequently traditional balance-of-power theories are talking

about essentially quantitative relationships, even though they present them informally and in everyday language rather than in symbols. This is true, for example, of the geopolitical treatments of the way military strength varies with distance, that underlie some of the familiar notions of spheres of influence. So, for example, Spykman: "Power is effective in inverse ratio from its source"[25]; and Kennan: "... the effectiveness of the power radiated from any national center decreases in proportion to the distance involved."[26]

The assumption of a sharp weakening of strength with distance underpins much of the recent discussion of the need to reduce American commitments (though, of course, the motivation of the debate has less to do with theory than with the frustrations of the Vietnamese war). The theory runs: Great powers can use force to keep distant great challengers at a distance from areas near their border, their "sphere of influence"; this makes possible a balance which is best left alone; it protects at the same time as it limits the interests of opposing states, and in any case it cannot successfully be upset.

It is both a strength and a weakness of this traditional theory of a proportionate weakening of strength with distance that its purity is marred by qualifications about differences in the variation of strength over air, sea, and land distances. References to "air powers" or "naval powers" versus "land powers" make evident that the pure theory needs qualification, but do not make clear just how such qualification can he effected. Some of the more formal quantitative theories on the other hand are quite pure.

(2) Kenneth Boulding has formulated a general theory of conflict and defense that is intended to comprehend the relation to distance of both classical or conventional strength and the strength of current forces of "world-wide range."[27] (The traditional theory I have outlined contemplates classical strength only.) His theory states in brief: In the classical case the amount of strength provided out of given resources decreases, or the cost of maintaining a fixed amount of strength increases, linearly with distance; stable equilibria between widely separated large and small powers are therefore possible; but in the case of contemporary delivery technology, the loss of strength with distance vanishes, as does also the chance of stable systems of national defense.

Boulding's mathematical model is derived from models developed by Harold Hotelling and Arthur Smithies for the analysis of the spatial competition between economic firms distributed in a line. It involves some simple linear differential equations, for which he offers as one interpretation: two countries, with their homes at points A and B respectively, each have a certain number of men who can be devoted to fighting; at a point outside the home countries, say between A and B, some out of the total number of men that each can muster have to be devoted to supporting the fighters, leaving fewer to fight; the farther out from A and nearer to B the fighters from A go, the more bearers are needed and so there are fewer fighters. ("Bearing" or "supporting" can be used inclusively to mean all activities other than fighting needed to make fighting possible.) If the forces available to A at home are larger than those available to B at home, they may still reach some point of equality in number of fighters at some point in between that is nearer to B. Though the theory is essentially a logistic one, it is assumed that at the point of equality the conflict is going to be a tie, hence an equilibrium point.

Boulding's model is static as well as linear. It has the virtue, however, of being more precisely simple than the traditional theory, which it generalizes slightly. Like the traditional theory, it assumes that strength is one-dimensional. (Boulding recognizes at one point that strength is really multi-dimensional, but dismisses this as a second-order effect,[28] as he dismisses deviations from linearity as minor.[29])

(3) It is possible to look more closely at various components of strength and how they vary with distance and to pay attention to a host of variables absent or implicitly held constant in a simple model, formal or informal. For either classical or nuclear strength one can examine not merely logistics or combat delivery, but also the attempts to interdict supplies and to use offense or defense to blunt opposing fire. And even so far as logistics is concerned, one can look at the alternative systems of transport available at any given time, at the result of varying allocations of resources to the purchase of lift or other support capabilities, and at changes in the technology of transport and communications at a distance. If one does this, in realistic, empirical detail, it is apparent that the linear picture of one-dimensional strength declining with distance is not merely a vast oversimplification of reality; it is wrong. In the first place, at any given time, and especially today when the range of possible sorts of conflict has increased dramatically, strength (as we have suggested) cannot be measured by a single arithmetic quantity, but by a sequence of many; and so for loss of strength. This is by no means a second-order effect. Equilibrium points that balance the strengths of two nations with respect to one component of the vector will not in general coincide with points that equalize

strength with respect to other components. And problems of the stability of equilibrium are much more complicated for both theory and practice.

Second, even when we look at components of strength, neither nuclear nor nonnuclear components behave like the simple linear picture. I shall sketch the results of some relevant close analyses of nonnuclear cases in the 1960s: the support capabilities in possible wars in Himalayan India and in Thailand by China on the one hand and the United States on the other. And I shall also outline a few of the results of an extensive nuclear study — the variation with critical distances of various sorts of nuclear strength during the 1950s.

Take the nonnuclear cases. Following Boulding, the linear model of decrease of strength with distance may be represented in the case of two powers with unequal home strength as a kind of lopsided M with legs of different heights representing the strengths of each of the two powers at home, and with the two slanting members meeting at a point nearer the shorter leg. Something like:

$$\mathsf{M}$$

The vertical legs represent the strengths at home of the two countries; the slanting lines show how the strength declines at various distances away from home toward the adversary. The point at which they meet is their equilibrium point.

This simple picture, I believe, is a fair representation of what a good many columnists and members of Congress have in mind when they talk of comparative disadvantages to the United States in fighting eight or ten thousand miles away from home against an adversary whose home base is near the scene of conflict. A curve representing the lift capability of the United States from its borders to the China-India border in the Himalayas and a Chinese capability from Cheng-tu-Szechwan to the same points in the Himalayas looks very different. It is both nonlinear and discontinuous. One such curve is shown in the accompanying Figure 1. Another such curve in Figure 2 shows the change in support capability of each side as a function of distance from home to battle on the Thai-Laos border.

The most striking fact displayed by these figures, however, is that the long-distance lift capacity of each side massively exceeds

148

their short-distance lift inside the theater, especially in the very short ranges in which the battle would be joined. But these bottlenecks inside the theater are to a very considerable extent determined by local factors: harbors, ports and loading facilities, railroad and road capacities, etc. They are not a function of the long-haul distances. The dramatic sweep of the curves showing, for example, the first 8,100 miles of hauling from the United States, while it catches the headlines and affects intuitive judgments, hardly determines the results. The bottlenecks are inside the theater. The important factors are the unimportant-looking little ripples in the cascade at the bottom of the chart which are so small that, in the Indian case, we have used a balloon within a balloon to magnify them enough to be visible. Nearly the same is true in the Thai-Laos case, where the United States from 8,500 miles away can lift four times as much to the Thai-Laos border as China can from 450 miles off; and U.S. capability in the combat zone is a small fraction of its long-haul capability.

If one looks at it in cost terms, the minor importance of the long haul appears even more vividly. It can be shown that adding several thousand miles to the distance at which remote wars are fought adds a very tiny percentage to the cost of fighting such wars.

The curves displayed, it should be stressed, are the result of a great deal of grubby, inglorious empirical work using a variety of detailed operational models to calculate the capacity of road nets in various seasons and a host of other laborious but necessary inquiries. One might be tempted to dismiss such labors as of little theoretical importance. However, they are important both for policy and for theory. Intuition on such matters is not enough, even when presented in formal mathematical dress. The curves show this.

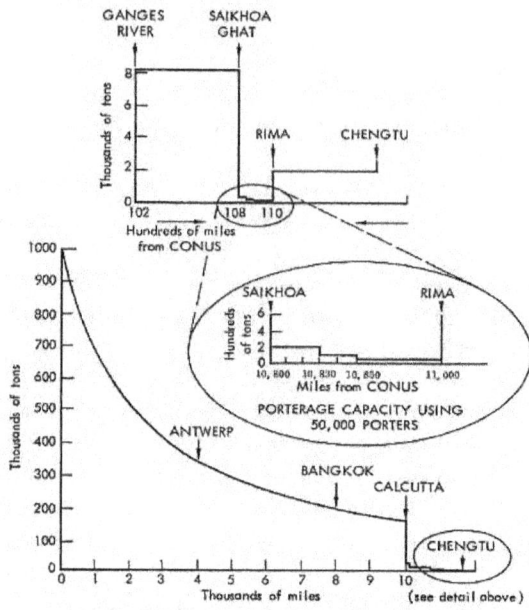

FIG. 1. Lift from United States mainland and from Szechwan to Orient-India border.
(Wohlstetter and Rainey, 1906.)

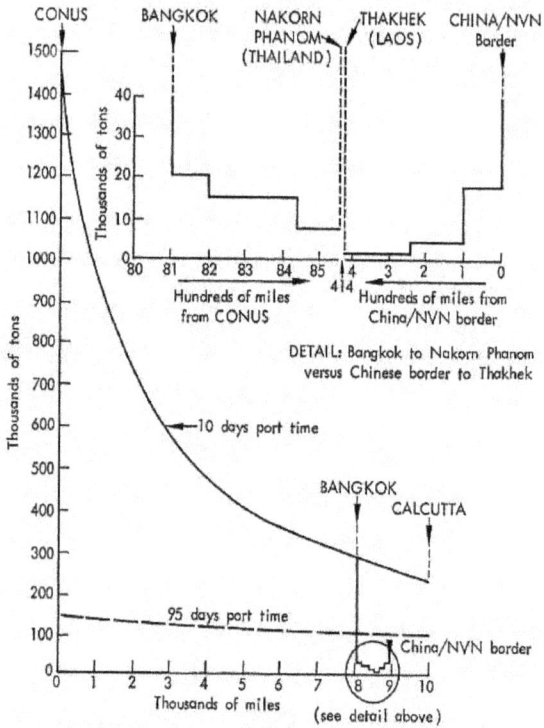

FIG. 2. Lift from United States mainland and China border to Thai-Laos borders.
(Wohlstetter and Rainey, 1906.)

The nuclear case also behaves quite differently from the assumption. First, if we neglect opposition by offense or defense, the costs of nuclear strength on the linear model should not increase significantly with distance. In fact, they do, and more than linearly; that is, more than the model suggests even for nonnuclear strength. (The formal linear model of strength weakening with distance also neglects opposition.) Cost curves for the 1950s generation of subsonic turbojets have an J-shaped form, rising asymptotically at points less than the maximum base-target distance, and costs of tanker refueling systems increase in steps at an increasing rate. Ground refueled systems increase in steps modestly. (Among other things, this suggests the wide variation *at any given time* in cost-radius curves depending on the choice of system.)

In the nuclear case, if one takes into account opposition by offense and defense—which means examining a very large number of potential conflicts and the interdependent choices of both sides in these conflicts—then the situation is reversed; it is even further from the simple linear model. Then the costs of a nuclear second-strike capability in the 1950s *decrease* sharply and effectiveness *increases* if operating bases are kept far back at intercontinental range. The decrease in costs and the increase in effectiveness, however, are not monotonic. While an overseas base system close to adversary attack was vulnerable, as well as difficult to support, an intermediate operating base system was even more costly and almost as vulnerable, with nearly all of the defects of the overseas base system plus a good many others of its own (extremely high aerial refueling costs, etc.). In fact, the intermediate operating base system combined the defects of the vulnerable overseas operating base system with the defects of an extremely high-cost, exclusively air-refueled intercontinental system. The latter was considered and rejected as an alternative to an intercontinental ground-refueled system. Against moderate enemy offense the least costly system was the intercontinental ground-refueled system. The advanced overseas base system was some 50 percent higher, and an intercontinental air-refueled system was roughly double the cost. The intermediate system was nearly triple the cost. Against a more formidable enemy offense the advanced overseas operating base system became about as expensive as the exclusively air-refueled intercontinental system. The intercontinental ground-refueled system remained cheapest and the intermediate system remained worst, being more than three times as costly for a given performance.

The importance of distance for the determination of nuclear strength is not merely a phenomenon of the 1950s. While the nature of the dependency changes, some large country examples (like the American extended-range Minuteman III and the enormous expenditures to increase the range of submarine-launched missiles) show the continuing importance of such complex dependency in the 1970s. And the troubles to be experienced by the medium-sized and smaller nth countries illustrate the continuing importance of distance even more vividly.

Sociologists and students of international politics have frequently referred to the maximum range of individual aircraft or missiles and the growth of this maximum range over calendar time as an indicator of the increasing capabilities for projecting military strength or civilian transport and travel and the consequent increasing interdependence of the world. Boulding's use of this parameter is then a familiar one.[30] However, while maximum delivery range or maximum speed of individual aircraft or maximum destructive radius of current explosives are suggestive, they are inadequate measures of strength. They deal with performance only crudely and leave out costs altogether. There is, for example, no direct connection between the maximum range of individual vehicles and national capabilities to do battle at a distance. Even if one neglects the subtler considerations of performance affected by interactions with adversaries, the factor of cost is essential. The nuclear propelled airplane, for example, a vehicle of very extended range, could be established in the 1950s as a poor way of projecting strength, one that would lower capabilities for fixed resources. This became obvious when one considered even a crudely measured performance for an entire system to be bought and operated out of a given budget. The unit costs were so high that adopting the system would have meant, for a fixed expenditure of resources, a decided reduction in the strength we could project even nearby.

Finally, the belief that stable nuclear equilibria are impossible owes its origin to some of the hoariest conceptions of the nuclear age. It neglects, among a good many other critical matters, the difference between first- and second-strike capabilities. Such stabilities are feasible, but limited and uncertain and not automatic.

I have tried to describe some of the features of opposed-systems analyses, and some of their chief limitations to date, and I have used as illustration some results that bear on variations of strength with distance. The models used in opposed-systems · design are plainly not intended to cover all the characteristics of all possible relations among nation-states from the Treaty of Westphalia on, nor all of the data that have been generated by agencies reporting on one or another aspect of the various nation-states or their intercourse. They are limited and partial. It is sometimes suggested by writers on some future international theory that one has the alternative of constructing a partial or limited theory on the one hand, or a total or general theory on the other. However, no theory is "total" in the sense that it deals with all possible traits of any given subject matter, and the notion of "generality" is an ambiguous one. Sometimes when one says that theory T_1 is more general than theory T_2, one means that T_2 is a special case of T_1 and deducible from it. T_1 is more powerful, has more content. On the other hand, sometimes one says T_1 is more general than T_2 when it is a proper part of T_2—as a geometry may be a proper part of a physical theory, and so may have less content. Or one may call a theory general because it has some undetermined parameters. In that case it is not an empirical statement. It might become one if operationally meaningful constants are substituted for the parameters, or if the parameters can be "bound," that is, said to hold for all or some values. For such parameters are, of course, really variables. They are blanks, pronouns without antecedents. Like some economic models, some of the formal models in international politics may be of this character.

Boulding's own general theory is general in this sense. A great deal of it consists in elementary truths of analytic geometry. These identify various regions of a quarter plane as regions of stability or instability. Though such statements yield categories of possible systems, they have no empirical content specific to international conflict. And the curves that divide the quarter plane, like the straight lines we have examined, have slight empirical relevance. In fact, the notion of "strength" as such is given no operational content. A typology of possible systems may be of use, but it is important to be clear that one is dealing with taxonomy, not with theoretical laws (much less "the great law of diminishing strength with distance"[31]). It is all too easy in constructing such a model, as I have remarked elsewhere, to get the exhilarating feeling that one is filling holes when one is only outlining them. Boulding contrasts his own theoretical bias with the sociological and taxonomic bias of political scientists working on types of international systems. He exaggerates the contrast. There is nothing wrong with taxonomy. It can be a most useful stage in preparation for the formulation of laws, but for this purpose one has to be clear about the difference.

The work of the Quaker physicist, L. F. Richardson, after some vicissitudes of attempted statistical testing, tends now also to be reduced to typology. Richardson started out by formulating differential equations of a very simple form, relating the rate of increase of arms expenditures of each side in any arms competition to the amount of the expenditures of the other side. The equations are essentially the same as the Lanchester equations described earlier except that the variables refer not to initial forces of each side but to the annual arms expenditures, and the right-hand side of the equation is positive. The familiar solution is an exponential, suggesting that arms expenditures lead to explosive arms races and (with some lacunae in the inference) to wars. Richardson began with this simple relationship about the time of World War I, but in the course of the interwar debates introduced extra terms and parameters into his equations to take into partial account such countervailing influences as budget constraints. There are enough terms and parameters in the equations to make them fit just about any actual configuration of arms expenditures. And the theory, which has been revived in recent years and is now rather frequently cited,[32] has become essentially a taxonomy, a way of classifying stable and unstable parameter values.

Richardson was an original and able research man. But there are some rather large drawbacks in the typologies obtained from the use of his equations. Constraints like those of a budget are introduced only in a very inadequate and unrevealing way, with no explicit reference to alternative choice. On the other hand, I know of no persuasive historical example of the simple sort of explosive arms process he had originally in mind where the extra terms are of minor importance. The one historical case that some contemporary commentators have called a "fairly successful"[33] application involved, among other substantial defects, only five observations in all on annual differences in arms expenditures before World War I. Hardly enough to be convincing. It will be no fault of Richardson's if, out of our madness for method, we accept the forms of these equations as a substitute for substance, and make them a permanent addition to our gadgetry.

Fundamental theories with a very wide range of reference may be based on common experience rather than on systematic empirical tests, and they may say very little about any particular subject matter. But they nonetheless can have great importance. It is not my intention to disparage them. On the contrary, several theories with a much wider range than any we have discussed throw light on the structure of interdependent choices much more fundamentally and inclusively than any study of national or international choice. For example, the mathematical developments of von Neumann, or more recently of Lloyd Shapley and others in game theory, or the less rigorously formal theories of bargaining and strategy of conflict in the sense of Schelling: these again are much more general than a study of international politics.

Nonetheless, it would be a rather arbitrary usage to limit application of the term "theory," still more of "explanation," to works of such a high degree of generality; still more arbitrary to limit it to models with undetermined parameters, sentential functions rather than completed universal "if..., then..." statements. Discussions of this subject tend to be muddled by a dichotomy sometimes used between the "nomothetic" or law-like and the "idiographic" that concerns particular, named objects, "some." However, it is apparent that no statement—not even a singular statement about individual objects—is idiographic in the sense that it only concerns particulars. We say, for example, that such-and-such an individual object bears some relation to such-another one: "Jill tumbles after Jack." If we aspire to say something rather than mutely to point, we have to ascribe properties, class membership, relationships. And, on the other hand, very many quite respectable laws contain references to particulars. They contain the operator "all" in uneliminable fashion. But they also use the operator "some," and may name individual objects. Kepler's laws for solar orbits, for example, make up an important theory, even though they refer to a subject restricted both in space and time. Moreover, though this theory seems obvious to us now (every new idea, Whitehead reminds us, has been called obvious by someone who did not discover it), it was in fact a most precarious inference from the astronomical observations available at the time. Peirce found that there were 79 alternative theories that Kepler tried before hitting on one that worked. Kepler's theory is less general than Newton's, whose inverse-square law later showed that bodies would move in an orbit that is a conic section, with the origin of the central force at the focus. But even then, to derive the elliptical form of solar orbits one needs to know the relative masses and the relative velocities of the sun and the planets — all individuals — and to neglect perturbing effects of some distant masses. It is even possible, if we accept a hypothesis propounded by the French physicist Duhem and also by Peirce, that all the laws of nature, such as Newton's and quantum mechanics, hold within the margin of error of our observations only for very, very long historical epochs. It is conceivable that the relations are slowly changing. In that case, of course, all laws would be restricted in space and time.

The word "theory" is used in the field of political science rather differently from its most familiar usage in the natural sciences, or in economics. It is frequently reserved for very basic studies in the philosophy of politics, and sometimes for studies in the history of the philosophy of politics. These seem to me to be valid enterprises, interesting and rewarding. And, though the word "theory" has, at least in academic circles, a eulogistic character, it would be a waste to spend much time arguing for the title.

Like some of the more general empirical theories, and unlike some of the crude empirical statistical associations, the models used in opposed-systems analyses are essentially general. A good many of the statements in them refer to domains of potential operations and cannot be reduced to statements about individuals. They are idealizations. They are hypothetical, like some of the more general theories. However, if I may borrow a phrase from Marianne Moore, these are "imaginary gardens with real toads in them." The restriction in time permits great specificity in input, the use of laws with bound variables and genuine constants rather than sentential functions, and a richness in detailed conclusions.

Very general theories and some simplified small-group experiments are sometimes used to justify policy conclusions, even though some essential specifics are lacking. Much of the discussion of the state of strategic forces on the international scene is discouragingly innocent of an awareness of even the relevance of specific information, not to say of the information itself. It makes a good deal of difference whether a strategic force is based on 400 bases or on 28. It makes a difference whether a third of the force is in the air at all times, with fuel tanks full enough to complete a combat mission, armed with all the necessary electronic equipment and other preparations; or only four percent of the force, and that almost entirely on training missions, unarmed, and on the average inadequately fuelled for combat. It makes a difference whether the tactical warning provided by radars along feasible routes and profiles of attack matches the degree of readiness and speed of response of the forces warned. In the 1950s a great many members of the academic community, as well as journalists and members of governments, were in error on each of these and a good many other essential factors affecting capacities for second strike, and yet spoke rather blithely about policy on the subject. Many analyses of the Cuban missile crisis are affected by the same carefree indifference to essential features of the military stance of each side. Some of these data are, of course, governed by rules of secrecy and, even with all the data available, inference must be uncertain. However, such uncertainty can be reduced with information, and on a good many critically important military relations among states, the effects that dominate results are gross enough to show up in public data, provided these are gathered diligently and analyzed systematically and with care. Some very interesting things can be said, for example, about nth countries only on the basis of such empirical analysis, and on the basis of using a logical apparatus considerably more refined than a few bare distinctions like that between "vulnerable" and "invulnerable" force.

An opposed-systems analysis is at the level of generality appropriate to policy choice. This is, of course, not surprising, since that is how opposed-systems analysis got started. I have said very little about the relationship of policy to valid theory. In the field of international politics, an interest in policy hardly needs justification. Just about everyone in the field is interested in policy. I am using the word "interest" in both of its meanings: they are fascinated by it and have a stake in it. I believe that the likelihood of useful analyses for the choice of ends — and of means for achieving such ends — is enhanced if the analyses are systematic and explicit about objectives as well as instrumentalities; for one thing, they are then open both to self-criticism and to public examination. How analyses performed to aid policy might affect policy is a subject that has received extended comment. I would like to close with a speculation on the theoretical potential of policy designs.

There is, of course, an old academic snobbery about applied science in general. Applied science is distinctly lower-class. Such snobbery affects the social sciences, too. It is clear that work on policy needs theory. The fact that this can be a two-way street, while sometimes recognized in the natural sciences, seems much less frequently, if at all, to be recognized in the social sciences. It is familiar to historians of science that, in the words of the philosophical biologist, L. J. Henderson, thermodynamics owes more to the steam engine than the steam engine owes to thermodynamics. This is evident in the work of Sadi Carnot. It seems plausible to me that something of the same sort might happen in social science. It may be that well-evidenced generalizations will be easier to come by where they concern or stem from alternative designed operations and social structures — especially where these structures involve complex interdependencies of men and machines — than where they stem from the haphazard reports of the workings of unpremeditated institutions that have grown mostly without intent. In the latter case, research men are sometimes reduced to correlating each time-series so gathered with every other time-series in their possession. Though designed social structures or policy alternatives are normally quite complex in the field of political-military affairs, they may be rather better understood or more accessible to understanding than the unpremeditated complexities normally dealt with in the social sciences. On the other hand, they may be more interesting because they are complex and have more direct social relevance than small-group experiments. While such experiments are, of course, the work of design, and may be of great interest, it is sometimes rather hard to make the inferential jump from the small experimental group to the large social or political groupings that concern us.

There is no single best path through the tangle of international politics to basic theory. One useful trail may lead through the analysis and design of complex systems that are viable in a world of partially hostile and independent states.

ENDNOTES - Wohlstetter - Theory and Opposed-Systems Design

Note: The original version of this essay contains in-text citations and a list of works cited at the end. In this version, in-text citations were converted into endnotes. Text bounded by square brackets generally indicates such a conversion.

1. [Burton Marshall, "Waiting for the Curtain," *SAIS Review*, Vol. 10, No. 4, Summer 1966, p. 21.]

2. The term "essentially general" is adapted from C. G. Hempel. [Hempel, *Aspects of Scientific Explanation*, New York, NY: Free Press, 1965, pp. 338*ff*.] An elaboration of this initial statement is made later in the section entitled "Specifics and the General: Imaginary Gardens with Real Toads." For those familiar with the symbolism of mathematical logic, a partial and summary statement can be made at this point: essentially general statements include, besides those containing no individual names and only universally bound variables, some that may refer to individual objects, as Kepler's laws refer to the sun and its planets: they may for example, be of the form "(x)Rxa." Or they may use existential quantifiers such as the word "some" or the symbol "(∃x)": they may be of the form "(x) (∃y)Rxy." But they also irreducibly involve universal quantifiers like the words "all" or "every" or the symbol "(x)."

3. See [Albert J. Wohlstetter, Fred S. Hoffman, Robert J. Lutz, and Henry S. Rowen, *The Selection of Strategic Air Bases*, R-244-S, special staff report, Santa Monica, CA: RAND Corporation, March 1, 1953, TOP SECRET, declassified on July 1, 1963, available from *www.albertwohlstetter.com/writings/19530301-AW-EtAl-R244S.pdf*]; and [Albert J. Wohlstetter, Fred S. Hoffman, Henry S. Rowen, and Robert J. Lutz, *The Selection and Use of Strategic Air Bases*, R-266, final report, Santa Monica, CA: RAND Corporation, April 1954, TOP SECRET, declassified circa 1961, available from *www.rand. org/pubs/reports/R0266/*].

4. [Albert J. Wohlstetter, Fred S. Hoffman, and Henry S. Rowen, *Protecting U.S. Power to Strike Back in the 1950s and 1960s*, R-290, staff report, Santa Monica, CA: RAND Corporation, September 1, 1956, TOP SECRET, declassified circa 1960s, availabl e from *www. albertwohlstetter.com/writings/19560901-AW-EtAl-R290.pdf*]

5. [Albert J. Wohlstetter and Fred S. Hoffman, *Defending a Strategic Force After 1960: With Notes on the Need by Both Sides for Accurate Bomb Delivery, Particularly for the Big Bombs*, D-2270, Santa Monica, CA: RAND Corporation, February 1, 1954, available from *www.albertwohlstetter.com/writings/19540201-AW-FH2270.pdf*.]

6.[F. W. Lanchester, *Aircraft in Wartime: The Dawn of the Fourth Arm*, London, UK: Constable, 1916.]

7. [R. E. Bach, L. Dolansky, and H. L. Stubbs, "A Loss Minimizing Extension of the Lanchester Theory of Combat," *Sc. Rpt.*, No. 3, Contract AF 19 (604)-4573, AD 235019, AFCRC-TN-60-168, Northeastern University, January 31, 1960]; [P. M. S. Blackett, "Operational Research," *Quarterly Journal of the British Association for the Advancement of Science*, No. 5, 1948, pp. 26-38]; [H. Brackney, "Dynamics of Military Combat," *Operations Research*, No. 7, 1959, pp. 30-44]; [R. H. Brown, *A Stochastic Analysis of Lanchester's Theory of Combat*, ORO-T-323, AD 82944, Operations Research Office, Johns Hopkins University, December 1955]; [S. J. Deitchman, "A Lanchester Model of Guerrilla Warfare, *Operations Research*, No. 10, 1962, pp. 818-827]; [J. H. Engel, "A Verification of Lanchester's Law," *Operations Research*, No. 2, 1954, pp. 163-171]; [G. A. Gamow and R. E. Zimmerman, *Mathematical Models for Ground Combat*, ORO-SP-11, Operations Research Office, Johns Hopkins University, April 1957]; [T. Ganelius, "Mathematical Treatment of Combat," *Artilleri Tidskrift*, No. 3, 1955, p. 84]; [B. O. Koopman, *Quantitative Aspect of Combat*, Office of Scientific Research and Development, AMP Note No. 6, August 1943]; [F. W. Lanchester, *Aircraft in Warfare: The Dawn of the Fourth Arm*, London, U.K.: Constable, 1916]; [P. M. Morse, "Mathematical Problems in Operations Research," *Bulletin of the American Mathematical Society*, No. 54, 1948, pp. 619-621]; [C. Tompkins, "Probabilistic Problems and Military Evaluation: An Example," *Logistics Papers*, No. 2, George Washington University, 1950]; [H. K. Weiss, *Requirements for a Theory of Combat*, BRL Memo Report No. 667, Project No. TB 3-0102, Ballistic Research Laboratory, Aberdeen Proving Ground, April 1953]; [Weiss, "Lanchester-type Models of Warfare," *Proceedings of the First International Conference, Operations Research*, December 1957, pp. 82-99]; [Weiss, "The Fiske Model of Warfare," *Operations Research*, No. 10, 1962, pp. 569-571]; and [D. Willard, "Lanchester as a Force in History: An Analysis of Land Battles of the Years 1618-1905," AD 29735L 63-1-5, Div. 18A, Bethesda, MD: Research Analysis Corporation, November 1962 (Limited distribution: Request approval of: Office, Chief of Research and Development, Department of the Army, Washington, DC, Attn: Research Planning Division)].

For a critical statement, see [Albert Wohlstetter and Richard B. Rainey, Jr., *Distant Wars and Far Out Estimates*, unpublished paper prepared for presentation at the American Political Science Association (APSA) meetings in New York, NY, on September 8, 1966; and at the Strategic Studies Conference, sponsored by MIT, Endicott House, Dedham, MA, September 9 to September 11, 1966, revised 1967], and especially [Charles Bernstein, "Reconsidering Systems Analysis of Theater Air," paper presented at NATO Symposium on Defense Resource Allocation, Paris, France, September 20-22, 1966].

8. [J. H. Engel, "A Verification of Lanchester's Law," *Operations Research*, No. 2, 1954, pp. 163-171.]

9. [Moshe Dayan, *Diary of the Sinai Campaign*, London, UK: George Weidenfeld and Nicolson, 1966, p. 5.]

10. [*The Military Balance, 1966-1967*, London, UK: Institute of Strategic Studies, 1967.] There is an error in the addition in the figures for Israeli aircraft.

11. [Albert Wohlstetter, *Strength, Interest and New Technologies*, opening address before *The Implications of Military Technology in the 1970s*, the Institute for Strategic Studies' ninth annual conference, Elsinore, Denmark, September 28 to October 1, 1967, D(L)-16624-PR, Santa Monica, CA: RAND Corporation, January 24, 1968, available from *www.rand.org/about/history/wohlstetter/DL16624/DL16624.html*. The address was also published as Wohlstetter, *Strength, Interest and New Technologies*, in *The Implications of Military Technology in the 1970s*, Adelphi Papers No. 46, London, UK: Institute for Strategic Studies, March 1968.]

12. [Charles J. Hitch, "On the Choice of Objectives in Systems Studies," P-1955, Santa Monica, CA: RAND Corporation, March 1960, p. 2.]

13. See [Albert Wohlstetter, "The Non-Strategic and Non-Existent," in Kathleen Archibald, ed., *Strategic Interaction and Conflict: Original Papers and Discussion*, Berkeley, CA: Institute of International Studies, University of California, Berkeley, 1966, pp. 107-126., esp. pp. 112-13]; also [Wohlstetter, "Defense Decisions: Design Versus Analysis," IFORS Conference, Aix-en-Provence, 1960]; [Wohlstetter, "Analysis and Design of Conflict Systems," in E. S. Quade, ed., *Analysis for Military Decisions*, Chicago, IL: Rand

McNally & Co., 1964, pp. 103-148]; [E.S. Quade, "Introduction" and "The Selection and Use of Strategic Air Bases: A Case History," in Quade, ed., *Analysis for Military Decisions*, pp. 2-12, 24-64.]; [Alain C. Enthoven, "Systems Analysis and the Navy," *Naval Review*, Annapolis, MD: United States Naval Institute, 1964, pp. 98-117]; [Hitch, "On the Choice of Objectives in System Studies"]; [Henry S. Rowen, "Improving Decision-Making in Government," lecture for the Budget Bureau's 1965 summer seminar on systems analysis and program evaluation]; and [Fred S. Hoffman, "PPB, Its Place in the Sun," speech at the American Bankers Association, December 1967].

14. The point of view expressed here is developed at considerably greater length in [Wohlstetter, "Analysis and Design of Conflict Systems"].

15. Aaron Wildavsky, no radical critic, suggests the method *is* tied to the existing political structure. See [Wildavsky, "The Political Economy of Efficiency," *The Public Interest*, No. 8, Summer 1967, pp 30-48].

16. One might distinguish the theory or design of *strongly* opposed systems from that of *weakly* opposed systems. In this paper I have dealt mainly with the kind of potential opposition familiar among nation states. While such opposition is only partial it may lead to actual combat and this possibility is a classic defining trait of the anarchic system of nation states. (See the section, "Potential Wars.") Where internal dissent from the institutions of the nation is large and powerful enough to interfere in essential ways with their operation or possibly to effect a change in them by force, much the same sort of analysis we have described as opposed systems design is relevant both for the dissenter and for the authorities. We might better call the subject matter of such theory and design, in both the international and national cases, "strongly opposed systems." But in the national case there are some useful analogies even where governmental or factional policies are more weakly opposed, where they do not threaten internal war. Even then policy in some areas may be best formulated with possible counter moves in mind. So, for example, policies aimed at desegregating schools (by bussing nonwhites to white schools or the reverse, or reducing the grade span of the city schools so as to widen and make more varied the ethnic catchment

area from which pupils for any given school are drawn, and so on) may be met by a movement of the more privileged whites into private schools or out to the suburbs. Policies may be deliberately chosen so as to minimize the effects of such countermeasures. In designing systems that are "weakly" opposed, the opposition may be dealt with by methods that stress conciliation, compromise, and bargaining even more than in international affairs. But of course the difference is one of degree, and in the international case, too, compromise and conciliation are important modes of resolving differences.

17. A much more extended discussion is contained in [Wohlstetter, "Analysis and Design of Conflict Systems"].

18. For an extended analysis of the B-36 history, see [*ibid.*] .

19. For a detailed account, see [William Emerson, "Doctrine and Dogma," *Army*, June 1963, pp. 818-827]. See also my essay in the Kaplan volume referred to under Falk (to be published). [Albert Wohlstetter, "Theory and Opposed Systems Design," in Morton A. Kaplan, ed., *New Approaches to International Relations*, New York: St. Martin's, 1968, pp. 19-53.]

20. [R. N. Rosecrance and J. E. Mueller, "Decision-Making and the Quantitative Analysis of International Politics," *London Year Book of World Affairs*, 1967.]

21. See [Richard Falk, "New Approaches to the Study of International Law," in Kaplan, ed., *New Approaches to International Relations*, p. 27].

22. See, for example, the cogent critiques by [Ernst B. Haas, "The Balance of Power: Prescription, Concept or Propaganda?" *World Politics*, No. 5, July 1953, pp. 442-477]; [Inis Claude, *Power and International Relations*, New York, NY: Random House, 1962, esp. chs. 2 and 3]; and [A. F. Pollard, "The Balance of Power," *Journal of the British Institute of International Affairs*, No. 2, March 1923, pp; 51-64].

23. [Wohlstetter and Rainey, *Distant Wars and Far Out Estimates.*]

24. See, for example, *The Federalist No. 6,* by Alexander Hamilton: "To look for a continuation of harmony between a number of unconnected sovereigns, situated in the same neighborhood, would be to disregard the uniform course of human events." [*The Federalist,* Cleveland, OH: Meridian, Books, 1961, p. 28.]

25. [Nicholas John Spykman, *America's Strategy in World Politics,* New York, NY: Harcourt, Brace and World, 1942, p. 448.]

26. [George Kennan, *Russia and the West under Lenin and Stalin,* New York, NY: Mentor Books, 1962, p. 261.]

27. [Kenneth E. Boulding, *Conflict and Defense,* New York, NY: Harper and Row, 1962.]

28. [*Ibid.,* p. 241.]

29. [*Ibid.,* p. 231.]

30. See [*ibid.,* p. 272]. For a more or less standard sociological example, see [Hornell Hart, "Social Science and the Atomic Crisis, *Journal of Social Issues,* Supplement Series No. 2, April 1949]. Compare also [Bruce M. Russett, *Trends in World Politics,* New York, NY: Macmillan, 1965, esp. ch. 1]. Mr. Russett, however, avoids the extrapolations into the future characteristic of Hart and others.

31. [Boulding, p. 244.]

32. [Boulding, esp. ch. 2]; [Dean C. Pruitt, "Definition of the Situation as a Determinant of International Action," in Herbert C. Kelman, ed., *International Behavior,* New York, NY: Holt, Rinehart and Winston, 1965, pp. 422*ff*]; [Anatol Rapoport, *Fights, Games and Debates,* Ann Arbor, MI: University of Michigan Press, 1960]; and [Rapoport, "Lewis Richardson's Mathematical Theory of War," *Journal of Conflict Resolution,* Vol. 1, No. 3, September 1957, pp. 249-299].

33. [Boulding, p. 34]; [Pruitt, p. 423].

II. NUCLEAR DETERRENCE

Commentary: *On Nuclear Deterrence*

Alain C. Enthoven

Albert Wohlstetter was the most important strategic analyst and thinker of our time. His ideas were the foundation of the overall nuclear strategy of the John F. Kennedy and Lyndon B. Johnson Administrations. His insights, recommendations, and ensuing policies greatly reduced the otherwise high danger of a thermonuclear war.

On a more personal scale, Albert was one of the most important influences in my life: father-figure, teacher, mentor, and friend. He was the intellectual godfather of the Systems Analysis Office that I created and led in the 1960s under the direction of Charles Hitch and Robert McNamara.[1]

Albert's effect on defense policy was profound and far-reaching. He was the father of strategic analysis based on systematic, empirical, and interdisciplinary studies. Indeed, he raised the standards for what could pass as an analysis of a policy issue in subsequent years. Albert searched out and asked the most fundamental questions. He insisted that the actual details — missile accuracies, reliabilities and payloads, bomb yields, blast resistance, bomber ranges, operating characteristics, costs, and much more — mattered and must be factored carefully into a systems analysis. Nuclear deterrence could not be dealt with sufficiently at a level of generality that did not consider such details.

Economics typically focuses on analyzing choice among a defined set of choices. For Albert, however, *out of analysis* emerged new choices. Analysis was as much about the invention of new solutions as it was choice among known alternatives.

While others made comparable contributions in the realms of politics and management, and may get the recognition in the history books, Albert's unique and essential contribution was in building the intellectual foundations of American strategy and defense policy, and how it must be studied. There, he had no equal.

The Basing Study.

The high point of Albert's early work was the "Basing Study," in which he led an unusually talented team including economists Fred Hoffman and Harry Rowen, and aeronautical engineer Bob

Lutz. With the Basing Study's two main reports — the 1953 staff summary report, *The Selection of Strategic Air Bases* (R-244-S),[2] and the 1954 final report, *The Selection and Use of Strategic Air Bases* (R-266)[3] — he turned the thinking on strategic air power on its head. He grasped the full significance of atomic and thermonuclear weapons. He and his team saw that the role of strategic air power could not be to carry on a protracted bombing campaign, a World War II with bigger bombs as envisioned in what was the doctrine at the time.[4] Such a war would be so destructive as to be not worth winning. But even this type of war couldn't be fought with the Strategic Air Command (SAC) based soft and concentrated on relatively few overseas bases. After a Soviet attack on our bases, there would be no SAC.

However, the Basing Study's most original insight was that the role of SAC should be to deter attack, and that required SAC to be able not only to survive a Soviet attack designed to destroy it, but also to strike back — in short, to acquire a "second-strike capability." And then he found that survival for a second-strike was itself a very large challenge. Albert inspired and led a great deal of research, ingenuity, and creativity to find solutions to that problem. The whole idea of survival, second strike, *and* deterrence came out of Albert's work and thinking.

In the decade after World War II, perhaps understandably, there were many views extant regarding the significance of nuclear weapons. Many thought that thermonuclear war would be so destructive as to be unthinkable, and therefore could not happen. Deterrence would be automatic. Albert and his team found that deterrence was far from automatic and far from easy to assure.

The Vulnerability Study.

Albert went on with the same team to do the follow-up "Vulnerability Study," an extension of his analysis into the missile age. With the Vulnerability Study's 1956 report, *Protecting U.S. Power to Strike Back in the 1950s and 1960s* (R-290), he showed how numerical superiority did not guarantee a credible deterrent:

> The criterion of matching the Russians plane for plane, or exceeding them, is, in the strict sense, irrelevant to the problem of deterrence. It may even be, as has been asserted, unnecessary to achieve such parity so long as

we make it crystal clear to the enemy that we can strike back after an attack. *But then we do have to make it clear.* Deterrence is hardly attained by simply creating *some* uncertainty in the enemy's attack plans, that is, by making it somewhat a gamble. The question is, *how much* of a gamble? And what are his alternatives?[5]

R-290 demonstrated the need to base and operate America's nuclear-armed bomber forces in ways that were not merely better protected and more capable of surviving surprise attack, but also much less accident-prone and much more controllable by the political leadership, in peacetime and especially in times of deep international crisis.

One of the many valuable activities that grew out of the vulnerability inquiry was Harry Rowen's study of how to put intercontinental ballistic missiles (ICBMs), the first of which were based in vulnerable clusters *above* ground, in better protected silos underground. These ideas of survival and second strike eventually passed into our security culture, and became the basis of defense policy. But they certainly were not obvious at the time. They were intensely controversial in several respects. For example, many authorities were *sure* that hardening bombers in underground shelters and missile silos to the required degree was impossible. I remember conferences where such judgments were expressed most forcefully. So, Albert went out and found Paul Weidlinger, a brilliant architect-engineer, who developed solutions to the problems of blast resistance. In the case of the missile silos, Weidlinger's engineering and Rowen's systems analysis were accepted and became the basis for our deployment of *Minuteman* ICBMs.

Challenging Dominant Paradigms: "The Delicate Balance" and After.

In the 1950s, people assumed that thermonuclear was so horrible that nobody would start one. Except that *we would*, if our NATO allies were attacked by the apparently overwhelming Soviet army. Most people, though, were oblivious to the implications of the vulnerability of SAC at the time. This vulnerability could have invited attack in a crisis, especially a crisis in which the Soviets thought we would carry out our threat, in which case their least worst alternative might be to launch a preemptive surprise attack. Albert published his memorable article, "The Delicate Balance of Terror," in *Foreign Affairs* to explain the problem to a wider audience.[6]

Despite the Eisenhower Administration's acceptance of many of Albert's programmatic recommendations for reducing vulnerability, it remained for the new Kennedy Administration to accept the broader strategic implications of his work. Whether in the military, government, academia, or other professions, there are such things as institutional interests and dominant paradigms that are very hard to change. It's hard to just tear up the plans and premises you have been acting on for years and admit that you were wrong. Albert was fearless and relentless in his attack on dominant paradigms when thorough analysis revealed they were wrong. Wasn't there a bumper sticker that said, "Attack the dominant paradigm"? If there was, it surely would have been the right one for Albert's car.

Fortunately for America—and the world—presidential candidate John F. Kennedy picked up on Albert's themes, and his first acts as President of the United States included accelerating the *Minuteman* as an underground-based ICBM, and the *Polaris* sea-launched ballistic missiles in submarines. President Kennedy personally changed the name of what were previously known as "strategic offensive forces" to "strategic retaliatory forces" to clarify the mission.

The Limits of Strategic Deterrence.

In the decade after World War II, the declared American policy for deterring a Soviet non-nuclear attack on our NATO allies was, as previously noted, to threaten an all-out thermonuclear attack on the Soviet bloc. Albert addressed this policy in "The Delicate Balance of Terror":

> But the notion of massive retaliation as a responsible retort to peripheral provocations vanished in the harsh light of a better understanding here and abroad that the Soviet nuclear delivery capability meant tremendous losses to the United States if we attacked them. And now Europe has begun to doubt that we would make the sacrifice involved in using SAC to answer an attack directed at it but not ourselves.

The many critics of the massive retaliation policy who advocate a capability to meet limited aggression with a limited response are on firm ground in suggesting that a massive response on such an occasion would be unlikely and the threat to use it therefore not believed. Moreover this argument is quite enough to make clear the critical need for more serious development of the power to meet limited aggressions.[7]

John F. Kennedy borrowed this idea in his campaign and denounced the massive retaliation policy as confronting the President with a choice of "Suicide or Surrender; Humiliation or Holocaust."[8] Albert himself, and through his disciples who went on to serve in the Pentagon, expressed profound concern about the uncontrolled, indiscriminate use of force. His studies led him to recommend control and deliberation — and, later, discriminate weapons such as accurate "smart weapons" and restraint in targeting. Albert's ideas had a large impact on the thinking of Secretary Robert McNamara. In the early years of the Kennedy Administration, Albert's ideas won out, and the very great danger of nuclear war was drastically reduced.

Albert was also very interested in NATO strategy, and very influential in its development. He understood that the *other* best way to reduce the danger of nuclear war was to eliminate our need for the threatened first use of nuclear weapons by acquiring adequate and effective non-nuclear forces.[9] Implementing this idea took a longer struggle than gaining acceptance of the need for a second-strike capability, but it was eventually successful.

Albert also directed attention to the flanks of NATO, and to potential attacks outside the NATO area. In August 1990, Iraq's surprise invasion of Kuwait fulfilled his prophecies.

Contemporary Relevance.

Albert's strategic views were "fact dependent," and facts change. As noted above, the actual technical factors mattered. So his legacy is as much in his intellectual standards and methods of analysis as it is in specific strategic doctrines. One of the most significant of Albert's legacies was to demonstrate the importance of what can be accomplished by rigorous, diligent, uncompromising search for truth in complex issues of public policy. He was skeptical of policy conclusions that rested on

171

uncertain intelligence estimates, and sought solutions that didn't depend on them even when they supported his case; he was openly critical of official estimates on occasions when he believed they reflected a policy bias. One cannot help wishing that such an analytical attitude had prevailed concerning the supposed presence of ongoing WMD programs in Iraq before President Bush's 2003 decision to invade. Among the many and large negative consequences of that error was the severe blow to the credibility of U.S. intelligence capabilities and top-level government decision-making processes.

Beyond that, the importance of Albert's insistence on secure and survivable command, control, and communications capabilities persists, as well as his insistence on the importance of a high level of security of nuclear weapons. We now find it clearly in our interest to help other nuclear powers maintain the security of and national control authority over their weapons so that they will not fall into the hands of nonstate actors who cannot be deterred, or will not be used in unauthorized ways in a crisis. Thus, we ought to be sure we are devoting adequate resources to that end. Moreover, with nearly 18 years having elapsed since the end of the Cold War, it is past time for publicly abjuring a policy that Albert always opposed, maintaining ICBM forces in a posture of readiness to launch on warning of an attack. He attacked that reckless policy during the dangerous days of the Cold War; he would certainly favor distancing ourselves from it now.

Albert's emphasis on the importance of and difficulty of deterrence remains relevant in the case of nuclear-armed states. Some may think that Iran can be deterred from attacking our vital interests with nuclear weapons. But we must face the difficult question of what would be an appropriate response. Surely, the idea of an all-out nuclear counterattack on Iranian cities would raise doubts in the minds of many reasonable people. Albert's insistence on the importance of control and deliberation, discrimination, and proportionality of response as a basis for a credible deterrent, remains relevant.

The problem of nuclear deterrence is enormously more complicated today than it was in the 1950s and 1960s when we faced essentially a bipolar world, and we believed the Soviets would act rationally in the interests of their own survival. (The bipolar world model may have oversimplified things.) Now we face a multipolar world, one in which nuclear weapons directed at our cities may not have a clearly marked return address in a nation-state. There now appears to be a significant danger that a nuclear weapon might be obtained by nonstate actors who want or are willing to die in an effort to deliver it to an American or European city. This problem needs to be analyzed with the same relentless determination, rigor, and thoroughness that Wohlstetter and his associates applied in the 1950s. Such analyses might point to important new technologies that need development.

Lessons from Wohlstetter's work include the fact that there is usually a lot of superficial, fuzzy, and wrong thinking extant. Just because 95 percent of people believe something to be true, including high-ranking authorities who have access to classified information, doesn't mean that it is true. For example, K. Wayne Smith and I debunked the widely accepted myth of overwhelming Soviet superiority in conventional forces in Europe in our book *How Much is Enough?* which we like to think was in the Wohlstetter tradition.[10] Fortunately, McNamara and both his presidential bosses also doubted that myth.

Complex problems of strategy must be approached by relentless pursuit of insight and truth, by people with access to relevant detailed information. As Albert believed, the numbers usually do matter. This makes it all the more important for our government to make such informed but independent analysis possible. This experience reflects creditably on the United States Air Force and the Eisenhower Administration who continued to support RAND's independence even when Wohlstetter and his team reached conclusions that were at variance with their policies. In an era marked by so much political cronyism and parochialism, it is important for our society to develop institutions that can conduct such analyses with the necessary degree of independence.

Not Just a Strategic Analyst.

On a more personal note, Albert was a remarkable person. He didn't suffer fools gladly, but he was as hard on himself as on others in the relentless search for valid insight and truth, and he appreciated good work and good policy analysis when he saw it. I felt the lash of his criticism for work not well thought through, and also the warmth of his appreciation for good work. Albert was a superb teacher.

Beyond the professional sphere, Albert was a great human being, with a wide range of friendships and interests. He loved life, music, art, poetry, felicitous toasts, flowers, architecture, food, and dance—"George Balanchine and Szechuan cuisine." He could speak intelligently on a vast range of topics.

Albert's judgment was never employed to better effect than in his choice of Roberta as his wife. The affection between them was evident to all who knew them well; but so was the importance of Roberta to Albert's professional achievements. The smoothly functioning domestic life she gave him allowed him the freedom to devote himself to his work and indulge his aesthetic tastes. She was also his closest colleague with outstanding accomplishments of her own, in an area that complemented his interests. He often acknowledged his dependence on her judgments of people and situations. More important, her prize-winning work on the problems of response to ambiguous intelligence warnings was central to his approach to the difficulty of strategic deterrence.[11]

This was a man of many facets and virtues. We miss his presence. Our world is a far better place for his work.

ENDNOTES - Enthoven

1. The Office of the Assistant Secretary of Defense for Systems Analysis, subsequently renamed Office of the Assistant Secretary of Defense for Program Analysis and Evaluation, is still in existence 40 years later.

2. Albert J. Wohlstetter, Fred S. Hoffman, Robert J. Lutz, and Henry S. Rowen, *The Selection of Strategic Air Bases*, R-244-S, special staff report, Santa Monica, CA: RAND Corporation, March 1, 1953, TOP SECRET, declassified on July 1, 1963, available from *www.albertwohlstetter.com/writings/19530301-AW-EtAl-R244S.pdf.*

3. Albert J. Wohlstetter, Fred S. Hoffman, Henry S. Rowen, and Robert J. Lutz, *The Selection and Use of Strategic Air Bases*, R-266, final report, Santa Monica, CA: RAND Corporation, April 1954, TOP SECRET, declassified circa 1961, available from *www.rand.org/pubs/reports/R0266/.* The follow-up Vulnerability Study's most representative report is: Wohlstetter, Hoffman, and Rowen, *Protecting U.S. Power to Strike Back in the 1950s and 1960s*, R-290, staff report, Santa Monica, CA: RAND Corporation, September 1, 1956, TOP SECRET, declassified circa 1960s, available from *www.albertwohlstetter.com/writings/19560901-AW-EtAl=R290.pdf.*

4. For more on this topic, see Albert Wohlstetter's "Letter to Michael Howard," November 1968, which is included in this edited volume.

5. Wohlstetter, Hoffman, and Rowen, *Protecting U.S. Power to Strike Back in the 1950s and 1960s*, p. 6.

6. Albert Wohlstetter, "The Delicate Balance of Terror," *Foreign Affairs*, Vol. 37, No. 2, January 1959, pp. 211-234. Although *Foreign Affairs* published an abridged version of "The Delicate Balance of Terror," this edited volume includes the unabridged version: Wohlstetter, *The Delicate Balance of Terror* (unabridged version), P-1472, Santa Monica, CA: RAND Corporation, November 6, 1958, revised December 1958, available from *www.rand.org/about/ history/wohlstetter/P1472/P1472.html*.

7. *Ibid.*

8. President John F. Kennedy, "Diplomacy and Defense: A Test of National Maturity," a speech at the University of Washington's 100th Anniversary Program, November 16, 1961. An audio recording and transcript of this speech is available online at the JFK Library at *www.jfklibrary.org/Historical+Resources/Archives/ Reference+Desk/Speeches/* Albert, while strongly supporting this position, was nonetheless critical of the Kennedy campaign's exploitation of the alleged "missile gap" to criticize the Eisenhower Administration. He rejected the argument on the sufficient grounds that it relied on the view that the strategic balance depended on the size of the opposing strategic forces rather than on their ability to survive and respond after a surprise attack.

9. See especially Albert Wohlstetter and Henry S. Rowen, "Objectives of the United States Military Posture," RM-2373, Santa Monica, CA: RAND Corporation, May 1, 1959, available from *www.rand.org/about/history/wohlstetter/RM2373/RM2373.html*; and Dean Acheson (with Albert Wohlstetter *et al.*), *A Review of North Atlantic Problems for the Future*, the Committee on U.S. Political, Economic and Military Policy in Europe's Policy Guidance to the National Security Council, March 1961.

10. Alain Enthoven and K. Wayne Smith, *How Much is Enough? Shaping the Defense Program, 1961-1969,* New York, NY: Harper & Row, 1971. A new edition of this book was recently published as: Enthoven and Smith, *How Much is Enough? Shaping the Defense Program, 1961-1969,* Santa Monica, CA: RAND Corporation, 2005.

11. Roberta Wohlstetter, *Pearl Harbor: Warning and Decision,* Stanford, CA: Stanford University Press, 1962.

The Delicate Balance of Terror (1958)

Albert Wohlstetter

P-1472, Santa Monica, CA: RAND Corporation, November 6, 1958, revised December 1958, available from *www.rand.org/about/history/wohlstetter/P1472/P1472.html*. Courtesy of the Wohlstetter Estate.

I. INTRODUCTION

The first shock administered by the Soviet launching of Sputnik has almost dissipated. The flurry of statements and investigations and improvised responses has died down, leaving a small residue: a slight increase in the schedule of bomber and ballistic missile production, with a resulting small increment in our defense expenditures for the current fiscal year, a considerable enthusiasm for space travel, and some stirrings of interest in the teaching of mathematics and physics in the secondary schools. Western defense policy has almost returned to the level of activity and the emphasis suited to the basic assumptions which were controlling before Sputnik.

One of the most important of these assumptions—that a general thermonuclear war is extremely unlikely—is held in common by most of the critics of our defense policy as well as by its proponents. Because of its crucial role in the Western strategy of defense, I should like to examine the stability of the thermonuclear balance which, it is generally supposed, would make aggression irrational or even insane. The balance, I believe, is in fact precarious, and this fact has critical implications for policy. Deterrence in the 1960's will be neither inevitable nor impossible but the product of sustained intelligent effort, attainable only by continuing hard choice. As a major illustration important both for defense and foreign policy, I shall treat the particularly stringent conditions for deterrence which affect forces based close to the enemy, whether they are U.S. forces or those of our allies, under single or joint control. I shall comment also on the inadequacy as well as the necessity of deterrence, on the problem of accidental outbreak of war, and on disarmament.[1]

II. The Presumed Automatic Balance

I emphasize that requirements for deterrence are stringent. We have heard so much about the atomic stalemate and the receding probability of war which it has produced, that this may strike the reader as something of an exaggeration. Is deterrence a necessary consequence of both sides having a nuclear delivery capability, and is all-out war nearly obsolete? Is mutual extinction the only outcome of a general war? This belief, frequently expressed by references to Mr. Oppenheimer's simile of the two scorpions in a bottle, is perhaps the prevalent one. It is held by a very eminent and diverse group of people—in England by Sir Winston Churchill, P. M. S. Blackett, Sir John Slessor, Admiral Buzzard and many others, in France by such figures as Raymond Aron, General Gallois and General Gazin, in this country by the titular heads of both parties as well as almost all writers on military and foreign affairs, by both Henry Kissinger and his critic, James E. King, and by George Kennan as well as Mr. Acheson. Mr. Kennan refers to American concern about surprise attack as simply obsessive,[2] and many people have drawn the consequence of the stalemate as has Blackett, who states: "If it is in fact true, as most current opinion holds, that strategic air power has abolished global war, then an urgent problem for the West is to assess how little effort must be put into it to keep global war abolished."[3] If peace were founded firmly on mutual terror and mutual terror on symmetrical nuclear powers, this would be, as Churchill has said, "a melancholy paradox"; nonetheless a most comforting one.

Deterrence, however, is not automatic. While feasible, it will be much harder to achieve in the 1960's than is generally believed. One of the most disturbing features of current opinion is the underestimation of this difficulty. This is due partly to a misconstruction of the technological race as a problem in matching striking forces, partly to a wishful analysis of the Soviet ability to strike first.

Since Sputnik, the United States has made several moves to assure the world (that is, the enemy, but more especially our allies and ourselves) that we will match or overmatch Soviet technology and, specifically, Soviet offense technology. We have, for example, accelerated the bomber and ballistic missile programs, in particular, the intermediate-range ballistic missiles. The problem has been conceived as more or better bombers—or rockets; or Sputniks; or engineers. This has meant confusing deterrence with matching or exceeding the enemy's ability to strike first. Matching weapons, however, misconstrues the nature of the technological race. Not, as is frequently said, because only a few bombs owned by the defender can make aggression fruitless, but because even many might not. One outmoded A-bomb dropped from an obsolete bomber might destroy a great many supersonic jets and ballistic missiles. To deter an attack means being able to strike back in spite of it. It means, in other words, a capability to strike second. In the last year or two there has been a growing awareness of the importance of the distinction between a "strike-first" and a "strike-second" capability, but little, if any, recognition of the implications of this distinction for the balance of terror theory.

Where the published writings have not simply underestimated Soviet capabilities and the advantages of a first strike, they have in general placed artificial constraints on the Soviet use of the capabilities attributed to them. They assume, for example, that the enemy will attack in mass "over-the-Arctic" through our Distant Early Warning line, with bombers refueled over Canada—all resulting in plenty of warning. Most hopefully, it is sometimes assumed that such attacks will be preceded by days of visible preparations for moving ground troops. Such assumptions suggest that Soviet leaders will be rather bumbling or, better, cooperative. These are best called "Western-preferred-Soviet strategies." However attractive it may be for us to narrow Soviet alternatives to these, they would be low in the order of preference of any reasonable Russian planning war.

III. The Quantitative Nature of the Problem and the Uncertainties

In treating Soviet strategies it is important to consider Soviet rather than Western advantage and to consider the strategy of both sides quantitatively. The effectiveness of our own choices will depend on a most complex numerical interaction of Soviet and Western plans. Unfortunately, both the privileged and unprivileged information on these matters is precarious. As a result, competent people have been led into critical error in evaluating the prospects for deterrence. Western journalists have greatly overestimated the difficulties of a Soviet surprise attack with thermonuclear weapons and vastly underestimated the complexity of the Western problem of retaliation.

One intelligent commentator, Richard Rovere, recently expressed the common view: "If the Russians had ten thousand warheads and a missile for each, and we had ten hydrogen bombs and ten obsolete bombers," . . . "aggression would still be a folly that would appeal only to an insane adventurer." Mr. Rovere's example is plausible because it assumes implicitly that the defender's hydrogen bombs will with certainty be visited on the aggressor; then the damage done by the ten bombs seems terrible enough for deterrence, and any more would be simply redundant. This is the basis for the common view. The example raises questions, even assuming the delivery of the ten weapons. For instance, the targets aimed at in retaliation might be sheltered and a quite modest civil defense could hold within tolerable limits the damage done to city targets by ten delivered bombs. But the essential point is that the weapons would not be very likely to reach their targets. Even if the bombers were dispersed at ten different points, and protected by shelters so blast resistant as to stand up anywhere outside the lip of the bomb crater — even inside the fire ball itself — the chances of one of these bombers surviving the huge attack directed at it would be on the order of one in a million. (This calculation takes account of the unreliability and inaccuracy of the missile.) And the damage done by the small minority of these ten planes that might be in the air at the time of the attack, armed and ready to run the gauntlet of an alert air defense system, if not zero, would be very small indeed compared to damage that Russia has suffered in the past. For Mr. Rovere, like many other writers on this subject, numerical superiority is not important at all.

For Joseph Alsop, on the other hand, it is important, but the superiority is on our side. Mr. Alsop recently enunciated as one of the four rules of nuclear war: "The aggressor's problem is astronomically difficult; and the aggressor requires an overwhelming superiority of force."[4] There are, he believes, no fewer than 400 SAC bases in the NATO nations alone and many more elsewhere, all of which would have to be attacked in a very short space of time. The "thousands of coordinated air sorties and/or missile firings," he concludes, are not feasible. Mr. Alsop's argument is numerical and has the virtue of demonstrating that at least the relative numbers are important. But the numbers he uses are very wide of the mark. He overestimates the number of such bases by more than a factor of ten,[5] and in any case, missile firings on the scale of a thousand or more involve costs that are

180

by no means out of proportion, given the strategic budgets of the great powers. Whether or not thousands are needed depends on the yield and the accuracy of the enemy missiles, something about which it would be a great mistake for us to display confidence.

Perhaps the first step in dispelling the nearly universal optimism about the stability of deterrence would be to recognize the difficulties in analyzing the uncertainties and interactions between our own wide range of choices and the moves open to the Soviets. On our side we must consider an enormous variety of strategic weapons which might compose our force, and, for each of these, several alternative methods of basing and operation. These are the choices that determine whether a weapons system will have any genuine capability in the realistic circumstances of a war. Besides the B-47E and the B-52 bombers which are in the United States strategic force now, alternatives will include the B-52G (a longer range version of the B-52); the Mach 2 B-58A bomber and a "growth" version of it; the Mach 3 B-70 bomber; a nuclear-powered bomber possibly carrying long-range air-to-surface missiles; the Dynasoar, a manned glide-rocket; the Thor and the Jupiter, liquid-fueled intermediate range ballistic missiles; the Snark intercontinental cruise missile; the Atlas and the Titan intercontinental ballistic missiles; the submarine-launched Polaris and Atlantis rockets; the Minuteman, one potential solid-fueled successor to the Thor and Titan; possibly unmanned bombardment satellites; and many others which are not yet gleams in anyone's eye and some that are just that.

The difficulty of describing in a brief article the best mixture of weapons for the long-term future beginning in 1960, their base requirements, their potentiality for stabilizing or upsetting the balance among the great powers, and their implications for the alliance, is not just a matter of space or the constraints of security. The difficulty in fact stems from some rather basic insecurities. These matters are wildly uncertain; we are talking about weapons and vehicles that are some time off and, even if the precise performances currently hoped for and claimed by contractors were in the public domain, it would be a good idea to doubt them.

Recently some of my colleagues picked their way through the graveyard of early claims about various missiles and aircraft: their dates of availability, costs and performance. These claims are seldom revisited or talked about: *De mortuis nil nisi bonum*. The errors were large and almost always in one direction. And the less we knew, the more hopeful we were. Accordingly the missiles benefited in particular. For example, the estimated cost of one missile increased by a factor of over 50 — from about $35,000 in 1949 to some $2 million in 1957. This uncertainty is critical. Some but not all of the systems listed can be chosen and the problem of choice is essentially quantitative. The complexities of the problem, if they were more widely understood, would discourage the oracular confidence of writers on the subject of deterrence.

Some of the complexities can be suggested by referring to the successive obstacles to be hurdled by any system providing a capability to strike second, that is, to strike back. Such deterrent systems must have (a) a stable, "steady-state" peacetime operation within feasible budgets (besides the logistic and operational costs that are, for example, problems of false alarms and accidents). They must have also the ability (b) to survive enemy attacks, (c) to make and communicate the decision to retaliate, (d) to reach enemy territory with fuel enough to complete their mission, (e) to penetrate enemy active defenses, that is, fighters and surface-to-air missiles, and (f) to destroy the target in spite of any passive civil defense in the form of dispersal or protective construction or evacuation of the target itself.

Within limits the enemy is free to use his offensive and defensive forces so as to exploit the weaknesses of each of our systems in getting over any of these hurdles between peacetime operation and the completion of a retaliatory strike. He will also be free, within limits, in the Sixties to choose that composition of forces for offense, and for active and passive defense, which will make life as difficult as possible for the various systems we might select. As I stressed earlier, much of the contemporary Western confidence on the ease of retaliation is achieved by ignoring the full range of sensible enemy plans. It would be quite wrong to assume that the uncertainties I have described affect a totalitarian aggressor and the party attacked equally. A totalitarian country can preserve secrecy about the capabilities and disposition of his forces very much better than a Western democracy. And the aggressor has, among other enormous advantages of the first strike, the ability to weigh continually our performance at each of the six barriers and to choose a precise known time and circumstance for attack which will reduce uncertainty. It is important not to confuse our uncertainty with his. The fact that we may not know the accuracy and number of his missiles will not deter him. Strangely enough, some military commentators have not made this distinction and have actually founded their belief in the certainty of deterrence on the fact simply that there are uncertainties.[6]

The slender basis for Western optimism is displayed not only in the writings of journalists but in the more analytic writings of professionals. The recent publications of General Gallois[7] parallel rather closely Mr. Alsop's faulty numerical proof that surprise attack is astronomically difficult—except that Gallois' "simple arithmetic," to borrow his own phrase, turns essentially on some assumptions which are at once inexplicit and extremely optimistic about the blast resistance of his dispersed missile sites to enemy attacks from nearby.[8] Mr. Blackett's recent book, *Atomic Weapons and East-West Relations*, illustrates the hazards confronting a most able analyst in dealing with the piecemeal information available to the general public. Mr. Blackett, a Nobel prize-winning physicist with wartime experience in military operations research, mustered a lucid summary of the public information available at the time of his writing on weapons for all-out war. He stated:

> It is, of course, conceivable that some of the facts have been kept so secret that no public judgment of military policy can have any great significance; in fact, that the military authorities have up their sleeve some invention or device, the possession of which completely alters the military situation. On reflection we can see that it is fairly safe to disregard this possibility.[9]

But unfortunately his evaluation of the use of intercontinental ballistic missiles against bomber bases shows that it was not at all safe to "disregard this possibility." Only a few pages further on, he said:

> It has recently been stated that some new method has been devised in America by which the H-bombs can be made small enough to be carried in an intercontinental missile. This seems unlikely.[10]

Mr. Blackett's book was published in 1956. It is now widely known that intercontinental ballistic missiles will have hydrogen warheads, and this fact, a secret at the time, invalidates Mr. Blackett's calculations and, I might say, much of his optimism on the stability of the balance of terror. In sum, one of the serious obstacles to any widespread rational judgment on these matters of high policy is that critical elements of the problem *have* to be protected by secrecy. However, some of the principal conclusions about deterrence in the early Sixties can be fairly firmly based, and based on public information.

IV. The Delicacy of the Balance of Terror

The most important conclusion runs counter to the indications of what I have called "Western-preferred Soviet strategies." It runs counter, that is, to our wishes. A sober analysis of Soviet choice from the standpoint of Soviet interest and the technical alternatives, and taking into account the uncertainties that a Russian planner would insure against, suggests that *we must expect a vast increase in the weight of attack which the Soviets can deliver with little warning, and the growth of a significant Russian capability for an essentially warningless attack. As a result, strategic deterrence, while feasible, will be extremely difficult to achieve, and at critical junctures in the 1960's we may not have the power to deter attack.* Whether we have it or not will depend on some difficult strategic choices as to the future composition of the deterrent force and, in the years when that force is not subject to drastic change in composition, hard choices on its basing, operations, and defense.

The bombers will continue to make up the predominant part of our force in the early 1960's. None of the popular remedies for their defense will suffice—not, for example, mere increase of alertness, the effects of which will be outmoded by the growth of a Russian capability for attack without significant warning, nor simple dispersal or sheltering alone or mobility taken by itself, or a mere piling up of interceptors and defense missiles around SAC bases. A complex of measures is required. I shall have occasion to comment briefly on the defects of most of these measures taken singly. Let me suggest at this point the inadequacy of the popular conception of the airborne alert—an extreme form of defense by mobility. The impression is rather widespread that one-third of the SAC bombers are in the air and ready for combat at all times.[11] This belief is belied by the public record. According to the Symington Committee Hearings in 1956, our bombers averaged 31 hours of flying per month, which is about four percent of the average 732-hour month. An Air Force representative expressed the hope that within a couple of years, with an increase in the ratio of crews to aircraft, the bombers would reach 45 hours of flight per month — which is six percent. This four to six percent of the force includes bombers partially fueled and without bombs. It is, moreover, only an average, admitting variance down as well as up. Some increase in the number of armed bombers aloft is to be expected. However, for the current generation of bombers, which have been designed for speed and range rather than endurance, a continuous air patrol for one-third of the force would be extremely expensive.

On the other hand, it would be unwise to look for miracles in the new weapons systems, which by the mid-1960's may constitute a considerable portion of the United States force. After the Thor, Atlas, and Titan there are a number of promising developments. The solid-fueled rockets, Minuteman and Polaris, promise in particular to be extremely significant components of the deterrent force. Today they are being touted as making the problem of deterrence easy to solve and, in fact, guaranteeing its solution. But none of the new developments in vehicles is likely to do that. For the complex job of deterrence, they all have limitations. The unvaryingly immoderate claims for each new weapons system should make us wary of the latest "technological breakthroughs." Only a very short time ago the ballistic missile itself was supposed to be intrinsically invulnerable on the ground. It is now more generally understood that its survival is likely to depend on a variety of choices in its defense.

It is hard to talk with confidence about the mid- and late-Sixties. A systematic study of an optimal or a good deterrent force which considered all the major factors affecting choice and dealt adequately with the uncertainties would be a formidable task. In lieu of this, I shall mention briefly why none of the many systems available or projected dominates the others in any obvious way. My comments will take the form of a swift run-through of the characteristic advantages and disadvantages of various strategic systems at each of the six successive hurdles mentioned earlier.

The *first hurdle* to be surmounted is the attainment of a stable, steady-state peacetime operation. Systems which depend for their survival on extreme decentralization of controls, as may be the case with large-scale dispersal and some of the mobile weapons, raise problems of accidents and over a long period of peacetime operation this leads in turn to serious political problems. Systems relying on extensive movement by land, perhaps by truck caravan, are an obvious example; the introduction of these on European roads, as is sometimes suggested, would raise grave questions for the governments of some of our allies. Any extensive increase in the armed air alert will increase the hazard of accident and intensify the concern already expressed among our allies. Some of the proposals for bombardment satellites may involve such hazards of unintended bomb release as to make *them* out of the question.

The cost to buy and operate various weapons systems must be seriously considered. Some systems buy their ability to negotiate a given hurdle—say, surviving the enemy attack—only at prohibitive cost. Then the number that can be bought out of a given budget will be small and this will affect the relative performance of competing systems at various other hurdles, for example penetrating enemy defenses. Some of the relevant cost comparisons, then, are between competing systems; others concern the extra costs to the enemy of canceling an additional expenditure of our own. For example, some dispersal is essential, though usually it is expensive; if the dispersed bases are within a warning net, dispersal can help to provide warning against some sorts of attack, since it forces the attacker to increase the size of his raid and so makes it more liable to detection as well as somewhat harder to coordinate. But as the sole or principal defense of our offensive force, dispersal has only a brief useful life and can be justified financially only up to a point. For against our costs of construction, maintenance and operation of an additional base must be set the enemy's much lower costs of delivering one extra weapon. And, in general, any feasible degree of dispersal leaves a considerable concentration of value at a single target point. For example, a squadron of heavy bombers costing, with their associated tankers and penetration aids, perhaps a half a billion dollars over five years, might be eliminated, if it were otherwise unprotected, by an enemy intercontinental ballistic missile costing perhaps sixteen million dollars. After making allowance for the unreliability and inaccuracy of the missile, this means a ratio of some ten for one or better. To achieve safety by *brute* numbers in so unfavorable a competition is not likely to be viable economically or politically. However, a viable peacetime operation is only the first hurdle to be surmounted.

At the *second hurdle*—surviving enemy offense—ground alert systems placed deep within a warning net look good against a manned bomber attack, much less good against intercontinental ballistic missiles, and not good at all against ballistic missiles launched from the sea. In the last case, systems such as the

186

Minuteman, which may be sheltered and dispersed as well as alert, would do well. Systems involving launching platforms which are mobile and concealed, such as Polaris submarines, have a particular advantage for surviving an enemy offense.

However, there is a *third hurdle* to be surmounted — namely that of making the decision to retaliate and communicating it. Here, Polaris, the combat air patrol of B-52's, and in fact all of the mobile platforms — under water, on the surface, in the air and above the air — have severe problems. Long-distance communication may be jammed and, most important, communication centers may be destroyed.

At the *fourth hurdle* — ability to reach enemy territory with fuel enough to complete the mission — several of our short-legged systems have operational problems such as coordination with tankers and using bases close to the enemy. For a good many years to come, up to the mid-1960's in fact, this will be a formidable hurdle for the greater part of our deterrent force. The next section of this article deals with this problem at some length.

The *fifth hurdle* is the aggressor's long-range interceptors and close-in missile defenses. To get past these might require large numbers of planes and missiles. (If the high cost of overcoming an earlier obstacle — using extreme dispersal or airborne alert or the like — limits the number of planes or missiles bought, this limitation is likely to be penalized disproportionately here.) Or getting through may involve carrying heavy loads of radar decoys, electronic jammers and other aids to defense penetration. For example, vehicles like Minuteman and Polaris, which were made small to facilitate dispersal or mobility, may suffer here because they can carry fewer penetration aids.

At the *final hurdle* — destroying the target in spite of the passive defenses that may protect it — low-payload and low-accuracy systems, such as Minuteman and Polaris, may be frustrated by blast-resistant shelters. For example, five half-megaton weapons with an average accuracy of 2 miles might be expected to destroy half the population of a city of 900,000, spread over 40 square miles, provided the inhabitants are without shelters. But if they are provided with shelters capable of resisting pressures of 100 pounds per square inch, approximately 60 such weapons would be required; and deep rock shelters might force the total up to over a thousand.

Prizes for a retaliatory capability are not distributed for getting over one of these jumps. A system must get over all six. A serious study of the competing systems in the late Sixties, as I stressed earlier, will have to consider the fact that a sensible enemy will design his offense and his active and passive defense so as to exploit the known weaknesses of whatever systems we choose. This sort of game, as anyone who has tried it knows, is extremely difficult to analyze and necessitates caution in making any early judgment as to the comparative merits of the many competing systems. The one thing that is apparent on the basis of even a preliminary analysis is that getting a capability to strike second in the late Sixties means running a hard course.

I hope these illustrations will suggest that assuring ourselves the power to strike back after a massive thermonuclear surprise attack is by no means as automatic as is widely believed. What can we say then on the question as to whether general war is unlikely? The most important thing to say perhaps is that it doesn't make much sense to talk about whether general war is likely or not unless we specify a good deal else about the range of circumstances in which the choice of surprise attack might present itself to the Russians. Deterrence is a matter of comparative risks. How much the Soviets will risk in surprise attack will depend in part on the vulnerability of our future posture. These risks could be smaller than the alternative of not striking.

Would not a general thermonuclear war mean "extinction" for the aggressor as well as the defender? "Extinction" is a state that badly needs analysis. Russian fatalities in World War II were more than 20,000,000. Yet Russia recovered extremely well from this catastrophe. There are several quite plausible circumstances in the future when the Russians might be confident of being able to limit damage to considerably *less* than this number — if they make sensible strategic choices and we do not. On the other hand, the risks of *not* striking might at some juncture appear very great to the Soviets, involving, for example, disastrous defeat in peripheral war, loss of key satellites with danger of revolt spreading — possibly to Russia itself — or fear of an attack by ourselves. Then, striking first, by surprise, would be the sensible choice for them, and from their point of view the smaller risk.

It should be clear that it is not fruitful to talk about the likelihood of general war without specifying the range of alternatives that are pressing on the aggressor and the strategic postures of both the Soviet bloc and the West. The balance is not automatic. First, since thermonuclear weapons give an enormous advantage to the aggressor, it takes great ingenuity and realism at any given

188

level of nuclear technology to devise a stable equilibrium. And second, this technology itself is changing with fantastic speed. Deterrence will require an urgent and continuing effort.

V. The Uses and Risks of Bases Close to the Soviets

It may now be useful to focus attention on the special problems of deterrent forces close to the Soviet Union. First, overseas areas have played an important role in the past and have a continuing though less certain role today. Second, the recent acceleration of production of our intermediate-range ballistic missiles and the negotiation of agreements with various NATO powers for their basing and operation have given our overseas bases a renewed importance in deterring attack on the United States — or so it would appear at first blush. Third, an analysis can throw some light on the problems faced by our allies in developing an independent ability to deter all-out attack on themselves, and in this way it can clarify the much agitated question of nuclear sharing. Finally, overseas bases affect in many critical ways, political and economic as well as military, the status of the alliance.

Let me say something to begin with about the uses and risks of basing SAC bombers overseas, first, on the costs of operating at great range. Suppose we design a chemically fueled bomber with the speed and altitude needed to penetrate enemy defenses and we want it to operate at a given radius from target without refueling. The weight of such a bomber along with the cost of buying and operating it will increase at a growing rate with the length of the design radius. Or, taking a specific bomber with a fixed radius, the cost of extending its radius by buying and operating aerial tankers will also grow at an increasing rate, with additional air refuelings to extend radius. The state-of-the-art during the past decade or so has been such that this has meant a drastic rise in costs at distances less than those from bases well within the United States to targets well within Russia. Or, looked at another way, for a fixed budget this means a smaller number of bombers capable of operating from far off than from close in to Russia. Indeed, with the actual composition of our tanker and bomber force, only a small proportion could be operated from the current continental United States base system to our Russian targets and back without *some* use of overseas bases.

At the end of the last decade, overseas bases appeared to be an advantageous means of achieving the radius extension needed by our short-legged bombers, of permitting them to use several axes of attack, and of increasing the number of sorties possible in the course of an extended campaign. With the growth of our own thermonuclear stockpile, it became apparent that a long campaign involving many re-uses of a large proportion of our bombers was not likely to be necessary. With the growth of a Russian nuclear-delivery capability, it became clear that this was most unlikely to be feasible.

Our overseas bases now have the disadvantage of high vulnerability. Because they are closer than the United States to the Soviet Union, they are subject to a vastly greater attack by a larger variety as well as number of vehicles. With given resources, the Soviets might deliver on nearby bases a freight of bombs with something like 50 to 100 times the yield that they could muster at intercontinental range. Missile accuracy would more than double. Because there is not much space for obtaining warning — in any case, there are no deep-warning radar nets — and, since most of our overseas bases are close to deep water from which submarines might launch missiles, the warning problem is very much more severe than for bases in the interior of the United States.

As a result, early in the Fifties the U.S. Air Force decided to recall many of our bombers to the continental United States and to use the overseas bases chiefly for refueling, particularly post-strike ground refueling. This reduced drastically the vulnerability of U.S. bombers and at the same time retained many of the advantages of overseas operation. For some years now SAC has been reducing the number of aircraft usually deployed overseas. The purpose is to reduce vulnerability and has little to do with any increasing radius of SAC aircraft. The early B-52 radius is roughly that of the B-36; the B-47, roughly that of the B-50 or B-29. In fact the radius limitation and therefore the basing requirements we have discussed will not change substantially for some time to come. We can talk with comparative confidence here, because the U.S. strategic force is itself largely determined for this period. Such a force changes more slowly than is generally realized. The vast majority of the force will consist of manned bombers, and most of these will be of medium range. The Atlas, Titan, and Polaris rockets, when available, can of course do without overseas bases. (Though it should be observed that the proportion of Polaris submarines kept at sea can be made larger by the use of overseas-based submarine tenders.) This is not true of the Thor and Jupiter. But in any case, strategic missiles will be in the minority. Even with the projected force of aerial tankers, this means that most of our force, which will be manned bombers, cannot be used at all in attacks on the Soviet Union without at least some use of overseas areas.

We might distinguish varying degrees in the intensity of such use. (1) At one extreme overseas bases could be simply places to land bomber crews by parachute. (2) Or they might provide emergency landing facilities for the bombers returning from target. (3) They might support the landing of tankers after they have fueled the bombers and so permit the transfer of larger amounts of fuel. (4) They might be used to help stage the bombers back to the United States (possibly to be turned around for another sortie). (5) They might be used for staging bombers on the way to as well as from the target. (6) They might support one or two such "turn-arounds." (7) At the other extreme, they might support continuous operation up to the outbreak of the war. The last of these types of use (involving continuous close-in operation and exposure before the outbreak) is, of course, the most vulnerable. Five and six, which involve exposure intermittently only, and after the start of war, are less vulnerable but nonetheless problematic. In the case of the first four, an attack on the base would not prevent the fulfillment by the bomber of at least a single mission of retaliation.

The essential point to be made is that to use the majority of our force will involve at least minimal employment of overseas areas for the early Sixties. In this period *some* U.S. bombers will be able to reach *some* targets from *some* U.S. bases within the original forty-eight states without landing on the way back. On the other hand, some bomber-target combinations are not feasible without pre-target landing (and are therefore doubtful). However, most of the bombers in the early Sixties will require some sort of touch down of the bomber or the tanker or both on the way back to the United States after fulfilling their mission.

In this section we have been discussing what I listed earlier as the fourth hurdle, the problem of reaching enemy territory with fuel enough to complete the mission. This is clearly an important hurdle in the early Sixties. But how important is it that the majority of the U.S. force of strategic vehicles be able to surmount this obstacle? This depends essentially on how well the rest of the force, which does not have range extension problems, can get over each of the other five obstacles: for example, the problem of surviving attack on the continental United States and penetrating enemy passive and active defense. What I have said already will suggest that these difficulties are large enough to make one hesitate to throw away lightly a capability that might be obtained by some form of radius extension overseas. Some touch down overseas will remain useful to most U.S. bombers, which will make up the greater part of the deterrent force in the early Sixties. On the other hand, because these bases are within range of so large a proportion of Russian striking power and subject to attack with so little notice, their use by bombers will be severely limited in form.

What of the bases for Thor and Jupiter, our first intermediate-range ballistic missiles? These have to be close to the enemy, and they must of course be operating bases, not merely refueling stations. (This is one of the many differences between the missile and the aircraft. Contrary to the usual belief, quite a few, though not all, of these differences favor the aircraft as far as ground vulnerability is concerned.) The Thors and Jupiters will be continuously in range of an enormous Soviet potential for surprise attack. These installations therefore reopen, in a most acute form, some of the serious questions of ground vulnerability that were raised about six years ago in connection with our overseas bomber bases. The decision to station the Thor and Jupiter missiles overseas has been our principal public response to the Russian advances in rocketry, and perhaps our most plausible response. Because it involves our ballistic missiles it appears directly to answer the Russian rockets. Because it involves using European bases, it appears to make up for the range superiority of the Russian intercontinental missile. And most important, it directly involves the NATO powers and gives them an element of control.

There is no question that it was genuinely urgent not only to meet the Russian threat but to do so visibly, in order to save the loosening NATO alliance. Our allies were fearful that the Soviet ballistic missiles might mean that we were no longer able or willing to retaliate against the Soviet Union in case of an attack on them. We hastened to make public a reaction which would restore their confidence. This move surely appears to increase our own power to strike back, and also to give our allies a deterrent of their own, independent of our decision. It has also been argued that in this respect it merely advances the inevitable date at which our allies will acquire "modern" weapons of their own, and that it widens the range of Soviet challenges which Europe can meet. But we must face seriously the question whether this move will assure either the ability to retaliate or the decision to attempt it, on the part of our allies, or ourselves. And we should ask at the very least whether further expansion of this policy will buy as much retaliatory power as other ways of spending the considerable sums involved. Finally, it is important to be clear whether the Thor and Jupiter actually increase the flexibility or range of response available to our allies.

One justification for this move argues that it disperses retaliatory weapons and that this is the most effective sanction against the thermonuclear aggressor. I have already anticipated this claim in my earlier discussion of the limitations of dispersal. At this point, however, it is useful to comment on one variant of the simple dispersal argument which is usually advanced in connection with overseas bases, namely that they provide a *widespread* dispersal and this in particular imposes insoluble problems of coordination. This argument needs examination. There is of course something in the notion that forcing the enemy to attack many political entities increases the seriousness of his decision. (However, (a) this can't be very persuasively argued as the justification for the IRBMs since they will add few if any new political entities to our current manned aircraft base system which would have to be attacked by the Russians in order to destroy our bombers; and, as we shall discuss, (b) where location in a foreign country means joint control, we may not be able to use the base in retaliation.) There is nothing on the other hand, or very little, in the notion that dispersal in several countries makes the problem of destruction more difficult in the military sense. Dispersal to increase enemy force requirements does not involve separation by oceans — just by the lethal diameters of enemy bombs. And the coordination problem referred to is very widely misunderstood. The critical part of the bomber coordination problem depends especially on the time spent within warning nets rather than simply the time of travel, and warning, as I have stressed, is difficult to come by close to the Soviets. Moreover there is not very much difference for the enemy in the task of coordinating bomber attacks on Europe and the eastern coast of the United States, say, and the job of coordinating attacks on our east and west coasts.

But the case of an enemy ballistic missile attack is most illuminating. These missiles are launched vertically and, so to speak, do not care in which direction they are told to proceed — their times on trajectory are eminently calculable and, allowing a cushion for failures and delays, times of firing can be arranged for near-simultaneous impact on many dispersed points, on Okinawa and the United Kingdom as well as on California and Ohio. Moreover, it is relevant to recall that these far-flung bases, while distant from each other and from the United States, are on the whole close to the enemy. They require for their elimination therefore a smaller expenditure of resources on the part of Russia than targets at intercontinental range. For close-in targets the Soviets can use a larger variety of weapons carrying larger payloads and with improved accuracies.

The seeming appositeness of an overseas-based Thor and Jupiter as an answer to a Russian intercontinental ballistic missile stems not so much from any careful analysis of their retaliatory power under attack as from the directness of the comparison they suggest: a rocket with a rocket, an intercontinental capability with a base at closer range to the target. In this respect the ready optimism on the subject reflects the basic confusion, referred to at the beginning of this essay, as to the nature of the technological race. It conceives the problem of deterrence as that of simply matching or exceeding the aggressor's capability to strike first. A surprising proportion of the debate on defense policy has betrayed this confusion. Matching technological developments are useful for prestige, and such demonstrations have a vital function in preserving the alliance and in reassuring the neutral powers. But propaganda is not enough. The only reasonably certain way of maintaining a reputation for strength is to display an actual power to our friends as well as our enemies. We should ask then whether further expansion of the current programs for basing Thor and Jupiter is an efficient way to increase American retaliatory power. If overseas bases are considered too vulnerable for manned bombers, will not the same be true for missiles? The basis for the hopeful impression that they will not be is rather vague, including a mixture of hypothetical properties of ballistic missiles in which perhaps the dominant element is their supposed much more rapid, "push-button" response. What needs to be considered here are the response time of such missiles (including decision, preparation, and launch times), and how they are to be defended.

The decision to fire a missile with a thermonuclear warhead is much harder to make than a decision simply to start a manned aircraft on its way, with orders to return to base unless instructed to continue to its assigned target. This is the "fail-safe" procedure practiced by the U.S. Air Force. In contrast, once a missile is launched, there is no method of recall or deflection which is not subject to risks of electronic or mechanical failure. Therefore such a decision must wait for much more unambiguous evidence of enemy intentions. It must and will take a longer time to make and is less likely to be made at all. When more than one country is involved, the joint decision is harder still, since there is opportunity to disagree about the ambiguity of the evidence, as well as to make separate considerations of national interest. The structure of the NATO decision process on much less momentous matters is complicated, and it should be recognized that such complexity has much to do with the genuine concern of the various NATO powers about the danger of accidentally starting World War III. Such fears will not be diminished with the advent of IRBMs. In fact, the mere widespread dispersion of nuclear armed missiles raises measurably the possibility of accidental outbreak.

Second—the preparation and launching time. It is quite erroneous to suppose that by contrast with manned bombers the first IRBMs can be launched almost as simply as pressing a button. Count-down procedures for early missiles are liable to interruption, and the cryogenic character of the liquid oxygen fuel limits the readiness of their response. Unlike JP-4, the fuel used in jet bombers, liquid oxygen cannot be held for long periods of time in these vehicles. In this respect such missiles will be *less* ready than alert bombers.

Third—the warning available. My previous comments have suggested that warning against both manned bomber and ballistic or cruise missile attack is most difficult overseas in areas close to the enemy. But this is related also to a fourth problem, namely that of active defense. The less warning, the more difficult this problem is. And the problem is a serious one, therefore, not only against ballistic missile attacks but, for example, against low-altitude or various circuitous attacks by manned aircraft.

And finally, passive defense by means of shelter is more difficult given the larger bomb yields, better accuracies, and larger forces available to the Russians at such close range. And if the press reports are correct, the installations planned do not contemplate bomb-resistant shelters. If this is so, it should be taken into account in measuring any actual contribution to the United States retaliatory power. Viewed as a contribution to deterring all-out attack on the United States then, the Thor and Jupiter bases seem unlikely to compare favorably with other alternatives. If newspaper references to hard bargaining by some of our future

195

hosts are to be believed, it would seem that such negotiations have been conducted under misapprehensions on both sides as to the benefits to the United States.

But many proponents of the distribution of Thor and Jupiter — and possibly some of our allies — have in mind not an increase in U.S. deterrence but the development of an independent capability in each of several of the NATO powers to deter all-out attack against themselves. This would be a useful thing if it can be managed at some supportable cost and if it does not entail the sacrifice of even more critical measures of protection. But aside from the special problems of joint control, which would affect the certainty of response adversely, precisely who their legal owner is will not affect the retaliatory power of the Thors and Jupiters one way or another. They would not be able to deter any attack which they could not survive. It is curious that many who question the capability of American overseas bases (for example, our bomber bases in the United Kingdom), simply assume that, for our allies, possession of strategic nuclear weapons is one with deterrence.

It remains to examine the view that the provision of these weapons will broaden the range of response open to our allies. The proponents do not seem to regard an addition of capability for NATO at the all-out end of the spectrum as the required broadening; but if they do, they are faced with the question previously considered: the actuality of this all-out response under all-out attack. Insofar as this view rests on the belief that the intermediate range ballistic missile is adapted to limited war, it is wide of the mark. The inaccuracy of the IRBM requires high-yield warheads, and such a combination of inaccuracy and high yield, while quite appropriate and adequate against unprotected targets in a general war, would scarcely come within even the most lax, in fact reckless, definition of limited war. Such a weapon is inappropriate for even the nuclear variety of limited war, and it is totally useless for meeting the wide variety of provocation that is well below the threshold of nuclear response. On the other hand, though a contribution of American aid, it may not be without cost to the recipient. Insofar as these weapons are expensive to operate and support, they are likely to displace a conventional capability that might be genuinely useful in limited engagements. More important, they are likely to be used as an excuse for budget cutting. In this way they will accelerate the general trend toward dependence on all-out response and so will have the opposite effect to the one claimed.

Nevertheless, if the Thor and Jupiter have these defects, might not some future weapon be free of them? Some of these defects, of course, will be overcome in time. Solid fuels or storable liquids will eventually replace liquid oxygen, reliabilities will increase, various forms of mobility or portability will become feasible, accuracies may even come down to regions of interest in limited wars. But these are all years away. In consequence, the discussion will be advanced if a little more precision is given such terms as "missiles" or "modern" or "advanced weapons." We are not distributing a generic "modern" weapon with all the virtues of flexibility for use in a wide range of attacks and invulnerability in all-out war. Finally, even with advances in the state-of-the-art on our side, it will continue to be hard to maintain a deterrent, and even harder close in under the enemy's guns than further off. Some of the principal difficulties I have sketched will remain and others will grow. This is of particular interest to our allies who do not have quite the same freedom to choose between basing at intercontinental and point-blank range. The characteristic limitations of "overseas" basing concern them since, for the most part, unlike ourselves, they live "overseas."

It follows that, though a wider distribution in the ownership of nuclear weapons may be inevitable, or at any rate likely, it is by no means inevitable or even very likely that the power to deter an all-out thermonuclear attack by Russia will be widespread. This is true even though a minor power would not need to guarantee as large a retaliation as we in order to deter attack on itself. Unfortunately, the minor powers have smaller resources as well as poorer strategic locations.[12] A multiplicity of such independent retaliatory powers might be desirable as a substitute for the principal current function of the alliance. But they will not be easy to achieve. Mere membership in the nuclear club might carry with it prestige, as the applicants and nominees expect, but it will be rather expensive, and in time it will be clear that it does not necessarily confer any of the expected privileges enjoyed by the two charter members. The burden of deterring a general war as distinct from limited wars is still likely to be on the United States and therefore, so far as our allies are concerned, on the alliance.

In closing these remarks on the special problems of overseas bases, it should be observed that I have dealt with only one of the functions of these bases: their use as a support for the strategic deterrent force. They have a variety of military, political and economic roles which are beyond the scope of this paper.

Expenditures in connection with the construction or operation of U.S. bases, for example, are a form of economic aid and, moreover, a form that is rather palatable to the Congress. There are other functions in a central war where their importance may be very considerable. In case deterrence fails, they might support a counterattack which could blunt the strength of an enemy follow-up attack, and so reduce the damage done to our cities. Their chief virtue here is precisely the proximity to the enemy which makes them problematic as a deterrent. Proximity means shorter time to target and possibly larger and more accurately delivered weapons—provided, of course, the blunting force survives the first attack. This is not likely to be a high confidence capability of the sort we seek in the deterrent itself; but it might make a very real difference under some circumstances of attack, particularly if the enemy attack were poorly coordinated, as it might be if the war were started by an accident. In this case the first wave might be smaller and less well organized than in a carefully prepared attack. The chance of even some of our unprotected planes or missiles surviving would be greater. Moreover a larger portion of the attacker's force would remain on base, not yet ready for a following attack. Using some portion of our force not in retaliation but to spoil the follow-up raid by killing or at least disrupting the matching of bombers with tankers, bombers with bombers, bombers with decoys, and bombers with missiles, could reduce both the number of attackers reaching our defenses and the effectiveness of their formation for getting through. It would be a fatal mistake to count on poor planning by an aggressor, but, given the considerable reduction in damage it might enable, it is prudent to have the ability to exploit such an error.

One caution should be observed. A force capable of blunting a poorly started aggression and equipped with information as to enemy deployments, might destroy a poorly protected enemy strategic force *before* the latter got started. Missiles placed near the enemy, even if they could not retaliate, would have a potent capability for striking first by surprise. And it might not be easy for the enemy to discern their purpose. The existence of such a force might be a considerable provocation and in fact a dangerous one in the sense that it would place a great burden on the deterrent force which more than ever would have to guarantee extreme risks to the attacker—worse than the risks of waiting in the face of this danger. When not coupled with the ability to strike in retaliation, such a capability would suggest—erroneously to be sure in the case of the democracies — an intention to strike first. It would tend to provoke rather than to deter general war.

One final use for our overseas bases should be mentioned, namely their use to support operations in a limited war. Their importance here is both more considerable and likely to be more lasting than their increasingly restricted utility to deter attack on the United States. Particularly in conventional limited wars, destructive force is delivered in smaller units and, in general, requires a great number of sorties over an extended period of time. It is conceivable that we might attempt the intercontinental delivery of iron bombs as well as ground troops and ground-support elements. The problem of intercontinental versus overseas bombers is mainly a matter of costs, provided we have the time and freedom to choose the composition of our force and our budget size. But there would be enormous differences in costs between distant and close-in repeated *delivery* at a given rate of high explosives.

I hope that my focus so far on the critical problem of deterring central war has not led the reader to believe that I consider the problem of limited war either unimportant or soluble by use of the strategic threat. Quite the contrary is the case. In fact it would be appropriate to say something about the limitations as well as the necessity of strategic deterrence in this as well as other connections. But first let me sum up the uses and risks of bases close to the Soviet Union. These bases are subject to an attack delivering more bombs with larger yields and greater accuracies and with less warning than bases at intercontinental range. Whether they are under American command, or completely within the control of one of our allies or subject to joint control, they present the severest problems for the preservation of a deterrent force.

VI. THE INADEQUACY OF STRATEGIC DETERRENCE, AND ITS NECESSITY

The inadequacy of deterrence is a familiar story. Western forces at the end of the war were larger than those of the Soviet Union and its satellites. We demobilized much more extensively, relying on nuclear weapons to maintain the balance of East-West military power. This was plausible then because nuclear power was all on our side. It was *our* bomb. It seemed only to complete the preponderance of American power provided by our enormous industrial mobilization base and to dispense with the need to keep it mobilized. It would compensate for the extra men kept under arms by the East.

199

But the notion of massive retaliation as a responsible retort to peripheral provocations vanished in the harsh light of a better understanding here and abroad that the Soviet nuclear delivery capability meant tremendous losses to the United States if we attacked them. And now Europe has begun to doubt that we would make the sacrifice involved in using SAC to answer an attack directed at it but not at ourselves.

The many critics of the massive retaliation policy who advocate a capability to meet limited aggression with a limited response are on firm ground in suggesting that a massive response on such an occasion would be unlikely and the threat to use it therefore not believed. Moreover this argument is quite enough to make clear the critical need for more serious development of the power to meet limited aggressions. Another argument, which will not hold water and which is in fact dangerous, is sometimes used: Little wars are likely, general war improbable. We have seen that this mistakes a possibility for its fulfillment. The likelihood of both general and little wars is contingent on what we do. Moreover, these probabilities are not independent. A limited war involving the major powers is explosive. In this circumstance the likelihood of general war increases palpably. The danger of general war can be felt in every local skirmish involving the great powers. But because the balance of terror is supposed, almost universally, to assure us that all-out war will not occur, advocates of graduated deterrence have proposed to fix the limits of limited conflict in ways which neglect this danger. A few of the proposals seem in fact quite reckless.

The emphasis of the advocates of limitation has been on the high rather than on the low end of the spectrum of weapons. They have talked in particular of nuclear limited wars on the assumption that nuclear weapons will favor the defender rather than the aggressor and that the West can depend on these to compensate for men and conventional arms. Perhaps this will sound reminiscent to the reader. These are, evidently, *our* tactical nuclear bombs. I am afraid that this belief will not long stand the harsh light of analysis and that it will vanish like its predecessor, the comfortable notion that we had a monopoly of strategic nuclear weapons and that these only completed the Western and, specifically, the American preponderance. I know of no convincing evidence that tactical nuclear weapons favor the defender rather than the aggressor if both sides use such weapons. The argument runs that the offense requires concentration and so the aggressor necessarily provides the defender with a lucrative atomic target. This ignores the fact that, in a delivered nuclear weapon itself, the offense has an enormous concentration of force. The use of nuclear weapons in limited wars might make it possible for the aggressor to eliminate the existing forces of the defender and to get the war over, reaching his limited objective before the defender or his allies can mobilize new forces. Like all-out nuclear war it puts a premium on surprise and forces in being rather than on mobilization potential which is the area in which the West has an advantage.

I am inclined to believe that most of those who rely on tactical nuclear weapons as a substitute for disparities in conventional forces have in general presupposed a cooperative Soviet attacker, one who did not use atomic weapons himself. Here again is an instance of Western-preferred Soviet strategies, this time applied to limited war. Ironically, according to reports of Soviet tactical exercises described in the last few years in the military newspaper, *The Red Star*, atomic weapons are in general employed only by the offense, the defender apparently employing Soviet-preferred Western strategies.[13] The symmetry of the optimism of East and West here could be quite deadly.

Whether or not nuclear weapons favor the West in limited war, there still remains the question of whether such limitations could be made stable. Korea illustrated the possibility of a conventional limited war which did not become nuclear, though fought in the era of nuclear weapons. It remains to be seen whether there are any equilibrium points between the use of conventional and all-out weapons. In fact the emphasis on the gradualness of the graduated deterrents may be misplaced. The important thing would be to find some discontinuities if these steps are not to lead too smoothly to general war. Nuclear limited war, simply because of the extreme swiftness and unpredictability of its moves, the necessity of delegating authority to local commanders, and the possibility of sharp and sudden desperate reversals of fortune, would put the greatest strain on the deterrent to all-out thermonuclear war.

For this reason I believe that it would be appropriate to emphasize the importance of expanding a conventional capability realistically and, in particular, research and development in non-nuclear modes of warfare. These have been financed by pitifully small budgets. Yet I would conjecture that if one considers the implications of modern surface-to-air missiles in the context of conventional war in which the attacker has to make many sorties and expose himself to recurring attrition, these weapons would look ever so much better than they do when faced, for example, with the heroic task of knocking down 99 percent of a wave of, say one thousand nuclear bombers. Similarly, advances in anti-tank wire-guided missiles and anti-personnel fragmentation weapons, which have been mentioned from time to time in the press, might help redress the current balance of East-West conventional forces without, however, removing the necessity for spending more money in procurement as well as research and development.

The interdependencies of limited and total war decisions make it clear that the development of any powerful limited war capability, and in particular a nuclear one, only underlines the need, at the same time, for insuring retaliation against all-out attack. An aggressor must constantly weigh the dangers of all-out attack against the dangers of waiting, of not striking "all-out." Sharp reversals in a limited war can increase the dangers of waiting. But finally there is no question at this late date that strategic deterrence is inadequate to answer limited provocation.

Strategic deterrence has other inadequacies besides its limitations in connection with limited war. Some of these concern air defense. The power to deter a rational all-out attack does not relieve us of the responsibility for defending our cities in case deterrence fails. It should be said at once that such a defense is not a satisfactory substitute for deterring a carefully planned surprise attack since defense against such an attack is extraordinarily difficult. I know in fact of no high confidence way of avoiding enormous damage to our cities in a war initiated by an aggressor with a surprise thermonuclear attack. The only way of preventing such damage with high confidence is to prevent the war. But if we could obtain a leakproof air defense, many things would change. A limited war capability, for example, would be unimportant. Massive retaliation against even minor threats, since it exposed us to no danger, might be credible. Deterring attack would also not be very important. Of course if both sides had such defenses, deterrence would not be feasible either, but this again would be insignificant since strategic war would be relatively harmless — at least to the targets on both sides if not to the attacking vehicles. It is a curious paradox of our recent intellectual history that, among the pioneers of both the balance of terror theory of automatic deterrence and the small nuclear weapon theory of limited or tactical war were the last true believers in the possibility of near perfect defense—which would have made deterrence infeasible and both it and the ability to fight limited war unimportant. However, in spite of the periodic announcements of "technological breakthroughs," the goal of emerging unscathed from a surprise thermonuclear attack has gotten steadily more remote.

On the other hand, this does not mean that we can dispense with the defense of cities. In spite of deterrence a thermonuclear war could be tripped by accident or miscalculation. In this case, particularly since the attack might be less well planned, a combination of spoiling counterattacks and active and passive defenses might limit the size of the catastrophe. It might mean, for example, the difference between fifty million survivors and a hundred and twenty million survivors, and it would be quite wrong to dismiss this as an unimportant difference.

If strategic deterrence is not enough, is it really necessary at all? Many sensitive and serious critics of Western defense policy have expressed their deep dissatisfaction with the strategy of deterrence. Moreover, since they have almost all assumed a balance of terror making deterrence nearly effortless, their dissatisfaction with deterrence might very well deepen if they accept the view presented here, that deterrence is most difficult. Distaste for the product should not be lessened by an increase in its cost. I must confess that the picture of the world that I have presented is unpleasant. Strategic deterrence will be hard. It imposes some dangers of its own. In any case, though a keystone of a defense policy, it is only a part, not the whole. The critics who feel that deterrence is "bankrupt," to use the word of one of them, sometimes say that we stress deterrence too much. I believe this is quite wrong if it means that we are devoting too much effort to protect our power to retaliate, but I think it quite right if it means that we have talked too much of a strategic threat as a substitute for many things it cannot replace. Mr. Kennan, for example, rejects the bomb as salvation, but explicitly grants it a sorry value as a deterrent. (In fact he grants it rather more than I since in his policy of disengagement it seems that he would substitute a threat something like that of massive retaliation for even conventional American and English forces on the Continent.)

On the whole, I think the burden of the criticism of deterrence has been the inadequacy of a thermonuclear capability and frequently of, what is not really deterrence at all, the threat to strike first. But it would be a fatal mistake to confuse the inadequacy of strategic deterrence with its dispensability. Deterrence is not dispensable. If the picture of the world I have drawn is rather bleak, it could nonetheless be cataclysmically worse. Suppose both the United States and the Soviet Union had the power to destroy each others' retaliatory forces and society, given the opportunity to administer the opening blow. In this case, the situation would be something like the old-fashioned Western gun duel. It would be extraordinarily risky for one side not to attempt to destroy the other, or to delay doing so. Not only can it emerge unscathed by striking first; this is the only way it can have a reasonable hope of emerging at all. Such a situation is clearly extremely unstable. On the other hand, if it is clear that the aggressor too will suffer catastrophic damage in the event of his aggression, he then has strong reason not to attack, even though he can administer great damage. A protected retaliatory capability has a stabilizing influence not only in deterring rational attack, but also in offering every inducement to both powers to reduce the chance of accidental detonation of war. Our own interest in "fail-safe" responses for our retaliatory forces illustrates this. A protected power to strike back does not come automatically, but it can hardly be stressed too much that it is worth the effort.

There are many other goals for our foreign as well as our military policy which have great importance: the strengthening of the alliance and of the neutral powers, economic development of the less advanced countries, negotiations to reduce the dangers of deliberate or accidental outbreak, and some attempts to settle the outstanding differences between the East and West. These other objectives of military and foreign policy are important and many of them are vital. But an unsentimental appraisal suggests no sudden change in prospect and in particular no easy removal of the basic East-West antagonisms. Short of some hard-to-manage peaceful elimination of the basic antagonisms, or a vast and successful program of disarmament, it would be irresponsible to surrender the deterrent. But in fact progress in disarmament too will be made easier if it is complemented by a defense against aggression.

VII. Deterrence, Accidents, and Disarmament

A deterrent strategy is aimed at a rational enemy. Without a deterrent, general war is likely. With it, however, war might still occur. This is one reason deterrence is only a part and not the whole of a military and foreign policy.

In fact, there is a very unpleasant interaction. In order to reduce the risk of a rational act of aggression, we are being forced to undertake measures (increased alertness, dispersal, mobility) which, to a smaller extent but still significantly, increase the risk of an irrational or unintentional act of war. The accident problem, which has occupied an increasingly prominent place in newspaper headlines during the past year, is a serious one. It would be a great mistake to dismiss the recent Soviet charges on this subject as simply part of the war of nerves. In a clear sense the great multiplication and spread of nuclear arms throughout the world, the drastic increase in the degree of readiness of these weapons, and the decrease in the time available for the decision on their use must inevitably raise the risk of accident. Though they were not in themselves likely to trigger misunderstanding, the B-47 accidents this year at Sidi Slimane and at Florence, South Carolina, and the recent Nike explosion (of which an Army officer in the local command said, "A disaster which could not happen did.") suggest the problem. And they are just the beginning.

There are many sorts of accidents that could happen. There can be electronic or mechanical failures of the sort illustrated by the B-47 and Nike mishaps; there can be aberrations of individuals, perhaps, quite low in the echelon of command; and, finally, there can be miscalculations on the part of governments as to enemy intent and the meaning of ambiguous signals. (With the rising noise level of alarms on the international scene and the shortening of the time available for such momentous decisions, this possibility becomes more real; with the widespread distribution of nuclear weapons with separate national controls, it is possible that there will be separate calculations of national interest. These could indicate a cause for all-out war to some nation doing the calculating which, from our standpoint, would be quite inadequate. That is, from our standpoint, a "miscalculation.")

What I have said does not imply that all deterrent strategies risk accident equally. The contrary is the case. One of the principles of selecting a strategy should be to reduce the chance of accident, wherever we can, without a corresponding increase in vulnerability to a rational surprise attack. (The problem of obtaining warning of a surprise attack, deciding on a response and communicating the decision — which last is especially acute for the mobile systems — would be very much easier if we did not have to be concerned with both goals: to deter a rational act of war and to reduce the chance of its happening by accident.) This is the significance of the recently adopted "fail-safe" procedures for launching SAC which came to the public notice in connection with the U.N. debates last May. Such a procedure requires that bombers, flushed by some serious yet not unambiguous warning, return to base unless they are specifically directed to continue forward. If the alarm is false, the bombers will return to base even if there is a failure in radio communications. If the alarm was in response to an actual attack and some radio communications should fail, this failure would mean only a small percentage diminution of the force going on to target. The importance of such a procedure can be grasped in contrast with the alternative. The alternative was to launch bombers on their way to target with instructions to continue unless recalled. Here, in case of a false alarm and a failure in communications, the single bomber or handful of bombers that did not receive the message to return to base might, as a result of this mistake, go forward by themselves to start the war. Of all the many poor ways to start a war, this would be perhaps the worst. Moreover, when one considers the many hundreds of vehicles involved, the cumulative probability of accidental war would rapidly approach certainty with repeated false alarms. Or the planes would have to be kept grounded until evidence of an attack was unambiguous — which would make these forces more vulnerable and, hence, such an attack more probable. A fail-safe procedure extends the period for final commitment.

While "fail-safe" or, as it is now less descriptively called, "positive control" is of great importance, it by no means eliminates the possibility of accident. While it can reduce the chance of miscalculation by governments somewhat by extending the period of final commitment, this possibility nonetheless remains.

The increased readiness of strategic forces affects the disarmament issues and therefore our allies and the neutral powers. Here it is important to recognize the obsolescence of some of the principal policies we have enunciated before the U.N. The Russians, exploiting an inaccurate United Press report which suggested that SAC started en masse toward Russia in response to frequent radar ghosts, cried out against these supposed Arctic flights. The United States response and its sequels stated correctly that *such flights had never been undertaken except in planned exercises — and moreover would not be undertaken in response to such high false-alarm rate warnings.* We pointed out the essential role of quick response and a high degree of readiness in the protection of the deterrent force. The nature of the fail-safe precaution was also described.

We added, however, to cap the argument, that if the Russians were really worried about surprise attack they would accept the President's "open skies" proposal. This addition, however, conceals an absurdity. Aerial photography would have its uses in a disarmament plan—for example, to check an exchange of information on the location of ground bases. However, so far as surprise is concerned, the "open skies" plan would have direct use only to discover attacks requiring much more lengthy, visible, and unambiguous preparations than are likely today.[14] The very readiness of our own strategic force suggests a state of technology which outmodes the "open skies" plan as a counter to surprise attack. Not even the most advanced reconnaissance equipment can disclose an intention from 40,000 feet. Who can say what the men in the blockhouse of an ICBM base have in mind? Or, for that matter, what is the final destination of training flights or fail-safe flights starting over the Pacific or North Atlantic from staging areas?

The actions that need to be taken on our own to deter attack might usefully be complemented by bilateral arguments for inspection and reporting and, possibly, limitation of arms and of methods of operating strategic and naval air forces. But the protection of retaliatory power remains essential; and the better the protection, the smaller the burden placed on the agreement to limit arms and modes of operation and to make them subject to inspection. Relying on "open skies" alone to prevent surprise would invite catastrophe and the loss of power to retaliate. Such a plan is worthless for discovering a well prepared attack with ICBMs or submarine-launched missiles or a routine mass training flight whose destination could be kept ambiguous. A tremendous weight of weapons could be delivered in spite of it.

Although it is quite hopeless to look for an inspection scheme which would permit abandonment of the deterrent, this does not mean that some partial agreement on inspection and limitation might not help to reduce the chance of any sizable surprise attack. We should explore the possibilities of agreements involving limitation and inspection. But how we go about this will be conditioned by our appreciation of the problem of deterrence itself.

The critics of current policy who perceive the inadequacy of the strategy of deterrence are prominent among those urging disarmament negotiations, an end to the arms race, and a reduction of tension. This is a paramount interest of some of our allies. The balance of terror theory is the basis for some of the more light-hearted suggestions: if deterrence is automatic, strategic weapons on one side cancel those of the other, and it should be easy for both sides to give them up. So James E. King, Jr., one of the most sensible writers on the subject of limited war, suggests[15] that weapons needed for "unlimited" war are those which both sides can most easily agree to abolish, simply because "neither side can anticipate anything but disaster" from their use. "Isn't there enough stability in the 'balance of terror'," he asks, "to justify our believing that the Russians can be trusted—within acceptable limits—to abandon the weapons whose 'utility is confined to the threat or conduct of a war of annihilation'?"

Indeed if there were no real danger of a rational attack, then accidents and the "n-th" country problem seem the *only* problems. In fact, they are very prominent in the recent literature on the subject of disarmament. As I have indicated, they are serious problems and some sorts of limitation and inspection agreement could diminish them. Almost everyone seems concerned with the need to relax tension. However, relaxation of tension, which everyone thinks is good, is not easily distinguished from relaxing one's guard, which almost everyone thinks is bad. Relaxation, like Miltown, is not an end in itself. Not all danger comes from tension. The reverse relation, to be tense where there is danger, is only rational. If there is to be any prospect of realistic and useful agreement, we must reject the theory of automatic deterrence. The size and degree of protection of our retaliatory forces in any limitation arrangement would in good part determine the size of the force that a violator would have to hide. If the agreed-on force were small and vulnerable, no monitorable scheme would be likely to be feasible. Most obviously *"the abolition* of the weapons necessary in a general or 'unlimited' war"* would offer the most insuperable obstacles to an inspection plan since the violator could gain an overwhelming advantage from the concealment of even a few weapons. The need for a deterrent, in this connection too, is ineradicable.

VIII. SUMMARY

What can we say then, in sum, on the balance of terror theory of automatic deterrence? It is a contribution to the rhetoric rather than the logic of war in the thermonuclear age. In suggesting that a carefully planned surprise attack can be checkmated almost effortlessly, that in short we may resume our deep pre-Sputnik sleep, it is wrong and its nearly universal acceptance is terribly dangerous. Though deterrence is not enough in itself, it is vital. There are two principal points.

First, even if we can deter general war by a strenuous and continuing effort, this will not be the whole of a military, much less a foreign policy! Such a policy would not of itself remove the danger of accidental outbreak or limit the damage in case deterrence failed, nor would it be at all adequate for crises on the periphery. Moreover, to achieve deterrent balance will entail some new risks requiring insurance—in any case, some foreign policy reorientation.

Second, deterring general war in both the early and late Sixties will be hard at best, and hardest both for ourselves and our allies wherever we use forces based near the enemy.

A generally useful way of concluding a grim argument of this kind would be to affirm that we have the resources, intelligence and courage to make the correct decisions. That is, of course, the case. And there is a good chance that we will do so. But perhaps, as a small aid toward making such decisions more likely, we should contemplate the possibility that they may *not* be made. They *are* hard, involve sacrifice, are affected by great uncertainties, concern matters in which much is altogether unknown and much else must be hedged by secrecy; and, above all, they entail a new image of ourselves in a world of persistent danger. It is by no means *certain* that we shall meet the test.

ENDNOTES - Wohlstetter - The Delicate Balance of Terror

1. I want to thank C. J. Hitch, M. W. Hoag, W. W. Kaufmann, A. W. Marshall, H. S. Rowen, and W. W. Taylor for suggestions in preparation of this article.

2. George F. Kennan, "A Chance to Withdraw Our Troops in Europe," *Harper's Magazine*, February 1958, p. 41.

3. P. M. S. Blackett, *Atomic Weapons and East-West Relations,* Cambridge Univ. Press, 1956, p. 32.

4. Joseph Alsop, "The New Balance of Power," *Encounter*, May 1958, p. 4. It should be added that, since these lines were written, Mr. Alsop's views have altered.

5. *The New York Times,* September 6, 1958, p. 2.

6. This is not a new error: in an interview with the press on December 3, 1941, Air Chief Marshal Sir Robert Brooke-Popham, Commander-in-Chief, Far East, for the British forces stated, "There are clear indications that Japan does not know which way to turn. Tojo is scratching his head." As Japan did not have a definite policy to follow, irrevocably, step by step, said Sir Robert, "there is a reassuring state of uncertainty in Japan." O. Dowd Gallagher, *Action in the East,* Doubleday, p. 94.

7. General Pierre M. Gallois, "A French General Analyzes Nuclear-Age Strategy," *Réalités,* November, 1958, pp. 19-22, 70-71; "Nuclear Aggression and National Suicide," *The Reporter,* September 18, 1958, pp. 23-26.

8. See endnote 12.

9. Blackett, *op. cit.,* p. 34.

10. *Ibid.,* p. 53.

11. See, for example, "NATO, A Critical Appraisal," by Gardner Patterson and Edgar S. Furniss, Jr., Princeton University Conference on NATO, Princeton, New Jersey, June 1957, p. 32: "Although no one pretended to know, the hypothesis that one-third of the striking force of the United States Strategic Air Command was in the air at all times was regarded by most as reasonable."

12. General Gallois argues that, while alliances will offer no guarantee, "a small number of bombs and a small number of carriers suffice for a threatened power to protect itself against atomic destruction." (*Réalités, op. cit.,* p. 71.) His numerical illustrations give the defender some 400 underground launching sites (*ibid.,* p. 22 and *The Reporter, op. cit.,* p. 25) and suggest that their elimination would require between 5,000 and 25,000 missiles—which is "more or less impossible"—and that in any case the aggressor would not survive the fallout from his own weapons. Whether these are large numbers of targets from the standpoint of the aggressor will depend on the accuracy, yield

and reliability of offense weapons as well as the resistance of the defender's shelters and a number of other matters not specified in the argument. General Gallois is aware that the expectation of survival depends on distance even in the ballistic missile age and that our allies are not so fortunate in this respect. Close-in missiles have better bomb yields and accuracies. Moreover, manned aircraft—with still better yields and accuracies—can be used by an aggressor here since warning of their approach is very short. Suffice it to say that the numerical advantage General Gallois cites is greatly exaggerated. Furthermore, he exaggerates the destructiveness of the retaliatory blow against the aggressor's cities by the remnants of the defender's missile force—even assuming the aggressor would take no special measures to protect his cities. But particularly for the aggressor—who does not lack warning—a civil defense program can moderate the damage done by a poorly organized attack. Finally, the suggestion that the aggressor would not survive the fallout from his own weapons is simply in error. The rapid decay fission products which are the major lethal problem in the locality of a surface-burst weapon are not a serious difficulty for the aggressor. The amount of the slow decay products, strontium-90 and cesium-137, in the atmosphere would increase considerably more than the amounts that have been produced by the rather large number of megatons already detonated in the course of testing by the three nuclear powers. This might for example, if nothing were done to counter it, increase by many times the incidence of such relatively rare diseases as bone cancer and leukemia. However, such a calamity, implying an increase of, say, 20,000 deaths per year for a nation of 200,000,000 is of an entirely different order from the catastrophe involving tens of millions of deaths, which General Gallois contemplates elsewhere. And there are measures that might reduce even this effect drastically. (See The RAND Corporation Report R-322-RC, *Report on a Study of Non-Military Defense,* July 1, 1958.)

13. I am indebted to an unpublished paper of Mr. Constantin Melnik for this reference.

14. Aerial reconnaissance, of course, could have an indirect utility here for surveying large areas to determine the number and location of observation posts needed to provide more timely warning.

15. James E. King, Jr., "Arms and Man in the Nuclear-Rocket Era," *The New Republic*, September 1, 1958.

Excerpts on "Missile Gap" from
General Comments on Senator Kennedy's
National Security Speeches (circa 1960)

Albert Wohlstetter

Excerpted from Albert Wohlstetter, "Some General Comments on Senator [John F.] Kennedy's National Security Speeches," circa 1960, available from Hoover Institution Archives, Albert and Roberta Wohlstetter Papers, Writings, Box 148, Folder 10. Courtesy of the Wohlstetter Estate.

The defense speeches are, on the whole, sound. The sense of what Mr. Kennedy has to say on national defense can be improved in detail and conceptually (for example, the analysis of the so-called missile gap), but the principal problem they present is that there are inconsistencies between the national defense speeches and the speeches on disarmament.

Discussion:

The defense speeches on the whole are sound in emphasizing:

1. That there are serious deficiencies in our national defense posture both for central war and for theater warfare. (The emphasis on conventional forces for theater is especially good as is the emphasis on a second-strike capability for central war and the mention, however brief, of the need for active and passive defense of our cities.)

2. That the expenditure of several billion dollars a year more on national defense is necessary and can be made without great sacrifice.

3. That the purpose of our military policy (that is, our national defense) is peaceful.

4. That the likelihood of concluding an arms agreement with the Russians is increased by a strengthening of our military posture—"we arm to parley."

There are some inaccuracies and unclarities in the defense speeches themselves, and in particular there are several points at which their most important insights are lost. For example, the missile gap speech in 1958 recognizes that retaliatory power depends on not just the number of offense vehicles on both sides but also the active and passive defenses of both sides. However, other parts of this speech and other speeches suggest that the problem is one of simply a disparity in the number of vehicles and is soluble completely by an increase in the number of our Polaris and Minutemen. The name "missile gap" itself was suggested by an anticipated difference between the number of missiles in our force and the number of missiles in the Russian force in the early 60's. There are several things that are wrong with the notion of missile gap, some of which are summarized in another attachment.

*****

The Concept of the "Missile Gap"

The phrase "missile gap" came into use to express the anticipated difference between the number of missiles anticipated for the Russian force and the number programmed for our own in the early 60's. It is evident that the more rapid growth of the Russian missile force is connected with some of our defense troubles, but nonetheless the notion of missile gap has many deficiencies for the purposes of describing what that trouble is.

1. The missile gap is the result of a direct comparison between pre-attack forces of the Soviet Union and pre-attack forces of the United States. In this case, missile forces. Similar direct comparisons of pre-attack forces figured in earlier Congressional and Administration debates, for example, an earlier flurry about an expected gap between the number of Russian heavy bombers and American heavy bombers led to an increase in our B-52 program. The Congressional critics have, especially until very recently, compared pre-attack numbers of U.S. bombers with pre-attack numbers of Russian bombers or pre-attack numbers of U.S. missiles with Russian missiles, etc. The Administration answers at first consisted in simply broadening the basis of comparison, for example, to the total of pre-attack missiles, and bombers (medium and heavy), in the U.S. force with the analogous total in the Russian force.

2. Strictly speaking, neither the critics nor the administration respondents were in point when they matched pre-attack forces to demonstrate either that there was a deficiency or that there was

214

not. The problem so far as deterrence is concerned is to assure retaliation which, of course, is a matter of a second-strike capability, and it is possible for the victim of aggression to have a larger pre-attack force than the aggressor and little or nothing to strike back with after the aggression. This is so if his forces are sufficiently concentrated, soft, easy to target, lacking in penetration capability, etc. And on the other hand it is possible for the reverse to be true. In fact the administration program for the 60's is inadequate to assure deterrence, but an analysis that shows this has to be subtler than a mere matching of pre-attack capabilities for both sides. The administration in this last year changed its line of response to its critics, and instead of saying that while we would have fewer missiles we would have as many or more missiles as bombers in total, it said correctly that matching is irrelevant. And it asserted that there would be no "deterrence gap." There is nothing wrong with the logic of this last argument. It is simply factually in error. To demonstrate it requires an analysis of the interactions of Russian and U.S. forces assuming various reasonable strategies for both sides and considering warning and response time, the problems of command and control, and the cumulative problems of keeping a relatively accident-safe peacetime operation of the force, [and keeping] the capabilities to survive the opening blow, to decide on the transition from peace to war, and to penetrate active and passive defenses.

The gap concept simply ignores the complexity of the problem and was open to counter by the increased sophistication of the administration's response.

3. The adjective in "*missile* gap" suggests that the problem arrived with the advent of long-range ballistic missiles, and the noun "gap" suggests that it is a transient phenomenon. This is also suggested in the first item that we have to get successfully through the gap. In fact the problem of deterrence became a difficult one before the advent of the ballistic missile and stemmed basically from the failure to *protect* our strategic force as distinct from simply increasing it. (In fact viewing it as a problem of matching pre-strike forces encourages a continuance of this bad habit.) Finally, the gap notion, in suggesting that there is a trouble period of more or less definite short duration, is excessively cheery. A "gap" would seem by definition to have something solid on the other side. Unfortunately there is not. It will take continuing ingenuity and effort in light of changing technology to get a stable deterrent. In some respects, far from getting easier in the late 60's

as some people think, deterrence, though achievable and critically important, will get harder.

4. The near side as well as the far side of the gap raises problems which are best avoided. They are of two sorts. If the vulnerability should come close enough to make it hard to remedy in time, there would be valid security and policy questions in focusing on this near border of the gap. The second problem is related. In speeches which mention the exact year [the gap is to begin], one tends successfully to put off the date at which the gap is supposed to start. So the missile gap speech of 1958 said without qualification "the gap will begin in 1960." The Investment for Peace speech delivered in 1960 qualifies this by suggesting that the matter will "become critical in 1961, 1962 or 1963." For such reasons it seems more sensible to talk about a less precisely delimited period beginning with the time our actions can take effect and continuing indefinitely to require ingenuity and effort.

On the Genesis of Nuclear Strategy:
Letter to Michael Howard (1968)

Albert Wohlstetter

Excerpted from Albert Wohlstetter, *On the Genesis of Nuclear Strategy*, unpublished, expanded version of Wohlstetter's unpublished November 6, 1968, letter to Michael Howard, with additional materials and commentary by James Digby and Arthur Steiner, and a note by Michael Howard, revised circa April 1986, available from Hoover Institution Archives, Albert and Roberta Wohlstetter Papers, Writings, Box 187, Folder 22. Courtesy of the Wohlstetter Estate, the Digby Estate, and Arthur Steiner.

November 6, 1968
1550 North State Parkway
Chicago, Illinois 60610

Michael Howard
All Souls College
Oxford, England

Dear Michael:

Let me begin with some comments on a few specific points in your paper on the history of nuclear strategy. I shall deal with the timing and logical content of concepts and doctrine, the role of physicists, "academic" historians and social scientists, and the then "unacademic" systems analysts whose work used actual military deployments, plans and operations; also with the actual relations of nuclear forces in the 1950s. My comments concern not only those concepts and strategies in whose development I was personally engaged, but also some earlier history that is traceable in the Special Collection on atomic scientists in the Harper Collection at the University of Chicago and similar collections at the U.S. Atomic Energy Commission.[1] I shall be using my as yet unpublished lecture notes on the history of nuclear strategy — and especially the notes relevant to the statements in your paper about how nuclear weapons were seen to affect and how they affected the stable deterrence of war; and the genesis of the first-strike, second-strike distinction.

First, your pages 4ff:[2] You contrast the lay notion that nuclear weapons would transform the entire nature of war with the judgment of professionals:". . . for the professional they made remarkably little difference. . . ." You suggest that the professional, including not only the military but also scientists who had long experience of military planning, held the latter view, and cite Blackett and Bush as examples.[3] Then you contrast a few "academics" who were thinking ahead of what you assume to have been the state of the art for the ten years following the initiation of planning in NATO at the end of the 1940s.

However, the very first contrast made — that between the professional and the layman — will not sustain examination; and the state of the art in the 1950s was not what you suggest. The physicists connected with the Manhattan Project (including some fitting your description as experienced with military planning) were the first to see that nuclear weapons made a great difference — though their understanding was understandably deficient. The "difference" made is actually multiple and complex. Some differences were critical much earlier than you suggest. NATO plans in 1949 and later did not recognize the impending technical environment in which they would operate in the 1950s. Finally, academic social scientists and historians, like Viner, Brodie, and Fox,[4] did indeed have important insights in 1945 and 1946, but they did not foresee the possibility that nuclear attacks on nuclear strategic forces raised an entirely new order of problem requiring a major distinction between "first-strike" and "second-strike" forces. Indeed, in some respects, they were even further from seeing the problem than the physicists — who caught inconsistent glimpses of it.

As my brief talk at Oxford indicated, it was mainly those rival institutions who didn't have the bomb at the war's end (such as the Navy, the ground Army — and the Russians) who then said it made little difference. And politicians and professionals associated with these bombless ones said the same. Military professionals connected with the Army Air Corps, and those concerned with strategic bombing in particular took an opposite view. (The War Department public statements uneasily tried to bridge its air and ground advocates' views.)

The physicists connected with the Manhattan Project at first almost unanimously held that the bomb changed things completely. Item 1 in the four-point "Creed" of the Federation of American Scientists read: "1. The bomb is a revolutionary weapon." But then after 1946 these scientists began to associate themselves with one side or another in the factional disputes. The majority gradually reversed the absolutist position they had previously taken that there was no defense against nuclear weapons, that it was "one world or none."[5] But this was after the end of 1946 when the Russians turned down the Baruch Plan and it was clear that there was not going to be one world. The physicists then looked more soberly at the "many-world" alternative to none. For the first half of the 1950s, in fact, the majority faction of physicists swung to the opposite of their first extreme. Vannevar Bush, whose 1949 views you cite, illustrates perfectly both the initial position and the change. His memoranda[6] on September 30, 1944, stated that nuclear weapons were of world-shaking importance, that they would soon place every population center in the world at the mercy of the nation that struck first, etc.

Let me expand a little on the initial position of the natural scientists and engineers connected with the Manhattan Project. And then let me treat the views of Viner, Brodie, and Fox in relation to those of the Manhattan Project scientists. I think it is clear that each of these groups had vital insights. Neither, however, can genuinely be said to have understood "the whole concept of a stable balance of second-strike forces" (your p. 5)[7] in the plain sense in which the phrase is used today and in which it was defined. Moreover, when looked at historically it is possible to see why, for all the honors they deserve, they were not likely to have foreseen the relations of forces that called forth the distinction in the early 1950s.

THE MANHATTAN PROJECT SCIENTISTS

A good place to begin with the early views of the atomic scientists is the "Prospectus on Nucleonics" by a committee headed by Zay Jeffries that included Enrico Fermi, James Franck, T. R. Hogness, R. S. Mulliken, R. S. Stone, and C. A. Thomas. It was dated September 1944. It contains several ideas that became commonplace immediately after Hiroshima.[8]

The first was the recognition of the enormous increase in destructiveness enabled by nuclear weapons, and, coupled with this recognition, the insight that simply overmatching an adversary's bombs is not strictly in point.

> A nation, or even a political group, given the opportunity to start aggression by a sudden use of nuclear destruction devices, will be able to unleash a "blitzkrieg" infinitely more terrifying than that of 1939-40. A sudden blow of this kind might literally wipe out even the largest nation — or at least all its production centers — and decide the issue on the first day of the war. The weight of the weapons of destruction required to deliver this blow will be infinitesimal compared to that used up on a present day heavy bombing raid. . . .

The second was the idea of the prospect of nuclear retaliation as, it is to be hoped, something that might paralyze an aggressor.

> The most that an independent American nucleonic rearmament can achieve is the certainty that a sudden total devastation of New York or Chicago can be answered the next day by an even more extensive devastation of the cities of the aggressor, and the hope that the fear of such a retaliation will paralyze the aggressor.

On both counts, the Jeffries Committee deserve very early credit. Yet, if one examines the statements closely, both analytically and in their historical context, some essential limitations emerge.

First, like almost everyone else for years to come, members of the Jeffries Committee were thinking primarily of production centers and cities as the natural targets for nuclear attack. Your quotation from Vannevar Bush in 1949 (and Bush's 1944 memoranda as well) display the same presumption: "They could undoubtedly devastate the cities and the war potential. . . ." For a good many reasons, some of which I have described elsewhere,[9] the notion was ingrained very early that an atomic weapon is essentially a weapon of "mass destruction" or "terror" to be used as the Americans used it at Hiroshima. Eugene Rabinowitch, the editor of the *Bulletin of the Atomic Scientists*, and two other physicists from the Metallurgical Laboratories in Chicago wrote that "Atomic bombs are weapons used only against large cities and industrial centers. Therefore, if both sides in a conflict have enough atomic bombs to wipe out each other's cities, they are in approximately equal position, even if the one has three times more bombs than the other." (*Life,* October 29, 1945, p. 46.) The famous Franck Report, which was dated June 11, 1945, proceeded on the same assumption: "Atomic bombs containing a larger quantity of active material but still weighing less than a ton may be expected to be available within ten years which could destroy over ten square miles of a city. A nation able to assign 10 tons of atomic explosives for the preparation of a sneak attack on this country can then hope to achieve the destruction of all industry and most of the population in an area from 500 square miles upwards." (Signed by J. Franck, D. J. Hughes, J. J. Nickson, E. Rabinowitch, G. T. Seaborg, J. C. Stearns, and L. Szilard.)[10] Whether cities were the only targets or just the preeminent ones, phrases like "weapons for mass destruction" came to be used as synonyms for "atomic weapons." So they entered the language and so they continue to color our thought, even though we have long since come to see the critical importance of other targets quite detached from masses of people. As might be expected, Oppenheimer in 1945 summarized with characteristic eloquence the essentially universal view of an atomic weapon: "Surprise and... terror are as intrinsic to it as are the fissionable nuclei."[11]

Oppenheimer's understanding had been formed in the circumstances of the original use of the weapon. The Interim Committee and the Scientific Panel, of which Oppenheimer was a member, were seeking as a target "a vital war plant employing a large number of workers and closely surrounded by workers' houses."[12] As was not infrequently the case in the strategic bombing debate between the wars, there was a certain ambivalence about the purpose of destroying "closely surrounding" civilian workers and their houses in addition to the "vital war plant." The flow of products from a war plant, however "vital," supported the war only by way of a pipeline of material to the fighting. Interrupting the material flow would reduce stocks and have an indirect and delayed effect. So also for the plant workers taken simply as a factor of production. But the sudden act of annihilating the plant and the workers could shock and inspire terror and so have a direct and immediate effect on the popular and governmental will to continue the war. Standard doctrine of strategic bombing, both English and American, stressed not only the destruction of war-supporting industry, but also the weakening of an adversary's will to resist. Though the Interim Committee and the Scientific Panel agreed that "the United States ... could not concentrate on a civilian area," it chose a war plant closely surrounded by workers' houses "to make as profound a psychological impression on as many of the inhabitants as possible," to administer "the maximum surprise shock."

Surprise at Hiroshima had then a function quite different from its role in surprise attack on nuclear forces. It reduced the probability that the active defenses would be alerted and the single unescorted plane carrying the A-bomb intercepted. But even more important, since delivery could have been assured by other devices — for example, by an escort of hundreds of planes — surprise was an intrinsic element in the terror and shock aimed at and achieved. It is easy to see why terror, and surprise in relation to terror, were seen not only by prominent members of the Scientific Panel, but also by the Manhattan Project physicists and by a wider public, as the essentials after Hiroshima and Nagasaki. The A-bomb was preeminently a weapon to be used against population centers or against industry embedded in population centers.

That this was an almost universal view of the Manhattan Project physicists I can confirm on the basis of an examination of hundreds of their statements made from 1944 to 1946. This view led to other consequences I cannot elaborate on in this letter. For example, it displaced the matching of weapons against weapons with an equally mechanical numerical matching of bombs against cities. This in turn led to the stereotypes of "overkill" in which numbers or total yield of bombs are compared with total population (now usually the population of the world). And it led natural and social scientists to take degree of urbanization as the measure of a country's vulnerability. In 1945 and 1946 this was taken to imply the intrinsic disadvantage to the United States in an arms race with the Soviet Union; and when after 1946 physicists began to think of defense as an alternative to world government, they thought of defending cities and began by talking especially of one most costly and implausible measure — namely to outrace bomb stockpiles by multiplying and dispersing cities.

However, what is essential for this letter is the way their view of the bomb as preeminently a city-destroyer blinkered them as to the possibilities of using it to destroy strategic nuclear forces. Perhaps the most revealing testimony in this respect is that of the Nobel Laureate Irving Langmuir.[13] I mentioned it in my talk at Oxford. He pictures four stages in an arms race:

1. We alone have atomic bombs. We are then secure at that time. 2. Other nations also have atomic bombs, but they haven't enough to destroy all our cities; but we have enough to destroy all of theirs. We are still relatively secure, and nobody is likely to start an attack under those conditions. 3. Two or more nations have enough bombs to destroy all cities, perhaps 10,000 bombs of the kind that we have now. That will probably come in an armament race. Retaliation, however, would be expected and that would be a deterring factor, but perhaps not decisive.

As was mentioned yesterday, and I think discussed by General Groves, 40,000 people might be wiped out in the United States by an attack of that kind, and it would not help us much to destroy 40,000,000 people in the nation of attack. . . .

There is, however, a fourth stage which would automatically come sooner or later in any unlimited armament race. We can confidently assume that there are going to be discoveries made in this field. They may be made 4 to 5 years hence. They may be made 10 or 15 years hence, but it is almost certain that we will have atomic bombs a thousand times as powerful as those that now exist by means that are now undiscovered.

It could be done by a cheaper means of production. Instead of producing 10,000 bombs, it is conceivable that by cheaper means of construction you could have 300,000 bombs.

That would be enough to treat every square mile in the United States the way Hiroshima was. There would then be no retaliation. There wouldn't be 60 percent of the people left; there might be 2 percent of the people left, and under those conditions you can see what happens in the world.

In short, so fixed was the notion that cities or production centers were the primary targets for nuclear weapons that Langmuir could only foresee nuclear damage to nuclear retaliatory forces when there would be enough bombs to cover the entire country — and so inevitably, as a by-product, nuclear strike forces too! The 300,000 bomb calculation is quite typical of the gross computations of the time. Langmuir took the 10 square mile damage area sometimes[14] roughly estimated for Hiroshima and, assuming square bombs, divided it into the 3 million square mile area of the United States. A good many of Blackett's calculations in his first book are of the same order of precision.

This suggests some limitations on the physicists' understanding of the problems of retaliation and its virtues. If, in fact, nuclear weapons to all intents and purposes were usable only against cities and industry, nuclear retaliatory forces would be intrinsically quite safe. Effortlessly safe, since they wouldn't be attacked. Retaliation would be assured. There would be, essentially, no distinction between striking first and striking second (and therefore no need for a first-strike, second-strike distinction.) And this automatically suggests, especially today, the prospect of deterrence. And, especially today, this doesn't seem the worst of all possible worlds. To us, it suggests at least a limited but important kind of stability. However, it would be a mistake to read our views into the writings of the physicists at the time. In fact, the Jeffries Report didn't think much of "the hope that the fear of such a retaliation will paralyze the aggressor." It went on to say, "The whole history of mankind teaches that this is a very uncertain hope, and that accumulated weapons of destruction 'go off' sooner or later, even if this means a senseless mutual destruction." The Jeffries Committee, then, uttered one of the earlier versions of the apocalyptic argument about the inevitability of nuclear war through some irrational act: "sooner or later." (Observe that Langmuir, too, refers to the deterring prospect of retaliation, but without enthusiasm.)

Moreover, in between the two paragraphs [of the Jeffries report] I have cited earlier, which drew the picture of a nuclear war as a sequence in which an aggressor destroyed the cities and production centers of his adversary, who in turn inflicted a similar mass destruction on the aggressor, the authors of the report included a fascinating analogy of the nuclear dilemma with the situation of two men equipped with machine guns in a room of 100 x 100 feet. The first to attack would not only destroy the other but, provided he attacked soon enough, emerge unscathed. Here the difference between striking first and striking second is all important, and there is an enormous incentive to preempt, a maximum of instability. (The close machine gun duel analogy has been attributed to Eugene Wigner[15] and used by other physicists as well.)

The Jeffries Report, then, contains side by side two incompatible pictures of the revolution wrought by nuclear weapons. In the one picture, striking first is of no advantage, since the other side inevitably could retaliate in kind. In the other picture, striking first is decisive, since neither side could retaliate. These incompatible pictures were not *seen* to be incompatible. Each existed, so to speak, by itself. And, by itself, neither would indicate any urgent need for a first-strike, second-strike distinction of the kind that grew out of the Base Study.[16] Neither picture called for basic choices and difficult efforts in the design and construction of a nuclear force specifically to survive nuclear attacks.

If we were to use the latter distinction, we might say that, in the one picture of the nuclear world, *neither* side could have a capacity for striking second; in the other picture of the nuclear world, with both sides directing their attacks on cities, *each* side with nuclear weapons had a capacity for "striking second," that is, retaliating against the other *automatically*. However, that is to use the words quite differently from the way they were defined when I introduced the distinction at the start of the 1950s. There *the capacity to strike second plainly referred to the ability of a nuclear force to strike back after the force itself had been subject to nuclear attack.* To find it urgent to make the distinction, one had to perceive both that it was possible and useful to get a second-strike capability and that it was neither inevitable nor easy. In a sense, the Manhattan Project physicists missed the target on both sides, as the Jeffries Report and many other documents illustrate. The world of the two close machine gunners missed it on the left by failing to see the measure of stability that might be brought by making even sudden attack highly risky. And a world in which one nuclear country would open a war with a nuclear attack only on a second nuclear country's cities and production centers missed it on the right by making nuclear retaliation automatic, or a minor problem. Surprise and striking early were vital in the first world; they were secondary in the second world of terror bombing of cities.

The fascinating thing is that these two worlds existed side by side without jostling, not only in the Jeffries Report, but for more than two years following, in the statements of the Manhattan Project physicists. In nuclear weapons, [as noted above, Robert Oppenheimer said] in 1945, "the elements of surprise *and* of terror are as intrinsic to it as are the fissionable nuclei." But if the element of terror were primary, the element of surprise would be important only insofar as it seconded the shock of terror visited on the population attacked. A city nuclear attack, unlike the surprise at Pearl Harbor which the physicists frequently cited, would ignore direct military targets, except as incidents or by-product.

It might destroy war industry and so prevent mobilization. But it would not prevent an already mobilized strategic force, separate from the victim's own cities, from retaliating against the attacker's cities and war-supporting industry. The temptation to aggression is then hard to see. "They are weapons," said Oppenheimer, "of aggression, of surprise, and of terror." There was a latent contradiction in the physicists' view.

It is this contradiction that Jacob Viner observed. It is easy for us to see it today. It was by no means easy then. Viner deserves great credit. By the same token, the physicists whose lack in this respect Viner observed nonetheless deserve high honors for having generated some of the basic issues and above all for having recognized that nuclear weapons were revolutionary. It is not, after all, surprising that they understood only a small part of what this revolution meant. They did not see that if nuclear forces were, as they assumed, safe from nuclear attack, surprise was by definition of little advantage. Neither did they pursue the line of analysis suggested by the machine gunners in a small room. The analogy is notable precisely because in it the gunners are not safe and there is no distinction between the safety of the "population" and the retaliatory force. The scattered insights of the Manhattan Project physicists did not penetrate any significant distance into the possibility that nuclear forces themselves were not easily made safe from one another, and that in *their* case being surprised might be fatal. However, Viner and the other social scientists and historians in the late 1940s did not see this either, and in fact they were in some ways further from seeing it than the physicists because they followed only the "unattacked-retaliatory-force" branch of the physicists' thought, with its implicit relative optimism.

The Social Scientists and Historians

Viner's extraordinary paper on "The Implications of the Atomic Bomb for International Relations" took off from the physicists' assumptions that nuclear weapons were city-destroyers, but rejected their apocalyptic conclusion — since

the atomic bomb, unlike battleships, artillery, airplanes, and soldiers, is not an effective weapon against its own kind . . . it does not much matter strategically how much more efficient the atomic bomb can become provided superiority in efficiency affects chiefly the fineness of the dust to which it reduces the city upon which it is dropped. . . . There seems to be universal agreement that under atomic-bomb warfare there would be a new and tremendous advantage in being first to attack and that the atomic bomb therefore gives a greater advantage than ever to the aggressor. I nevertheless remain unconvinced. . . . What difference will it then make whether it was country A which had its cities destroyed at 9 a.m. and country B which had its cities destroyed at 12 a.m., or the other way round?

Viner read his paper on November 16, 1945.[17] He must have written it only a couple of months after he first heard of the bomb when it exploded over Hiroshima, and on all counts this paper, to which Brodie and Fox acknowledged their indebtedness, must be seen as one of the landmarks in the history of the development of strategic doctrine.[18]

What is more, Viner not only detected one crucial strand of inconsistency in the strategic thinking of the Manhattan Project scientists; he brought to the political issues a kind of sophisticated awareness of the character of the international system which was quite beyond the physicists. His remarks on the dim prospects of early world government are the sort of thing that one might have expected from a distinguished student of both international relations and international economics. And Bernard Brodie and William Fox, and several others of like training, made very important similar points, points that were very rare at the time.

There are many other matters of interest in Viner. Viner's is the first, and in some ways still the best, statement of Pierre Gallois's position on the stabilizing effect of the spread of nuclear weapons.[19] Wrong, I think. Its error is, of course, pardonable in November 1945; it flowed from the fundamental assumption of great stability because of the automatic or nearly automatic invulnerability of strategic forces, and from a belief that they would therefore be "equalizers," restoring in fact essential features of the 18th and 19th century international system.

Viner's insights were limited by the scant information he had derived from the physicists. He was aware of this and said specifically that he was working with "a few facts and a few surmises about the military effectiveness and the cost of atomic bombs": information that he deliberately exposed to his audience, including many of the most famous physicists associated with the Manhattan Project.

> The bomb has a minimum size, and in this size it is, and will remain, too expensive — or too scarce, whether expensive or not — to be used against minor targets. Its targets therefore must be primarily cities, and its military effectiveness must reside primarily in its capacity to destroy urban population and productive facilities. Under atomic bomb warfare, the soldier in the army would be safer than his wife and children in their urban home.

In this set of assumptions and in drawing inferences from them, Viner observed one inconsistency of the physicists but shared some inconsistencies with the physicists. He assumed that the bomb would be too expensive for even the superpowers to acquire enough of them to use against targets other than cities. Yet he assumed that they would be cheap enough so that even small powers could acquire them in substantial numbers. (In fact, the physicists sometimes explicitly talked of the bomb as cheap, especially when they were stressing the dangers of the spread of nuclear weapons.) But the principal upshot of Viner's analysis was to suggest that nuclear weapons would, *in the nature of the case,* be rather stabilizing, that they would *reduce* the importance of surprise and restore military significance to the weaker countries.

Viner has one sentence that refers in passing to the possibility of atomic or other attack on nuclear forces. But his perfunctory dismissal of this possibility is entirely characteristic and displays as much as anything else how far he was from recognizing the essentials of surprise nuclear attack. He says, "No country possessing atomic bombs will be foolish enough to concentrate either its bomb-production and bomb-throwing facilities or its bomb stockpiles at a small number of spots vulnerable to atomic bomb or other modes of attack." In fact, a policy of simply multiplying the number of points containing these nuclear facilities could hardly hope to match the means of destroying these facilities, among other reasons because such simple multiplication if very extensive is very costly. However, if Viner did not think seriously of the problem of nuclear attack on nuclear forces at that time, it is hard to find anyone else who did.

Brodie starts from Viner's notion that since a nuclear exchange would be directed at cities and industry, the element of surprise is not as important as the physicists assumed. In fact, he cites Viner as having first suggested and elaborated the idea (see pp. 73, 74 of *The Absolute Weapon*).[20] And, as he says, his paper is plainly in debt to Viner in numerous ways. Like Viner, he is thinking of nuclear weapons as being primarily directed at cities and industry, and for much the same reason.

> The enormous concentration of power in the individual bomb, irreducible below a certain high limit except through deliberate and purposeless wastage of efficiency, is such as to demand for the full realization of that power targets in which the enemy's basic strength is comparably concentrated. Thus, the city is a made-to-order target, and the degree of urbanization of a country furnishes a rough index of its relative vulnerability to the atomic bomb (p. 99).

His First Postulate, in the preceding chapter, reads that:

> The power of the present bomb is such that any *city* in the world can be effectively destroyed by one to ten bombs . . . (p. 24, emphasis added).

Any damage done to a retaliatory capability he thinks of as a by-product of the nuclear attack which the aggressor would have directed at cities. This is plain on pp. 88 and 89, but at many points elsewhere. And he is thinking of the problem of retaliation essentially as that of maintaining the nuclear retaliatory force in isolation from the disaster areas that the cities would become under nuclear attack; and of protecting it [the retaliatory force] from conventional ground forces.

> *The ability to fight back after an atomic bomb attack will depend on the degree to which the armed forces have made themselves independent of the urban communities and their industries for supply and support.* The proposition just made is the basic proposition of atomic bomb warfare. . . . (p. 88, emphasis in the original).

In fact, Brodie considers and dismisses the "private arguments" of "certain scientists" that nuclear attack on nuclear launch sites might be effective without ground force seizure of the launch sites.

> Certain scientists have argued privately that . . . a nation committing aggression with atomic bombs would have so paralyzed its opponent as to make invasion wholly superfluous. It might be alleged that such an argument does not give due credit to the atomic bomb, since it neglects the necessity of preventing or minimizing retaliation in kind. If the experience with the V-l and V-2 launching sites in World War II means anything at all, it indicates that only occupation of such sites will finally prevent their being used. Perhaps the greater destructiveness of the atomic bomb as compared with the bombs used against V-l and V-2 sites will make an essential difference in this respect, but it should be remembered that thousands of tons of bombs were dropped on those sites (pp. 91 and 92).

However,

> An invasion designed to prevent large-scale retaliation with atomic bombs to any considerable degree would have to be incredibly swift and sufficiently powerful to overwhelm instantly any opposition. Moreover, it would have to descend in one fell swoop upon points scattered throughout the length and breadth of the enemy territory. The question arises whether such an operation is possible, especially across broad water barriers, against any great power which is not completely asleep and which has sizable armed forces at its disposal (pp. 92 and 93).

And

> The invasion and occupation of a great country solely or even chiefly by air would be an incredibly difficult task even if one assumes a minimum of air opposition (p. 93).

Brodie regarded ground force occupation of strategic air bases as necessary to prevent retaliation, but infeasible. However, he regarded ground force invasion as both feasible and necessary to consolidate the effects of atomic bombardment of cities and industry. Much the same view is reflected in the official Air Force position expressed by General H. H. Arnold at about that time.[21]

The realistic insights of Viner, Brodie, and Fox are best appreciated as a contrast with the utopianism of the scientists at the end of the war. The Manhattan Project physicists (and a good many others who knew about the Manhattan Project early and felt that it had revolutionary implications for warfare) believed that it made both necessary and possible a revolutionary change in international relations. They were thinking of something like world government, or at least very extensive international control, and frequently said that it was feasible just because it was urgent and necessary. The apocalyptic predictions they made tended, therefore, to have a hortatory character. They were appeals for a soul change in world statesmen. Publicists like Norman Cousins in his *Modern Man Is Obsolete* accepted the essentials of their apocalyptic view.[22] Viner, Brodie, and Fox were particularly discerning and incisive in their perception that, on one hand, ways of organizing the world for perfect peace were not then available, nor would be in the foreseeable future, and that, on the other hand, the alternative of nuclear annihilation was not inevitable, that there were some elements of stability implicit in the scientists' own picture of nuclear relations, or rather in one of their pictures.

In sum, Viner, Brodie, and Fox made many cogent points of great importance. But none seriously considered the problem of designing a nuclear force to survive a major nuclear surprise attack, nor did they show any awareness that this was a problem at all, much less a basic one. In fact, they were further from seeing this than *some* of the scientists — inconsistently to be sure, in writing and in "private arguments" — were at least *some* of the time.

THE MILITARY VIEWS AND THE MILITARY STANCE

As I have mentioned, the Manhattan Project physicists, once they had abandoned hope for early agreement on international control of atomic energy, tended to line up with one faction or another of the military. After the Russians turned down the Baruch proposal, some physicists, like Edward Teller, thought about fusion weapons and improvements of the strategic offense. Many more, like Bush, Oppenheimer, Rabinowitch, and Rabi,[23] turned to the defense of cities and the problems of battlefield war. Project East River considered civil defense. The Lincoln Summer Study focused on the active defense of the industrial heartland of the United States and on providing early warning for fighter interceptors.[24] Project Vista proposed battlefield nuclear weapons for the defense of Europe. It is familiar now that the factional disputes among the scientists, and the corresponding ones within and among the services, were bitter and destructive. Perhaps the most fascinating aspect of these disputes (one that has not been observed) is their total neglect of the increasingly serious problem of the vulnerability of strategic forces, of the problem of obtaining a defended offense. This neglect affected both the military and the scientists, including all the principal factions of each.

The service positions on the A-bomb in the immediate postwar period were predictable. The War Department held that the A-bomb "has given the offensive a marked advantage, at least for the time being, over the defensive." (*Bulletin of the Atomic Scientists*, June 1947, reprinting *Army Navy Journal* for April 12, 1947.) The Navy Department, on the other hand, had it that "the present technological trend is decidedly in favor of the defense." It "decidedly favors the defense of large centers of population and industry." (*Bulletin of the Atomic Scientists,* July 1947.) This disagreement deepened and culminated in the B-36 Hearings at the end of the decade, where the Navy said that the bomb had little chance of getting through and that it would do little harm if it did. (I mentioned the brave naval officer who said one could stand at one end of the runway at Washington National Airport "with no more protection than the clothes you now have on, and have an atom bomb explode at the other end of the runway without serious injury to you.")[25] And LeMay[26] affirmed that the bomber always gets through.

However, the Navy never brought up the subject of the liability of nuclear bombers to be destroyed before takeoff on the ground by enemy nuclear bombers; and neither did the War Department, nor its Air Force split-off. General Arnold (then Air Force Chief of Staff) early in 1946 argued for the possibility, though not the certainty, of an atomic stalemate through mutual fear:

> Now the arguments given above are not intended
> to comfort us with the thought that, if all nations had
> atomic weapons no nation would use them for fear of
> retaliation. All they show is that there is a *possibility* of

232

stalemate with respect to destruction of cities by atomic bombs (*One World or None*, p. 32, emphasis in the original).

He *was* thinking of cities, though with the usual ambiguities about industrial support of military strength, and the "will to resist" (see p. 27). His view was less downright and abstract, though not unlike that of Viner:

> Our defense can only be a counteroffensive; we must be prepared to give as good as we take or better. Should we ever find ourselves facing an aggressor who could destroy our industrial machine without having his destroyed in turn, our defeat would be assured. Thus our first defense is the ability to retaliate even after receiving the hardest blow the enemy can deliver. This means weapons in adequate numbers strategically distributed so that no enemy is better situated to strike our industry than we are to strike his (*One World or None*, p. 31).

The war would be an exchange of blows against cities and industry.

I had intended to describe in some detail the characteristic developments in the nuclear doctrines of each of the services. Unfortunately, there isn't time for that. Nor is there time to say much on the history of the actual plans and operations of the Strategic Air Command and the Air Defense Command.[27] However, I will say a little about actual deployments, operations, and plans for most of the 1950s.

A rough way to characterize the nuclear *offense* stance is to say that it was focused on the problem of coordinating an immense attack capable of penetrating Russian area and local active defenses in order to deliver a decisive blow, primarily to the industrial heartland of the Soviet Union. The planning for this was ingenious and efficient—given time to get the attack under way undisturbed. And almost the only sorts of disturbance that had been seriously considered were those that might have been by-products of a Russian attack on American cities, or sabotage, or conventional ground attack. Such "by-product" disturbances to SAC were, correctly, not anticipated to be large or extremely difficult to overcome. In this respect, the active offense stance reflected a view similar to that of Viner and Brodie.

233

A rough way to characterize the *defense* stance against nuclear attack would parallel this focus of the offense force on the enemy active defense of the enemy heartland. Our defense was focused on the problem of intercepting Russian bombers before they reached the bomb release line over American cities and war-supporting industry. The contiguous radars were deployed primarily in the Northeast industrial heartland and near our coastal cities. Though they had a variety of problems, including that of saturation by a large raid employing electronic countermeasures, the radar and air defense bomber system was able to detect and track bombers and guide fighters toward the interception of a massive raid in particular.

Our offense and our defense stances changed over time as our own and the Russian stocks of nuclear weapons swelled. But in some essentials they changed not at all. Viner, an excellent economist, had derived from the physicists and chemists in 1945 the assumption that A-bombs would always be expensive and scarce because fissile material was scarce. (Eugene Rabinowitch's writings at the time offer examples.) However, an elementary economic operation — raising the price of uranium — offered incentives to a great many uranium prospectors and it soon became clear that bomb stockpiles could be greatly expanded and that there were bombs enough for military targets in addition to cities and industry. As our stockpile expanded, military targets, including strategic bases, were added to our attack plans. And in a symmetrical way the Air Defense Command assumed that with expanding Russian stockpiles a massive Russian attack directed at the American industrial heartland would add on some bombs and bomb carriers directed at our nuclear force.[28] However, in both cases these extra targets were attachments to attacks directed basically at cities and industry. This was a quite natural way to see the problem, given the history of views I have already outlined, but it is important to note that it had a critical effect on the chance that the vulnerability of SAC would be observed. For the U.S. defenders anticipated a massive Russian attack of anywhere from 500 to over 1000 bombers directed at cities and industry and using techniques of saturation rather than the methods of minimizing warning possible for a smaller force directed solely or mainly at SAC.[29] So massive a Russian attack was likely to provide strategic warning and would quite reliably have given extended tactical warning — enough tactical warning, perhaps, to be useful to even a very ponderous and complex strategic force. This was by no means true, however, for an adversary who designed his first raid specifically to disrupt and destroy a strategic retaliation. Surprise turned out to be as important as the Manhattan Project physicists had assumed, but for very different reasons.

SAC bases, unfortunately, were located primarily outside the radar cover that had been designed for the defense of cities and industries: they were mainly not in the Northeast, but in the South and West, where the flying weather for training is good, and for the most part where they would not be engulfed in a disaster of the cities. The bombers and tankers were concentrated on a few crowded and shelterless bases (some holding a total of about 120 bombers and tankers). The bases in the continental United States expanded slowly in number, reaching about 28 or 29 in 1956. Other, equally indispensable elements of the force, such as the stockpiles of bombs and command and control, were even more concentrated. The bombers normally were stripped down and in maintenance, a state that enabled very high availability rates, given notice of a day or two, but extremely low readiness for the first six hours after receiving warning. However, even an improved warning network, designed specifically for the protection of SAC, could not have assured anything like that much warning. But the warning network had been designed primarily for the protection of cities and industry. If the strategic force could have survived a modest attack on its home bases, the plans called for an immensely complex operation of coordinating slow tankers and bombers, picking up [nuclear ordnance] at bomb stockpile sites generally far from the home base, and finally deploying to overseas bases, which were far more vulnerable than the home bases left behind. Fred Hoffman remarked during the Base Study that the problem of the analyst looking soberly at the vulnerability of SAC sometimes boiled down to propping SAC up over one barrier so that it could be knocked down at the next, so many were the alternative, entirely feasible, ways of destroying it.

At several points in your paper you suggest that the Russians had no capability for attacking the United States until rather late—until after they had acquired a stock of thermonuclear weapons, or after they had acquired very long-range aircraft or possibly after Sputnik and the intercontinental missile. In fact, before 1955 the Russians had enough planes with adequate range and enough bombs with adequate yield to have done a great deal of damage to American cities, if not intercepted. This was understood and displayed in all of the intelligence estimates during a period when

235

intelligence generally underestimated the Russians. *Even more important, only a fraction of their estimated capability was enough to dispose of SAC.*

Finally, the Russian force itself was even more concentrated and vulnerable than the American strategic force. Neither side had a second-strike capability, in the sense in which I defined it.

I said at the meeting in Oxford that the vulnerability of SAC had nothing to do with Air Force stupidity, or folly, or anything of the sort. Nuclear weapons were new; their implications were little understood; and the strategic force planners tended to examine the meaning of nuclear weapons to see how they affected the answers to the questions of strategic bombing as these questions had been understood previously. (See my comments in "Analysis and Design of Conflict Systems," pp. 109ff and 125ff.)[30] Moreover, the Navy and ground Army themselves failed to see that nuclear weapons raised new questions of the vulnerability of retaliatory forces before launching. And the limitation was not simply military; it affected natural and social scientists as well. Nor were these matters obvious to able systems analysts, who had access to data and worked on other closely related questions.

SYSTEMS ANALYSTS

At the end of the 1940s and in the early 1950s there were a good many analysts working in operational research organizations attached to the Strategic Air Command or the Air Defense Command. They dealt with important but relatively restricted questions that had to be answered to improve decisions by the operational commanders: questions such as techniques for the offense for penetrating defenses; alternative ways of releasing weapons over target, such as high altitude versus low altitude bomb release; and techniques for the defense system for sifting out potentially hostile attacks from the normal air traffic patterns displayed on radar. For this purpose they used actual data on the performance of men and equipment and the actual detailed geography.

At Rand this sort of study was extended to include a much wider and longer range of choices, involving choices among equipments that would be available several years hence and that would alter significantly current operational performance, such as speed, altitude, range of bomber aircraft, performance of defense radars, and a host of other matters. Some of these studies were excellent. The systems studies for active defense led by Barlow and Digby (R-227 in 1951 and R-250 in 1953)[31] were particularly impressive. Impressive and serious treatments of the functioning of immensely complicated systems of interdependent elements were done in very realistic and objective fashion on the basis of a very large effort by many researchers closely aware of current military operations as well as of impending changes in the state of the art. These persistent and careful efforts contrasted greatly with crash campaigns like the Lincoln Summer Study, which exploited the famous names of Manhattan Project physicists to sell some gadgetry such as the DEW line and the Whirlwind computer, or later the SAGE system, as handy-dandy solutions to the problem of getting nearly perfect active defense of cities and industry. If the subject of this letter were the problem of limiting damage in case deterrence fails, there would be a good deal to say about the Barlow-Digby study. Moreover, unlike minimum deterrence theorists, I regard active defense as a subject of continuing interest.

However, I am dealing here mainly with the development of our understanding of problems of stable deterrence. The most important observation to be made in this respect about the offense bombing systems analyses — such as that of Quade-Shamberg-Specht, *A Comparison of Airplane Systems for Strategic Bombing,* September 1950 (R-208)[32] and the defense systems analyses led by Barlow and Digby — is that, as far as the problems of deterrence and retaliation were concerned, these studies exhibited exactly the same tunnel vision as did the military plans and the informal utterances and essays of the natural and social scientists. The offense systems analyses examined systematically alternative equipments and methods for American bombers to penetrate Russia's defense of her heartland. They matched American bombers against Russian fighters and surface-to-air missiles. The defense systems analyses, on the other hand, essentially matched Russian bombers against American interceptors and local defenses; moreover, even when they added our SAC bases in the United States to the Russian list of offense targets, as in the case of our military plans, this was done simply as a perturbation of an attack directed essentially at crippling population and industry. The defense analyses never therefore considered attacks specifically designed for the purpose of surprising and destroying the strategic force.

The systems analysis embodied in the Base Study addressed that problem. It observed that surprise had a different and greater significance for the possible nuclear destruction of the retaliatory force than it did for an attack on cities and industry.

> The advantages of mounting the first surprise attack of a war (little or no warning of city populations, confusion of defenses) have been generally recognized. The surprise attack is doubly important for attack on strategic bases, since many of the most vital and vulnerable elements on these bases are mobile, and, if the attack comes as no surprise, aircraft, personnel and essential material may have been evacuated from the bases before bomb release. . . . The surprise attack, large or small scale, must be regarded as a major threat to SAC survival (p. 233).[33]

Exploiting the information, expertise, and methods that had been developed in the offense and defense analyses, it matched enemy offense and defense against our own offense and defense in potential attacks designed specifically to destroy an inadequately defended offense. The results were a shock. The authors knew the results in a preliminary way by the start of 1952 but spent the following fifteen months systematically checking and testing the conclusions, as well as refining them and designing improvements. When I briefed the results internally to the Rand Management Committee at the end of 1953, even though there had been quite a few rumors and preliminary indications, the shock was quite as great. Though the results seem painfully obvious now and were overwhelmingly evidenced then, the fact that the study caused this shock suggests how completely the prior strategic focus and assumptions had precluded an understanding of how hard it was to design a strategic force capable of surviving a nuclear attack directed at its destruction. For the same reason, the results of the study had to be briefed over 90 times to the military and particularly to audiences of specialists in related plans and operations.

There are a few observations worth making. First, these studies deliberately understated the vulnerability of the programmed systems. R-244S and R-266[34] showed the deadly results of attacks using as few as 30 bombs of 40-kiloton yield, at a time when intelligence estimated that the Russians would have 400 bombs, many in the megaton range. Against the programmed system it employed mostly medium-range Russian piston-engine bombers, the TU-4, modeled on our own B-29 and B-50. These were times when intelligence, moreover, was underestimating the Russians. (After Sputnik, intelligence frequently went to the opposite pole; but before that it underestimated how rapidly the Russians would get the A-bomb, jet-fighters, the H-bomb, long-range turbo jet and turbo-prop bombers, and how rapidly they would expand their stockpile of weapons.) The conservatism is also illustrated by comparing the forces presumed by the Base Study for 1956 with those actually revealed by intelligence in 1956 to be operational. This comparison can be made by examining R-290's section on "current vulnerability" (that is, 1956 vulnerability).[35] It can also be shown by comparing the 1961 capabilities presumed in R-290 with the capabilities which were public knowledge by 1961. For example, the best accuracy assumed in R-290 to be available to the Russians for attacking the programmed strategic force in 1961 was 2 nautical miles (see p. 27). But President Eisenhower revealed before 1961 that the Russians and we had achieved accuracies of 1 mile. This makes quite a difference. The number of weapons needed to destroy a target varies essentially as the square of the median miss-distance. This means roughly that when circular error probable, or CEP (that is, median miss-distance), is halved, the salvo needed for destruction is divided by four. The curve on p. 27 with this adjustment looks even worse. But R-290 showed that it was feasible to destroy the force programmed for 1961 using only *manned aircraft*. The results in no way depended on a "missile gap." The entire method of both studies, however, was to show that even with the most favorable assumptions for our side, the situation was extremely bad. We therefore omitted in the printed version and for large audiences some even more extreme vulnerabilities.

Third, we studied attacks on all nuclear forces capable of retaliation, including carrier task forces. (See pp. 11ff and 30ff of R-290.)

Fourth, the data and the reasoning of the study were subjected to intensive review by experienced military officers, who were by no means eager to accept these painful conclusions. This was done not only in the course of the long series of briefings for the specialists but during months of examination by an ad hoc committee of the Air Staff which included as members officers from Plans, Logistics, Operations, and other parts of the Air Force. Even if we had been able to guess *a priori* the results of the study, we would never have been able to persuade any substantial number of military men whose *a priori* guesses had been quite the contrary.

But finally an examination of the Base Study, and of the study that followed it after another three years of work, should make clear that *a priori* reasoning on these matters could hardly hope to yield convincing conclusions.

When I suggest that a systems analysis was necessary, I am referring not so much to the sort of training in a specific traditional discipline that was required; I refer rather to a kind of activity or function. The systems analysts in studying the potential interactions of military forces to aid military decision, used extensive data on peacetime operations and logistics, data on the actual geographical and temporal distribution of forces and equipment, and data derived from state-of-the-art studies and theoretical analyses of equipment design, including data both for ourselves and for our adversary. Some first-class systems analysts, like Jim Digby and Ed Barlow, were electronic engineers; or like Robert Lutz, a co-author of the Base Study, an aeronautical engineer; like Bruno Augenstein, a physicist. Some were mathematicians, like Ed Quade, or mathematical statisticians, like Andy Marshall, or mathematical logicians, like myself and Norman Dalkey. Some had training in more than one discipline; Marshall and I had worked in economics, Marshall also had done work in physics, and I in industrial engineering. Harry Rowen was trained in engineering and economics. Or, like Fred Hoffman, they were trained mainly in economics. Economists played a key role. But at least one sociologist-demographer, Fred Iklé, did a partial systems analysis of great importance on the problem of reducing the chance of nuclear accidents and unauthorized acts. Bill Kaufmann, so far as I know, is the only political scientist with traditional training who undertook and successfully executed a concrete analysis of the potential operations of actual military systems, and he did this around 1960. It is not strictly correct to contrast systems analysts with physicists or social scientists or engineers. Some of each of these have been systems analysts.[36]

What these men had in common is that they were dealing with actual operational, design, and plans data. They were not basing evaluations on simple models and *a priori* guesses as to the performance of the interacting strategic offense and defense of both sides.

This line of attack stemmed from operational research during World War II. Pat Blackett deserves an honored place as progenitor of this method in his work during World War II, along with Harold Larnder and several others in the United Kingdom and in the United States.[37] He used methods that later were greatly

240

extended for the more complex military decisions on equipment and operations in the postwar period, when many more variables were open.

Blackett, in a well-known paper on operational research[38] written during World War II, gave some illustrations of why it was absurd to hope to reach reasonable conclusions on the typical problems of potential interactions among military forces unless one had access to operational data — data, he was constrained to point out, that even physicists working on secret research and development problems normally could not and did not have. He considered the case of the anti-U-boat operations by aircraft. "The yield of the operations . . . will depend at least on the following variables: *U-boats* — number operating, tactics, defensive strength, offensive armament, geographical distribution, state of training and morale of crews, efficiency of look-outs; *Aircraft* — number and duration of sorties, search tactics, height of patrol, attack tactics, bomb load, accuracy of bombing, geographical and temporal distribution, performance, camouflage of aircraft, performance of radar, site of training and fatigue of crews; *Weather Conditions* — state of the sea, cloud height and amount, visibility." He concluded: "To attempt an *a priori* solution of this problem is clearly absurd." One needs data.

But it is even more plainly absurd to suppose that one can determine *a priori* whether the American strategic force in the mid-1950s, say, was vulnerable to attack by a Russian strategic nuclear force, or whether the strategic force planned for the 1960s was likely to be easily destroyed. The absurdity is plainer because there are many more variables involved in a systems analysis of the problem of nuclear retaliation than the twenty-one listed by Blackett for the anti-U-boat operation. And, in fact, some of the individual *components* of the second-strike problem are of an order of complexity like that of the anti-U-boat case.

The point that Blackett made about the need for classified operational data for wartime operational research can easily be misunderstood, as can my similar point about the design and analysis of complex opposed systems in the postwar period. It might be taken as a sort of obscurantism, a suggestion that the people with "inside dope," and only such dopesters, have sound conclusions about the critical, potential interactions of military forces in the period under discussion. However, that is not his meaning; nor is it mine.

First, one can have access to secret "inside information" and make no use of it — or make very poor use of it. Just as a library card or other access to the *Bibliothèque Nationale*, the British Museum, and the Library of Congress does not automatically assure that its holder has made a study of the historical documents they contain, or, if he has, that he has done it competently and written an able history; so a clearance providing access to secret operational as well as design data is very far from assuring that its holder has used such data in a competent, serious analysis. In fact, the frequent assurances by an electronics engineer such as Jerry Wiesner or a physicist such as Herbert York in October 1964 that no important technological changes were likely to affect the strategic offense or the strategic defense demonstrate that even design and development data, not to say operational complexities, may be ignored by people with access, especially when they have an ideological axe to grind.[39]

They said this when it was already clear that multiple, independently aimed reentry vehicles and increased precision could work revolutionary changes in the offense, and that phased array radars, advances in the computer art, and new weapons effects that greatly increased the lethal volume of defense warheads, could revolutionize active defense against ICBMs. Moreover, these changes did not simply cancel each other, they affected the relations between large, sophisticated and small, less-advanced nuclear forces. Even more than such failures to use access to development data to anticipate technological changes, there are failures to analyze the strategic military consequences of such technological changes — even when participants in the strategic debate have, so to speak, their "library card," that is, could get access to the data but do not go through the laborious analysis required. To me, it has been simply appalling how much of the debate proceeds in terms of the scholastic absurdities of *a priori* models, whether the debaters have access or do not. Among those who do not have access, Blackett has the smallest excuse for such *a priori* reasoning since, when not consumed by political passions, he knows better.

Second, the point against simple *a priori* models that pretend to cover interactions involving several dozen variables can be made in another, somewhat more explicit, way. No conclusion at all is possible except by picking values for the many variables involved. One has to determine the range, the speed, the altitude, the radar cross-section of the offense vehicles, their precision in navigation and bomb delivery, the yield of the weapons, and many other matters on the offense side; and one must determine the location in space and time of the vehicles under attack, their degree of readiness, protection against blast and other weapons effects, etc. If one determines these values arbitrarily, one can get any conclusion desired. It will depend simply on the arbitrary choice. If one determines it by rumor—the rumor that the B-47s used three or four hundred bases (see Raymond Aron, *Paix et Guerre*),[40] or the rumor that one-third of SAC was armed, combat ready, and in the air at all times (see Patterson and Furniss, *NATO, A Critical Appraisal*),[41] or, even more farfetched, that there was, in the 1950s, a continuous air-alert of short-range fighter bombers, as Blackett suggests—then one can emerge only with a conclusion as valid as the rumors themselves.[42] All these and many other rumors, however, were quite false. One must agree with Blackett's original position that it is hopelessly absurd to judge the outcomes of such complex interactions without access to actual operational data, plans, and deployments. Such access is a necessary, though not a sufficient, condition for *concrete* judgments about the stability of nuclear deterrence at any particular time. There seems to me to be a very grave lack of understanding of this point today in the European and British discussions of strategy, not to say the American ones.

I do not by any means reject the importance of the more philosophical and conceptual analyses of strategy, but they are severely limited by a lack of empirical concreteness as to what they can say about the actual relations among opposing military forces in any given historical period. I am sure that as a historian, you find no difficulty in distinguishing essays on the philosophy of history by Isaiah Berlin or E. H. Carr or M. G. White, however valuable, from concrete historical studies such as your monumental work on the Franco-Prussian war, or Carr's history of Russia.[43]

I would distinguish my own essays on matters of principle and basic concepts, such as "The Delicate Balance of Terror"[44]— which was *not* about the vulnerability of strategic forces in 1958— from the detailed, empirical studies, consuming years for their completion, of the operations of deterrence in the 1950s, or the operations of deterrence in the late 1950s and the 1960s.

I say this even though the concepts elaborated in my own public essays were developed for the most part as working tools—e.g., the second-strike concept, the idea of deterrence as a matter of comparative risks, and the recognition that a stable deterrence was feasible, but hard, and that its stability was subject to technological upset. When "The Delicate Balance..." stated that:

> it is not fruitful to talk about the likelihood of general war without specifying the range of alternatives that are pressing on the aggressor and the strategic postures of both the Soviet bloc and the West. Deterrence is a matter of comparative risks. The balance is not automatic. First, since thermonuclear weapons give an enormous advantage to the aggressor, it takes great ingenuity and realism at any given level of nuclear technology to devise a stable equilibrium. And, second, this technology itself is changing with fantastic speed. Deterrence will require an urgent and continuing effort.[45]

It reflected a concrete judgment made earlier in R-290, pp. 40-41:

> The attacks described here, and many others studied, clearly indicate the present vulnerability of our strike force. They do not, of course, imply that a Russian attack is imminent. Nor do we think it is. That is a matter of Soviet intention rather than Soviet capability, and such intent would be affected in the first instance by Soviet knowledge of our vulnerability and in the second instance by the comparative gains and risks of alternatives to central war. Nonetheless it is a painful fact that the risks to the Soviets of attempting a surprise attack on the United States are much lower than are generally estimated. We would like this course of Soviet action to be a worse alternative to almost any other they might contemplate — including, for example, the acceptance of defeat in some limited or peripheral war. But the sober and careful scrutiny of the present vulnerability of our strike force to feasible Russian attacks, and realistic tests of the plans for its future defense, show the seriousness of the problem.

And the reference to the possibility of technological upset was not hypothetical. It was based on the fact that by the time the Base Study was finished and some, though not all, of its principal recommendations were accepted, I knew that it had no more than seven years or so to run. In the 1960s, vehicles traveling 4 miles per second would make warning and alert measures inadequate. Fred Hoffman and I wrote "Defending A Strategic Force after 1960" (D-2270)[46] and put it out on February 1, 1954, as the first rough cut at the problem of protecting SAC in the ballistic missile era. It was the precursor of R-290, which was not issued for two and a half years, but this precursor of the second study showing the technological limits of the first study was put out before the final report of the first study was issued in April. Moreover, it proposed the system of hardening adopted for the 1960s, but foresaw that hardening would be enough for only a finite time—that in the 1970s precision was likely to have increased enough to make it inadequate even though still useful. (Today an ABM defense of hardened ballistic missiles seems a very likely way of maintaining stability of the deterrent in the 1970s, but that can be accepted or rejected only on the basis of a detailed system analysis.)

It is conceivable that these particular concepts might have been arrived at *a priori* but I'm rather skeptical. In any case, it should be plain from the history I have tried to document why the discovery of the vulnerability of SAC, the development of the first-strike/second-strike distinction, and the recognition of the feasible but limited and difficult stability of deterrence, owe substantially nothing to the strategic writings of the natural and social scientists. I was not familiar with these writings, and if I had been they could hardly have led me to make the conclusions that emerged from empirical study. I am afraid that your footnote 41, p. 15, and your paragraph beginning "Not until thermonuclear weapons . . ." on p. 6 are misleading.[47] The work at Rand that you refer to did not study the implications of Brodie's ideas. The work was quite unconscious of these early ideas of Brodie and Viner. Moreover, the study came to precisely the opposite conclusions from those implied by Viner and Brodie. The timing and direction of influence suggested in your footnote 41 and your p. 15 seem then in error. The analysis of the vulnerability of strategic forces was clear to the authors of the Base Study by the beginning of 1952, and the first summary printed report (R-244-S) was formally presented to the Air Force on March 1, 1953. Morgenstern, Schelling, and Brodie all had read, as consultants or staff members of Rand, some or all of the sequence of papers and reports on the subject.[48] This is by no means to minimize the great importance of Schelling's keen analysis of the relations of the problems of surprise attack, deterrence, and disarmament. His essay was an illuminating example of the sorts of basic clarification that can proceed without new empirical effort on the foundation of intuition, common sense, and previous empirical work. But the discovery of the vulnerabilities of strategic forces owes its primary debt to the tradition of operational research and empirical systems analysis. Hence, the acknowledgments at the beginning of the Base Study to J. F. Digby, E. J. Barlow, E. S. Quade, P. M. Dadant, E. Reich, *et al.*[49] Because their contributions to strategy have been classified, they are largely unknown. This is true even of the important contributions of men like Fred Hoffman and Harry Rowen which are a little better known.[50] They are largely unsung heroes of strategy in the nuclear age.

I must apologize for the extreme length of this "letter." And for the corresponding length of time it has taken me to get it off. It is focused on one central problem, that of the stability of nuclear deterrence. Your paper quite rightly deals with many other problems besides this one. I hope, however, the material I have drawn from my lectures on this one subject will be useful.

ENDNOTES - Wohlstetter - On the Genesis of Nuclear Strategy

Note: Unbracketed endnotes are Wohlstetter's. Endnotes in square brackets were added in by April 1986 by James Digby and Arthur Steiner. Endnotes in double-square brackets were added in 2008 by Robert Zarate.

1. [These collections are now in the Joseph Regenstein Library at the University of Chicago, the Historian's office of the U.S. Department of Energy, and the U.S. National Archives.]

2. [In the Adelphi Paper version this becomes pp. 19ff.] [[See Michael Howard, "The Classical Strategists," Adelphi Paper No. 54, London, UK: Institute for Strategic Studies, 1969; and "The Classical Strategists," in Howard, ed., *Studies in Peace and War*, New York, NY: The Viking Press, 1971, pp. 154-183.]]

3. [P. M. S. Blackett, British Nobel Laureate physicist, pioneer in operational research, was author of *Fear, War, and the Bomb*, published in the United States by McGraw-Hill in 1949. Vannevar Bush, electrical engineer, was head of the Organization for Scientific Research and Development during World War II, making him, in effect, the nation's chief scientist for the war effort.

He wrote *Modern Arms and Free Men,* published by Simon and Schuster in 1949.]

4. [Refers to Jacob Viner, Chicago economist and specialist in international trade; Bernard Brodie, political scientist at Yale, 1945-51, and later at Rand; and William T. R. Fox, political scientist and associate of Brodie at Yale in the late 1940s, later at Columbia.]

5. [The title of a book edited by Dexter Masters and Katharine Way, *One World or None,* New York: McGraw-Hill, 1946.]

6. These documents are in the Atomic Energy Commission collection. See p. 329 of the Hewlett and Anderson official history. [Richard Hewlett and Oscar Anderson, *The New World: Vol. 1 of a History of the U.S. Atomic Energy Commission,* University Park: Pennsylvania State University Press, 1962. One of the three similar memoranda of that date, signed by Bush and James Conant, was published as an appendix to Martin J. Sherwin, *A World Destroy*ed, New York: Knopf, 1975. The three original memoranda can now be found in the National Archives.]

7. [Adelphi version, p. 21. See editors' preface, above, for a note on how this was changed by Howard.]

8. [All signers of the Jeffries report were senior scientists at the Metallurgical Laboratory, University of Chicago. For background on the "Prospectus on Nucleonics," see Hewlett and Anderson, *op.cit.*, pp. 324-325, and Alice Kimball Smith, *A Peril and a Hope,* Chicago, IL: University of Chicago Press, 1965, pp. 19-24 and 539-559. Most of the text is reprinted in Smith, *ibid.*; the full text is in the National Archives.]

9. [Here Wohlstetter was referring to unpublished writings that are still not generally available.]

10. [The Franck Report, a report to the Secretary of War, is reprinted as an appendix in Smith, *op.cit.*, pp. 560-572. For background, see *ibid.*, pp. 41-52, and Arthur Steiner, "Baptism of the Atomic Scientists," *Bulletin of the Atomic Scientists,* February 1975, pp. 21-28.]

11. "Atomic Weapons," paper presented at a Symposium of the American Philosophical Society on Atomic Energy and Its Implications, Philadelphia, November 1945. [See *Proceedings of the American Philosophical Society*, Vol. 90, No. 1, January 29, 1946, The American Philosophical Society, Philadelphia, 1946.]

12. [Quoted in] Hewlett and Anderson, p. 358. [The Interim Committee was set up by Secretary of War Stimson in May 1945 to advise him on atomic energy policy. Its scientific panel was composed of Oppenheimer, Fermi, Lawrence, and Arthur H. Compton. The minutes of the meeting that included the Scientific Panel have been published as an appendix in Sherwin, *op.cit.* The original is in the National Archives.]

13. [The quoted passage is from *Atomic Energy, Hearings on S. Res. 179*, Special Committee on Atomic Energy, U.S. Senate, 79th Congress, First Session, Part I, U.S. Government Printing Office, 1946.]

14. Sometimes 4 [square] miles was estimated for total destruction. [The U.S. Strategic Bombing Survey report, *The Effects of Atomic Bombs on Hiroshima and Nagasaki*, U.S. Government Printing Office, 1946, pp. 3 and 30, cites "4.4 sq mi which were almost completely burned out" at Hiroshima and 9.9 sq mi as the area within which wood frame buildings were damaged at Nagasaki.]

15. [Wigner was a Manhattan Project physicist, later a Nobel Laureate.]

16. [Albert Wohlstetter, Henry S. Rowen, Robert Lutz, and Fred Hoffman, *Selection and Use of Strategic Air Bases*, Rand Report R-266, 1954 (declassified in 1962). Publicly released in 1985, a number of copies have been in scholarly hands for some time; for a description of its methodology, see E. S. Quade, *Analysis for Military Decisions*, Chicago: Rand McNally, 1966, Chap. 3, pp. 24-63. See also Bruce L. R. Smith, *The RAND Corporation*, Cambridge, MA: Harvard University Press, 1966, Chapt. VI.]

17. At the same symposium that included Oppenheimer's paper on "Atomic Weapons," and also a short, less explicit version by Langmuir of his four-stage atomic arms race. ["The Implications of the Atomic Bomb for International Relations,"

Proceedings of the American Philosophical Society, Vol. 90, No. 1, January 1946. Viner's paper is also available in his *International Economics,* Glencoe, IL: The Free Press, 1951, pp. 300-309.]

18. Not that it was unanticipated. The University of Chicago scientists had met on September 20, 1945, and concluded that "The atomic bomb makes surprise an unimportant element of warfare. Retaliation in equal terms is unavoidable, and in this sense the atomic bomb is a war deterrent, a peace-making force" (Box 28, Folder 25, Harper Collection). Viner, however, unlike the physicists, noticed the inconsistency with some of the principal themes these same physicists were advancing at the time. [Viner attended the conference and read an early version of his paper. The Harper Collection is now in the Regenstein Library, University of Chicago.]

19. [Gallois retired from the French air force and became an advocate of a French nuclear capability. For a summary of his early views, see Howard's Adelphi version, p. 29.]

20. [Bernard Brodie, ed., *The Absolute Weapon: Atomic Power and World Order,* New York: Harcourt, Brace, 1946. Brodie contributed Chaps. I and II, pp. 21-107.]

21. [See Masters and Way, *op.cit.,* pp. 26-32.]

22. [See Norman Cousins's editorial in *The Saturday Review of Literature,* August 18, 1945, pp. 5-9. Cousins's editorial preceded the scientists' public statements.]

23. [I.I. Rabi, Nobel Laureate physicist, was a consultant to the Manhattan Project and a member of many governmental advisory committees after World War II.]

24. East River and Lincoln came at the start of the 1950s and were accompanied and followed by a great flurry of concern in the universities and in the intellectual community about urban defense. It was reflected in the *Bulletin of the Atomic Scientists* and in the liberal and popular magazines and newspapers at the time, and it culminated in the disasters of the Oppenheimer Hearings. [U.S. Atomic Energy Commission. *In the Matter of J. Robert Oppenheimer,* MIT Press, Cambridge, MA, 1971. See index

for many references to Lincoln, East River, and Vista.] [[Digby and Steiner's index is not included in this edited volume.]] Your statement, p. 14, about the timing of the public concern is almost the reverse of what actually happened. Sputnik occurred near the end of the campaign for civil defense by the MIT, Harvard, Cal Tech, and etc., faculty members, who then switched back to the notion that there was no defense and that defense indeed might be destabilizing. Teller and others tended to change places with their physicist opponents in a kind of minuet. But they never commanded the support of the intellectual community that Oppenheimer, Bethe, Rabi, Rabinowitch, *et al.*, had. [The reference to p. 14 was to material on p. 26, Adelphi version.]

25. Statement of Eugene Tatom, Commander, U.S. Navy. *The National Defense Program-Unification and Strategy,* Hearings before the Committee on Armed Services, House of Representatives, 81st Congress, First Session, October 1949, U.S. Government Printing Office, Washington, 1949, p. 170. Compare Blackett, a Navy opponent of strategic bombing, in 1948: "The power of human beings to 'stick it' is immense; a determined folk will learn to stand atomic bombardment, if that is their fate, just as Germans learnt to stand ordinary bombing on a scale up to fifty times larger than that which the enthusiasts for strategic bombing thought would bring about the collapse of their war effort." (*Military and Political Consequences of Atomic Energy,* London, 1948, p. 56.) Blackett, of course, was also then a supporter of the Soviet position on atomic energy at the United Nations.

26. [General Curtis E. LeMay, former Commander-in-Chief, Strategic Air Command and Chief of Staff of the Air Force during the early 1960s. LeMay was noted for his enthusiastic advocacy of long-range strategic bombers.]

27. [In recent years, several secondary sources have explored the declassified original documents. See David Alan Rosenberg, "The Origins of Overkill," *International Security,* Spring 1983, Vol. 7, No. 4, pp. 3-71. See also Fred Kaplan, *The Wizards of Armageddon,* New York: Simon & Schuster, 1983. A complete annotated war plan of the late 1940s can be found in Anthony Cave Brown, *DROPSHOT,* New York: Dial Press/James Wade, 1978.]

28. [For example, in "Summary Evaluation of the Net Capability of the U.S.S.R. to Inflict Direct Injury on the United States up to July 1, 1955," NSC140/1 (May 1953), it is assumed that a mid-1955 attack by the Soviets would allocate 80 atomic weapons against the U.S. atomic air defensive capability worldwide, 151 against urban industrial targets, and hold 60 in reserve. Printed in U.S. Department of State, *Foreign Relations of the United States, 1952-1954,* Vol. II, part 1, Washington, U.S. Government Printing Office, 1984, pp. 328-349.)]

29. [For example, JCS 1924/76, October 30, 1953, in the National Archives, assumed a Soviet attack with 700 aircraft at the end of 1957.]

30. [The page numbers refer to the version included in E.S. Quade, ed., *Analysis for Military Decisions,* Chicago: Rand McNally and Company, 1964.]

31. [Edward J. Barlow and James F. Digby, eds., *Air Defense Study,* Report R-227, The Rand Corporation, Santa Monica, October 15, 1951; Edward J. Barlow, *Active Defense of the United States 1954-1960,* R-250 (Abridged), December 1, 1953. R-227 is not yet publicly released.]

32. [According to the Rand Publications Department, R-208 is not yet publicly released. Edward Quade was a mathematician, Richard Schamberg an aeronautical engineer, and Robert Specht a mathematician at Rand.]

33. [See R-266, *op.cit.*]

34. [R-244-S is not yet generally available. It reported in summary form the conclusions of Wohlstetter's team. For a discussion, see Bruce L.R. Smith, *op.cit.,* pp. 218-219. R-266, previously cited, was a more comprehensive report.]

35. [Albert Wohlstetter, Fred Hoffman, and H.S. Rowen, *Protecting U.S. Power To Strike Back in the 1950s and 1960s,* Rand Report R-290, The Rand Corporation, Santa Monica, 1956. This report is not yet generally available.]

36. [All of the people referred to in this paragraph were colleagues of Wohlstetter at Rand during much of the 1950s.]

37. [Harold Larnder was an English scientist who had worked on Britain's early radars before immigrating to Canada after World War II. He saw much of Rand analysts during the development of the North American Air Defense Command. Wohlstetter held him in especially high regard.]

38. [Patrick M. S. Blackett, "Operational Research," *The Advancement of Science*, Vol. V, No. 17, April 1948; reprinted in Blackett, *Studies of War*, Edinburgh: Oliver and Boyd, 1962, p. 188.]

39. [Jerome B. Wiesner and Herbert F. York, "National Security and the Nuclear Test Ban," *Scientific American*, October 1964, pp. 27-35.]

40. [Raymond Aron, *Peace and War*, trans. by Richard Howard and Annette Baker Fox, New York: Praeger, 1967, p. 422.]

41. [Gardner Patterson and Edgard S. Furniss, Jr., "NATO, a Critical Appraisal," Princeton University Conference on NATO, Princeton, June 1957, p. 32 (cited in "The Delicate Balance of Terror," *op. cit.*, p. 218).]

42. [Others may not interpret Blackett's words in quite the same way. Cf. Blackett, *Studies*, p. 133.]

43. [E. H. Carr was a British diplomat turned historian; Berlin is a British, and White an American, philosopher.]

44. [*Op. cit.*, pp. 211-234.]

45. [*Op. cit.*, p. 222.]

46. [This internal Rand document has not been formally released, but copies have been in the hands of some scholars. It is cited, for example, in Fred Kaplan, *The Wizards of Armageddon*, pp. 118-119. Wohlstetter himself quoted from this document in his testimony favoring the proposed "Safeguard" anti-ballistic missiles system. Today he continues to believe that stability would be enhanced by active defenses, and therefore supported proposals

for active anti-missile defenses. (See U.S. Senate, Committee on Armed Services, Hearings, *Authorization for Military Procurement Research, Fiscal Year 1971* and *Reserve Strength,* Ninety-First Congress, Second Session, Part 3, May 19, 1970, pp. 2249-2250.) Herbert York, an opponent of Wohlstetter on the ABM issue, referred to D-2270 as "This remarkably prescient study" in *Race to Oblivion,* New York: Simon & Schuster, 1970, p. 183.]

47. [See pages 27 and 21, respectively, of the Adelphi version. Howard made no change in footnote 41. The paragraph on old page 6 was slightly changed to read ". . . the full implications and requirements of his ideas, *and others current in the United States' academic community* were to be exhaustively studied." (The italicized phrase was added in the Adelphi version.) In footnote 11, Howard added the sentence (referring to Brodie), "He did not, however, deal with the problem of vulnerability of retaliatory forces and the consequent dependence of stability on an effective second-strike capability."]

48. [Oskar Morgenstern was an economist at Princeton and a Rand consultant; Thomas Schelling, a Harvard economist, spent a year at Rand in 1959-1960. This led to his important book *The Strategy of Conflict,* Cambridge, MA: Harvard University Press, 1960.]

49. [Digby, Barlow, and Dadant were engineers at Rand who worked on air defense analyses in the early 1950s; Quade and Reich were mathematicians.]

50. [Hoffman and Rowen, both economists, were and are Wohlstetter's long-time collaborators.]

III. NUCLEAR PROLIFERATION

Commentary: *Timely Warnings Still —*
The Wohlstetters and Nuclear Proliferation

Henry Sokolski

Strike up a serious discussion in Washington regarding the spread of nuclear weapons, and there's a good chance the works of Albert and Roberta Wohlstetter will be invoked to add an air of authority to whatever is being said. Those citing the Wohlstetter's works, however, do so as if Albert and Roberta were only of historical interest.[1]

Certainly, the Wohlstetters understood far better than most officials do today how the spread of nuclear weapons, even to friendly states, could undermine our security and international stability. That's why they detailed the security risk of the United States and other states supplying dangerous nuclear technologies and materials for civilian purposes under loose safeguards. They also understood the inherent dangers of additional states making nuclear fuels or using nuclear weapons-usable fuels, and how inspections by the International Atomic Energy Agency (IAEA) could provide little warning of diversions of these materials and activities to bomb-making.

For these reasons and others besides, they objected to interpreting the Nuclear Nonproliferation Treaty (NPT) as if it recognized the *per se* right of signatories to make or stockpile nuclear weapons-usable fuels. Here, they were attentive to the notion, heralded in the NPT, that it was the "benefits" of peaceful nuclear energy that were to be promoted, not money-losing, dangerous activities that brought states to the brink of acquiring bombs. That's why they made such painstaking efforts to clarify which nuclear activities and fuels were economical and safe, and which ones were not.

Finally, although the Wohlstetters were skeptical of arms control and nonproliferation schemes that thought "minimum deterrent" nuclear stockpiles were justifiable for states to threaten each others' cities with, they were open to sounder arms control proposals. Here, they felt more comfortable promoting restraints that focused on economics and approaches that might increase the number of states that could veto the access of nations to dangerous materials and activities rather than elaborate civilian nuclear supply "grand bargains" whose success depended on unverifiable "peaceful" end-use pledges.

The analyses and key conclusions of the Wohlstetters are still timely today. A brief review of their key works on nuclear proliferation clarifies why.

N + 1 Problems.

Since 9/11, it's been fashionable to see U.S. nonproliferation efforts as turning upon the distinction between friends and adversaries. The United States should worry about hostile states like Iran getting nuclear arms, it is argued, but support the nuclear activities of possible friends, such as India. It makes sense to help our Middle Eastern friends to develop "peaceful" nuclear energy, but there is a problem with North Korea or Syria doing so.

This line of reasoning is plausible. The Wohlstetters certainly were no friends of Communist North Korea or revolutionary Iran. But to an extent rarely expressed in Washington today, they also worried about friendly countries acquiring nuclear weapons. As Albert made clear in "Nuclear Sharing: NATO and the N+1 Problem" (1961), alliance members that try to acquire nuclear weapons, even with U.S. help, can significantly reduce alliance cohesion *and* defense capabilities against first-tier competitors (such as Russia and China today) or even second-tier competitors (such as a possible nuclear-armed Iran). In his view, it was a major mistake for the prospective or newly nuclear-armed state and its friends to view proliferation as being a problem limited to the next country that acquired nuclear weapons after them (that is, the "N + 1" problem country). Instead, in Albert's view, alliance and security headaches arose from the prospective or newly nuclear-armed state (or the "Nth" problem country) itself.

The Wohlstetters certainly were much more skeptical than most officials and academics, then and today, of the ability of smaller states — France in the 1960s, India in the 1970s, and beyond — to make their nuclear forces any more than net liabilities to a security alliance relationship. As Albert noted in *Strength, Interest and New Technologies* (1968), Russia needed to dedicate only a small percentage of its strategic offensive and defensive forces to neutralize France's entire *force de frappe*. Moreover, France would constantly be pressed financially and technologically to make its nuclear forces even minimally credible without simultaneously drawing down critical conventional force capabilities:

A small nuclear force . . . is hardly likely to make any country that has it the equal of any other in deterring attack on itself. And the technological defects of small nuclear forces limit their potential for protecting their possessors indirectly by triggering one major power against the other. However, even if these defects did not obtain and any country with nuclear weapons could thereby get direct or indirect protection for itself, there would still remain the need to protect non-nuclear countries from nuclear coercion. And giving bombs to everybody hardly seems the way to do it.[2]

These points should raise more than a few questions for U.S. and allied policymakers today. Just how much of a headache might India and Israel create for the achievement of U.S. and allied security goals *because* of their nuclear forces?[3] What assistance might each demand of the United States to maintain their force's survivability and effectiveness against improved Chinese and Pakistani forces and, in Israel's case, against its neighbors with nuclear ambitions? Might Israel ask the United States for intelligence or other help in bombing future threatening "peaceful" nuclear sites in Iran, Syria, Egypt, or Saudi Arabia? How critical might the American role be in keeping the peace between New Delhi and Islamabad? Failing this, how automatic might deterrence between India and Pakistan be? What advanced offensive and defensive strategic weapons technologies might India or Israel ask the United States to share in order to assure these countries' nuclear strategic freedom of action? How much assistance will the United States be asked to lend to the respective conventional forces of India, Israel, and Pakistan as each of these countries tries to cope with the constant technical and financial demands of keeping their strategic deterrents credible against key adversaries?

This, then, brings one to questions touching on U.S. foreign policy. How might attending to these demands detract from other U.S.-allied security objectives? Will India or Israel ever be able to keep their nuclear forces sufficiently survivable or effective to suit their own views of what is required for their national security? How might trying to fulfill their requests for strategic assistance (or failing to do so) affect Washington's ability to shore up allied counterinsurgency, counterterrorism, and state-building efforts in Iraq or Afghanistan, or America's need to maintain sound relations with Pakistan in the war on terror? Given the questions with these states, how eager should the United States be to humor or support the military nuclear musings of Australia, Brazil, Turkey, Ukraine, Japan, Saudi Arabia, Egypt, South Korea, or Taiwan? What headaches for U.S. security might these nations' efforts to go nuclear pose? Should we simply assume that these nations will go nuclear no matter what we do, or should we instead try to discourage them by offering—or strengthening existing— security arrangements?

Safe or Dangerous?

The next set of issues that the Wohlstetters' nuclear studies highlighted is the imprudence of nuclear-supplier states spreading dangerous civilian nuclear technology under loose safeguards. Here, the Wohlstetters were the first to seriously analyze and question the nonproliferation merits of the Nuclear Nonproliferation Treaty, the International Atomic Energy Agency's Statute, and the IAEA's nuclear materials accountancy system.[4] None of these nonproliferation[5] measures, the Wohlstetters concluded, would do anything but *spread* the means to make bombs unless they did a much clearer job of defining what is—and is not—"peaceful," "beneficial," and "safeguardable."

The Wohlstetters certainly were clear about the dangers of allowing for the transfer of nuclear weapons-usable fuels and nuclear fuel-making plants to states that did not have nuclear weapons. They also were firm in their opposition to moving toward commercial use of plutonium-based fuels, even if such fuels were "lightly" irradiated to reduce partially their usability in weapons. Today, the Global Nuclear Energy Partnership (GNEP) proposes to share virtually identical plutonium-based fuels. Such fuels, it is claimed, can be made sufficiently "proliferation resistant." But how likely is this? Already, the backers of GNEP promise only to make fuels that might be difficult for terrorist organizations to divert for bomb-making. GNEP fuel recycling, they concede, would be risky to share with other states that do not already make their own nuclear fuels because it might allow them to break out and make bombs quickly.[6]

Then, there is the whole question of the ability of IAEA safeguards to keep track of such fuel and fuel-making activities in order to warn against possible military diversions in a timely manner. The Wohlstetters were particularly wary of attempts to use Article IV of the NPT to justify the further spread of plutonium-based fuels, centrifuge plant technologies for uranium enrichment, and reprocessing. It was fashionable in the 1970s, as it is again today, to insist that the NPT recognizes that all states have a *per se* right to any and all declared and inspected nuclear technologies and materials so long as they have some conceivable civilian application. Yet, as the Wohlstetters detailed in, "Signals, Noise, and Article IV" (1979), for historical, technical, economic, and legal reasons, asserting such a *per se* right is both dangerous and untenable.

One reason why is the clear limit of protection that international inspections can afford against the diversion of civilian nuclear programs to military uses. No inspections system, the Wohlstetters noted, could possibly afford timely warning of military diversions from fuel fabrication and production plants where materials directly usable to make bombs were being generated or handled. These facilities, and materials in them, literally could bring states within days—or hours—of acquiring nuclear weapons. Again, the only safe locations for such plants or materials, the Wohlstetters noted, locations in states that already had nuclear weapons.

Unfortunately, this point—which the Wohlstetters amplified in "Spreading the Bomb without Quite Breaking the Rules" (1976), *Swords from Plowshares* (1979), *Towards a New Consensus* (1979), and many other works—has yet to sink in. President Bush, for example, proposes to make nuclear fuel accessible at "reasonable prices" to any states that do not now make nuclear fuel as a way of discouraging them from making their own nuclear fuel. Both the State Department and former Senator Sam Nunn, chairman of the Nuclear Threat Initiative, back such fuel offers, along with power reactor assistance in general. They warn, however, that we will fail to get states to use such fuel services unless we reassure them that by taking our assistance, they will in no way jeopardize their "inalienable right" to make such fuel on their own if they subsequently should choose to do so. European supporters of such assurances even insist that offers of such assistance will be believable only if the fuel is produced in facilities built in states that don't currently make nuclear fuel.

None of this is likely to reduce the spread of nuclear weapons capabilities. As the Wohlstetters noted in their analyses, there is no reliable, timely way to detect military diversions from centrifuge enrichment plants or reprocessing plants. These facilities could quickly convert fresh or spent power-reactor fuel into bomb-usable plutonium or uranium. Nor did the Wohlstetters see any reliable way to prevent or detect in a timely manner the gradual or quick diversion of nuclear weapons-usable and near weapons-usable fuels to make bombs.

None of these points are getting their due today. There is renewed interest in negotiating a "verifiable" military fissile material production cutoff treaty, but there really is no way to verify such a treaty effectively, not only because covert bomb-fuel plants cannot be detected reliably, but because a military cutoff treaty would still allow states to make nuclear fuel for "peaceful" purposes. Insisting that these civilian plants can be safeguarded in weapons states will inevitably lead nonweapons states to insist that they can be safeguarded everywhere. Even now, one hears desperate talk of somehow limiting Iran's nuclear enrichment activities so that they might be safeguarded. Sadly, this is not feasible.

For these and other reasons, the Wohlstetters were eager to discourage states from pursing dangerous nuclear activities. They also were skeptical of regionalizing them. Where were these regional fuel-making centers to be located? Who would build, run, and own them, and what would be charged for the fuel produced? Would such services increase or decrease the number of states that could acquire nuclear weapons, or simply be used as yet another reason for states to acquire large, uneconomical reactor programs of their own?

These questions bring us back again to current proposals to make nuclear fuel available at "reasonable" prices from international or regional nuclear fuel banks. Wouldn't subsidizing the fuel simply encourage more states to pursue nuclear energy programs? Each reactor would require tons of fresh low enriched uranium, and would make many bombs worth of weapons-usable plutonium annually. What would prevent these states from using these materials to make highly enriched uranium or separated plutonium? As already noted, the official U.S. position is that all states retain their "right" to make such materials at any time. What is to keep them from exercising this "right"?

Atoms for Peace.

This, then, brings us to a related problem that Roberta Wohlstetter spotlighted in her detailed Energy Research and Development Agency study, *The Buddha Smiles: Absent-Minded Peaceful Aid and the Indian Bomb* (1976): the tendency of American and allied officials to oversell the "control value" of various civilian nuclear initiatives. This point is all too painfully clear when examining the U.S. nuclear cooperation agreements and disputes with India, which arose from Canada's and America's concessionary diplomacy of the 1950s and 1960s. Here, American and Canadian diplomats thought that they had secured clear, "peaceful" end-use pledges from New Delhi that would prevent India from ever misusing the nuclear goods that they might receive. The pledges, instead, were fatally vague. India, in fact, insisted that it had done nothing wrong in using this aid to detonate what it called a "peaceful" nuclear explosive device.

Diplomatic failures of this sort—the result of haste and inattention—are still prevalent today. Certainly, many of the contentious Indian demands made during the 1950s and 1960s regarding the CIRUS and Tarapur reactors are all too similar to those more recently raised during the negotiation of the U.S.-Indian civilian nuclear cooperative agreement. If the U.S. Executive Branch is not lucky, it may yet see India test nuclear weapons and again have to defend such action against Congressional demands that Washington suspend further U.S. nuclear co-operation.[7]

This helps explain why the Wohlstetters were so hard-nosed when it came to nuclear restraints and economics. They understood the power of economics, and believed that it was a mistake for any government to pay extra to produce strategic forces or nuclear electricity or fuels if, in the process, it only reduced security. They both went to great lengths to analyze the economics of different types of nuclear power fuels and reactors, and to detail the high economic and security costs of creating even a "small" nuclear force.

This analysis complemented their insight that the best proposals for restraint played to the natural tendencies of states to defend themselves and to surrender only that which was safe to give up. Rather than relying heavily on efforts to bribe specific states into "doing the right thing" (*e.g.*, Agreed Frameworks, Iranian nuclear incentive packages, and other "grand bargains"), the Wohlstetters preferred to develop country-neutral rules that played to states' clear security interests.

In this vein, Albert sketched out a worthy proposal in a brief memo entitled "Nuclear Triggers and Safety Catches, the 'FSU' and the 'FSRs'" (1992). The memo addressed the potential problems posed by Russian nuclear weapons in post-Soviet Ukraine. Albert asks: Instead of trying to reduce the number of nations with their finger on the nuclear "trigger" (*i.e.*, demanding that Ukraine give up its nuclear weapons to Russia), why not secure the weapons and increase the number of states — starting with Ukraine, Russia, and the United States — that would have a veto over the Ukraine's ability ever to regain access to the weapons? In discussing this idea further, Albert was quite willing to see his idea expanded to cover other nuclear problem sets — for example, to weapons-usable nuclear materials.[8] Why not get Japan, North Korea, and China to surrender whatever direct-use nuclear materials they felt comfortable to declare to be in surplus (including highly enriched uranium, plutonium-based fuels, and separated plutonium) and make access to this material by any of these states contingent upon total agreement among and consent from all of these states? Initially, one might simply put the material under safe storage with state-of-the-art cipher locks. Later, one could remove the material to some safer, more remote location (*e.g.*, Greenland) with much greater physical barriers and protections. The idea would be to increase the number of states whose fingers would be on the "safety catch" rather than reduce the number of states whose fingers were on any nuclear trigger, and also to increase the holdings kept under such safety arrangements.[9]

Conclusion.

Albert was fond of arguing that it would be nice if we could somehow stop making our mistakes hereditary. What he was referring to, of course, was the diplomatic tendency not only to grandfather past errors, but to insist that we repeat them in the future so that no one might notice the original mistake. What's worrisome about this practice is that it generally works. In time, we accept our past policy choices as absolutes and actually stop thinking about reversing course — even when it makes sense to do so.

There's no question but that if the Wohlstetters were alive today, they would continue to push for clear changes in U.S. and allied policies regarding civilian nuclear energy and nonproliferation. They certainly would be dismayed by the current enthusiasm to use plutonium-based fuels commercially and to subsidize further capital-intensive nuclear energy projects. They would object to the U.S.-Indian nuclear deal, as well as to nuclear cooperative efforts with states in the unstable Middle East, and would be sharp critics of the way the United States and its allies have handled the North Korean and Iranian crises. What would distinguish them from other such critics today, however, would be that their objections would not be partisan, but would be consistent with many decades of sound research. We could do much worse than to read them either again — or for the first time.

ENDNOTES - Sokolski

1. E.g., see Brad Roberts, "Rethinking N + 1 Proliferation of Nuclear Weapons," *The National Interest,* Spring 1998; and David Santoro, "Of the Utility of the Non-Proliferation Regime: The Essential Dialectic between Supply and Demand," in *Strengthening the Global Nonproliferation Regime: Views from the Next Generation,* Brad Glosserman, ed., Washington, DC: Pacific Forum CSIS Young Leaders, May 2006, available from *www.tinyurl.com/6bqak9.*

2. See Albert Wohlstetter, *Strength, Interest and New Technologies,* opening address before *The Implications of Military Technology in the 1970s,* the Institute for Strategic Studies' ninth annual conference, Elsinore, Denmark, September 28 to October 1, 1967, D(L)-16624-PR, Santa Monica, CA: RAND Corporation, January 24, 1968, available from *www.rand.org/about/history/wohlstetter/DL16624/DL16624.html.* The address was also published as Wohlstetter, *Strength, Interest and New Technologies,* in *The Implications of Military Technology in the 1970s,* Adelphi Papers No. 46, London, UK: Institute for Strategic Studies, March 1968.

3. We have more than an inkling of what the Wohlstetters' views of the Israeli and Indian nuclear programs were. In *Moving Toward Life in a Nuclear Armed Crowd?* (1976), the Wohlstetters were quite clear about the high costs and negative security value of nuclear weapons for smaller states such as Japan. They spotlighted the great expense smaller nations would have to pay in order to make their nuclear forces truly survivable and effective against large and small competitors. Regarding Israel, Professor Wohlstetter published little but detailed before a student seminar held in 1976 — years before it was publicly clear that Israel had nuclear weapons — the "mistake" Israel made in acquiring its own nuclear forces. His key arguments were that Israel would gain little in possessing its own nuclear force, that maintaining sound relations with the U.S. would otherwise provide security, and that Israel would run severe strategic risks if these relations soured. The reason why was simple: Israel (and other states, including

nations as large as Japan) could hardly make its nuclear forces truly competitive against major powers, whose favor Israel's security would ultimately rely upon.

4. The best known of these studies was *Moving Toward Life In a Nuclear Armed Crowd?* a Pan Heuristics report completed for the U.S. Arms Control and Disarmament Agency in 1976 and subsequently published by the University of Chicago Press in 1979 as *Swords from Plowshares: The Military Potential of Civilian Nuclear Energy.*

5. Albert Wohlstetter once warned his University of Chicago class against thinking that "deterrence" was always a very clear thought. "Turning a verb into a noun," he warned, "was rarely a good idea." With this in mind, one would have to wonder about the clarity of "nonproliferation," which is a verb ("proliferate") turned into a noun, and with a prefix ("non") attached to it.

6. On these points, cf. the U.S. Department of Energy's website, *www.gnep.energy.gov*; Edwin Lyman and Frank von Hippel, "Reprocessing Revisited: The International Dimensions of the Global Nuclear Energy Partnership," *Arms Control Today,* April 2008, available from *www.armscontrol.org/act/2008_04/ LymanVonHippel.asp*; and Committee on Review of DOE's Nuclear Energy Research and Development Program, National Research Council, *Review of DOE's Nuclear Energy Research and Development Program*, Washington, DC: National Academies Press, 2007, esp. "Minority Opinion: Dissenting Statements of Gilinsky and Macfarlane," pp. A1-A6, available from *www.nationalacademies. org/morenews/20071029.html*.

7. On these points, see Victor Gilinsky, "Nuclear Consistency: "The U.S.-India Deal and Our Approach to Rogue Nuclear Powers Is Threatened by Double Standards," *National Review Online*, April 30, 2007; and Roberta Wohlstetter, *The Buddha Smiles: Absent-Minded Peaceful Aid and the Indian Bomb*, PH-78-04-370-23, final report prepared for the U.S. Energy Research and Development Administration in partial fulfillment of E (49-1)-3747, Los Angeles, CA: Pan Heuristics, November 15, 1976, revised November 1977, available from *www.npec-web.org/essays/19771100-RW-BuddhaSmiles-Revised.pdf*, courtesy Joan Wohlstetter.

8. Author's private conversation with Albert Wohlstetter at his California residence, spring 1992.

9. This idea should be seen as still ahead of its time. A similar proposal recently was suggested by Robert Einhorn at an international conference hosted by the Nuclear Threat Initiative and the Norwegian Government held in 2008 in Oslo, Norway.

Nuclear Sharing: NATO and the N + 1 Country (1961)

Albert Wohlstetter

Spreading the Bomb without Quite Breaking the Rules (1976)

Albert Wohlstetter

From *Foreign Policy*, No. 25, Winter 1976, pp. 88-94 and 145-179. Courtesy of the Wohlstetter Estate.

The basic problem in limiting the spread of nuclear weapons is that in the next 10 years or so many countries, including many agreeing not to make bombs, can come within hours of a bomb without plainly violating their agreement—without "diverting" special nuclear material and, therefore, without any possibility of being curbed by "safeguards" designed to verify whether material has or has not been diverted.

This development would lower the political and economic price of nuclear weapons and at the same time greatly increase the incentives to acquire them. The legal acquisition of concentrated fissile material by regional powers will increase the desire of regional adversaries to do the same. Such a development is encouraged by the incoherence and carelessness of the policies of the United States and other nuclear exporters which allow material easily turned into bombs by government nuclear laboratories to be used or produced during the course of civilian research or the generation of electricity.

The problem in the present export rules can be made vivid by a comparison. Under these rules a non-weapon state can come closer to exploding a plutonium weapon today without violating an agreement not to make a bomb than the United States was in the spring of 1947, when the world considered us not only a nuclear power but *the* nuclear power. The plutonium bombs of the time were primitive in design and crated in knockdown form. The very bulky high explosives had to be glued together piece by piece with slow-drying adhesives to form an implosion system. The fusing and wiring circuits were much more primitive than those commercially available today, and even a skilled team would have required several days to put a weapon together. In the spring of 1947, moreover, we had no skilled teams. Yet some believe our nuclear force to have been the main obstacle to an adversary reaching the English Channel, and others believe it to have been the backup for "atomic diplomacy." It should make suppliers thoughtful that their nuclear exports might bring a non-weapon state closer to exploding a plutonium bomb today than the United States was in 1947.

From the outset of the nuclear age it has been clear that designing a bomb and getting the nonnuclear components are much easier than getting fissile material in high enough concentration for an explosive. Research on bomb design and testing of nonnuclear bomb components are not prevented by agreements on nuclear cooperation, and can proceed in parallel with the accumulation of fissile material. Fissile uranium (in particular, uranium-235) or fissile plutonium (especially plutonium-239) concentrated enough to need no isotope separation[1] and only a modest amount of chemical separation are then the main hard steps on the way to a nuclear bomb.

The fresh fuel used in the present generation of power reactors is either natural uranium, which is almost all uranium-238 with less than 1 percent of the fissile isotope uranium-235, or low enriched uranium with only 3 percent to 4 percent of uranium-235. Such fresh fuel with less than 20 percent of uranium-235 cannot be used in an explosive without isotopic separation. But the irradiated or "spent" uranium fuel contains, along with other by-products, significant quantities of plutonium which result from the absorption of neutrons by the uranium-238. The plutonium so generated along with electricity has upward of 70 percent of the fissile isotopes of plutonium and requires no isotopic, but only chemical separation to be used in an explosive. Some "critical experiments" use large amounts of plutonium and uranium in metal form needing little further change.

To avoid putting fissile, that is, readily fissionable, material into the hands of non-weapon states, we deny licenses on facilities for isotope separation which could produce highly enriched uranium. So also on reprocessing plants for chemically separating plutonium. In the nuclear suppliers group, according to news accounts, we argue in principle against any other country making such exports even under International Atomic Energy Agency (IAEA) "safeguards." While we so far haven't won on the general principle, we have successfully opposed French sales of reprocessing plants to Taiwan and South Korea. And though not successful in our opposition, we say we objected to the German sale of enrichment and reprocessing plants to Brazil as well as to the French sale of a reprocessing plant to Pakistan. We used to refuse to license the export of uranium enriched to more than 20 percent in uranium-235, whatever the inspection arrangements. All of this recognizes, sometimes explicitly, that safeguards imply timely warning and that material that is weeks, days, or hours from incorporation in a bomb therefore cannot be effectively safeguarded.

On the other hand, we have for some time exported to non-weapon states, for use in research, both separated plutonium and highly enriched uranium, which bring them closer to the bomb than do the facilities for separating such material. For example, from mid-1968 to spring 1976, we exported 697 kilograms of highly enriched uranium and 104 kilograms of separated plutonium to Japan and 2,710 kilograms of highly enriched uranium and 349 kilograms of separated plutonium to the Federal Republic of Germany.

And we continue to offer nuclear assistance to countries that plan to acquire fissile material, and even to a country like India which has already detonated a nuclear explosive in defiance of explicit Canadian and U.S. statements over the past decade that no nuclear explosive is exclusively peaceful within the meaning of their agreements on nuclear cooperation. We say that that is what our agreements have always meant (and it is indeed their commonsense implication),[2] and we try to make this obvious meaning explicit in new agreements. Nonetheless, for old agreements we content ourselves with statements of U.S. unilateral understandings on this subject, and continue nuclear exports to countries that have refused to endorse our unilateral interpretation.[3]

The State Department assures the Congress that such unilateral understanding is binding enough, but after the Indians made a nuclear explosive using Canadian and U.S. peaceful assistance, we denied that the Indians had violated anything but the Canadian unilateral understanding and went through extraordinary contortions to hide the fact that they had used U.S. heavy water. We raised no objections when the French sold a reprocessing plant to Japan. Indeed, in 1972, before that sale, we had authorized U.S. companies to sell a reprocessing plant to Japan under stricter safeguards than the Japanese were willing to accept, but apparently no stricter than those they actually accepted later for the French sale.

Our policies at that time did not recognize, as they do now, that the sale of reprocessing plants is mistaken even if safeguarded. The South Koreans observe that we treat Japan differently from them when it comes to reprocessing. The French comment sardonically that we make a great fuss about the sale of a reprocessing plant to Pakistan, even though our representative to the IAEA approved the Agreement between Pakistan, France, and the IAEA on the transfer and safeguarding of that plant. And apparently not all American officials, and evidently not the most important ones, opposed the West German sale to Brazil in tones audible at the highest level of the German government. Chancellor Schmidt told the press in June 1975 that he regretted criticism by U.S. journalists and politicians but that "he knew of no criticism by the U.S. government."

We get then the worst of both worlds: In the end we refused to supply reprocessing or enrichment facilities to the Brazilians, knowing that though nominally civilian, such facilities could bring Brazil close to a bomb. But because we never formulated a coherent policy explaining that, it was easy for the Federal Republic to tell itself that we were simply sore losers in a business deal and that clinching the deal by giving the Brazilians a "sweetener" in the form of the principal ingredient of a nuclear explosive was perfectly all right.

Our agreements on nuclear cooperation abound in clauses that presume that the importing country will separate and recycle plutonium and that stocks of plutonium may in principle be effectively safeguarded. Moreover, we have talked of separating and recycling plutonium as if they were essential to the future of nuclear power both here and abroad, and have allowed the myth to persist that power-reactor plutonium cannot be used as an explosive. We have recently made the recycling of plutonium a "key initiative" in our energy conservation program. The Nuclear Regulatory Commission (NRC) has only recently shown signs of considering the international consequences of recycling to be a factor in the U.S. decision to license it domestically. As for uranium, sometime in the 1960s our attention wandered and we began to ship highly enriched uranium to non-weapon countries. We appear to have shipped some five tons overseas — perhaps 300 bombs worth of readily fissionable material. Our confusion has been durable and bipartisan.

How We Got Into This Fix

The extensive fundamental overlap of the paths to nuclear explosives and to civilian uses of nuclear energy has been recognized since the mid-1940s.[4] The "heart of the problem" of international control, according to Robert Oppenheimer, was "the close technical parallelism and interrelation of the peaceful and the military applications of atomic energy." We have almost from the start said that the military and civilian atoms were substantially identical yet, paradoxically, that we wanted to stop one and to promote the other. The paradox was present in the Truman-Atlee-King Declaration of October 1945, and we made our most valiant effort to reconcile these opposing aims in the Acheson-Lilienthal Report and the Baruch Plan of 1946.

The Acheson-Lilienthal Report tried to resolve the dilemma by proposing to "denature" plutonium: that is, to spoil it as an explosive. This was to be accomplished by leaving the fuel to be irradiated in the reactors long enough so that the fissile isotope, plutonium-239, generated in the uranium fuel rods, would in turn generate a large portion of higher isotopes of plutonium and, in particular, a large fraction of plutonium-240, which had serious drawbacks from the standpoint of the art of weapons design of the time. The idea had been advanced in March 1945, by Leo Szilard, quite tentatively. (The troubles with plutonium-240 had been discovered only in the summer of 1944.) The Franck Report proposed denaturing less cautiously in June 1945.

Discussion was necessarily muted and limited by the requirements of secrecy, by the bounds of the current state of the art, and by the limitations of current understanding of that state of the art. The initial report was predicated on the belief that denaturing would interpose the high barrier of isotopic separation between the use of plutonium for civil and military ends. This, given the elaborate mechanism of international control called for in the Acheson-Lilienthal Report, would assure some two to three years warning. The report itself exhibited some uncertainty and ambivalence[5] about the hope for denaturing and the hope was almost immediately modified by a committee of distinguished Manhattan Project scientists to suggest that such plutonium could be used in a weapon, but would be very much less effective.[6] Even the qualifications immediately introduced, we now know, were not strong enough. Yet the initial hope for denaturing has generated a long and inconsistent trail[7] of statements which still have their effect in encouraging the belief that plutonium left in the reactor long enough to become contaminated with 20 to 30 percent of the plutonium-240 or plutonium-242 would be unusable or, at any rate, extremely ineffective when used in a nuclear explosive. Since power reactors operated "normally" were expected for reasons of economics to achieve maximum "burnup" of fuel by leaving the fuel rods in the reactor long enough to so contaminate the rods, a kind of denaturing was hoped for as a result of standard procedures. However, this hope turned out to be a slender reed.

The Baruch Plan would have given sovereign states control only of "safe" civilian activities. They would have gotten all of their fissile material in denatured form, separated from spent fuel in plants owned by an international authority. That authority was to have a monopoly of all "dangerous" activities: that is, all those that could quickly be turned to the manufacture of explosives. The plan rejected as unworkable any reliance on inspection rather than on ownership and control of dangerous activities.

The Soviets turned down the Baruch Plan. Since then we have come to rely on exactly the scheme regarded as unworkable by the authors of the Acheson-Lilienthal Report and the Baruch Plan. We rely in essence only on accounting and inspection of dangerous activities in non-weapon states. We are encouraged to do so by remnants of the belief that plutonium from a power reactor is not very dangerous.

But why was it important that plutonium be made safe for civilian use? The short answer is that we were powerfully impelled after the horrors of Hiroshima to believe that nuclear energy had a constructive use in electric power as spectacular as its use in military destruction. And we believed, on the basis of our initial understanding of the scarcity of uranium, that plutonium was essential to the future of nuclear electric power. The known reserves of natural uranium in the late 1940s were a mere 2,000 short tons. Since natural uranium contains only a tiny fraction of the fissile isotope, uranium-235, converting the more abundant uranium-238, which is not itself fissile, into fissile plutonium seemed a logical way to extend the scarce supply of fissile material for electric power. (From the first, we had contemplated using plutonium not only in breeders, but also in present-day reactors.)

And the natural impulse to find civilian use for this enormous force led statesmen frequently to talk as if the civilian use were a substitute for the military one: The more we used atoms for peace, the less we would use them for war. We subsidized the spread of civilian nuclear technology not simply in the hope for spectacular economic benefits, but as if it were a decisive measure of nuclear disarmament. We dispersed "research" reactors in the Third World as a substitute for sending a symbolic "atomic peace ship" around the world rather than as a matter of hard economics for development, and were embarrassed to find that we had made it a matter of international prestige to have a research reactor, even for countries that had no trained personnel to use it. We made concessionary loans for power reactors almost as tenuously based in economics, and we did this as if they were necessarily advancing the cause of peace.

Robert Oppenheimer was quite right in saying that, unlike the Acheson-Lilienthal Report or the Baruch Plan, the Atoms for Peace program had no "firm connection with atomic disarmament" and that its bearing on the prospect of nuclear war was "allusive and sentimental" rather than "substantive and functional." This symbolic use of atomic energy antedated the Atoms for Peace program and relates to our earliest habits of talking about promoting the peaceful uses of the atom as if they would automatically displace the military use.

However, it can be said of the pioneers of the nuclear age that though they sometimes talked as if there were a dichotomy, they also saw that the heart of the problem was a large overlap between civilian and military applications of nuclear energy, and they grasped very firmly the point that keeping the two sorts of activities separate means more than simply detecting a violation of an agreement. It means early detection of the approach by a government toward the making of a bomb in time for other governments to do something about it. This principle has been reaffirmed recently by the president, by the assistant administrator for national security of the Energy Research and Development Administration (ERDA), and by the inspector general of the IAEA. But, in practice, the point has a way of getting lost in the middle reaches of both national and international bureaucracies.

It was only to be expected that over two decades of Atoms for Peace programs would result in the formation of large groups of professionals in industry, in nuclear engineering departments of universities throughout the world, in governments, and in regional and international agencies. All of these groups have a strong interest in the "enlargement and acceleration" of the use of nuclear energy and a much milder concern with such long-term problems as the disposal of radioactive waste or the spread of nuclear explosives. They tend to identify any restraints to control the dangers of proliferation as simply — dread word — "antinuclear." The hostility has been worsened by some of the extremists of the environmentalist movement, who seem dedicated to stopping and dismantling all civilian nuclear power rather than controlling its dangers and encouraging the development of safe forms of nuclear and nonnuclear energy. The nuclear energy faction inside large industrial corporations in turn feels embattled by any attempt at further restriction, precisely because reactor manufacture has so far involved great business losses in spite of subsidy. The nuclear debate degenerates into a dog fight between extremes, with the accusations by Squeaky Fromme and the Manson Family about a nuclear power conspiracy almost mirrored in the dark hints by the beleaguered industrial bureaucracy.

For example, delegates to a meeting in Vienna last spring of the International Union of Producers and Distributors of Electrical Energy suggested that the holdups in separating plutonium to "close" the fuel cycle are due to "subversive elements" at work among groups opposing nuclear development.[8] At a conference in Düsseldorf earlier that week the chief executive of VEBA, a leading West German energy concern, indicated that the nuclear opposition was heavily backed with cash "from across the border."[9] But from the standpoint of reactor manufacturers whose profits are all still in the future, less sales promotion and a more sober look at the social and even the entrepreneurial risks would be salutary for the industry itself. Treating as the enemy all doubters of nuclear market and cost-benefit studies encourages badly timed investments and the present industry troubles.

However we got into our present fix, we still have to ask what the fix portends for the future of proliferation, if we do nothing.

Is the Spread Likely?

Past predictions of immediate spread have, for the most part, been false alarms. So, immediately after the war, scientists who had figured in the Manhattan Project predicted that, unless there were very drastic international controls, bombs would spread rapidly. Harold Urey forecast a half dozen countries entering the nuclear club in as few as five years. Irving Langmuir predicted that Russia would get nuclear weapons very quickly, but would be beaten in the race by Canada and England. And the general public reflected this pessimism. Intelligence estimates in 1948 were more hopeful (excessively so in predicting when the Soviet Union would get the bomb), but official predictions have had their ups and downs.

A second flurry of alarm came in the late 1950s as the military potential of the Atoms for Peace programs began to be visible. Officials predicted, for example, that not only Canada and Sweden would get nuclear weapons in the early 1960s but, unless there were a multilateral nuclear force, West Germany would too. Perhaps the best known study done then was by the American Academy of Arts and Sciences and the National Planning Association (NPA): it suggested that without international control there might be as many as 10 new nuclear powers in five years. This study was summed up somewhat incautiously by C.P. Snow's famous statement in 1960 that all physical scientists ". . . *know* that for a dozen or more states, it will only take perhaps six years, perhaps less" to acquire fission and fusion bombs. Nothing of the kind happened. By comparison with these early alarms, the actual increase in the number of countries testing nuclear explosives has been very slow. Three additional countries tested at intervals of eight, four, and 10 years in the 22 years following the British nuclear explosion.

There is a lesson to be drawn from a close examination of these past apocalyptic predictions. They assumed essentially that, in the absence of some quite extreme and politically implausible change in circumstance, countries that could get nuclear weapons would do so, and would do so more or less in the order of their technical and industrial competence. The incentives and drawbacks for proceeding with a nuclear weapons program were in all essentials neglected. However, political will is the key, rather than mere competence. The demand for weapons was softened by a system of working alliances and explicit or implicit guarantees that applied to most of the then likely prospects for an independent nuclear capability. The price and risks in undertaking a nuclear weapons program were also higher than most of the prophets had recognized. It is important today, as then, to look soberly at incentives and disincentives for the spread and how they might be affected. We should not easily assume inevitability.

Some students of proliferation, however, observe that three countries tested in the first decade, two in the second, one in the third, and are made excessively cheery by the diminishing sequence. But changes are taking place beneath the placid surface, which is presently undisturbed by new countries testing weapons. These changes are much less cheering. Under the present rules, civilian nuclear energy programs now under way assure that many new countries will have traveled a long distance down the path leading to a nuclear weapons capability. The distance remaining will be shorter, less arduous, and much more rapidly covered. It need take only a smaller impulse to carry them the rest of the way. There is a kind of Damoclean overhang of countries increasingly near the edge of making bombs.

For convenience, distinguish three conditions in which plutonium might be found in the course of generating nuclear electric power. The first is the accumulation of plutonium in irradiated or "spent" uranium fuel which is now a normal by-product of any operation of our current reactors. The second condition, much closer to being usable in a nuclear weapon, would be that of plutonium in fresh mixed plutonium and uranium oxide fuel rods. Even if a country did not separate plutonium or manufacture such mixed oxide fuel rods itself, it could have plutonium in this second form in reloads of mixed oxide fuel at the input end of reactors. Plutonium in the third condition would be found already separated in the form of plutonium dioxide or plutonium nitrate. In this form, it could be found at the output end of a separation plant, or at the input end and in stocks-in-process in facilities that manufacture mixed plutonium and uranium fuel rods. Plutonium in these three conditions comes successively closer to a nuclear explosive. The last two conditions need occur only if plutonium recycling becomes general.

At present, our agreements on cooperation in general leave title to the spent fuel and all its products in the importing country. For governments accumulating the spent fuel, the barrier to obtaining a high enough concentration of fissile plutonium will be the need to separate the plutonium chemically. This is a less formidable obstacle than isotopic separation, the facility for which costs billions of dollars using present techniques and would take years to construct. Nonetheless, chemical separation is substantial barrier and perhaps the most important one remaining, if nuclear suppliers do not secure the return of spent fuel. Getting spent fuel is a considerable stride along the road to nuclear weapons, compared to the position of the weapon states which started from scratch. But spent fuel still needs to be reprocessed, and that involves delay and then remote manipulation of extremely toxic, radioactive substances, facilities with six or seven feet of shielding, lead glass windows, etc. Tons of spent fuel must be handled to produce kilograms of plutonium.

At the other extreme is the plutonium that would be stored at the output or "back" end of reprocessing plants and at the input or "front" end of plants fabricating plutonium or "mixed oxide" fuel. Such plutonium in the form of plutonium dioxide or plutonium nitrate could be converted to plutonium metal using generally known methods and without remote handling equipment or extensive shielding and the like, but only a glove box. It should take no more than a week in a facility covering 3,600 square feet and costing about $1,400,000.

Plutonium would also be found, if it is recycled, in fresh unirradiated fuel rods at the input end of the reactor. Extracting plutonium from such mixed oxide fuel would be very much easier than taking it out of the irradiated spent uranium fuel. Plutonium is more concentrated in the mixed oxide fuel rods (4.5 percent compared to .7 percent). Unlike irradiated fuel, it is not highly radioactive and would require no delay, no "hot cells" with heavy shielding, no remote manipulation, and no removal of fission products. A facility for separating 5 kilograms per day and converting it to plutonium nitrate might exist in a 1,400 square foot laboratory and might cost $235,000. This is trivial by comparison with the cost of a facility for deriving comparable quantities of plutonium nitrate from the spent uranium fuel. The latter might cost from $75 million to $100 million. The difference is important, because today many proposals would ban separating plutonium in non-weapon states, but not recycling it in mixed plutonium and uranium fuel. So, for example, early drafts of U.S. agreements of cooperation with Egypt and Israel.

We can measure the advance toward the ability to manufacture nuclear explosives implicit in recent civilian nuclear electric programs, as of 1975, by showing first the number of countries, including the present weapon states, that would have enough separable but possibly unseparated plutonium for a few bombs between now and 1985. Second, the large number of countries with various quantities of plutonium in fresh reloads of unirradiated plutonium fuel if plutonium recycling should become general, and even if these countries do not themselves separate plutonium or manufacture plutonium fuel rods. Third, the number of countries that have planned to have a capability to separate that much plutonium by 1985. The results of these three sets of calculations are displayed respectively in Figure 1, Table 1, and Figure 2.

311

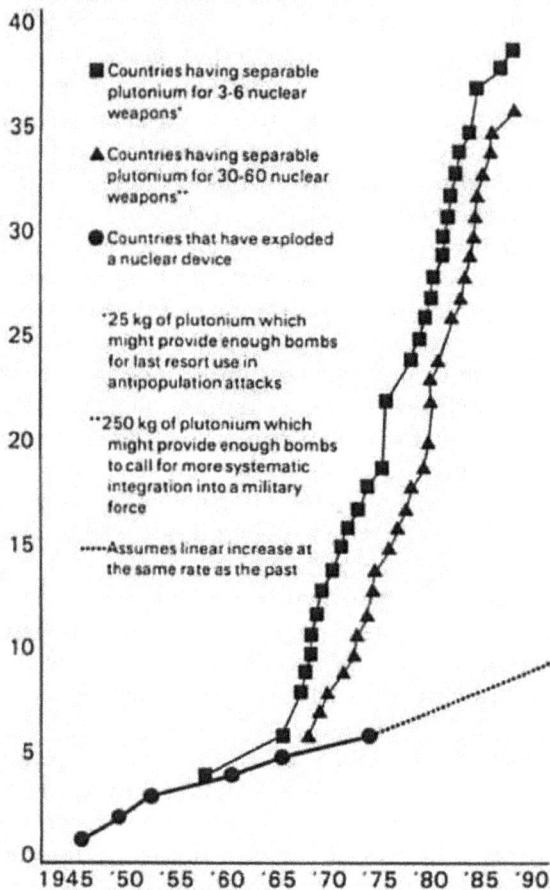

Figure 1
The overhang of countries with enough separable plutonium for primitive or small military forces
Vertical scale: number of countries

■ Countries having separable plutonium for 3-6 nuclear weapons*

▲ Countries having separable plutonium for 30-60 nuclear weapons**

● Countries that have exploded a nuclear device

*25 kg of plutonium which might provide enough bombs for last resort use in antipopulation attacks

**250 kg of plutonium which might provide enough bombs to call for more systematic integration into a military force

·····Assumes linear increase at the same rate as the past

Figure 1.

Table 1
Plutonium Available
from Reloads of Mixed Plutonium
and Uranium Oxide (MOX) Fuel
in the Early 1990s*

	kg of Pu[a] (Plutonium)	Number of Bombs' Worth[b]
Austria	400	46
Belgium	2,800	325
Brazil	500	58
West Germany	11,700	1,357
India[c]	360	42
Iran	3,200	371
Italy	2,100	244
Japan	9,000	1,044
South Korea	900	104
Mexico	800	93
Netherlands	400	46
Philippines	1,000	116
Spain	5,600	650
Sweden	4,800	557
Switzerland	3,200	371
Taiwan	3,200	371
Yugoslavia	500	58
Egypt	700	81

* Using only indigenously produced plutonium and assuming that one reload is always kept at each reactor. Any country without its own MOX fuel fabrication facilities could justify stocking one reload. A single MOX reload might contain 350-900 kg of plutonium (40 to 104 bombs worth). Countries that fabricate MOX fuel would have still more plutonium available in process.

[a] Assuming 580 kg per 1,000 megawatt boiling water reactor reload and 770 kg per 1,000 megawatt pressurized water reactor reload, linear scaling for other reactor sizes. See U.S. Atomic Energy Commission, Generic Environmental Statement Mixed Oxide Fuel (GESMO), Vol. III, August 1974, p. IV C-65.

[b] 8.62 kg Pu per bomb assuming 5kg fissile Pu/bomb and assuming MOX Pu is 58 per cent fissile Pu.

[c] The figures for India are the result of direct calculation.

Table 1.

313

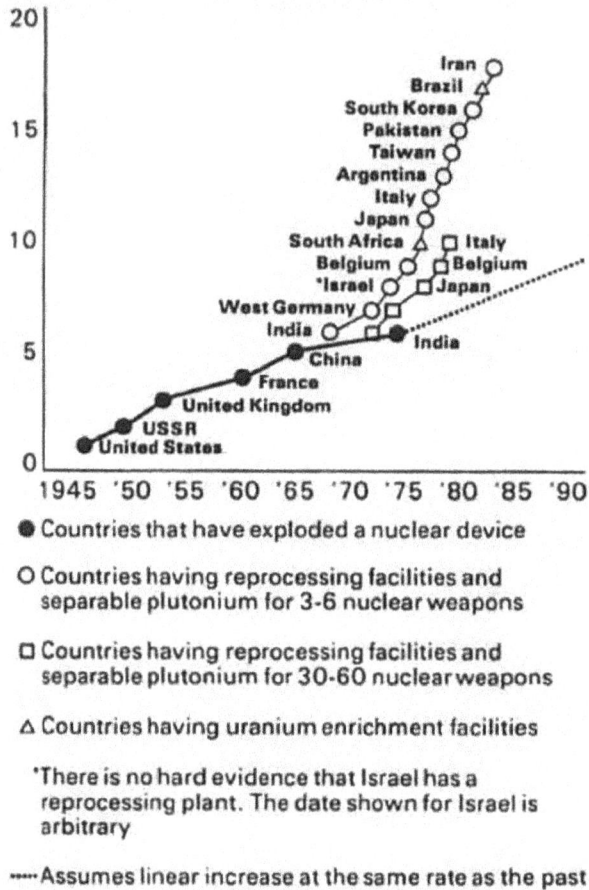

Figure 2
Countries planning to have plants for
separating plutonium or enriching uranium in
quantities enough for several bombs
Vertical scale: number of countries

● Countries that have exploded a nuclear device

○ Countries having reprocessing facilities and
separable plutonium for 3-6 nuclear weapons

□ Countries having reprocessing facilities and
separable plutonium for 30-60 nuclear weapons

△ Countries having uranium enrichment facilities

*There is no hard evidence that Israel has a
reprocessing plant. The date shown for Israel is
arbitrary

····Assumes linear increase at the same rate as the past

Figure 2.

The first thing to be said about the numbers in these charts is
that they are very large ones. Chemical separation of plutonium
and the enrichment of uranium are civilian activities which have
long been regarded as "normal," if not yet operational, parts of
the nuclear electric fuel cycle. They may sometimes and in some

314

places be discouraged by various ad hoc national policies, but they have not been subject to a clear-cut international or universal national prohibition by supplier countries. The problem of inhibiting or reducing the size of this burgeoning capacity is not merely then a matter of an improved watch, to see that a clearly agreed prohibited line is not crossed. Among other things it would involve defining and moving such a clearly agreed boundary to preclude activities which cannot provide adequate warning. And for whatever dangerous activities remain on the permissible side of the agreed boundary, we need to elaborate a consistent national policy to discourage them and encourage other safer alternatives.

The second thing to be said is that this large growth is not inevitable. It presumes the carrying through of plans, negotiations, and constructions not yet firmly committed; some, like the Korean and Taiwan separation plants, have had setbacks. The growth, moreover, is open to further influence, a subject for the elaboration of policy of supplier as well as recipient governments. But American influence on the policies of various importing and exporting countries is limited by the confusion and arbitrariness of our policy on access to fissile material. Figures 1 and 2 and Table 1 are not unconditional forecasts, but indications of what may happen if conditions are not altered.

The gist of these figures is that, under the present rules of the game, any of a very large number of countries may take these further long strides toward the production of nuclear weapons in the next 10 years or so without violating the rules — at least no vigorously formulated, agreed-on rules.

These paths toward producing weapons are in addition to paths which exploit the weakness of sanctions against breaking the Treaty on Non-Proliferation of Nuclear Weapons (NPT) or bilateral rules, and in addition to paths open to those governments which have not ratified the NPT. Extending the NPT to more countries or increasing the efficiency of "safeguards" or physical security measures would not, therefore, block these paths. The recent interest in measures against "diversion," while useful in itself, distracts attention from the steady spread of production capacities within the rules.

Some part of the stocks of fissile material might always be diverted within the limits of error of material unaccounted for by any inspection system. In the future, when these stocks are very large, diverting even a small percentage would yield sizable absolute amounts. This tends therefore to be the focus of most attention. Yet it is much less important than the possibility of piling up significant stocks of fissile material legally, without diversion, for use later in explosives.

I have distinguished for convenience four kinds of nuclear explosive capacity. The first is the sort of capacity which has been much in the public eye in the last year or two, due especially to the efforts of Dr. Theodore Taylor to make clear its dangers. It would consist in the manufacture of a crude device derived from stolen fissile material, perhaps not using plutonium metal, but plutonium dioxide powder, yielding as little as 10 or 100 tons of energy, and designed for terrorist use by some nongovernmental group, or possibly even a single individual. It might use poorly separated material and be dangerous not merely if exploded in anger, but to store and handle.

The second capacity would rely on a few explosives, perhaps implosion weapons in the kiloton or greater range. They might be used by governments as a desperate last resort threat against populations (or transferred by some governments to terrorists). The third capacity I have taken arbitrarily as consisting in perhaps 50 such devices, enough to call for plans to incorporate them into a military force. The fourth would be much more sophisticated. It is the kind that an industrial power like Japan might contemplate, if it made the decision to become a military nuclear power in the 1980s or 1990s. It would require very sophisticated fission and fusion weapons with predictable yields and with more advanced and protected delivery capabilities.

This article focuses especially on the second sort of capability. It imposes no stringent requirements for delivery. (These requirements are very stringent for a middle power to get a serious and responsible force in the 1980s.) I do not, however, mean to imply that the capacity to produce a few bombs for use as a last resort will actually realize the hopes some government might place in it. It is likely to be extremely inflexible, vulnerable, and available only for suicidal use. Nonetheless, some governments might take this route.

However, the nuclear energy bureaucracy, and statesmen informed by it, have been cheerfully arguing that the recycling of plutonium will not make the spread of weapons more likely. Their arguments are residues of the initial faith in denaturing. They are saying that power reactor plutonium would be contaminated in normal reactor operations and abnormal operations would be quickly detected and punished; that power reactor plutonium cannot be used as an explosive; or if so used, it would be ineffective, with generally low yields and highly variable ones; that only sophisticated nuclear weapon countries like the United States and the Soviet Union, with many years in the business, could so derive weapons that have any genuine military use; and finally, with a touching bathos, that power reactor plutonium is anyway less than optimal for weapons.

It is surprising that the faith in denaturing of plutonium, however plausible initially, could have survived for more than three decades. Since this belief explicitly or implicitly rationalizes so much carelessness, it is important, before putting it to rest, to offer some current examples. "Both Framatome and French officials," according to *Nucleonics Week*, June 3, 1976, "deny the [South African] deal is conducive to weapons building. 'The worst way to make a bomb is to buy an LWR (light water reactor) for 5 billion francs,' commented Leny. Abourdarham [also of Framatome] added, 'To get clean Pu-239 from our type of reactor, you'd have to lower the burnup rate and discharge the reactor not once a year but about twice a month.' The higher the burnup the more contaminated the spent fuel is with Pu-240." The new French foreign minister, while ambassador to the United Nations, told the Security Council flatly that plutonium so derived "could not be used for military purposes."[10] In Germany, officials of Kraftwerk Union have suggested that weapons-grade plutonium must be 98 percent pure plutonium-239, and that anything less could be used not in a military weapon, but only in "terrorist explosive devices" of low and uncertain yield, which in any case would be extremely hard for terrorists to make.[11] The Swedish government committee on radioactive wastes (the Aka Committee) reports that "The plutonium . . . produced in Swedish power reactors contains as much as 25 percent to 30 percent of plutonium-240 [and] . . . can only be utilized in weak and probably unreliable nuclear charges of highly questionable military value."[12]

In the United States, the president of the Atomic Industrial Forum says that if nuclear reactors are "run on an economic fuel cycle—that is, long irradiation times—the plutonium produced is readily used only for making explosive devices which are hardly military weapons."[13] He goes on to suggest that only very sophisticated weapons countries like the United States and the Soviet Union are able to overcome the difficulty by special design. The Forum's Committee on Nuclear Export Policy concludes that

317

we should promote peaceful nuclear electric power only to the extent consistent with the goal of eliminating proliferation, but they do not think that should impose much constraint, since, ". . . power reactors are not a practical or economic vehicle for producing weapons-grade plutonium. The processing of fuel from a power reactor at low irradiation levels would be costly and revealing of intentions, thus jeopardizing the supply of new fuel. On the other hand, the use of reactor-grade plutonium of high irradiation levels for weapons purposes presents formidable technical challenges."[14]

And finally American government officials in agencies granting loans and subsidies to countries like India which have or propose to get reprocessing plants take comfort from the fact that, "While the plutonium produced by these reactors could be used in an inefficient and unsophisticated explosive program, it is not optimum material for explosive uses because of the high percentage content of the nonfissionable plutonium isotope plutonium-240."[15]

But all of this is quite misleading. For one thing, a non-weapon country can operate a power reactor so as to produce significant quantities of rather pure plutonium-239 without violating any agreements or incurring substantial extra expense. This would involve departing from theoretical "norms" for reactor operation, but a look at the actual operating record of reactors in less developed countries suggests how theoretical these norms are. Even in America in the early 1970s, leaking fuel rods caused Commonwealth Edison to discharge the initial core of its Dresden-2 reactor early, with nearly 100 bombs-worth of 89 to 95 percent pure fissile plutonium.[16] (In India, as of September 1975, 97 percent of the fuel discharged from its Tarapur reactors had leaked.) Countries like Pakistan and India, with smaller electric grids and poorer maintenance, have operated much less and much more irregularly than the steady 80 percent of the time originally hoped for; and have irradiated their fuel and contaminated the plutonium in it less. Since it is neither illegal nor uncommon to operate reactors uneconomically, governments may derive quite pure plutonium-239 with no violation nor much visibility.

What is more, there is plainly a considerable latitude in the degree of purity actually required for explosives. The discussion in the European nuclear industry frequently assumes that "weapons-grade" plutonium must be 98 percent pure plutonium-239.[17] In this country, however, under present classification guidance, the fact that plutonium containing up to and including 8 percent plutonium-240 *is* used in weapons is unclassified as is the fact that more than 8 percent plutonium-240 (reactor-grade) *can* be used to make nuclear weapons.

Most significantly, 20 years of Atoms for Peace programs have dispersed well-equipped and well-staffed nuclear laboratories among nonnuclear weapons states throughout the world. (For example, by 1974 the United States alone had trained 1,100 Indian nuclear physicists and engineers. The Shah of Iran plans to have 10,000 trained.) Many of these laboratories would be quite capable of designing and constructing an implosion device and of studying its behavior by nonnuclear firings. It is true that if they were to use power reactor plutonium with 20 to 30 percent of the higher isotopes, they would be likely to obtain a lower expected yield and a greater variation in possible yields than if they should use more nearly pure plutonium-239. (Of course a nonnuclear component could fail, but this has nothing to do with the grade of plutonium used.) However, they could build a device which, even at its lowest yield level, would produce a very formidable explosion. This may be seen from the record (now public) of the characteristics of the Nagasaki plutonium bomb.

The Fat Man and the Little Boy

The first American implosion design, "Fat Man," was used in the Trinity test and the Nagasaki bomb. It had a finite probability of predetonating even though it used an extremely high percentage of plutonium-239. Plutonium-239 itself emits neutrons spontaneously, though five orders of magnitude less so than an equal quantity of plutonium-240. More important, though the Trinity and Nagasaki devices used exceptionally pure plutonium-239, they had a significant fraction of plutonium-240. They had a definite chance, then, of detonating prematurely, that is, between the time the rapidly assembling fissile material first became critical and the time that it might have arrived at the desired degree of supercriticality; and the less supercritical, the lower the yield.

In a memorandum to General Farrell and Captain Parsons immediately after the Trinity test, and before the use of Fat Man at Nagasaki, Oppenheimer wrote, "As a result of the Trinity shot we are led to expect a very similar performance from the first Little Boy (the gun-assembled uranium weapon used at Hiroshima) and the first plutonium Fat Man. The energy release of both of these units should be in the range of 12,000 to 20,000 tons and the blast should be equivalent to that from 8,000 to 15,000 tons of TNT. The possibilities of a less than optimal performance of the Little Boy are quite small and should be ignored. The possibility that the first combat plutonium Fat Man will give a less than optimal performance is about 12 percent. There is about a 6 percent chance that the energy release will be under 5,000 tons, and about a 2 percent chance that it will be under 1,000 tons. *It should not be much less than 1,000 tons unless there is an actual malfunctioning of some of the components. . . .*" (italics added)[18]

Indeed General Groves, like Oppenheimer writing between the Trinity test and the actual use of the implosion weapon at Nagasaki, anticipated an increase in the fraction of plutonium-240 in later weapons. He wrote, "There is a definite possibility, 12 percent rising to 20 percent as we increase our rate of production at the Hanford Engineer Works, with the type of weapons tested that the blast will be smaller due to detonation in advance of the optimum time. *But in any event, the explosion should be on the order of thousands of tons.* The difficulty arises from an undesirable isotope which is created in greater quantity as the production rate increases" (italics added).[19]

The essential point to be made is that even if a device like our first plutonium weapon were detonated as prematurely as possible – at a time when the fissile material was least supercritical – its would still be in the kiloton range. Apart from a modest degradation in the quality of the fissile material employed, and hence in the size of the expected yield, all that a higher fraction of plutonium-240 in such a first implosion device could do is increase the probability of obtaining a yield smaller than the optimal, but still as large or larger than that already enormously destructive minimum.

The lowest yield of such a weapon can by no stretch of the imagination be called "weak." Moreover, by comparison with the average or even the maximum yield possible in that implosion design (or by any standard), it would by no means be contemptible. In fact, only 7 months before Trinity, the first implosion weapons were expected to yield much *less* than one kiloton.[20] A reduced yield would not mean a proportionate reduction in damage. The area destroyed by blast overpressure diminishes as the two-thirds power of the reduction in yield, and the reduction in prompt radiation – which is the dominant effect on population of a low-yield weapon — is even smaller. (If the expected yield were eight kilotons, and the less probable but actual yield were "merely" one kiloton, the blast area would be reduced not by seven-eighths, but only by three-fourths and the region in which persons in residential buildings would receive a lethal dose of prompt radiation would only be halved.) The lethal area would still be nearly a square mile.

Variability in yield would be a drawback for an advanced industrial country preparing the sort of force I have referred to as of interest to an industrial power like Japan in the 1980s or 1990s. Such a power might want a theater weapon that minimized collateral damage if only for the protection of its own troops. However, for a last resort weapon used against a distant population, it is important only that the blast effect of the yield be formidable; and if in fact more destructive energy is released than anticipated, this would only reinforce the destruction intended.

Finally, the variations in damage due to differences in the purity of the plutonium are likely to be much less than the variation in damage due to the differing operational circumstances in the use of the weapon. The Nagasaki plutonium implosion bomb had an estimated yield of 21 kilotons. The Hiroshima uranium gun weapon is now estimated to have released 14 kilotons. Yet, due to differences in terrain, weather, accuracy of delivery, and the distribution of population, the Hiroshima bomb killed twice as many people as the Nagasaki weapon.

As for the argument that military men would never use a device whose result was not precisely predictable, this is not very persuasive. If so, military men would hardly ever enter battle. The uncertainties of surviving ground attack, of penetrating air defense, and of delivering weapons on target are cumulatively larger than the uncertainties in the yield of a bomb made with power-reactor plutonium. Plans for delivering the first nuclear weapons were going forward before any test, and during a period when the Manhattan Project scientists had highly varied estimates of their yield.

In sum, no one should believe that power-reactor plutonium can be used only in a feeble device too unreliable to be considered a military weapon, or that recycling plutonium is therefore safe.

Recently, as some of the examples I have cited suggest, the bureaucracy has taken a slightly different tack: power-reactor plutonium can be used as an explosive, it is admitted, but would-be nuclear countries won't use it that way. They can get better plutonium more cheaply and easily by buying reactors specifically for the purpose of producing plutonium and not for generating electricity. However, if one already has paid for an electric power reactor, the relevant economic figure is not the total, but the marginal, or extra, cost to get bomb material, given the fact that one has paid anyway for the reactor. In fact, if recycling is accepted as essential for the fuel cycle, the cost of separation plants would be charged to the generation of electricity and would involve no incremental cost for getting separated plutonium for weapons. Getting impure plutonium in this way would be nearly costless. Getting a significant quantity of rather pure plutonium would involve some fuel and operating costs, but these would be small by comparison with the expense of a program to produce and separate plutonium exclusively for weapons.

The more important costs are political for any program designed overtly to get plutonium for a weapon. That could be why the Pakistanis, the Koreans, the Taiwanese, and others deny that they are doing any such thing. It would hurt them militarily, economically, and politically. They can more easily get the financial and technical assistance and trading relations necessary for a power reactor. The political costs would be high for the exporting country too.

Finally, what the bureaucracy seems to miss altogether is that a non-weapon state under the present rules can proceed down the path toward making a weapon without deciding to do so in advance. It doesn't have to start out as a "would-be nuclear country." It can change its mind or it can make up its mind later. It doesn't have to get a production reactor.

Of course a production reactor might be disguised as a vague sort of "research" reactor, though this is likely to yield smaller quantities of plutonium. In fact, the rules governing research reactors and "critical experiments" have been even more careless and need tightening even more than those governing power reactors. But this second line of argument is hardly a cheery confirmation that the rules make the spread unlikely. It has the opposite sense. It has led industry representatives to suggest that the spread is inevitable "sooner or later" and we will just have to live with it.[21]

Would the Spread to More Countries be Bad?

As we and other supplier countries continue to subsidize the export of materials, equipment, and information needed for making nuclear explosives, the bureaucrats in industry and government associated with these programs tend more and more to tell themselves and everyone else that the spread of nuclear explosives may not be so bad after all: governments that get nuclear weapons will themselves behave more cautiously; their nuclear weapons will inspire caution in their neighbors; this in turn might free the United States from the burden of defending some troublesome allies.

However, the spread of nuclear weapons to many countries will disperse not only instruments of deterrence and prudent behavior, but also means of coercion and reckless or deliberate devastating attack. Not all threats of nuclear aggression will be neatly offset and canceled by convincing promises of nuclear response. The risks will rise very high. In unstable parts of the world, the disasters possible in short conflicts will increase enormously. In the Middle East, for example, before outside powers could stop the conflict, as a result of an exchange involving a few bombs the Arabs might suffer several million and the Israelis a million dead in contrast with the thousands killed in the October war. In a conventional war, it takes a very long time or huge resources to kill the number of people that would be destroyed by a few nuclear weapons in a matter of hours. The spread of nuclear weapons will reduce our ability to control events. It will have a dissolvent effect on alliances, expose our own forces overseas to huge new risks, and ultimately impose large costs in shaping our own offense and defense to protect the continental United States against small terror attacks by national, as well as subnational groups. Even distant small powers using freighters and short-range missiles, such as the Soviet SCUD, will be within system range of the United States.

Even if such a development were, as it is claimed, inevitable "sooner or later," later would be better than sooner, and less better than more.

What Can We Do to Limit or Slow the Spread?

The characteristic view in the bureaucracy is that we have no leverage. We can't prevent foreign suppliers from selling nor importers from buying nuclear technology on terms even less constraining then ours. It's unfair then to burden our nuclear exporters. Besides, we can retain our influence on non-weapon states only by continuing to supply them with nuclear services, equipment, and materials without interruption.

There is an obvious muddle in the bureaucracy's view that we can't influence events on the one hand, but on the other hand that we do have an important influence that we can retain only by continuing to export and – to make the muddle muddier – by continuing to export to buyers, no matter what their behavior, no matter what moves they make toward nuclear explosives. For the bureaucracy, in short, we can retain our leverage only it we never use it. A lever is a form of abstract art rather than a tool giving us a mechanical advantage.

All this is plainly disingenuous: We've talked of the inevitable while actively promoting nuclear energy in non-weapon states in forms that permit access to readily fissionable material, subsidizing the financing of these sales, giving away research reactors with highly enriched uranium cores, assisting "critical experiments" that involve hundreds of kilograms of separated plutonium and highly enriched uranium, urging that non-weapon states recycle plutonium, training engineers from non-weapon states in how to separate plutonium, arguing for domestic recycling as an essential to the future of all nuclear electric power, and in general setting an example to non-weapon states that suggests that the stocking of fissile material is both necessary and safe.

The State Department argues that we must supply nuclear services, equipment, and material "reliably" – by which it means that we should supply them steadily and indiscriminately to importers who do and to those who do not live up to an obligation to avoid getting explosives, or materials quickly convertible to nuclear explosives. Such "reliable" supply, it claims, will enable us to influence the importers. Exactly the opposite of the truth. Importers will be influenced to stay away from stocks of explosive material only if it costs them something not to do so, and only if our threats or sanctions are taken seriously. The Indian use of Canadian and American help for "peaceful uses only" in order to make nuclear explosives illustrates the point marvelously. The Indians guessed right in not taking the constraint seriously. Their explosion inspired only ingenious apologies for them in our State Department.

One token of our lack of seriousness is the piecemeal way we decide on licensing exports without considering the cumulative effect of our own and other suppliers' individual decisions in enabling an importing country to get explosive material. For example, we limit the amount of highly enriched uranium in the core of an individual research reactor we have given away, but place no constraint on the total amount of highly enriched uranium the importing country might gather from several sources. In this and other ways, we set a confused and incoherent example for other suppliers.

But other supplying countries have an interest in avoiding the spread of weapons to more states. The French government doesn't like the prospect of Spanish nuclear weapons, and neither the Germans nor the French could afford explicitly to use bombs as sweeteners for reactor sales, even if they wanted to. The French and Germans point out correctly that they now impose more stringent safeguards on exports than the IAEA requires, but they do not recognize, nor do we point out, that safeguards cannot be effectively applied to fissile material only a few hours away from a bomb; that is, such "safeguards" cannot give timely warning.

The principal precondition for us to influence other suppliers as well as importers is a clear, consistent policy: a set of signals which are green on some activities, red on others. We now flash red, yellow and green on practically everything.

But there are clear signals we can send and effective levers we can press. On the political and military side, we can help countries defend themselves against nonnuclear attack without resort to nuclear weapons. Our military sales program should be designed to discourage a nuclear defense and to make nonnuclear defenses more effective. And our alliance policy can strengthen guarantees against nuclear adversaries. For example, we can supply the South Koreans with improved short-range surface-to-air missiles and short-range precision guided nonnuclear weapons, and discourage their attempts to convert Nike Hercules into 200-mile surface-to-surface rockets which would be effective only with nuclear warheads and only against population targets.

On the economic side, we can design our export and export financing policy to affect an importing country's energy program considered as a whole, not piecemeal, by encouraging the use of nonnuclear energy and of comparatively safe forms of nuclear energy and by discouraging or penalizing the dangerous forms of nuclear energy that permit access to fissile stocks.

The effectiveness of the levers at our disposal can be illustrated by the extreme sensitivity of various programs in the non-weapon states of the Third World (where the impending spread is now most threatening) to simple alterations in the terms of financing. Korea, for example, has drastically cut back its nuclear program in response to a slight hardening in Canadian and American financial terms. And the effectiveness of our political and military levers is illustrated by the cancellation of the Korean reprocessing plant.

In sum, statements that we have no leverage mean that we don't want to press the levers we have, that we are not serious about proliferation. We don't think about the international consequences of digging ourselves deeper into a commitment to recycle plutonium, for example, by bailing out Allied General from its costly investment in reprocessing at Barnwell. We prefer to hang on to some quite inessential outworn conceptions of the nuclear fuel cycle and we are moving toward competing with the French and the Germans by giving away para-bomb capabilities.

Other governments have reason to doubt our claim that we unequivocally oppose proliferation. But actions against proliferation do cost something. It is only fair to ask whether they are worth the cost.

Will Slowing the Spread Cost More than It Is Worth?

Slowing the spread means reducing the demand for nuclear weapons by intelligent policies of alliance and of military sales and assistance. It means reducing the supply of nuclear weapons materials by sensible nuclear energy policy for our domestic as well as our foreign sales. On the supply side in particular, restrictions are often thought of as depriving us and other suppliers of enormous market benefits and imposing energy shortages on all of us, including the Third World countries now in the market for nuclear energy that is at least overtly civilian.

Nuclear energy has an important role to play, but its positive contributions will not make the difference between heaven and hell on earth. Its benefits have been puffed up from the start in ways that have greatly distorted its performance and made national energy programs follow something much less than the best path and timing for introducing nuclear energy into the total energy mix. A more sober program would benefit the security interests of the United States and ultimately the economic interests of the industry. Without the extensive conversion of uranium-238 into plutonium and the separation of plutonium from spent fuel, we can have enough coal and enough of the fissile isotope uranium-235 at reasonable prices to last us well into the second quarter of the twenty-first century. By then we should be able to make an intelligent transition to the use of abundant or renewable resources: a safe and economic breeder; or a safe form of fusion; or solar energy, whether in the form of solar electric power, biomass, or some other. We have time.

The contrary claim that we need immediately to add to the reserves of uranium-235 by the extensive use of separated plutonium in the current generation of light water reactors, and that we should now contract into the early use of the plutonium breeder, is based on bad economics. It ignores the way an increase in market prices generates a larger supply of specific scarce resources (by making them worth finding and exploiting), or a supply of substitutes, and at the same time reduces the demand.

In fact, the nuclear industry has suffered chronically from premature commitments based on exaggeration of energy demand, the demand for electric power, in particular the demand for nuclear electric power, and the derived demand for uranium and for enrichment services. This exaggeration applies to overseas as well as to domestic demand. And the impression of crisis has been encouraged further by understatements of the supply that might be made available at various prices and by the discouragement of supply that has followed from the wild swings in demand when excessive hopes have been deflated. In 1975, the AEC predicted 450 GWe[22] of nuclear capacity operating in the United States in 1985. In 1970, it predicted 300 GWe by that date. Today, on the basis of actual construction and orders, the Federal Energy Administration (FEA) expects 145 GWe or less. Given varied technical assumptions appropriate for the dates when the forecasts were made,[23] these predictions imply a cumulative need respectively for about one million, 500,000, or 220,000 tons of fresh uranium yellow cake if there is no recycling. The 80,000 tons that would be needed annually by the year 1985, if the AEC's 1970 nuclear power forecasts were right and we did not recycle, far exceeds the supply of low cost uranium that might be available at that time. The 33,000 tons that would be needed to fulfill the more sober FEA schedule during the year 1985 is quite in line with what is in prospect. ERDA has estimated that a rate of 33,000 tons can be available in the early 1980s at the low forward cost of $15 per pound.[24]

Much the same can be said about inflated forecasts of the need for uranium enrichment services; and about the longer term forecasts until the end of the century for both uranium and enrichment. European, Japanese, and Third World nuclear power forecasts have been similarly inflated. In 1957, Euratom forecast about 15 GWe of nuclear power in 1967 and about 50 GWe in 1975. In actuality there was 1.6 GWe in 1967 and at the end of 1976 there will be only about 12.2 GWe.[25] The Japanese in 1970 expected 60 GWe by 1985. They have officially cut this to 49 GWe and some Japanese experts expect it to be as low as 30 GWe.

The nuclear bureaucracy believes that overstating demand is much less harmful than understanding it.[26] This is not so. The exaggeration has severely damaged both national policy and the profitability of industry. Exaggerated uranium demand biases decisions toward plutonium recycling in the current reactors as well as in breeders. The inflated domestic demand for enrichment led us in 1974 to ban any new enrichment commitments to foreigners. This led to the present scramble overseas to get enrichment capabilities independent of the United States with an obvious resulting loss of U.S. control. Inflated market expectations have also cost the industry money. Chronic premature commitment has meant, in the United States, a loss to General Electric of $500 million to $600 million on 13 turnkey contracts; a loss of $.5 to $2 billion by Westinghouse depending on how it settles the legal claims of public utilities on its forward sale of uranium that it used to sweeten its reactor sales. Royal Dutch Shell and Gulf Oil, the two owners of General Atomic, have lost over one billion dollars on the latter's high temperature gas-cooled reactor.

It is hard to disentangle losses on commercial nuclear sales in company statements that, in general, merge those losses with profits on fossil fuel plants, military nuclear sales, or other industrial products. But it appears that Babcock and Wilcox, and Combustion Engineering, the other two major U.S. reactor manufacturers, have suffered respectively a cumulative loss on nuclear sales of about $100 million and $150 million; for 1976 each will have an estimated $10 million pre-tax loss. General Electric's pre-tax loss on nuclear sales in 1976 will be about $40 million. AEG Telefunken, part owner of Kraftwerk Union, lost DM 685 million ($274 million) on nuclear sales in 1974, and expected losses in "three figure millions" marks in 1975.[27] It is harder to determine Framatome's losses. As for reprocessing of light water reactor fuel, though very little has been performed, the losses have been impressive. General Electric's Morris, Illinois, plant which cost $64 million had to be abandoned without ever going into operation.[28] The Allied General Nuclear Services plant at Barnwell, owned by Allied Chemical, Royal Dutch Shell, and Gulf Oil, originally estimated to cost about $50 million actually has cost $250 million so far, and may take about a billion dollars in total to complete in accordance with current requirements. Getty's Nuclear Fuel Service plant in West Valley, New York, shut down for modification after about $30 million in gross sales. It might require some hundreds of millions just to dispose of the radioactive waste from its previous work. Getty wants to cancel some $180 million in reprocessing contracts it has accepted, since it estimates it will take $600 million to fulfill the contracts within regulatory requirements. The government-owned plant in Windscale, England, had troubles with the head end. The Eurochemic plant in Belgium has been shut down, and Europeans now judge that the recycling of plutonium will exceed the cost of getting fresh uranium fuel and that if reprocessing should be necessary for waste disposal, it will require subsidies from public utilities.[29]

In general it is plain that for the nuclear industry as a whole, profitability is still a vision of the future. Immense losses could be avoided by greater realism.

The collapse of expectations in domestic markets unfortunately has led to an aggressive campaign to sell to the less-developed countries (LDCs), where, in general, nuclear power is least economic: Nuclear electricity is highly capital intensive, efficient only in very large sizes and requires continuing highly sophisticated maintenance. The LDC reactor market, which the industrial powers might fight to share, is quite small, and the market for reprocessing plants is even smaller—1 percent or 2 percent of the reactor market. The heavily subsidized initial sales have been made on terms which worsen the problem of proliferation without any realistic prospect that the ambitious LDC long-term nuclear programs will be fulfilled. Yet in the past the French have talked of sales to the Third World of plutonium breeders which are more damaging and even less plausible for LDCs than the present generation of reactors which [the breeders] will exceed in capital costs, diseconomies of small scale, and sophistication.

The most urgent issue, if we are to restrict access to fissile material, is the use of plutonium as a fuel in current reactors. This has been argued for on grounds that it would (1) save a lot of money, (2) save much scarce uranium, (3) be essential for permanent disposal of radioactive wastes, and (4) be required now in order to get the plutonium breeder on present schedules. None of this is true. On the first point, the estimates of costs for separating plutonium and making it into fuel rods have multiplied tenfold in 10 years and are still highly uncertain and in controversy. On Vince Taylor's calculations, they exceed the estimated costs of fresh uranium fuel rods. Most important, even if plutonium separation were costless, it could make only a 1 percent or 2 percent difference in the delivered kilowatt hour cost of nuclear electricity.

As for point two, the conservation argument should be related to the economics: We are not impelled to extract plutonium from spent uranium fuel any more than we are presently moved to extract the enormous quantities of uranium from sea water. It depends on the costs. Fissile material is present in spent fuel in more concentrated form than in ore, but, by comparison with uranium ore, it is enormously radioactive. There are cheaper ways of getting uranium, by mining and even by a change in U.S. enrichment policy. (In unpublished work, Vince Taylor of PAN Heuristics has shown that the apparent uranium shortage of the 1980s has been effectively created not only by inflated projections of nuclear power and the derived demand for uranium but also by U.S. policies that (1) envision adding substantially over the next 10 years to an already immense government stockpile — worth $8 billion at current prices — of enriched and natural uranium, (2) leave an excessive amount of uranium-235 in the waste streams of the enrichment plants, thus inflating the amount of natural uranium that must be fed into the plants, and (3) force customers to stick to schedules for delivering uranium for enrichment which they contracted for before the recent substantial cutbacks in nuclear power programs both here and abroad.) But even if one were absurdly optimistic about the costs of using plutonium fuel for light water reactors, the private cost savings would be trivial. The political and social costs plainly dominate.

As for point three, plutonium separation would remove most of the longest-lived radioactive actinides, and so, it has been hoped, would economize in packaging and compacting wastes. However, spent uranium fuel can be stored without reprocessing and recent study indicates that the process of separation will contaminate much of the equipment, filters, solvents, etc. used and that the total volume and heat content of the waste so created and of the spent plutonium fuel which will require remote handling and geologic isolation will exceed those of the unreprocessed spent fuel.

On point four, the present schedule calls for ERDA recommendations on a commercial breeder in 1986. If the decision is positive, it is hoped that the first commercial breeder will start operating in the mid-1990s. We can, therefore, defer the decision on plutonium separation for at least five years.[30] In fact, the spent fuel would cool enough in that period to make separation easier and the savings would nearly pay for the storage costs. This fourth argument is, however, revealing. It is motivated in good part by a desire to force a positive decision on a commercial plutonium breeder — another case of premature commitment. The domestic U.S. decision on plutonium separation has obvious international implications and it is these that will impose the largest political and social costs.

Policies

The last year has seen a salutary ferment about changing policy so as to discourage nuclear proliferation. Proposals range from David Lilienthal's recommendation at one end, to stop all nuclear exports, through the bureaucracy's at the other, which suggests that we continue pretty much as we are. Rather than engage in a detailed analysis of this wide range of proposals, I will set down summarily a program indicated by my argument so far.

On the Demand Side

Slowing the spread of nuclear weapons means reducing the demand for them as well as restricting the supply of nuclear weapons material. Political and military policy on alliances, on nuclear guarantees, and on non-nuclear military sales and assistance should be directed to help in non-nuclear defense against non-nuclear threats and to provide nuclear guarantees against threats of nuclear coercion or attack. I have illustrated the sort or thing needed in my earlier remarks about South Korea. But such a policy has to be shaped country-by-country and does not lend itself to easy summary.

On the Supply Side

1. Deny access to readily fissionable material. We need to state as a general guide for U.S. domestic as well as export policy that it is our plain purpose to deny access by individual terrorists, either here or abroad, and to deny access by governments of non-weapon states to nuclear materials that can be readily converted to explosive use. This principle should be the basis for our negotiations in the suppliers group where we will then be able to say we not only advocate it but illustrate it. The general principle has implications spelled out in many more detailed policy suggestions.

2. Delay for at least 5 or 10 years any decision to separate plutonium in the United States.

3. Press actively for fuel cycle designs which would eliminate access to highly enriched uranium or chemically separated plutonium in power reactors and research reactors. Up to now, this has not been part of any design criterion.

4. Continue to deny export licenses for isotope enrichment facilities and plutonium separation plants.

5. Provide to any non-weapon state low-enriched uranium services at nondiscriminatory prices provided that the importer agrees (a) not to acquire further enrichment facilities or plutonium separation facilities, (b) to place all its nuclear facilities under IAEA safeguards, (c) not to acquire nuclear explosives, and (d) not to acquire fissile material quickly convertible to explosive use. We should make new commitments for the sale of nuclear technology only under these conditions. Though we have no shortage of enrichment capacity, it may be prudent to expand our enrichment capacity because it is critical for exercising control, and for assuring supplies of low-enriched uranium to importers who live up to their agreements. We should alter our perverse enrichment policy which has done much to create the appearance of a shortage of uranium and of enrichment. We should first start to reduce our $8 billion stock of natural and low-enriched uranium; second, permit customers to cancel or defer dates for delivering uranium to be enriched; and third, start operating our enrichment plants, subject to capacity constraints, so as to minimize the amount of uranium needed to produce nuclear fuel for our customers.

6. Where we supply low-enriched uranium to non-weapon states, either lease it or otherwise arrange for its return. (The Soviet Union apparently does this.) Spent fuel so returned would make

up a small percentage of the enormous radioactive wastes from our military program and our own domestic power program.

7. In the future, when centrifuge or laser separation facilities might otherwise become widespread, consider transfers of enrichment technology to an international or multinational center that would provide only low-enriched uranium (and not plutonium fuel) services to non-weapon states. However, do not encourage plutonium separation in such centers with or without the fabrication of mixed plutonium and uranium oxide fuel. If such centers shipped out separated plutonium to non-weapon states, it would be immediately available for explosives. And plutonium is much more easily separated chemically from fresh unirradiated mixed oxide fuel than from spent fuel. Low-enriched uranium is not an explosive. Plutonium separated from reactor fuel is.

8. Deny further assistance for critical experiments in national laboratories of non-weapon states, since these experiments involve access to unirradiated or only lightly irradiated, readily fissionable material. Where warranted, provide for U.S. or possibly multinational or international facilities for the conduct of critical experiments by non-weapon states.

9. Deny licenses for the export to non-weapon states of research reactors with highly enriched uranium cores or significant plutonium output unless the total nuclear program for an importing country will not permit it to derive enough readily fissionable materials for weapons.

10. Change Export-Import Bank policy so that its loans and the private loans it guarantees will support rather than defeat the preceding recommendations.

11. Offer further financial and technical assistance to IAEA to improve safeguards, but alter trilateral agreements to permit and require IAEA to report on the location, size, and chemical and physical composition of all stocks of readily fissionable material monitored under these agreements. The improvements in IAEA inspection to detect violations will be useful if, and only if, export agreements are altered so that accumulating readily fissionable material becomes a violation, whether accounted for or not. Presently, IAEA centers its attention on the "limits of error in material unaccounted for" ("LEMUF" in the jargon) without reporting on the legal accumulation of explosive materials.

The best maxim to keep in mind is that of Florence Nightingale: "Whatever else hospitals do, they shouldn't spread disease." On these complex issues it has been all too easy to advance resounding programs to slow the spread of weapons which actually speed it. That is how we got into the present fix. So Atoms for Peace, and so some of the incompatible clauses of the NPT. Using the eighteenth century language of natural law from our Declaration of Independence, the NPT asserts the "inalienable right" of all countries to peaceful nuclear energy — which includes, some exporters apparently feel, reprocessing. We have then the new natural right to Life, Liberty, and the Pursuit of Plutonium.

And now most recently each side in the last presidential campaign showed how the multinational form can distract from substance in slowing the spread. Each sometimes contemplated not only the return of spent uranium fuel but using multinational centers for making and distributing fresh mixed plutonium and uranium oxide fuels. Yet, plutonium for use in explosives is much more easily extracted from the fresh mixed oxides than from the spent uranium fuel. The word "multinational" tends to give many opponents of the spread a warm feeling all over, unless it is followed immediately by the word "corporation." But this cure would simply spread the disease. Here it is essential to focus our aim precisely on the substance rather than the symbol. Multinational centers for the distribution of bomb material will not help.

ENDNOTES - Wohlstetter - Spreading the Bomb

1. Isotopes of the same heavy element, such as uranium-235 and uranium-238, undergo the same chemical reactions at almost the same reaction rates and therefore cannot be separated by any known conventional chemical means, but so far only by an expensive, difficult, and time-consuming physical process that exploits slight differences in atomic mass. The fissile isotopes are those that are readily fissionable by slow or thermal neutrons as well as fast neutrons.

2. U.S. Senate, Committee on Government Operations, Hearings on S. 1439. testimony by Robert J. McCloskey, Department of State, June 16, 1976, p. 811.

3. Indeed, we attached a "related note" to our agreement with Spain of March 20, 1974, which said, "It is understood that the material subject thereto will not be used for any nuclear explosive device, regardless of how the device itself is intended to be used. . . ." We signed the note, but Spain did not.

4. For a more extended analysis, see Chapter III of *Moving Toward Life in a Nuclear Armed Crowd?* a Pan Heuristics report to the Arms Control and Disarmament Agency. A revised edition will be published by the University of Chicago Press.

5. For example, it said ". . . the development of more ingenious methods . . . which might make this material effectively usable is not only dubious, but is certainly not possible without a very major scientific and technical effort" (pp. 26-27), but also unequivocally that "the limit between what is safe and what is dangerous . . . will not stay fixed" in "what is sure to be a rapidly changing technical situation" (p. 30). U.S. Department of State, Publication 2497, March 16, 1946.

6. The committee included Oppenheimer and C. A. Thomas, who among the authors of the Acheson-Lilienthal Report were the two qualified to speak on the subject. Its statement was issued on April 9, 1946.

7. The ambivalence and inconsistency were present at the start. Like Szilard, who had been cautious about denaturing a few months earlier, Glenn Seaborg, whose team had discovered plutonium in 1941, signed the final draft of the Franck Report which stated flatly that "denaturalization of pure fissionable isotopes . . . [would] make them useless for military purposes."
Yet Seaborg, commenting on early drafts, had written, "Can't denature 49 by dilution with stable isotopes." "Forty-nine" was the wartime code for the element 94, plutonium. The James Franck papers, University of Chicago Regenstein Library.

8. "Nuclear Experts Give Warning on Build-up of Untreated Waste Fuel," *The Times*, London, May 25, 1975.

9. Guy Hawtin, "East Bloc Aids Bonn Anti-Nuclear Groups," *Financial Times*, London, May 22, 1976.

10. Address by Louis de Guiringaud, June 19, 1976, New York: *Service de Presse et d'Information,* 1976, No. 76/95, p. 3. In September 1976 the French cabinet reconsidered such dangers, though not as a result of any clear message from the State Department. Michel Tatu, *Le Monde*, September 9, 1976.

11. Lecture entitled, "The Fuel Cycle and the Export Situation," by Dr. G. Hildebrand, to visiting embassy representatives at the Kraftwerk Union plant in Mülheim, West Germany, on April 30, 1976.

12. "Spent Nuclear Fuel and Radioactive Waste," Statens Offentlige Utredningar, Document No. 32, Stockholm: Libervorlag, 1976, p. 43.

13. Carl Walske, "Nuclear Energy Environment in the United States," a paper presented at a conference in Madrid, Spain, May 4, 1976.

14. The Atomic Industrial Forum's Committee on Nuclear Export Policy, *U.S. Nuclear Export Policy*, July 21, 1976, p. 3.

15. Letter to Congressman Findley from Denis M. Neill, Assistant Administrator for Legal Affairs, Agency for International Development, Department of State, August 18, 1975.

16. The spent fuel had 13 kg of plutonium that was 95 percent, 110 kg that was 93 percent, and 331 kg that was 89 percent purely fissile.

17. Hildebrand, *op. cit.*

18. Memorandum from Oppenheimer to Farrell and Parsons, 23 July 1945, Top Secret; Manhattan Engineering District Papers, Box 14, Folder 2, Record Group 77, Modern Military Records, National Archives, Washington, DC. Declassified in 1974.

19. Memorandum to the Chief of Staff by General Leslie Groves, 30 July 1945. *Ibid.*, Box 3, Folder 5B. Declassified in 1972.

20. See Richard G. Hewlett and Oscar F. Anderson, Jr., *The New World, 1939/1946, Volume I, A History of the United States Atomic Energy Commission*, University Park, PA: The Pennsylvania State University Press, 1962, p. 321.

21. See, e.g., Walske, *op. cit.*, and Hildebrand, *op. cit.*

22. "GWe" means gigawatts, that is, thousands of megawatts of electrical capacity.

23. Estimates of uranium requirements vary with precise assumptions as to the percentage of uranium-235 left in the tailings by the process of enrichment, the rate of growth in reactors, the capacity factor or percentage of time the reactors are generating electricity; and such technical characteristics of reactor operation as fuel enrichment levels, fuel burnup levels, and frequency of reloads. These earlier estimates assume 80 percent capacity factors. The 1976 forecast assumes a 70 percent capacity factor. I assume .2 percent tails assay throughout.

24. John Patterson, chief of the Supply Evaluation Branch, Division of Fuel Cycle Production, "Uranium Supply Developments," a paper presented at the Atomic Industrial Forum Fuel Cycle Conference, Phoenix, Arizona, March 22, 1976. More recently ERDA has estimated an "attainable" U.S. production capacity of 47,000 tons of yellow cake at the $15 cost level by 1985 and 60,000 tons by about 1990. According to *Nucleonics Week*, September 23, 1976, ERDA summed up, "The information we have today indicates that there is a good possibility that uranium will be available at reasonable prices."

25. End 1976 estimates are taken from *Nuclear News*, "World List of Nuclear Power Plants," August 1976, pp. 66-79.

26. See U.S. Congress, Joint Committee on Economics, *Review and Update of Cost-Benefit Analysis for the Liquid Metal Fast Breeder Reactor*, May 27, 1976, Washington, DC: U.S. Government Printing Office, 1976, p. 18.

27. *Financial Times*, London, December 9, 1975. American loss estimates by R. Cornell of E. F. Hutton.

28. *Chemical Engineering*, January 6, 1975, p. 68.

29. *Nucleonics Week*, July 22, 1976, p. 8.

30. On ERDA's projections the plutonium then available from

light water reactor fuel will be over three times more than the amount needed by breeders at the end of the century. Moreover, even ERDA's low growth projections for the breeder presume an unrealistically early and rapid build-up of commercial breeders.

The Buddha Smiles:
U.S. Peaceful Aid and the Indian Bomb (1978)

A Summary

Roberta Wohlstetter[1]

From Albert Wohlstetter, Victor Gilinsky, Robert Gillette
and Roberta Wohlstetter, eds., *Nuclear Policies: Fuel
without the Bomb,* Cambridge, MA: Ballinger Publishing
Co., 1978, pp. 57-72. Courtesy of the Wohlstetter Estate.
The unabridged version of this report is available from
www.albertwohlstetter.com/writings/BuddhaSmiles.

THE PATH TO THE INDIAN NUCLEAR EXPLOSION

The Indians decided in 1956 to produce and separate plutonium long before they decided to make a nuclear explosive. So
did the British, and so did the French. The Indians had separated
plutonium in their Phoenix reprocessing plant by 1965, years
before they had any power reactors in operation, and the decision
to separate plutonium had no persuasive economic justification.
It was tied to plans in the 1950s for developing an Indian breeder
reactor that is still remote in the 1970s. However, India's plans to
produce plutonium, with only a tenuous and vague relation to a
realistic program of power production, were not very different
from the vague expectations of the United States and the United
Kingdom in the 1940s and the 1950s about the utility and even the
necessity of plutonium in the production of electric power.

Whether or not Indian plutonium ever became important
in the generation of electricity, the separated plutonium would
carry India most of the way toward a nuclear explosive. The same
would be true for any country acquiring substantial amounts of
separated plutonium. Neither our export policy nor that of any
other country had recognized this fact, or seriously tried to cope
with its consequences, until President Ford's *Statement on Nuclear
Policy* of October 28, 1976.

First Steps to a Bomb

It appears on the basis of public evidence that sometime in late
1964 Prime Minister Shastri had given Homi Bhabha, the director

339

of the Indian Atomic Energy Commission (IAEC), permission to reduce the critical time needed to make a nuclear explosive. Bhabha had stated some time before his death early in 1966 that India could make a bomb in eighteen months, and by the spring of 1966 some Indians were claiming it could be done in six months. Evidently Shastri's permission set in motion work on design of an explosive system and preparation for testing of the nonnuclear components. This preliminary activity would still leave open the question as to whether India would assemble a nuclear explosive, and also the question of whether, with the explosive at hand, India would choose to detonate it. Shastri's private relaxation of his public stance was motivated primarily by concern about China, and the decision to go ahead with military components was given greater impetus by the withdrawal of American military aid in the fall of 1965.[2]

Shrinking Critical Time Versus Preserving the Option

India illustrates that, with cumulating changes that shrink the critical time, only a minor event is needed to tip the decision in the timing for exploding a nuclear device: for example, a mere "tilt" toward Pakistan by the United States rather than a reversal of alliance, or a need for a distraction from transient domestic economic troubles such as a railroad strike. The basic decision to come close to making a bomb has to do with more fundamental, long-term interests.

One frequently talks of a given government trying to preserve the option to become a military nuclear power. But the phrase is misleading. A sovereign government cannot surrender such an option in perpetuity, even if it renounces the possibility with fewer qualifications than in the Nonproliferation Treaty (NPT). It can always change its mind and, starting from where it stands in nuclear technology, proceed to get weapons. The Indian case, however, illustrates the more important phenomenon, namely, that a government can, without overtly proclaiming that it is going to make bombs (and while it says and possibly even means the opposite), undertake a succession of programs that progressively reduce the amount of time needed to make nuclear explosives, when and if it decides on that course. This can be done consciously or unconsciously, with a fixed purpose of actually exploding a device or deferring that decision until later. But it is more than holding out the option. It involves steady progress toward a nuclear explosive.

The Indian program also illustrates the linkage of decisions among antagonists to get nuclear explosives, and also the fact that the linkage is not a mechanical phenomenon but is related to a network of competing national interests and domestic factions. The Chinese nuclear explosion in October 1964 followed the Sino-Indian conflict in 1962, which itself had been a flaring into the open of the rivalry between the two Asian powers previously smothered in the rhetoric of coexistence. The Chinese explosion generated a policy debate among Indian domestic factions that led more or less steadily to a nuclear explosion nearly ten years later. The beginnings of the nuclear explosive program were clearly visible for at least eight years. The Indian explosion in turn, following Pakistan's disasters in the 1971 war, may confirm Pakistan's decision to get nuclear explosives, "even if," as Prime Minister Bhutto said, "we have to eat grass."[3] The consequences of both the Chinese and Indian explosions involved not only such direct links, but a more generalized lowering of the taboo.

The Rhetoric of Peace and Economic Development

The rhetorical separation, as if in a dichotomy, of peaceful and military uses of nuclear energy, as well as the rhetorical identification of investments in civilian nuclear energy with economic development and catching up with the advanced countries, form a substantial part of the background of cumulative changes that made India's nuclear explosive program easier.

The identification of civilian nuclear energy with economic progress is sometimes made in self-consciously symbolic terms with no pretense at hard economic argument, but merely as an invocation to modernity. Nuclear technology, it is said, is the most important or most characteristic development of the present age—the "nuclear age." Therefore it becomes the essential component for catching up with the advanced countries, from which India and other less developed countries have only recently been liberated. Dr. Bhabha, the first director of India's nuclear energy program, argued steadily in this vein against the economic arguments of Francis Perrin, I. M. D. Little, and others. He was aided by the rhetoric of Atoms for Peace, and his early implementation of the Indian civilian nuclear program found strong support in the U.S. Agency for International Development (USAID) and the U.S. Atomic Energy Commission (USAEC) of the 1950s as part of a general and generous U.S. policy to aid Third World development.

341

The Rhetoric of Disarmament

The Indians also use the rhetoric of nuclear disarmament and "general and comprehensive" disarmament as ultimately justifying their production of nuclear bombs: (a) nuclear armament would put them in a powerful position to argue for nuclear disarmament (a standard argument by intending nuclear powers), and (b) the only alternative to India's nuclear armament is unattainable, namely, the disarmament of the superpowers and of their own major antagonist China. Indian rhetoric here exploits the insincerities and the hopes expressed in the rhetoric of the weapons powers themselves. Off-the-record interviews at crucial periods make plain, however, that Indian officials would put no trust even in an agreement by China to disarm totally. No such promise to disarm will substitute for an Indian nuclear weapons program because, they say, there is no way of verifying the nonexistence of Chinese bombs in the vastness of China's territory.

This is the reality underlying India's part of the debate on Article VI of the Nonproliferation Treaty.

In spite of the long gestation period, when the Indians were plainly moving toward a nuclear explosive, U.S. experts both inside and outside the government have tended to take Indian arms control rhetoric at face value. One excellent student of proliferation (Harold Feiveson) reported in 1973, shortly before the explosion, on a consensus of U.S. experts that the Indians would not explode a nuclear device.

National Sovereignty in the Less Developed Countries

Frequently in arms control negotiations we think of countries like India as hostile to any surrender of sovereignty in an alliance, but as quite willing to accept limitations by a truly universal international authority. The Indians, as they prepared their nuclear program, were sedulous attendees at Pugwash conferences, as well as highly vocal participants in the Eighteen-Nation Disarmament Committee. However, it is apparent that India, like many other less developed countries, has been among the most jealous of surrendering any part of its sovereignty to an international inspectorate. It has fought against potential harassment by IAEA inspectors and used some of the indirectness of the trilateral relationship to keep as much freedom of action as possible, and specifically freedom from restrictions imposed by suppliers. Its agreement on nuclear cooperation with the United States and the IAEA is unique in that safeguards apply only to the enriched uranium fuel supplied by the United States and not to equipment.

Ambiguities, Ambivalence, and Sanctions

The ambiguities of agreements on the Indian nuclear program are central to the problem. Did the Indians violate any agreement in literal terms? Even if they have not violated the exact terms of an agreement, or even if they can argue that they did not, did their actions represent a dangerous shrinking of critical time?

The U.S. government has made clear since 1966 that there is no distinction between a peaceful and a military explosive. But the Indians act as if the nonexclusive "and/or" were in fact a dichotomous "either military or peaceful, but not both." This poses problems for sanctions.

Precisely because Indian behavior did not overtly and plainly violate the letter of agreements as the Indians chose to construe them, the decision to impose sanctions was vulnerable to arguments that the sanctions imposed costs not only on the Indians but on the United States as well. U.S. suppliers were heavily involved, following the spirit of the original open-handed Atoms for Peace program and later of Article IV of the Nonproliferation Treaty, which promised "the fullest possible exchange" to help civilian nuclear energy programs. (Even though Article IV was directed especially at parties to the Nonproliferation Treaty, it also stipulated "due consideration for the needs of the developing areas of the world." And though the rights and duties under Article IV are limited by the obligation in Article I, "not *in any way* to assist non-nuclear weapons states to manufacture or otherwise acquire ... nuclear explosive devices," many nonnuclear weapons states in this context conveniently forget Article I and the fact that this is a nonproliferation treaty, not a nuclear development treaty.) The machinery of grant aid and concessionary loans was nowhere more utilized than in the Indian case. In its agreement with India the United States also undertook various obligations to send enriched uranium for reloads frequently enough to keep the reactors operating, and to provide continuing technical assistance. These are contingent, of course, upon India's fulfilling its own obligations. However, if India does not do so, and if the United States stops assistance, it does so at some domestic cost to American business. At the very least American business will be smaller than if we take a relaxed view of the customer's obligation to eschew nuclear activities with a potential for military application.

Besides American business, there might also be objections from members of the relevant congressional committees and the media, who would feel, after the so-called Pakistani tilt, that the U.S. government was picking on India. Other factors also reinforce the reluctance to impose sanctions: some members of the U.S. bureaucracy think that the Indians were right; some were involved in negotiating the original agreements with all their ambiguities; and some, as always, find it pleasanter to distribute rewards rather than punishments and dislike being cast in the role of "heavy," perhaps especially with respect to a less developed country that seems intermittently to be on the brink of famine, and find the specter of responsibility for bringing on such a famine hard to live with. For example, a breakdown in electric power might decrease fertilizer production, which in turn might affect the crops in Gujarat.

Although the United States had and continues to have considerable leverage in the continuing Indian need for help from General Electric when India runs into trouble with operating the boiling-water reactors at Tarapur, and in the Indian need for slightly enriched uranium, heavy water, and other supplies, it is easy to understand why we have been reluctant to use the leverage.

U.S. Ambivalence

There is in any case an ambivalence in U.S. policy. We have been against proliferation in general, but not necessarily in particular. Nonproliferation is only one of a number of foreign policy goals, and those who stress it excessively tend to be regarded as fanatics, "one-issue men." If in fact the occasions for application of sanctions are blurred by ambiguity, and the effectiveness of the sanctions themselves seems weakened because we no longer hold a monopoly on the services we might threaten to withhold, and because our influence over other suppliers is limited, policy is likely to be affected by a feeling of the inevitability of the spread. From there it is a short step to reviving the comforting doctrines, popular especially in the late Fifties, that the spread would not be so bad anyway. If we do not actually enjoy it, we might at least relax.

Our own ambivalence and that of other supplier countries and the implicit rivalries among them make for a failure to press for very clear bilateral understanding as to what is proscribed. Canadian and U.S. temporizing in the mid-1960s illustrates this point. Unilateral understandings, no matter how explicitly transmitted, are no substitute. Trudeau's plain talk to Indira Gandhi is one example. Mrs. Gandhi was not talking — and not listening either. Canada's recent decision to stop aid on the RAPP II reactor has finally drawn a clear line between safe and dangerous activities. Its actions clearly say that a nuclear explosive is not exclusively peaceful.

The U.S. intelligence function is weakened by the fact that it is not very clear about what should be looked for (a violation? a legitimate activity that is "unsafe"?) and whether there is much point in looking for it, for there may be no clear policy to do something with the information and no urgent need expressed in advance. May 18, 1974, marks a failure to clarify our policy on response more than a failure of intelligence.

Nuclear Versus Conventional Forces

The Indian program proceeded slowly over a very extended period under a nominal cover, but with many obvious indications that India intended at least to explode a device and get a few primitive weapons. Partly because of this manner of proceeding, the Indians are a long way from having a serious nuclear capability against their major adversary, China. Moreover, they suffer from many geographical strategic asymmetries for this purpose. It is conceivable that they may proceed with a missile program at the same stately pace. On the other hand, they do have sizable ambitions in the world strategic environment (the title of their defense journal is *India in the World Strategic Environment*). Though extremely poor on a per capita basis, the country is large enough to have a gross national product that can support a substantial military program, and possibly in the future a much more extensive military program than a simple last-resort capability usable only in response to an overwhelming conventional attack and with little hope of surviving nuclear attack. It might even go for a blue-water navy.

The Indian conventional forces have been considerably strengthened. The military in the mid-Sixties plainly regarded nuclear weapons as a rival to such conventional expansion and therefore did not support it. But as such conflicts frequently are resolved, the military got its conventional expansion and the Foreign Office and the Atomic Energy Department got their nuclear explosives, with consequent increasing military support for the nuclear program. An expanded military nuclear program might in the future get wide general support.

Nonalignment and Joint and Individual Guarantees

The Indians continued to maintain a nonaligned stance in the mid-Sixties long after the conflict with China and regional antagonisms had transformed the meaning of nonalignment. Nonetheless, it made them reluctant to try to get an unequivocal unilateral guarantee from the United States, which might appear to line them up with the United States. They actively sought a joint guarantee from the Soviet Union and the United Slates, even though some high officials recognized that such guarantees among potential adversaries are worth considerably less than alliance guarantees. In the end the Nonproliferation Treaty was followed by an extremely weak statement of guarantee by the weapons states that they would take "appropriate action" according to the decision of the U.N. Security Council. When the treaty was passed in the Security Council, India as well as France abstained, though it was the end point of a sequence of actions seeking a guarantee in which India had played a leading role.

POLICY IMPLICATIONS OF THE INDIAN-CANADIAN-U.S. EXPERIENCE IN NUCLEAR COOPERATION

This case history has implications (a) for decisions on future U.S. cooperation with India itself and these are of course the policy choices most directly illuminated; and (b) for the choice of policies for stopping the spread of nuclear weapons to other countries as well as India, and this more general application of the U.S.-Indian experience is perhaps even more important.[4]

Some causal connection naturally exists between the policy we adopt toward India in the future and the influence we can exercise on other countries. Our policy toward India sends a message to other countries that may be more persuasive than declaratory statements about the rewards and penalties for actions that might violate the letter or spirit of our antiproliferation policy. But even apart from this direct effect of our Indian policy on our policies elsewhere, it is apparent that the sequence of events leading up to the Indian explosion in May 1974 had a widespread and immediately recognized significance as a major challenge to policies that had been directed at transferring nuclear technology for peaceful uses only while discouraging or preventing its military application. In the four years since the Indian explosion international awareness of this challenge has deepened. It has not, as some expected, dissipated. In fact, in spite of all that has been written about the Indian nuclear program, the implications of its history are not yet widely understood. Yet they are directly relevant for much of the current debate on nuclear export policy.

Stopping Drifting Governments vs. Stopping Governments That Are Committed from the Start

It is frequently argued today that there is no point in constraining exports of plutonium separation plants or uranium enrichment facilities or even in limiting exports of plutonium or highly enriched uranium themselves. There is no point, and it may even be bad, the argument runs, because almost any country committed to getting nuclear weapons can get them by itself, for example by designing and building a production reactor.[5] After such a facility (say, a simplified version of the Brookhaven Graphite Research Reactor taking four or five years to build and using natural uranium) is fully operational, it will produce plutonium in the spent fuel that might yield material for one or two bombs a year.[6] Such a country could also design and build a reprocessing facility for extracting plutonium from the irradiated fuel rods.[7] If we do not export facilities for producing such highly concentrated fissile materials or the materials themselves to such countries that are intent on getting nuclear weapons, we will compel them, it is said, to do it on their own. It would be better for the United States to supply these under safeguards.

This line of reasoning, which is sometimes buttressed by a reference to the Indian example, has many weaknesses. In fact, an examination of the Indian experience reveals a key flaw in the argument. It is essential to consider not merely governments that have made up their minds to get nuclear weapons and to get them perhaps at any cost. That list is likely to be very small indeed

347

at the present time, as it has been in the past. More important is the much larger list of governments that at any given time have not made up their minds at all, or that have not even seriously considered a nuclear weapons program, or that have considered it and quite sincerely rejected it.

That larger list is the one that policy must principally address: the countries that can drift toward a military capability without any intention of arriving at it, and yet that may adopt a civilian program that ultimately places them within days of acquiring material for nuclear explosives. The Indian experience illuminates that process of drifting toward a bomb. Canadian and U.S. help — transfers of facilities, equipment and material, advisory scientific and engineering services, training of Indian personnel, financial subsidies and loans—formed a major ingredient of the Indian program that was shortening critical time to make an explosive. And this help was given before and after the Indians revealed a strong interest in nuclear explosives. It continued after the time when Indian officials were formally and informally issuing statements that the Indian nuclear program had shortened the time remaining before they could get an explosive, and while the time announced was growing shorter and shorter.

During this period both the United States and Canada made public announcements indicating that "exclusively peaceful applications" excluded by definition explosives of any kind, and the Canadians made many private reminders of this point. However, in advance of the actual Indian explosion, neither Canada nor the United States insisted that the Indians themselves publicly agree with them, and still less did either government demand that India eschew forms of nuclear research and nuclear electric power activity that would provide them with stocks of plutonium or simple compounds of it, and thus bring them closer to a nuclear explosive. Nor did the United States or Canada ever explicitly say that stocking plutonium was illegitimate.

Canada waited until after the explosion to insist on India's disavowal of a nuclear explosive program, and it was only in 1976 that both governments indicated that civilian activities involving stocks of plutonium might themselves have to be banned. The latter course of action finally faces up to the question of stopping a drift toward the bomb by countries not yet committed.

Current Pure Intentions Are Not Enough

A point closely related to the preceding one is also clearly confirmed by the Indian experience: The fact that a government receiving nuclear transfers has the purest of motives at the time of receipt, that it intends to use this aid solely for purposes of advancing civilian electric power, and that it abhors nuclear weapons, offers no assurance that it will not change its mind, and provides no warrant therefore for favored treatment in granting aid which will shorten the time to make an explosive. Because such aid makes it technically easier and cheaper to get nuclear weapons and means that the progress toward nuclear weapons can be more ambiguous, or concealed, and politically less risky, it also facilitates a change in intention responding to new external or internal pressures. Only a policy that restricts the forms of nuclear energy (in research or in production of nuclear power) to those that exclude national control of highly concentrated fissile material can deal with future intentions to make nuclear weapons and make it less likely that present good intentions will change.

This particular lesson is relevant today to the situation of several countries (Japan, Sweden, West Germany) whose current intentions are on all the evidence exemplary, but whose programs of nuclear cooperation with us and other suppliers involve an accumulation of plutonium and highly enriched uranium.

"Safeguards" are Necessary but Not Sufficient

Bilateral and international safeguard systems are essentially arrangements for accounting and inspection. They are intended to deter bomb manufacture by assuring early warning and permitting timely counteraction.[8] The Indians resisted safeguards with very substantial, though partial success. Some of their facilities are not or will not be safeguarded at all, even though they involve technology that is at least directly descended from some Canadian and U.S. imports: for example, the heavy-water reactors under construction at Madras. Other facilities given them by Canada and materials given them by the United States, though restricted to peaceful uses, were unsafeguarded: so CIRUS and the U.S. heavy water used in it. Nonetheless even if this unfortunate laxity had been avoided, safeguards would not have been effective in fulfilling the purpose of providing timely warning, if the Indians had been permitted to separate plutonium, to fabricate it into mixed plutonium and uranium oxide fuel and in the course of these activities, to stock significant quantities of plutonium or simple compounds of it under their control for use either in electric power or research. To prevent the sudden manufacture of a nuclear explosive without warning requires not only safeguards on essentially all research and power facilities that could contribute substantially to the eventual accumulation of fissile material, but restrictions on the accumulation itself.

The mixed plutonium and uranium oxide fuel requirements implied by such extensive nuclear electric power programs as those of Japan, Spain, and many other countries that do not have nuclear weapons today are very large, and the plutonium or simple compounds of it (such as mixed plutonium and oxide fuel) are very quickly usable in an explosive. Any attempt therefore to limit the working stocks of such plutonium under national control to an amount that would be strategically insignificant is bound to be unacceptable. Such restrictions would make these countries much more dependent and their reactor operations much more liable to interruption than they are presently or would be with slightly enriched uranium fuel.

Fresh low enriched uranium stocks under national control are more likely to be susceptible to limitations satisfying both the user's desire for adequate working stocks and the international community's desire to keep stocks of highly concentrated fissionable material out of the hands of non-weapon states. It is also true that international control and also close, even continuous inspection of spent uranium fuel would intrude less into the essential operation of reactors.

Policy Toward Countries That Make Nuclear Explosives in Spite of an Agreement to Restrict Nuclear Activities to Peaceful Uses Only

The Indians used a facility given by Canada and some U.S. heavy water to make and test a nuclear explosive. They did this in both cases under a peaceful uses-only agreement, and the U.S. State Department makes clear that our agreements had always intended to exclude such a development.[9] Nonetheless we are faced with the fact that, whatever our or their good intentions, they have produced at least one nuclear explosive. What should be our course of action?

On one side it can be argued that the damage is done. India has carried through the program, and we might just as well, as in the case of the French, acknowledge the fact and treat India as a full-fledged member of the club, along with the preceding five members. Or we might reduce our embarrassment somewhat by accepting India's distinction between peaceful and military explosives and, to preserve the fiction, provide them, so to speak, with only an associate membership in the club. If we do not do so, India can go ahead with its own program, having advanced so far, and moreover, as a potential supplier of nuclear technology, India could proceed to help other countries to follow in its footsteps with a nuclear explosive program. There is no point simply in punishing India, and encouraging it to be irresponsible.

On the other hand, such arguments, though tempting, have disturbing implications for future aspirants to nuclear weapons. For what it will suggest to them is that we will oppose their getting nuclear weapons and even threaten dire consequences if they do, but should they be successful in ignoring our opposition and our threats, we will never execute the threats, and never impose any sanctions, but only reward them with membership or associate membership in the club. If in addition we permit civilian activities that bring countries close to manufacture of nuclear explosives in any case, then the interval of unpleasant opposition from us before we reward them will be gratefully short. The truth is that we oversimplify when we say that "the damage is done" as soon as a country explodes a nuclear device. Much more damage will be done if we do nothing to make the country regret its action. This is especially true if there has been a violation of the sense of an agreement. But even for those few countries that have never disavowed an interest in nuclear bombs, we should make clear in advance that in case they do, success will not be met by a welcoming committee. It will cost them something.

Policy Towards Countries That Do Not Disavow Intentions to Make Nuclear Explosives, "Peaceful" or Otherwise

There are about a half-dozen countries of importance that have refused to ratify the NPT or to make a separate statement that they will forgo even "peaceful" nuclear explosives (India, Pakistan, Argentina, Brazil, Israel, Egypt). The Indian case illustrates the dangers of continuing nuclear cooperation with such countries and remaining content with unilateral statements to the effect that such nuclear cooperation is premised on the recipient's not making nuclear explosives at all or at least not making them with the aid furnished in a specific U.S. nuclear agreement. I believe that U.S. policy should refuse nuclear cooperation unless these countries give up nuclear explosives altogether, and not just nuclear explosives made using our help. This means no slightly enriched uranium, no heavy water, no reactor sales, no advisory services, no nuclear transfers of any sort.

A Policy for Both India and Pakistan

Indian military concern centered primarily on China rather than Pakistan, and in fact as distinct from rhetoric, not at all on a threat from the two superpowers. Indian arguments in international forums about superpower disarmament were in good part a way of justifying India's own armament and nuclear explosive program. The Indians were interested in help from the superpowers against China, and superpower disarmament was rather irrelevant or inconsistent with that goal. Although they have made constant reference to the evils of vertical proliferation from the mid-Sixties on, the evidence suggests that this was merely a debating point. It is, moreover, doubtful that substantial superpower disarmament would in general influence a country not to undertake a nuclear weapons program, if it is concerned about nuclear threats from other sources.

The Indian experience confirms that countries that by choice or circumstance stand outside alliance systems are particularly liable to decide to make nuclear explosives, if it is easy for them to do so and if the international environment changes adversely. The Indians' cautious attempts to get nuclear guarantees jointly or separately from the United States and the Soviet Union yielded nothing very substantial, and U.S. conventional military assistance was withdrawn just about the time that Indian concern about the Chinese nuclear explosive program was most acute. A policy to discourage nuclear proliferation has to deal with legitimate or perceived military challenges, both direct and indirect, to the countries concerned.

The new administration in India has begun with a rejection of nuclear weapons and an expression of doubt about the usefulness of "peaceful" nuclear explosives for India. Morarji Desai seems likely to be skeptical of the sort of technocratic idyll that has animated the nuclear energy program in India in general and that in particular might give some shred of plausibility to such dubious gadgetry as Plowshare.[10] The nuclear bureaucracy in

352

India has been most closely linked with the Congress Party, with Nehru and with Mrs. Gandhi. This is a particularly opportune time, then, to induce a revision in Indian thinking and to move it away from nuclear explosives.

However, there are obstacles other than the Indian nuclear bureaucracy. First of all, our own nuclear industry and bureaucracy fostered many of the Indian positions on nuclear energy and rationalized them for the American Congress. A change in policy in India presupposes a very clear-cut change in American policy at the working level, as well as at the top. Second, India has some legitimate defense concerns, and insofar as it has any continuing worry about a Chinese nuclear threat, it may require some sort of assurance of help. For the United States to provide this assurance may be hard to manage. Third, India nonetheless has an interest in seeing to it that Pakistan, an irredentist power with respect to parts of India, and an adversary with whom India has been engaged several times in the short history of Indian independence, does not itself get nuclear weapons. There is no doubt that Pakistan has been powerfully moved to get nuclear explosives by India's own explosive program, and that Pakistan's desire to improve its conventional forces is motivated mainly by its adversary relation with India.

All of this suggests that it is essential to try to use a formal abandonment of India's nuclear explosive program as a lever to get a similar commitment from Pakistan about nuclear explosives, and vice versa. And in a similar way, it is important to try to arrange for the simultaneous abandonment by Pakistan of its plans for a reprocessing plant and for the abandonment or indefinite deferral by India of its plans to reprocess spent fuel.

We should assure India of nuclear material equivalent in amount to that which it might derive from reprocessing spent fuel. This equivalent would be in the form of natural or slightly enriched uranium. We should also offer to take back India's spent uranium fuel, and to lease rather than sell slightly enriched uranium fuel rods in the future.

The plutonium content of the spent fuel has an uncertain value that will depend on the relative costs of deriving fissile material from spent fuel, compared to the costs of freshly mined uranium. It may have a negative value. We should offer India, if it likes, an equity interest in any use of its spent fuel to extract fissile material. That is, if in the future it is profitable to extract plutonium from spent fuel, we should give India a credit for the positive value of the plutonium as an offset for the cost of the slightly enriched uranium which we supply as a substitute. If this risky venture of reprocessing is nevertheless undertaken and there are losses, India, with an equity stake, would have a debit to add to the price of slightly enriched uranium. India should not be obliged to take the equity risk in reprocessing, but making it clear that India has the opportunity will make it clear also that it is highly uncertain that plutonium embodied in spent fuel has a positive value.

If India does not explicitly disavow a nuclear explosive program, and if it does not accept full fuel-cycle safeguards, the United States should stop nuclear cooperation with India.

If India does disavow nuclear explosives and accepts full fuel-cycle safeguards, we should supply it with slightly enriched uranium and heavy water only if it also agrees not to accumulate plutonium or highly enriched uranium, and not to maintain facilities that could quickly provide stockpiles of such highly concentrated fissile material. A more restricted immediate policy initiative would ask India to defer any further contracting into a program yielding stocks of highly concentrated fissile material, while we negotiate with it to provide equitable less dangerous substitutes for the highly concentrated fissile material or the facilities yielding it.

ENDNOTES - Roberta Wohlstetter - The Buddha Smiles

1. I want to thank Professor Albert Wohlstetter, as well as several participants in the seminar where this paper was first presented, in particular, Professor Robert Bacher of the California Institute of Technology, Professor Leo Rose of the University of California at Berkeley, and Professor Stanley Wolpert of the University of California at Los Angeles.

2. For expansion and documentation of these points, see Chapter 5, "From Civilian Power to Military Power," in *The Buddha Smiles: Absent-Minded Peaceful Aid and the Indian Bomb*, Monograph E-3, Los Angeles: Pan Heuristics, April 1977, available from *www.albertwohlstetter.com/writings/Buddha Smiles*.

3. A statement by Bhutto in 1965 when he was Foreign Minister quoted by Patrick Keatley, *The Guardian* (London), March 11, 1966.

4. I draw here on Albert Wohlstetter, *The Spread of Nuclear Bombs: Predictions, Premises, Policies*, Monograph E-1, Los Angeles: Pan Heuristics, November 1976, revised 1977.

5. See for example the views of Peter Hermes, State Secretary of the Foreign Ministry, West Germany, and Hans-Hilger Haunschild, State Secretary of the Research and Technology Ministry, as summarized in *Nucleonics Week*, February 10, 1977, p. 9:

> Bonn hopes that Washington will see the [Brazil-German] deal in a different light after a more detailed study of its safeguards, which as German government officials are quick to emphasize, go beyond those of the non-proliferation treaty. German philosophy is that *a country really wanting the nuclear bomb will get it anyway.* The Bonn belief is that it is better to extend cooperation at a time when it is still possible to persuade the recipient country to accept international controls rather than turn down the threshold country's request for technology, letting it reach its nuclear goals through its own development work, without IAEA inspections. As it is, "the [German-supplied] Brazilian nuclear facilities will be fully subject to IAEA controls."

See also C. Starr, W. Haefele, and E. Zebroski, draft paper on "Nuclear Power and Weapons Proliferation," March 1976; E. Zebroski, contribution to panel on "U.S. Nuclear Policy and International Security," California Seminar on Arms Control and Foreign Policy, December 7, 1976; and a 58-page Westinghouse study cited by *Nucleonics Week*, March 31, 1977, as showing that there are "multiple avenues" other than by way of LWR plutonium that can be followed by a "*determined* non-nuclear weapons state" (italics added).

6. John Lamarsh, "Construction of Plutonium-Producing Reactors by Small and/or Developing Nations," April 30, 1976, reproduced by the Library of Congress, Congressional Research Service, June 4, 1976.

7. John Lamarsh, "On the Extraction of Plutonium from

Reactor Fuel by Small and/or Developing Nations," July 19, 1976, reproduced by the Library of Congress, Congressional Research Service, October 14, 1976.

8. *Laws and Regulations Governing Nuclear Exports and Domestic and International Nuclear Safeguards*, Message from the President of the United States, May 6, 1975, Washington, DC: U.S. Government Printing Office, 1975, p. 35; General Alfred Starbird, Assistant Administrator for National Security, Energy Research and Development Agency, "Statement before the Senate Committee on Government Operations," January 29, 1976, in *Hearing on S-1439: The Export Reorganization Act 1975*, Washington, DC: U.S. GPO, 1976, p. 408; International Atomic Energy Agency, INFCIRC/153 (1971); B. Sanders and R. Rometsch, "Safeguards against Use of Nuclear Materials for Weapons," *Nuclear Engineering International*, September 1975, p. 683; and Chapter 3 of Albert Wohlstetter *et al.*, *Moving Toward Life in a Nuclear Armed Crowd?* report to the Arms Control and Disarmament Agency, Los Angeles: Pan Heuristics, April 1976, p. 72.

9. Robert J. McCloskey, U.S. Senate Committee on Government Operations, *Hearings on S-1439*, p. 811.

10. Morarji Desai has been on record for some time against nuclear weapons for India. He is quoted as saying, "We can drive out any aggressor even without the bomb." He adds: "If China were to throw an atomic bomb on the Indian border, she would create an impenetrable barrier for herself." See Hari Ram Gupta, *India-Pakistan War 1965*, Vol. 2, Delhi, India: Hariyana Prakashan, p. 100.

In his first public press conference since his election as Prime Minister he also expressed doubt as to whether a nuclear explosive program would be useful for India and advised returning to "cottage industry." See Morarji Desai, quoted by *Newsweek*, April 4, 1977, p. 36.

Signals, Noise and Article IV (1979)

Albert Wohlstetter, Gregory S. Jones, and Roberta Wohlstetter

Excerpted from *"Why the Rules Have Needed Changing,"* in *Towards a New Consensus on Nuclear Technology*, Vol. 1, Summary Report Prepared for U.S. Arms Control and Disarmament Agency, Los Angeles, CA: Pan Heuristics, July 6, 1979, pp. 32-45. Courtesy of the Wohlstetter Estate and Gregory S. Jones. The report from which this essay is excerpted is available from *www. albertwohlstetter.com/ writings/NewConsensus*.

Military Signals and Civilian Noise

The problem presented by the spread to many countries of civilian stocks of highly enriched uranium or plutonium, or facilities that could quickly produce these materials, is that such stocks would carry these countries so far along the path that leads also to nuclear explosives that from the moment that their military purpose became unambiguous, the additional time to get nuclear explosives would be too short for any feasible inspection system to provide timely warning. And timely warning, it has long been recognized, is the most that a feasible international inspection system can provide. The International Atomic Energy Agency (IAEA) has no police force. Moreover, one of the major factors affecting a government's decision to make a nuclear explosive will be not only the extra time from the point at which its military purpose becomes clear, but also the additional political risks and indeed the increment in resource costs above the costs expended for at least a plausibly pure civilian commercial activity.

The timely warning concept is not an innovation recently thought up by President Ford near the end of his term in office. It is an essential part of what is meant by "effective safeguards." It was universally recognized as such in the 1940s when civilian nuclear power first came to be talked about seriously. It was intermittently forgotten in the 1950s but restored to a central place in the 1960s, and in particular when the IAEA began to elaborate its Nuclear Nonproliferation Treaty (NPT) safeguard system in detail. Safeguards do not mandate any penalties but *only* timely warning. That is what affords at least the possibility of counteraction. Without even timely warning, we would have little besides reminiscence.

What is new so far as the public (and even many public officials) is concerned is the official acknowledgement[1] in explicit quantitative terms that power reactor plutonium is *not* safe but can be used to make nuclear explosives reliably yielding 1 to 20 kilotons in even a very simple implosion device. The implication immediately follows that the timely warning requirement precludes the accumulation of stocks of separated plutonium or simple compounds of it in non-weapon states. This should also remind us that the same preclusion applies even more obviously to highly enriched uranium.

Since the central aim of "effective safeguards" as explicitly defined in the IAEA information circulars on NPT safeguards[2] is timely warning, signals of a military program must be detected and identified early enough; but they must also be unambiguous enough, that is, stand out clearly enough from the noisy background of civilian activity, to permit response either by international agencies, by regional allies, or by regional adversaries who have been relying on promises that the country observed will not acquire nuclear weapons. Programs and facilities overtly "dedicated" (to use the current jargon) to the purpose of getting bomb material present of course the least ambiguous signals. Some nuclear activities, facilities and equipment that are regarded as having legitimately "civilian" applications may nonetheless advance a country significantly toward a military weapons capability. That is to say, they diminish the additional costs entailed by a decision to get the bomb. They reduce the remaining time it would take to get nuclear explosives, and they reduce also the additional political risks of exposure and counteraction. For usable warning time must be measured at best from the moment that identification or differentiation from the noise is *reliably* made. For some sorts of response, the signals have to be not merely unambiguous enough, but they must also be public, *i.e.*, usable without excessive risk of destroying sources.

Confusions of "Peaceful Use" with "Exclusively Peaceful Use"

The rhetoric of Atoms for Peace has tended, for countries aspiring to or undecided about whether to get nuclear weapons, to enhance the political utility of the ambiguity inherent in nominally civilian activities which in fact have a dual military and civilian character. With the one explicit exception of Plowshare (nuclear explosives for civil engineering), Article IV of the NPT is frequently interpreted as conferring legitimacy on all civilian activities, simply because they have some civilian function.[3] This is so even if they are not exclusively civilian in their import. As a result, Article IV is often interpreted as obliging all advanced countries to transfer any civilian technology except Plowshare, no matter how far such transfer might carry the recipient country toward a military nuclear capability. Even some *Agreements on Nuclear Cooperation* between countries have been rather careless in failing to include or to stress the adverb "exclusively." And the trouble goes back to the beginning of the nuclear era, when we formed the habit of talking as if a civilian use automatically substituted for military utility, rather than sometimes complementing or enhancing it.

However, the legislative history of the IAEA Statute shows that "peaceful" was intended to mean "exclusively peaceful," as well it might in the commonsense interpretation. In the United States, for example, the legislative history makes clear that U.S. Senators have always been concerned that a civilian use should not also assist a country to get nuclear bombs. One illustration is the exchange between Senator Sparkman and Secretary of State Dulles in the 1957 *Hearings* on the IAEA. The Senator asked, "Just what certainty is there that a particular peacetime project might not have a future military use as well as a peaceful one?" Secretary Dulles deferred to Atomic Energy Commission Chairman Strauss but gave his

> untutored impression that since the material furnished will not itself be of weapon quality, and since the making, converting of it into weapon quality or the extraction of weapons quality material out of it as a byproduct would be an elaborate and difficult and expensive operation, that could not occur without the knowledge of the agency and that the violation would be detected.

According to the Secretary's impression, in short, the material furnished, or derived from what was furnished, would be "denatured."

Senator Sparkman's concern addressed the plain common sense meaning of "Atoms for Peace" and of various *Agreements on Nuclear Cooperation*. He assumed, but wanted to be assured, that the material would have only a peaceful use. In the same way, in reading the Nonproliferation Treaty, we ought to keep in mind that the peaceful uses it wants to encourage are intended to be exclusively peaceful, not also military.

Now Article IV of the NPT refers to the undertaking by all parties to the Treaty "to facilitate" and the right of all parties "to participate in the fullest possible exchange of equipment, materials and scientific and technological information for the peaceful uses of nuclear energy." Indeed, it refers to such rights to the peaceful pursuit of nuclear energy, in the language of 18th-century natural law, as "inalienable." The contention was made by many of the delegates to the Iran Conference on Transfer of Nuclear Technology at Persepolis in the spring of 1977 that this "inalienable right" includes the stocking of plutonium or other highly concentrated fissile material and was therefore violated by President Carter's proposal to delay commitment to unrestricted commerce in plutonium. This particular Third World rebellion might have been a little more convincing if the President of the American Nuclear Society had not played a leading role in the writing of their declaration, and if some of the countries complaining most bitterly about a supposed violation of a most sacred part of the NPT had not themselves neglected ever to sign or ratify the NPT.

However, Article IV explicitly states that the inalienable right of all parties to the Treaty to the peaceful use of nuclear energy has to be in conformity with Articles I and II, and it is these Articles that are what make the Treaty a treaty against proliferation. In Article I the nuclear weapons states promise not to transfer or "in any way to assist, [or] encourage ... any non-nuclear weapons state to manufacture" nuclear explosives. If the "fullest possible exchange" were taken to include the provision of stocks of highly concentrated fissile material within days or hours of being ready for incorporation into an explosive, this would certainly "assist" an aspiring nonnuclear weapons state in making such an explosive. No reasonable interpretation of the Nonproliferation Treaty would say that the Treaty intends, in exchange for an explicitly revocable promise by countries without nuclear explosives not to make or acquire them, to transfer to them material that is within days or hours of being ready for incorporation in a bomb. Some help and certainly the avoidance of *arbitrary* interference in peaceful uses of nuclear energy are involved. However, the main return for promising not to manufacture or receive nuclear weapons is clearly a corresponding promise by some potential adversaries, backed by a system to provide early warning if the promises should be broken. The NPT is, after all, a treaty against proliferation, not for nuclear development.

At the *Windscale Inquiry* in 1977, British Nuclear Fuels Limited (BNFL) and the U.K. Department of Energy took the position that England was obligated under Article IV to perform plutonium separation services for non-weapon states.[4] And Mr. Justice Parker, in his Report on the Inquiry, agreed with BNFL. He said in fact that the NPT is "on its face a straightforward bargain"[5]: an exchange of every assistance by the nuclear weapons states in the development of nuclear energy for a promise by the nonnuclear weapon states not to make or get nuclear weapons. This assumes, among other things, that the non-weapon states have no interest of their own in seeing that other nonnuclear weapon states do not acquire nuclear weapons, that South Korea does not care if North Korea has the bomb, that Syria is unconcerned about a nuclear Iraq, that Iraq is not concerned about Iran, that Pakistan is not worried about India, and that Belgium is not concerned about the Federal Republic of Germany. This, of course, is an absurdity, since it is not hard to find recent statements to the contrary in almost all of these countries. Moreover, it flies in the face of the actual history of the genesis of the NPT, which started as a rather straightforward bargain, proposed by the Irish Republic, *among non-weapon states* to increase their safety by mutual agreement to abstain from getting nuclear weapons.[6] Article IV was one of the embellishments added in the course of negotiation.

There are, of course, powerful commercial incentives for suppliers who are engaged in selling nuclear services and various nuclear materials and facilities to interpret Article IV as imposing as little constraint as possible. In the short term at least, the "fullest possible exchange of equipment, materials and services" is the greatest encouragement to nuclear sales. The purchasers might have mixed motives. Some, as President Carter himself suggested on April 7, 1977, clearly have used or intend to use civilian facilities to develop a nuclear explosive capability. Some, undoubtedly, believe that civilian nuclear transfers will be of enormous economic benefit or, perhaps, that they can stave off economic disaster. They may be interested in the fullest possible exchange, especially if Article IV can be interpreted as requiring nuclear suppliers to subsidize these transfers. During the negotiation of the treaty, in fact, Italy proposed inserting language to that effect, but the motion was defeated.

The report of the *Windscale Inquiry* insisted that the nuclear weapon states have the obligation, even if it might involve some expense or loss.[7] By great good fortune it happens that Britain's fulfillment of its obligation, as interpreted by Mr. Justice Parker, is alleviated somewhat by the fact that the billion dollar contract it has arranged with the Japanese involves a cost plus commitment by the Japanese. The loss sustained then can only be negative.

Time, Warning Time and Article IV

The interpretation of Article IV is by no means a trivial matter. If, in fact, technological transfers can bring a "non-nuclear weapon state" within weeks, days or even hours of the ability to use a nuclear explosive, in the operational sense that "non-nuclear weapon state" will have nuclear weapons. The point is even more fundamental than the fact that effective safeguards mean timely warning. A necessary condition for having timely warning is that there be a substantial elapsed time. But if there is no substantial elapsed time before a government may use nuclear weapons, in effect it *has* them.

Consider, for example, the situation of a government engaged in a very short war with an adversary that has no nuclear weapons. If its adversary appears to be winning, and [if] the government has plutonium in explosive concentrations and the capability of assembling an implosion system developed by years of experiments with nonnuclear explosives in the rapid compression of heavy metal, then from the standpoint of the adversary who had been winning, it would be facing a government which to all practical effect had nuclear weapons.

Or, consider the case of a government which is not at war, but is capable of quickly assembling a nuclear device to use or threaten to use against another government without such a capability. Once again, there is no practical difference between the coercion it could use or the threat it could execute from what a nuclear power might manage.

Or, one might even consider a case where both of two adversaries were that close to potential assembly and use. The instability might be at least that which we associate with some possible confrontations between two vulnerable nuclear powers.

The point may be driven home if we recall that in 1947, for example, the United States stored its plutonium weapons in disassembled form. Moreover, since the design was quite

362

primitive and used much more inconvenient components than are commercially available today, the process of putting the weapon together took many hours. In fact, it took a longer time than would be needed today by a well prepared government laboratory to make highly concentrated fissile material ready for insertion in a nonnuclear assembly for compressing it rapidly.[8] The United States did have nuclear weapons in 1947. And if the rules are relaxed enough, so can nonnuclear weapon states today.[9]

There have been a number of recent statements suggesting as implausible "an overnight scenario" by which is meant apparently a contingency in which a non-weapon state assembled a weapon in less than a day or so.[10] There is, of course, nothing magical or even anything of critical importance in the interval of 24 hours. For purposes of policy against the spread of nuclear weapons, it would be bad enough if a prospective nuclear power were able to get ready in a few days or a few weeks. In suggesting that it would be a great failure in proliferation policy if the rules made it legitimate for a non-weapon state to come within a day or so of readiness to use nuclear weapons, we surely do not imply that having months or years of warning would not be valuable. Nonetheless, it is worth noting on the plausibility of the overnight scenario that the United States assembled the very first nuclear bomb for the Trinity test in 26 hours and this included time out to get some sleep.[11]

At the *Windscale Inquiry*, representatives of BNFL suggested, as an alternative to dependence on slightly enriched uranium, that those governments (which BNFL said were moved by a concern for "energy independence" and a desire to obtain the conservation benefits of plutonium) be allowed to purchase plutonium separation services, but that the plutonium be sent out in the form of plutonium fuel rods, perhaps pre-irradiated or made radioactive in some other way; and in any case, that such fuel be placed under strict international storage and control and released only according to international criteria. The report of the *Windscale Inquiry* in paragraph 17.6 seems to accept this suggestion as a partial alleviation of the fact, which it there recognizes, that plutonium fuel would bring non-weapon states closer to nuclear weapons.

But this proposal has several difficulties, including some that involve an intolerable legal tangle in the interpretation of Article IV and some that would involve difficulties intolerable to the purchaser.

To illustrate the latter point, this proposal would make these countries more rather than less dependent on outside sources for an uninterrupted fuel supply, and their reactor operations would be much more liable to shutdowns than with the slightly enriched uranium fuel which it would be feasible and safe to supply.[12] Presumably, BNFL's proposal would mean keeping *strategic* quantities of plutonium out of the hands of governments that do not have nuclear weapons. If such arrangements were practicable at all, keeping the amount of plutonium under national control to less than a bomb's worth or a few bombs' worth would allow these countries almost no working stocks of MOX or separated plutonium under their own control. With only one MOX reload as a working stock for each reactor, and assuming they do not fabricate their own MOX fuel, in the 1990s Japan and the Federal Republic of Germany would each have more than 1,000 bombs' worth of plutonium quickly accessible and even Spain would have 650 bombs' worth.[13] (That is, on their plans up to recently. If they fabricated their own MOX fuel they would have even more plutonium, in forms still more directly usable in nuclear weapons.) But less than one thousandth or one 650th of a country's annual reload requirement could hardly be called a working stock.

The American experience with India offers strong evidence that even supplies of slightly enriched uranium fuel that would have been enough to guarantee operation of the Tarapur reactor for over two years have been deemed by the Indian government to be below emergency levels, dictating resupply by air and other speedy action.[14] Moreover, the debate in the 1950s on the draft of the IAEA Statute focused on similar though less drastic proposals for deposit of fissionable materials with the IAEA. Even then it was made clear that to give such powers to the IAEA was unacceptable to governments like India, as threatening their economic life and their independence.[15] It seems extremely unlikely that governments trying to secure a little more energy independence by the use of plutonium fuel than if they only used natural or slightly enriched uranium would accept a new international institution depriving them of any significant national control of such plutonium, thus making them more rather than less dependent on outside powers for continuity of supply.

Fresh low enriched uranium stocks under national control are more likely to be susceptible to limitations satisfying both the user's desire for adequate working stocks and the international community's desire to keep stocks of highly concentrated fissionable material out of the hands of non-weapon states. It is also true that international control and close, even continuous, inspection of spent uranium fuel would intrude much less into the essential operation of power or research reactors, yet serve an important function in providing early warning of diversion.

The proposal also makes a chaos out of the interpretation of Article IV proposed by BNFL and Justice Parker (and most of the vocal attendees at the Persepolis Conference). That interpretation of Article IV, it will be recalled, had it that "every assistance" — that is, any transfer whatsoever except for an actual weapon — was required by Article IV. Even though the first paragraph of Article IV states that the use of nuclear energy it contemplates must be "in conformity with Articles I and II of this Treaty," which prohibits transfers that would "in any way … assist … non-nuclear weapon states to manufacture or otherwise acquire nuclear weapons," Justice Parker's report says that this does not exclude the transfer of the service of separating plutonium. Mr. Parker says quite correctly that at the time of the signing of the Treaty, many of the parties to the Treaty believed that the development of nuclear energy contemplated under Article IV included the production of plutonium. In fact, it is not hard to find documentation for that statement, including statements specifically mentioning the transfer of *metallic* plutonium. The fact that the parties to the Treaty did not understand that power reactor plutonium was not and could not be "denatured," explains how they could have accepted both Article IV and Articles I and II, to which Article IV is subject. However, it is also obvious that many parties to the Treaty believed that they would not be subject to any of the constraints involved in the technical "fixes" BNFL and the report propose. Surely no government expected to receive fuel in pre-irradiated form and many, if not most, expected to fabricate plutonium fuel themselves, and to be handling metallic plutonium. The government of Canada, for example, a non-weapon state which is a party to the Treaty, fabricated plutonium fuel in the early 1960s for use in its NRX research reactor. To insist that governments be deprived of plutonium except in the form of already fabricated fuel rods, would be to deny them "every assistance."

The only way out of this dilemma is to recognize that "a non-proliferation treaty should not contain any provisions which would defeat its major purpose."[16] That statement was made during the hearings on the NPT before the Senate Foreign Relations Committee by the U.S. spokesman who apparently himself did not understand that power reactor plutonium metal was directly usable in the bomb, and had mentioned it as one of the things he thought was consistent with Article IV.

The operational meaning of Article IV is not an academic matter. If suppliers could legitimately make any nuclear transfer other than that of a fully assembled weapon, then this would radically transform the situation both of warning signals and of the sanctions they might evoke. For there to be a signal of a violation, the activity signaled has to be illegitimate. But if Article IV is not subject to the constraints of Articles I and II, in effect there may be no violations.

As for sanctions, the implications here are worth stressing.

Sanctions and Article IV[17]

Ambiguities as to whether an activity is "safe" and civilian, or "dangerous" in its military implications, not only confuse and reduce warning. They weaken and can totally frustrate sanctions.[18]

For a dozen years now, U.S. spokesmen have indicated that our agreements on the peaceful use of nuclear energy have always implicitly excluded the manufacture of nuclear explosives.[19] The Canadian government has said the same. When the Indians conducted a nuclear explosion, they described it as "peaceful," and not a violation of any agreement either with Canada or with the United States. The Canadian government, adhering to the commonsense meaning of its agreements on nuclear cooperation with India, took immediate steps to administer sanctions. They stopped essentially all nuclear cooperation not only under the agreement covering the CIRUS research reactor, but also on those covering the CANDU power reactors at Rajasthan. The United States, on the other hand, did not follow suit. It continued its nuclear cooperation with India, and indeed in 1976 Hearings before the Nuclear Regulatory Commission, the Department of State held that if the United States did not continue its shipments of slightly enriched uranium to India under its *Agreement on Cooperation* covering the Tarapur reactors, the *United States* would be in violation; and that this would free the government of India to do whatever it wanted to, not only with the future plutonium it might accumulate from that reactor, but also with the plutonium it had accumulated in the past.[20] The present as well as the past Indian administration has indicated it takes a similar position.

In fact, a casual survey of the debates in Parliament and the Indian press revealed the prevalence of the view in India that the United States is or would be in violation, but failed to turn up any suggestion that the Indian government had violated the agreement on CIRUS in making and testing its nuclear explosive.

Of course, most of our agreements now explicitly exclude the manufacture and testing of a completed nuclear explosive. The point of this example, however, is more general. If an activity that brings a country very close to a nuclear weapon, and that stops just short of its assembly, is legitimate, then by assumption, there is nothing wrong with it. The government of that country has not violated the agreement. Moreover, *it is the application of sanctions by the supplier that would be a violation of the agreement.*

Increase of Civilian Nuclear Noise through Laxity in Project Economics

The practice of promoting and undertaking civilian nuclear activities which may confer prestige but have no strict economic justification has increased the noise background which serves as a potential cover for military activities. The IAEA has as part of its charter the mission of accelerating and enlarging the benefits of civilian uses of nuclear energy, with special regard for the developing countries. It is worth observing, however, that the principal international agency charged with financing international economic development, namely, the International Bank for Reconstruction and Development, has refused to finance nuclear projects in the less developed world (and not only the most dubious projects like small reprocessing plants or the cumulation of fissile stocks likely to be idle for decades) because it wants to support economic development rather than status or prestige. Nuclear electric power is in general highly capital intensive, efficient only in very large sizes and requires continuing highly sophisticated maintenance, characteristics which do not in general fit the needs of less-developed countries. Expenditures for using plutonium fuel in breeders are in general even more inappropriate. However dubious the civilian value of some nuclear projects, their military applicability may be quite definite. The most familiar example is Plowshare, which has yet to demonstrate a realistic economic application, but which — because of the laxity of economic analysis applied to such projects — has served as a nominally civilian cover for an activity with obvious military implications. In this case, the lack of rigor in the economic analysis, indeed the nearly total absence of any economic analysis at all, has reinforced the error involved in ignoring the point that "Atoms for Peace" means "exclusively for peace." These particular atoms for "peace" are in fact likely to be useful exclusively for war. Article IV of the NPT therefore excludes "peaceful" nuclear explosives.

Plowshare, however, is merely the most familiar case. The careless way in which nuclear establishments in the mid-1950s and at the beginning of the 1960s decided to separate plutonium and to accumulate it for the distant and uncertain date at which it might be used for the initial load of a breeder reactor, ignored any rigorous economic criterion for investments over time. A rigorous criterion would maximize the productive use of current resources and so increase the resources available for future generations. When India decided in the mid-1950s to invest in a separation facility and in stocks of plutonium which in essence would be economically idle for many decades — until the hoped-for appearance of a thorium breeder, or near-breeder — this was a waste of capital in a developing country where capital is particularly scarce. Yet the activity served to increase the noise level and the opportunities and ease for a decision to make military nuclear explosives when circumstances changed.

Take the example of India: It has frequently been said that there is very little connection between programs for nuclear electricity and the spread of nuclear weapons to more countries. And the prime example of this lack of connection is sometimes said to be the Indian bomb program, which used plutonium from their CIRUS research reactor. On the contrary, the Indian program illustrates the connection. The CIRUS reactor was intended from the beginning to produce plutonium as well as to offer facilities for research and training. Both the plutonium and the research and training were connected with nuclear electric power plans. The research and training were, as one might expect, connected indirectly. For a large-scale power program, men needed to be trained in operating reactors, in handling radioactive materials, in fabrication of fuel, in safety measures, and in understanding the physics and engineering of related nuclear processes. CIRUS was an important part of that. Moreover, the Indians intended to develop their own natural uranium burner reactors on the Canadian model, moderated by heavy water, and studies and experiments with CIRUS were part of the program of designing such power reactors. Finally, the plutonium was intended from the start to be separated and stocked for use in near-breeder and breeder power reactors.[21] In short, the CIRUS reactor and the Phoenix separation plant were, from the beginning, part and parcel of an ambitious nuclear electric power program.

These long range plans paralleled in a general way (with some modifications for exploitation of specifically Indian resources of thorium) the model of nuclear power development current in the industrial countries: to begin with burner reactors, and to make a transition to breeders, using the plutonium from the burner reactors for the initial fuel loading of the breeders. The fact that such production and separation of plutonium followed the general model of Canada and the U.S. itself in this respect gave the Indian plans an apparent legitimacy. It made less likely that anyone would question whether the plutonium would be used in an explosive. Later, after the Sino-Indian war and the Chinese bomb test (and after nuclear explosives for civil engineering had been presented by the U.S. as a plausible agenda item at the Second International Conference on Peaceful Uses of Atomic Energy), the Indians contemplated the use of the plutonium from CIRUS under the alternative, apparently legitimate rubric of "Plowshare." (By as early as 1966 Canada and the U.S., in response to rumors of Indian interest in "peaceful" nuclear explosives, said in public that any nuclear explosive had a clear military use.)

In the case of Plowshare, the cover of legitimacy was too transparent to escape international notice and eventually a sizeable international response. The Indian explosion provoked a more immediate response, particularly by Canada. However, the apparent legitimacy of the initial plans for the use of plutonium from the CIRUS reactor for a future breeder served very well in bringing the Indians to a position where they required very little additional effort to shift to "peaceful" nuclear explosives from plutonium stocked for breeder power reactors. The fact that such plutonium stocks were justified by a quite unrealistic economic and technical program for an early breeder did not distinguish it sufficiently from India's other nuclear programs with a civilian purpose; and the universality of similar long-range programs in other countries helped explain why it was never noted that such programs were not exclusively civilian in the technologies they made accessible.

Finally, such neglect of the military potential implicit in these civilian programs is made easier by the fact that the transfers involved are small ones, shipments of heavy water and the like, and training in reprocessing for small numbers of nuclear engineers. These can be handled at middle or even lower levels of the bureaucracy, where high policy is rarely in mind. When the transfers come up for approval at higher levels, their small scale is reassuring to the policymaker. Surely they do not constitute a mortal danger. In fact, they seem like a reasonable item or trinket for barter for the good will of a friendly country, and the good will of one's counterpart in the bureaucracy or political hierarchy of that country.

But it is precisely in this way that the policy on spreading civilian nuclear energy as a substitute for military nuclear energy dissolved into incoherence and the furtherance of military nuclear activity during the late 1950s. And it is always in danger of dissolving.

Plowshare has for a long time been a rather transparent cover for a military purpose. However, it seems that decisions to stock separated plutonium for the breeder began as sincerely but badly conceived economic measures. Many other countries besides India, including Japan, decided very early to accumulate plutonium, not for recycle in light water reactors, but for the breeder. These early decisions were made with little economic analysis, on the basis of quite unrealistic anticipations of the dates at which breeders might be of commercial importance. In India, however, these early decisions made on other than military grounds served to prepare for a program of nuclear explosives. More recent decisions to acquire either stocks of plutonium separated elsewhere, or a national separation plant, are likely to be from the outset more self-consciously related to military plans. For example, Pakistan, which has no reactors requiring fuel enriched by either uranium or plutonium, sometimes insists that the separation plant it is purchasing from France is purely civilian in intent, and on the other hand sometimes says that she will be glad to give up plutonium separation, provided that the superpowers abandon their own nuclear weapons.[22] Which rather directly, if inconsistently, acknowledges that Pakistan's purpose in separating plutonium is only to make nuclear weapons to balance those of "Nuclear Powers" and that this purpose would be served equally by the destruction of everybody else's nuclear weapons.

ENDNOTES - Wohlstetter *et al.* - Signals, Noise and Article IV

1. "Reactor Plutonium and Nuclear Explosives," briefing paper by Robert W. Selden reported by Robert Gillette as presented to representatives of nuclear industry and foreign governments, November 1976, Meeting of the American Nuclear Society and Atomic Industrial Forum, Washington, DC. See Gillette, "Military Potential Seen in Civilian Nuclear Plants," *Los Angeles Times*, June 26, 1977.

2. International Atomic Energy Agency, Information Circular/153, p. 28; and *Safeguards Technical Manual*, IAEA-174, 1976.

3. See Arthur Steiner, "Article IV and the 'Straightforward Bargain'," PAN Paper 78-832-08, in Wohlstetter *et al.*, *Towards a New Consensus on Nuclear Technology*, Vol. 2: *Supporting Papers*, ACDA Report No. PH-78-04-832-33, Marina del Rey, CA: Pan Heuristics, July 6, 1979.

4. The BNFL view of Article IV reflects this interpretation widely preferred by the nuclear industry and nuclear agencies of other countries as well. See, for example, "U.S. Nuclear Export Policy," statement by the Atomic Industrial Forum's Committee on Nuclear Export Policy, July 21, 1976. It also appears to be the view of the Director General of the IAEA.

5. *Report by the Hon. Justice Parker*, presented to the British Secretary of State for the Environment, in *The Windscale Inquiry*, Vol. 1, Report and Annexes 3-5, London: Her Majesty's Stationery Office (HMSO), January 26, 1978.

6. See Steiner, "Article IV and the 'Straightforward Bargain'."

7. *Windscale Inquiry*, p. 18.

8. Albert Wohlstetter, "Spreading the Bomb without Quite Breaking the Rules," and History of the Strategic Air Force, typescript, Vol. 1, unclassified portion in Air Force history archives.

9. On this point, see Albert Wohlstetter *et al.*, *Swords from Plowshares, op. cit.*

10. See, for example, Carl Walske, "Nuclear Power and Proliferation," speech delivered to the International Conference on Nuclear Power and the Public: A European-American Dialogue, Geneva, Switzerland, September 27, 1977.

11. Arthur Steiner, "Trinity, the First Overnight Bomb," Pan Heuristics Paper 78-832-09, February 1978.

12. Our comments here do not address the question as to what extra costs would be imposed on the purchaser by the various methods of making the fuel radioactive, nor the question as to how effective such technical "fixes" might be.

13. Chap. 1, "The Military Potential of Civilian Nuclear Energy," in *Swords from Plowshares.*

14. March 25 Order By the Nuclear Regulatory Commission in the Matter of India, to Export Special Nuclear Material, Docket XSNM 805, KSNM 845, Transcript, pp. 4ff.

15. Dr. Bhabha rejected the draft proposal which gave the IAEA the power "to approve the means to be used for chemical processing of irradiated materials recovered or produced as a by-product, and to require that such special fissionable materials be deposited with the Agency except for quantities authorized by the Agency to be retained for specified nonmilitary use under continuing Agency safeguards." (AEA/CS/OR/28, p. 6.) "In our opinion," Dr. Bhabha continued, "the present draft gives the Agency the power to interfere in the economic life of States which come to it for aid. . . . It therefore constitutes a threat to their independence, which will be greater in proportion to the extent that this atomic power generation is developed through Agency aid" (IAEA/ CS/OR/7, pp. 49-50).

16. Hearings on the NPT before the Senate Foreign Relations Committee, July 1968, p. 39.

17. See Arthur Steiner, "Safeguards, Sanctions and Signals," PAN Heuristics Paper 78-832-08, April 1978; and "Article IV and the 'Straightforward Bargain'," *op. cit.*

18. On this, see Wohlstetter *et al.*, *Swords from Plowshares, op. cit.*

19. See testimony of Robert J. McCloskey, U.S. Senate, Committee on Government Operations on S.1439, June 16, 1976, p. 811.

20. Acting Assistant Secretary, Bureau of Oceans and International Environment and Scientific Affairs.

21. See Roberta Wohlstetter, Seminar on U.S. Peaceful Aid and the Indian Bomb, Santa Monica, CA: Seminar on Arms Control and Foreign Policy, December 1976, revised August 1977; "The Buddha Smiles: Absent Minded Peaceful Aid and the Indian Bomb," Monograph 3 in *Can We Make Nuclear Power Compatible with Limiting the Spread of Nuclear Weapons, op. cit.*; and *Swords from Plowshares, op. cit.*

22. See, for example, *Dawn Overseas*, Islamabad, June 19, 1977: "Mr. Bhutto said Pakistan was ready to cancel its deal with France if the Nuclear Powers gave a solemn pledge to destroy each and every nuclear weapon."

Nuclear Triggers and Safety Catches, the "FSU" and the "FSRs" (1992)

Albert Wohlstetter

Unpublished note, February 6, 1992, available from the Hoover Institution Archives, Albert and Roberta Wohlstetter Papers, Notes, Box 121, Folder 1. Courtesy of the Wohlstetter Estate.

February 6, 1992

The U.S. and other Western leaders have been celebrating the breakup of the evil empire, the Former Soviet Union, or "FSU"; and the end of the Soviet nuclear threat to the West. But they sometimes seem to be continuing to try nostalgically to keep the old Empire—or most of it—together, under Moscow's control. They seem even to be trying to preserve the General Staff and the unified Soviet military responsible, if at all, to Moscow. Or if not, to that quite insubstantial ghost of Empire, the Commonwealth of Independent States (the CIS). Which is to say, responsible to no one. The Soviet General Staff seems to be the only entity of the FSU which doesn't need the qualifier "Former."

Aside from nostalgia, it is the fear that the disintegration of the FSU might quicken the spread of nuclear and other weapons of mass destruction that most often motivates Western efforts to keep Moscow in charge. We should indeed worry about an increase in the number of centers capable of deciding independently to launch nuclear weapons. But our leaders' fears aren't that precise. *That's* part of the trouble.

In its vague form, this fear was one of the main justifications for their support of Gorbachev and Communist rule. They needed same existing national entity that could sign nuclear arms control agreements. Lithuania, Latvia, Estonia, Ukraine, *et. al.* weren't national entities. Now that the former Soviet republics (the FSRs) do exist, and we recognize them, Western leaders continue to support Moscow. They have substituted Yeltsin (or possibly the General Staff) for Gorbachev, and the Russian Republic for the Soviet Union.

They have been pressing the non-Russian FSRs to transfer all nuclear weapons to the Russian Republic. The FSRs such as Ukraine plainly don't feel they need nuclear weapons to deter an unprovoked nuclear attack by the United States. (That was never a plausible fear in the Soviet Union itself.) Many of the political leaders of the FSRs have indicated they want to be free of nuclear weapons. However, several of the FSRs are uneasy about allowing the Russian Republic, whose dominance they have only just escaped, to be the only FSR which could make an unimpeded decision to launch—or threaten to launch—nuclear weapons. They see that as a threat to their continuing independence.

Ukraine, for example, has for decades been a site for the development and manufacture of nuclear weapons, not to mention chemical and biological weapons. Ukraine is likely to want to maintain some of the facilities they have, or build similar ones in the future. It seems the arrangements the U.S. government has been pushing offer incentives for the spread of independent decision centers for the production and use of weapons of mass destruction. The Administration doesn't want Ukraine *et al.* to have nuclear weapons, but apparently it *does* want Russia to have them.

The Administration has made statements to the effect that it wants to see Russia keep nuclear weapons, even if they're aimed at us.

In December 1991, Secretary Baker wound up in Brussels at the end of a long trip that took him to Moscow, Bishkek, Alma Ata, Minsk and Kiev. He held a press conference where he was asked,

> Mr. Secretary, you said a minute ago that you were not unambiguously in favor of Russia becoming a non-nu-clear power because you said you weren't prepared to walk away from the concept of deterrence. Can you be a little more specific as to who the Russian nuclear weap-ons are deterring?

Secretary Baker answered:

> No, and I won't right now be any more specific with you about whom our weapons are deterring. But over the past forty years they have served as a substantial and significant deterrent, and I would like to see zero weap-ons targeted on the United States, but I'm not prepared today here, having said that, to subscribe to the philoso-phy of de-nuclearization. That's all I was saying.

How's that again? He and some of his advisors, like the Director of Policy Planning, have been clearer. However, on the subject of the spread of nuclear weapons in general, the fog at Foggy Bottom has been dense for many years. And it's been pretty cloudy about American interests in the disposition of the nuclear weapons, materials and facilities that are now distributed in the territory of several of the FSRs.

It may be that some members of our Foreign Service feel that the Administration's reluctance to see the republics abandon nuclear weapons is because America *needs* adversaries armed with nuclear weapons in order to deter them from an attack on us. But then it's hard to see why we can't fortify our deterrence by letting *other* FSRs have the ability to launch weapons independently, so we could deter *them*. It's hard to see, then, why we should worry about Iran and Libya, or even Saddam. Poor Saddam, he's been trying so hard to get a nuclear force which we could also deter!

Nuclear weapons are likely to spread further, without U.S. encouragement, and to countries that might use them or threaten to use them for purposes hostile to American interests. They'll be forces to exercise U.S. capabilities for deterrence. On the whole, it's a better idea to slow or to reduce their increase as much as possible. But policy in this connection will be better if the U.S. is clearer.

It's in the U.S. interest, of course, to see as many of the nuclear weapons in the former Soviet Union disabled and destroyed as is feasible. But that process will take a lot of time. Put that aside for the moment and consider the control of those weapons that are not scheduled for destruction.

We need to make at least one basic distinction: that between "control" meaning the power to decide to launch a nuclear weapon; and "control" meaning the power to *veto* a decision to launch a nuclear weapon. There's a difference between a finger on the trigger and a finger on the safety catch. The "trigger" or the "safety catch," like the "button," of course is a metaphor. But a useful one in this case.

When we say we want to "concentrate" "control" in order to reduce the number of decisionmakers who control nuclear weapons, we mean we want to have as few fingers as possible on the "trigger." (Or: When one talks of reducing the number of people in "control" of nuclear weapons, it's the number of fingers on the trigger that's contemplated.) We mean we want to minimize the number of those who can, without interference or veto, launch any of the nuclear weapons in the territory of the FSU. From the standpoint of the prospective targets, maximum safety would be achieved when the number of fingers on the trigger is zero.

As for fingers on the "safety catch," the more the merrier.

The United States had many weapons overseas under multi-key arrangements. From the standpoint of the United States, it seemed important that such weapons couldn't be used without a U.S. representative turning a key or inserting one essential part of the combination. Host countries, on the other hand, in general didn't want weapons launched from their territory without consent. They didn't want the weapons launched unless they had turned *their* key or inserted *their* part of the combination. Such arrangements can be made so that the weapons are not usable (without the efforts of a national laboratory) unless all combinations are inserted from remote sources.

Neither Russia nor the non-Russian republics are worried about an American or French or British threat. They may worry about threats from each other that might come up in the course of the painful process of the division of assets, populations, etc., in which differences might be settled or strongly influenced by the potential use of weapons of mass destruction.

From the American standpoint, but also from the standpoint of the FSRs, the best way to avoid those problems is to distribute vetoes over decisions to use nuclear weapons, wherever they are, rather than to distribute nuclear weapons or see their spread as counters to each other.

IV. ARMS RACE MYTHS VS. STRATEGIC COMPETITION'S REALITY

Commentary: *Arms Race Myths vs. Strategic Competition's Reality*

Richard Perle

"All this is familiar, but is it true?" was Albert Wohlstetter's response to widely accepted ideas about the U.S.-Soviet arms race in 1976, ideas he proceeded to demolish—but only after adumbrating them with a precision that eluded the officials, academics, and intellectuals who held them.

Racing Forward? Or Ambling Back? (1976) was vintage Wohlstetter: precise, masterfully argued with clarity, logic, masses of evidence, wry humor, and great elegance. Albert puts the arguments he knocks down far better than their adherents, sharpening the vague notions that formed the core of thinking about arms control into well-defined propositions that could be tested against the evidence, the facts and logic on which they were based.

Of course, he had been doing this for years, examining complex issues by breaking them down into their components, testing those components, gathering all the available relevant facts (and doing basic, original research to establish facts that were not readily available), reading everything connected to the subject, and rendering the whole into a rich, original, and rigorous analysis.

In an unpublished note, Albert points to the importance of philosopher Karl Popper's insistence that meaningful statements must be open to disconfirmation. As Albert put it: "If a statement cannot conceivably be refuted by any observation or test, it has no meaning. Such statements are impregnable but empty."[1] He regarded the vague provisions commonly found in arms control agreements as dangerously empty because they were too imprecise to be tested. From this observation he concluded— and subsequent history proved him right—that it would be extraordinarily difficult to reach clear and convincing conclusions about arms control violations, even when they occurred.

While Albert's focus was principally on the nuclear arms control agreements of the 1970s and 1980s, the pitfalls of vaguely worded agreements—an inability to verify and therefore to force compliance—are as relevant to deals with Iran or North Korea today as they were for deals with the Soviets during the Cold War.

Albert was at his best when the conventional thinking he challenged was most widely accepted: the greater the number of proponents, especially if they were widely read and admired, the more pleasure Albert took in the rigorous examination, and frequent refutation, of their views. And when he could group a gaggle of respected commentators into a chorus singing from the same flawed sheet of music, he did so with good-natured glee. That is why in *Racing Forward? Or Ambling Back?* he quoted so many "experts" saying the same thing. After all, two or three quotations from Morton Halperin or Jeremy Stone would have sufficed to demonstrate that conventional thinking about the "arms race" held it to be the product of over-estimation and reciprocal over-reaction. He hardly needed to add statements to the same effect from Jerome Wiesner, Leonard Rodberg, Herbert Scoville, Leslie Gelb, Robert McNamara, Stanley Hoffman, and Paul Warnke. But these were *the* authorities in the arms control field, and Albert was determined to corral them all before leading them to slaughter.

For Albert, the field of "arms control" was almost wholly lacking in intellectual content. The popular press, drawing its information from conventionally thinking "experts," had largely succeeded in establishing the "fact" of a U.S.-Soviet arms race in the minds of policymakers as well as the broad public. Albert understood that the arms race theorists' underlying misconception would make it difficult to gain support for policies that could enhance American safety and security. So while he enjoyed demonstrating that there was in fact no such thing as a spiraling "arms race," he regarded the belief that there was as deadly serious. If a mistaken belief in a mythical mechanism called the "arms race" meant that the United States might not make prudent investments in secure and discriminate strategic forces, or might turn to fragile agreements rather than measures of self-defense, well, he would have to begin at the beginning and put the concept of the "arms race" under the microscope.

And what a sharp, rigorous element his microscope had. Take, for example, Albert's treatment of the issue of over or under prediction of Soviet nuclear forces. Contrary to the widely held belief that we had chronically under-estimated the future size of Soviet arsenals, Albert's meticulous audit shows the opposite. Having won the point, he goes on to tease out and dissect yet another error—the mistaken belief among those who grudgingly acknowledged a history of *under*-estimations—that estimates got better with time and experience. This apparent but wrong finding was the product of a flawed methodology, which he takes pains to explain:

> Some analysts now grant that we underestimated, but claim that we improved with time. They ignore the important difference between predicting a *cumulative* total of vehicles that will have been deployed at some future time, most of which are known to be already completed or in process at the time when the prediction is made, and predicting a *change* from this known state. This accurately-known past makes up an increasing portion of the cumulative total. Nonetheless, those who detect an improvement in forecasts compare predicted with actual totals, not predicted with actual change from what was known; and so swamp unpredicted new starts in the steadily increasing total of launchers known to be started or completed.

Albert was intrigued by the pattern of under-estimation he so carefully documented and searched for an explanation. When he found it, he put it succinctly:

> Part of the pressure to conform by underestimating was very likely a reflex, over-correcting for the "missile gap" that had publicly embarrassed the intelligence community.

Re-reading that, I could not help thinking of the December 2007 National Intelligence Estimate (NIE) on Iran's nuclear weapons program. Could the intelligence community be over-correcting for the infamous 2003 Iraq NIE that caused the nation and the world such grief? And if Albert were alive and serving on the President's Foreign Intelligence Advisory Board, as he once did, would the CIA and the other intelligence agencies have gotten away with the Iraq estimate in the first place? Or the Iran estimate now?

As a member of the Pentagon's Defense Policy Board, I sat through a number of intelligence briefings following the attacks of September 11, 2001. Some of them had to do with Iraq and its weapons of mass destruction. Now, with the advantage of hindsight, I can see how imprecision about what we actually *knew* – as opposed to what we believed could be reliably *inferred* – led to the mistaken conclusion that Iraq had a stockpile of weapons of mass destruction. The careless acceptance in the Iraq NIE of information that required establishing the reliability of informants was not inevitable. But the now famous case in which an Iraqi defector in Germany was never interviewed by U.S. intelligence, leaving his false claims simply taken at face value, would have astonished even Albert, who was a frequent critic of intelligence estimates. Albert served on the Defense Policy Board for many years, but not as the nation contemplated its response to 9/11.

We will never know whether his relentless questioning of everything and everyone would have teased out the hidden assumptions and flawed inferences in the Iraq NIE. (Or, for that matter, whether he would have seen the possession of *stockpiles* of WMD as the central issue. He was, as so much of his writing makes clear, always mindful of how rapidly things can change and how quickly civilian programs – to say nothing of unilaterally abandoned military ones – can be activated for military purposes.)

Neither will we enjoy the benefit of Albert's critique of the Iran NIE. I imagine it would zero in on the apparent inconsistency of Iran's sustained, costly, and challenging ballistic missile development with the regime's claim not to have a nuclear weapons program. I know he would be wary in the extreme of the idea that the way to deal with a future Iranian nuclear weapon is to sign an agreement in which the regime in Teheran promises to restrict itself to only "peaceful" uses of nuclear materials.

If we were to think as Albert would about the issues flowing from Iran's current position with respect to nuclear power (they insist on it) and nuclear weapons ("we don't want and have no program to get them"), we would do well to study his important discussion of the multiple applications of a single technology or the multiple technologies instrumental in the achievement of a single purpose. Albert believed that both phenomena rendered arms control dangerously ineffective in all but a few very special cases.

In the case of the Iran NIE, and in other intelligence products not yet even conceived, we should resolve to apply the Wohlstetter four-word test: "But is it true?"

384

Albert's disdain for arms control theory reflected his concern that ineffective agreements would substitute for hard thinking and hard choices about how to protect the nation in the era of the "delicate balance of terror." That was the title he gave to a brilliant, widely discussed article in *Foreign Affairs* in 1959 that introduced the broad public to the key concepts of strategy in the nuclear age, many of which were conceived and articulated during the course of his highly classified research at the RAND Corporation. He was especially emphatic in later years that careless thinking about arms control could drive strategic policy even further in the direction of accepting "mutual assured destruction" (MAD) as the key to American security.

Much of Albert's critique of arms control refers to what he calls "MAD-based arms control" because its main objectives were premised on the idea that (a) stable nuclear deterrence was easy to achieve; (b) the way to achieve it was to build only a minimum deterrent force that could confidently destroy Soviet (or, for the Soviets, American) cities in a massive retaliatory attack; and (c) since both the United States and the Soviet Union accepted (a) and (b), agreements in which each pledged not to acquire capabilities beyond those defined in (b) could, and should, be negotiated. But when one examined the arguments for the arms control agreements beginning with the (subsequently violated) moratorium on nuclear testing and continuing through the ABM Treaty and the SALT and START treaties, they invariably presupposed the desirability of a strategic balance based on the threat to destroy cities.

So, at the core of Albert's disparagement of arms control is his view that the underlying rationale for treaties limiting the numbers, types, and technologies of strategic forces served only to reinforce MAD doctrine, a doctrine he deplored on both prudential and moral grounds. After all, the idea that it was desirable to reduce our strategic arsenal to the lowest number of weapons required for massive retaliatory attacks against Soviet cities meant that if deterrence failed, we might someday be forced to choose between doing nothing or killing millions of innocent civilians. Throughout his life and writings, Albert argued the moral obtuseness of the physicists, clergymen, politicians, and intellectuals who so readily embraced MAD. (Once, observing a group of women marching in an antimissile defense demonstration in Washington, DC, Albert remarked: "They must call themselves 'mothers for offensive forces only'.")

Responding to Henry Kissinger's rhetorical question, "What in God's name is superiority at these levels?", Albert comments:

> I am all for probing the premises of thought on arms and arms-control which the Secretary is said to want. But that can only start when we face up to evasions making "murder respectable" in such chaste phrases as "counter-value attacks" and in all the unreflective vocabulary of the arms race. This is an important part of rethinking policy about our relations with allies and adversaries, long overdue and essential for reducing the present chaos.

Albert's deep skepticism about the utility of arms control agreements did not lead him to oppose them in principle, although he was frequently described as among a group of analysts who were "opposed to arms control." While many of the arms control enthusiasts Albert assessed never met an agreement they didn't like, it could not be said that Albert opposed all agreements. To be sure, he set a much higher standard than the arms control professionals — negotiators, analysts, politicians, and professors — by insisting that only certain types of agreement were worth having. The criteria he set out are as relevant today as when he argued for them over a long career — and they tend to be ignored by diplomatic professionals who frequently lose sight of an agreement's purpose in their zeal to get an agreement for agreement's sake.

The idea that arms control agreements should have limited purposes and should be of limited duration reflected Albert's view that "comprehensive" agreements were bound to invite evasion through the exploitation of loopholes or, worse, out-and-out violations. He opposed permanent agreements because he knew that the considerations underlying any agreement would change in unpredictable ways: today's technological *cul de sac* would become tomorrow's super highway.

He knew that, once in place, arms control agreements were nearly impossible to vacate, even if they had clear termination clauses (indeed, even when they had expiration dates). And he knew that agreements were not self-enforcing. He scoffed at the claims of arms controllers that "if the other side violates the agreement, we will withdraw from it immediately." He had seen too many instances in which it was difficult or impossible to prove that a violation of a vaguely worded provision had taken place, or in which a questionable interest in keeping a violated agreement trumped even a legal exit, or in which the hope that yet another agreement could be reached led governments to turn a blind eye to the violations of the agreements already in place. He summarized his view of an agreement worth having this way:

> For this reason, one should reject the argument made by many proponents of arms control today that a treaty of permanent duration will confer stability, because it will enable us and our adversaries to plan with certainty. On the contrary, it is a sure recipe for instability because in general we cannot anticipate such further changes long enough in advance, and a permanent treaty would prevent us from making incremental adjustments when it becomes clear that they are about to occur. We should look for an agreement which is not only monitorable, but one which we can enforce unilaterally, and one that provides strong incentives for us to enforce compliance. In fact, we want the incentives for our enforcing the agreement to exceed the incentives for looking the other way.

Disappointment with the use of military power in Iraq has led to another of what have become recurrent surges in the idea that "diplomacy" can achieve what the force of arms cannot, and that agreements with adversaries are the highest expression of diplomacy. Thus we are deeply engaged in negotiations with Iran and North Korea in which Albert's high standard defining a good agreement will almost certainly not be met. And the search is on for other partners, venues, and contexts in which to negotiate the cooperation of other states in solving the problems we face.

How will we approach an end to the uranium enrichment demands of the Iranians? How will we define the prohibited activities of the North Koreans under an agreement to cause them to abandon their nuclear weapons program? How should we respond to Putin's rants about ballistic missile defense or his threats to abandon arms control agreements reached during the Soviet period? Can the limitation of greenhouse gases be limited most effectively by constraints on the consumption of fossil fuels or by technological innovation?

Albert would certainly not approve relying solely, or even significantly, on arms control agreements with the Iranians or

387

the North Koreans as a means of halting their nuclear programs. And, having never been enthusiastic about the ABM Treaty or the agreements limiting conventional forces, I suspect he would treat Putin's threats and posturing with benign neglect. As for global warming, Albert would place a large bet on technology. He would look at the numbers, the costs of limiting consumption, the likelihood that our restraint would be vitiated by the behavior of others, the tradeoffs between limiting economic growth and investing in technology, and he would look beyond current thinking for new solutions. And he would be right.

ENDNOTES - Perle

1. Albert Wohlstetter, "On Disconfirmability: A Karl Popper Sort of Observation on the Troubles with 'Verification'," unpublished, revised December 20, 1984, p. 1, available from the Albert and Roberta Wohlstetter Papers, Notes, Box 102 Folder 5.

The Case for Strategic Force Defense (1969)

Albert Wohlstetter[1]

From Johan J. Hølst and William Schneider, Jr., eds., *Why ABM?: Policy Issues in the Missile Defense Controversy*, New York: Pergamon Press, 1969, pp. 119-142. Courtesy of the Wohlstetter Estate.

THE ROLE OF ABM IN THE 1970'S

Since I believe the Safeguard program warrants the sums involved, and I support it, perhaps I should begin by saying that I am entirely sympathetic to a rigorous review of the Defense Budget. I favor getting our safety as cheaply as we can. Moreover, I believe the Defense Budget has a good deal of fat that can be cut without substantial harm. I would recommend, for example, a careful look at the equipment and support costs of our ground forces, and at our tactical air forces, both land and sea-based. Some of these seem ineffective, or leveled at threats that are poorly defined or not grave enough to be worth the cost.

Sensible efforts to reduce the Defense Budget, however, would not center on the strategic offense and defense force. There are, of course, arguable choices about strategic offense and defense. But the eight billion dollar plus strategic budget makes up a small part of the total Defense Budget. It has a paramount importance for the safety of the country and, indeed, of international society. Deterring nuclear coercion and nuclear attack on ourselves and our allies, [and] reducing the damage done in case deterrence fails, are complex and uncertain functions; but because they are crucial, the part of the Defense Budget devoted to them has been the most studied and is better understood than any of the rest.

Nonetheless, sizable uncertainties are intrinsic. They affect the predictions of scientists as well as the military and limit the reductions we can make without excessive risk. The strategic forces will need continuing adjustment to predicted and to some unanticipated changes in the state of the art. But such adjustments need not entail drastic changes up or down in long term levels of spending.

A start in deploying ABM [anti-ballistic missile defenses], I believe, is a prudent response to changes in the state of the art

389

available to ourselves and to our adversaries. As strategic systems go, it is a modest program. It is subject to review and can be halted or stretched out. The average annual cost of the completed program on a five year basis is less than one-fifth of what we were spending for active defense against manned bombers at the end of the 1950's. Nor is it at all likely to start a quantitative arms spiral. Indeed, despite the stereotype, there has been no quantitative arms race in the strategic offense and defense budget, no "ever-accelerating increase," nor, in fact, any long term increase at all. The budget for strategic offense and defense forces in fiscal 1962 was 11.3 billion dollars.[2] The proposed fiscal 1970 budget, as of June, comes to about 8 billion dollars. Adjusted for price changes, the 1962 figure was well over fifty percent higher than that for 1970, perhaps even as much as two-thirds higher.

There is an important difference between making qualitative adjustments to technical change and expanding the number of vehicles or megatons or dollars spent. The difference has been ignored in a debate on ABM that seems at the same time impassioned and very abstract, quite removed from the concrete political, economic, and military realities of nuclear offense and defense and their actual history. For example, one alternative to protecting Minuteman is to buy more Minutemen without protection. But adding new vehicles is costly and more destabilizing than an active defense of these hard points, since it increases the capacity to strike first. A one-sided self-denial of new technology can lead simply to multiplying our missiles and budgets, or to a decrease in safety, or to both.

Active defense against ballistic missiles in the 1970's will have an important role to play in maintaining a protected and responsible second-strike capacity. The projected Safeguard defense of the national command authority and of the bomber and Minuteman bases are directed to this end. And it has a useful function in providing an area defense against attacks involving modest numbers of apparent incoming missiles.

There have been so many charges that the Safeguard program was invented in bad faith in March of this year as a gimmick to answer critics of the Sentinel city defense that I would stress that in 1967, long before the present Administration quite independently decided on Safeguard, the evidence of advancing technology convinced me that ABM in the 1970's would have essentially the uses the Administration suggests for Safeguard, and in the same order: to defend the offense and, given this, at a small extra cost to provide a light area defense of population.[3] In fact, there is a substantial continuity between the ABM decisions of the present and past Administrations. The last Administration called for an ABM area defense but said it would furnish an economic basis for defending Minuteman if the threat grew. It had been weighing and it continued to weigh this decision for some time—indeed itself requested some funds for hardpoint defense in its own version of the 1970 fiscal budget.

Like the Republicans now, the Democrats in 1967 were charged with directing their ABM decision against the opposing party. I would recommend to opponents of ABM that they contemplate the possibility that the decisions were made in good faith in both cases, and that we turn to the substance of the issues.

There are other political and military functions of an ABM system than protecting the offense and offering an area defense of civilians against light attack. I would like to say something about each of these two latter roles and also something about the doctrine of Minimum Deterrence on which much opposition to the ABM is based, but time permits comment mostly on the protected offense function.

ABM as a Part of a Second-Strike Force in the 1970's

For one superpower as against another, getting and keeping a responsible second-strike force is feasible but hard. It requires thought, effort, and continuing realistic adjustments to technological change. Minimum Deterrence theorists, who call for no defense of our civilians and nearly total reliance on a threat to bombard enemy civilians, have always claimed that the attacker inevitably must expend many strategic vehicles to destroy only one of the vehicles attacked. No such generalization holds. It has depended and always must depend on the changing capabilities of the offense and on the kind and degree of protection of the force attacked. At one time, for example, both we and the Russians had very many unprotected aircraft concentrated on a base within the lethal radius of a single bomb. On a two-wing base, for example, we had as many as one hundred thirty aircraft; on a one-wing base sixty-five medium bombers and tankers. And the planned response time was too slow for the reliable warning likely to be available. Small numbers of vehicles could have destroyed much larger numbers of the vehicles they attacked. Under some realistically determined conditions, the ratio would have favored the attacker by one to eight or more. These vulnerabilities had nothing to do with the supposed missile gap. In fact they preceded such predictions.

There is always a temptation in such circumstances to resort to responses that are automatic or that bypass national command. Advocates of sole reliance on city bombardment forces have from the time this doctrine first gained currency been tempted to prove that response was certain by making it automatic, by shortcutting responsible political decision.[4] But the decision to launch ICBM's against Russian cities would be perhaps the most momentous choice ever made in all of history. It would be the decision for World War III. If this awful decision is ever made it should be based on as much information as we can get and it should be made by as high a political authority as possible. It is the last decision we should contemplate delegating to a computer.

The revival today, by several distinguished senators and some able physicists opposing ABM, of the suggestion that, rather than defend ICBM's [intercontinental ballistic missiles], we should launch them at Russian cities simply on the basis of radar represents a long step backward. If we were willing to do this, we would dispense with silos or Poseidon submarines or any other mode of protecting our missiles. And we would increase the nightmare possibility of nuclear war by mistake.

Understanding of the complex problems of designing a protected and responsible nuclear strategic force has grown slowly among scientists as well as laymen, civilians as well as soldiers, Democrats as well as Republicans. But it has grown, and decisively. The United States has designed and deployed a second-strike force capable of riding out an attack, and there have been large improvements in protecting responsible command. This was accomplished not by merely expanding nuclear bombardment forces, but in essence by shifting to forces with protection against the changing threat. The stereotype repeated throughout the 1960's that our security has declined while our strategic force grew at an accelerating rate is grossly wrong on both counts. In the past some key programs increased the protected second-strike capacity of the force, while cutting at the same time billions of dollars from the spending projected.

In the 1970's unless we continue to make appropriate decisions to meet technological change, once again the viability of a large part of our second-strike force will be put in question. Several related innovations, but in particular the development of a rocket booster carrying many reentry vehicles each aimed precisely at a different target, raise once again the possibility of attack ratios favoring the attacker. One reentry vehicle may kill a booster carrying several. One booster can carry the means of destroying many boosters.

Raising a question about the future second-strike capacity of any part of our strategic force implies nothing about the present intentions of an adversary to strike first or even to be able in the future effectively to strike first. The recent debate on whether the Soviet missile, SS-9, is a "first-strike weapon" or whether the Russians intend it to be seems beside the point. If by maintaining our second-strike capability we can make the risks of striking very great, this can affect an adversary's intentions favorably to ourselves. It can deter him even in a crisis, like the one over missiles in Cuba, when the alternative to striking may look bad, but not, if we are careful, as bad as striking. Moreover, we ought not to talk of "first-strike weapons" and "second-strike weapons" as if this could be settled simply by looking at the weapons on one side. Whether or not a weapons system can preclude substantial retaliation will depend on many uncertain future performance characteristics of the forces on *both* sides. The test of whether one has a responsible second-strike capacity is whether one can, under nuclear attack, preserve vehicles, decision centers, and the flow of communications among them, whether one can transmit the order to retaliate and penetrate adversary defenses to reach targets. If we were unwilling even to entertain the hypothesis of a first-strike, we would do nothing to protect any part of our strategic forces or its control centers by making them mobile or hard or defended by ABM. Some leading scientists who oppose currently deploying ABM say they will favor it for the defense of Minuteman when precise MIRV's [multiple independently targetable reentry vehicles] and the related offense technologies are likely to be available to the Russians. That calendar date, and not present Soviet intent, is then a major substantive issue for these opponents. And their position recognizes that we want to maintain the second-strike capacity—not of just one, but of all major vehicle types in our strategic force: Minuteman, bombers, and Poseidon.

In designing a second-strike force, there are excellent reasons for making it a substantial mixture of vehicles of several quite different types: land as well as sea-based, manned as well as unmanned, each with its own mode of protection. Such systems have differing limitations, are subject to varied and independent uncertainties, require distinct modes of attack and, if each type is protected, greatly complicate the attack. It is a serious matter, then, if a large part of this mixture is badly affected by changing adversary forces and technologies. The forces deployed and the state of the art available to the Russians will influence other parts of our strategic force than Minuteman silos. And ABM has a role to play, for example, in protecting the important fixed elements of a mobile force, including the politically responsible command centers. Preserving command, control and communications is always hard, and particularly so for mobile sea-based systems.

My remarks, however, center, so far as the second-strike function of ABM is concerned, on the problem of protecting Minuteman. We have good cause to preserve the second-strike capability of so large a proportion of our strategic force. Even if it were true that the United States needed only a few strategic vehicles surviving, buying and paying for the operation of a great many that had become vulnerable to attack would be a very poor way to obtain those few surviving. There are safer and cheaper ways of getting a force of a given size than to buy a much larger one, most of which is susceptible to annihilation.

How does the planned timing of our ABM deployment compare to the date when it is reasonably likely that Russian offense technology could badly worsen the effectiveness of our projected Minuteman III? The first point to note is that the proposed Safeguard deployment has extended lead times. It can stretch out further if continuing review of intelligence suggests it should, but the shortest schedule calls for completing this program early in 1976. If, as ABM opponents stress in other connections, there is likely to be a substantial shakedown period, we are talking of 1977 or later. If, as has been suggested, we delay decision for another year or more and then proceed to design and develop an entirely new ABM, we are talking of the 1980's.

Second, predicting exact calendar dates at which technologies will be available to adversaries and what their strategic significance will be is very hard, and we are not very good at it. Moreover, we have erred not only on the side of overestimating Russian capabilities, but often by underestimating them. At earlier dates we were surprised by the rapid Soviet achievement of the A-bomb, the H-bomb, advanced jet engines, long-range turbo-prop bombers, airborne intercept radars, and large-scale fissile-material production. And scientists have been surprised, not only military men.[5]

Third, the public discussion has not stressed how sensitively the accuracy of attack affects the viability of the hardened force attacked. Accuracy affects the number of weapons required to destroy a hard target very much more than the bomb yield or the overpressure resistance of the target. Roughly speaking, for such targets, improving accuracy by a factor of slightly more than two is the same as increasing bomb yield tenfold and serves essentially to offset a tenfold increase in overpressure resistance.

I have tried to reconstruct various numerical proofs recently presented or distributed to the Congress that purport to show that Minuteman will be quite safe without any extra protection; these proofs depend heavily on optimistic estimates of limitations in Russian delivery accuracies, reliabilities, and associated offense capabilities and sometimes on very poor offense tactics.[6] Suppose, however, that by 1976 when Safeguard is deployed, or by 1977 when it may be shaken down, the Russians have:

1. accuracies like those of the systems we are deploying now[7]
2. over-all reliabilities currently attributable to them
3. methods familiar to us for using extensive and timely information as to which missiles have failed so that others can replace them
4. continued production of SS-9 boosters at past rates
5. modest numbers of MIRV's per booster (e.g., the three five-megaton reentry vehicles stated by Secretary Laird for the SS-9).

Then the percentage of the Minuteman force that would be destroyed, if undefended, comes to about ninety-five percent.

These results are based on quite moderate assumptions about Russian capabilities. Better accuracies, for example, may be expected in the late 1970's, and higher degrees of MIRVing. Reliabilities of any given offense missile system improve with use. Do those who favor a hardpoint defense but would postpone a start really consider these Russian capabilities I have outlined "extremely implausible"? Or at *all* implausible?

There is a striking inconsistency in the way ABM opponents treat the Chinese and the Russians. In contemplating the possibility of a Russian offense against our Minuteman, they assume that Russians who cannot by 1976 or 1977—twenty years after Sputnik—do what we know how to do now. When considering the ability of the Chinese to penetrate an ABM defense, they attribute to them penetration systems that cost us many billions of dollars, a dozen years of trials and many failures to develop, and they assume this for the first generation Chinese missiles. These are rather backward Russians and very advanced Chinese. Moreover since in the Russian case we are considering a potential threat to our second-strike capability and we want this to be highly reliable, we want particularly to avoid underestimating the threat. But we should undertake a modest defense of population if it works in the expected case, even if on extremely pessimistic assumptions it might not. Here again it seems to me the ABM critics get things exactly backwards.

Finally, the fact that such impending developments in Russian offense may make it necessary to do something more to protect the fixed elements of our force should come as no surprise. It was the sensitive effects of missile inaccuracy that in the early 1950's suggested to the original proponents of programs for hardening strategic vehicles against ICBM attack that

a. hardening would be an important and effective method of protection against ICBM attack in the 1960's; and that
b. by itself hardening would not be adequate for much past the 1960's.

The ICBM's then expected in the 1960's were, of course, enormously faster than manned bombers, and therefore would out-mode some programs that served very well in the 1950's; but the early ICBM's were likely to be much less accurate than the manned bombers. They were expected to have inaccuracies measured in miles, perhaps, it seemed then, as large as five miles, compared to the quarter of a nautical mile or fifteen hundred feet median miss distance associated with manned bombers. Since just doubling inaccuracy could affect weapons requirements by a factor of four, hardening clearly seemed a good idea. The paper proposing hardening for the 1960's was entitled "Defending a Strategic Force after 1960" and was put out on February 1, 1954. That paper included a very short section called "After After 1960" that is quite relevant for understanding why we should expect that we will have to adapt the current Minuteman to impending changes in opposing offense technology. The section read in full:

The foregoing also suggests that even against the ballistic missile this defense would have a finite life. The

missile might improve drastically in accuracy and payload. However, the date at which the Russians will have
a missile capable of carrying a 25 MT bomb with a 1500
ft. CEP [circular error probable] appears sufficiently far
removed to make the defense good, let's say, until the
end of the Sixties (p. 91).

That the numbers cited in this paper of February 1954 so closely
match some of those being talked of for the SS-9 is, of course,
purely a coincidence. They were performance characteristics of
bombers then current. However, the quotation illustrates that,
from the outset, it was to be expected that sooner or later and
probably in the 1970's, hardening would not be enough by itself.
The discussion also suggests that to depend merely on further
hardening would make the system vulnerable to further improvements in accuracy.

Hardening can be outpaced by further development in precision. This does not mean that for some possible threats a combination of ABM and extreme hardening might not be useful. It
might. But as a complete substitute for ABM extreme hardening
has drawbacks. It is subject, in my opinion, to much larger uncertainties as to both performance and costs than the ABM.

The major components of the Safeguard system have received
elaborate study and testing. Ideas for brand new ABM systems
to defend hard points that I am familiar with are not serious
competitors in this time period. We should start deploying the
system now on the schedule suggested and we should expect, as
in the case of every other offense and defense system, that we
shall learn a great deal from operational experience, make some
changes and retrofits. This seems to me a sound way to supplement
the protection of the Minuteman in a period when we can expect
it to be endangered.

ON THE COUNTERFORCE CALCULATIONS OF SOME
PROMINENT ABM OPPONENTS[8]

In preparing the preceding portion of this chapter on the role
of ABM in the 1970's, I undertook to review and test my past
views on the subject and once again to form my own independent
judgment. I, therefore, did not rely on calculations of either the
government or its critics. I took the relevant classified and public
data and performed my own analysis.

The kind of analysis involved in obtaining a protected and responsible strategic force has been my principal concern for eighteen years starting with the study that gave rise to the first-strike/second-strike distinction and to a good many other concepts and modes of protecting and controlling strategic forces cited by both sides in the present debate. The ABM has other functions that I support, but my chapter in the space available focused on its role in defending Minuteman. As I stressed there, these are complex and intrinsically uncertain matters. Where scientists differ on them, laymen may be tempted simply to throw up their hands and choose to rely on the authority of those scientists they favor. I feel, however, that the substantive differences among the scientists, if carefully explained, are quite accessible to interested readers and that such careful explanation can help them form their own judgment as to which conclusions are sound.

On the Safely of Minuteman

In my statement to the Senate Armed Services Committee on April 23, I said, "I have tried to reconstruct various numerical proofs recently presented or distributed to the Congress that purport to show our Minuteman will be safe without any extra protection; these proofs depend heavily on optimistic estimates of limitations in Russian delivery accuracies, reliabilities, associated offense capabilities, and sometimes on poor offense tactics." In response to questions from members of the Committee, I illustrated several troubles with these attempted proofs of the safety of Minuteman, but there was no time to explain their defects adequately. I would like to try to do that now, and to comment specifically on the calculations of Dr. Rathjens, Dr. Lapp, and of the Federation of American Scientists. Some of the comments, particularly those of Dr. Lapp, bear also on some unevidenced statements on this subject by Prof. Chayes and Dr. Panofsky and, more recently, by Dr. Wiesner.

Though my own calculations were based on classified as well as public data, my summary of results, like that of Dr. Rathjens, was unclassified and so are the comments I am about to make. This will prevent explicit specification of some of the numbers assumed by Dr. Rathjens and by myself and inevitably it forces some roundaboutness of expression. I am able to state, for example, that Dr. Rathjens and I assume the same accuracy for the Russian SS-9 in the mid- and late 1970's. I can say that the SS-9 is now expected (and, before the Nixon Administration, was expected) to achieve that accuracy years in advance of this late time period. And I can say, as Dr. Rathjens did, that the accuracy we have assumed for the Russians, in this late time period, is essentially the same as that estimated for our own MIRV carrying missiles, namely Poseidon and Minuteman III.[9] But I cannot say what that accuracy is.

I, therefore, submitted a classified statement in which the essential numerical assumptions are explicit and related to intelligence estimates. However, even without the classified statements, some essential defects of the calculations of Dr. Rathjens, Dr. Lapp, and the Federation of American Scientists can be made clear.

Dr. Rathjens' Calculations

Dr. Rathjens has stated, "Even if the Soviet SS-9 missile force were to grow as rapidly as the Defense Department's most worrisome projections, even if the Soviet Union were to develop and employ MIRV's with those missiles and even if they achieved accuracies as good as we apparently expect with our MIRV forces (according to figures released in late 1967 by former Deputy Secretary of Defense Nitze), a quarter of our Minuteman force could be expected to survive a Soviet preemptive SS-9 attack. That quarter alone would be more than enough to inflict unacceptable damage on the U.S.S.R."[10]

My own parallel calculations for the mid- and late 1970's, using what I described as moderate assumptions, show about five percent surviving. What explains the difference? Since Dr. Rathjens and I compared notes on April 22, I am able to fix quite precisely where we agreed and where we differed.

Our assumptions agreed in the accuracy assumed for the SS-9, in the overall reliability rate, in the numbers of SS-9 boosters (500) and in the use of several independently aimed reentry vehicles in each booster. Our assumptions differed on three key points: in the degree of blast resistance assumed for our Minuteman silos, in the yield of the Russian reentry vehicles, and in the use or non-use by the Russians of substantial information about what missiles are unready at launch or fail in early stages.

On the first point, I have explained that Dr. Rathjens assumed that Minuteman silos were two-thirds more blast resistant than I did, and two-thirds more blast resistant than they are officially estimated to be. He derived his assumption by reading several points off an unclassified chart showing the probability of a Minuteman silo being destroyed as a function of accuracy for various bomb yields. Then by using standard rules for weapons effects he inferred the overpressure resistance of Minuteman silos. However, the curves on the unclassified chart cannot be correctly read to imply the overpressure resistance Dr. Rathjens infers. His reading of the curves was in error.

Second, I assumed three 5-megaton reentry vehicles for each SS-9, as in Secretary Laird's public statements. Dr. Rathjens assumed four 1-megaton reentry vehicles. More than four reentry vehicles can be fitted on the SS-9, if the payload is only one megaton. However, the three 5-megaton reentry vehicles, given the accuracy we both assume, and given the actual blast resistance of the Minuteman, do enough for the attacker. Using his lower Russian bomb yield and his overestimated Minuteman blast resistance, Dr. Rathjens derived a probability of about sixty percent that one arriving Russian reentry vehicle would destroy one Minuteman silo. If he had used the officially estimated 5-megaton reentry vehicle and the actual blast resistance of the Minuteman silo, the probability would have been nearly ninety-nine percent. If he had used three 5-megaton reentry vehicles per booster for the SS-9 and the correct estimate for blast resistance, he would have found only sixteen percent, instead of twenty-five percent of the Minuteman force surviving. Alternatively, if he had used the classified estimates of the number of 1-megaton reentry vehicles that can be fitted on an SS-9 booster, his calculations would have shown about 7.3 percent surviving. The combined significance of these first two points of difference between Dr. Rathjens and myself is then considerable.

The third point of difference between our calculations is that Dr. Rathjens assumes that the Russians would have to salvo all of their missiles with no information as to which had been unready or failed in time to be discovered, or at any rate with no use of such information. However, it is familiar that better methods are available and are of considerable utility for an offense that wants to assure a very high percentage of destruction of the force attacked. Most missiles that are counted as "unreliable" (excluded from the figure of overall reliability) are either not ready for launch or fail at launch, and this information can be made available immediately. A substantial additional fraction that fail do so at burnout, and information as to whether burnout velocity is within expected

TABLE I

CALCULATIONS ON THE VULNERABILITY OF THE
MINUTEMAN FORCE IN THE LATE 1970's
IF NO EXTRA PROTECTION

*Difference Between Assumptions Used by
Dr. Rathjens and Myself*

Number of SS-9's	: Same (500)	
Over-all reliability	: Same	
Accuracy	: Same	•
Minuteman Blast Resistance	{ Dr. Rathjens' }: { Mine	: 2/3 higher than official estimate : Official estimate
SS-9 payload	{ Dr. Rathjens' }: { Mine	: 4 reentry vehicles at 1 MT (less than SS-9 capability) : 3 at 5 MT (SS-9 capability)
Use of partial information on missile malfunctions	{ Dr. Rathjens' }: { Mine	: Not used : Used

*Effect of Assumptions on
Minuteman Survivability*

	Minuteman Surviving
Dr. Rathjens' result	25%
Adjust for correct Minuteman blast resistance and three 5 MT MIRV per SS-9	16%
Alternatively adjust for correct Minuteman blast resistance and number of 1 MT MIRV warheads the SS-9 is capable of carrying	7.3%
Using correct Minuteman blast resistance, three 5 MT MIRV per SS-9, and information as to missile malfunctions before or during launch only	8.7%
Using correct Minuteman blast resistance, the correct number of 1 MT warheads per SS-9, and information as to missile malfunctions before and during launch only	6%
Using correct Minuteman blast resistance and *either* the 5 MT MIRV or the 1 MT MIRV option, and information as to missile malfunctions including one-half those that fail after launch	5%

The table above summarizes the differences between Dr. Rathjens'
and my calculations.

tolerances can also be made quickly available. For radio-guided missiles this is almost automatic, but inertial systems can also radio this information back, as the telemetering in a missile flight test program shows. Later flight information is also feasible. While some fraction of the failures will remain unknown, a large proportion can be known. Therefore, instead of salvoing all extra missiles blindly, to make up for all unreadiness and all failures without knowing where they occur, one can reprogram some extra missiles to replace the large proportion of known failures. Using a current planning factor for the proportion of the unreliable missiles that cannot be replaced on the basis of timely information, the calculations using three 5-megaton reentry vehicles show considerably greater destruction. Instead of sixteen percent surviving, the approximate five percent survival that I mentioned previously results. It should be observed that this ability of the 5MT force to destroy five percent of the Minuteman force presumes that only about one-half the failures after launching are replaced — a figure well within the state of the art. Moreover, even limiting the use of information to missile malfunctions before or during launch, the 5MT MIRV force would leave only eight or nine percent surviving.

Finally, such techniques of using substantial timely information as to which missiles cannot be relied on are less important for cases where smaller yields and larger numbers of reentry vehicles per booster are used. For the 1-megaton multiple reentry vehicle case I have referred to, the expected number of Minutemen surviving reduces from approximately 7.3 percent without using such techniques, to five percent using them. The errors in Dr. Rathjens' calculations are not amended simply by taking into account the possibility of reprogramming.

Dr. Lapp's Calculations

Dr. Ralph Lapp's calculations were not presented at a Senate Hearing. However, one set of his calculations was presented as a two page appendix to his statement called "The Case Against Missile Defense," and they were featured in front page stories early in April in leading newspapers, describing Dr. Lapp as science advisor to the Senate opposition. These calculations attacking the credibility of a threat to the Minuteman itself apparently achieved widespread credence. They contain several grave errors, some of which have been pointed out independently by myself on April

23, 1969, before the Senate Armed Services Committee, by Dr. Lawrence O'Neill before the House Armed Services Committee, and by Professor Eugene Wigner before the American Physical Society on April 29th. Yet these statements pointing out Dr. Lapp's errors have received little or no newspaper notice. It is therefore worth reviewing Dr. Lapp's calculations, particularly so since one of his most blatant errors appears to have been adopted uncritically by some of the other witnesses before the Committee, specifically Professor Chayes and Dr. Panofsky.[11]

Dr. Lapp states that his calculations are based on "maximum values" for Soviet capabilities. He shows seventy-six percent of the Minuteman surviving, compared to Dr. Rathjens' twenty-five and my five percent. Moreover, he has several assumptions that agree with my own:

1. Three 5-megaton reentry vehicles per SS-9, and
2. An accuracy estimate derived, like Dr. Rathjens', from public indications of the great precision of our Poseidon or Minuteman MIRV's.

His combined assumptions about the yield and accuracy of an SS-9 reentry vehicle and the blast resistance of the Minuteman result in very high probabilities that a single arriving reentry vehicle will destroy a Minuteman silo.

He suggests that two and one-half warheads of 5-megaton power with a half nautical mile inaccuracy or CEP[12] are needed to destroy a 200 psi target with a ninety-five percent probability, and 1.1 warheads would have that probability if the CEP were a quarter of a nautical mile. In fact, using standard methods of calculation, at a half-mile inaccuracy, two warheads would yield a ninety-six percent destruction probability and at a quarter of a mile inaccuracy one warhead would have a more than ninety-nine percent probability of destroying a 200 psi target. Either Dr. Lapp's calculations are based on some rather exotic and unspecified method, or they are in error. But in any case it is apparent that, even using his methods, he derives a very high single shot kill probability, roughly comparable to my own.

How then does Dr. Lapp's Minuteman force, faced by supposedly "maximum" Russian capabilities, come out so much better than even Dr. Rathjens' Minuteman force? First, Dr. Lapp assumes a much smaller number of SS-9's than Dr. Rathjens and I. He assumes three hundred thirty-three SS-9's. This is hardly a maximum force. It is less than the number that would be produced at past rates by continuing production into the relevant 1976-77 time period. At three reentry vehicles per booster, Dr. Lapp's assumption would give the Russians about one thousand reentry vehicles.

Second, he assumes that the Russians would use only three-fourths of their SS-9 force, that is, about two hundred fifty SS-9's (or 750 reentry vehicles). This extraordinary failure to use a fourth of the force most adapted to the purpose of destroying Minuteman is attributed to a supposed universal rule that military strategists always keep forces in reserve. This may or may not be true for tank battles or aircraft attacks in a conventional war. (The June 1967 war in the Middle East suggests it is not a sound generalization even about attacks with aircraft at the start of a non-nuclear war.) But as a universal rule for a nuclear first-strike? Dr. Lapp does not say for what these SS-9's would be reserved.

Most important, Dr. Lapp forgets that the Soviet Union has a great many intercontinental missiles besides the SS-9 and exceeding the SS-9 in numbers by a large amount. These missiles would seem to furnish a reserve that might satisfy a military strategist.

Third, he assumes overall reliabilities that are quite a bit lower than the reliabilities that Dr. Rathjens and I assumed, also lower than those attributed to the SS-9. As a result of the three assumptions, Dr. Lapp's Russians would have substantially less than half as many reliable arriving reentry vehicles as our thousand Minuteman silos. More than half the Minuteman force would then be untouched by SS-9 reentry vehicles.

Finally, Dr. Lapp makes an assumption that is plainly absurd. He supposes that even though each warhead has a very high probability of destroying a single silo, "any military realist" would fire two of his outnumbered attacking reentry vehicles at each silo that is attacked. This would leave three-fourths of the silos untouched. But if each warhead has a ninety-nine percent probability of destroying a single silo, firing two at one silo would merely increase the probability of destroying that specific silo to 99.99% but would make it quite certain that a silo that could have been destroyed will go unscathed. If a more sensible tactic were followed, namely to fire each of the two missiles at a different silo, there would be a probability of ninety-eight percent of destroying both silos and a probability of 99.99% that at least one of the two would be destroyed. (This latter is the same probability that Dr. Lapp would have achieved against the specific one that he was aiming at.) In short, Dr. Lapp's tactic would greatly reduce the expected level of destruction achieved by the attack, and it would not increase the probability of achieving some minimum level of destruction. I know of no military realist who would regard Dr. Lapp's tactic as a sensible one for the attacker. I must agree with Dr. Wigner that Dr. Lapp has presumed that his adversary would be unbelievably stupid.

It should be observed that the absurdity of the tactic is not dependent on the roughly ninety-nine percent single shot kill probability implicit in Dr. Lapp's accuracy, yield and resistance assumptions. If one were to use a ninety-five percent shot destruction probability, the point is equally obvious. In this latter case, an adversary who assigned one missile to each of two targets would have a better than ninety percent chance of getting them both and a probability of 99¾% of getting at least one; and he could get no better than a 99¾% probability of getting one silo if he sent both missiles against one silo. In the latter case, however, he could destroy at *most* one silo.

Professor Chayes and Dr. Panofsky have made statements suggesting they also accept the principle of sending at least two missiles to each silo. Professor Chayes said in his statement to the Senate Armed Services Committee on April 23:

> ... it is agreed that the attacker would need at the very minimum 2,000 accurate warheads—two for every one of our silos—before being able to think about a first strike.

Professor Panofsky in his statement to the Senate Armed Services Committee on April 22 stated:

> Moreover, an attacker would have to compensate for the limited reliability of his force by targeting at least two and possibly more warheads against each of the 1,000 Minuteman silos.

The reason behind these two statements is less explicit than Dr. Lapp's. Dr. Panofsky is talking about compensating for unreliability rather than inaccuracy, but it seems plain that no such universal rule makes sense.

Dr. Lapp has a second set of calculations published on May 4, 1969, in *The New York Times Magazine*.[13] There he assumes the Russians may have five hundred rather than three hundred thirty-three SS-9's. Since he again assumes three reentry vehicles per booster, this makes a total of 1,500 reentry vehicles. He apparently avoids the obviously bad strategies of reserving a quarter of the force, and then using the remainder to attack only half the targets they are capable of destroying with high probability. Nonetheless, once again his calculations show very high survival rates: "500 to 750 operable Minuteman." With these changed assumptions, how does the outcome continue to remain so favorable to Minuteman's survival?

Dr. Lapp has made some other changes. He has reduced the yield of the SS-9 reentry vehicles by twenty percent, increased his estimate of the hardness of the Minuteman by fifty percent, and, most important, he now uses very large inaccuracies for the SS-9, 3,600 feet in one case and 5,500 feet in the other. The latter great inaccuracy assures him his seven hundred fifty operable Minuteman surviving. But there is no justification for assuming such great inaccuracies in the mid- and late 1970's. One of the few constants in Dr. Lapp's various calculations appears to be his conclusion.

Calculations of Dr. Steven Weinberg and Dr. Jerome Wiesner (in *ABM: An Evaluation of the Decision to Employ an Anti-Ballistic Missile System,* edited by Abram Chayes and Jerome Wiesner, New York, 1969)

Dr. Weinberg and Dr. Wiesner present variants of the same calculation to show the safety of the Minuteman force. Dr. Weinberg supposes that at least 2,100 reliable arriving reentry vehicles "with megaton yield and high accuracy" would be needed to destroy all but 42 of our 1,050 ICBM silos. He appears to assume an eighty percent single shot kill probability. Dr. Weinberg doesn't indicate the exact blast resistance, yield, and inaccuracy assumptions that go into his eighty percent hypothetical kill probability, and the testimony of Deputy Secretary Packard that he cites in that connection offers no basis for such a determination.[14] Mr. Packard there shows for three different bomb yields a spectrum of probabilities varying from less than ten percent to one hundred percent as accuracy varies from a mile or so down below one-tenth of a mile. Mr. Packard does not say what the accuracy of any SS-9 reentry vehicle is expected to be so that no specific single shot kill probability can be inferred from his testimony.

Dr. Wiesner assumes five hundred reliable SS-9's, each carrying three MIRV's; or more exactly fifteen hundred reliable MIRV's. And he also assumes an eighty percent kill probability for each arriving reentry vehicle. He justifies this with the statement that a 5-megaton reentry vehicle would have to be used and that "at best the MIRV guidance system will be accurate enough to give only a 0.8 kill probability for the unit."[15] One can read directly from Deputy Secretary Packard's chart that Dr. Wiesner is thus implying that accuracies less than about 2,400 feet are not possible in the time period in question. Dr. Wiesner has given no technical argument to support this assertion; it is at variance with expected accuracies for our own MIRV systems, and it is at variance with the accuracy that the intelligence community has *for some time* expected the SS-9 to achieve years before the late 1970's time period, and with the accuracy assumed by Dr. Rathjens. At the 5-megaton yield and with the expected SS-9 accuracy the single shot kill probability for each reliable arriving reentry vehicle would be very much higher than eighty percent as I have already pointed out elsewhere.

If Dr. Wiesner had used three 5-megaton reentry vehicles, the expected accuracy of the SS-9's and, furthermore, had incorporated expected reliabilities, his calculations would have shown only sixty-three out of 1,100 hard targets surviving, that is 5.7%. Or if he had used the expected accuracy and reliabilities and the number of 1-megaton vehicles deliverable by the SS-9, he would have arrived at substantially the same result: sixty-eight out of 1,100 surviving.

There are a number of less critical flaws in Dr. Weinberg's and Dr. Wiesner's calculations. The essential, however, is that they both assume combinations of accuracy, yield, and number of reentry vehicles per booster that are less effective than intelligence expects (and for some time has expected) of the SS-9.

The Calculations of the Federation of American Scientists (FAS), March 8, 1969

These calculations of the FAS were published nearly a week before the President's decision on the Safeguard System was announced. The FAS statement was intended to refute in advance the need for extra protection of the Minuteman force. However, the calculations it presents are basically irrelevant since they use only the Russian force "at the present time," and they assume larger inaccuracies than intelligence attributes to the Russians' SS-9's for the later time period. They do not use MIRV's and in fact, according to their author, they do not use the SS-9 at all.

In the first section of this chapter,[16] I said that the many confident assertions current that Minuteman will be safe without extra protection in the late 1970's are unjustified. These supplementary comments have illustrated and analyzed some essential flaws in these assertions: they depend on erroneous estimates about the blast resistance of our own forces or wishful estimates about Russian lacks either in accuracy or in other capabilities or in competent tactics in that time period; they do not, as they claim, use "the most worrisome projections" and the "maximum capabilities" for Russian forces. In fact even my own calculations showing that the Minuteman will be vulnerable if extra protection is not provided do not use "maximum" Russian capabilities. Greater accuracies, for example, are quite feasible in the late 1970's for the Russians. I have used the CEP attributed to the SS-9 in the early 1970's. If the SS-9's CEP should be two-hundred fifty feet smaller than that estimate, then only four-hundred SS-9's using megaton range reentry vehicles would destroy about ninety five percent of the Minuteman force. Or with the larger force even greater percentages of the Minuteman force could be destroyed if we do nothing to supplement its protection. As I emphasized in my statement on April 23rd, the expected vulnerability of a hardened force is extremely sensitive to the accuracy of the force attacking. The accuracy assumed by Dr. Rathjens and myself is not only attributed to the SS-9 in the early 1970's, it is also the accuracy we estimate for our own MIRV's. Programs for achieving still greater accuracies for some of our MIRV's have been drawn up though not funded.

I have focused on the problem of protecting Minuteman, because, as I have stressed, we need a mixed force and have good reason to preserve the second-strike capability of so large a proportion of our strategic force. Even if it were true that the United States needed only a few strategic vehicles to survive, buying and paying for the operation of a great many that had become vulnerable to attack would be a very poor way to obtain those few surviving. There are safer and cheaper ways of getting a force of a given size than to buy a much larger one, most of which is susceptible to annihilation. To maintain a force most of which could be used only in a first-strike, hardly contributes to stability.

It is sometimes said that such analyses of the potential vulnerability of Minuteman are like the talk of the bomber gap in the early 1950's and the missile gap at the end of the 1950's. Nothing could be further from the truth. Most of those who talked of bomber gaps and missile gaps raised these possibilities to argue for expanding the number of our own bombers or missiles to close the gap. They thought of the problem as one of matching first-strike forces. But how to maintain a second-strike force cannot be adequately understood in these terms. Whether or not we have it depends, as I have said, not simply on the relative size of two opposing forces, but on a great many characteristics of the attacking force and of the force attacked and its protection. It is the opponents of the ABM today who, rather than defend the offense, would simply expand it. Moreover, many of these same opponents of the ABM were among the chief propounders of the missile and bomber gaps in the past; some scientists are now willing to state that they helped "create the myth of the missile gap." My own record on this matter is quite clear. Throughout the 1950's I pointed out the essential irrelevance of matching first-strike forces and of all the gap theories that flowed from such matching. For example, in 1956 I wrote:

> Exaggerated estimates of Russian force size, for example, might be used directly to suggest emulation. But we have already made clear that determining who has the best or second best Air Force in being in advance of attack by simply matching numbers or quality is not to the point. Those who assert that we may have fewer and perhaps inferior planes than the enemy and still have a deterrent force must also recognize that we may have more and even better vehicles and yet have inadequate deterrence.[17]

The propensity simply to list Russian and American pre-attack forces measured in various arbitrary ways continues to be exhibited on both sides of the present debate. On one side, first-strike capabilities are sometimes matched against adversary cities in the discussions of "overkill." On the other side, first-strike forces of Russia and the United States are sometimes matched against each other to show "superiority" or "inferiority" or "parity" or the like. My point is quite different. Foreseeable technical change in the 1970's compels sober thought about improving the protection of crucial elements in our strategic force. Such change can affect our second-strike capability. In that connection, I have centered my discussion on the protection of the Minuteman, but the problem of protecting our bombers is also important, and, even more, we must improve our protection of the national political command vital to the control of sea as well as land-based strategic forces.

ENDNOTES - Wohlstetter - The Case for Strategic Force Defense

1. This chapter constitutes a slightly edited version of my Statement to the Senate Armed Services Committee, April 23, 1969, and a supplement submitted on May 23, 1969.

2. *DoD Appropriations for 1969*, Hearings, Part I. Financial Summary. Expenditures in the 1950's were not then broken down by mission, but strategic budgets were even higher in the late 1950's than in 1962. In constant prices, for example, 1959 was more than double 1970.

3. ". . . *First,* an offense force with such increased accuracies and reliabilities and with an extensive use of MIRV's is very much more efficient in attacking the fixed offense force or the important fixed elements of the mobile force of an adversary. . . . *Second,* one result of this sort of change in Russian offense forces is to make improved antiballistic missiles (rather than simply more hardening or more missiles) an economic way for the United States to protect the hard fixed elements of a strategic force. . . . *Third,* at a minor increment in the modest cost of a hard-point ABM defense, it is possible to make available a light ABM for defense of civil societies against a small submarine or land-based missile force or part of a large one launched by mistake or without authorization. . . ." See Albert Wohlstetter, "Strength, Interest and New Technologies," Address to the September 1967 Institute of Strategic Studies Conference on the Implications of Military Technology in the 1970's at Elsinore, Denmark, in *Adelphi Papers,* No. 46, p. 4.

4. See, for example, one of the first classic sources of Minimum Deterrence Doctrine: *1970 Without Arms Control,* Special Committee Report, Planning Pamphlet No. 104, Washington, DC: National Planning Association, 1958, pp. 32-33, and 44.

5. We have not been very good at predicting our own or our adversary's technologies. These matters are intrinsically uncertain. Eminent scientists at the end of the 1940's predicted that fusion weapons would be infeasible, and, if feasible, undeliverable, and, if delivered, of no strategic significance, since it was thought (erroneously) they could be used only against cities. Some of those who then thought the threat of fusion bombs against cities neither moral nor important strategically now take it to be both. Compare, for example, Hans Bethe's present views with those in "The Hydrogen Bomb," *Scientific American*, Vol. 182, No. 4, April 1950, pp. 18-23. In February 1953 an important scientific study group expected the Soviets would have no ICBM's before the late 1960's—a prediction plainly in error by the end of the year. See the final report of the Lincoln Summer Study, among whose prominent members were James Killian, Jerome B. Wiesner and Carl Kaysen. Writing in October 1964, Jerome B. Wiesner and Herbert York, "National Security and the Nuclear Test Ban," *Scientific American*, Vol. 211, No. 4, October 1964, pp. 18, 27-35, were quite sure that no technological surprises could substantially change the operational effectiveness of intercontinental delivery systems, and thus entirely missed the major strategic potential of precisely aimed MIRV's, a concept that had already emerged in the classified literature. These were able and informed men. But exact prediction on these matters defies confident assertion.

6. See [this essay's] next section, "ON THE COUNTERFORCE CALCULATIONS OF SOME PROMINENT ABM OPPONENTS," for elaboration.

7. Poseidon and Minuteman III have been test flown and are in the process of deployment (the first of these should be operational in about a year and a half).

8. This section is a slightly edited version of a May 23, 1969, supplement to my April 23, 1969, Statement to the Senate Armed Services Committee.

9. See endnote 7 above.

10. Testimony of April 23, 1969, before the Senate Armed Services Committee. See also Wohlstetter testimony of March 28, 1969, Part 1, p. 359, of *Strategic and Foreign Policy Implications of ABM Systems,* Hearings before a subcommittee of the Senate Committee on Foreign Relations.

11. It is an error that is repeated also in Abram Chayes and Jerome B. Wiesner, eds., *ABM: An Evaluation of the Decision to Deploy an Anti-ballistic Missile System,* New York: Harper & Row, 1969.

12. CEP is the acronym for "Circular Error, Probable," a commonly used measure of the inaccuracy of weapon systems. In repeated firings, 50% of the weapons would miss their targets by less than the CEP (or median miss distance) and 50% would miss by more than the CEP. A frequent misinterpretation assumes that all weapons miss their targets by a distance equal to the CEP— which is like assuming that all students score at the 50th percentile on an exam. A nautical mile is 6,080 feet. It, rather than a statute mile, is a standard dimension for measuring CEP or median miss distance.

13. Ralph E. Lapp, "From Nike to Safeguard: A Biography of the ABM," *The New York Times Magazine,* May 4, 1969.

14. Chayes and Wiesner, eds., *op. cit.,* pp. 86-93.

15. Johan Hølst and William Schneider added the following commentary in 1969: Professor Wohlstetter's critique is based upon the manuscript version of the book which was distributed prior to its publication. In book form, Dr. Wiesner replaced the explicit .8 kill probability with a vague reference to an "accuracy estimated by Secretary Laird." In the manuscript, he incorrectly calculated (on the basis of a .8 kill probability) that 270 missiles would survive (the correct number is less than 150). The book version retains the "conclusion" of 270 survivors but does not make any explicit probability assumption—and thus now assumes a kill probability of about .65. See Chayes and Wiesner, eds., *op. cit.,* p. 73.

16. I.e., my testimony on April 23, 1969.

17. Albert J. Wohlstetter and F. S. Hoffman, *Protecting U.S. Power to Strike Back in the 1950's and 1960's*, R-290, Santa Monica, CA: The RAND Corporation, September 1, 1956.

Racing Forward? Or Ambling Back? (1976)

Albert Wohlstetter[1]

Not long ago the *Bulletin of the Atomic Scientists*, which since 1945 has kept time on the arms race, moved its famous clock ominously closer to midnight. The familiar reasoning is that American and Soviet negotiators at Geneva have failed to reach agreement on limiting strategic arms and so the race continues. The United States has forced the pace by overestimating the Soviet threat, and then, to play safe, spends more resources than are needed to meet even a menace so inflated. In this way we have given the U.S.S.R. no alternative than to react by spending in its own self-defense — which, in turn, we meet by still more "worst case" analyses, increased spending, and so on and on in the deadly "action-reaction cycle." The superpowers are engaged in a mortal contest, each provoking the other into piling up arms endlessly, wasting scarce resources, increasing the indiscriminate destructiveness of weapons, lessening rather than adding to their security, and moving the world closer to nuclear holocaust.

Secretary of State Kissinger has recently adopted one variant of this reasoning that puts the blame on technology. He has said that military technology has developed a momentum of its own, is at odds with the human capacity to comprehend it, is simply out of control, or is in imminent danger of getting beyond political control. Thus we must restrain not only the number of arms but their qualitative improvement. For it seems that the very effort to design new and better techniques to protect ourselves against adversaries makes things worse for both sides and mankind.

All this is familiar, but is it true? Is it true, for example, that we chronically overestimate what the Russians will deploy and that this is the source of an "action-reaction" chain, driving the Russians and ultimately ourselves to disaster? Whatever is the case for the Soviet strategic budgets and forces, has the United States in any clear sense been racing at all? Is it true, as is claimed, that U.S. technical innovation, in particular, has spurred us to higher and higher levels of strategic spending, destructiveness, and instability?

In fact, none of this is true. Starting in the early 1960s, we systematically *under*estimated how much and how rapidly the Soviets would increase their strategic offense forces. Moreover, for an even longer time, our own spending on strategic forces has been "spiraling" down rather than up. U.S. strategic program budgets ("Program I" as it is called) in real terms fell from a plateau at the end of the 1950s that was three and a half times the present size. In fact, the peak in strategic spending occurred in fiscal year 1952 when the budget was about 4.25 times the fiscal 1976 level (in 1976 U.S. dollars the strategic program budget in FY52 was 32.6 billion compared to 7.7 billion in FY76). Finally, the net effect of major innovations in our strategic force since the 1950s was to reduce not only its cost but also its indiscriminate destructiveness, and its instability or vulnerability to attack. These actualities seem to contrast so sharply with the standard saying about Soviet-American competition that we need:

First, to recall and document what the stereotypes about the strategic arms race have been;

Second, to contrast the standard view that we chronically overestimate Soviet offense deployments with the facts about what Soviet offense forces we predicted in the 1960s and how these predictions turned out;

Third, to contrast the theory that our strategic spending has been going up with the actual declining costs;

Fourth, to consider briefly the concrete effects of qualitative improvements on U.S. strategic forces and budgets.

Finally, to ask how we could have been repeating obvious untruths for so long without embarrassment. Answers to this last question must necessarily be speculative. I'll suggest some as I go along.

I

The Standard View of the "Arms Race"

Contemporary stereotypes about the strategic arms race resemble the arms-race doctrines of Lord Grey, Bertrand Russell, Lewis Fry Richardson, and other doctrines that flourished in England between two world wars and can be traced back at least to Cobden in the mid-nineteenth century. These doctrines suggested that each side in an arms race sees as a threat an increase in arms by the other side that is intended merely for defense. Lord Grey, who had been Foreign Minister when the Great War broke out, wrote:

> The increase of armaments, that is intended in each nation to produce consciousness of strength, and a sense of security, does not produce these effects. On the contrary, it produces a consciousness of the strength of other nations and a sense of fear.... The enormous growth of armaments in Europe, the sense of insecurity and fear caused by them — it was these that made war inevitable.[2]

The Quaker physicist, Richardson, put such views into differential equations relating the rate of increase in defense budgets, on one side, to the level of spending on the other with a resulting exponential increase of budgets for both.

The doctrines of the strategic "race" that have prevailed for more than 15 years add a few new twists to the old theory. First, they talk not simply of an exaggerated fear about the intent of an opponent in amassing armaments, but about exaggerated estimates of the size of these armaments and about plans to meet the opposing side's increase which would be overcautious (assuming the "worst case") even if the estimates of the range of possibilities were correct. Second, the British theorists between the wars adopted a certain Olympian even-handedness in describing the reciprocal fears generating the race. (Richardson talks of the mistaken fear of the "Minister of *Jedesland* [every country].") But current American doctrines, like revisionist history, frequently place on America the main responsibility for the rate and scale of the arms race. Third, the current doctrines stress the instabilities brought about by technology. And fourth, they locate the source of the race especially in efforts to defend civilians and destroy offensive military forces, and see the force driving the quantitative spiral to be not merely qualitative military change, but, in particular, improved technologies for destroying not people but weapons, whether in place or already on their way to target. This perverse doctrine, widely prevalent among theorists of the arms race since Sputnik, has been summarized by a sympathizer to the view in the "frosty apothegm": "Killing people is good; killing weapons is bad."[3]

Arms race dogma about "runaway technology," "exaggerated threats," "worst case analysis," "explosive increases," "uncapped volcanoes," "action-reaction," "treadmill to nowhere," etc., so pervades the statements on SALT and strategic interaction by Cabinet members, Congress and its staff, public interest lobbies, the academics, and the news media, that selecting a few out of a mass of citations may seem redundant; it risks bruising individual sensibilities.

But as Leon Festinger, a student of apocalyptic prophecies, reminds us, prophets and their disciples often deny they meant what they said, or even that they said it. So also, the apocalyptic prophets of the race to nuclear oblivion, when confronted with an empirical test and refutation of their beliefs: they have responded by denying that they or anyone else hold the dogma.[4] Here then is a sample of views documenting the points challenged.

Take the exaggerated threat "worst case" dynamic. In its more moderate form, this dogma holds that our planners have a systematic bias towards exaggerating — expecting our adversary to do more than he does — and that they compound this error by designing our force to meet a force greater than we expect — a "worst plausible case." It is this minimal form I show to be in error, not only the more obviously wrong extreme that talks of "invariable overestimation" or "worst possible case."

Morton Halperin and Jeremy Stone, as if arguments can be directed only at the extreme, say the notion that "arms race analysts believe in a myth of invariable U.S. overestimation" is a "straw man." It is "obviously unlikely," they say, that "analysts believe anything is invariable." They want quotations.

For the extreme, one can introduce the flesh and blood Jeremy Stone to the straw Jeremy Stone, who has written:

> The department invariably exaggerates the Soviet threat
> to obtain public and congressional support for weapons
> that will undermine the Soviet deterrent.[5]

417

And less or equally extreme:

> **Jerome Wiesner** — We always underestimate our own capabilities and overestimate those of the other fellow.[6]

> **Leonard Rodberg** — Even though the Soviets invariably lag far behind these predictions, our own programs go forward as if the forecasts were accurate....[7]

> **Herbert Scoville** — We should not again fall into the trap of perennial, compulsive reaction to timeworn exaggerated threats.[8]

> **Leslie Gelb** — The common practice, as I think we all know, has been to exaggerate and overdramatize.[9]

> **Robert McNamara** — ...a strategic planner must be "conservative" in his calculations; that is, he must prepare for the worst plausible case.[10]

> **Stanley Hoffmann** — The whole history of the postwar arms race is one of... preemptive escalation based on a worst case hypothesis which assumes the adversary's capacity and will to go ahead full speed.[11]

> **Paul Warnke** — ... in determining relative strategic balance, the other side, just as we do, must use worst case analysis.... They are not going to overestimate their potential and underestimate ours. If any, the error will be in the other direction.[12]

Such a belief is distinct from, but frequently associated with, a view that the United States is the catalyst for the race. Halperin and Stone observe sagely that the two views are distinct, but seem to doubt the currency of the second view as well. We might begin the list once more with a characteristically temperate quote from Stone:

> The Department of Defense has become an inventor and a merchandiser of exaggerated fears ... an unscrupulous lobbyist to get the weapons to answer these fears. Worst

of all, through the action-and-reaction phenomenon, its aggressive pursuit of the arms race has greatly undermined the security of the nation by unnecessarily stimulating Soviet efforts to keep up.[13]

Edgar Bottome — It is my contention that with minor exceptions, the United States had led in the development of military technology and weapons production throughout the Cold War.... The Soviet Union has been placed in a position where all it could do was react to American initiatives in bomber or missile building programs. This American superiority, along with the highly ambitious nature of American foreign policy, has placed the United States in a position of being fundamentally responsible for every major escalation of the arms race.[14]

William Epstein — American scientists seem to have the edge in technology and to lead the way in developing new weapons, particularly in the nuclear field, but Soviet scientists follow close behind in the action-reaction chain.[15]

Bernard Feld — History guarantees that new American technology will certainly be followed ... by Soviet emulation.[16]

Marshall Shulman — This commitment ... has led us to force the pace of the strategic arms race, and it inescapably leads to an uncontrolled military competition with the Soviet Union.[17]

John Newhouse — America's forces apparently served as both model and catalyst for the Russians.... Such is the action-reaction cycle as perceived by many scientists and bureaucrats.[18]

Newhouse adds that other scientists argue, "It is the impulse of technology, not an action-reaction cycle, that drives the arms race...." Most scientists in my collection see the impulse coming from us *and* technology. So, to quote Rodberg, "...we have used our own superior technology to drive the arms race forward."[19] But the malign role of technology is particularly important in the dogma and deserves illustration. "Is Jerome Wiesner," Michael Nacht has demanded, choosing an evidently far-fetched case, "a modern-day Luddite?" Consider the following from a committee Wiesner headed:

> It is, after all the *continuing competition to perfect and deploy new armaments* that absorbs quantities of time, energy, and resources that no static environment would demand; that exacerbates U.S. and Soviet relations with unreal considerations of strategic advantage or disadvantage; that keeps political leaders in both great powers off-balance and ill-prepared for far-reaching agreements; that fixes the attention of both sides on the most threatening aspects of the opposing posture; and, especially, that provides heightened risks of a violent *spasm of procurement — one spurring to new levels the cost, distrust, and the explosive dangers of an unending competition in arms* (italics added).[20]

The explosive dangers feared, Wiesner makes clear elsewhere, involve "an ever-increasing likelihood of war so disastrous that civilization, if not man himself, will be eradicated."[21] Anyone who holds that military innovation has a *net* bad effect (my definition of a Luddite in the military field) — let alone the effect of ultimate catastrophe — should want to impose general restraints on it. So, to quote Herbert York:

> The recent small successes in controlling the quantitative side of the arms race also call for renewed efforts to control its qualitative side, to slow down the rate of weapons innovation, and hence to reduce the frequency of introduction of ever more complex and threatening weapons.[22]

Examples could be multiplied. But we need not leave Cambridge, Massachusetts. Consider George Kistiakowsky and George Rathjens:

> ... any understanding that slowed the rate of development and change of strategic systems would have an effect in the right direction.[23]

And take Harvey Brooks, who argues that "the most promising lines of action for controlling the qualitative arms race probably lie in mutually agreed limitations on testing," but also suggests agreements to forgo specific improvements and general declarations against destabilizing developments, even if both would be hard to interpret or verify — particularly "in closed societies."[24] Even unverifiable agreements would provide arguments in internal bureaucratic debate to those who oppose such developments — at least in open societies. Or take Paul Doty:

> ... even better would be the adoption of a generalized
> set of restraints that would slow the whole development
> and deployment process.[25]

These would have an effect in the right direction, if qualitative change has a net bias toward making strategic forces more costly, more indiscriminately destructive, more vulnerable, and harder to control. But if not, you wouldn't slow things down generally. Nor try merely to stop "unfavorable" developments (always a good idea). You would encourage the development with all deliberate speed of technologies that reduce costs, increase discrimination, and make forces less vulnerable and easier to control.

I will present evidence that, whatever the false starts and mistakes in detail, the net effects of our major technological choices from the 1950s to the present were exactly the reverse of the Luddite stereotype. Generalized restraints would have been a bad idea.

II

U.S. Predictions and Soviet Realities

Systematic or even invariable overestimation need not lead to an arms spiral. If one's aim to counter a given threat is made extremely costly by expected adversary moves, because the threat is very large and the advantage is all on the other side, the game may not be worth the candle. This was in fact Secretary McNamara's chief argument against undertaking a thick ABM defense against the Soviets. In short, the larger the threat, the more futile a response may seem. The logic that overestimating an adversary drives one to race him is not compelling. Nonetheless, it is important to ask whether the U.S. government has in

421

fact systematically overestimated Soviet missile and bomber deployments — an assertion central to the dogma of a spiral driven by exaggerated estimates and mistaken fear.

The "missile gap," as is well known, was a U.S. overestimate after Sputnik of the number of intercontinental ballistic missile (ICBM) launchers that the Russians would deploy in the early 1960s. Indeed, the trauma of discovering the error formed the basis of many of Mr. McNamara's generalizations about our tendency to exaggerate and then to respond to anticipated larger threats rather than to what the Soviet leaders actually turned out to do. The missile gap has also generated a substantial confessional literature on the part of current proponents of the doctrine of an explosive arms race about their own role in creating the myth of the missile gap, and a substantial academic industry in doctoral theses and articles explaining this particular overestimate and the supposedly general and plainly evil habit of overestimating. A few comments, therefore, are in order on the missile gap before making a broader test of the habit. (Perhaps it is worth saying that I am on record, before and after Sputnik, as having steadily opposed evaluating force effectiveness on the basis of bomber or missile gaps.)

First, the "missile gap," a brief period in which the Soviets were expected to but did not deploy ICBMs more rapidly than we did, was an ICBM gap rather than a general missile gap. During the same period, in fact, we regularly and greatly underestimated the number of *intermediate and medium range* ballistic missile (IRBM/ MRBM) launchers that the Russians would deploy at the end of the 1950s and in the early 1960s. For example, our underestimate of the number of IRBM and MRBM launchers that the Russians would deploy by 1963 roughly offset our overestimate of the number of ICBM launchers they would deploy. In short, we misunderstood or reversed the priorities the Russians assigned to getting capabilities against the European as distinct from the North American part of NATO. This piece of ethnocentrism on our part was characteristic. We also greatly underestimated Soviet aircraft systems directed primarily at Europe rather than ourselves.

Second, predicting the size and exact mixture of a potential adversary's weapon deployments several years hence is a hard line of work. It is intrinsically uncertain, reversible by the adversary himself between the time of prediction and the actual deployment. Moreover, an adversary may want his opponent to estimate wrongly, either up or down. In the specific case of the missile gap, Khrushchev did what he could to make the U.S. and the rest of the world believe that the Soviets had a larger initial program of ICBMs than they actually had; and he succeeded.

Whatever the source and nature of our misestimation, it helped generate the belief that we invariably expect the Russian programs to be larger than they turn out to be, that we compound this overestimate by deliberately designing our programs to meet a Russian threat that is greater even than the one we expect, and then, when the Russian threat turns out to be less rather than greater than expected, the damage is done; the overlarge U.S. force is already a reality or irreversibly committed.

It is a good idea, then, to subject to systematic test this claim of regular overestimation. It is a major element of the current dogma, repeated endlessly since 1961. In fact, the nearly universal acceptance of this belief has emerged from constant repetition of tags like "the mad momentum," "we have invariably overestimated" or "we are running a race with ourselves," etc., rather than from any systematic numerical comparison with reality.[26] Figures 1 to 3 sum up[27] the results of a search for all of the long-term predictions of Soviet strategic missile and bomber deployment that could be found in the annual presentation of programs and budgets to Congress by the Secretary of Defense from the start of 1962 to the start of 1972, and a comparison of these predictions with what the Russians actually deployed by mid-1972 — the last date referred to in the predictions that could be checked at the time the analysis was completed.

Aside from their comparative accessibility, several reasons governed the choice of these predictions from the Defense Secretaries' formal statements, rather than from Army, Navy, Air Force, CIA, Bureau of Intelligence Research in State, or other estimates.

First, during this extended period the Secretary of Defense did, regularly, every year, make predictions precise enough to be proved wrong and precise enough for measuring how much they had missed the mark. The possibility of determining error here requires not only that the predictions be specific as to time and quantity, and not excessively hedged by "might" or "may conceivably," but also that the adversary realities referred to in the predictions be open to observation and highly reliable measurement by the U.S. *after the fact*. Not all *objects* nor all characteristics predicted nor all predictors meet these requirements. Far from it.

Second, these predictions of the Secretary of Defense form a well-defined, substantial population of estimates—which is not the case for intelligence predictions in general.

Third, these estimates were presented as authoritative and official.

Fourth, they were given particular prominence in the programming and budgeting process by the fact that the Secretary used them directly to support his program. And finally these particular forecasts relate directly to the Secretary's judgment and that of the Congress on the five-year defense program. They are therefore most relevant for analyzing possible relations between defense programs and defense budgets and the impetus these programs might be given by forecasts as to the future enemy force deployments. Defense systems take many years to become operational, and the forces they will confront are necessarily the subject only of long-term conjecture. In presenting these estimates the Secretary emphasized this point. For example, in 1963 he testified:

> Because of the long leadtimes involved in making these weapon systems operational, we must plan for our forces well in advance of the time when we will need them and, indeed, we now project our programs at least five years ahead of the current budget year. For the same reason we must also project our estimates of the enemy's forces at least five years into the future, and for some purposes, even beyond. These longer range projections of enemy capabilities are, of course, highly conjectural, particularly since they deal with a period beyond the production and deployment lead-times of enemy weapon systems. Therefore, we are, in effect, attempting to anticipate production and deployment decisions which our opponents, themselves, may not yet have made. This fact should be borne in mind as we discuss the intelligence estimates and our own programs based on them.[28]

The first eight charts, Figures 1a to 1h, compare U.S. predictions of Soviet ICBM launchers to be deployed with the actuality as estimated after the fact.[29] The vertical arrows indicate the date at which the prediction was made (e.g., February 1962 in Figure 1a). The dashed line or lines indicate the range from high to low of what was predicted (in Figure 1a, a high of 650 and a low of 350, by mid-1967, five and a half years later). Later projections usually included (as in Figure 1b) a high and a low for more than one year. This is shown in the shaded portion. The steeply rising solid line which is the same in all the charts shows the number the Russians actually completed, as estimated after the fact.

Though the claim about invariable overestimation posits that at least the middle of the range between high and low always exceeds the reality, it will be apparent that even the high end of the range seldom did that, and then only at the start of the period — and even then just barely. For ICBMs the "highs" reached as high as reality only twice in 11 times. The prediction made in 1965 (Figure 1d) is typical. Figures 2 and 3 illustrate analogously typical long-run predictions of future Soviet submarine-launched missiles deployed and future Soviet bomber deployments. The middle of the predicted range of the number of sub-launched missiles deployed was about three-quarters of the eventual reality. In the case of the bombers, we continued to believe that the Russians were going to phase them down and most drastically in the case of the medium bombers; but the Soviets never came down to our expectations. Tables 1 and 2 sum up some principal results. Out of 51 predictions, the low end of the range *never* exceeded the actual; the mean between the high and low exceeded it only twice in 51 times; our highs reached reality only nine times! Hardly a record of overestimation. Moreover, the ratios of projected-to-realized future values of the Soviet strategic force in operation display the fact that the underestimates were very substantial and that even the average of the highs was under the reality. It will be evident also that there was no systematic learning from the past as information accumulated.

In fact, since the numbers shown refer to estimates of the *cumulative* number of strategic vehicles in operation at future dates, and since the later predictions were based on much more extensive knowledge of what was already deployed or at least started in construction at the time of the prediction, the degree of bias can be made even plainer. There are several points.

Table 1

1962–1971 U.S. Predictions that Exceed the Actual
Soviet Strategic Deployment *

	ICBMs	Sub-launched Missiles	Heavy Bombers	Medium Bombers	Total
Low Predictions that exceed Actual	0 of 11	0 of 15	0 of 14	0 of 11	0 of 51
Mid-Range of Predictions that exceed Actual	0 of 11	1 of 15	1 of 14	0 of 11	2 of 51
High Predictions that exceed Actual	2 of 11	3 of 15	2 of 14	2 of 11	9 of 51

Table 2

Average Ratios of Predicted-to-Actual Cumulative Numbers *
(Numbers in parentheses compare predicted to actual *change*)

	ICBMs (11 Estimates)	Sub-launched Missiles (15 Estimates)	Heavy Bombers (14 Estimates)	Medium Bombers (11 Estimates)
Lower Predictions	0·53 (0·16)	0·64 (0·12)	0·85	0·67
Mid-Range of Predictions	0·67 (0·33)	0·74 (0·47)	0·91	0·77
High Predictions	0·80 (0·50)	0·84 (0·82)	0·98	0·87

* Predictions exclude short-term estimates of ICBMs and sub-launched missiles that are limited essentially to completion of launchers already started.

First, our means of acquiring information improved greatly over the period. Second, in the later years a much larger proportion of the cumulative total in operation was already in operation at the time predictions were made. And third, we had information not only about the number of launchers completed and in operation (displayed in the rising curves of Soviet ICBM and SLBM launchers) but also about the substantial numbers of launchers that had been started but not completed at the time the prediction was made. We knew that ICBMs started would generally be completed, say, in about a year and a half, and submarine-based missile launchers in about two and a half years, but in any case well before the dates in our long-run predictions. In fact, estimates of the missile launchers already started that were expected to be completed by a given time were, at the midrange, only 3 percent below the actual number for ICBMs and 2 percent above it for submarine-launched missiles. If we make a rough adjustment for this fact on the one hand and on the other allow for some delay in acquiring and processing information by the date predictions were made, if we assume generously a seven-month delay, the degree of understatement will be more apparent. In effect, what was being predicted was an *increment* in the force then in operation or under construction. It is appropriate to compare that increment with the actual amount newly started and completed in the ensuing interval.

Figure 1a
ICBM Prediction Made in 1962

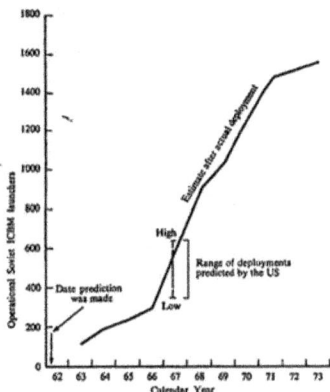

Figure 1b
ICBM Predictions Made in 1963

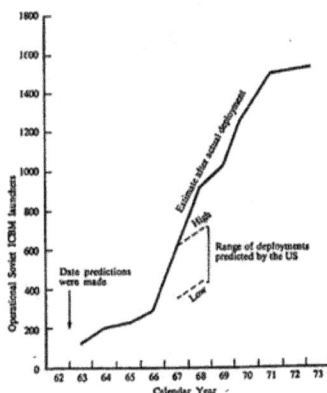

Predictions in Figures 1a-1b exclude short-term estimates that are limited essentially to the completion of launchers already started.

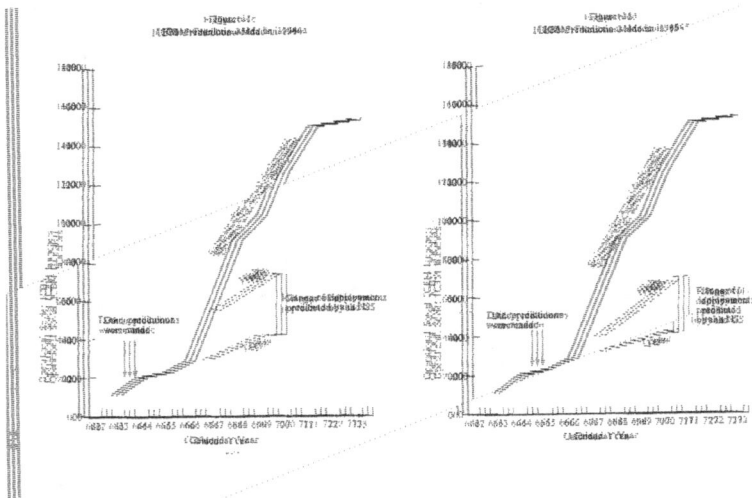

Figure 1e
ICBM Prediction Made in 1966

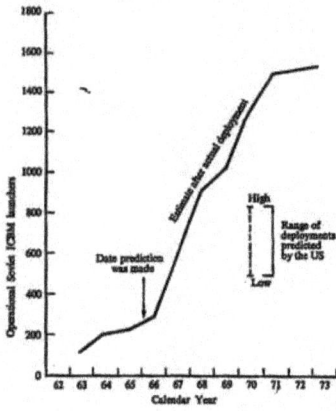

Figure 1f
ICBM Prediction Made in 1967

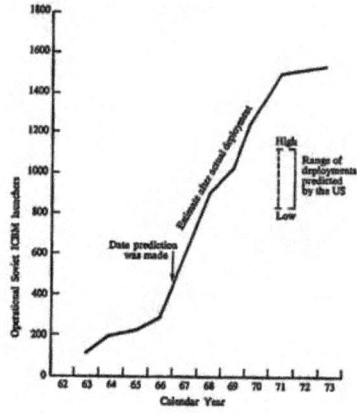

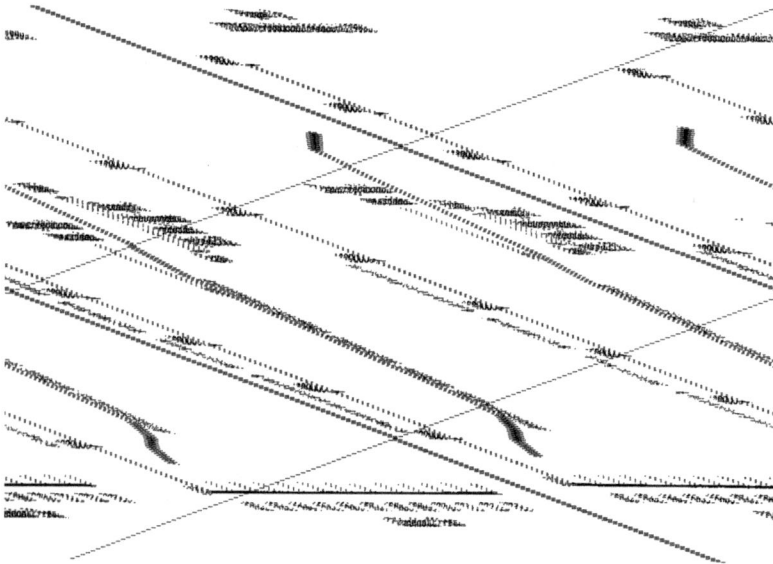

Figure 2
Operational Soviet Sub-launched Missiles
1965 US Long Term Prediction Compared to the Actual Number *

Figure 3
Operational Soviet Bombers
1966 US Predictions Compared to the Actual Number

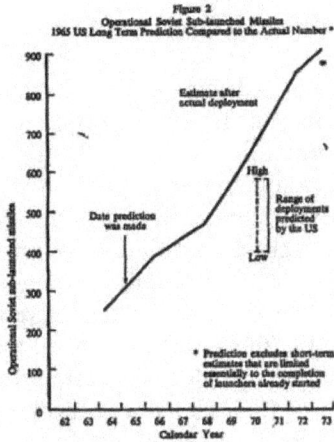

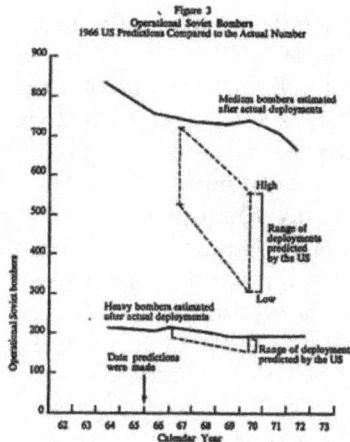

Burying Wrong Predictions in the Known Past

Our longer-term predictions about the Soviet strategic triad were under the mark for 11 years. The long-term ICBM projections presented in Figures 1a-1h were made during the eight years from 1962 to 1969. (Later ones referred to dates well after SALT I numerical limits on missiles took effect.) Did these eight years of long-range ICBM predictions show systematic learning?

It would not be surprising if they did, or even if, after eight years of trying, ICBM predictions finally touched reality. Programs do, in the end, level off; and the forecaster who year after year predicts they will, sooner or later, like a stopped watch, will be right. What is surprising is that these forecasts got worse, not better.

Some analysts now grant that we underestimated, but claim that we improved with time.[30] They ignore the important difference between predicting a *cumulative* total of vehicles that will have been deployed at some future time, most of which are known to be already completed or in process at the time when the prediction is made, and predicting a *change* from this known state. This accurately-known past makes up an increasing portion of the cumulative total. Nonetheless, those who detect an improvement in forecasts compare predicted with actual totals, not predicted with actual change from what was known; and so swamp unpredicted new starts in the steadily increasing total of launchers known to be started or completed.

429

Suppose every year a forecaster regularly predicted that during the next 12 months an adversary was going to add 10 more missile launchers; and every year, without fail, the adversary added 100. At the end of 10 years, the adversary would have built up a force of 1,000 launchers. But in the beginning of the tenth year, with 900 in place, the forecaster, undaunted, might predict, once more, that in the *next* period the adversary would build only 10 more, so reaching a cumulative total of 910. If one used Nacht's ratio of the predicted-to-actual cumulative number deployed, it would appear that the forecaster's skill in prediction was steadily improving. In the first year the predicted-to-actual ratio was 10/100, in the second year 110/200 — and so on until the great success of the tenth year, when the predicted-to-actual ratio would be 910/1,000. A success ratio of 0.91 seems a marvelous improvement over 0.10. However, year after year he would have been undershooting reality in the same way. The *difference* between the predicted and actual cumulative numbers would have been the same — namely 90 — and the *ratio* of predicted-to-actual *increments* would have continued to be one-tenth. The forecaster would have learned nothing about how better to anticipate the future. The cumulative ratios, as in Figure 4a, miss this essential point.

Figure 4a
Ratios of Predicted to Actual Cumulative Totals of Soviet ICBM
Silos (Burying the Future in the Known Past) *

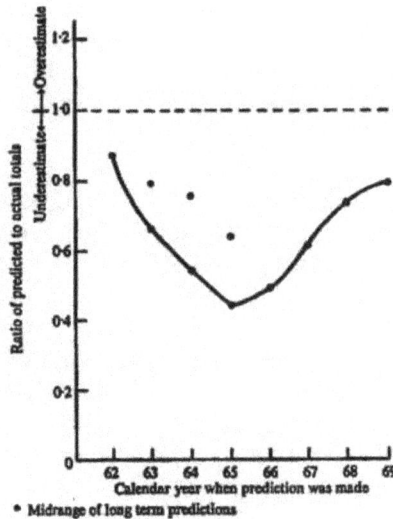

* Midrange of long term predictions

430

Moving from hypothetical to actual history, if we exercise a little care, it is easy to see that our long-run predictions of net future change were getting no better, that if anything they were worsening. The most direct way to establish that fact is suggested by our hypothetical example, where the difference between prediction and reality remains constant while the cumulative ratios suggest an apparent improvement.

Figure 4a[31] presents a scatter diagram that buries errors about the future in statements that are mostly about the known past. It shows ratios of predicted-to-actual cumulative totals of finished silos. The Secretaries made these long-term predictions during the eight-year period 1962 to 1969. All refer to dates no later than mid-1972. Each dot represents one such cumulative ratio calculated at the mid-range of each prediction. In each of three of the years, the Secretaries made two long-range predictions. I have connected the subset of eight dots that maximize the impression that the worsening was reversed.[32]

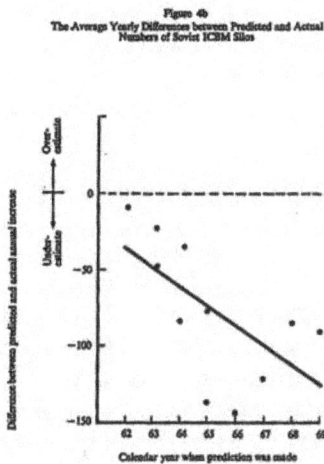

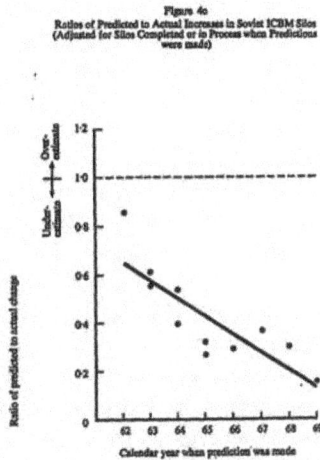

Figure 4b
The Average Yearly Differences between Predicted and Actual Numbers of Soviet ICBM Silos

Figure 4c
Ratios of Predicted to Actual Increases in Soviet ICBM Silos (Adjusted for Silos Completed or in Process when Predictions were made)

In the more appropriate Figure 4b each dot represents the mean amount per year by which the mid-range between high and low of a long-term prediction missed reality. All of the dots throughout the entire period are below zero. All undershoot reality. The average difference between predicted and actual silos was -80.1. Second, the dots drift downward quite steeply; that is, the underestimates tended to get much worse year by year. A trend line fitted in the standard way to the points representing underestimates slopes downward at the rate of -12.59 silos per year. For the period as a whole the evidence indicates not "learning," but "unlearning." During the later subperiod starting in 1965 (the year some analysts think of as the worst), tests do not show improvement: there is no statistically significant trend towards reducing the differences between predicted and actual. A variety of statistical tests indicates worsening.[33] Moreover Figure 4b still neglects knowledge of launchers in process. On the whole, then, the evidence provided by a study of differences between predicted and actual numbers of silos suggests both underestimation and *increasing* underestimation.

That evidence can be greatly reinforced by a closer look at ratios, provided however that one looks at ratios of predicted-to-actual *changes* from the accurately known past. At the time when predictions were being made, the forecaster had hard data not only on (a) silos completed at that time, but also on (b) those that were in process of construction. Figure 4c presents ratios adjusted both for silos completed and for those in process of construction. Since the predicted numbers were less than the actual numbers, the ratios are all less than one; all are underestimates. The predictions averaged roughly a third of the actual number. The median ratio is .34. The ratios drift downward with time, worsening at a rate of about eight percentage points a year.

In sum, the long-term U.S. projections of Soviet ICBM silos were not only underestimates, but also deteriorating underestimates. The phenomenon cries out for explanation.

The distinction between predicting cumulative totals and predicting changes in these totals may explain not only recent errors in analyzing history; it may also be part of the explanation for the slowness of the forecasters themselves to recognize a drift away from reality while it was happening. For even though the use of cumulative totals of finished launchers (and especially of ratios of predicted-to-actual totals) has its hazards in an analysis of the success of predictions, such totals have an obvious current operational importance for those who are charged with planning for the contingency of combat. Adversaries must fight with the stocks they have ready at the time a war breaks out. "Orders of battle" are given in terms of such total stocks. For many current purposes, therefore, it is entirely natural to formulate predictions in such terms.

Nonetheless, when predictions are formulated mainly in this way—as they are—systematic forecasting errors will tend to be buried in the larger totals, and corrections are likely to be discovered later than if forecasts were made in terms of the changes expected during the prediction interval. Someone planning to buy additional forces or to phase some out, should focus on long-term *changes* in adversary forces. Failure to center on change is only part of the explanation. Much remains to be explained. But underestimation of bomber and missile deployments for a very long time plainly persisted. That is the main point

So far I have focused on the important set of predictions cited by the Secretaries of Defense. While these plainly played a key role in the planning and budgeting process, one might well ask whether they were typical of the intelligence community. Those reluctant to give up the myth of chronic overestimation in particular ask this question, and have in mind the official consensus and, even more, the widely reported excesses of the Air Force. In fact it is familiar that during the "missile gap" Army and Navy estimates were under, and the Air Force over, the consensus. To judge how widespread underestimation became during the 1960s, it is worth comparing Air Force long-range ICBM predictions with the official consensus starting in the autumn of 1961, and comparing both with the Soviet realities counted in post-deployment estimates.

The Air Force, the Consensus, and Reality

In the first two years (Figures 5a and 5b), the Air Force did indeed exceed both the consensus and the reality. In autumn 1962 the mid-range of the consensus was below the 1967 reality and the "high" barely reached it. In autumn 1963, the Air Force predictions still greatly exceeded the consensus, but the two began to converge. There was some overlap between them in the early years referred to in the prediction, and in the more distant years, when the Air Force outbid the consensus, even its high dropped below reality. In autumn 1964 the Air Force and official predictions came close together and overlapped for the first time in predictions about the more distant years. For these more distant years, even the Air Force highs were below reality, though the Air Force still exceeded the consensus. In autumn 1965 and 1966 (Figures 5e and 5f) underestimation worsened with further convergence. Finally, in autumn 1967, convergence was total. The Air Force endorsed the consensus on condition that the Soviets would deploy MRVs (Multiple Re-entry Vehicles — unlike MIRVs, *not* aimed independently), which they did. The highs of the long-term forecasts in these last years till mid-1967 were invariably under reality, and both the consensus and the Air Force assumed an ultimate leveling off of the Russian program well below what happened. In autumn 1968 the Air Force concurred with the consensus on the assumption, now clearly conservative, that MIRVs would be deployed by mid-1978.

Figure 5a
Air Force and Official Consensus Predictions Made in Autumn 1961

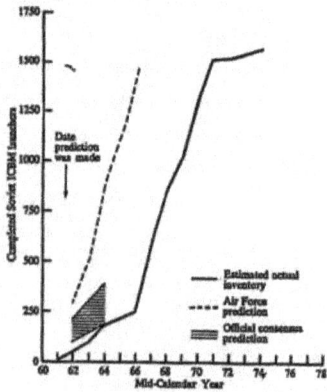

Figure 5b
Air Force and Official Consensus Predictions Made in Autumn 1962

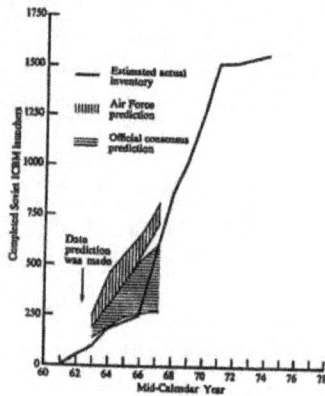

Figure 5c
Air Force and Official Consensus Predictions Made in Autumn 1963

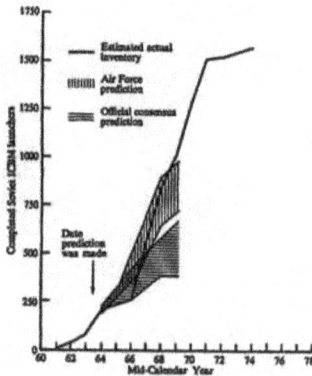

Figure 5d
Air Force and Official Consensus Predictions Made in Autumn 1964

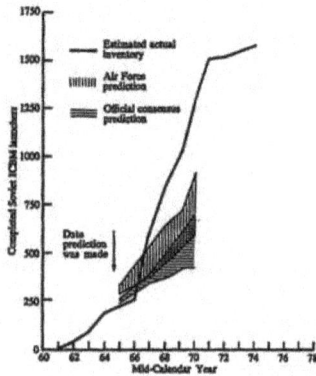

Figure 5e
Air Force and Official Consensus Predictions
Made in Autumn 1965

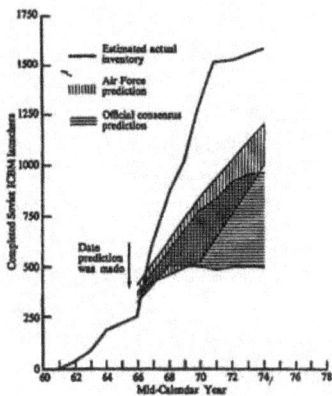

Figure 5f
Air Force and Official Consensus Predictions
Made in Autumn 1966

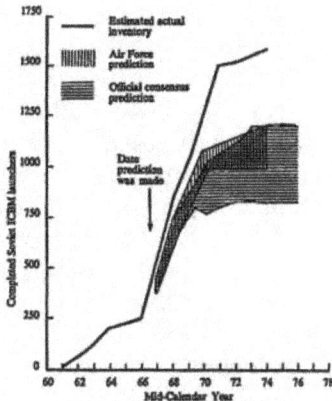

Figure 5g
Air Force and Official Consensus Predictions
Made in Autumn 1967

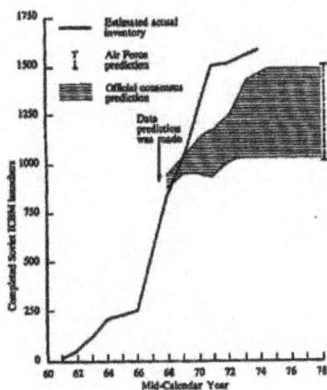

Figure 5h
Air Force and Official Consensus Predictions
Made in Autumn 1968

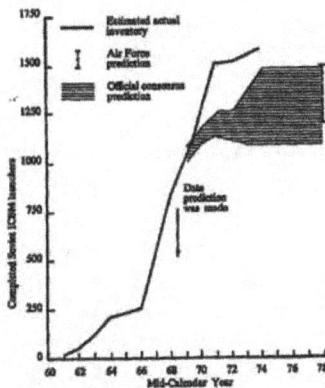

The steady movement towards the official forecasts suggests the power of consensus. That power is particularly impressive since final convergence occurred in autumn 1967, which (as McNamara observed the following January) marked a 380-silo jump from autumn 1966. Deviation from the consensus on the high side went out of style just as it became objectively most plausible.

Why?

Pressures for conformity in the 1960s tended to operate against overestimating offense deployment. Overestimating rather than error had become disreputable. For example, the Secretary, in January 1964, stressed that "these longer-range projections of enemy capabilities must necessarily be highly uncertain," but, "indeed the record shows that in the last several years we have consistently *over*estimated Soviet ICBM strength" (italics added). He then cited three forecasts made in 1959, 1960, and 1961, during the "missile gap," about Soviet ICBMs expected in mid-1963. All three, of course, were far above the mark. He warned, "These facts should be borne in mind as we discuss the estimates for the 1967-69 period." But the 1964 estimate about 1967, to which he attached this caveat, turned out to be not above but way below the mark—120 silos below at mid-range. Moreover, while in the preceding two years predictions about 1967 were also below, the 1964 prediction was worse. And the 1965 prediction about 1967 was worse still. As 1967 got closer, our aim at it sank steadily further beneath the bull's eye.

Part of the pressure to conform by underestimating was very likely a reflex, over-correcting for the "missile gap" that had publicly embarrassed the intelligence community. But this could hardly explain the extraordinary persistence and even worsening of the errors, as evidence to the contrary began to pour in. It is interesting that the Secretary brought up the "missile gap" in 1964 to reinforce his caveat against overestimation. The "gap" had been given public burial in the autumn of 1961. The Defense Report had not bothered to mention it in 1962 or 1963. The Report revived the horrible example as part of the budget battle and issued ominous strictures against exaggeration as a way of cutting the ground from under importunate service demands based on anticipated large Soviet capabilities.

As for Soviet "capabilities," when the Secretary used that phrase, or "Soviet ICBM strength," as in the passage quoted, he referred explicitly to the *number* of vehicles deployed. These numbers are what the forecasts were overwhelmingly about, just as the forecasts during the "missile gap" had been. It was only when the number of Soviet silos completed or in process came close to catching up with the ceiling we had chosen for our ICBM force that the Secretary began to put some stress on "qualitative superiority." In effect, he asserted by way of comfort, the Soviets may get nearly as many missiles, but ours will be better. But his FY 1968 Report insisted that especially if we counted in the SLBMs, we were still ahead even in numbers—"as of now." "As of now, we have more than three times the number of intercontinental ballistic missiles (i.e., ICBMs and SLBMs) the Soviets have. Even by the early 1970s, we still expect to have a significant lead over the Soviet Union in terms of numbers... and," the Secretary added, in a vague but dazzling phrase, able to comfort even today, "a very substantial superiority in terms of overall combat effectiveness."

But in 1971, the Soviets had the lead in numbers. Looking on the bright side—"quality"—may have dazzled perceptions of our failure to predict the numerical shift. The Defense Reports in fact contain a treasure trove of methods of bucking us up while blurring our view. Their very vagueness soothes. "By and large," said the Secretary in 1965, "the current estimates... projected through mid-1970 are of the same order of magnitude as [last year's] projections through mid-1969." And in 1966, with reassuring familiarity: "By and large the current estimates projected through mid-1970 are of the same general order of magnitude as those which I discussed here last year." In 1967, he reported that the current estimates were "generally in line" with the preceding year. "Order of magnitude" is particularly mind-boggling, but strictly implied only that this year's estimates were within one-tenth to 10 times as much as last year's. Which is less reassuring. In any case, the estimates were wrong and getting worse.

In 1968, after the huge 380-silo jump in one year, McNamara said, "We believe the Soviet ICBM force will continue to grow over the next few years, but at a considerably slower rate than in the recent past." But the rate specified fell far below the one later observed. In 1969, Secretary Clifford continued in the same cheery vein. The Soviet force has grown "well over threefold in a ... little more than two years. The rate ... has been somewhat greater than estimated a year ago. However, we believe [it] will be considerably smaller over the next two or three years." But once again the expected rate of new starts formed a small fraction of the actual. Such muffled disappointments scarcely perturbed the theory, pushed hard in 1969 and 1970, that exaggerations drove a race.

It would be wrong, I think, to conclude that the Defense Reports display a conscious effort to obscure our failure to anticipate rapid Soviet increase. More likely, wishes and policy leanings shaped—and lowered—consciousness. But much remains to be explained. Undoubtedly, various leanings—some to expand, some to cut or reallocate strategic spending—influenced estimates of contending factions. But then we need to ask not only "*cui bono* [to whose advantage]?" but which estimates matched reality. Factions in or out of government have *some* compatible interests. Aside from a joint interest in accurate assessment for the common defense, all factions have at least an occupational self-interest in *not* making forecasts that fail disastrously.

Underestimates persisted for an extraordinarily long time after the error of the missile gap in part because they were fortified by an American strategic view that Americans often attributed also to the Soviets. (These were "projections" in the psychoanalyst's, as well as the forecaster's sense.) That view suggested that the Soviets did not need a large expansion of forces in order to be able to destroy a few American cities and therefore did not intend to undertake it.[34]

It was common in and out of government through the mid-1960s to hold that the Soviets wanted only a minimum deterrent, a couple of hundred missiles aimed at cities (roughly the actual number of Soviet ICBMs in 1964-65), and that they would not try to catch up.[35] We clung to this belief after they had started enough launchers to make it untenable. Then we shifted to saying they wanted *only* to catch up, just as they were passing us on the way to getting 50 percent more. "Rough parity" can be quite rough.

Action-reaction language is vague enough to rationalize events after the fact. It was a glass through which we saw darkly. It not only led us to wrong predictions about the Soviet actions, but it made inaction on our part seem reasonable. The Russians would not act to catch up, because they knew we would react to counter them, and since they would not act we did not have to. But in fact, they acted and we did not. And sometimes the Secretary argued that if we were to increase our active defense, the Russians would inevitably react by vastly increasing their offense so that in the end we would not only have wasted the money, but would end up with a net increase in the number of fatalities we might suffer. In other words, if we acted, the Russians would react; therefore there was no point in taking action.

Unfortunately, a distorting and wishful myopia followed from the close polemical focus of factions in and out of government on the very latest incremental change in Soviet force dispositions and its implications for the current year's U.S. budget, as compared to that of the preceding year. Momentary pauses in Soviet construction of launchers for one missile type, perhaps because new improved systems were being readied for deployment or because of bad weather, were seized on by outside advisers and by unnamed "highly placed officials" as an indication that Soviet programs were "tapering off," "leveling off," "slowing down," "petering out," "grinding to a halt."[36] Since, characteristically, massive Soviet efforts in research, development, testing, and evaluation parallel a countercycle in deployment, and since Russian weather is notoriously intemperate, especially during their long winters when our budget debates start, there was plenty of room for confusion, ambiguity, and self-deception inside and outside the U.S. government.

As for the public view, it was only to be expected that statements about increased Soviet missile deployments would be dismissed with a kind of naive cynicism: the slickers in the Pentagon are using their annual scare tactics in support of bigger budgets. Some outside advisers protested the government's "'most outrageous' statements about the alleged buildup by Russia," whereas in fact we were told, "The Soviet arms capability actually is tapering off." Dissonant sounds of reality were hardly audible in Establishment study groups meeting in Washington, Cambridge, and New York. The successful attempt to save the predictions and the dogma on which they were based is quite as instructive as the performance of Sabbatai Zevi's followers, a sect that managed to survive and reinterpret a public prediction that the world would end in 1648 and even to acquire new and more enthusiastic adherents; or the Millerites who gathered new followers after the world failed to end as Miller had predicted by March 21, 1844.[37] Students of the subject have observed that when predictions fail, this may only increase fervor and proselytizing for the dogma that led to the prediction. After all, it is in just such adversity that a dogma needs all the recruits it can get. Editorials and articles appear with ritual regularity in *The New York Times,* the *New Republic,* the *Christian Science Monitor, Scientific American,* and elsewhere warning of the Pentagon's ritual exaggeration of the threat and presenting in full-blown form a generalized doctrine that it is just such exaggerations that accelerate the fatal spiral.

Though holders of the dogma of regular U.S. overestimation protested against excessive secrecy, they were in good part protected by it. Exact quantitative comparisons of past predictions with reality take time and would have met much resistance even in private; in public a systematic, long-term check was impossible. However, enough has long been public to undermine the theory of regular overestimation. We have had open official statements reflecting classified estimates that the Russians would not try to get as many missiles as the U.S., that they were stopping or slowing down; and equally public figures on the actual growth of Russian strategic forces. The contrast was plain, or rather would have been plain, if only we had been taking a long hard look; or even looking. More important, the reality of understatement should have destroyed the generalized theory of overstatement, but it did not.

It would be unfortunate if we should now swing from understatement to the opposite extreme. It would be nice, though far from easy, to get it nearly right. Even if we do, the implications for our strategic budgets will by no means be simple. Sober consideration, however, will discount the threat that invariably overestimating Soviet threats drives us to exponential increases and the notion that only throwing caution to the winds can stop the "race." The threat of invariable overestimation is one that is plainly exaggerated.

Some of these policy decisions, I believe, were justified on other grounds. But prevailing doctrine offered a generalized rationale for cutting rather than expanding. That is what happened, but we didn't notice. Our perceptions of actual U.S. past declines have been as confused as our view of supposed future Soviet increases.

III

Mythical U.S. Increases and Actual U.S. Declines

Whatever the explanation offered for the strategic race—invariably overestimating and worst-case analysis, bureaucratic politics, technology out of control, etc.—there is a prior question as to whether or not there has been a race. To justify the term "race," any side that is racing has at least to be rapidly increasing its strategic budgets and forces. Even if the increase does not proceed at an increasing rate, for the name "race" to make any sense at all, there would have to be at the very least an increasing trend. An examination of American strategic budgets and forces since the mid-1940s suggests that on the principal relevant measures the trend is down. And an examination of the net effect of qualitative innovation in the strategic forces over the same time period equally refutes the stereotype about the net destabilizing effect of technical change. First, look at our supposed quantitative upward spiral in the total explosive energy that could be released or in its capacity for indiscriminate destruction.

Total Explosive Energy and "Overkill"

The total explosive energy that could be released by the strategic stockpile is a measure frequently used to compare U.S. and Soviet forces by conservative organizations, such as the American Security Council. It also appears in the popular vivid comparisons of the total explosive yield of all the bombs dropped in Korea (200,000 tons) or in the Second World War (5,000,000 tons) with the explosive yield (measured in tons of some non-nuclear chemical explosive such as TNT) of a single nuclear warhead, several of which might be carried in one vehicle today. However, the drawbacks of such a measure are clear and most obvious in the vivid comparisons. A single bomb releasing five million tons of explosive energy (i.e., a five megaton weapon) is incapable of doing anything like the damage done worldwide from Japan and Burma to West Europe and Russia by the many tens of thousands of bombs exploded in the Second World War, even if the total energy yield were the same. In general, one large warhead with twice the energy yield of two smaller weapons, unlike them, cannot be used to attack two very widely separated targets.

Moreover, it was understood at the dawn of the atomic age that, even though the Hiroshima bomb had roughly one thousand times the explosive yield of one of the largest Second World War blockbusters, it would not do structural damage to an area one thousand times the size, but roughly one-tenth of that. By comparison with the smaller bomb, some 90 percent of its energy would be "wasted" in "overhitting" or "overdestroying" or "overkilling" the nearby area.[38] For that comparison then, not 1,000, but its two-thirds power, 100 is a roughly correct approximation for determining relative structural damage. And even in comparing the destructive effect of stocks of bombs that are less varied in yield, some such adjustment is essential.

However, it is not only conservative polemic that exploits the misleading measure of gross "megatonnage" of explosive energy. Some of the crudest polemical uses are by opponents of increases in military budgets. In talking of "overkill," they usually divide the total population of the world into the aggregate explosive energy in the stockpile to arrive at some such figure as 10 tons of TNT equivalent for every man, woman, and child in the world. Such a measure makes exactly the confusion that the original discussions of overhitting or overdestruction of the area near the target were designed to avoid. And it adds several other more potent confusions besides. It implies that the purpose of stocks of weapons is and should be exclusively to destroy population, that what is wrong is not the killing of populations, but their overkilling. It is not strictly related to hypotheses about a spiraling increase in total explosive yield, or still less a spiral in the damage that might be done. However, by suggesting that the stocks are now far too large, it makes plausible the notion that there has been a steady exponential increase. In fact, nuclear weapons are directed at any of a large variety of military targets, and there is no simple rule for deciding whether one has too many or too few. That is a problem we need not address here.[39] The question we are asking is whether on this measure there has been an exponential increase.

Figure 6
Combined US Strategic Offense and Defense Megatons

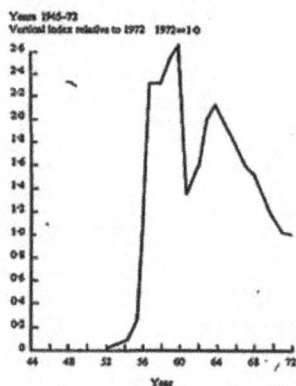

Years 1945-72
Vertical index relative to 1972 1972=1·0

Figure 7
Combined US Strategic Offense and Defense Warheads

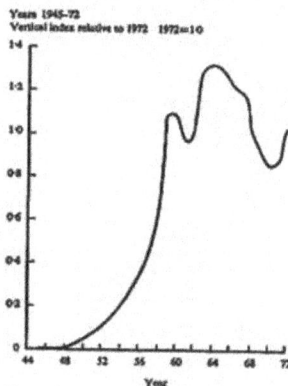

Years 1945-72
Vertical index relative to 1972 1972=1·0

The answer indicated in Figure 6 is "clearly not." After an initial sharp increase, the total explosive energy yield declined from a peak two-and-a-half times the 1972 figure. And 1972 was about at the level of 1955. While this aggregate includes, appropriately for contemporary arms race theories, strategic defense as well as offense warheads, the decline is about the same for the aggregate explosive yield of the offense warheads alone.

The Number of Strategic Warheads

At the opposite extreme from totting up the energy releasable by all strategic warheads is a measure that ignores the yield altogether and counts simply warheads. The smallest strategic defense warheads differ from the largest strategic offense warheads by many orders of magnitude, but even if we were to limit ourselves to strategic offense warheads, merely counting warheads while neglecting yield involves a heroic distortion. In fact, the largest offense nuclear warhead is roughly a thousand times the smallest offense nuclear warhead[40] — the same as the difference between the Hiroshima bomb and the largest non-nuclear blockbusters of the Second World War! Counting the largest and the smallest each as one — with even-handed justice — would then be exactly like dismissing the first two nuclear weapons as of negligible importance since they increased the stocks of "block-busters" by only a fraction of a percent.

While there is no adequate single common measure for so heterogeneous a collection of vehicles and weapons, clearly something better is possible than a simple count of warheads.[41] That the latter is used so uncritically is one of the intellectual scandals of the current debate on SALT. Nonetheless one may ask whether the number of strategic offense and defense warheads has spiraled. And as Figure 7 shows, for this disparate aggregate, the answer is that it has not. It peaked in 1964 at roughly 30 percent higher than in 1972 which was about the 1960 level.[42]

The sense of post-Sputnik arms race doctrine, with its central strictures against all weapons aimed at weapons and therefore against active defense as particularly destabilizing, plainly calls for including the Spartan, Sprint, Nike-Hercules, Falcon, and all other defense warheads in the total. However, given the opportunism of the current debate, it is hardly surprising that, when convenient, the distortion involved in counting warheads is compounded by excluding the supposedly most destabilizing — the defense warheads. In fact, one great oddity is that in spite of all the fire leveled at active defense, the debaters hardly notice that U.S. defense warheads, interceptor aircraft, surface-to-air missiles, and air-to-air missiles have decreased drastically. The number of offense warheads has increased over time, but their average yield has decreased even more. From 1958-60 to 1972 they increased roughly by half. But their average yield was divided by four-and-a-half (Figure 8). It is essential then to consider some measure in between counting megatons and counting warheads. We turn now to a measurement widely used for that purpose in the defense and arms control technical community.

Measures of Relative Destructive Area ("EMT")

No single number adequately measures the destructive power of military weapons, still less other important attributes of military forces — their susceptibility to attack, their safety from "accidental" or mistaken or unauthorized use, their political controllability, their capability for discriminating between nonmilitary and military targets, and between friend and foe, their flexibility in a variety of political-military contingencies, etc. Nonetheless, as we have said, it is not hard to do better than counting warheads or counting megatons, and for comparing highly varied stocks of weapons at two different times or in two different countries, an index known (misleadingly) as "equivalent megatonnage" (EMT) has come into widespread technical use. It counts the number of weapons and their yields but makes a rough adjustment for the relative waste of explosive energy by the larger weapons through over-concentration near the target. Taking a one-megaton weapon as standard, it measures any given stock of weapons in terms of the number of such one-megaton weapons that under a variety of relevant conditions would do structural damage over an equal area.[43]

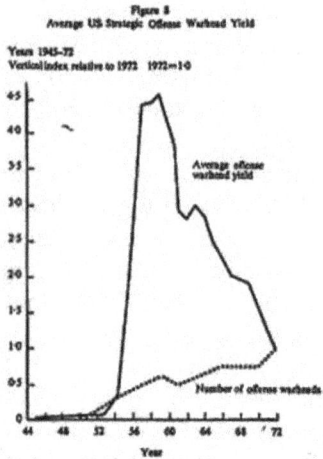

Figure 8
Average US Strategic Offense Warhead Yield

Years 1943–72
Vertical index relative to 1972   1972=1·0

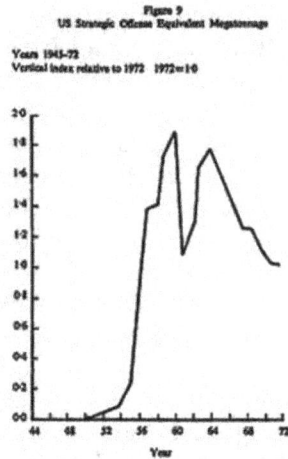

Figure 9
US Strategic Offense Equivalent Megatonnage

Years 1943–72
Vertical index relative to 1972   1972=1·0

EMT, like all other indexes, has its limitations, but it captures some essentials missed in simply adding unadjusted megatons or warheads. Figure 9 shows a dramatic decrease since 1960 in the relative destructiveness, so measured, of the U.S. strategic force. At its peak it was nearly double the 1972 figure; and 1972 was roughly at the 1956 level! In any case, no spiral. This measure is relevant among other things to test the arms race argument that the uncontrolled destructiveness of U.S. strategic forces has increased. It has not. The area that might sustain structural damage has been halved and there has been a similar decline in potential fallout.

Offense and Defense Budgets

I could reinforce these results using curves on further physical measures. Instead I turn now to measures of the resources used in deploying a strategic force. Since these resources must be diverted from important alternative civilian uses, such measures are properly at the heart of the defense debate. In any case, they are central to arms race doctrines. Expenditures on strategic forces are most frequently identified as the variable that is supposed to be accelerating.

Figure 10
Combined US Strategic Offense and Defense
Obligational Authority

Fiscal years 1945-76
Vertical axis in billions of dollars

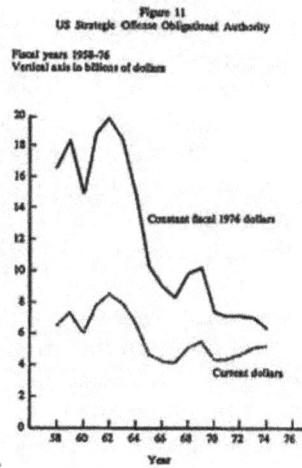

Figure 11
US Strategic Offense Obligational Authority

Fiscal years 1958-76
Vertical axis in billions of dollars

Figure 10 shows the total strategic budget as measured in the Defense Department Program I,[44] extending back to the Second World War. The top curve shows that the strategic budget in 1976 dollars declined from a peak of $32.6 billion in FY 1952 to $7.7 billion in FY 1976. Strategic expenditures have fluctuated, with a brief sharp decline and recovery after Korea, to very high levels varying between $24 and $28 billion in the seven years beginning in 1956; and then a more or less steady drastic decline to the recent low levels. In short, in real terms the strategic budget was well over four times higher during the Korean War and about three times as high at the end of the Eisenhower Administration as in 1976. This scarcely looks like an exponential increase in strategic budgets — more like an exponential decrease.[45] For the 24 years from 1952 to 1976, the average rate of decline was about 5 percent. For the 15 years from FY 1961 to FY 1976, there was a decline averaging 8 percent per year. I want to stress that this long-term decline is not simply [measured] as a percentage of GNP but in real terms. It is an absolute decline. Since real GNP was rising while strategic budgets in real terms were declining, strategic spending declined even more as a percentage of GNP. In percentage of GNP it was nearly seven times higher in the early 1950s and about five times higher in the late 1950s than in FY 1976 (3.2 percent and about 2.5 percent compared with .48 percent).

How is it possible for the constantly expanding literature on ever-accelerating strategic budgets to ignore this increasing divergence between doctrine and reality?

First, exponents using the doctrine as a weapon in budget battles handle rather carelessly the familiar distinction between real and inflated dollar costs. This can hide somewhat the drastic extent of the decline, but not the decline itself. Even in current, depreciating dollars the budget dropped from generally high levels in the 1950s and a peak of $12.1 billion in 1961 to $7.7 billion in 1976.[46]

Secondly, the curves show minor local peaks and dips. Men concentrating on the immediate budget fight may easily take an ant's eye view. Looking forward from the bottom of a shallow local dip, the future looks all uphill. This opportune but myopic focus has tended to obscure the very trends that any arms race doctrine would have to confront. Such doctrines after all do not pretend to be concerned only with the brief rise, say, from 1960 to 1961. An intense focus on the current year's budget battle also leads to a related confusion: comparing the new budget request not with last year's request, but with the actual amount approved by Congress in the prior year — which can be considerably less. For example, for the defense budget as a whole, the total obligational authority approved in 1973 was $3.6 billion less, and in 1972 $4.1 billion less, than the amount requested. For the FY 1974 strategic program the net difference between the requested and total obligational authority appears to be about $0.5 billion.

Thirdly, the drastic fall in strategic budgets measured in Program I may be partially obscured by adding in a rising but quite arbitrary "overhead" figure.[47] The program budgets for strategic or for general purpose forces aim to include all the cost of equipment, *matériel*, and personnel that can be directly attributed to the program mission, including all support costs that "follow directly from the number of combat units."[48] Overhead allocations, whatever their accounting uses, are by definition arbitrary, and those now current have little or no causal relation to past or future reductions in the number of strategic combat vehicles. These arbitrarily allocated costs have tended to remain the same or to rise even though the strategic forces and their direct costs have been greatly reduced.

The formula for budgets that the Brookings Institution uses, which we call "Method I," would assign to the strategic forces an amount of overhead equal to less than half their direct costs during the 1950s, and over one-and-a-half times their direct costs in 1974.[49] Meanwhile, direct costs of general-purpose forces have varied in size from less than one-and-two-thirds to nearly five times the direct costs of the strategic forces, and the formula, year after year, splits the Intelligence and Communications budgets evenly between them. Of course, it has always been clear that some of these "overhead" costs may vary inversely with direct costs. Take Intelligence for example. Large SALT (or unilateral) reductions might call for greatly increased national means of monitoring variations in adversary forces, since marginal absolute changes make a larger proportional difference in small forces. (Dr. Wiesner in the past has suggested that inspection might have to double if the forces were halved, and so on linearly.) But then one should expect future cuts in the direct costs of strategic forces to be partly offset by increases in Intelligence costs.

If one considers not merely what causes changes in "overhead," but also what the effects are of increases in overhead on an adversary, it is hard to see how these programs, many

447

of which could well be classified under Human Resources or Social Welfare, would strike terror in the heart of an enemy. For example, CHAMPUS (Civilian Health and Medical Program of the Uniformed Services) includes such items as medical care for retirees, their dependents, and survivors. A drastic cut in the number of strategic combat vehicles would hardly decrease these costs, and their increase should hardly seem menacing to the Soviet Union.

Nonetheless, even if these arbitrary costs are added on, they can only partially obscure the drastic decline. Using the formula Brookings applies to past budgets, the FY 1962 strategic forces budget was nearly double that in FY 1976 (this is displayed in the dashed line in Figure 12). The method Brookings applies to future projected budgets is less reducible to formula and involves more subjective judgment and even larger uncertainties.[50]

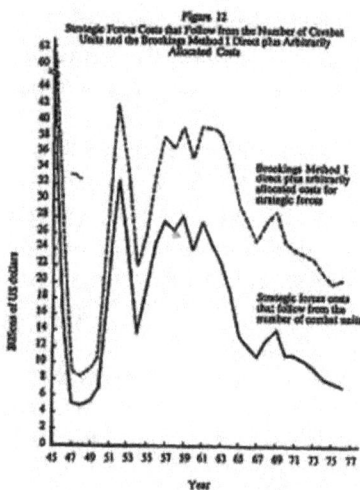

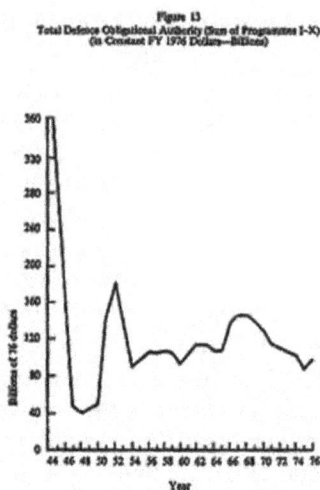

Figure 12
Strategic Forces Costs that Follow from the Number of Combat Units and the Brookings Method I Direct plus Arbitrarily Allocated Costs

Figure 13
Total Defense Obligational Authority (Sum of Programmes I–X) (In Constant FY 1976 Dollars—Billions)

If that method were applied to determine past trends, however, the decrease would be more drastic. Still other allocation methods, all necessarily arbitrary, show declines from a peak more than double the present budget. So for example, a method used by the Department of Defense shows a decline in FY 1976 dollars of over $2 billion in the late 1950s from a peak 2.5 times as high as the FY 1976 budget including overhead. With recently improved deflators the decline would be even larger.[51] Overhead allocations have their uses, but they are limited. All of them distribute some unallocatable costs. When added to program costs without any breakdown, they obscure more than they illuminate change. Nonetheless, no overhead allocation with which I am familiar can hide the sharp declines in strategic budgets. Whether the decline is from a peak over four or two-and-a-half or twice recent levels, that should be fatal to the dogma about "ever-accelerating spending."

Nonetheless that dogma does die hard. Paul Warnke, for example, has agreed that some facts do damage the arms race figure of speech. But he talks of our continuing tendency "to spend these steadily increasing billions" and of our "formula for endless escalation in defense costs." Indeed, Warnke is so seized by the idea that the U.S. strategic budget and the defense budget as a whole have been steadily climbing that he can read a long document devoted to showing that both budgets have been sinking for years, with plunging graphs to illustrate, and not notice.[52] He did not, for example, notice the point of the article which painstakingly showed evidence of the drastic fall in the strategic program budget in real terms over the preceding 14 years. (The defense budget as a whole had been declining for a shorter time – since 1968.) He understands it to be saying that the United States and the Soviet Union have both been increasing strategic spending, but at different rates. Running at different speeds, he thinks, might still be a race. However, we have been moving not only at different speeds, but in opposite directions. If that doesn't do lethal damage to the arms race metaphor, nothing will.[53]

Fourth, in spite of the fact that arms race theorists take strategic defense along with counterforce as the villain in the piece and the principal force driving the race, they sometimes look for exponential increases in strategic budgets that cover only offense and allow for no compensating decreases in strategic defense. However, in 1962 the budget for offense taken alone was over three times its 1976 level.[54]

Fifth, I suspect the major reason for failure to observe the decline is that public debate usually concentrates intensely on the initial decision to buy and deploy a new system; much less on the operation and maintenance of the system once in; and hardly at all on its phasing out. In particular, the present exponents of arms race doctrines have had their gaze focused on the introduction of new systems – in line with their dominant preoccupation with innovation. As advocates they have been very much in on the beginnings, in favor of the new systems in the 1950s and generally against them in the 1960s. But the phasing out seems to escape their attention.

Systems starting from zero or near it are likely to grow very rapidly in the initial phases; they can scarcely go down. It is easy apparently to slip into the belief that there has been an "across-the-board growth of our own strategic forces."[55] However, an examination of the components of the strategic budget and an analysis of the entry into the force and the exit of various combat vehicles suggests the broad solution to the puzzle as to how this popular impressionistic doctrine can fit the facts so poorly.

U.S. strategic forces have not grown "across the board." On the contrary, as new systems were brought in, many others, including some very expensive ones, were taken out. At the end of FY 1956, for example, the strategic force included nearly 1,500 B-47 and RB-47 medium bombers, some 270 B-36 and RB-36 heavy bombers, a remnant of the B-50s and B-29s, and nearly 850 KC 97 and KC 29 tanker aircraft, all of which have since made their exit, along with or preceded by a drastic reduction in overseas strategic operating bases and a multi-billion dollar cut in overseas stocks for strategic forces. Between 1956 and the late 1960s the B-58 supersonic bomber, the Snark intercontinental cruise missile, the Atlas ICBM, and the Titan I ICBM have come and gone. So also have the Bomarc area defense missile and most of the Nike-Hercules and fighter interceptors. In fact, air defense vehicles, promoted so vigorously in the 1950s by many who oppose them today as destabilizing, show an exponential decline from a peak of over 8,000 in 1959 to a force less than one-seventh as large in 1972; and to less than that now.

The terms of the public debate have been scandalously loose and they have received very little critical attention from the media. SALT rhetoric and headlines linking new strategic programs to "Record Defense Spending" help the impression that strategic budgets especially must be out of control, since they are spotted as the main culprit in the general increase. In real terms, however, there has been no general increase in defense spending since 1968. Witness Figure 13. Picking on the strategic budget as the guilty party in the nonexistent general increase in the defense budget as a whole seems particularly absurd, since the strategic decline has been larger, more consistent, and more durable. But guilt by association has its effect because the smaller decline in total defense budgets is more easily obscured by neglecting inflation.

It is hard to fault the media when academics and politicians who specialize in defense and arms control matters themselves make such blunders, but even so the media's handling of the defense budget in recent years needs some comment. Take the distinction between real and inflated changes in dollar amounts. Although there are some sophisticated questions about methods of allowing for inflation, the gross sense of the distinction is not at all arcane. Newsman handle it all the time without stumbling. When in a recession year, 1970, the American gross national product neared $1 trillion ($970.1 billion) by comparison with $930.3 billion the preceding year, no headline greeted the news by announcing a record advance in production. On the contrary, the press observed that the GNP in 1970 was lower in real terms than it had been the year before. But year after year of Defense Department requests for budgets lower in "real" terms than the 1968 peak have been announced as "record budgets," apparently because in this case the media regard the distinction as unreal. And a press that with some justice prides itself on its energetic factual investigations is considerably weaker on analysis and reflection about even moderately complex matters. There, predisposition is more likely to hold sway.

The sloppiness is suggested in the largely unconscious predispositions implicit in the way the data are described or pictured. One can find examples among good journalists and excellent newspapers. Take the following case shown in Figure 14 of the *Los Angeles Times* announcing the new defense budget request in February 1974. The article headlines "Record Defense Spending" and suggests the primary cause for the increase in new strategic nuclear weapons of the kind that SALT is supposed to limit. Thus the lead paragraph states, "... a defense budget surpassing the peak spending period of World War II and laying the foundation for a new generation of nuclear weapons...." Only later in the article is it acknowledged that inflation might have something to do with the budget increases, and even then in wording that suggests this may just be a Pentagon claim — "While the research on new nuclear weapons systems could portend massive new spending several years hence, the $6.3 billion increase in the Pentagon's new budget largely was attributed to pay increases and in higher costs across the board for hardware and supplies."

LOS ANGELES TIMES   FEBRUARY 5, 1974

Record Defense Spending Plan Includes New Nuclear Systems

BY RUDY ABRAMSON
Times Staff Writer

WASHINGTON—President Nixon Monday sent Congress a defense budget surpassing the peak spending period of World War II and laying the foundation for a new generation of nuclear weapons as insurance against the failure of strategic arms talks with the Soviet Union.

"If negotiations fail and the Soviet Union seeks military advantage," Mr. Nixon said in his budget message, "the United States must be prepared to increase its forces quickly and effectively."

"Because the time required for development and deployment of major weapons systems is long, decisions made today will shape the ability of the United States to maintain its strength 5 to 10 years from now."

In asking a record defense outlay of $87.7 billion in the year beginning

next July 1, the Administration proposed an $3.4 billion Pentagon research and development program plus more than $1 billion for the Atomic Energy Commission's nuclear weapons and propulsion projects.

Besides continuing work on the new B-1 strategic bomber and the giant Trident missile-firing submarine, the Defense Department asked Congress for $249 million for research and development on:

—Larger warheads for intercontinental ballistic missiles.

—Improved accuracy for ICBMs.

—A new missile-firing submarine smaller than those in the current Polaris-Poseidon fleet.

—Mobile ICBMs, which would be

Please Turn to Page 21, Col. 1

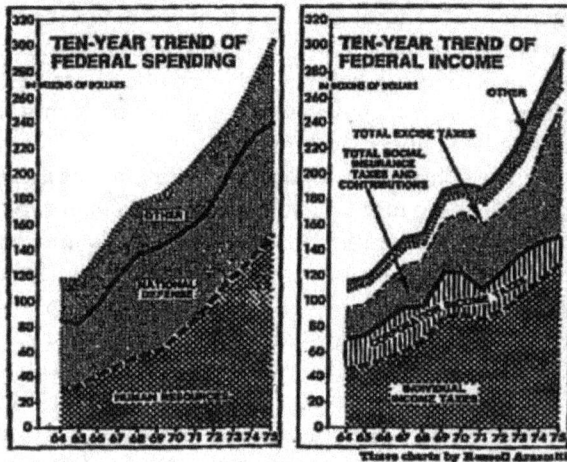

Figure 14

The graph, "Ten Year Trend of Federal Spending," accompanying in the article, not only reinforces the impression that national defense expenditures have been steadily climbing; it also suggests to the casual reader that they are the primary reason for the growth in the total federal budget. This effect results from piling the "National Defense" expenditures on top of those for "Human Resources."

Figure 15 is a redrawing of this chart for clarity, and Figure 16 shows exactly the same data as Figure 15 at exactly the same scale.[56] The only change is that National Defense is now presented on the bottom rather than Human Resources.

The resulting chart gives quite a different and more accurate impression than that in the article. It shows that the major source of the increase in federal spending has been increases in Human Resources, not National Defense.

But even Figure 16 is misleading, since it is in current dollars and hence ignores the effects of inflation. Figure 17 presents the data of Figure 16 adjusted for inflation, i.e., in dollars of constant purchasing power. We now see a *downward* trend in National Defense spending that is more than overcome by an *upward* trend in spending for Human Resources. (In fact, more authoritative results indicate a sharper downward trend for National Defense expenditures than is shown in Figure 16. The data in the original article contain some anomalies. Retirement pay seems to have been included in the "National Defense" category, and this would help to explain the slower decline shown.)

Belief in an exploding arms race is so ingrained by now in the way the media look at things that it seems even the chartmakers and layout men make their own *trompe l'oeil* [deceive the eye] contribution to its existence.

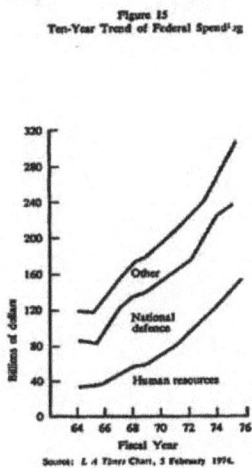

Figure 15
Ten-Year Trend of Federal Spend'g

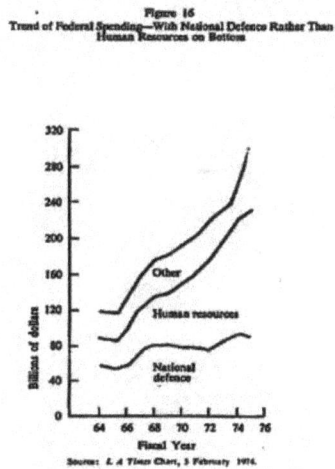

Figure 16
Trend of Federal Spending—With National Defence Rather Than Human Resources on Bottom

However, the regular annual alarms in the press about an up-ward trend in the strategic budget can often point to economic projections *for several future years,* based on gleanings from testi-mony before Congress on Defense Department and service plans. Such indications of plans can mislead in the same way as compar-ing this year's budget request with the last enacted budget, but even more so, since the long-term plans are even more tentative and subject to attrition than requests formally submitted to Congress. They must run a recurring gauntlet through many stages of bargaining and review within Defense, Budget, the White House,

453

and Congress. It is appropriate to study the uncertain long-term costs implicit in various defense plans, but not to treat them as if they reflected the likely course of defense spending. Brookings says as much: "A note of warning must be emphasized. The projections should not be taken as predictions of future defense budgets. . . ."[57] As with drugs and cigarettes, however, users may ignore the warning label. (Even Brookings, normally more careful than its readers, sometimes forgets its own warning.) In any case, Figure 18 shows vividly that year after year Brookings' projections of strategic cost have sloped steeply upward, as year after year the actual budgets have continued to decline. This perpetual picture, so useful in budget battles, of a strategic budget on the point of exploding, sticks in our mind rather than any glimpse of actual history.

Figure 17
Trend of Federal Spending—Adjusted for Inflation
(Constant FY 1974 Dollars)

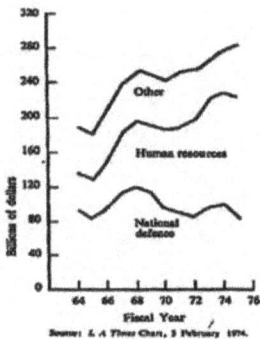

Figure 18
Brookings' Historical versus Brookings' Projected Strategic Costs
(Including "Overhead")

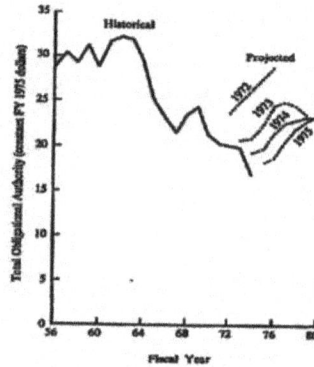

There is an amusing paradox, intelligible only in political debating terms, about the one-eyed vision displayed by exponents of arms race doctrines. On the one hand they fail to observe the increasingly obvious fact that in spite of their theory of invariable American overestimation of the size of Russian strategic forces, these forces have for many years systematically exceeded our expectation. Their one good eye in this case is focused on any momentary pause in the continuing deployment and expansion of existing strategic weapons systems. They turn a blind eye when the Russians start new systems. They see the Russians stopping, seldom starting. On the other hand, when it comes to U.S. strategic

454

forces, they can barely preserve their belief that the American strategic budget is rising at an accelerating rate by fixing their gaze narrowly on the phasing in of new systems or their continuance and by neglecting the phasing out of the old. For the Americans, it seems, they notice the starts, not the stops. If they cannot find a trend of increase in the plunging figures of the last 24 years, they find it in rosy service visions of the future, undampened by Executive or Congressional budget considerations.

However one explains the failure of arms race theorists to note the deviation of reality from their theory, it is quite plain that reality has diverged massively—not only in the facts of *under*estimation that destroy a principal element of the supposed dynamics of the arms race, but also in the plain fact that the United States has not been running a quantitative strategic race.

It would be possible to present similar results for many others measures: for example, while strategic defense vehicles have declined for a decade and a half from a peak more than *seven* times their present number, offense vehicles have remained roughly the same for many years. The total of strategic vehicles therefore has gone down. The point should be very clear. There is no serious evidence of a quantitative strategic spiral.

That is quite a different point from saying that as a result of these declines, we are uniformly worse off. While I have differed with many specific development and deployment decisions, on the whole my view is that the net effect of changes over this long period, from the mid-1950s through the 1960s to the present time, has been an improvement in our force in key respects. *My view is indeed the opposite of the commonplace about the exponential arms race which has it that as we have spent more and more on our strategic forces, our security has steadily declined.* To evaluate the commonplace we need to consider the nature of the major qualitative innovations in strategic forces and their net effect.

IV

The Net Effect of Qualitative Change

Theories of the quantitative strategic race are an extraordinary muddle of errors and self-deceptions. Yet notions about "qualitative races" may be even worse off. In fact the Secretary of State recently expressed a longing for a "conceptual breakthrough" that would bring our understanding of qualitative races up to the present standard on the quantitative strategic race. Heaven forefend! The modesty of this desire, however, may measure the current confusion about qualitative competition.

Though discussion is far from rigorous, the kinds of changes usually thought of as "qualitative" are alterations in some relevant unit performance characteristic. The most obvious historical example is the thousand-fold increase in the average unit explosive yield accomplished by the first A-bombs. A second, almost equally famous, example is the introduction of the H-bomb in the 1950s which, as originally envisaged, was expected to multiply the yield of a single A-bomb again a thousand-fold. Another equally crucial case is the increase in the average speed of a strategic vehicle from about 500 to 13,000 miles per hour, made possible by the development of intercontinental rockets. Other unit performance characteristics affected by innovation have been mentioned earlier—blast resistance, concealability, accuracy, reliability, and controllability, or resistance to "accidental" or unauthorized use.

Some technical changes, it seems obvious, might worsen the position of everybody. Indeed, many now think that typical even of civilian technology, which is increasingly assigned all the hyperbolic traits recently attributed by the Secretary of State to military technology: it has "developed a momentum of its own," is "at odds with the human capacity to comprehend it," is, in brief, "out of control." Shades of Friedrich Juenger. Or Jacques Ellul, who holds: "Technique itself... selects among the means to be employed. The human being is no longer in any sense the agent of choice," and "everything which is technique is necessarily used as soon as it is available, without distinction of good or evil. This is the principal law of our age."[58] The use of the A-bomb for Ellul only illustrates this law and is a symbol of "technical evolution" in general. Such symbols recall the cloudy determinism of Oswald Spengler's portentous "that which is a possibility is necessity."

For environmentalists today, as for Juenger, a civilian technology out of control is the source more typically for polluting than humanizing the environment. We owe the environmental movement a debt for stressing that it is important in choosing among technologies to take into careful account the indirect, long-term, and public costs as well as the direct, immediate, and private costs of technical change. It has unfortunately also encouraged the revival of a more general Luddite view of technology as a threat to us all. The Luddite view, moreover, is particularly tempting when it comes to military technology. Most of us have little affection for weapons; and weapons improvements are likely to arouse a good deal less enthusiasm than technical advances generally. It is easy to believe that such "improvements" might make things worse all around.

However, just as in the civilian case one can only choose technologies and it is highly unlikely that existing technologies are ideal, so also in the military case it is extremely implausible that current technologies are optimal, that they fit our political purposes beyond any possibility of improvement. We have to choose and we do. But the conditions of thoughtful choice are only obscured by the immoderate rhetoric, characteristic of Ellul, and also typical of the arms debate in the post-Sputnik era. So Lipton and Rodberg talk of the "mystique of technological progress within the defense establishment, where feasibility is equated with obligation, where if we can build it, we must."[59] A purple passage of that sort is expressive. But what is its meaning? It has no plain application to the real world in which a very long list of development projects was cancelled after much spending, but before deployment.[60] And many more development ideas were stillborn before any substantial money had been spent in their pursuit.

Moreover, it is clear that qualitative changes need not affect both sides badly. Some changes might benefit one side primarily as radar favored the British more than the Germans in the Second World War. Still others might conceivably help both, since the two sides have some objectives in common. So, for example, fail-safe techniques that prevent a war from starting by mistake through a failure of communication or a false alarm, or Permissive Action Links that prevent local arming of weapons without a release from a remote responsible command center, and modes of protection that make it possible to ride out an attack and depend less on hair-trigger response. Neither side would like to see a nuclear war start by "accident" or through some unauthorized act.

The problem of judging the effect of a specific qualitative change in key performance parameters is complicated by the fact that it may be ambiguous. It may serve the interests of just one adversary in some particular respect and in another respect the interests of both. For example, improvements in reconnaissance may permit more precise location and destruction of a target, but also may reduce collateral damage and serve as a key national means of verifying that alterations in an adversary's force are no more menacing than is permitted by an arms treaty. The SALT agreements would be infeasible without precise national means of surveillance other than ground inspection. No case-by-case analysis of qualitative changes since the mid-1950s can be given. However, it is unnecessary for the purpose of evaluating the Luddite stereotype in the contemporary debate. According to that stereotype, major innovations (1) lead to new and higher levels of strategic expenditure, (2) make strategic forces more destructive, (3) make them less secure, and (4) make them harder to control politically. To test this familiar view, it is important to look broadly at the net outcome of such major technological innovations as the development of fusion weapons and strategic rocketry.

Before forming some judgment on this subject, it may provide perspective to observe that the view of innovation as generating an unstable arms race, though widespread in recent times, is by no means universal. One of the few serious studies of arms races, that by Samuel P. Huntington, held that military innovation was fundamentally benign, among other reasons because it enabled the redeployment rather than the increase of arms budgets.[61] Moreover, since it did not increase the share of national resources devoted to defense, it did not produce the strains leading to war, but in fact made war less likely.

Huntington's hypothesis about the effect of technological change, though it runs counter to the present fashion, is by no means implausible. A qualitative improvement has to do with some relevant performance characteristics of a weapon. Painting bombs blue, for example, would not generally qualify as an improvement. Increasing the explosive yield for a given weight or the accuracy of delivery would. Such changes mean that effectiveness per unit or per dollar is increased and this implies in turn that a given task might be done with fewer units or at less expense.

To meet an adverse change in a potential enemy's force, then, a government has the alternative, through qualitative change, to redeploy resources, just as Huntington asserts, rather than simply to multiply them. He also points out that a self-imposed or a treaty constraint on improving qualitative performance may impel a simple multiplication of units — that is, it may generate a quantitative race. Moreover, though it is possible that opposing governments may blindly introduce changes that worsen the position of both sides, and though it is surely true that governments make a lot of bad choices, they have plenty of incentives for looking beyond the immediate consequences of a procurement decision. And not all of their choices have been grossly wrong. It is not hard to dig up governmental analyses, good and bad, that look well beyond the next immediate step.

Conventional arms race theory presupposes a totally mechanical or instinctual behavior, that reacts only to the immediate move, never looking forward. But it is by no means clear that governments are as fatally concentrated on the immediate as arms race theorists debating the current budget. Both the U.S. and the Russians introduced (in good part independently) the revolutionary technologies of rocketry and fusion weapons. But we made adaptations in our force that exploited these technologies precisely to avoid the kind of deterioration the dogma suggests is automatic.

The main methods worked out in the early 1950s for protecting the strategic force based in the United States for the rest of the decade depended on tactical warning and a rapid, safely repeatable response by our force that did not commit it to war on the basis of substantially uncertain warning. These methods could work reasonably well, so long as the speed of attacking vehicles was that typical of manned aircraft. But it soon became clear that strategic rockets were likely to be a feasible operational component of strategic forces in the 1960s.

Rockets, because of their speed, might, in current jargon, have been described as "intrinsically destabilizing." However, no single performance characteristic taken in isolation, whether speed or accuracy or whatever, can be so established. If one had believed that speed was intrinsically destabilizing, one might conceivably have tried to get an agreement banning rockets altogether; or tried to increase their travel time by getting agreements to use extreme lofted trajectories; or—still more far-fetched—an agreement to orbit them several times before landing; or (as discussed in the 1958 Surprise Attack Conference) to construct an elaborate international warning system shared with adversaries in order to preserve the possibility of timely, secure response. Instead of trying simply to stop or slow down technology, the tack taken to maintain an improved second-strike capability was to make unilateral adaptations that exploited both the initial limitations of the new rockets, specifically their great inaccuracy, and also their substantial advantages for defense penetration and for developing new, cheaper, and better modes of protection against attack, including mobility. Useful adaptations of the new techniques were feasible, even though our understanding of them was only partial and uncertain. Our adjustments to them did not have to be made all at once. They were made incrementally as various pitfalls and opportunities presented by these techniques became plainer.

In short, in spite of the recent as well as the age-old romantic antagonism to technology and the belief expressed by such critics of technology as Jacques Ellul, we are not slaves to technique. We can and do make technical choices, and in doing so sometimes improve matters. The alternative is an indiscriminate hostility to innovation *per se*, but that rests on the implicit assumption that the point at which we have arrived cannot possibly be improved — a rather odd view for the critics of technology to hold, who otherwise stress the arbitrary and irrational process by which past decisions on development have been made. In effect, an antagonism to all innovation amounts to a sentimental attachment to older technology rather than a hostility to technique in general.

A study of the major changes in technologies from the 1950s to the present and their effects on the strategic force supports the view that whatever the false starts and mistakes in detail, on the whole the outcome was exactly the reverse of the stereotype in the four respects listed above.

Much of this is implicit in the analysis of quantitative changes already offered. So I can be brief. First, strategic spending did not rise to new levels. From the late-1950s it fell almost by two-thirds. Second, the relative destructiveness of our strategic forces as measured by EMT declined. Moreover, in precise contradiction to the standard view, this decline responded in good part to the increased size and effectiveness of actual and anticipated Soviet active defenses. On the whole, the shifts in the American force from gravity bombs to air-to-surface missiles carried on strategic aircraft and to ICBMs and SLBMs themselves were in the first instance basically a response to the formidable growth of Russian air defenses. But these as well as later developments meant a drastic reduction in total and average explosive yield and in EMT. Third, through such devices as placing rockets on submarines moving continuously underwater or in highly blast-resistant complex silos, the strategic forces became less vulnerable than they had been in the 1950s — with a resultant increase in stability. In the mid-1950s our strategic forces were concentrated at a few points, were soft, slow to respond, inadequately warned, and inadequately protected by active defense.[62] The Soviet forces were even more vulnerable, and remained so much longer, but greatly improved in this respect in the mid-1960s. Fourth, the controllability of the force was improved by the very methods of protection adopted, which made hair-trigger response unnecessary; also by a variety of fail-safe devices and arrangements permitting positive control and by improving the protection of the command and control arrangements themselves.

Finally, many of the measures that so improved the strategic force were adopted self-consciously as alternatives to simply multiplying the force and increasing budgets. They did not undertake the hopeless task of stopping qualitative change. Rather, they adapted qualitative change roughly to our purposes, not all of which are incompatible with those of potential adversaries.

The combination of fusion weapons and missiles that enabled us to choose cheaper, safer, less destructive and better-controlled strategic forces were some of the very technologies that were thought at the time inevitably to have the opposite effects. Fusion warheads and the vastly increased speed of strategic rockets in particular made obsolete existing methods of protecting strategic forces, but they opened up new opportunities to increase the stability of the force. The principal effect of fusion technology was not so much to make weapons higher in yield, but to make low- and medium-yield weapons smaller, lighter and cheaper. This in turn made it possible to put them in rockets more easily protected by blast shelters or in constantly moving submarines. An attempt simply to stop or slow this technology would have reduced the survivability of deterrent forces and therefore diminished international stability.

Increasing the Choices

Perverse current dogmas center most of all on an attempt to stop or slow technologies of discrimination and control. However, the remarkable improvements in accuracy and control in prospect will permit non-nuclear weapons to replace nuclear ones in a wide range of contingencies. Moreover, such improvements will permit new forms of mobility for strategic forces, making it easier for deterrent forces to survive. More important, they will also increase the range of choice to include more discriminate, less brutal, less suicidal responses to attack— responses that are more believable. And only a politically believable response will deter.

Some technologies reduce the range of political choice; some increase it. If our concern about technology getting beyond political control is genuine rather than rhetorical, then we should actively encourage the development of techniques that increase the possibilities of political control. There will be a continuing need for the exercise of thought to make strategic forces secure and discriminatingly responsive to our aims, and to do this as economically as we can. Agreements with adversaries can play a useful role, but they cannot replace national choice. And neither the agreements nor the national choices are aided by the sort of hysteria implicit in theories of a strategic race always on the point of exploding.

Language and the Present Political Chaos

> Political language—and with variations this is true of all political parties, from Conservatives to Anarchists— is designed to make lies sound truthful and murder respectable, and to give an appearance of solidity to pure wind.

Orwell, who said that, prescribed never using a metaphor you are used to seeing in print as his very first rule for reducing the decay. That would cut the vast clutter of images about racing and uncapped volcanoes that we use in order to hide from ourselves what has been happening and what the issues are. In the chaotic "debate" about Vladivostok, the proponents claimed it would put a "cap" or "lid" on the explosive increase. Opponents, from Senator Jackson to the Left, said it wouldn't: like SALT I it would only force the continuing of the spiral in strategic spending. But before and after SALT I, the spiral was pure wind; and it will be wind in the present political circumstance with or without SALT II. For the United States, one might conceivably talk about a "shoe" or a "floor," but hardly a "cap." Vladivostok also illustrates the absurdity of the exaggerated threat/"worst case" dynamic. Here, overblown estimates of future Russian programs may lend a specious urgency to rapid agreement—another "miracle" for the Secretary.

And when Secretary Kissinger asks, "What in the name of God is strategic superiority... at these levels?" he seems to be saying that it does not make any difference how many more missiles the Russians have than we—in which case it is hard to see any urgency in agreement. He sometimes explicitly means that it makes no difference, because each side now can—in the stereotype—kill every man, woman, and child several times over. But that is an example of exactly the use of language Orwell had in mind. For it implies in fine moral tones that we should measure the adequacy of our weapons in terms of the number of civilians they can kill. The Secretary, however, does not believe that. He has also said that attacks on population are a "political impossibility, not to say a moral impossibility." I am all for probing the premises of thought on arms and arms control which the Secretary is said to want. But that can only start when we face up to evasions making "murder respectable" in such chaste phrases as "counter-value attacks" and in all the unreflective vocabulary of the arms race. This is an important part of rethinking policy about our relations with allies and adversaries, long overdue and essential for reducing the present chaos.

ENDNOTES - Wohlstetter - Racing Forward? Or Ambling Back?

1. I am indebted to many colleagues but especially to David McGarvey, Steven Honda, Gregory Jones, Robert Raab, Arthur Steiner, and Zivia Wurtele.

2. Sir Edward Grey, *Twenty-Five Years, 1892-1916*, Vol. 1, New York: Frederick A. Stokes Company, 1925, pp. 89-90.

3. John Newhouse, *Cold Dawn: The Story of SALT*, New York: Holt, Rinehart and Winston, 1973, p. 176.

4. See, for example, Morton H. Halperin and Jeremy J. Stone, "Rivals but No Race: Comment," *Foreign Policy*, No. 16, Fall 1974, pp. 88-92, and the views represented in Michael L. Nacht, "The Delicate Balance of Error," *Foreign Policy*, No. 19, Summer 1975, pp. 163-177.

5. Jeremy Stone in Erwin Knoll and Judith Nies McFadden, eds., *American Militarism 1970*, New York: Viking Press, 1969, p. 71.

6. Jerome Wiesner and Donald Brennan, eds., *Anti-Ballistic Missile: Yes or No?* New York: Hill and Wang, 1969, pp. 13-14.

7. Nancy Lipton and Leonard S. Rodberg, "The Missile Race — The Contest with Ourselves," in Leonard S. Rodberg and Derek Shearer, eds., *The Pentagon Watchers*, Garden City, New York: Doubleday, 1970, p. 303.

8. Quoted from U.S. Congress, Senate, Committee on Armed Services, *Fiscal Year 1972 Authorization for Military Procurement: Hearings,* May 3, 1971, Part 2, 92nd Congress, 1st Session, p. 1767.

9. Quoted from U.S. Congress, House of Representatives, Subcommittee on National Security Policy and Scientific Developments of the Committee on Foreign Affairs, *National Security Policy and Changing World Power Alignment: Hearing-Symposium,* May 31, 1972, 92nd Congress, 2nd Session, p. 98.

10. Robert S. McNamara, "The Dynamics of Nuclear Strategy," speech, September 18, 1967, *Department of State Bulletin,* Vol. 57, No. 1476, October 9, 1967, p. 445.

11. Quoted from U.S. Congress, Senate, Committee on Foreign Relations, *Strategic Arms Limitation Agreement: Hearings,* June 28, 1972, 92nd Congress, 2nd Session, p. 193.

12. Quoted from U.S. Congress, Senate, Committee on Foreign Relations, Subcommittee on Arms Control and International Organizations, *Arms Control Implications of Current Defense Budget: Hearings,* July 13, 1971, pp. 205-206.

13. Knoll and McFadden, eds., *op. cit.,* p. 68.

14. Edgar M. Bottome, *The Balance of Terror: A Guide to the Arms Race,* Boston: Beacon Press, 1972, pp. xv-xvi.

15. William Epstein, "Will the Russians Play 'American Roulette'," *Saturday Review World,* June 29, 1974, pp 7-8. Epstein is the former Director of the UN Secretariat Disarmament Division.

16. Bernard T. Feld, "The Sorry History of Arms Control," *Bulletin of the Atomic Scientists,* Vol. 26, No. 7, September 1970, p. 26.

17. Quoted from U.S. Congress, Senate, Committee on Foreign Relations, *Strategic Arms Limitation Agreement: Hearings,* June 26, 1972, 92nd Congress, 2nd Session, p. 139.

18. John Newhouse, *op. cit.,* p. 133.

19. Nancy Lipton and Leonard S. Rodberg, *op. cit.,* p. 303.

20. Quoted from National Citizen's Commission, Report of the Committee on Arms Control and Disarmament, White House Conference on International Cooperation, November 28-December 1, 1963.

21. Jerome Wiesner, Foreword, in Donald G. Brennan, ed., *Arms Control, Disarmament and National Security,* New York: G. Braziller, 1961, p.14.

22. Herbert F. York, "Controlling the Qualitative Arms Race," *Bulletin of Atomic Scientists,* Vol. 29, March 1973, p. 4.

23. George Kistiakowsky and George Rathjens in *Scientific American,* Vol. 222, No. 1, January 1970, p. 27.

24. Harvey Brooks, "The Military Innovation System and the Quantitative Arms Races," revised draft distributed at Aspen Conference on Arms Control, August 1974.

25. Quoted from U.S. Congress, Senate, Committee on Foreign Relations, *Détente: Hearings,* September 1974, 93rd Congress, 2nd Session, p. 195.

26. E.g., Nancy Lipton and Leonard S. Rodberg, "The Missile Race—The Contest with Ourselves," in *The Pentagon Watchers, op. cit.,* p. 303; Dr. Jerome Wiesner, *ABM: Yes or No,* Santa Barbara, CA: Center for the Study of Democratic Institutions, 1969, p. 18; Dr. W. K. H. Panofsky, "Roots of the Strategic Arms Race: Ambiguity and Ignorance," *Bulletin of the Atomic Scientists,* Vol. XXVII, June 1971, p. 15.

27. For the data on the statistical distribution of predictions on which Figs. 1-3 are based, see *Strategic Review,* Fall 1974, U.S. Strategic Institute Report 75-1.

28. *Statement of Secretary of Defense Robert S. McNamara before the House Armed Services Committee, the Fiscal Year 1964-68 Defense Program and 1964 Defense Budget,* Office of the Secretary of Defense, January 1963.

29. Predictions in Figures 1a to 1h exclude short-term estimates that are limited essentially to the completion of launchers already started.

30. See, for example, Nacht, *op. cit.*

31. This figure is based on Nacht, *op. cit.*

32. In this, we follow Nacht.

33. Impressions from even a relevant picture, such as Figure 4b, can stand supplementing by the computation of a few statistics and the summary of the results of a variety of statistical tests on the differences between predicted and actual silos: (a) The mean underestimate of -80.1 silos per year is significant (using the Student's t-test) at the .001 level using the more rigorous "two-sided" criterion, that is, assuming appropriately that predictions can exceed as well as understate the reality. (b) The least squares trend line has an r^2 equal to .40, but its slope, -12.59, is significant at the .05 level. (c) There is no significant trend up or down at the .05 level for the sub-period 1965-1969. (d) The worsening displayed is confirmed by the Student's t-test for the difference between the sample means for 1962-1964 compared with 1963-1969. (The difference between predicted and actual is worse for the second sample at the .01 level.) (e) And finally, the Wilcoxon two-sample test, a robust "distribution-free" test, using only rank orders, also shows that later sample to be worse than the earlier at the .05 significance level. All of the above tests are two-sided.

34. Such a view was never consistently adopted by Mr. McNamara. He came to use action-reaction language, and often talked as if the adequacy of strategic forces could be measured solely in terms of their use to destroy cities. However, he brilliantly attacked the overkill theory and continued through his last Posture Statement to insist that we keep the objective of limiting damage in case deterrence failed.

35. See, for example, "The Soviets... are not seeking to engage us in ... the quantitative race.... There is no indication that the Soviets are seeking to develop a strategic nuclear force as large as ours." "Interview with Robert S. McNamara, Defense Secretary,"

U.S. News and World Report, April 12, 1965, p. 52. Compare the *Military Balance, 1962-1963,* London, Institute of Strategic Studies, p. 2: "The Soviet Union thus appears committed to a policy of 'minimum' or counter-city deterrence in relation to the United States, though the large medium range missile force it has now developed and deployed against targets in Europe and Japan may serve as both." This view was held by men with little else in common. So, Hedley Bull: "... The Soviet Union did not embark upon the massive programme of intercontinental missile construction that had been anticipated, but seemed to settle for the sort of capability that in the United States is associated with the policy of 'minimum deterrence.'" *The Control of the Arms Race,* New York, 2nd ed., p. xxii; and Richard J. Barnet and Marcus G. Raskin: "... Where we once believed that the Soviets were bent on surpassing the U.S. in military power, it now appears that ... they are quite willing to put up with a missile gap: Indeed, we have been running much of the arms race with ourselves." *After Twenty Years: Alternatives to the Cold War in Europe,* New York: Random House, 1965, p. 4.

36. For this focus on the momentary or partial causes, see, for example, *The New York Times,* April 27, 1969; *Chicago Sun Times,* April 22, 1970; *Milwaukee Journal,* April 26, 1970; *SIPRI Yearbook of World Armaments and Disarmament, 1969-1970,* New York: Humanities Press, 1970, p. 53; *Wall Street Journal,* December 17, 1970; *Manchester Guardian,* November 7, 1971; and *Survival,* September/October 1972.

37. These two cases of failed predictions are described in Leon Festinger's *When Prophecy Fails,* Harper Torch Book, 1964; and in his *Theory of Cognitive Dissonance,* Stanford, 1967. Festinger's model of cognitive dissonance fits the history of the theory of systematic overestimation rather well.

38. For an early appreciation of this point, see, for example, P. M. S. Blackett, *Fear, War and the Bomb: Military and Political Consequences of Atomic Energy,* London, 1948.

39. I address it briefly in Fred Warner Neal and Mary Kersey Harvey, eds., *Pacem in Terris III, Vol. II, The Military Dimensions of Foreign Policy,* Santa Barbara: Fund for the Republic, Inc., 1974. I favor a U.S.-Soviet reduction to equal lower totals. That is quite

independent of the question as to whether the U.S. totals have increased exponentially or at all.

40. Even this fact (and not merely its implications for the incomparability of the elements in the aggregate of offense warheads) is not always recognized. It is sometimes said that U.S. strategic warheads in general are in the megaton range. See, for example: *Arms Control: Readings from Scientific American*, San Francisco: W. H. Freeman and Co., 1973, p. 179.

41. One argument for simply counting warheads is the notion that the dangers of an accidental detonation increase linearly with that number. However, this is plainly false. The probability of an accidental, unauthorized detonation depends among other things on arrangements for weapons safety and for the centralization of control and command over these weapons.

42. The curves on numbers of warheads (Figure 7 and bottom of Figure 8) are smoothed in order to approximate the calculated data points, but closely enough so that deviations from the trends discussed are not significant.

43. The EMT of a weapon is computed by raising its yield, expressed in megatons, to the two-thirds power.

44. Program I refers to Strategic Forces. Program II refers to General Purposes Forces. We have used unpublished computer tabulations dated July 24, 1975, available from the Office of the Assistant Secretary of Defense, Comptroller (Programs and Budget) of Total Obligational Authority by Program, which were extended back beyond FY 1956 only recently.

45. The decreasing exponential fit is rather good. The r^2 for the period 1952 is .75, and the r^2 for the period FY 1961-76 is .88.

46. Recent Department of Defense computer tabulations have revised upward the 1961 current dollar estimate from its earlier-reported level of $11.5 billion.

47. See, for example, "The Advocates," WETA-TV, Washington, DC, February 14, 1974.

48. Martin Binkin, "Support Costs in the Defense Budget," Washington, DC: Brookings Institution Staff Paper, 1972, pp. 45-46.

49. The Brookings Institution uses a different method, which we call "Method II," when estimating the effects on overhead of future reductions in the strategic combat forces. We are indebted to Barry Blechman for generous help in explaining Brookings' methods.

50. If I were to suggest changes to Brookings, one would be to display separately, in past and future budgets, the overhead fraction. For future budgets especially this would help. It is easy to expect greater overhead savings from direct program cuts than are likely: total overhead and the direct program budgets have moved in opposite directions. Yet Brookings' overhead formula for past budgets, like most such allocations, assumes that overhead costs vary in a straight line with direct or operating costs without any time lag. And it loads an increasing proportion of total overhead onto the strategic budget. For such reasons I present figures on the strategic budget *with and without* Brookings' overhead allocation.

51. Recent improvements in deflators for Total Obligational Authority take into account the fact that a substantial fraction of the funds authorized in a given year are spent in later years.

52. Paul C. Warnke, "Apes on a Treadmill," *Foreign Policy*, No. 18, Spring 1975, pp. 12-29.

53. Maybe nothing will. As an even more striking example of how hard the dogma dies, consider the following statement by Bernard Brodie written after I had assured Mr. Warnke that I was indeed saying that the total cost of our strategic force has gone down, not up. "We should note here Albert Wohlstetter's denial that there is an arms race between the two superpowers, though he concedes there is an arms competition which raises costs on both sides." Mr. Brodie cites not only my original paper which documented the decline in U.S. strategic costs, but also a reply to Mr. Warnke in which I said again that U.S. strategic costs had not "escalated" but had gone down. "On Clarifying Objectives of Arms Control," ACIS Working Paper No. 1. Program in Arms

Control and International Security, University of California at Los Angeles, April 1976, p. 22.

54. Arms race theorists, faced recently with the divergence of strategic budgets from their theory of how they should behave, have suggested that the decline in the total strategic budget since it includes defensive forces merely displays the benefit of SALT I, which limited ABM. But the May 1972 agreements could hardly have affected anything before FY 1973, and the strategic defenses declined drastically many years before that. See, for example, "The Advocates," WETA-TV program cited above.

55. Nancy Lipton and L. S. Rodberg, "The Missile Race – The Contest with Ourselves," in *The Pentagon Watcher*, New York, 1970, p. 301.

56. Figures 15 and 16 were drawn by first reading the data points on the graphs in the original article as carefully as possible using a ruler and set square. I do not know the source of the data used or kinds of budget moneys employed (e.g., obligational authority, expenditures, or other); or what definitions were used for the three categories displayed, and I have made no attempt to justify the data or explain the anomalies in it. In particular, I am at a loss to explain why National Defense expenditures show a decline from 1974 to 1975, even though the article talks about a $6.3 billion increase.

57. B. M. Blechman, E. M. Gramlich, and R. W. Hartman, *Setting National Priorities; the 1975 Budget*, Washington, DC: Brookings Institution, 1974, p. 306.

58. Jacque Ellul, *The Technological Society*, New York: Vintage Books, 1964, pp. 80, 99; cf. Friedrich Juenger, *The Failure of Technology*, Chicago: Gateway Editions, Inc., Henry Regnery Co., 1956, pp. 163-164.

59. Lipton and Rodberg, *op. cit.*, p. 302. Cf. Richard Barnet, "The National Security Bureaucracy and Military Intervention," paper delivered at Adlai Stevenson Institute, June 3, 1968, p. 27.

60. Nuclear-propelled aircraft, started in 1951 and cancelled 10 years later; the XB-70 bomber started in 1958 and cancelled in

1967; the Hard Rock Silo project started in 1968 and cancelled in 1970; the SCAD Armed Decoys begun in 1968 and cancelled in 1973; the Navajo ramjet intercontinental missile begun in 1954, cancelled in 1957; the Rascal, the Skybolt, the mobile medium range ballistic missile, Regulus II, the Manned Orbiting Lab, and so on.

61. Samuel P. Huntington, "Arms Races: Prerequisites and Results," *Public Policy*, Vol. 8, in Carl J. Friedrich and Seymour E. Harris, eds., Cambridge: Harvard University Press, 1958.

62. For a contemporary analysis of the vulnerability of strategic forces in 1956, see, for example, Wohlstetter, Hoffman, and Rowen, *Protecting U.S. Power to Strike Back in the 1950s and 1960s*, RAND, R-290, September 1956, pp. 30, 41. For earlier analyses by the same authors, see *The Selection of Strategic Bases*, R-244-S, April 1953; and *The Selection and Use of Strategic Air Base Systems*, R-266, March 1954.

On Arms Control: What We Should Look for
in an Arms Agreement (1985)

Albert and Roberta Wohlstetter

Unpublished draft essay, May 20, 1985, available from the Hoover Institution Archive, Albert and Roberta Wohlstetter Papers, Notes, Box 118, Folder 16. Courtesy of the Wohlstetter Estate.

The agreement should serve some clear military purpose, if only a limited one. Sometimes, to avoid an agreement for which there is much public and bureaucratic pressure, but which would plainly do us harm, one might be tempted to make a proposal in the expectation that it will be turned down. However, such proposals have a way of being modified so as to be acceptable to the Soviets without removing the harm they might do to us. And they often appear unconvincing until they are modified. It's safer to back a proposal which would clearly be of some definite military use; this is not *always* incompatible with being useful to the Soviets too.

The agreement should aim *only* at a limited purpose. The implications of even a limited agreement are hard to predict. Comprehensive agreements are even harder. Moreover, they are almost surely unlikely to be verifiable. And even less likely to be enforceable.

It's best to try for an agreement in an area where it is hard to accomplish our purposes by unilateral efforts. An example that will be developed at some length is a carefully restricted agreement for "keep-out" zones around selected satellites, permitting the owner of a satellite to destroy any objects in that zone, or in some cases more restrictively, any object traveling in that zone at the same velocity as the protected satellite. A carefully designed agreement might help with the problem of space mines, for it is particularly hard to deal with that problem solely by unilateral efforts. However, even a well-designed agreement will not *replace* all unilateral effort. This is true in general, and not just for dealing with space mines, as is suggested by the preceding points, namely that agreements should be seen as limited and supplementing unilateral efforts, not replacing them.

Agreements should be of a finite and short duration. It is hard to end any agreement, even one that is explicitly temporary, but a short agreement is important if we are to make essential adjustments for unanticipated changes in the state of the art and in geopolitical circumstances. Unilateral defense decisions are hard enough even though they are incremental and can be changed year by year as we understand their consequences better. An agreement of indefinite duration wagers a great deal on our being able to predict technical and geopolitical changes and to understand the strategic consequences of such changes in the long run. We are good at neither.[1]

For this reason, one should reject the argument made by many proponents of arms control today that a treaty of permanent duration will confer stability because it will enable us and our adversaries to plan with certainty. On the contrary, it is a sure recipe for instability because in general we cannot anticipate such further changes long enough in advance, and a permanent treaty would prevent us from making incremental adjustments when it becomes clear that [such changes] are about to occur.

We should look for an agreement which is not only monitorable, but one which we can enforce unilaterally, and one that provides strong incentives for us to enforce compliance. In fact, we want the incentives for our enforcing the agreement to exceed the incentives for looking the other way.

As the case of the German violations of the Versailles Disarmament Clause illustrates, democracies have powerful incentives to ignore violations, even when they are quite plain and widely known. Versailles provided arrangements for inspection on the ground and other intrusive arrangements which are extremely unlikely to be obtained in any agreement with a closed society like the Soviet Union. Moreover, British and French inspectors and political figures knew of the violations, but did nothing — for fear of making it harder to negotiate a new disarmament agreement; or because political leaders feared the domestic political consequences of *appearing* to be insufficiently enthusiastic about a potential disarmament agreement.

Strategic arms agreements proposed by American advocates of a declaratory policy of deterrence based on suicidal threats to destroy Soviet population centers ("Mutual Assured Destruction," or MAD) tend also to be premised on the notion that no one can survive a nuclear war and on the notion also that introducing new systems to protect population would be wrong. So, the National Campaign to Save the ABM Treaty states with approval that "the fundamental premise underlying the Anti-Ballistic Missile

Treaty was that nuclear war is not survivable and that a search for technological solutions to alter this reality would be both futile and dangerous."[2] Agreements based on such a premise are an outstanding example of the wrong kind of arms agreement. They assume that "the mad momentum of the race" is driven by American technical innovation, especially one that would protect population. And, therefore, to stop the "race" they would impose compliance on the U.S., no matter what the Soviets do. However, that removes Soviet incentives to comply. It encourages passive acceptance, if not total neglect, of Soviet cheating and especially Soviet interpretations of an agreement that defeat its overt purpose and, in particular, defeat our purpose in signing the agreement.

While arms control doctrines based on MAD seem designed to discourage our responding to adversary violations of agreements, their laxity is not unique. Today the media have made it a notorious sin not to display total and uncritical enthusiasm for past as well as future agreements; they take any U.S. government report of a Soviet violation of current agreements as proving that the U.S. government doesn't "seriously" want arms control. Powerful forces of inertia in the bureaucracy, including the service bureaucracies, tend in the same direction. Administration leaders have told the Congress and the public that the Soviets have violated SALT I and SALT II and many other agreements as well; but have not indicated that we will or should do anything if the Soviets do not take "corrective action." That presents a serious domestic problem.

The MAD Momentum of MAD-Based Arms Control

The "MAD momentum of the strategic arms race," talked about by Robert McNamara and other proponents of MAD beginning in the early 1960s, was pure talk. The Soviet Union raced forward while we moseyed back. They tripled their spending on strategic forces — accelerating after SALT I. We cut ours by two-thirds. There has been no MAD momentum in U.S. strategic arms deployment. There has been a MAD momentum in the one-sided application of strategic arms control. Even though, today, it is easy to prove this (Harold Brown, after he was in office, said of Soviet arms, "When we go up, they go up, when we go down, they go up"), the administration has not been able so far to deal adequately with these domestic pressures. We continue to cripple or slow down our own innovations and continue to tolerate Soviet advances. A more sophisticated and carefully modulated policy is needed to redress this asymmetry.

The Example of German Violations of the Versailles Disarmament Clause and British and French Complaisance in the 1920s

Negotiations for an arms agreement usually carry with them a certain amount of euphoria about the ability to enforce even a vaguely worded agreement. That is part of selling the agreement to a domestic public in a democracy. It is said that if an adversary violates the agreement then the world will know, and fear of world opinion will deter him or shame him into ending the violation; or, if not, we will end the agreement. Our current agreements emerge from negotiations entered into voluntarily by sovereign undefeated states where our means of monitoring are limited. The means of monitoring and enforcing the provisions of a treaty imposed by a victor over a much feared adversary would seem to furnish much more powerful incentives and a much more favorable environment for enforcing compliance. But history tells a different story and should temper any hopes we may have today. The French and British victors in World War I had the means to enforce compliance by a defeated but dangerous Germany, but did not use them. Clandestine German rearmament of the 1920s is a less familiar story of violation than in the 1930s, but it is quite as illuminating.

The Versailles Treaty was meant to disarm a defeated Imperial Germany. The successor government of the Weimar Republic subscribed with overt wholeheartedness to this goal. Karl Joseph Wirth, then Chancellor of the Republic, was the official who signed Weimar's acceptance of the Versailles Treaty. The acceptance said in part: "The German Government is determined ... to carry out without reservation or delay the measures relative to the disarmament of military, naval and aerial forces as specified in the memorandum by the Allied Powers dated 21 January 1921." The memorandum specified that the "manufacture of arms, munitions or any war material, shall only be carried out in factories or works, the location of which shall be communicated to and approved by the Governments of the Principal Allied and Associated Powers, and the number of which they retain the right to restrict." It prohibited "importation into Germany of arms, munitions and war material of every kind" and the dispatch "to any foreign country" of "any military, naval, or air mission."[3] These regulations followed

475

the scrapping of machines, and machine tools in munitions factories like the Krupp Works, and the destruction of existing munitions stockpiles. Moreover, it would seem that whether or not the leaders of the Weimar government really intended without reservations to disarm as specified by the Allied Powers, the allies did not have to rely on their good faith. The Allied Control Commission had very extensive powers of inspection on the ground over a defeated Germany, which exceeded by far any that would ever be agreed to voluntarily by an independent but hostile and closed society entering into an arms agreement during a long period of peace.

On the face of it, one might believe an ideal state of disarmament existed in the 1920s in Germany under a new idealistic government. Unfortunately at the moment of signing Chancellor Wirth was already violating his agreement. In a letter to Gustav Krupp he recalls "with satisfaction" the years from 1920 to 1923 when he and Krupp director Dr. Wiedfeldt were cooperating "to lay new foundations for the development of the German armament technique." President Von Hindenburg, he wrote, "had been informed.... His reaction was also very creditable, though nothing of this has yet been disclosed to the public...." Wirth wished to add this information to his earlier accomplishments "on account of my initiative as the Reich Chancellor and Reich Minister of Finance, by releasing considerable sums of the Reich for the preservation of German armament techniques."[4] "Preservation" was perhaps the wrong word. The government was helping to finance an entirely new line of armaments, since destroyed industries were obliged to start afresh. And facilities were being provided not only by traditional neutrals — the Dutch, the Danes, the Swedes — but also by the Soviet government. To cite only one example, Krupp's development of a new tough steel permitted the manufacture of machines for grenades which turned out one grenade every 12 minutes as compared to 220 minutes earlier.

In Germany, of course, complicated financial maneuvering became necessary, but double books were not the only means for eluding a conscientious Allied Control Commission. German deception became a fine art, even including infiltration of the Commission so that factories would have adequate warning of inspection visits. The French representative was especially vigilant, since for the French government at this time German rearmament remained an ever present threat. But even the French representative, who was aware of the deception, was unaware of its magnitude.

The Allied Control Commission as a whole knew of the deception. It had discovered and reported many evasions of the Versailles Treaty on the part of industry as well as in the armed forces. Within the army these included numerous paramilitary units, which were secretly equipped and armed, a large expansion in the numbers of police who were housed in barracks, an illegal General Staff which went under the name of *Truppenamt* or Troops Office (which supposedly took care of general *Reichswehr* organizational matters), the covert training of pilots in the Soviet Union, the growth of a military air force within the civilian air transport industries, a device of short-term enlistments, an expansion in the number of NCOs, the use of wargames and command post exercises to give officers training in handling strategies for large armies, etc. Within the Navy one of the most flagrant evasions was construction of submarines under secret contracts with Spain and Finland. The Allied Control Commission's final report in 1927 concluded, "Germany had never disarmed, had never had the intention of disarming, and for seven years had done everything in her power to deceive and 'counter-control' the Commission appointed to control her disarmament."

"Control" has two meanings: one to monitor or observe, the other to regulate or enforce behavior according to rule. The Allied Control Commission monitored. It did not compel, nor did it lead the allied governments to enforce—for all the debate over verification.

Why were these numerous evasions disregarded by the governments in question? There are a number of reasons which will remind us of the situation today, and some that are peculiar to this period of the Twenties.

First, the Commission itself was divided. Some of its members were uninterested and performed perfunctorily. Others welcomed German rearmament as a counter to the French. For example, a senior naval inspector at the time of the dissolution of the Commission in 1927, a Commander Fenshaw, told retired Lt. Renken, his German opposite number, "Both you and I are glad that we are leaving. Your task was unpleasant and so was mine. One thing I should point out. You should not feel that we believed what you told us. Not one word you uttered was true, but you delivered your information in such a clever way that we were in a position to believe you. I want to thank you for this."[5]

477

Commander Fenshaw's view was shared by many of his British countrymen, who regarded French statesmen as paranoid on the subject of a revival of German militarism. Edouard Herriot is quoted as saying to Austen Chamberlain, "I look forward with terror to her making war upon us again in ten years." And Raymond Poincaré, who resented strongly British indifference to the risks of a German revival, was regarded as personifying a French aggressiveness that was a greater threat to European and world stability than anything likely to emerge from Germany.

Anglo-French antagonisms were reinforced by a feeling on the part of many in England that Germany was being punished too severely for her part in the war not only from the point of view of ethics or justice, but also because the success of the Russian Revolution had alarmed a good many of these officials. The specter of communism had begun to haunt Europe and even before Chancellor Wirth had laid his elaborate plans for deception, the first President of the German Republic, the Socialist Friedrich Ebert, recognized that the Social Democrats might suffer the fate of Kerensky's government if the Spartakist faction gained control of the Social Democrats and if the armed forces disintegrated as they had in Russia. The danger of revolution was real. Liebknecht and Luxemburg on the steps of the Imperial Palace had declared a Soviet Germany when General Groener stepped in with an offer to preserve order and maintain discipline with what was left of the armed forces. Ebert accepted with relief. General Groener interpreted his mandate to be combating the revolution "without reservation" and that meant among other things getting rid of the Workers' Councils and the Spartakists, and he accomplished this in January 1919. His volunteer Free Corps, one of the first fronts for a clandestine Army, crushed the local Communist movement. But in the meantime collusion between parts of the Weimar government and officers of the German Army ensured the quiet return of both the Army and its new arms, while the British government looked the other way. A justified fear of communism motivated the Social Democrats to restore the army to a key role in the state and this led to the systematic deception in rearming. A less urgent fear of communism in part motivated British acceptance of the deception.

As Wheeler-Bennett put it in his heavily documented analysis of the German Army in politics:

> ... in 1919 the majority of the leading statesmen of the world were more afraid of Communist Russia—a new

phenomenon of evil—than of a possible revival of the old Adam of German nationalism, and those who were shaping the new policies of Germany were quick to take advantage of the opportunity presented by this aberration....

... It was, in effect, the only common ground which existed between victors and vanquished, and already at Weimar there appeared that same line of propaganda which, twenty years later, was to be used by Hitler—and, thirty years later, by Dr. Adenauer and Herr Schumacher—namely, that Germany constituted Europe's first bastion of defence against Bolshevism.[6]

Another motive for failure to enforce the Treaty was the hope that a new disarmament agreement might be reached which would reduce the need for each nation to rebuild armaments after the war. In England people had had enough of war. The Bloomsbury elite were a symptom of this war weariness. They combined fatigue and a "habit of indecision" with what Wyndham Lewis called "gilded Bolshevism," a hope and trust that the Soviet experiment was ushering in a brave new world. When the Armistice was signed, they celebrated "not so much the victory of the allies, as Lenin's wisdom in signing a separate peace to 'create and fashion a new God'."[7]

Even the most farsighted and thoughtful of men, Winston Churchill, who was among the earliest and surely was the most outstanding person to recognize the dangers of German rearmament and the menace of the Axis powers, was at the start of the 1920s preoccupied with other matters. As the 1921 Minutes of the Committee of Imperial Defence (CID) illustrate, he was disposed to consider the need for social programs to deal with social unrest after the long hardships of World War I and the rising danger of communism; and to worry about the serious debt problem of England. Therefore in defense matters he focused on ways to reduce British defense spending especially by reducing the British navy and its ability to defend the Far East. (Churchill, for many years after this, discounted any Japanese attack in the Far East as inconceivable in his lifetime. He considered expedients for defending the Middle East, such as those proposed by Air Marshall Trenchard, to use strategic bombers to keep the natives in line cheaply. And he, like others much less foresighted, adopted the Ten Year Rule that Britain could count on their being no war for the next ten years.)

With domestic problems primarily on his mind he raised no serious objections to the views advanced by Trenchard and others that the French air force and French submarine force, not the German armed forces, were the main threat. He also took part in meetings of the Committee of Imperial Defence (CID) and made no principled objection to the view that disarmament agreements, under the aegis of the League of Nations, would help solve the financial problems of Britain, in effect by reducing the main threat, namely that of France.

Churchill, even in 1921, was more circumspect about the French threat than Trenchard, but he did suggest in these meetings that, "while it was undesirable to fall out with France on this question [i.e., the French air menace to Britain] if it could be avoided ... if France were disagreeable to us in regard to other matters [i.e., the repayment of their debt to Britain], we might bring up the question of the strength of Air Forces" (CID #146, October 2, 1921, p. 3).

Perhaps one of the most fascinating aspects of these meetings of the CID in 1921 is the way that disarmament agreements, the financial difficulties of England, and the need for social programs came up simultaneously with discussions of the use of strategic bombing as a cheap way of bringing an enemy to sue for peace quickly. Trenchard, who at other times talked of attacking only legitimate military targets of war-supporting industry and avoiding innocent bystanders as much as is feasible, read a paper in the 139th meeting of the CID on May 27, 1921, which made clear that he thought of strategic bombing (and especially strategic bombing that would have to be faced by England) as having as its purpose "to drive home the fear of personal injury and loss to every individual." It is not clear that he is advancing here the position he frequently took that the only good defense in the Middle East was to drive home the fear of personal injury and loss to every individual on the other side even more quickly. But there is little evidence that he displayed interest in discrimination and precision in that meeting.

Churchill, in the late 1920s, long before it was common, saw clearly that disarmament negotiations raised more problems than they solved. "We always seem to be getting into trouble over these stupid disarmament manoeuvres," he wrote to Donald Ferguson on September 9, 1928. "And personally I deprecate all these premature attempts to force agreements on disarmament." In particular, Churchill recognized (as in his splendid "disarmament fable" which anticipated Salvador de Madariaga, see Appendix A) the arbitrariness and ambiguity of the capabilities each of the powers wanted to restrict in others and allow for itself and, most important, he recognized that France was not the greatest threat, and that Germany was going to be. He stressed that weakening France compared to Germany by forcing it to cut its army in half while allowing the Germans to double theirs in the name of giving the Germans "equality" was a very bad idea. However, Churchill's views in 1928 were rare in Britain.[8]

In Germany, Foreign Minister Streseman pressed continuously for a decision to withdraw the Allied Control Commission, and he finally accomplished his goal on December 11, 1926. He had acted in conjunction with the French Foreign Minister, Aristide Briand, and his British counterpart Austen Chamberlain. Briand had always been impatient with the "petty details" brought forward by the Commission, and it is significant of the temper of the time that he and Stresemann shared the 1926 Nobel peace prize. The Commission's final report about German non-compliance with the old disarmament agreement was either ignored or suppressed.[9] It was subordinated to flourishing hopes for a new disarmament agreement—hopes which finally culminated in the Geneva Disarmament Conference of 1932. Sir John Simon, the British Foreign Secretary at that time, was an urgent advocate for rapid and comprehensive disarmament. In the event this resulted in great pressure on France to reduce its defense expenditures and the size of its army, in order—in Sir John's words—"to allow the fair meeting of Germany's claim to the principle of equality." Under his aegis, the disarmament plan finally submitted to the House of Commons proposed the approximate halving of France's army and a doubling of the German army.

One of the members of the Allied Control Commission, Major General Temperley, who had been painstaking in his observation and recording of German violations of the Versailles Treaty, became the principal military expert for Great Britain at the Geneva Disarmament Conference of 1932. In spite of his earlier experience, he did all in his power to promote a new agreement. The French delegates, on the other hand, concerned about the growing military strength of their neighbor, had at hand a dossier listing the continuing German deceptions, which they were planning to present to the Conference. General Temperley wrote, "I was in possession of our own [dossier] which was not less an indictment of German good faith, backed up by unimpeachable evidence." However, he felt that "the past was past and we saw no particular point in raking it up ... so long as there was a chance of getting an agreement, I used what influence I possessed against bringing up the 'secret' dossier. In fact it never was made public...."[10]

We are seeing the same reactions today to the U.S. government's publication of Soviet violations of U.S.- Soviet arms agreements—a plea to forget our past experience and to stop rocking the boat. We are reminded of Churchill's words in an article he wrote for *The Daily Mail* in the spring of 1932:

> There is such a horror of war in the great nations who passed through Armageddon that any declaration or public speech against armaments, although it consisted only of platitudes and unrealities, has always been applauded; and any speech or assertion which set forth the blunt truths has been incontinently relegated to the category of "warmongering."[11]

Arms Agreements Based on MAD, by Paralyzing U.S. Response to Soviet Union Arms Expansion, Encourage It

The idea that has governed the elite view of arms control in the U.S. since the mid-1960s proceeds on the assumption that the U.S. has been driving "an ever accelerating nuclear arms race" in the strategic field, forcing an increase by the Soviet Union—which would otherwise be satisfied with a minimal force designed only to deter U.S. attack by threatening U.S. cities. It assumes:

a) that the U.S. can reliably deter any Soviet use of nuclear weapons against a major Western country by threatening to bomb Soviet cities, and that this can be done cheaply without continuing innovation in nuclear forces and with a much smaller, exclusively offensive force.

b) the U.S. not only need not defend its population but that spending for that purpose would be bad since it would deprive the Soviet Union of the ability to destroy our cities and so provoke the Soviet Union into new and ever higher levels of arms spending and possibly into an actual attack.

c) spending money on preserving *control* of our nuclear offense forces would not only waste resources but provoke the Soviet Union.

Our elites recommend avoiding waste and provocation by foregoing defense of our population or any attempt to secure the ability to keep our offensive forces under control in the event of war. In fact, even if the Soviets introduce more weapons or new weapons, it would make no difference. "Neither side can alter the situation decisively by any foreseeable deployment or technological breakthrough."[12] As President Nixon put it at the time of SALT I: "The change required to upset the balance is so large that it cannot be achieved by limited means."[13]

Nominally Bilateral Arrangements Actually Reduce U.S. Arms One-Sidedly

MAD theory would seem to say that the U.S., by unilaterally renouncing any nuclear capability other than the capability to bomb Soviet cities, can both end the arms competition and be safer against nuclear attack. We can reduce our spending unilaterally. That would seem to make negotiations on arms agreements restricting the Soviet Union quite unnecessary, and certainly not urgent. However, our elites are sophisticated fellows and recognize that the Congress and the American public and even perhaps the Executive are all too primitive to accept such unilateral disarmament if it is explicit. They therefore need arms negotiations and agreements which are superficially bilateral to get the Congress and the Executive branch to make the necessary reductions on our side. For that purpose, however, an agreement need not restrict the Soviet Union—which, they assume has in any case, no ambitions which would be served by maintaining an effective nuclear force other than to deter us from attack, and which has only been forced by *us* to increase its nuclear arsenal. An agreement which tolerates Soviet violations, and indeed cripples our own ability to enforce their compliance, they believe, does us no essential harm. In short, arms negotiations and agreements based on MAD serve the practical political function of restricting us while only nominally (but supposedly safely) restricting the Soviets.

In fact, MAD theories of *deterrence* focus almost exclusively on making sure that U.S. political leaders will never use nuclear weapons first or second, early or late: They stress (most obviously in recent years) that any nuclear exchange will mean universal ruin and that we therefore should not take part in any such exchange. MAD declaratory policy undermines our ability to deter Soviet attack by relying on a suicidal threat we plainly would not (and should not) execute if deterrence fails. An arms control agreement based on MAD, on the other hand, undermines our ability to restrain a Soviet arms buildup in violation of the agreement by making it hard to reply with a buildup of our own, since that too would be in violation of the agreement.

Advocates of MAD never face the problem of how to deter or respond to a Soviet limited use of nuclear weapons which would leave the U.S. and other Western countries a large stake in not sacrificing their populations. They make any response suicidal and incredible. Similarly, theories of arms control based on MAD focus almost exclusively on making sure that the U.S. will comply not only with the letter of that agreement but with the spirit of the agreement, that we will avoid anything that could be possibly interpreted as an infringement of the rules; on the other hand, they sometimes rather explicitly make it safe for the Soviets to violate the agreement or so to interpret the agreement as to subvert its nominal purpose in controlling them as well as us. They prepare an advance apology for Soviet noncompliance.

Such Nominally Symmetrical Arrangements are a Pragmatic Political Device Justifying Actual Asymmetry

It is hard to say how much is self-conscious in this manipulatory view of the role of arms controllers as a way of getting Congress and our political leaders to go along with what are effectively one-sided restraints on us and using the bureaucracy in a way that enforces American but not Soviet compliance.

However, the arms control community has developed some legalistic technical arguments which are sometimes quite explicit on the possibility of exploiting the inertia of bureaucracies to enforce our compliance and at the same time to predispose the bureaucracy, the Congress and the political leadership to tolerate violations by the Soviet Union. For example, Abram Chayes in an article in *Harvard Law Review*, March 1972, written shortly before the ratification of SALT I, argued that "the inertia and imperatives of bureaucratic operations under a treaty and the contemplated mechanisms for verification and enforcement" would generate "forces for compliance." He applies this not only to treaties but also to informal understandings and moratoria. Mr. Chayes gives us a splendid example of such forces for compliance on our side operating in the nuclear moratorium of 1958.

> After President Eisenhower proclaimed a moratorium on nuclear testing in 1958, the AEC and Defense Department sharply reduced what had been a routine activity: cranking out test plans and programs. It was no longer very profitable, from an agency viewpoint or in terms of the career line of an official, to sit around thinking up ideas for interesting weapons tests or planning their execution. As a result, when the U.S.S.R. resumed atmospheric testing in September 1961, the United States was not ready to respond in kind. It took six months just to complete the physical operations. But even when the logistics were all worked out, no significant tests and experiments had been developed. The tests that were actually carried out were not very productive for purposes of science or weapons technology—they were essentially political.[14]

Mr. Chayes believes that this shows that once a treaty or informal understanding goes into effect "all the classical defects of bureaucracy become virtues from the point of view of arms control. Rigidity, absence of imagination, initiative, creativity, unwillingness to take risks, operations by the book—all are enlisted in aid of compliance with the agreement (pp. 935-936)."

The example of the test moratorium, however, brings out an essential flaw in this line of reasoning and this style of arms limitation. It may seem a minor problem in a theory presented so grandly and in such general terms about compliance by *any* party to *any* arms agreement. However, it should be enough to spoil the euphoria. Apparently the familiar rigidity of the Soviet bureaucracy, which we know is impressive, did not operate to force the Soviets to comply with the moratorium in either the letter or the spirit. The Soviet breakout was not a sudden decision, but as Hans Bethe pointed out in indignation at the time,[15] it followed elaborate preparations for the sudden conduct of such tests on a massive scale. The Soviet bureaucracy was not generating forces for Soviet compliance, but proceeding on the orders of their political leadership and under an elaborate cover and deception plan to generate a test program. And, in general, the troubadours who sing the virtues of bureaucratic irrationality would mislead themselves less if they used fewer abstract nouns like "compliance" and more verbs like "complying" or "violating" or "deceiving" with names of real countries as subjects and objects of the verbs. But of course that would reveal to themselves and to the public that they are really talking about forcing U.S. compliance and making it difficult for the U.S. to penalize Soviet noncompliance.

Roger Fisher, also of the Harvard Law School, has talked about a zone of doubtful conduct which establishes "a precautionary rule" — "some distance back from the interest we are trying to protect, so that a breach of the rule does not necessarily offend that interest" (*op. cit.*, p. 937). It is true that the United States has taken such precautions to avoid infringements on the unratified threshold Test Ban. But the Soviets have exploited the uncertainty in the other direction, in order to exceed the threshold. In this they rely on the inertia of our bureaucracies to escape any sanctions or denunciations of the informal understanding.

In fact, Professor Chayes himself observes the Soviets are "strict constructionists" who interpret a limitation in such a way as to restrict themselves as little as possible. That is, anything that is not very plainly prohibited by the agreement, they take as permissible:

> "The very meaning of a line in the law is that anyone may get as close to the line as he can if he keeps on the right side." (Quoted from Justice Holmes, 1916.) In fact, this view finds expression in Soviet strict constructionist doctrine, which holds that a government is bound only to the extent of its express consent.[16]

In brief, the Soviets will tend to stay as far as possible on the noncompliance side of the line, secure in the knowledge that the U.S. advocates of arms agreements will keep the U.S. as far as possible on the compliance side. And all this can take place without any clear violation of the letter of the agreement, regardless of what damage it does to the "spirit."

However, the Soviets can, and have, plainly violated even the letter of agreements with impunity. This has involved the masking of signs of what they were doing, but no great risk when the mask is dislodged or removed. The inertia of Western political leaders and Western bureaucracies makes the job of an adversary interested in deception easier. He need not suppress all signals of his violation. He can in fact avoid sanctions even if agencies of the U.S. government are aware of "probable" violations, or "almost certain" violations, or just plain violations. The Soviets have been able to depend on the desire of Western decisionmakers to avoid denouncing violations for fear of spoiling the possibility of future agreements, or out of fear of being accused of *wanting* to spoil arms control.

The U.S. tends to avoid obtaining a capability which may be extremely important for the purpose of the agreement (for example, a precise non-nuclear missile, that could replace the sort of nuclear missile restricted by the agreement) if that capability (e.g., the same precise missile, but with a nuclear as distinct from a nonnuclear warhead) also permits activities of a kind restricted by the agreement. In fact we often avoid attaining a capability which would further the overt *purpose* of an arms agreement because it would make it possible for us to avoid the *letter* of the agreement. (We have avoided or delayed developing precise non-nuclear missiles which could *replace* missiles with nuclear warheads and so reduce our reliance on nuclear weapons on the ground that such nonnuclear missiles *could* carry nuclear warheads. So the now expired moratorium on cruise missiles in SALT II.)

At the same time we tolerate Soviet forces which are easily capable of functioning in ways restricted by the agreement, so long as the Soviets claim that their purpose in fielding these particular forces is not incompatible with the agreement. And in fact there may be some "Functionally Related Observable Differences" (FRODs) which they point to as indicating their benign intent. The differences displayed in "FRODs" usually are trivial and seldom seriously restrict the Soviet's ability to defeat the agreement.

Professor Chayes notes that "in the recent Cold War period, the rubric has been that since it was impossible to be sure of the other side's intentions, policy decisions should be based on capabilities." In brief, Professor Chayes thinks we should take a more relaxed attitude towards a Soviet capability to shoot down, say, one of our ICBMs or SLBMs even though it might seem to violate the ban on defense against strategic ballistic missiles. We should depend rather on being able to predict whether or not the Soviets will expand that capability and use it in that particular way. The supporters of MAD declaratory policy, and of arms negotiations based on the assumptions of that policy, have been singularly unsuccessful in predicting Soviet behavior — or even in noticing what Soviet behavior has been in past Soviet deployment—and especially poor in noticing how badly our predictions of Soviet deployments have matched the realities that eventuated. There is no reason to believe that their ability to predict will improve enough to reassure us that a violation is insignificant. However, once again it appears that this sort of relaxed view of Soviet compliance in letter or spirit is not matched by an equally relaxed view about American compliance among American elites who base their arms control policy on MAD. There are some immediate important current examples.

Alan B. Sherr, who heads the Lawyers Alliance for Nuclear Arms Control, published a brief in June 1984 on "Legal Issues of the 'Star Wars' Defense Program." He says,

> A major perceived loophole in the ABM Treaty is that weapons development which clearly would be prohibited if intended for use in an anti-ballistic missile system can proceed unhindered if intended for use, at least initially, in an *anti-satellite (ASAT) system*. As a matter of law and sound policy, however, *capability*, rather than *intent* is the applicable standard. As a factual matter, it appears that some projects have an *ABM capability* even though they are currently referred to as serving an "ASAT role." Contrary to current practice, therefore, the development, testing and deployment of such weapon systems or components are barred by the ABM Treaty independent of whether they are "tested in an ABM mode" (pp. 15-18).

In short, however benign our apparent intentions (and Mr. Sherr regards us as suspect), it is enough that we *could* use a capability actually designed to destroy Soviet satellites (a capability not restricted by SALT I) to commit the cardinal sin of destroying a Soviet ICBM on its way to destroy an ICBM base in the U.S. or to annihilate an American city (a sin which is drastically restricted in SALT I).

The Soviets, as might be expected, take a different view. They now have ways of destroying (or disabling for critical periods) American satellites. And under the Anti-Satellite Treaty they propose they could continue to have such capabilities. No problem. They would not use them that way, and even if they did, once they had destroyed our satellites, we could always verify that our satellites had been destroyed. Academician Velikov recently said,

> You can kill with a hammer. So it is logically stipulated that you'll be punished not because you have a hammer but because you try to kill with it. The same reasoning applies to the treaty on antisatellite weapons that we propose. Of course, there exist ways of destroying satellites, any stupid ways [sic]. If we can dock with a satellite, then clearly we can dock with an American satellite, but a bit carelessly, and thus destroy it. But the idea of our proposal is that there is no problem in verifying whether or not a satellite has been destroyed.[17]

Of course, that verification might come a little late.

Mr. Sherr, one may predict, is unlikely to insist on strict banning of the Soviet *capability* to destroy our satellites in some future ASAT treaty. However, he does insist that developing U.S. capabilities now, when there is no ASAT treaty, has already violated the ban on developing and testing a capability to defend against Soviet strategic ballistic missiles.

Since No Military Capability is Unambiguous, MAD-Based Agreements Tolerate a Pervasive Asymmetry between the Soviet Union and the U.S.

An offensive force can be used in a preventive war to preclude attack; or as a deterrent and to retaliate to attack. A defensive force can be used to preserve the ability to respond to an attack by an aggressor and contain the catastrophe to civil society wreaked by his attack; or it might be used to supplement an offense force in an aggression by interposing an extra barrier to the victim's response.

Attempts at qualitative disarmament or freezes today which act as if one could tell whether a system or a performance characteristic has a "first-strike character" or a "second-strike character," simply by inspection without looking at the many uses in differing contexts, misunderstand the first-strike/second-strike distinction. Such attempts repeat the interwar confusions of the "qualitative disarmament" which tried hopelessly to distinguish between "offensive weapons" and "defensive weapons." It is

489

worth quoting Winston Churchill once again on the subject of such qualitative disarmament:

> The Foreign Secretary told us that it was difficult to divide weapons into offensive and defensive categories. It certainly is, because almost every conceivable weapon may be used in defence or offence; either by an aggressor or by the innocent victim of his assault. To make it more difficult for the invader, heavy guns, tanks, and poison gas are to be relegated to the evil category of offensive weapons. The invasion of France by Germany in 1914 reached its climax without the employment of any of these weapons. The heavy gun is to be described as "an offensive weapon." It is all right in a fortress; there it is virtuous and pacific in its character; but bring it out into the field — and, of course, if it were needed, it would be brought out into the field — and it immediately becomes naughty, peccant, militaristic, and has to be placed under the ban of civilisation. Take the tank. The Germans, having invaded France, entrenched themselves; and in a couple of years they shot down 1,500,000 French and British soldiers who were trying to free the soil of France. The tank was invented to overcome the fire of the machine-guns with which the Germans were maintaining themselves in France, and it saved a lot of lives in clearing the soil of the invader. Now, apparently, the machine-gun, which was the German weapon for holding on to thirteen provinces of France, is to be the virtuous, defensive machine-gun, and the tank, which was the means by which these Allied lives were saved, is to be placed under the censure and obloquy of all just and righteous men....
>
> A truer classification might be drawn in banning weapons which tend to be indiscriminate in their action and whose use entails death and wounds, not merely on the combatants in the fighting zones, but on the civil population, men, women, and children, far removed from those areas. There, indeed, it seems to me would be a direction in which the united nations assembled at Geneva might advance with hope....[18]

Present discussions of qualitative arms control in some ways are even more far-fetched than the interwar efforts which tried to restrict offensive weapons and encourage defensive weapons. The present efforts actually treat defensive weapons as more malign. But, in any case, like the earlier efforts they vastly oversimplify the problem by ignoring ambiguities that are intrinsic. Churchill's comment that we'd be better off trying to restrict weapons that are indiscriminate or that indiscriminately kill civilians is even more applicable today.

A research reactor using natural uranium as a fuel might serve as an aid in designing power reactors; or as a means of accumulating and separating plutonium for producing plutonium fuel for a civilian breeder reactor in the future; or as a means of accumulating and separating plutonium for a nuclear explosive. A nuclear explosive might be used to destroy an adversary's military facilities or population centers; or to dig a canal. There have been several clear-cut violations of agreements on the peaceful uses of atomic energy and also violations of the nonproliferation treaty. These have been known to other parties to the atomic energy agreements, and in particular the United States government. And they have also been known to the IAEA. Compliance has not been pressed, nor in general has cheating been acknowledged for fear of jeopardizing past or future agreements. Instead, ambiguities have been used, even where interpretation is far-fetched, as equivocations in order not to disturb the inertia of bureaucracies.

A large phased-array radar may be used to track space "junk" or for early warning if it is placed near the periphery of a country looking outwards towards a probable attacker; or it may be used for battle management to guide interceptor missiles to destroy an incoming ballistic missile. ABM may defend missile sites (which MAD doctrine might be expected to regard as a good thing just as shelter for a missile is supposed to be good); or it might be used to defend population (which MAD doctrine supposes to be bad, just as it supposes civil defense shelters to be bad). During the negotiations for the ABM treaty there were some internal papers within the U.S. government proposing that defense against ballistic missiles might be permitted, but limited to missile sites remote from cities — in the Soviet Union west of the Urals and in the United States east of the Rockies. This was rejected in internal debate because it was said that even such circumscribed site defense remote from cities might conceivably be extended and thickened so as to defend populations though such an extension and thickening would take many years and would be quite visible. But the ABM treaty went to great lengths to make certain that no development, testing or deployment of an ABM other than a quite trivial deployment on a single site would be allowed. As anticipated, that destroyed any strong incentives on the American side to carry out a vigorous research and development program on ballistic defense of any sort. But not on the Soviet side. Nor did it stop the Soviets from deploying radars at Krasnoyarsk which almost certainly are likely to have a battle management capability.

To compensate for the restraint on active defense in ABM missile sites, SALT I relied on restraining the dimensions of the silos so as to limit the number of Soviet heavy missiles, and so, it was thought, their capacity to destroy our ICBMs. (They used techniques for launching that ignited the booster after the missile had been expelled from the silo and so were able to fit heavier missiles in the silo.) In any case, a limitation on the size of missiles did not prevent their increasing the precision of missiles and so in this way gaining the ability to destroy our missile sites. In short, SALT I did not prevent an active Soviet research and development program on ABM and it did not prevent their increasing their offensive capability so as to make our fixed land-based force obsolete. (See Appendix B.)

The Advocates of Arms Agreements Based on MAD Prefer Arms Agreements of Indefinite Duration Because They are Harder to Alter Even When Circumstances Alter

Agreements that do not terminate automatically at a given time are hard to terminate at all, even when wisdom suggests they should be ended because changes in the state of the art unanticipated in drafting the agreement or Soviet infringements of the agreement make it obsolete. Given the intrinsic difficulties of anticipating technical change and the especially poor record of arms controllers in making such predictions, it is essential that any serious agreement be limited in duration if we are to avoid serious instabilities.

APPENDIX A

Returning from the Paris negotiations, Churchill reflected on what he saw as the folly of premature disarmament, and on October 25, 1928, during a speech in his constituency, he told what he called a 'disarmament fable.' The tale was as follows:

> Once upon a time all the animals in the Zoo decided that they would disarm, and they arranged to have a conference to arrange the matter. So the Rhinoceros said when he opened the proceedings that the use of teeth was barbarous and horrible and ought to be strictly prohibited by general consent. Horns, which were mainly defensive weapons, would, of course, have to be allowed. The Buffalo, the Stag, the Porcupine, and even the little Hedgehog all said they would vote with the Rhino, but the Lion and the Tiger took a different view. They defended teeth and even claws, which they described as honourable weapons of immemorial antiquity. The Panther, the Leopard, the Puma and the whole tribe of small cats all supported the Lion and the Tiger. Then the Bear spoke. He proposed that both teeth and horns should be banned and never used again for fighting by any animal. It would be quite enough if animals were allowed to give each other a good hug when they quarrelled. No one could object to that. It was so fraternal, and that would be a great step towards peace. However, all the other animals were very offended with the Bear, and the Turkey fell into a perfect panic.
>
> The discussion got so hot and angry, and all those animals began thinking so much about horns and teeth and hugging when they argued about the peaceful intentions that had brought them together that they began to look at one another in a very nasty way. Luckily the keepers were able to calm them down and persuade them to go back quietly to their cages, and they began to feel quite friendly with one another again.

Quoted in Martin Gilbert, *Winston S. Churchill*, Vol. V, 1922-1939 (Boston, MA: Houghton Mifflin, 1977).

Ambiguities and the Soviet Destruction of SALT I

Part of the problem of arms control is, first, that every military weapon or weapons system can be used for several functions, and, second, that any specific function can be performed in several ways by various alternative military systems. These two difficulties have affected our negotiators and our actual agreements. The first difficulty has operated as a broad constraint on the United States, leading us to forego the development and deployment of systems with several useful and in some cases extremely important military functions in order to make sure that the noxious function is banned. We have interpreted the constraints upon ourselves very broadly.

The second difficulty, namely that a function can be performed by several military systems, has operated so as at most to keep the Soviets from using only one specified way of performing the banned function, but leaving them free to adopt several other alternatives for doing so. We have interpreted the constraints on the Soviets very narrowly, making it possible for them to defeat the overt purpose of the agreement. And that is what they have done.

Both difficulties are illustrated in SALT I. First, we surrendered the important possibility of actively defending the missile silos — a purpose which both sides agreed would be legitimate — because we thought that such defenses might be amplified to perform another function, that of defending population, even though this sort of transformation could hardly have been done without easy detection. For the second difficulty, we cut off one way for the Soviets to destroy our Minuteman silos, but left other ways open for them to develop a formidable array of silo destroyers, and so defeated the major purpose of the agreement.

SALT I

Language worked out in Helsinki probably assures adequate protection against any increase in the number of missiles in the SS-9 class; but it is nonetheless a bit vague and incomplete, lacking, for example, a definition of what constitutes a 'heavy' missile. The Soviets were determined to keep it that way. And they did. Still, any violation of the spirit of this language, let alone the letter, would probably oblige the United States to withdraw from the agreements. Moscow understands that.

John Newhouse's account, which is quoted above, of how the American negotiators of SALT I regarded the probable response of the U.S. to Soviet violations of the spirit of the SALT I offense agreement is accurate. Newhouse also correctly reports what the U.S. delegation *thought* the Soviets believed we would do. Unfortunately the delegation was wrong on both counts. The Soviets violated the letter and above all the spirit and purpose of the agreement. They anticipated apparently that the U.S. would *not* withdraw. And the U.S. has not withdrawn.

The offense agreement and the Treaty on Anti-Ballistic Missile Defense were supposed to complement each other. For the ABM treaty to be viable, the offense agreement had to work, or better, be replaced by a treaty that could accomplish at least the same thing more desirably. The ABM treaty limited any defense against ballistic missile attack to trivial levels. Moreover it limited *not only* ballistic defense of cities, in accordance with the ideology of MAD which regards killing people as good and defending people as bad (to use language which Newhouse has also faithfully quoted in describing the beliefs of the U. S. delegation). It also limited the defense of Minutemen missile sites against Soviet ballistic missile attack.

On the face of it that last limitation seems cockeyed, even if one were to accept the simpleminded theory of stability held by advocates of MAD: They believe that killing *weapons* is bad, just as killing people is good; therefore *defending* weapons is supposed to be good and "stabilizing." However, the advocates of MAD were so bent on preventing the defense of population against missile attack that they drastically limited the defense of Minutemen missile sites so as to exclude even the far-fetched possibility that the site defense might be expanded secretly and rapidly to include a thick defense of population throughout the country. Such expansion of Safeguard ballistic missile defense of Minuteman sites would have taken five to ten years and would have been easily open to observation and interruption. Moreover, it was possible to make that sort of breakout even more remote (as some of us suggested at the time, even though we did not accept the premises of MAD) by constraining the defense of missile sites to regions east of the Urals and West of the Rockies which are very far from population centers.

Instead of a site defense which could have been made increasingly sophisticated over time, the negotiators of SALT I proposed to defend the Minuteman (MM) sites by limitations embodied in the offense agreement. These, it was believed, would prevent any addition to the number of Soviet offense ballistic missile warheads capable of destroying our MM silos. They assumed that it was only the large yield five-megaton warheads on the "heavy" SS-9 missiles which could destroy silos, and that there were at the time only 924 of these warheads, three apiece for each of the 308 SS-9 missiles in the silos we had counted by satellite. Our negotiators, therefore, tried to accomplish this purpose in the agreement by restricting the number of "heavy" missile silos to 308.

There were lots of troubles with the assumptions underlying the agreement which were easily exploited to defeat its purpose. First, the accuracy of the missile is much more important than the yield in destroying a small target like a silo. If we consider only blast overpressure, an improvement in accuracy, in fact, is worth roughly the cube of an increase in yield. An improvement in accuracy by a factor of two offsets a decrease in yield by a factor of eight; an improvement in accuracy by a factor of five offsets a 125-fold change in yield.

For some targets including silos, we must consider in addition to the transient blast overpressure another factor, namely, the duration of the impulse. Larger yield weapons have a larger impulse and therefore are more than proportionately destructive. However, even with this qualification, the importance of changes in accuracy far exceeds that of differences in yield. The Soviets did not need a five megaton warhead to destroy a MM silo. More accurately delivered warheads could be lighter and smaller, and of very much smaller yield. They could be carried on light missiles or you could have many more than three such silo-destroyers on a heavy missile.

The Soviets did improve their accuracy by a factor of five and therefore a warhead of less than 100 kilotons could be as effective as the SS-9 five megaton warhead. A "heavy" missile could carry many more than three of the silo destroyers and so even could a light missile.

Second, the constraint in the agreement applies to silos which we can observe, not to the number of missiles which we cannot. The Soviets have some missiles which are not in silos. They have some missiles that can be reloaded into reusable silos. Some might

496

be fired not from silos, but from launchers concealed in wooded areas or under sliding roofs.

Third, even for warheads of substantial yields, constraints on silos are quite inadequate for imposing limitations on the number of warheads. We don't know how to monitor the yield and numbers of reentry vehicles so we might think of restricting throw weight. But we don't know how to do that directly either, so we might think of restricting the volume of the missile. But even here the delegates failed to observe what was plain at the time, that the Soviets could squeeze larger missiles into silos of a given size if, instead of igniting the booster in the silo, they expelled the missile first from the silo, and then ignited it. That is the way we launch missiles from submarine tubes. In fact, the Soviets exploited these "cold launch" techniques, as some of us predicted. They squeezed much "heavier" SS-18s into SS-9 size silos and they squeezed much heavier missiles into SS-11 size silos that we had taken as the standard for defining a "light missile silo," as differentiated from a "heavy missile silo."

The Russians refused to define a heavy missile silo. (That should have given us a hint as to their behavior under the Treaty.) We stated what we understood it to be, and said that any new silos that were 10-15 percent larger in dimensions would violate the agreement. There was a great deal of vagueness and confusion in our definition. The 10 percent, of course, was not operative. In talking of 10-15 percent, it is obvious that only the 15 percent could operate as a constraint. (The 10 percent was like the 50 percent in advertisements of fire sales with discounts of *up* to 50 percent.) But the initial phrasing of our understanding did not make clear as to whether the 15 percent applied to the length or the cross-sectional area or the volume, that could make a difference between a 15 percent and 50 percent increase in volume. Moreover in testimony before the Senate on SALT I, it was clear that there were differences among principal negotiators as to what that constraint meant.

But it is unnecessary to focus on the detailed ambiguities in the letter of our "unilateral understanding" or in the letter of the main body of the agreement itself. The gist of the matter is that the Soviets exploited these ambiguities so as to vastly increase the number of their warheads capable of destroying our MM silos. The SS-19 which counts as a light missile, for example, has *three times* the throw weight of the SS-11 which was supposed to be the standard for a light missile! It has six accurate reentry vehicles and warheads capable of destroying MM silos, compared to the three in the "heavy" SS-9. The SS-18 has ten.

The upshot of these changes is that the SS-18 missiles and the SS-19 missiles in silos now have nearly six times as many warheads capable of destroying Minuteman as the 924 MIRVs in the 308 SS-9 missiles which our negotiators thought were the threat to Minuteman. The language at Helsinki did not "assure adequate protection against any increase in the number of missiles in the SS-9 class."

In short, whatever the details, the Soviets defeated the principal purpose of the agreement on offensive missiles. They violated the spirit in a quite material sense. The U.S. did *not* feel obliged to withdraw. And the Soviets were *not* wrong in anticipating that we would not withdraw, that they could defeat the overt purpose of the agreement with impunity. They predicted our behavior better than we did.

ENDNOTES - The Wohlstetters - On Arms Control

1. Many present-day advocates of permanent treaties based on MAD have been unable to predict technical changes or their strategic consequences or even their own strategic views six months in advance: they switched from advocating in 1957 in the Gaither Report a huge program for civil and active defense including the defense of populations against ballistic missile attacks, on the ground that it would increase stability, to the other extreme some six months later, that maintaining even a modest defense of population would be destabilizing.

2. "Statement in Support of the ABM Treaty," National Campaign to Save the ABM Treaty, 1324 Connecticut Avenue, NW, Washington, DC, p. 1. See also, the conclusions on page 37 of their "Report on the Impact of U.S. and Soviet Ballistic Missile Defense Programs on the ABM Treaty."

3. Quoted in William Manchester, *The Arms of Krupp, 1587-1968*, Boston, MA: Little Brown and Company, 1964 [1968], p. 342.

4. *Ibid.*, p. 343.

5. Navy Captain Schussler, "The Fight of the Navy Against Versailles, 1919-1935" in *Trials of War Criminals before the Nürnberg*

Military Tribunals, Vol. X, Washington, DC: USGPO, 1951, pp. 433-465.

6. John W. Wheeler-Bennett, *The Nemesis of Power: The German Army in Politics,1918-1945*, 2nd ed., London, UK: MacMillan & Co.; New York: St. Martin's Press, 1964, p. 40.

7. Paul Johnson, *Modern Times: The World from the Twenties to the Eighties*, New York: Harper & Row, 1983, p. 171.

8. Martin Gilbert, *Winston S. Churchill, The Prophet of Truth*, Vol. V, 1922-1939, Boston, MA: Houghton Mifflin, 1977, pp. 304-305.

9. Wheeler-Bennett, *op. cit.*, p. 185-186.

10. A. C. Temperley, *The Whispering Gallery of Europe*, London, UK: Collins, 1938, pp. 221-222.

11. Quoted in Martin Gilbert, *op. cit.*, p. 445.

12. Abram Chayes, "An Inquiry into the Writings of Arms Control Agreements," *Harvard Law Review*, Vol. 85, No. 905, 1972, p. 911.

13. *U.S. Foreign Policy for the 1970s*, a report to the Congress by the President, May 3, 1972, p. 232.

14. Chayes, *op. cit.*, p. 936.

15. "[T]he Russian procedure showed bad faith. Their test series was so elaborate that it must have been prepared for many months, perhaps longer. It is likely that they had started preparations by March when the test ban conference reconvened in Geneva; thus they negotiated for six months in bad faith. They did so at the time when we were showing most clearly by our attitude and proposals at Geneva that we were sincerely interested in the test ban...." Hans Bethe, "Nuclear Testing," lecture, Cornell University, January 5, 1962.

16. Chayes, *op. cit.*, pp. 937-338.

17. Interview with Yevgeniy Velikhov, vice president of the U.S.S.R. Academy of Sciences, Moscow Radio in English to North America, May 26, 1984, 2300 GMT, *FBIS Daily Report: Soviet Union,* June 6, 1984, p. AA 12.

18. Winston S. Churchill, Speech to the House of Commons, May 1932, in *The Gathering Storm,* Boston, MA: Houghton Mifflin, 1948, pp. 71-72.

Arms Control That Could Work (1985)

Albert Wohlstetter and Brian G. Chow

Op-ed, *Wall Street Journal,* July 17, 1985, p. 28. Courtesy of the *Wall Street Journal,* the Wohlstetter Estate, and Brian G. Chow. This op-ed summarizes Wohlstetter and Chow's *Self-Defense Zones in Space,* a study for Integrated Long-Term Defense Strategy in partial fulfillment of MDA903-84-C-0325, Marina del Rey, CA: PAN Heuristics, July 1986, available from *www.albertwohlstetter.com/ writings/SelfDefenseZones.*

The House has voted for a fiscal 1986 moratorium on U.S. testing of anti-satellite weapons (ASATs) against objects in space unless the Soviets resume their testing. The Senate version permits such tests. This week a conference committee will try to resolve this difference. The pious insincerities of Capitol Hill suggest the issue is to avoid militarizing the untouched heavens. But the U.S. and U.S.S.R. will use and have used space for 25 years to further their rival political and military ends. Over 70 percent of Soviet satellites are purely for military purposes. Many of the rest are for both military and civilian uses. In fact, even the House measure aims to encourage an agreement with the Soviets that would protect the many satellites that supply reconnaissance, warning, communications, navigation and guidance, and other critical information for the defense of the two superpowers and their allies. Can an agreement do that?

Some agreement with the Soviet Union conceivably could help the U.S. protect the functioning of key military satellites. But it will take a fresh approach. The standard sort of ASAT ban that is supposed to be a way of defending satellites would very likely end by preventing the U.S. from protecting them. Then many (not all) proponents of the treaty would ignore its disastrous failure to accomplish its purpose of helping satellites survive. They would instead celebrate the survival of the treaty. If that seems cynical, it shouldn't. That's essentially the story of the offense and defense controls imposed by SALT I as a way of ensuring the second-strike capability of U.S. intercontinental ballistic missiles. These controls ended up ensuring that the U.S. could not defend Minuteman silos and that the Soviets would be able to eliminate them. (They deployed nearly six times as many silo-destroying

501

warheads as U.S. negotiators expected.) Many proponents of the SALT I defense and offense restrictions celebrated SALT I as "the jewel in the crown" of arms control. Well, it's clear that the jewel was lost or stolen, if it was not paste in the first place.

More Than One Potential Use

The problem is that almost every military system has more than one potential use, and every prohibited military function can be performed in more than one way — often by permitted military systems or even by systems in civilian use. Satellites can be anti-satellites. So can devices that defend satellites. So, with changes in their guidance logic, can ICBMs and submarine-launched ballistic missiles. (In fact, the Soviets use ICBMs to launch their current ASAT interceptors.) Ban everything that can be used against satellites, and you might end up with no strategic offense ballistic missiles. And no satellites. Yevgeny Velikhov, vice president of the U.S.S.R. Academy of Science, is disturbingly reassuring on this: "If we can dock with a satellite, then clearly we can dock with an American satellite, but a bit carelessly, and thus destroy it. But the idea of our proposal is that there is no problem in verifying whether or not a satellite has been destroyed."

Verifying that U.S. satellites have already been destroyed in a surprise attack might be no problem. And recording that fact could help future historians, if any. However, it would hardly enable the U.S. to prevent the surprise attack.

Even complaining to the usual sluggish Standing Consultative Commission about suspicious satellites hovering near the U.S.'s own, or U.S. threats to renounce an ASAT ban, would not prevent a Soviet surprise attack. In fact a complete ASAT ban would fatally hamper acts of self-defense. To prevent a surprise attack on American satellites, the U.S. will need to respond in time with a combination of passive and active measures: hardening, maneuver, decoys, replenishment and jamming or destruction of enemy ASATs. For, just as ships at sea are liable to sudden attack by other ships staying close to them in peacetime, so critical U.S. satellites will be vulnerable to a simultaneous raid by apparently benign satellites pre-positioned to act as "space mines." Space mines exploit the time delays inherent in defense.

We propose a space agreement to facilitate unilateral defense against surprise attack on satellites. It resembles (but only slightly) the existing U.S. and Soviet agreement on Prevention of Incidents

On and Over the High Seas. Its basic idea is to specify a number of separate "Self-Defense Zones" for Western and Soviet satellites. Each side would have the right to inspect, expel or otherwise render harmless any invaders (should they exceed a safe number) moving through these zones.

Each could do so, of course, without harming any life, military or civilian. Unlike the agreement on Incidents at Sea that the Soviets violated during their search for the wreckage of KAL 007, this one would have automatic enforcement.

The Self-Defense Zones arranged for satellites would vary with their different orbits, since satellites differ in their orbital characteristics and some orbits are more densely populated than others. Here, we sketch only the agreement for the important geosynchronous orbits. The West has some 20 military and 30 civilian communication satellites in such orbits, and the Soviet Union a growing number. In the future, for an adversary to reach geosynchronous orbits (some 36,000 kilometers high) with hit-to-kill vehicles launched from the Earth's surface would be a slow business, taking over an hour. It would be especially hard for them to confidently manage a simultaneous raid on a sizable fraction of critical Western communication satellites. On the other hand, launching hit-to-kill vehicles (or other ASAT weapons) from satellites pre-positioned near the targeted satellites would leave almost no time for defense. But defense needs time. The West has yet to take this serious threat adequately into account.

Instead of attaching self-defense zones to satellites, advantage can be taken of the fact that geosynchronous satellites circuit the Earth roughly as it rotates and so appear almost stationary. Negotiators might designate, for example, 36 zones — bands 10 degrees wide and 7,400 kilometers across with 12 each for the West, the Warsaw Pact and neutral nations. Each zone would rotate with the Earth. Current and future satellites would enter the other side's zones at their peril. Satellites, once declared dead or uncontrollable, would be subject to the other side's disposal when they enter the other side's zones. Enforcing the agreement by defending one's satellites would not therefore involve abrogating it. Self-defense would be part of the agreement. The agreement would not replace unilateral defense. (Nothing will.) Rather, it would facilitate defense.

The cost of this would be low compared with its potential advantage. Initially, each side would need only to reposition a small number of its satellites that now happen to be in the other side's zones. Afterward, a small number of satellites stationed near the zone boundaries would require only occasional orbital adjustments to avoid slow drifting into the other's zones. Moreover, up to two live satellites could be permitted in the other's geostationary zones at any given time. This would reduce the frequency of those orbital adjustments and allow satellite operations (such as initial placement and subsequent repositioning, as well as inspection and collection of information about the other side's satellites) to be performed with few restrictions. At the same time, the small number of allowable transits would make simultaneous attacks much more difficult.

Unique Opportunity

Important Western navigation satellites at near semi-geosynchronous altitudes between 19,800 and 21,100 kilometers are already separated from Soviet navigation satellites orbiting more than 500 kilometers below them. Each side now orbits six to twelve of these satellites. Each is likely to double these numbers in the next few years in order to keep several visible at any given time for use by ships, aircraft and other vehicles requiring extremely precise navigation and guidance. An agreement would formalize this separation for purposes of self-defense.

This is the kind of agreement the U.S. should be discussing with the Soviets. A government concerned about protecting its satellites would want to use such measures of self-defense in any case. Negotiating for such an agreement would make apparent the mutual adjustments in peacetime deployments that would facilitate self-defense. The U.S. could benefit whether the negotiation failed or succeeded. Preparing and negotiating an agreement that includes enforcement would also offer a unique opportunity to inform domestic and allied publics (and allied leaders) of the intrinsic troubles that plague democratic governments (including the Reagan administration) in the standard agreements. Candor about these matters is urgent and is more easily feasible in the context of the design of a serious agreement aimed at coping with such problems explicitly. When our leaders are less than candid on these matters, they trap themselves. Being "serious" about arms control should not mean being unserious about restraining

Soviet behavior and energetic only about preventing a U.S. response. The ASAT ban, pushed by zealots for Mutual Assured Destruction, would paralyze the West, not the East. It would not verifiably prevent Soviet anti-satellite actions. It would prevent the U.S. from effectively defending its satellites.

Messrs. Wohlstetter and Chow are director of research and senior research specialist, respectively, at PAN Heuristics, a Los Angeles-area policy research firm.

V. TOWARDS DISCRIMINATE DETERRENCE

Commentary: *Towards Discriminate Deterrence*

Stephen J. Lukasik

Events in the 1950–1970 period shaped the nation's understanding of nuclear forces and added an experimental dimension to the interaction between the theory and practice. The interplay of external events with the structure and details of strategic forces was central at this early period, as both the United States and the Union of Soviet Socialist Republics (USSR) sought to understand the capabilities and challenges of nuclear weapons and to incorporate these weapons into national strategies.

During the first of these events, in the fall of 1950 when the People's Republic of China (PRC) intervened in North Korea, the United States considered the use of nuclear weapons to destroy the bridges over the Yalu River, but the tactical situation was too fluid for strike planning and delivery to be accomplished. Strikes against Chinese cities in Manchuria were seen as an unacceptable risk. Similar circumstances prevailed when the French asked for military assistance from the United States at Dien Bien Phu in 1954, but nuclear strikes against the rapidly closing perimeter would have decimated the defenders as well. This nuclear planning situation was played out 14 years later in the defense of Khe Sanh in 1968. By this point, apart from collateral damage to defenders, there was the issue of escalation in the face of substantial Soviet nuclear weapons and a now-nuclear PRC. In the case of Suez in 1956, U.S. strategic forces were put on alert but concerns over the possibility of intemperate action by Nikita Khrushchev leading to accidental war provided new appreciation of the downsides of nuclear weapons. Escalation control in Lebanon in 1958 was central to all alerting of nuclear forces, their movements, and attendant public statements. Cuba in 1962 illustrated in detail how actions by nuclear-armed states to secure strategic advantages could escalate to the point of unintended nuclear war. During the attack on the *Liberty* by Israel in 1967, U.S. carrier-based aircraft dispatched to its assistance were called back personally by the Chairman of the Joint Chiefs of Staff and the Secretary of Defense because the aircraft were armed with nuclear weapons and their intentions could have been misinterpreted by the USSR. This same situation was avoided in the *Pueblo* attack by North Korea in 1968 only because all U.S. aircraft in South Korea that could have intervened were nuclear armed and remained on the ground.[1]

While easy to view as a series of theoretical exercises, dependent on cost-benefit analyses, damage optimization, competitive advantage gaming, strategic balance calculations, and other technical factors, strategy is, in practice, experimental in nature and has features in common with biological evolution. The problem of strategy, as Albert Wohlstetter realized, was not optimization of a static system of forces but one of understanding their dynamics over time.

Lacking a calling to pursue technology as a weapon-developer or to employ its firepower as a weapon-wielder, Albert had spent his undergraduate and graduate years steeping in logic and data analysis, and his early professional years grappling with failures of technology to deliver on their promises—experiences which later distinguished him from many of his peers. Arms limitation negotiations that resulted in the Limited Test Ban Treaty in 1963 and the Nonproliferation Treaty in 1968 emphasized that limiting the potential damage from the downsides of nuclear technology was at least as important as realizing its power.[2] Thus limiting collateral damage, both physical and political, seeking stability between nuclear-armed states, and minimizing the risks of accidental war became central features of his strategic thinking.

Technology and Strategy

Albert was intensely interested in new technology. He extrapolated from how the new nuclear technology changed warfare and strategy, to an examination of other areas of technology that could have comparable impacts. It is this extrapolation that characterizes the papers discussed here.

Albert viewed technology as offering what became a favorite word of his, *alternatives*. The process began when he joined RAND and started his extensive work on the basing of bombers and their survivability. In a conversation years later, he noted potential points of failure in the alarm systems that activated bomber crews on strip alert, underlining his detailed concern with critical command and control procedures. During this period, two technological explorations at RAND sharpened his appreciation for the opportunities in command and control they offered. The first was a report in 1946, by a group of 18 in RAND's Missile Division, providing detailed technical studies of earth satellites, which were critical for reconnaissance and global communication.[3] The second came in 1960–64, when Paul Baran and two coworkers proposed a technology for survivable strategic communication based on digital packet technology.[4] In discussions, Albert often returned to the significance of this technology for strategic communication. This rationale was, in fact, dominant in the funding of the development and deployment of an experimental prototype network, the ARPANET, which I had a role in later in the decade.

These developments are mentioned briefly in the first of Albert's papers in this section of the edited volume.[5] The paper opens by asking, "In what ways will technical change alter the interests that join or divide various nuclear and non-nuclear countries, and how will it alter the likely outcomes of potential conflicts among them? In particular, how will new techniques transform the interest and ability to project strength to distant places, and so the worth of nuclear and non-nuclear commitments there?" Of particular note is his raising the question of the relative value of nuclear and conventional weapons.

Future Conflict

By the late 1960s, the Vietnam conflict stimulated rethinking on the circumstances in which U.S. forces would be committed to combat in the future. While World War II and Korea were "conventional" except for the Hiroshima-Nagasaki interlude in 1945, Cuba was a purely nuclear confrontation, with little room for conventional force considerations. But Vietnam added a new dimension to "conflict space." Nuclear weapons had been considered twice for use there, but their effects did not comport with tactical circumstances. The jungle environment precluded large ground force actions. There were no front lines on a map to measure progress in achieving war aims. What was needed was to locate fleeting targets undistinguishable from the neutral background, to interdict distributed bicycle-based supply lines, to deal with an enemy who occupied not only the surface but the subsurface as well, and to minimize collateral damage to the noninsurgent population. These issues challenged military thinking and the technical innovators who had served the United States so well in the past.

In an attempt to close such capability gaps, U.S. laboratories worked closely with the Department of Defense (DoD) to accelerate needed developments and move them into the theater.

The Office of the Secretary of Defense (OSD) established an office for Southeast Asia, and Military Assistance Command-Vietnam (MACV) was provided with a Science Advisor to define new military needs for the technical community, to suggest how technology could assist operations, and to coordinate trials of new equipments when they arrived.

Many avenues were pursued to improve the effectiveness of U.S. forces. Attempts were made to increase the precision of weapons through wire-guidance, radio-control, and laser target designators. All had their successes but none fully provided the capabilities needed. The war against a few rapidly moving targets embedded among many non-targets was too different from prior military actions. Fixed targets such as roads and bridges were easily reparable and the necessary labor and materials were widely available. Targets consisted of relatively low value components distributed at low densities over large areas. Heavy vegetation obscured both air and ground reconnaissance and impeded communication.

On returning from a tour as Science Advisor to General Creighton Abrams, Fred Wikner proposed to the Advanced Research Projects Agency (ARPA) and Defense Nuclear Agency (DNA) a study of R&D needs to address what were seen as major and long-lasting changes in military affairs. The study, eventually named the Long Range Research and Development Planning Program (LRRDPP), took as its starting point that nuclear parity existed between the United States and the USSR, but that deterring a wider range of more limited Soviet challenges must be addressed, particularly at low levels of conflict.[6] In Albert's terms, these were, in contrast to nuclear strikes, *realistic contingencies* to be addressed. Five categories were considered: (1) Soviet participation in wars between other nations; (2) Soviet aggression against nations peripheral to the USSR; (3) Soviet aggression against a single NATO nation; (4) Soviet aggression against NATO as a whole; and (5) selective Soviet threats against specific targets in the U.S. homeland. The second and third categories had been neglected in then-current political-military planning but would become a foundation for establishing future military requirements.

The methodology employed was to examine selected contingencies in great detail, detail sufficient to understand the forces driving the conflict and to develop requirements for technologies and systems that offered the greatest expectation of containing, and thus deterring, the threat. These contingencies were: an attack on Norway arising from a Soviet military exercise; an attack on Iran by Soviet and Iraqi forces; a ground and air attack on Yugoslavia by forces from Hungary, Romania, and Bulgaria; and a Soviet invasion of Japan to seize Hokkaido by air, airborne, and amphibious forces again starting from a military exercise. In all these cases, the Soviet objective was to advance rapidly before defensive forces could be mobilized. Several historical cases were also examined, including the Cuban crisis of 1962 and Linebacker II aerial raids on Hanoi in 1972.

The analyses proceeded by identifying military and industrial target sets intended to inflict the greatest damage with minimal forces in a short but decisive time. In all cases the "dual criteria" of killing targets and leaving nontargets undamaged were applied. Defensive weapons systems were of two types: precision conventional weapons and subkiloton nuclear munitions.

The program was organized into three panels supported by four industrial contractors to contribute expertise and advanced concepts in ground, air, and naval warfare, conventional and nuclear munitions, reconnaissance, command and control, and system integration. Albert chaired the strategic alternatives panel, Don Hicks the advanced technology panel, and Jack Rosengren the munitions panel.[7] Senior-level executives from OSD and the Services participated in panel sessions. The team members were selected for their in-depth knowledge as well as their skill in working as a multidisciplinary group, combining history, strategy, technology, military operations, and systems. In addition to Albert's broad skills, his ability to synthesize the essence of a problem and its solution and to communicate it to senior executives and political leaders was invaluable.

For a person of Albert's inclination, it was a superb opportunity to be instructed in the latest emerging technologies by these innovators, recreating his earlier RAND environment; to understand what each technology was, and was not, useful for; and to match offensive and defensive concepts with current needs and, more importantly, with presumed future needs as defined in a context of realistic relationships among nation states ranging from the largest nuclear competitor to the smallest ally or participant. It was a comprehensive military-strategic planning study combining both breadth and depth.

The technological scope of the study matched its strategic reach: precision-delivered ballistic and cruise missile warheads, terminal sensors across the entire electromagnetic spectrum for night and all-weather capability, low-yield shallow and deep-earth penetrators, microelectronics, data links, artillery-delivered warheads, rapid land and naval mining, and high-mobility ground vehicles.[8]

Albert's role was critical in reorienting thinking in several ways. Technical developers at the time focused entirely on killing targets, not on avoiding killing nontargets. Conflict scenarios were often sketchy, confined to whatever was adequate to justify the intended technical task. Nuclear weapons were seen as effective ways of delivering enormous firepower, with yield making up for poor delivery precision and uncertainties in target location and vulnerability. Development choices were often guided by the issue *du jour* and the evolutionary plans of weapon system suppliers and customers. Consequently new technology of uncertain performance went to the end of the queue in favor of what was familiar, always with the expectation that current deficiencies were fixable and would be fixed. Emerging problems also went to the end of their queue, overshadowed by the Fulda Gap problem and SIOP execution. Albert made it clear that this would simply not do. His quiet voice, distinguished demeanor, and kindly smile as he demolished an ill-conceived argument left many quietly embarrassed. Having gotten this far, Albert did not allow the flock to stray.

Another role of Albert's was shaping external arguments to support the direction the study was taking. The participants were quite prominent in their own right, but years of avoiding bureaucratic minefields had had its conditioning effect. Albert provided the intellectual discipline to see issues posed in terms of unrecognized future needs. More of the same was unacceptable when the same was not working. Albert was the tailor who sought to clothe the emperor.

The technological possibilities and their strategic impact examined in the LRRDPP, though well-founded, might have gone nowhere had they not been elevated for assimilation by higher levels of government. The social network established under the program, and its coverage of so many unexamined issues and opportunities, were factors guiding subsequent decisions to adopt "smart weapon" technology. Their introduction into force structures had a profound impact on the nation's military capability by the late 1980s. Since many of the innovations were based on computing hardware and software, they led to technical competitions with the Soviets where the United States had a comparative advantage, a view compatible with the developing concept of competitive strategies. While the subsequent story is too long to examine here (it is recounted by Andrew May and Bartlett Bulkley), the systems eventually developed first demonstrated their effectiveness in Kuwait in 1991.

Backing Away from Massive Retaliation

What is important in the present context is the technical ground the LRRDPP put under Albert's own thinking on the questionable utility of nuclear weapons. Albert asked, "Must we aim to kill noncombatants?" and "can we justify aiming our nuclear weapons at civilians simply because they're easy to reach and cheap to kill?"[9] He noted that "even if MAD were a persuasive deterrent to a thoroughly rational decision-maker, such rationality is hardly universal." Albert also quotes from the *Pacem in Terris* Encyclical: "The [MAD] conflagration may be set off by some uncontrollable and unexpected chance" and result in "an unprecedented mass slaughter of unoffending civilians." He concluded by pointing out that "in the long run, mutual threats to kill innocent populations seem an especially poor way of building a community of interests between the Soviet Union and the United States."

Such arguments slowly impacted U.S. strategic targeting doctrine. An early attempt was to offer the President a large number of strategic nuclear response options to a nuclear exchange. They sought to use reduced numbers of weapons to "signal" in an attempt to control and constrain a nuclear exchange. Of course, the scaled-down options remained huge in absolute terms, reflecting, say, a reduction from 1,000 to 500 thermonuclear warheads. The scaled-down options were apparently based on the logic that a smaller fraction of a poor idea might eventually become a good idea.

In the 1980s, a new issue arose to which Albert responded, in part for its own importance but also as an opportunity to continue his assault on massive retaliation. This was the proposal for a new technological approach to strategic defense, the strongly ridiculed and ultimately rejected Star Wars concept.[10] Albert used his effective technique of pointing out the inconsistent, paradoxical, or absurd consequences of the positions taken on both sides of the argument, in this case a pastoral letter on war and peace by American Catholic bishops. This approach has the effect of

515

clearing conceptual underbrush and defining the playing field. In public policy debates, where there are always strong views on both sides, it is not uncommon for all sides to start with their own preferred solution, often arrived at on political, ideological, theological, or even visceral grounds, and then to work backward from it to establish a supporting case. It is a process that often leads to logical difficulties highly vulnerable to Albert's "controlled burn" approach to strategic forestry.

Reacting to a writer on strategy, Albert notes that espousing massive retaliation while opposing the protection of one's people amounts to saying, "Offense is defense, defense is offense. Killing people is good, killing weapons is bad." Further, at the time he wrote those words there were at least six nations possessing nuclear weapons, and that "hardly anyone seriously expects that each and everyone . . . that have made nuclear explosives will destroy all their nuclear arms irretrievably and verifiably in a future near enough to govern our present actions." Thus alternative strategies were clearly in order. His prescription was to "rely less on threats of nuclear destruction and much more on improving conventional defenses; discourage the spread of nuclear weapons; and continue making nuclear weapons less vulnerable to attack, safer from 'accidental' detonation, and more secure against seizure and unauthorized or mistaken use."

Conventional Weapon Ascendancy

The prescription set forth above segued directly to new and unexploited technological opportunities. Since collateral damage increases with inaccuracy, not only will "[i]mproved accuracies make feasible greater discrimination as well as effectiveness in the use of nuclear weapons," but "they also make possible more extensive replacement of nuclear with conventional weapons," and thus greatly reduce unnecessary killing of bystanders. Albert argued that, against a small fixed target, an improvement in accuracy by a factor of 10 provided the same effectiveness as an increase in yield by a factor of 1,000. Put another way, exploiting the new technologies of precision allows drastic reduction in nuclear yields, and even brings needed capabilities into the range of conventional explosives. As John Foster once observed to me in a discussion of silo hardness, "10 kilotons on the roof does it every time." While not arguing for the complete replacement of nuclear with conventional weapons, Albert maintained that the effect will be to make it "more feasible to avoid crossing the divide between conventional and nuclear weapons. They give us choices."

The next paper in this section, Albert's final aria in the MAD opera, is an excerpt from *Discriminate Deterrence*, the report of the Commission on Integrated Long Term Strategy (CILTS).[11] CILTS, which Albert co-chaired with outgoing Undersecretary of Defense for Policy, Fred C. Iklé, started its deliberations in 1986 and published its report in early 1988. The opening paragraphs of the excerpt echo many of Albert's concerns, the first mentioned being technology, followed by basing, conventional arms in concert with nuclear arms, Third World conflicts, and low-intensity high-probability conflicts. It speaks to lesser powers acquiring advanced weaponry. A "wider range of contingencies," "discriminating non-nuclear force," "conventional and nuclear posture . . . based on a mix of offensive and defensive systems," "survivable communications and control of forces," and "discriminate nuclear attacks," are all pure Wohlstetter. It asks, "Can NATO rely on threats of escalation that would ensure its own destruction (along with that of the Soviet Union) if implemented?" The report broaches the possibility of economic collapse of the Soviet Union, increasing proliferation of nuclear weapons, and insurgencies and organized terrorism. It makes the case that gains in accuracy strongly support the case for discrimination.

But it argues for a Third World strategy where a combat role for U.S. armed forces is to be viewed as an "exceptional event." Its encouragement of support for anti-communist insurgencies, reflecting then current support in Afghanistan, misses the point of what happens when such friends, having vanquished one superpower, then turn on the other. The report worried greatly about a growing Soviet role in the Third World, and it speaks warmly of using Saudi bases. It points out the large disparity between U.S. and Soviet procurement of major weapon systems, the Soviet's increasing research, development, and testing expenditures, their greater pace of satellite launches, and their greater military capital stocks, compared to those of the United States.

As is typical of "commission reports," it is a compromise between sometimes opposing views, such as those of the Wohlstetter canon and those of the Soviet-oriented defense establishment. This is not to be critical. Even if the CIA had opened its files to CILTS, it would not have helped. The CIA also missed the impending dissolution of the USSR, which happened 2

517

years later. On the other hand, its plea for an integrated strategy is probably more relevant and important now than when the report was written. The Soviet Union did impose a degree of political and intellectual coherency on U.S. national strategy. As many security analysts have bemoaned, at least then we knew who the enemy was. The current uncertainty of who and where the enemy is has replaced the Cold War's simpler focus on what and when to strike. The Commission's prescriptions are still sensible.

In the final paper of this section, Albert returns, 24 years later, to the subject of his 1968 RAND publication dealing with technology.[12] In the interim a great deal of invention had occurred, particularly with respect to conventional weapons, some traceable to the LRRDPP in the early 1970s. A revolution had occurred in the acquisition, storage, analysis, and distribution of information, and these changes further shifted the balance from nuclear to conventional weapons. Large nuclear weapons, seen as far too large to be useful in realistic contingencies, now compete with far more acceptable precision conventional weapons, augmented by such technologies as stealth and networked battlefield surveillance. The consummate nuclear strategist says, "The technical changes [of the Information Revolution] are larger, and their effects more ramified, more closely interconnected, and much more important than the changes worked by fission and fusion." Albert recognized that rapidly increasing accuracy enabled by technology was far more important than the relatively slow growth in yield.

The paper is an indicator of where Albert would have gone in developing a strategy for precision weapons, networked military operations, and ubiquitous surveillance, all comparable to his earlier work in the 1950s on nuclear weapons. His difficulties with nuclear weapons that are so large and powerful as to cause as much damage to their user as to the targets have been noted earlier. From the standpoint of the 15 years that have elapsed since this presentation, the Information Revolution has gone far beyond that which provided the basis for Albert's assessment of the disutility of nuclear weapons. But he clearly appreciated that what he was seeing in the evolution of conventional weapons was only a start, and that many more evolutionary orders of magnitude, some of which have now been realized, lie in store.

Albert speaks positively of the implications of the wide dissemination of information, not only on the battlefield but also in the world of social and political discourse and economic development. He notes that decentralization results in competition

518

and establishes a basis for the spread of democratic processes that can replace the more arbitrary and less stable decisions of dictators.

Unexplored Downsides

In writing about the impacts of rapidly changing technology, Albert had the benefit of demonstrated capabilities, such as the development of the Internet, use of precision weapons in Operation DESERT STORM, and the collapse of the closed USSR in the face of vibrant open economies. But in part because he died a few years later, he did not have an opportunity to learn the downsides of the Information Revolution he was so enamored of.

He appears unaware of some of the other results of computer and communication-based networking. Computers and networks can be penetrated by adversaries as easily as armor-piercing ordnance can penetrate a tank. Malicious software can be introduced into systems to subvert their intent, and their content can be stolen or changed. Communication and sensing satellites can be jammed, their uplinks captured, and they can be destroyed in orbit. Networks can be saturated by computer-generated traffic, and the practical and technical overhead of encryption and access controls limit their wide adoption in real-time situations. Software is a beautiful logical construct, but the systems based on it are of such complexity that they defeat the full understanding and control by their designers and operators. And in networking all aspects of modern societies we create attractive new targets capable of system-wide failures.

Albert's final assessment—that "man is the species that can use information, reasoning, and insight to improve the odds [of avoiding an apocalyptic end]"—may be optimistic. In transforming nuclear confrontation to the domain of information, we are returned to the stage of nuclear strategy at the beginning of the Cold War. Albert was fortunate to be able to read the end of the "book" he started 40 years earlier, though what might have been the final chapter has not yet been written. Albert wanted to extend the concept of deterrence to the realm of conventional warfare. The Defense Nuclear Agency's New Alternatives Panel was one way to keep the idea alive, and some were considering a CIOP, a Conventional Integrated Operational Plan based on a one-to-one relation between a smart warhead and a pre-identified target.

While nuclear strategy emerged as Albert joined RAND, it is far from its end as a domain of central importance to the security of all nations. In 1950 the "nuclear problem" was one of managing U.S. strategic nuclear forces. Today the corresponding nuclear problem is that of "managing" a set of global nuclear powers, real and "virtual," the latter reflecting the circumstance that nuclear weapons and national nuclear forces not yet in being are as worrisome as those that are.

The focus of nuclear concerns changed in Albert's closing years. The collapse of the Soviet Union took the edge off the U.S.–USSR nuclear confrontation. Although strategic force levels did not change immediately, the shift to cooperation, even in such sensitive matters as the safeguarding of Russian nuclear materials, made much of past postures less relevant. Precision conventional weapons were used on numerous occasions in largely non-nuclear circumstances. Operation JUST CAUSE in Panama in 1990, Operation DESERT STORM in 1991, and various "peace operations" in Iraq, Somalia, Macedonia, Haiti, Bosnia, and Kosovo provided numerous opportunities to hone doctrine in the areas of precision weapons, net-centric operations, and coalition warfare.

During this period where explicit nuclear confrontations diminished, the global nuclear weapon landscape was "enriched" by the emergence of new nuclear nations. While South Africa dismantled its nuclear force in 1991, Iraq's nuclear program was an active concern until 2003. India had exploded a "peaceful" nuclear weapon in 1974 and both India and Pakistan announced their full nuclear status with back-to-back nuclear test series in 1998. Libya's nuclear ambitions were known, and it did not terminate its program until 2003. North Korea was actively pursuing nuclear weapons, with negotiations during this period to limit its development activities ultimately unsuccessful when it detonated a nuclear weapon in 2006. Iran, as early as the period of the Shah, was on a path to nuclear power and, according to public statements, intimated that nuclear weapons were a possible future goal.

As the domain of nuclear strategy has shifted from the management of credible deterrent forces in a two-sided balance, the lessons painfully learned and the doctrines and strategies put into place no longer suffice. Nuclear weapons have entered a "commodity" period. Pakistan disseminated its weapon technology as well as Chinese weapon designs. North Korea, Iran, and Syria are engaged in mutually-supporting programs in nuclear and missile technology. Industrial nations, despite the strictures of the *Treaty on the Nonproliferation of Nuclear Weapons* (NPT), provide technologies to would-be proliferators, some dual-use, some the result of inadequate technology export controls, and some simply illegal transactions. Non-nuclear signatories to the NPT engage in clandestine weapon development despite the efforts of the International Atomic Energy Agency (IAEA). Compliant signatories must reevaluate their options in the light of each new nuclear nation.[13]

One now parses the "nuclear problem" quite differently than was the case in 1950 and in the following 40 years. There are four aspects to the transformed problem. First is to reduce the complexity of the scene by discouraging non-nuclear nations from acquiring nuclear weapons, a matter addressed by the NPT, though not entirely successfully in view of the observed rate of one new country every nine years. The second is encouraging responsible stewardship of their nuclear forces by nuclear nations, an issue on which the NPT is silent. The third is devising a path for the complete elimination of nuclear arsenals by nations possessing them. While this is a stated goal of the NPT, it is *terra incognita* in a policy sense.[14] The fourth is preparing a global response in the event that a nuclear weapon is detonated, whether by accident, by unauthorized use, in an accidental nuclear war, or by explicit intent.

Were Albert alive, he would delight in dissecting these issues and nudging us in sensible directions.

Coda: Were Albert to read my introduction, I think he would be pleased. But here is how his reaction to me would be.

He would make some mildly positive statement that would amount to giving me an "A" for effort, or maybe just a "B+" overall. Then he would point out the most egregious error in my logic. There would be more errors in his mind, but he would be too polite to enumerate them, and after all, he would be privately pleased at the progress of a promising student.

ENDNOTES - Lukasik

1. William C. Yengst, Stephen J. Lukasik, and Mark A. Jensen, "Nuclear Weapons That Went to War," SAIC report prepared for the Defense Special Weapons Agency, DSWA-TR-97-25, October 1996.

2. There were a number of arms control agreements reached in this period that reflected widespread concern over the growing threats created by weapons of mass destruction. These included the Antarctic Treaty in 1959, the Moon, Space, and Other Celestial Bodies Treaty in 1967, the Latin America Nuclear Free Zone Treaty in 1967, the Seabed Treaty in 1971, SALT I in 1972, the Biological Warfare Treaty in 1972, the ABM Treaty in 1972, and the Threshold Test Ban Treaty in 1974.

3. *Preliminary Design of an Experimental World-Circling Spaceship*, SM-11827, Santa Monica, CA: Douglas Aircraft Company's Project RAND, May 2, 1946, available from *www.rand.org/pubs/special_memoranda/SM11827/*.

4. For more on Paul Baran's work on survivable strategic communications, see *www.rand.org/about/history/baran.html*.

5. Albert Wohlstetter, *Strength, Interest and New Technologies*, opening address before *The Implications of Military Technology in the 1970s*, the Institute for Strategic Studies' ninth annual conference, Elsinore, Denmark, September 28 to October 1, 1967, D(L)-16624-PR, Santa Monica, CA: RAND Corporation, January 24, 1968, available from *www.rand.org/about/history/wohlstetter/DL16624/DL16624.html*. The address was also published as Wohlstetter, *Strength, Interest and New Technologies*, in *The Implications of Military Technology in the 1970s*, Adelphi Papers No. 46, London, UK: Institute for Strategic Studies, March 1968.

6. The program's name was, in part, chosen to result in the unpronounceable acronym, one so long as to be dull and forgettable, in contrast to most government program acronyms that are chosen to be bold, inspiring, and self-defining, and to encourage funding. In this case the intent was to minimize attention until results were in hand.

7. The reports of the Panel on Remotely Piloted Vehicles, Defense Science Board Summer Study, July 19-31, 1971, and *Final Report of the Task Force on Remotely Piloted Vehicles*, August 1972, were significant inputs to this work.

8. The output of the program exists only in difficult-to-locate declassified documents. Two comprehensive summaries are *Summary Report of the Long Range Research and Development Planning Program*, draft final report prepared by D. A. Paolucci, Falls Church, VA: Lulejian & Associates, Inc., February 7, 1975, declassified by DNA on March 2, 1978; and Andrew May and Bartlett Bulkley, *The Pre-History of the Revolution in Military Affairs*, Unclassified Draft Report, McLean, VA: SAIC, Hicks and Associates' Strategic Assessment Center, February 2004.

9. Albert Wohlstetter's remarks in "The Military Dimensions of Foreign Policy," Fred Warner Neal and Mary Kersey Harvey, eds., Vol. II of four volumes edited from the proceedings of Pacem in Terris III, National Convocation to Consider New Opportunities for United States Foreign Policy, Washington, DC, 1973, Chap. II, "The Debate on Military Policy: How Much is Enough? How MAD is MAD?"

10. Albert Wohlstetter, "Bishops, Statesmen, and Other Strategists on the Bombing of Innocents," *Commentary*, June 1983.

11. *Discriminate Deterrence*, report of the Commission on Integrated Long-Term Strategy, co-chaired by Fred C. Iklé and Albert Wohlstetter, Washington, DC: U.S. Government Printing Office, January 1988, available from *www.albertwohlstetter.com/writings/DiscriminateDeterrence*.

12. Albert Wohlstetter, "RPM, or Revolutions by the Minute," presented at a meeting at the American Enterprise Institute, June 10, 1992.

13. These issues are examined in a working paper by Stephen J. Lukasik, "Dealing with the Proliferation of Nuclear Weapons: Plan B," October 2007.

14. For a recent affirmation of this goal, see George P. Shultz, William J. Perry, Henry A. Kissinger, and Sam Nunn, "A World Free of Nuclear Weapons," *The Wall Street Journal*, January 4, 2007.

Strength, Interest and New Technologies (1968)

Albert Wohlstetter[1]

[Opening address before *The Implications of Military Technology in the 1970s,* ninth annual conference of the Institute for Strategic Studies, Denmark, September 28 to October 1, 1967] D(L)-16624-PR, Santa Monica, CA: RAND Corporation, January 24, 1968, available from *www.rand.org/about/history/wohlstetter/DL16624/ DL16624.html.* Courtesy of the Wohlstetter Estate.

I

In what ways will technical change alter the interests that join or divide various nuclear and non-nuclear countries, and how will it alter the likely outcomes of potential conflicts among them? In particular, how will new techniques transform the interest and ability to project strength to distant places, and so the worth of nuclear and non-nuclear commitments there? What do they suggest about the realities that will confront some American and many European hopes for stable regional autarkies, including the hopes of the new isolationists?

II

The Receding Technological Plateau

These are large and uncertain questions. They raise a prior one: will there *be* major changes in military technology? During much of the last decade many theorists have presumed a plateau in the arts of nuclear offense and defense. They believed that a protected strategic force was not endangered by future changes in offense technology, that it would be threatened by a ballistic missile defense, but that such defense fortunately was unfeasible. Estimates of the unfeasibility of this supposedly destabilizing measure bolstered arguments against any investment in new active defense systems. But in fact major changes have been cumulating in both offense and defense. The plateau was a mirage.

In the early 1950's, estimates of the unfeasibility, and if feasible, the lack of any strategic utility for the H-Bomb, had been used in much the same way for an opposite end: to support arguments for active defense and against a focus on offense. It is a minor irony that many of the ardent defenders of defense in the 1950's are among those most offended by it now. Nor can the conversion be explained by changes in the technology.

In both the early 1950's and early 1960's, judgments on the technology as well as its strategic consequences were faulty. Fusion weapons were not merely feasible but had very large implications for delivery systems, their protection and mode of operation. And the 1960's have witnessed major changes in the arts of offense and defense that will be operational in the 1970's. Moreover, no simple hard and fast distinction divides the effects on stability of offense and defense, making offense changes good or innocuous and defense changes bad. The complexities are particularly apparent if one looks at the consequences, not for a hypothetical two-nation world, but for the real one with a great many non-nuclear countries and a handful or so of countries with nuclear weapons and grossly different resources and strategic situations.

The impending widespread appearance of civilian reactors is one of several important developments that will impose the need for more complex and varied policies than relying solely on international inspection against diversion of plutonium or simply deterring direct nuclear attack on oneself. For civilian reactors will greatly diffuse much of the essential material and knowledge and so reduce the extra cost and time to acquire nuclear weapons. By the end of the 1970's civilian reactors, on some official though uncertain estimates, will have as by-product about 10,000 bombs' worth of plutonium; in the following 20 or 30 years, perhaps a million bombs' worth doubling every ten years.[2] Drafts of nonproliferation and other arms control treaties specifically allow for parties to the agreements to exercise their sovereign national rights to withdraw, if on their own estimate extraordinary events endanger their supreme interest.[3] But policies that will keep this estimate of danger low among non-nuclear countries will involve responsible commitments on the part of at least some nuclear countries to non-nuclear countries that feel subject to coercion. Nuclear weapons will not make small and large powers equal, but they will increase the possibility of mischief, particularly in the coercion of non-nuclear powers.

The technological plateau in nuclear offense and defense has been assumed wishfully by many who hoped for early extensive disarmament and opposed the spread of nuclear weapons. However, the supposed plateau also encourages advocates of nuclear weapons in countries that do not now control them by suggesting that a force of super-power quality is a static goal, that it might be obtained at modest cost or perhaps by one supreme effort, and that then it is possible to rest. It isn't.

Technologies relevant for nuclear war have reached no flat level. They have been altering steeply, and affecting them unevenly. And technologies affecting interests and capabilities in classical engagements are changing too, significantly if less suddenly.

III

Some Technical Changes

Rapid changes in finished military systems stem from even more rapid changes in basic elements of these systems. For finished systems affecting the conduct of classical wars, I shall refer particularly to the large changes in communication, in control systems, and in transport. In the nuclear field, I shall refer to antiballistic missiles, to systems for gathering, processing and transmitting timely data on adversary offense and defense, and especially to the multiplication of armed offensive re-entry vehicles carried in a single launch vehicle (MIRVs), and the great improvements in offense accuracies and reliability. There are, of course, other changes in military technology, some with related implications, but the ones I have selected for brief analysis are perhaps the most immediately significant.

First, however, the basic elements of finished systems. Changes here, in themselves, make quite implausible the assumption of a plateau in finished military systems. Take computers, for example. They are essential instruments used in the process of designing weapons systems or their elements, such as nuclear warheads, and in designing logistics management for classical wars. Computers are also critical components of the weapons systems designed. They are essential parts of the airborne inertial guidance systems that keep offensive missiles pointing at targets. And they are parts also of the radars and defense missiles that might be used to shoot them down. The computer art changes at an extraordinary rate. Computers have and will become faster, cheaper, and more reliable. While terminal ends, the input-output

526

units that mate the computer to its user, permit fewer economies of scale and have improved much more slowly, the hardware for the highly repetitive central processing and memory has been multiplying in speed ten-fold every four years and costing only one-tenth as much every four years or less. They took one-tenth as much room after the last ten years and, in the next ten, they may shrink by a factor of one thousand.[4]

These improvements in computers result in good part from still more basic changes—massive changes in the art of solid state and micro-electronics. Order of magnitude improvements come even more swiftly in the tiny elements that form essential parts of computers, sensing and communications systems. It has been suggested that, as in nature, gestation periods shorten with decreasing size; and sizes are decreasing very rapidly. It appears now, for example, that it may be practical soon to pack as many as one hundred thousand transistors on a quarter-inch wafer. Such startling densities are promised by the techniques known as LSI or "large scale integrated circuitry." The packing not only cuts size, but perhaps more important, increases speed, and by reducing the number of wafers and critical interconnections, may vastly increase reliability and make new ranges of complexity workable. By "discretionary wiring," even if fewer than a third of the potential gates are working, paths of connection on the wafer may take advantage of the many alternatives to detour faulty gates. LSI and related techniques will affect almost every phase of electronics and, ultimately, the shape of military offense and defense systems. Antimissile systems, for example, greatly advanced in recent years, may be expected to become still faster-reacting and more effective for a given budget. Moreover, such improvements tend to reinforce each other. Improved missile-borne computers decrease guidance errors. Geodetic errors, another important component of missile inaccuracy, diminish with new basic data obtained by satellite. And satellites, of course, supply much precise information about target systems. Lighter guidance equipment and increases in explosive yield per pound of payload make it possible to cut the size of a re-entry vehicle that can destroy even resistant targets. This makes it possible in turn to carry on each launch vehicle many armed re-entry vehicles directed at widely separated targets.

The new technologies make it possible to do new things as well as to do the old things more cheaply or better. And while they make doing the old things accessible to more countries, this does not mean closing the gap between the largest countries and the smaller ones. In some respects they increase the disparity. For instance, the tremendous improvements in satellite, sensing and data processing technologies and reductions in their cost make feasible world-wide information gathering facilities where they were not possible at all before — but on a scale of resource expenditure not likely to be undertaken by medium or smaller size powers.

Transformations in finished system reliability, accuracy and destructive payload may be less rapid than in the small components of these systems: they are nonetheless impressive. Roughly speaking, over about a decade — depending on where one starts and how one measures the changes — failure probabilities of missile guidance systems have decreased by a factor of ten or more. So also has the resultant of intercontinental delivery errors of all types. When combined with increases in the number of armed re-entry vehicles carried in a launch vehicle, such order of magnitude changes have large strategic consequences. For a significant range of circumstances the number of weapons needed to destroy a target varies essentially as the square of the delivery inaccuracy and only as the two-thirds power of target resistance or megaton yield. Improving accuracy ten-fold or increasing yield 1,000-fold then amount to the same thing. To put this in perspective, the shift from the largest high explosive bombs of World War II to the Hiroshima fission weapon was roughly an increase of 1 or 2 thousand in yield. The important improvements in antiballistic missiles have been accompanied by less noticed but in some ways more dramatic changes in the advanced offense systems of the major powers.

IV

Changes in Nuclear Offense and Defense

Discussions of "offense" in general compared with "defense" in general yield slogans like "The best defense is a good offense" or the reverse; but almost no understanding. Offense and defense serve overlapping but partially distinct and important functions, and adversaries differ. U.S. defense against a Chinese offense in the 1970's or the viability of a French strategic force in the face of Russian offense and defense are quite different matters from the mutual relations of Russian and American strategic offense

528

and defense forces. Adversaries not only differ in resources, but also in the state-of-the-art of offense or defense available to them at any given time and in the marginal costs to buy and operate a given offensive or defensive unit. Given the high research and development and other capital costs of modern weaponry and the so-called learning curve effects, the small forces in particular are likely to have much higher unit costs than large ones. For such reasons, the "exchange ratios" of attacking vehicles expended as against those they can destroy, or the analogous offense to defense "exchange ratios" of an increment in the cost of attacking vehicles as against the extra cost of defense to knock down the attacking vehicles, all need to be used with a caution seldom observed in popular literature. In the space available here I can indicate only a few essential implications of the recent and impending changes for relations among the varied nuclear and non-nuclear nations.

First, an offense force with such increased accuracies and reliabilities and with an extensive use of MIRVs is very much more efficient in attacking the fixed offense force or the important fixed elements of the mobile force of an adversary. For some relevant circumstances which I shall illustrate, these offense improvements can drastically reverse the ratios of attacking missiles to missiles destroyed which in the hypothetical missile duels that fill the strategic literature are always shown to disfavor the attacker.

Second, one result of this sort of change in Russian offense forces is to make improved antiballistic missiles (rather than simply more hardening or more missiles) an economic way for the United States to protect the hard fixed elements of a strategic force. More hardening is outpaced by the offense changes since target resistance affects weapons requirements only as the two-thirds power. Simply adding more vehicles is costly and more destabilizing than an active defense of these hard points since increasing vehicles also increases the capacity to strike first.

Third, at a minor increment in the modest cost of a hard point ABM defense, it is possible to make available a light ABM for defense of civil societies against a small submarine or land based missile force or part of a large one launched by mistake or without authorization.[5] Its possessor can keep substantially free of damage from a desperate small attack issuing out of a crisis of escalation and can do this without starting nuclear war. By protecting against desperate acts, it reduces the effect of desperate threats, and so decreases the cost and increases the worth of commitments to third countries — especially those doubtful of their importance to the committed power. A light defense, as Robert Oppenheimer perceived years ago, can also help stabilize arms control arrangements against small non-signers or violators of the arrangements. It would leave essentially untouched the two principal powers' ability for major retaliation against each other, even if they failed to make minor adjustments in their offense. And, contrary to some claims, each of the major powers is quite capable of assessing the difference between an actual thin defense and a thick urban defense oriented effectively against each other. Moreover, given the very large disparities in resources available to the two largest powers on the one hand and to such countries as China on the other, they can continue to preserve offense capabilities against each other without an arms "spiral" and without becoming nearly as vulnerable to attack by such smaller powers. Arguments that an adversary is more likely to respond to defense improvements than to an increase in offense capability are implausible in general, and especially so as applied to the Russians, who have said exactly the opposite many times and have behaved as if they mean it. I agree with the Russians. Moreover it does neither the Russians nor the Americans any essential harm if each is defended against China, *as they are now.* Even more obviously, I should think, it does no harm to a country protected by the United States against Chinese nuclear threats if the United States can execute its commitment more safely, and hence more reliably. Relations of arms and arms control are not two-person games in which improving the position of one participant necessarily worsens that of the other.

Fourth, reliable mutual deterrence between the great powers and reliable commitments to protect other countries, to be stable in the face of changing technologies, cannot be technologically static. Trying to stop qualitative change would be like King Canute commanding the waves. Qualitative improvement does not, however, entail—in the uncritical stock phrase—an "ever-accelerating spiral" in arms budgets. The American strategic offense and defense "package" from 1961 to 1967 greatly improved in second-strike capability and in responsible control while its budget declined by at least 40%, from 11.7 billion to 7.1 billion in current prices. (In constant prices the decline was about 50%. The strategic budget was more than 2% of the GNP of 1961, less than 1% in 1967.) The stereotype repeated throughout the early 1960's that the strategic budget was accelerating while our actual security decreased is grossly in error on both counts. The annual cost of a useful ABM system that defends hard points and provides a thin shield for American civil society, when averaged over a ten-year period, comes to about one-tenth of the 5 billion dollars that the United States was spending annually on anti-bomber defense at the end of the 1950's. The thin defense of civil society, taken as an increment to the defense of hard points, will average about 200 million dollars annually out of a GNP approaching nearly a trillion.

Fifth, a smaller country, spending much less on research and development, conceivably might achieve technological equality with a much larger power. But the upshot of the foregoing is that there is no rest. So far, the smaller forces lag in performance as well as in size. Given advances in adversary offense and defense technology, the planned three generations of the French force, for example, may be negated by a few percent of the Russian resources devoted to strategic offense and defense.

Arguments for smaller strategic forces in large countries, or favoring the spread of nuclear weapons to medium and small countries, purport to show that even a small nuclear force is intrinsically capable of retaliation after attack by the largest nuclear countries. Typically these analyses take a simple model of a duel between two countries with sheltered forces. The attacking side launches its entire force against the force of an adversary who replies by launching the undestroyed remainder of his force against the attacker's cities. To have a high confidence of destroying the force attacked, it is usually said, sometimes as the result of calculation, that for every vehicle it destroys, the attacking force must expend many more of its own strategic vehicles. In the more euphoric versions of these attempted stability proofs, particularly those advanced in support of new national military nuclear programs as "equalizers," the exchange ratio of attacking vehicles expended as against those they can destroy is taken to be over 60 to 1 (25,000 vehicles to destroy 400). Or over 25 to 1. Or 16 to 1. In the last six or seven years these hypothetical duels assume more modest odds against the attackers: 5 or 3 to 1.

These highly simplified duels of vehicle against vehicle have many shortcomings for a realistic estimation of the complex problems of nuclear attack and response. (1) They omit completely attacks on the more concentrated but critical elements of a responsible system of deterrence, such as command, control, and communications; and in actual nuclear forces a good many even of the vehicles have been concentrated without adequate warning and unsheltered. (2) Given appropriate costing, exchange ratios may tell what adversaries have to spend to achieve given results, but not whether they can easily afford it. (3) Even in their own terms, the calculations seldom reflect the actual current technological, operational and cost factors. It is worth illustrating some of these points, since hypothetical demonstrations of the invulnerability of small forces have maintained a kind of invulnerability of their own by sticking to pure hypotheticals.

According to the press, the first generation French strike force consists in 62 Mirage IV bombers and 12 KC 135 tankers. The force is unsheltered and without any tactical warning of ballistic missile attack. In the unwarned state the operational part of the force is concentrated on about 10 points in the south and southwest of France. The probability that any of this force will survive can be made extremely low with a high confidence by reserving a force of about 20 early generation Russian missiles with a strategy of attack that uses extensive and timely information as to which attack vehicles have failed, but without MIRVs or advanced accuracies. The second generation French force was to add to the 10 soft points on which aircraft are concentrated 30 additional points, each with a single missile sheltered to resist 300 psi. Recent press reports[6] indicate that the addition will amount to 75 rather than 30. However, 20 or so attacking launch vehicles, each equipped with 10 reentry vehicles and an advanced guidance, could destroy the first and second generation forces with a confidence of .9. And higher confidences are quite feasible. In short, the changes taking place in the offense cancel these additions to a small nuclear strike force. Much more important than the offense-to-defense exchange ratio, 20 or 30 launch vehicles might be a bit more or less than 2 percent of the number of vehicles in a Russian strategic force.[7]

The part in movement underwater of a small third generation missile submarine force is not subject to straightforward ballistic missile attack. And submarines are hard to hunt and kill. However, a small missile submarine system taken as a whole is not immune to interdiction, in particular by an adversary with a large, varied and sophisticated offense and defense. A large adversary can launch missiles at the fixed elements: at the sizable fraction of the small submarine forces in port, and at the fixed command, control and communications that are a key element of a responsible strategic force. He can muster a much larger destroyer and submarine force to hunt the few submarines at sea and aid his hunt with complex mixtures of various sensors, data processing and communication. Finally, most important in the 1970's, he may interpose a thin antiballistic missile system that is extremely effective against small numbers of incoming objects.

In sum the theory that nuclear weapons are "equalizers," that, equipped with them, any country, no matter how small, can surely retaliate against any other country, no matter how large, is in error. The small forces we have examined would have little chance to survive a modest attack, much less a major sophisticated one. Neither past nor future technologies bear out the equalizer theory.

Sixth, subtler theories that take small nuclear forces, not as equalizers, but as "triggers," are also put in doubt by any concrete examination of technologies, operations, and costs. A triggering force too small in itself to deter a great power enemy is supposed to be able to release an unwilling strategic force of one of the principal nuclear powers against the other. Unlike the equalizer, such a triggering force then is not a substitute for alliance or unilateral commitments for protection, so much as a way of making these commitments operative. The trigger theory seems to be replacing that of the equalizer in Europe and perhaps also among advocates of national nuclear forces in India and Japan. While a subtler theory, it is less consistent and usually vaguer. Intuitively it would appear that a small force, prepared especially to compel a major ally to use nuclear weapons when that ally thinks it unwise, might *loosen* alliance bonds. It might offer some incentives to the ally to tie its fate less closely with the small power. And it might, on the whole, suggest to an adversary that the identification is less close. The mechanism linking the small trigger to the large force is extremely obscure and very seldom explained in operationally meaningful terms.

Where it is precise enough for close analysis, it may be rendered doubtful by the same technological and operational facts that call into question the equalizer theory. For example, the more rigorous formulation offered by Arthur Lee Burns covers two kinds of trigger, a passive and an active one. The passive trigger, while small, is supposed to be so protected that a major nuclear adversary could destroy it only by expending so much of his own force that he could no longer deter the small power's major ally. An active trigger could, by pre-empting, reduce the force of one of the major powers enough to make it vulnerable to attack by the other. The prospect of either sequence of events would deter the major adversary. But the small forces we have examined would be grossly inadequate in both an active and a passive role. They would add little to the force of a large nuclear ally attacking a big nuclear adversary, and their destruction would require their large adversary to expend only a tiny fraction of his total retaliatory force.

A force able to vie with or even to trigger a major nuclear strike force must change rapidly enough to keep up: the forces now planned by the smaller nuclear countries conceivably might, but do not accomplish this. In short, there is no rest.

Seventh, even if a small nuclear force were able to protect any country that had it, either because it was a trigger or an equalizer, this would still leave unsolved the problem of protecting non-nuclear countries from nuclear coercion. A small triggering force seems particularly inadequate for extending guarantees to non-nuclear countries. If it is unclear how it can protect its own possessor by manipulating the two largest nuclear powers, it is still more obscure how a triggering force can maneuver one of them to protect a fourth power against the other; or to protect any of some 130 non-nuclear powers.

Proponents of the equalizer theory on the other hand proceed from the assumption that commitments for nuclear protection by others are not merely unnecessary, but impossible, that no country will risk responding to a nuclear attack on someone else. In principle, if not always in practice, proponents of equalizers must conclude that either no sovereign country must have nuclear weapons or all of them should. Yet permanent and total nuclear disarmament hardly seems at hand. And even if a few intrepid proponents of nuclear equalizers might be ready to distribute nuclear bombs to everybody, to most of us the perils are plain in a spread of nuclear weapons rather less than world-wide.[8] Still, a country without nuclear weapons that feels menaced by a nuclear adversary is likely to seek nuclear weapons of its own unless it feels assured of nuclear protection by someone else. Moreover, since any country, nuclear or non-nuclear, is likely to have interests affected by the coercion of some non-nuclear nation, perhaps a neighbor, perhaps a more distant country, the issue of guarantees, of formal or informal commitments for nuclear protection, cannot be avoided.

In particular, long-range commitments and defenses that make the risks of commitment commensurate with what is at stake will continue to be essential for stability on the international scene. But in recent times distant commitments have become increasingly unpopular. This has been manifested in many diverse and incompatible ways in the United States as well as in Europe: rising nationalisms, a continental regionalism, a resurgence of moves towards protection in trade, disillusionment with foreign aid and with the turbulence and frustrations of the Third World, and a weariness with distant wars that affects hawks, doves, and some that fly dead center. But hopes for regional or national insulation ignore features of technology that have long been current and that will be greatly emphasized by developments in the future.

V

Distant Classical Wars, Old Geopolitics, and New Isolation

Revulsion against distant commitments may be based on an understandable fatigue or on unanalyzed feelings of the irrelevance of remote troubles; and sometimes on the estimate that an air or naval power can do little to affect remote land powers; or on the theory, as expressed by Mr. Kennan, that "the effectiveness of the power radiated from any national center decreases in proportion to the distance involved." Geopolitical theories of spheres of influence and stable balances of power between widely separated large and small countries frequently presume such proportional or linear decreases of military strength with distance.

Yet the relation has never been so simple. Logistic support by water has in general been cheaper and easier than over land. References in earlier geopolitical writing to continental land masses, islands and the like, have been in fact a crude means of characterizing some of the differences between water and land combat logistics. In discussing geography, geopoliticians at best have been talking about the technologies of communications or transport or weapons range. Maxims so derived, however, are not eternal. These technologies have been changing at a rapid clip.

Nonetheless the agonies of Vietnam have revived some rather old-fashioned geopolitics. Whatever one's view of Vietnam (and I have substantial differences with U.S. policy there), the isolationism it has encouraged receives no adequate support from such theories. Distance bears no simple relation either to interests or military strength. For nuclear relations, the defects of the old geopolitical treatment of distance are striking. However, its defects for describing variations in non-nuclear military strength with distance are also crucial.

It was rather common until recently to talk of the comparative disadvantage to the United States in fighting eight or ten thousand

535

miles from home against an adversary whose home base is near the scene of conflict. While these dramatic long-haul distances catch the headlines, neither in current nor in past technology do they determine the matter of comparative disadvantage. This has been documented in detailed studies of the comparative logistics at present levels of technology in several areas of possible non-nuclear conflict—in Thailand, in the Himalayas, in Iran and in Lebanon—and in the *actual* conflict in Korea.[9]

The most striking fact displayed by these studies is that the long-distance lift capacity of each side massively exceeds their short-distance lift inside the theater, especially in the very short ranges in which the battle would be joined. These bottlenecks inside the theater are to a very considerable extent determined by local factors: climate, terrain, harbors, port unloading facilities, railroad and road capacities, etc. They are not a function of the long-haul distances. The specific local circumstances may favor the combatant that starts from far-off; or the one that starts from nearby. (Moreover, the local circumstances may be more or less susceptible to change by the distant combatant, depending on his resources, technical level and the physical geography he confronts. They are likely to be changed by local, less-industrialized combatants, in any case with their further industrialization. But the supporting or combatant external powers will vary, before or during a war, in their ability to construct harbors, roads, etc.) On the Thai-Laos border the United States can lift, from 8,500 miles away, four times as much as China can from 450 miles off. Various potential combat areas in Iran would show a logistic standoff between the neighboring Soviet Union and the United States. In the Himalayas, support for Chinese and for opposing forces would be measured in tons per day: the 200,000 tons per day the United States might deliver over the long haul from U.S. ports to Calcutta are not the critical matter.

The figures above describe the rate at which supply can be lifted steadily after the initial build-up. If one looks at various rates of deployment and build-up, where stocks are accumulated in advance in a potential trouble area, the conclusions are not altered. Moreover, if one looks at the matter in cost terms, as distinct from capacity, the minor importance of the long haul appears even more vividly. Adding several thousand miles to the distance at which remote wars are fought increases the total cost of fighting such wars by only a very tiny percentage. It appears, for example, that if the support of U.S. forces in Korea had been

536

2,000 miles further away, it would have meant adding less than three-tenths of a percent to the total annual cost of the war.

The studies cited deal with recent past technology. The 1970's technology will decrease military communication and transport costs further, but especially long-distance costs. As in the case of computer technology described earlier, the terminal ends permit fewer economies of scale. Larger payload transport both on the surface and in the air will greatly reduce costs per ton-mile. Fast deployment logistic ships might (Congress and the established shipbuilders willing) combine with the planned massive increase in air cargo capacity to offer more efficient mixtures of pre-stockage and rapid deployment of men and material for the initial build-up. The C-5A will be operational in large numbers in the 1970's; it will have a ton-mile cost one-tenth that of the DC-3 and will carry 2-1/2 times the payload of the largest jet now flying. Synchronous communications satellites make the point even more clearly than improved transport.[10] It has long been true in telephony, for example, that a very large part of the costs of long distance service is traceable to such elements as local switching, operator charges and local lines. Communications satellites make unimportant the distance between transmitting and ground stations so long as both are within line of sight of the satellite, whereas undersea cables vary in cost directly with length. Such satellites may be on station over 50,000 miles above the earth. The difference will be negligible in miles, not to say elapsed travel time between electro-magnetic signals traveling between various pairs of points on earth by way of an over 100,000 mile trip to and from a satellite.[11] Satellites spanning the Atlantic and Pacific will greatly increase the capacity and reduce the costs of sending messages to far-off and isolated locations, and so will make possible a much more detailed and centralized control of classical wars in distant theaters.

If future technology reduces further the difference between fighting a war close by and far off, it can do this of course not just for the United States, but for other nations as well. This is only one reason that the technical developments should fortify no illusion of omnipotence. We may contest some sorts of war badly almost anywhere, in particular revolutionary wars where recently improved weapons technologies seem to me largely irrelevant (though no more so in Vietnam than they might be in Colombia or even in Cuba). Military strength is frequently a very poor and self-defeating way of protecting or fulfilling interests.

This applies to military strength used nearby as well as military strength used far off. It is plainly better not to have to fight at all. Even more plainly, an ability to fight with formal military force cannot be directly translated into political authority. Limits in the usefulness of American military strength are clear in relation to countries hostile in varying degrees to the United States, such as tiny nearby Cuba. Perhaps even more in relation to America's allies. In spite of rhetoric about slavery to American despotism, General DeGaulle always struck me as a rather masterful slave, long before he had even a façade of a *force de frappe*. The point can be made in reference to those allies most menaced and least able to defend themselves. Polemists using words like "puppet," Mr. McGeorge Bundy has said, have never been on the other end of the strings. It is rather more, I should think, like pushing than pulling strings. The fact that military technology can be projected by the United States and by others at great distances displays some critical connections between remote parts of the world, but lends no support to the mechanical extension of American political hegemony.

Furthermore, though we can affect matters in some places close to us or far off, we frequently have no discernible interest in doing so. And even where we do, improved technologies may not be the best vehicle for the influence we want to exert. In the last year, the isolationist debate has shifted somewhat from capabilities to interests. A good many places interest none of us very much, and some that interest us can take care of themselves. That's almost always better. No one on either side of the debate is for intervention all over or for total escape. The genuine issues concern the right extent and places of commitment. They cannot be clarified wholesale. And they have not been by the endlessly tedious repetitions and denials of the phrase "policeman to the world."

A great many things—historic, political, ethnic, cultural, sentimental—affect national interests, including a residue of past technologies like the methods of ocean transport that linked Great Britain, Spain, France, Portugal and the Netherlands durably to some of the remotest parts of the world. But future technologies will affect interests too; and on the whole in a direction that makes the new isolationism pure nostalgia. Let me say something on interests of nations in cultural contact, in trade and the movements of capital, and in national safety.

VI

Distant Cultural and Economic Interests

Cultural interests have never fallen off directly with distance. Englishmen and North Americans find Australians and New Zealanders quite accessible culturally, and are sometimes greatly puzzled by their immediate neighbors. French contacts with some parts of North America were always considerable and lately seem to be much on the increase. The vast improvements coming in long-distance communications and transport will multiply remote cultural contacts just as they will increase the capacity to project military strength. They will extend processes of education, learning and possibilities of cooperation in research. Civilian supersonic passenger planes, the subsonic high payload 747 stretch jets, a possible passenger version of the C-5, and the commercial satellites neatly parallel in the civilian field the military equipment that make the problem of getting to a theater of war small compared to getting about in it. Travelers are already used to the sharp contrast between the speed with which they can hurtle between distant airports and the maddeningly slow pace for getting to and from the airport, and queuing up for tickets, taxis, baggage, porters, and traffic lights.

High payload jets will cover great distances still more quickly and cheaply; but may increase the queues. Supersonic jets will be economic only on long trips. Their principal result will be to bring the remote places closer. It has been pointed out that if sonic booms prevent supersonic aircraft from flying over land, once again, as in the time before the building of the transcontinental railroad, New York will be closer to Europe than to Los Angeles. Passenger traffic in the Pacific should increase still more strikingly. Travel time from Los Angeles to Tokyo may be cut by nearly two-thirds. It will take perhaps forty minutes more than from Los Angeles to New York.

For civilian communications as for civil transport, the right map cannot be drawn in kilometers or miles, in what Francois Perroux calls "banal distance." Buenos Aires is closer now to Europe or the U.S. than to Caracas or Santiago. Telephone calls from Buenos Aires to Caracas go through New York. Calls between two points in Africa may go through switch points in both London and Paris. The new communications will alter optimal switching points and help local traffic, but in particular will bring together widely separated points.

From the standpoint of economic and strategic interests one important result of improvements in communications and transport will be to increase the geographical extent of interests and simultaneously to reduce the specific importance of what are now critical bottlenecks on transit points. Suez is an example: reducing very long-haul costs cuts the added expense of a detour.

Indeed, most of what I have said about effects on cultural contacts applies quite directly to economic interactions, that is, to the movements of commodities and capital and possibly seasonal labor. Air freight capacity has been increasing rapidly for high value commodities; the huge cargo aircraft coming will make distant air transport economic for new ranges of less valuable commodities. For bulky primary commodities, those that are lowest in value density, like oil, the development of super tankers drastically reduces long-haul costs. While there are diminishing returns to scale, the economies of scale are enormous. A tanker with a capacity for 150,000 dead weight tons can move crude oil 5,000 miles at $1.69 per ton compared to $7.29 for a 10,000 dead weight ton tanker. Construction costs decrease with increasing tanker size from $220.00 per ton at 20,000 dead weight tons to less than $70.00 at 300,000 dead weight tons. Operating costs decrease, too, in particular with increased opportunities for automation. In fact, the *Tokyo Maru*, a tanker of about 135,000 dead weight tons, will be operated by a crew of 29, while tankers of 50,000 dead weight tons may use 35 men or more. The Japanese in the early 1970's will be constructing 500,000 dead weight ton tankers, something like ten times the size of the largest tankers available during the Suez Crisis of 1956. As a result of such changes, not only are detours around gateways like Suez cheaper than they were; they may, because of the limitations of the gateways themselves, be cheaper than the direct route. Suez at present can handle fully loaded tankers only up to 70,000 dead weight tons.

There is a fruitful analogy with the discretionary wiring in micro-electronics to which I referred earlier. Just as the multiplication of gates on a tiny wafer permits a detour around ones that are not working, and so reduces the number of critical interconnections, so the lowered costs and increased capacity for both long distance transport and long distance transmission of messages increase the number of economic alternatives available and make it feasible to go around choke points. These communications and transport developments reduce interests in specific gateways to remote places, the points traditionally called "strategic," but not the interest in remote places themselves. On the contrary, to the extent that they make links to distant points more reliable, they spread interests more evenly but farther. For example, Japan's growing trade in manufactures with Europe will risk less from arbitrary interruption. In reducing the risks of war or peacetime interruption, these technical changes counter one of the chief traditional arguments for economic autarky.

One argument for autarky current in many variants for nearly 150 years rests on technology. Robert Torrens[12] predicted that the industrialization of additional countries, population growth and diminishing returns in primary products would reduce the basis for foreign trade. This hypothesis of course entails *as corollary* the declining importance of trade among already industrialized countries in particular. It is not an argument for intra-regional trade but for the autarky of nations even within the same region. In fact, it suggests reduction of trade among regions within a single nation as these "converge" in economic structure.

This venerable argument[13] has several essential theoretical flaws. Except in some extremely simplified economic models, a convergence in over-all average efficiency of trading countries does not entail a lessening of the possibilities of specialization in particular products. Some advantages of specialization flow not simply from economies of scale at fixed techniques, but from such other matters as the gains from learning which come with cumulatively great output. The argument neglects technical changes like the global extension of communications that tend to create world markets for specific products, and neglects techniques that increase the advantages of trade such as reduction in freight and communications costs. Increasing income itself creates a demand for variety and for products of higher value in which transport costs are in any case less important. Finally, like some sounder theories that oppose it, the Torrens and related hypotheses say nothing in principle about the way the benefits of trade vary with geographical distance, and in particular how transport costs as a complex function of distance may change and flatten over time with changing techniques. Even if in the absence of trade countries had marginal costs in identical ratio for their many highly differentiated products, there would be a basis for specialization and exchange, so long as some short or long run costs declined and transport expense did not wipe out cost differences. However, such identical ratios are implausible; the increased output permitted by specialization and trade almost surely for some commodities would be accompanied by a decline in costs in the short or long run; and transport costs are decreasing, especially for distant places.

Aside from its theoretical lacks, the belief that technology would reduce the role of trade does not square with available data, even though the benefits of trade are hampered by government barriers. World trade in manufactures in the 90 years after 1876, in spite of setbacks in the protectionist and depressed interwar period, increased per capita two or three times. Between 1950 and 1966 it has been increasing even faster than world production of manufactures — 7.3% compared to 5.3% *per annum*.[14] For the United States, in spite of claims to the contrary, from 1879 to 1960 neither exports nor imports declined relative to GNP in real terms.[15] Similarly within the United States, interregional trade, as Richard Cooper has shown, has grown more rapidly than total output, in spite of an apparent "convergence" in economic structure of the various regions.[16]

What is true of trade seems true also of the movements of capital, when not constrained by artificial barriers. Improvements in long-distance travel and telecommunications encourage distant foreign investment by making it easier to manage. Large-scale data processing may stimulate organizational innovation and in any case makes feasible much more detailed and far-flung control. All of this should continue to encourage the already significant growth of international corporations whose interests extend far beyond any narrow geographical region, and make economic autarky more inappropriate than ever. Distant interests should not be taken, however, as applying only to the capital-rich countries as an attribute of "imperialism." The underdeveloped world has perhaps even more obvious interests in distant developed countries as a source of aid and as a market for exports. Indeed, as Edwin Reischauer suggests, one of the more disturbing aspects of some of the new isolationism is an implication that "Asians, having their own distinctive cultures and special problems, should go their own way, presumably in poverty and turmoil, while we of the advanced nations go our own prosperous and peaceful way."

The revolution in transport and communications casts doubt not only on the new isolationism of a growing minority but also on the more respectable but rather mechanical regionalism that may frequently be found in both the Democratic and Republican establishments: the grand designs for Latin American common markets, Asian common markets, African unions, economic unities spanning the Middle East from Morocco to Afghanistan, and others. The composition of some of these groupings suggests how poor a criterion mere proximity is for association. Some have higher cost communication and transport links among themselves than to the outside world. They may be mainly rival exporters of the same commodities, those in which they have the greatest comparative advantage. Yet a mechanical regionalism is not exclusively American. The head of the Commission of European Communities recently expressed his conviction that the world will inevitably organize itself into continents just as it organized itself into nations five centuries ago. And there are crasser forms of isolationism in Europe as well.

At the start of World War II it was the isolationists like Charles Beard, Jerome Frank, Stuart Chase and many others who urged a self-sufficient, "continental" American policy. They argued in fact that elsewhere than in the United States continental integration was the wave of the future and the only way to peace in the world. Interventionists argued for the primacy of overseas links in cultural, economic and military terms. Naturally they had a great deal of support from the future allies overseas. It is remarkable that having successfully countered arguments for regional self-sufficiency, so many interventionists ended the war supporting one regionalism or another, and as technology moved further in the opposite direction, espoused regional solutions for more and more of the world.

Reducing trade barriers inside a region may permit important economies of scale and indirect benefits to future growth as well as direct gains in efficiency at a given time. But this applies also to reducing trade barriers among countries that are not contiguous and that may be very widely separated. From a cosmopolitan view, the direct gains from a customs union depend on whether the increased trade and specialization within the union would outweigh the decrease in division of labor as between the union and the countries outside; whether in short it involved a net shift to higher or lower cost sources. Some unions might represent a gain; some would surely be a loss, particularly if their composition were determined solely on the basis of criteria as unrelated to economic efficiency as contiguity. Many groupings of countries outside the

West seem little more than a literary or touristic convenience for Europeans and Americans, or a bureaucratic convenience for dividing up the work in their Foreign Offices. Various members of such a "region" may otherwise have had rather little economic or political interest in each other. Nor much interest in military cooperation.

Neighborhood, in international relations, as Jacob Viner has pointed out, has never guaranteed neighborly feelings, and often has prevented them. Writings on international relations in the 18th century and later often took proximity as one of the natural conditions of enmity. Indeed one of the largest defects of regionalism in the post-war period has been a frequent neglect of the hard truths of differences in political interest inside regions and the varying bonds of interests with countries outside. Regionalism which has seemed a half-way house between nationalism and a utopian universalism has itself sometimes been a kind of utopia for hard-headed *Realpolitikers*.

The historic antagonisms that divide a geographical region of course may be the very reason offered for a focus on regional association. But the network of conflicting and common interests extends far beyond a single region, and so do problems of conciliation. Today Germany is not the greatest menace to the English or the French. Just as generals are said to prepare always to fight the last war, so statesmen and social scientists may be prone to prevent the last war, but not the next.

The future increasing ease of communication and transport should not be taken as simply irenic, leading only to harmony and peace. On the contrary, it means an extension of the "neighborhood" to more remote areas, and such larger neighborhoods need not mean neighborliness any more than the small ones. The possibilities of coercion as well as cooperation increase. Which brings us back to the third interest, that of national safety.

VII

Interests in Safety

National safety is the most critical matter and perhaps the least understood by those who think of it in terms of 19th century and earlier technologies, or by those who conceive of it exclusively in terms of bilateral nuclear deterrence, the preoccupation of the mid-1950's. One essential here is that improvements in the technology of combat delivery and logistics support affect not merely one's own capabilities and those of one's friends, but those of potential adversaries as well. These changes then drastically extend the range at which potential adversaries can do harm. This is most obvious in the case of the technologies for nuclear war. Not only nuclear capabilities of the two largest powers, but also of others, will extend far beyond any single region, and will permit coercion if unopposed.

But improvements in technology extend the range at which classical, not just nuclear, conflicts may be fought. And as in the case of nuclear technologies such improvements apply to potential adversaries too. While neither for the nuclear nor the classical case is distance without effect, the effects are complex; and very much more complex than is recognized by linear theories of the weakening of strength with distance.[17] Nonetheless, the upshot of these considerations of 1970's technology is that basic interests in safety will extend farther out than they ever have before. And a great many of the new isolationists in the United States were interventionists in World War II because they recognized that even then interests in security extended far beyond one's hemisphere.

A second essential is that bilateral mutual deterrence is not enough to prevent the international system from deteriorating. A small nuclear force, we have seen, is hardly likely to make any country that has it the equal of any other in deterring attack on itself. And the technological defects of small nuclear forces limit their potential for protecting their possessors indirectly by triggering one major power against the other. However, even if these defects did not obtain and any country with nuclear weapons could thereby get direct or indirect protection for itself, there would still remain the need to protect non-nuclear countries from nuclear coercion. And giving bombs to everybody hardly seems the way to do it.

On the other hand, getting stable isolated nuclear balances in Asia or the Middle East or other areas that comprise diverse antagonisms and varying interests with respect to countries outside, will not be easy. Simple balances involving nuclear commitments from one or two member countries will be hard to make persuasive, and some of the members may feel more menaced by the regional nuclear capabilities than assured. Multiple regional nuclear balances would by definition involve an extensive spread of nuclear weapons with the attendant problems of a still further spread by a chain reaction with countries in and out of the region and increased probabilities of nuclear war by accident or design. Multilateral nuclear forces (MLF) for such diverse "regions" as Asia seem much less feasible even than the European counterpart. And an Arab-Israeli MLF seems rather far off in the future. Or even a Saudi-Hashemite-Algerian-Egyptian one.

While a variety of forms of cooperation among countries in and out of a particular region may be useful, long distance nuclear commitments by great powers have been essential at the very least to cancel long distance threats by others. The growth of new long distance nuclear forces like that of China will emphasize these.

Long distance commitments confer no perfect stability. But neither does any other alternative. I do not think that the deterrence between the United States and the Soviet Union is unconditional.

In a many-nation world including so far 5 countries that have exploded nuclear devices and about 130 that have not, unconditional deterrence, I would stress, is not a sensible goal. If each of the nuclear countries could unconditionally deter any other, this would mean the instability of nuclear peace, not stability. Any nuclear power could then threaten or safely use nuclear weapons against any non-nuclear one within range.

Commitments for protection against nuclear coercion or attack, whether tacit or explicit, formal or informal, unilateral or in alliance arrangements or in the form of a United Nations collective security agreement, are a necessary element of stability on the international scene. Long range commitments and defenses that make the risks of commitment commensurate with what is at stake are essential.

The word "commitment" may perhaps be traumatic, given all of the remote and uncertain conflicts in which so many of us have been engaged. A commitment, moreover, lessens autonomy in one way or another for both the party committed and the recipient of the commitment. The United States commits itself in NATO to regard an attack on Europe as an attack on itself. It has extended commitments in varying degrees to other allies and to some non-aligned countries. This is frequently painful but it is not quixotic. If we do not commit ourselves and keep it plain that the configuration of our interests and capabilities make the sacrifice smaller in fulfilling the commitment than in not fulfilling it, the countries in question would have to preserve their safety by their own means; and to try to obtain nuclear safety by nuclear means.

In a great many cases these are likely to be even less perfect than the long distance commitment. And the failure to make long distance commitments would reduce options by changing the international environment adversely.

In sum, neither military capabilities, nor economic interests, nor interests in cultural contacts, nor in national safety seem likely to be narrowly circumscribed by geography, to be contained, for example, by continents. Neither national nor regional autarkies look sensible in either strategic or economic or political terms. Orwell projected for 1984 a world split into a few huge blocs. I find such a prospect neither attractive nor likely to improve the chance of peace. Even inside a single nation sharp regional lines dividing the country into groups with different political, sentimental, ethnic, and economic interests make civil war more likely. On a world scale it would be more ominous. Orwell showed his insight by having his huge continental blocs constantly at war. The fact that, so far as technology is concerned, the 1970's do not seem to be marching toward 1984 strikes me then as all to the good. There are many forms of cooperation including, I would stress, some regional ones that are useful for specific and limited purposes. But perhaps it's just as well that the useful sorts of association are "cross-cutting," likely to vary in membership from one purpose to another.

We all believe in the importance of preserving options, of being able to defer decision in order to make a final resolve on the basis of the utmost information about alternatives. We feel uneasy about getting involved, "contracting in." Nonetheless, contracting out isn't genuinely feasible. Commitment, foreclosing some options, is essential if we want to keep others open in the future. Speaking here at Elsinore, Denmark, in Hamlet's shade, I find it appropriate to emphasize that decision cannot be postponed indefinitely, that putting off the awful day frequently makes things still more awful; that we must commit ourselves. The technologies of the 1970's suggest that many of the essential commitments will continue to be long distance.

ENDNOTES - Wohlstetter - Strength, Interest and New Technologies

1. Presented at Elsinore, Denmark, September 28, 1967, as the opening address of the 9th Annual Conference of the Institute for Strategic Studies on Military Technology in the 1970's. I am indebted to Paul Armer, Michael Arnsten, Dan Ellsberg, Malcolm Hoag, Oleg Hoeffding, A. W. Marshall, David McGarvey, Richard Nelson and Charles Wolf for their comments on an earlier draft, and to Miss Janina Bonczek for research assistance.

2. See Victor Gilinsky, "Fast Breeder Reactors and the Spread of Plutonium," RM-5148-PR, Santa Monica, CA: The RAND Corporation, 1967.

3. *Cf.* Leonard Beaton, "Nuclear Fuel-for-All," *Foreign Affairs*, Vol. 45, No. 4, July 1967, pp. 662-669.

4. This describes the changes only very grossly. For the source of these three estimates and for more detail, see Paul Armer, "Computer Aspects of Technological Change, Automation and Economic Progress," printed in "Technology and American Economy," the report of the National Commission on Technology, Automation and Economic Progress, Appendix, Vol. I, *The Outlook for Technological Change and Employment*, Washington, DC: U.S. Government Printing Office, February 1966, pp. I-205 through I-232.

5. Since this paper was written, the United States Government has announced that it will deploy a thin ABM system.

6. William Beecher, "Small Atomic Arms Being Developed by France," *The New York Times*, April 14, 1967.

7. The Institute of Strategic Studies, *The Military Balance*, has for some time now attributed to the Soviet Union well over 2,000 medium and long-range manned and unmanned strategic vehicles.

8. See Hedley Bull, *The Control of the Arms Race*, New York: Praeger, 1965; and Albert Wohlstetter, "Nuclear Sharing: NATO and the N+1 Country," *Foreign Affairs*, April 1961. In the latter

paper I tried to examine more inclusively the disincentives and incentives for acquiring a nuclear strike force, and in particular the high costs of small nuclear forces that seriously aim at surviving a major power attack. More recent cost study emphasizes the results presented there.

9. For more detail on these studies, see Albert Wohlstetter and Richard Rainey, "Distant Wars and Far Out Estimates," monograph presented at the APSA meeting, New York City, September 1966. *Cf.* also Albert Wohlstetter, "Theory and Opposed Systems Design," to be published in *New Approaches to International Relations*, Morton Kaplan, ed. In this connection we are indebted to the work of Mary Anderson, Wallace Higgins, L. P. Holliday, Norman Jones and John Summerfield.

10. I am indebted here to the work of Leland Johnson. See "Some Implications of New Communications Technologies for National Security in the 1970's."

11. This formulation was suggested to me by H.S. Rowen.

12. *Essay on the Production of Wealth*, London, 1821.

13. Frequently revived and modified by Werner Sombart at the turn of the century, by Keynes and D. H. Robertson in the 1930's, and more recently by Karl Deutsch and Alexander Eckstein.

14. For the years up to 1959 see Alfred Maizels, *Industrial Growth and World Trade*, Cambridge, UK: Cambridge University Press, 1963, pp. 79 ff. For an extension of these data through 1966, see "Monthly Economic Letter" of the First National City Bank, New York City, September 1967.

15. See Robert Lipsey, *Price and Quantity Trends in the Foreign Trade of the United States*, Princeton, NJ: Princeton University Press, 1963.

16. Richard Cooper, "Growth and Trade: Some Hypotheses About Long-Term Trends," *Journal of Economic History*, December 1964.

17. See Wohlstetter and Rainey, "Distant Wars and Far-Out Estimates," *op. cit.*, for the complex effects of distance on nuclear capabilities as well as classical strength. And for a very detailed empirical study of the effects of various critical distances on nuclear capabilities in the 1950's, see A. J. Wohlstetter, H. S. Rowen, F. S. Hoffman and R. J. Lutz, *The Selection and Use of Strategic Air Base Systems*, R-266, Santa Monica, CA: The RAND Corporation, 1954.

How Much is Enough? How Mad is MAD? (1974)

Albert Wohlstetter

From Fred Warner Neal and Mary Kersey Harvey, eds., *Pacem in Terris III,* Vol. 2: *The Military Dimensions of Foreign Policy,* Washington, DC: Center for the Study of Democratic Institutions, pp. 37-43. Copyright © 1974 Fund for the Republic. Reproduced with permission of NPQ/Center for the Study of Democratic Institutions.
Wohlstetter's remarks below respond to two addresses, Clark Clifford's "The National Interest and Military Power," and Herbert York's "Nuclear Deterrence: How to Reduce the Overkill."

On the important subject of deterrence, the two main speakers agree on relying on the "assured nuclear destruction" of civilians. I feel called upon to introduce a note of discord and to ask some questions. My questions center mainly on Herbert York's praiseworthy effort to make a little saner what he himself has called an essentially mad strategic doctrine, deterrence by threatening the mass destruction of civilian populations. However, in considering whether alternative forms of deterrence entail a strategic arms spiral, I shall question the received notions reflected by Mr. Clifford as well as by Mr. York, as to the nature and actual history of strategic arms competition.

The received strategic doctrine in the foreign policy establishments today calls not only for keeping civilians defenseless on both sides, but for deliberately aiming whatever strategic forces are available exclusively to kill the adversary's civilians; for avoiding military targets; and for shunning as much as possible any development of discriminateness, of an ability to destroy military targets without destroying civilians *en masse.* This doctrine of "mutual assured destruction," identified by its acronym "MAD," has never been officially accepted as the policy for using nuclear force by either the Soviet or the American government. Nor do the forces of either side conform to such a policy. The Soviet Union, for example, continues to spend roughly as much on defense of its civilian population as the United States spends on strategic offense and defense. Official statements on both sides insist that, whatever the capabilities for reciprocal mass civilian destruction, in the event of a nuclear war the governments would use their forces against a variety of military targets. As Mr. York has pointed out, accuracies, and therefore the ability to reduce unintended destruction, have improved dramatically, and are likely to continue improving on both sides.

Some systems analysts gave currency to the ghastly and most unassuring phrase "mutual assured destruction." They stressed, however, that this was an accounting device, measuring only how the forces could be used, rather than a reflection of the policy for their actual use in the event of war. The relevance and meaning of such macabre accounting are dubious. In any case, much is wrong with both the doctrines and the forces of the superpowers.

However, a responsible policy would move away from, rather than toward, the targeting of civilians. The diverse critics of MAD range from the respected Princeton theologian and student of the ethics of war, Paul Ramsey, to the current director of the Arms Control and Disarmament Agency, Fred Iklé, to Michael May, who, like Herbert York, formerly directed the Lawrence Livermore Radiation Laboratory. Mr. York accepts one of their most powerful objections, namely that even if MAD were a persuasive deterrent to a thoroughly rational decision-maker, such rationality is hardly universal. Even if no one "deliberately takes the responsibility for the appalling destruction and sorrow that war would bring in its train," as the *Pacem in Terris* Encyclical said, "the conflagration may be set off by some uncontrollable and unexpected chance." In that event, to execute the doctrine would mean an unprecedented mass slaughter of unoffending civilians.

Mr. York therefore proposes to limit the damage that would be done in such a case by altering not the aiming points but the size of the force aimed, leaving essentially intact the MIRVed (to use the jargon) missile force, Poseidon and Minuteman III. For these remaining missiles he would limit the yield of each warhead, if I understand him, to twelve-and-a-half kilotons. I presume he would welcome, if not insist, on cutting the Soviet force to the same total of small warheads.

Now I want to stress that I am completely sympathetic with attempts to modify so harsh a doctrine, though I never supported it in the first place. I favor reducing the weight of the explosives that can be launched by strategic forces. I would like to see each side with the same total, and that total much lower than the present U.S. capacity.

However, one must question Mr. York's reduced force on the following grounds: first, if it is deliberately aimed at killing civilians, will the reduction in fact significantly limit the slaughter? Second, would the alternative of aiming such a reduced force at military targets provide a useful deterrent and yet destroy fewer bystanders? As for the first question, even if the twelve-and-a-half kiloton limit were monitorable, the successful launching of three-quarters of Minuteman III missiles, and less than half the Poseidon, when aimed solely to kill Russian civilians, would promptly destroy nearly 100 million. The delayed effects from fallout would be small only in comparison with this enormous immediate slaughter. In short, simply reducing the force, as he proposes, would not accomplish Mr. York's goal. Even more drastic cuts in the strategic force to a size that still remains reasonably secure against attack in the face of uncertainties or unmonitorable increases, will not make it small enough to keep the slaughter less than catastrophic, so long as the force is aimed exclusively at defenseless population centers.

A nuclear war will in any case be terrible, but if deterrence fails, the alternative to aiming at civilians is to aim at military targets, to limit these targets in number, to choose them in part precisely for their geographical separation from civilian population centers so as to keep the destruction of civilians as low as one can; to select weapons and yields accuracies with that purpose in mind; and, specifically, to reduce fallout by using weapons with a lower fission fraction and by avoiding surface bursts. In fact, surface bursts in such military attacks are a doubly bad idea: they not only increase the *un*intended harm done by fallout; they also reduce the intended harm to military structures, both hard and soft, from blast overpressure—the most predictable weapons effect, and therefore the one that would be counted on by a conservative military planner. Further, the alternative is to maintain command and control of nuclear weapons throughout the conflict, to avoid destroying adversary command centers, and to try to bring the war to an end as rapidly as one can, with as much as possible left intact of civilian society.

This suggests an answer to the second question raised by Mr. York's proposal. There are tens of thousands of possible military targets, just as there are at least equal numbers of villages and farms containing civilians that could be attacked. But there is no legitimate military need to attack every single military target, not to say every civilian target. The force that Mr. York proposes, given the accuracies that he himself has predicted, could destroy any of several selected military systems, either long-range or general-purpose forces and their means of support. The loss of such massive and costly systems, especially along tensely disputed borders, would be felt as an enormous disaster by a given political-military leadership, leaving it and the nation naked to its enemies. Why wouldn't the prospect of such a loss be an excellent deterrent? Must we aim to kill noncombatants? I favor cutting the force to an agreed lower total, though I would specify the cuts differently. For reducing mass destruction of civilians, however, what is essential is how the force would be aimed and used.

Herbert York is concerned that if we aim at anything other than population centers this would mean more and larger weapons, and so more unintended damage to civilians than would be done deliberately by use of his proposed force. On the face of it, given the concentration of populations and their vulnerability to even a few weapons, this seems implausible. With the accuracies Mr. York and others expect, fewer and smaller weapons than those deployed in the present forces, which may be agreed to under SALT II, would do very well for attacking military targets. For one thing, SALT I already limits numbers, and SALT II can limit them further.

The hypothetical "spiral" models, popular in the academy, seem to me quite remote from the realities. For years claims have been repeated, without supporting evidence, that there has been a spiral increase in strategic budgets, in megatonnage, or in the area that could be destroyed by strategic weapons. And it has been argued that this spiral would continue upward unless civilians become the exclusive targets. These claims are simply inconsistent with actual U.S. history.

The United States has always aimed its nuclear arsenal at military targets, and this has not meant an exponential increase in destructive power in the past. In constant dollars, strategic budgets in the mid-1950s were two-and-a-half times what they are now. Strategic defense vehicles, which current arms race theory supposes to be particularly destabilizing, peaked at seven times what they are now. Offensive vehicles, as Messrs. Clifford and York observe, have been roughly constant.

Moreover, contrary to the stereotype, not only has strategic megatonnage declined drastically, but the geographical area that could be destroyed by the many smaller warheads has been declining for many years, and in 1972 was the same as in 1956. We may reach agreements, and I hope we do, on still lower strategic budgets. But can we justify aiming our nuclear weapons at civilians simply because they're easy to reach and cheap to kill? Because, so to speak, these noncombatant populations are available in the large, economy size? We should question not only the familiar arguments about budget instabilities occasioned by a supposed arms race, but also the argument that strategic forces aimed exclusively at civilians can provide a stable deterrent ("even one bomb aimed at one city," etc.), while a force aimed at military targets cannot.

To deter, one needs to possess not only a capability to destroy something that's important to an adversary, but also an ability to convince him that the capability would actually be used in response to the action one wants to deter. However, if the action to be deterred left our own civilian society essentially intact — as it would if the action were, for example, a nuclear attack directed at an ally in Europe or at Japan — would our promise to respond be convincing if our response would lead not only to the destruction of an adversary's civilians but also of our own? One of the many problems with MAD, when used as a threat, is that the destruction it promises would, in fact, be mutual and is therefore quite obviously unassured. On the other hand, a policy of attacking military targets that minimizes unintended civilian fatalities would offer incentives for an adversary to reciprocate under similar restraints by attacking military targets, thereby making unnecessary both mass homicide and mass suicide.

In any case, military attacks, even with the proposed reduced force, could scarcely remove the possibility of the urban destruction to which proponents of MAD cling. With Mr. York's proposed force of Minuteman III and Poseidon (assuming ten reentry vehicles per Poseidon, rather than fourteen), there would be 6,200 strategic warheads on each side. No one could dream of successfully destroying 6,199; for whatever that is worth, the possibility of one bomb on one city would always remain. A responsible deterrent calls for a less reckless, less homicidal, and less suicidal response.

One final point concerns détente. The process of constructing common interests and warranted mutual trust among sovereign nations with a long history of divergence is likely to be lengthy and painful. The *Pacem in Terris* Encyclical had something to say about the disabilities of threats and fears as a way of moving men toward common goals. In the long run, mutual threats to kill

555

innocent populations seem an especially poor way of building a community of interests between the Soviet Union and the United States.

Bishops, Statesmen, and Other Strategists
on the Bombing of Innocents **(1983)**

Albert Wohlstetter

From *Commentary*, Vol. 75, No. 6, June 1983, pp. 15-35.
Copyright © 1983 the American Jewish Committee. Reproduced with permission of *Commentary*.

Must the West threaten to bomb innocent bystanders in order
to deter nuclear war? Does the West itself need to be threatened
with annihilation of its civil society in order to be deterred?
President Reagan's speech of March 23, 1983, proposing a decades-
long research program to protect civilians against ballistic-missile
attack revived these questions. The instant hoots of ridicule and
references to *Star Wars* from many Senators and Congressmen
suggest that holding out the nightmare vision of last things, the
apocalypse, is now part of the nature of things; that the need to
threaten the end of the earth must dominate earthly policy.

In fact, the West has for years used apocalyptic threats as a
substitute for improving our capacity for discriminate response
and in particular for a conventional reply to conventional attack.
(The media hardly noticed the more immediate technical effort
urged in the President's speech—to improve conventional
technology.) Reckless nuclear threats and the intimidating growth
of both Soviet conventional and nuclear strength have had much
to do with the rise of the anti-nuclear movement here and in
Protestant Northern Europe. By revising many times in public
their pastoral letter on war and peace, American Catholic bishops
have dramatized the moral issues which statesmen, using empty
threats to end the world, neglect or evade. For the bishops stand
in a long moral tradition which condemns the threat to destroy
innocents as well as their actual destruction. They try but do not
escape reliance on threatening bystanders. Ironically, the view
dominating all their revisions reflects an evasive secular extreme
which, instead of speeding improvements in the ability to avoid
bystanders, has tried to halt or curb them. But because the bishops
must take threats seriously, they make more visible the essential
evasions of Western statesmen. That, however, is a kind of virtue.
The letter offers a unique opportunity to examine the moral,
political, and military issues together, and to show that, as the
President suggests, threatening to bomb innocents is not part of

the nature of things. Nor has it been, as is now widely claimed, an essential of deterrence from the beginning. Nor is it the inevitable result of "modern technology." It may be that our Senators and even some of our younger Congressmen haven't watched *Star Wars* closely enough.

The bishops have been sending a message to strategists in Western foreign-policy establishments—and to strategists in the Western anti-nuclear counter-establishments. It seems unequivocal: "Under no circumstances may nuclear weapons or other instruments of mass slaughter be used for the purpose of destroying population centers or other predominantly civilian targets." Though that only restates an exemplary part of Vatican II two decades earlier, it is far from commonplace. Nonetheless it should be obvious to Catholics and non-Catholics alike. Informed realists in foreign-policy establishments as well as pacifists should oppose aiming to kill bystanders with nuclear or conventional weapons: indiscriminate Western threats paralyze the West, not the East. We have urgent political and military as well as moral grounds for improving our ability to answer an attack on Western military forces with less unintended killing, not to mention deliberate mass slaughter.

The bishops *seem* to be countering the perverse dogma which, after the Cuban missile crisis, came to be used by Western statesmen eager to spend less on defense: that the West should rely for deterring the Soviets on the ability to answer a nuclear military attack by assuring the deliberate destruction of tens or even hundreds of millions of Soviet civilians; and that the United States should also, for the supposed sake of "stability," give up any defense of its own civilians and any attack on military targets in order to assure the Soviets that they could, in response, destroy a comparable number of American civilians. The long humanist as well as the religious tradition on "just war" stresses especially the need to avoid attacks on "open," that is undefended, cities. The new doctrine exactly reversed this; it called both for leaving cities undefended and threatening to annihilate them. John Newhouse succinctly states this dogma, to which he was sympathetic, in the "frosty apothegm": "Offense is defense, defense is offense. Killing people is good, killing weapons is bad." The late Donald Brennan, a long-term advocate of arms control to defend people and restrain offense from killing innocents, was not sympathetic. He noted that the acronym for Mutual Assured Destruction—MAD—described that Orwellian dogma.

Having observed long ago that not even Genghis Khan avoided combatants in order to focus solely on destroying noncombatants, I was grateful, on a first look at this issue in the evolving pastoral letter, to find the bishops on the side of the angels. Unfortunately, a closer reading suggested that they were also on the other side. For, while they sometimes say that we should not threaten to destroy civilians, they say too that we may continue to maintain nuclear weapons — and so implicitly threaten their use as a deterrent — while moving toward permanent verifiable nuclear and general disarmament; *yet we may not meanwhile plan to be able to fight a nuclear war even in response to a nuclear attack.*

Before that distant millennial day when all the world disarms totally, verifiably, and irrevocably — at least in nuclear weapons — if we should not intend to attack noncombatants, as the letter says, what alternative is there to deter nuclear attack or coercion? Plainly only to be able to aim at the combatants attacking us, or at their equipment, facilities, or direct sources of combat supply. That, however, is what is meant by planning to be able to fight a nuclear war — which the letter rejects.

Perhaps the bishops can work this out in later statements. But a close reading of their changing text, their congressional testimony, and the writings of their associates suggests that this is unlikely. For their struggle with conscience has led them to make only more explicit the widespread confusions and evasions of many secular strategists — including many statesmen, scientists, Senators, editors, and business leaders. Take John Cardinal Krol and Father Brian Hehir, who was staff adviser to the ad hoc committee drafting the pastoral letter. Cardinal Krol repeated in a sermon at the White House in 1979 what he and his associates had been saying in recent years: in brief, "possession, yes, for deterrence . . . but use, never." It is all right for the United States implicitly to threaten the use of nuclear weapons, but "at the point of such decisions, . . . political and military authorities are responsible to a higher set of values" and so "must reject the actual use of such weapons, whatever the consequences." Any consequence "whatever" includes giving up military resistance. But "the history of certain countries under Communist rule today shows that not only are human means of resistance available and effective but also that human life does not lose all meaning with replacement of one political system by another."

Father Hehir elaborates this view: (A) We should not get or keep an ability to attack combatants. (B) We may maintain an ability to attack noncombatants while waiting for nuclear disarmament, and (C) We may use that ability implicitly (though not explicitly) to threaten retaliation against noncombatants. (D) Indeed, to deter nuclear attack, we must *convince* other nations that our "determination to use nuclear weapons is beyond question." (E) We should never intend to use nuclear weapons. (F) Nor (to make the deception harder) *declare* an intent to use them even in reply to a nuclear attack. (G) We should never actually use them; that is to say, we shouldn't retaliate at all.

Precisely how this volubly revealed deception is to fool allies and adversaries "beyond question" has not itself been revealed. (Future sermons at the White House might have to be classified.) If the bishops could transmit that revelation, it would fortify a good many strategists in our foreign affairs establishment who want fervently to believe that we can safely deter an adversary solely by threatening the nuclear extermination of his cities while making clear to the entire world that we would never use nuclear weapons at all; and who also want firmly to believe we needn't spend much money on a less reckless defense. In sending that message to Western elites the letter only relays, amplifies, and broadcasts signals our elites have themselves been sending for years. The troubling obscurity of the letter reflects that establishment ambivalence and incoherence. On many matters of technical military and political fact, the bishops derive their views not from sacred authority but from a more doubtful range of secular strategists than they realize. Much of the letter, for example, stems from the strategists who hold that defense is offense and that killing people is good and killing weapons bad — the very strategists who would rely exclusively on threatening to destroy cities.

In invoking divine authority to sustain such lay strategies, the bishops' power seems dangerous to many Catholics who disagree. But their moral prestige alone gives weight to the bishops' strategic views with non-Catholics and Catholics. They reinforce the impassioned pacifist and neutralist movements that have been growing in Europe and in the United States, as well as the establishment strategies which helped to generate these protest movements.

* * * * *

For the bishops pass lightly over or further confound many already muddled and controversial questions of fact and policy. In a world where so many intense, deep, and sometimes mutually reinforcing antagonisms divide regional as well as superpowers, are there serious early prospects for negotiating the complete, verifiable, and permanent elimination of nuclear or conventional arms? If antagonists don't agree, should we disarm unilaterally? If we keep nuclear arms, how should we use them to deter their use against us or an ally? Might an adversary in some plausible circumstance make a nuclear attack on an element (perhaps a key non-nuclear element) of our military power or that of an ally to whom we have issued a nuclear guarantee? Might such an enemy nuclear attack (for example, one generated in the course of allied conventional resistance to a conventional invasion of NATO's center or of a critical country on NATO's northern or southern flank) have decisive military effects yet restrict side effects enough to leave us, and possibly our ally, a very large stake in avoiding "mutual mass slaughter"? Could some selective but militarily useful Western response to such a restricted nuclear attack destroy substantially fewer innocent bystanders than a direct attack on population centers? Would any discriminate Western response to a restricted nuclear attack — even one in an isolated area on a flank — inevitably (or more likely than not, or just possibly, or with some intermediate probability) lead to the destruction of humanity, or "something little better"? Or at least to an unprecedented catastrophe? Would it be less or more likely than an attack on a population to lead to unrestricted attacks on populations? Can we deter a restricted nuclear attack better by threatening an "unlimited," frankly suicidal, and therefore improbable attack on the aggressor's cities, or by a limited but much more probable response suited to the circumstance?

The bishops' authorities slip by or confuse almost all these questions. The bishops sometimes seem only to be saying that the extent of direct collateral harm done by a particular restricted attack is uncertain, quite apart from the possibilities of "escalation." At other times they are certain that restricted attacks will lead to an entirely unrestricted war. And they then suggest that the chance is "so infinitesimal" that any Western nuclear response to a restricted attack would end short of ending humanity itself, that we might better threaten directly to bring on the apocalypse. The bishops cite experts as authority for their judgment that any use whatever of nuclear weapons would with an overwhelming probability lead to unlimited destruction. And some of their experts do seem to say just that. But some they cite appear only to say that we cannot be quite sure (that is, the probability is not equal to one) that any use of nuclear weapons would stay limited. If any response other than our surrender is to be believed, it makes a difference whether we talk of a probability that is not quite zero or a probability that is not quite equal to one that any nuclear response would bring on a suicidally total disaster. Yet two successive paragraphs in the 1982 *Foreign Affairs* article by McGeorge Bundy, George F. Kennan, Robert S. McNamara, and Gerard Smith proposing "no first use" of nuclear weapons, which the bishops cite, assert each of a wide range of such differing possibilities without distinction. Most authorities relied on by the bishops are themselves not very discriminating about which point they are trying to make.

Some important components of conventional military power vulnerable to nuclear attack are close to population centers. Others, however, may be very far from them—for example, naval forces at sea; or satellites in orbit hundreds or even a hundred thousand miles above the earth, that may be expected to perform the essential tasks during a conventional war of reconnaissance, surveillance, navigation, guidance, and communications. These are more vulnerable to nuclear than conventional attack. If we have no way of discouraging a limited nuclear attack except by extracting a promise from an adversary that he will not attack, or by threatening that we will respond to such isolated attacks with a suicidal retaliation on his cities, an adversary might, in the course of a conventional war, chance a small but effective nuclear attack against such isolated military targets. Such an attack would do incomparably less damage to civilians in the West than any of the "limited" attacks discussed by the bishops' authorities. Is it really so evident that a similarly restricted Western nuclear response to such a nuclear attack would be nearly certain to escalate to the end of humanity? Wouldn't a restricted response doing minimal damage to civilians on either side be much less likely to escalate than an attack on cities? And wouldn't the ability to respond in a proportionate way be a better deterrent to an adversary's crossing the gap between nuclear and conventional weapons? The bishops' lay experts tend to see the Soviets as mirror images of themselves, but sometimes diabolize them. They argue as if the Soviets would not continue during a war to have the strongest possible incentives to keep escalation within bounds; and as if the Soviets would love every killing of a Western bystander exactly as much as the West values his survival; as if the Soviet interest were in annihilating rather than dominating Western society.

* * * * *

In fact, calculations cited by the bishops' authorities hardly probe the issue as to whether an adversary might use nuclear weapons that would destroy key components of a military force discriminately, leaving us a very large stake in making either a discriminate response or no response at all. The calculations published in 1979 by the Office of Technology Assessment (OTA), in answer to an inquiry by supporters of MAD on the Senate Foreign Relations Committee, deal with hypothetical "small" and supposedly "limited" attacks. However, OTA's "limitations" were not seriously designed to test the feasibility, now or in the future, of destroying military targets and *not* population. One of their "limited" cases involves direct attacks on the populations of Detroit and Leningrad. And OTA's most "limited" Soviet attack directed 80 one-megaton[1] nuclear warheads at oil refineries, including some inside Philadelphia and Los Angeles, in order "to inflict as much economic damage as possible" and "without any effort to maximize or *minimize* human casualties" (emphasis added). No one should be surprised that such a "limited" attack might kill about 5 million bystanders; or that a similar attack on Soviet oil refineries might kill 840,000 — a result which the influential English military historian, Michael Howard, describes as "little better" than "a genocidal pact" killing up to 160 million in each country and leaving the rest "to envy the dead."

The bishops rely heavily on a three-and-a-half page study embodying the views of fourteen scientists who seem mainly to be specialists in public health. The Papal Academy of Sciences convened this group from several countries, including the Soviet Union, "to examine the consequences of the use of nuclear weapons on the survival and the health of humanity." Like the Physicians for Social Responsibility in this country, the group considers (except for one paragraph) only the effects of intentionally bombing cities. It says that the consequences of such an attack on the survival and health of humanity "appear obvious." Indeed they have always been. That is the principal reason to reject MAD and avoid threatening cities.

The papal study devotes one paragraph to "a nuclear attack directed only at military facilities." Like the pastoral letter, that paragraph assumes that any nuclear attack by an aggressor anywhere or any response by his victim would be directed at *all* the adversary's military facilities, however minor or irrelevant to the immediate outcome of the conflict that generated the use of nuclear weapons. It also assumes there would be no attempt to explode the weapons at altitudes that avoided fallout and no attempt in any other way to confine destruction to targets critical to the conflict's outcome.

But such analyses dodge all the serious issues as to whether an adversary might, in the course of a conventional war, use some nuclear weapons with substantial military effect and yet deliberately leave us and our allies with very strong incentives to avoid mutual mass slaughter; and as to whether we should have no response to such an attack except bringing on the mass slaughter or surrendering; and no better way of deterring it than promising one or the other or even, like the bishops' strategists, *both* of these two incompatible bad alternatives.

Yet the problem of deterring nuclear coercion or attack on an ally will persist. Despite lip-service at Geneva and the United Nations, hardly anyone seriously expects that each and everyone of the six or seven or eight nations that have made nuclear explosives will destroy all their nuclear arms irretrievably and verifiably in a future near enough to govern our present actions. (The uncertainty as to the number of *present* nuclear powers suggests some of the difficulty we would have in getting actionable evidence that all of the existing nuclear powers had destroyed all of their weapons.) Nor are all prospective nuclear powers likely or even able to surrender the possibility of making the bomb. Moreover, the harm that these weapons can do is so great that merely reducing them to the numbers talked of by "minimum deterrers," who would use the remainder to threaten the mass slaughter of populations, would not remove and might increase the probability of an enormous catastrophe. And it would not prevent the potent use of threats of mass slaughter for coercing those who have disarmed. Pope John Paul II has observed that "a totally and permanently peaceful human society is unfortunately a utopia"; and that "pacifist declarations" frequently cloak plans for "aggression, domination, and manipulation of others" and could "lead straight to the false peace of totalitarian regimes." (The Pope has known that false peace personally.)

* * * * *

It has been obvious since the 1950's that the West needs: to rely less on threats of nuclear destruction and much more on improving conventional defenses; to discourage the spread of nuclear weapons; and to continue making nuclear weapons less vulnerable to attack, safer from "accidental" detonation, and more secure against seizure and unauthorized or mistaken use. The Soviet Union has its own reasons, as have we, for undertaking such measures unilaterally, with or without formal agreements or even "understandings." Formal agreements on these matters, in fact, have frequently defeated their overt purpose. Agreements, for example, that were supposed to encourage exclusively peaceful uses and research on nuclear energy have spread plutonium usable in explosives. The bishops call for "strengthening command and control over nuclear weapons" to make them more secure against unauthorized or inadvertent use, but call more strongly for agreement on a freeze — which would halt all current programs to replace aging nuclear weapons with ones that are not only more secure against seizure but safer against accidents, more discriminate, and less susceptible to attack.

What is more, the West has many excellent reasons for reducing the numbers and destructiveness of its nuclear weapons quite apart from any agreement. The indiscriminate destructiveness of the American stockpile (as measured in numbers of megatons) was four times higher in 1960 than in 1980. The number of weapons was one-third higher in 1967. The persistent failure of the bishops and other strategists who make a fetish of bilateral agreements to observe the unilateral decline in destructiveness and numbers in American nuclear stockpiles shows, at the very least, a certain lack of seriousness. In any case, if a freeze doesn't stop it from doing so, the U.S. can reduce further and drastically the numbers and destructiveness of its nuclear stockpile by exploiting the improved accuracies possible today. Improved accuracies make feasible greater discrimination as well as effectiveness in the use of nuclear weapons, and they also make possible more extensive replacement of nuclear with conventional weapons.

My own research and that of others has for many years pointed to the need for a much higher priority on improving our ability to hit what we aim at and only what we aim at. That would mean, in particular, that effective conventional weapons could drastically

565

reduce the West's reliance on nuclear force. Moreover, for years now, the thrust of technology, as in the electronics revolution, has been to improve the possibilities of discrimination and control. It can increasingly provide us with just such intelligent choices between using conventional or nuclear weapons, and between killing innocent bystanders with nuclear weapons or attacking means of aggression and domination.

The danger of Soviet aggression is more likely to be lessened by a Western ability to threaten the military means of domination than by a Western ability to threaten bystanders. First, the Soviets value their military power, on the evidence, more than the lives of bystanders. Second, Western nonsuicidal threats against legitimate military targets are more credible than threats to bring about the destruction of civil society on both sides. The latter have a negligible likelihood of being carried out by Western leaders, and therefore cannot be relied on to dissuade Soviet intimidation or aggression. Finally, it is even more absurd and dangerous to suppose that the only way to dissuade the U.S. from unleashing aggression is to help the Soviets threaten our civilians by leaving them defenseless and by leaving us no choices other than capitulation or an uncontrollably destructive offense against Soviet cities that would invite the reciprocal destruction of our own civil society.

Only some widely prevalent but shallow evasions and self-befuddlements, and not any deep moral dilemma or basic paradox, force us to threaten the annihilation of civilians in order to prevent nuclear or conventional war. The bishops are clear about rejecting the actual use of nuclear weapons to kill innocents. About *threats* to kill innocents, they are much less clear. Their obscurity mirrors an uneasy area of darkness at the core of establishment views.

II

Precisely because the bishops' views do not come from on high but are shared by many in the establishment, and also in the anti-nuclear and pacifist movements that shake the establishment, it is worth looking at their arguments on the morality of nuclear deterrence in the context of changing defense policies. Anti-nuclear arguments proceed from premises about the inevitable dependence of deterrence on threats deliberately or uncontrollably to kill innocents. To some degree, bluffs about bringing on the nuclear apocalypse helped generate the rise of the unilateral nuclear disarmers; and continuing reliance on such bluffs helps to disarm the establishment from answering the unilateral disarmers. The arguments of both undermine deterrence.

Many recent accounts of defense policy in the nuclear age rewrite history to lend an aura of inevitability to the extreme view that we can reliably deter a nuclear attack in any plausible circumstance solely by threats to kill innocents on both sides, threats which we plainly should never and would never carry out. Advocates of that dangerous self-paralyzing bluff claim that this extreme has been the essential base of Western defense policy since Hiroshima. It wasn't at the beginning. Nor was it the meaning of the second-strike theory of deterrence that originated near the start of the 1950's. The second-strike theory did not hold that we had to choose between deterring and being ready and willing to fight if deterrence failed. Americans who oppose unilateral disarmament have never split into a "party of deterrence" as distinct from a "war party" that prefers fighting to deterring a nuclear war. Advocates of MAD suggest as much. But MAD was not declaratory policy before the mid-1960's. And it has never been operational policy. Yet many liberal and conservative critics of the bishops, like the bishops themselves, are under the impression that it always has been. Many believe that MAD has kept the nuclear peace and is therefore necessary, at least as myth. But the evolution of doctrines and policies of deterrence needs to be seen in relation to the changing technologies of discriminateness and control as well as the technologies of nuclear brute force.

Mass Destruction and Initial Doubts about Stability

Manhattan Project scientists assumed immediately after Hiroshima[2] that the least destructive fission (or atomic) bomb would affect so large an area and the number of such bombs would always be so scarce that they were suited only to attacks on large population centers rather than military forces or war plants directly supporting them. Hence the standard description— weapons of "mass destruction" or "mass slaughter." Worse yet, the atomic scientists thought atomic deterrence extremely unstable. (Leo Szilard, for example, thought in 1945 that the odds for nuclear war in ten years were 9 in 10.) In short, the imminence of total destruction was so probable that nothing less than world government soon and total disarmament would permit survival. It was—in a slogan common in 1945 to which Jonathan Schell might now subscribe—"One World or None."

By the time it had become clear that we were not about to get one world, and that atomic weapons could be used effectively and in adequate numbers against military targets, the atomic scientists' movement had come to the view that they should be used *only* against military targets. By then, fusion weapons were in prospect and many of the same scientists assumed, as they had at first about the A-bomb, that the new H-bomb was suited only to destroy population centers and, at that, offered a net advantage over A-bombs only against a few of the largest population centers. Therefore, they opposed the H-bomb and advocated a vast expansion of the A-bomb stockpile to be used in fighting a ground war in Europe, in anti-submarine warfare, in continental defense, and against enemy bomber bases.

In 1952, thoughtful analysts of the implications of thermonuclear weapons like the economist Charles Hitch found that—contrary to many claims—H-bombs were indeed much more effective than A-bombs against military targets and war-supporting industry; but, like the atomic scientists, he was concerned that they raised the gravest problems of *unintended* collateral damage to noncombatants. To reduce civilian casualties one should give priority to targets outside cities and warn urban populations to evacuate. Like the physicists, Hitch considered mainly very large (25-megaton) H-bombs delivered with great inaccuracy, that is, with half the bombs missing by a radius of at least a half-mile and generally by well over a mile. Other writers on the H-bomb at the time, like Bernard Brodie, an international relations theorist who had once thought A-bombs were suited only to attack whole cities, sometimes agreed with Hitch that H-bombs made restraint essential and that war objectives had to be limited as well; at other times he talked of them as "city busters"; at still other times, he talked about their tactical advantage for use in Europe where they could destroy so large an area as to frustrate dispersion and concealment of ground forces.

Yet, whether one considered H-bombs or A-bombs, the trend in NATO policy — if only to keep defense budgets within domestic political bounds — was to rely increasingly on nuclear weapons in large numbers and to neglect the unintended harm they would do. Churchill, who justified British nuclear weapons in part because they would be able to destroy military targets of special interest to Britain, was so impressed by the destructive side-effects of the H-bomb soon to be acquired by both Britain and the U.S., that he talked vividly and hopefully of safety becoming the "sturdy child of terror." The Republicans, coming to power at the end of an unpopular and costly conventional war in Korea, talked of nuclear weapons as simply "modern weapons" which furnished a "bigger bang for a buck." They talked of massive retaliation against lesser threats; and the NATO Military Committee in 1957 formally adopted a strategy of threatening a "full" nuclear response even to a local persisting incursion into NATO territory.

Inevitably, uneasiness about the sturdiness as well as the morality of a balance based on threats of such massive destruction, however unintentional, led many sober critics to propose more limited applications of nuclear force, and especially the use of small nuclear weapons on the battlefield. But it soon became clear that nuclear weapons used on the battlefield in the center of Europe also had drawbacks as a replacement for adequate conventional force. The Carte Blanche exercise in 1955 indicated that the side effects of their early introduction might kill nearly 2 million West Germans and wound many others. Chancellor Konrad Adenauer therefore resisted an increased reliance on nuclear weapons and changed his mind only at the end of 1956, when he saw that a conventional build-up in West Germany would be drastically constrained by domestic political problems in getting eighteen-month terms for army conscripts. After that, the Germans and other West Europeans came more than any American President since 1961 to favor relying on nuclear weapons as a cheap substitute for conventional force.

Operational plans, however, have always differed from the rhetoric of indiscriminate threats. Certainly NATO has never planned to avoid military targets in order deliberately to kill innocents at long or short range. NATO plans have always included various restraints on the size of weapons used against military targets in Eastern as well as Western Europe. Nonetheless the problem of unintended harm to noncombatants on both sides remained and always cast some doubt about the sturdiness of deterrence and especially about the Western will to respond to limited or isolated nuclear attacks against the military forces of an ally. (Where that ally is a country on the northern or southern flanks of Europe, the doubt is most obvious; yet these "flank countries" are at present more endangered and more critical for the Alliance than ever. Doubts have increased, especially about the effectiveness of massive nuclear threats as a substitute for conventional force.)

Another line of research that was pursued intensively in classified form, beginning in 1951, disclosed a different but even more urgent range of problems about the sturdiness of nuclear deterrence. This research, which generated the second-strike theory of deterrence, looked at the vulnerabilities of all the essential elements of strategic nuclear forces under nuclear attack, and the problems these entailed for maintaining a convincing deterrent. These problems had been badly neglected in part because the original belief after World War II that nuclear weapons could be used effectively only against cities predisposed political and military leaders, as well as scientists, to overlook the possibility that our own nuclear force might come under attack; also because bombing doctrines during and before World War II had stressed that the chief aim of strategic forces was to destroy the centers of war-supporting industry and not the military forces themselves.

As a result, the force we had planned for the mid- and late-1950's, before the introduction of ballistic missiles, was much more vulnerable than is generally realized even today. That was dangerous in particular because NATO had always counted on the help of the Strategic Air Command (SAC) to deter or oppose an invasion of Western Europe and to reduce the intimidating political shadow cast by the possibility that an invasion might grow out of some future crisis. A strategic force, however powerful when left undisturbed to do its work, cannot deter an attack which it is unable itself to survive; and the studies showed that we needed to protect not only the vehicles but all the complex elements of an effective response, including in particular a politically responsible command-and-control. Moreover, preserving control required operating in peacetime in ways that avoid a large risk of lethal "accidents" or even more lethal mistakes in response to false alarms. It excludes, for example, "launching under attack," a euphemism for launching ICBM's on ambiguous electromagnetic signals.

Popularizations of the second-strike theory and some recent academic accounts distort history to make it seem essential deliberately to threaten innocents rather than military forces in order to deter. They frequently identify a second strike with attacks on civilians. In its origins the second-strike theory assumed no such identity. The study that generated the distinction [between first- and second-strike] and first specified requirements for a second strike, the Rand Base Study, in which I was engaged between 1951 and 1953 with Fred Hoffman, Harry Rowen, and Robert Lutz, made explicit that it would not deal with how to choose targets, but rather how to choose a protected mode of basing and operating a strategic force that would be best for any of several target systems. It looked at several target sets typical of the time: a quite limited number of key war plants supporting combat; military targets whose destruction might retard the advance of ground forces in Europe; and those that might blunt a continuing enemy strategic attack. It did so in order to show in all cases how best to reduce the vulnerability of our own strategic forces. That was the more important result, but the study also saved 9 billion 1953 dollars, showing that one does not have to aim to destroy cities only, or to destroy cities at all, to avoid "exponential" increases in defense spending, as one implausible rationalization for bombing innocents has it.

The authors' next long study, started at the end of 1953, was about defending a strategic force in the coming ballistic-missile era of reduced warning—then seven years or so off. It paid particular attention to "fail-safe methods" of avoiding war through mistaken responses to ambiguous signals and to the difficult issues of protecting political command-and-control. However, like the Base Study, it dealt only with the urgent problem of choosing responsible ways to protect SAC, not with choice among SAC's targets. Separating targets for SAC never looked harder than in the mid-1950's, since our bombs were then at their most destructive and expected inaccuracies near their anguishing worst. However, in successive later studies of strategic aims, the authors became increasingly clear that to have only the alternative of indiscriminate attack would seriously compromise the credibility that there would be any response at all. The two lines of research, one on targeting and reducing collateral damage and the other on protecting the strategic force, converged. It had become apparent that to have a persuasive deterrent, we had not only to be able to protect command-and-control, but also to have some alternatives which a responsible political leader would be willing to command.

Imprecision and Unintended Harm

The recognition at the end of 1953 that fusion warheads might be made small enough to be carried in ballistic missiles by the 1960's might have seemed to hold out the prospect for reducing collateral damage somewhat. For these first ballistic-missile warheads were expected to be substantially smaller than the gravity bombs carried in aircraft. (Later Navy SLBM warheads were about the same size as some early A-bombs, 40 kilotons. Even the first SLBM and ICBM warheads were about a half-megaton, much smaller than the H-bombs contemplated in the initial debate.) In fact, however, the prospect of the ballistic missile worsened expectations about collateral damage because the first generation of missiles was expected to be much more inaccurate than aircraft. The median miss distance then expected for the first ballistic missiles was anywhere from two to five miles. A five-mile median radius of inaccuracy meant that half the bombs would strike outside of an 80-square-mile area!

But inaccuracy determines the unintended harm done in destroying a small target more basically than does the explosive yield of individual bombs. It is the lack of technology smart enough, rather than the availability of large brute-force single weapons, that lies at the root of the problem of collateral damage. One makes up for incompetence in aiming by filling an enormous area of uncertainty either with a few large-yield nuclear weapons or, as the British did in World War II, with many thousands of small conventional bombs. When the British discovered in June 1941 that only a third of the bomber crews who thought they had bombed the target were within 80 square miles of it, they resorted to huge raids involving thousands of bombers with results that became visible in Hamburg and in Dresden. David Irving's estimate of the dead in Dresden came to 135,000 — much more than the official estimates of the Hiroshima dead. A single American conventional raid on Tokyo in March 1945 destroyed an area over three times that destroyed by the Hiroshima bomb (15.8 compared to 4.7 square miles) and nearly nine times that destroyed by the Nagasaki bomb (1.8 square miles). The average area destroyed in 93 conventional attacks against Japanese cities amounted to the same as that in Nagasaki.

During the postwar period the prospects for reducing collateral damage seemed at their worst in the late 1950's when the average explosive yield of a bomb was *ten* times the present level and when anticipated missile inaccuracies were also at their maximum. Some of the most familiar and perverse current views on nuclear deterrence, including those that have shaped the pastoral letter, were formed at that time. Since then, the prospects of hitting only what one is aiming at have changed by several orders of magnitude. That implies improvements in effectiveness against small, hard fixed targets that are in some ways more revolutionary than the transition from conventional to fission explosives or even fusion weapons. The fission and fusion revolutions blasted themselves, so to speak, into public awareness. Revolutionary improvements in our ability to focus destruction on targets alone have proceeded quietly and attracted less public notice and understanding.

The fact is, however, that a tenfold improvement in accuracy is roughly equal in effectiveness to a thousandfold increase in the explosive energy released by a weapon. Improving accuracy by a factor of 100 improves blast effectiveness against a small, hard military target about as much as multiplying the energy released a million times. The fission bomb at Hiroshima released about a thousand times more energy, and a 10-megaton fusion bomb can release a million times more energy, than a 10-ton conventional "block buster." A one-hundredfold improvement in accuracy roughly equals in effectiveness a millionfold increase in the release of destructive energy to enable the blast destruction of a small fixed target.

The Revolution in Precision

But while the improvement in effectiveness may be the same, these two technologies achieve it in essentially different ways. When one improves effectiveness by releasing more destructive energy, there is a corresponding increase in collateral damage. When one improves the ability to destroy a target by increasing one's accuracy, there is a corresponding decrease in collateral damage.

Improvements in guidance using midcourse adjustments have already reduced cruise-missile inaccuracies to 200 feet from the 12,000-30,000-feet average misses expected for ballistic missiles in the late 1950's. That improvement by a factor of 60 to 150 makes feasible radical reductions in collateral damage. Even more important, terminal guidance systems in development now that can be deployed in the late 1980's could further reduce inaccuracies at extended ranges by another order of magnitude. That would permit a conventional weapon to replace nuclear bombs in a wide variety of missions with an essentially equal probability of destroying a fixed military target. It would drastically raise the threshold beyond which one would have to resort to nuclear weapons in order to be effective. It would mean a much smaller likelihood of "escalation" and incomparably smaller side effects.

Destroying ground targets that might decide a conventional conflict could have much more troubling side effects even in relatively isolated areas than the destruction of equally decisive naval forces at sea or key satellites deep in space. Yet the situation has altered greatly here too. Most such land targets are less blast-resistant than ICBM silos. Yet attacking them effectively with the huge inaccuracies expected in the late 1950's would have meant filling an enormous area of uncertainty with destruction. That might typically have subjected an area of 1000 square miles or so to unintended lethal effects. By contrast, a current cruise missile, with midcourse guidance and a small nuclear warhead, could be equally effective against a military target while confining lethal damage to less than one square mile. Most important, improved terminal guidance in the next few years could enable a cruise missile with a suitable *non*-nuclear warhead to destroy a military target and reduce the area of fatal collateral damage to about one-thousandth of a square mile — an enormous contrast with World War II.

Some conservative critics counter the bishops' strictures against a nuclear response to conventional attack by suggesting that any "conventional war in Western Europe would almost certainly mean terror and destruction far in excess of World War II" — with perhaps 100 million dead; that, in short, any conventional conflict in Europe would bring on horrors hardly less terrible than nuclear war. Such expectations lead many Europeans to feel that even a conventional war would destroy Europe and end Western civilization. For the bishops, a policy of No-First-Use follows from the broader nuclear policy of "Use, Never." And both are only part of Cardinal Krol's injunction in his White House sermon against all war. ("No more war, war never again.") Through all the political compromises in various drafts, the bishops support conventional alternatives only grudgingly. But estimates of conventional damage by the bishops' critics have even less basis in evidence than those the bishops cite to show that nuclear damage would be unlimited. It is plain that the increasing advances in precision and control can be most fully exploited by suitably designed conventional weapons.

It is essential to emphasize that advances in our ability to reduce collateral damage and increase the effectiveness of conventional weapons do not blur the distinction between nuclear and conventional force. On the contrary, that remains vital. But these revolutionary changes make it much more feasible to avoid crossing the divide between nuclear and conventional weapons. They give us choices.

Discussions of the morality of bombing and deterrence today often proceed as if "the technical realities" foreclose choice (as one eminent physicist, Wolfgang Panofsky, suggests), as if "the mutual hostage relation" were not at all a "consequence of policy and therefore . . . subject to change," but a matter of physics — permanently determined by the technology for releasing nuclear energy. Yet the evolution since the 1950's of technologies other than the release of nuclear energy has altered the possibilities of discrimination and will not excuse us from the responsibility for preparing to keep violence from mounting without bounds.

III

With few exceptions, even the most thoughtful considerations of the morality of nuclear threats have been frozen in the technology of the late 1950's and specifically that of nuclear brute force. This can be shown by referring to the evolution of NATO policy, to the development of technologies of destruction and of discrimination and control, and to a sequence of substantial analyses of the morality and prudence of threats to bomb innocents between the end of the 1950's and the present.

Terror and Technology at the End of the 1950's

Robert W. Tucker's book, *The Just War* (1960), observed that the policy of nuclear deterrence in the 1950's had demonstrated "at least a striking verbal insensitivity" to the consequences of the defensive use of nuclear force. Indeed, "the more extreme versions" were "obsessed" with the idea that the deterrent threat would never have to be carried out and therefore regarded "the effectiveness of deterrence as directly proportionate" to its horrors. If one accepted this extreme, then one had to acknowledge that "in the nuclear age . . . virtually no substantive restraints . . . need to be observed by those waging a defensive war." But Tucker himself leaned toward the extreme, since he thought no restraints would be effective. He was writing when the average destructiveness of our weapons and the expected inaccuracies, and hence the probable unintended harm, were all near their peak.

575

Indiscriminateness, he suggested, is a "'necessity' that is inherent in technology." He rejected the position taken by the World Council of Churches in 1958 against "all-out" use of nuclear weapons. As Paul Ramsey observed, Tucker agreed with the pacifists that statecraft in the nuclear age entails using evil means — threats whose execution would inevitably exterminate civilians. He parted company with the pacifists because the pacifists would abandon statecraft. Tucker would rather abandon morality. His concluding paragraph argued: "There is something patently absurd in the complaint that a threat of extermination, even when restricted to preventing one's own annihilation, signifies a moral decline for which there is no explanation other than that men have deliberately chosen to abandon any sense of restraint. If men presently show less restraint in threatening their adversaries, it is largely because they are less secure than in an earlier age." But during the 1950's, doubts grew about the credibility and the political and military implications of threats of extermination and about whether there were no better choices.

The McNamara Doctrine of the First Two Years

The view dominant among the Kennedy administration and its advisers during its first two years embodied the two converging lines of research on the protection of the strategic force and its targeting. It put into effect many of the criticisms of massive retaliation that had accumulated during the 1950's. It stressed the importance of a second-strike capability, including a responsible command-and-control system with its vulnerabilities reduced, for example, by the use of airborne command posts. But it also called for a conventional build-up to reduce reliance on nuclear weapons and contemplated the use of nuclear force itself only with discrimination and restraint in the service of political ends. Both conventional and nuclear force, neither of which could substitute for the other, would have to be used in limited ways, if we were to deter aggression, or frustrate it should it occur.

Alain Enthoven defended the continuing relevance of the traditional Christian doctrine of "just war" in the context of the initial Kennedy policy. He explicitly rejected the "realist" and pacifist views of deterrence, both of which assume the incompatibility of morality and statecraft in the nuclear age. We do not, he said, have to choose one or the other. The realists would eliminate moral restraints because they believe them impossible or suicidal. The pacifists think that the impossibility of restraint in nuclear war proves what they had believed all along, that the only moral course is to disarm totally, even if unilaterally, and that this would bring universal peace.

Enthoven distinguished his view also from the obsessive extreme which Tucker had in mind—the position known sometimes by the euphemisms "Minimum Deterrence" or "Deterrence Only." Enthoven noted that this view, which had begun to take hold among academics after Sputnik (1957), resembled that of the pacifists in its belief that a lasting peace was feasible in the short term. But Deterrence Only would base stability on threats to respond to an attack on our strategic force by *deliberately* bombing enemy civilians, by avoiding enemy military targets, and by exposing our own civilians to attack. The core of this newer view, as he might have noted, was therefore an antithesis both of pacifist nonviolence and of the Christian and other ethical traditions of humane warfare.

It also differed drastically from preceding U.S. policy. In one sense the new dogma seemed to return to the immediate postwar understanding of nuclear weapons. But the typical view after Hiroshima held that the number of either side's nuclear weapons would be intrinsically so small and the individual bombs so destructive that they could be effective only against large population centers. An aggressor *could* effectively attack only cities. His victims *could* effectively retaliate only against the aggressor's cities. Deterrence Only, on the other hand, accepted the fact that strategic forces *could* bomb military forces, but held that we *should* threaten to respond to a nuclear attack only by bombing cities, and that we *should* leave our own cities undefended. It was remarkable not only for its extreme departure from humane ethics, but also because it represented a 180-degree turn by many of its main proponents, who, for nearly a decade before they adopted this dogma, had proposed using nuclear weapons only against military targets—in continental defense against invading bombers, against ground forces in Europe, and against combat ships at sea—and who had recommended immense deep-shelter programs for civil defense. Deterrence Only was an extreme minority view at the time of Enthoven's writing. After the Cuban missile crisis, it became an established ideology.

It was in a speech at Ann Arbor, Michigan, in June 1962 that Robert McNamara made public that, in a nuclear war growing out of a major attack on NATO, our main goal would be to destroy enemy military forces, not civilians. He added that we could reserve enough power to destroy the enemy's society, "if driven to it," and that threat would give him "the strongest imaginable incentive to refrain from striking our own cities." (This last resort, which some moralists questioned at the time, I believe was unnecessary: the Soviets have the strongest incentives to preserve their military power.) The part of McNamara's speech about restricting, so far as feasible, the use of strategic forces to military rather than civilian targets, was embedded in statements stressing that American military force was designed only to discourage aggression, not to change the status quo and never to initiate a war; and that the United States was reducing reliance on nuclear weapons in general and wanted to discourage their spread.

Despite these cautions, his speech produced a strikingly negative response from conservatives as well as liberals both here and abroad, and from keepers of the traditional morality of "just war." McNamara's harsh didactic style can hardly explain it. Rather, a certain ambivalence about, if not affection for, nuclear terror had become nearly universal. Franz Josef Strauss, then West German Defense Minister, made clear that he continued to believe that deterrence depended on threatening the immediate use of tactical nuclear weapons at the battle line, to be followed quickly by massive strategic retaliation. Senator Richard Russell and Senator Margaret Chase Smith, Democratic and Republican stalwarts respectively on the Senate Armed Services Committee, denounced McNamara's statement. Some scientists and engineers, who had only recently, in the aftermath of Sputnik, turned to relying on threats to bomb cities and away from advocating the use of nuclear weapons against military forces and from massive continental defense and deep-shelter programs, now pronounced any ability to attack military forces or to defend cities to be "destabilizing." With a rancor suggesting a bad conscience, they said that the very modest Kennedy fallout-shelter program, and the new official focus on military targets rather than massive retaliation, might influence American leaders to initiate preventive nuclear war. This, though members of the administration had abundantly stated the very opposite and had explicitly recognized that any nuclear war would be an "unprecedented catastrophe."

* * * * *

It was plainly silly to suppose that American political leaders
would be eager to unleash such an unprecedented catastrophe
simply because it might not be total. The reaction was all the
more striking since neither these critics nor anyone else had
ever suggested that the much more costly and supposedly more
effective programs the critics had been backing a few years earlier
(for nearly leakproof air defenses, a thick ballistic-missile defense
of population as well as of strategic forces, extensive deep shelters
for civilians, and the limitation of nuclear weapons to legitimate
military targets) would induce American leaders to undertake
preventive war. All in all, the venomous response, including that
of the media, was shallow, partisan, and, not infrequently, in
bad faith. Such venom unfortunately continues to poison current
debate as to whether there is an alternative to suicide or surrender.
It takes great civic courage to sustain that burden and, in the
détente that started after the missile crisis, the administration
did not show such courage. Nonetheless, every one of the last six
Secretaries of Defense has found it essential both to rely less on
nuclear weapons and to return to the subject of the limited use of
long- as well as short-range nuclear forces against military targets.
Much of Paul Ramsey's work on "just war" (brought together in
The Just War: Force and Political Responsibility, 1968) is related to
such a policy.

Ramsey's answer to Tucker states that the conduct of a nuclear
war need not—and, if it is to be moral, must not—"violate the
moral immunity of noncombatants from direct attack." Any harm
to noncombatants should at least be unintended. He implies,
moreover, that the conduct of nuclear war should involve a serious
effort to minimize such unintended damage. If he had been more
aware of the possibilities implicit in the electronic revolution, he
might have added that research and development need to aim
at improving the ability to discriminate. He insists that attacks
should not only attempt to discriminate but that the unintended
damage should be proportionate to any good that would come
out of the war.

In a chapter on "The Limits of Nuclear War," Ramsey
considers what actions in a nuclear war are "undoable" even if
they are "thinkable." He notes that McNamara's announcement
at Ann Arbor that our main aim in responding to an attack on the
Alliance should be to destroy the enemy's forces, not his civilian

population, had occasioned hardly a single amen on either side of the Atlantic. The only responses were stereotyped objections from defense establishments here and abroad, and the same from publications like the *Christian Century*, normally regarded as keepers of such a civilized rule. Ramsey proceeds with a brilliant support of such limitation and with a sympathetic but penetrating critique of Thomas Schelling and Herman Kahn, who favored limiting nuclear war, but included under those limits attacks on cities, and who held that it might be rational to threaten such attacks even though it would be irrational to execute them. Limited attacks on military installations and forces are both thinkable and doable, according to Ramsey; but a direct attack on innocent civilians to achieve some other goal, even a good goal, is wrong. Like art, a political action has consequences beyond itself, but, as Aristotle pointed out, an action is also right or wrong in itself. Attacking innocent civilians is wrong even to accomplish something else. Ramsey rejected the use of threats of even limited city attacks.

Enthoven criticized such threats on the ground also that they would not be believed; that policies based on "the rationality of irrationality" (on which Father Hehir and the bishops also rely) are not viable in the long run for a democracy, especially one with allies: "Rather, the most credible kind of threat is the threat that we will do what in the event will be most in our interest to do."

According to Michael Walzer, in *Just and Unjust War*, Ramsey relies on unintended "collateral civilian damage from counterforce warfare in its maximum form to deter potential aggressors." Walzer himself believes that to deter one must intentionally or unintentionally threaten to kill innocents. But Ramsey was not referring in that context to deterrence of the initial outbreak of an aggression. He was talking of the possibility that, *during a war waged against military targets on both sides*, both sides might avoid attacking cities and also avoid a maximum counterforce attack — in order to prevent the collateral damage that would ensue from attacking even military targets that are closely co-located with population centers. That is very different from saying that to deter an initial attack one must threaten civilians — even unintentionally. Nor does selectivity in attacks on military targets *during* a war mean threatening civilians, but rather the opposite. Ramsey did sometimes falter by recommending a "studied ambiguity" about our intentions to retaliate in kind to an attack on cities. Michael Novak's answer to the bishops also finds "the best of the ambiguous but morally good options . . . in a combination of counterforce and countervalue deterrence." Yet even he is affected by the insidious semantics of MAD: "countervalue" suggests the Soviets value only bystanders, not military force. But to deter we need rely neither on unintended harm nor on ambiguous intentions.

IV

McNamara, MAD, and MADCAP

One difficulty in getting the evolution straight of both official doctrines and operational policies on nuclear weapons is that the two have often diverged, and the statements of doctrine have often been designed for political combat within domestic bureaucracies rather than potential combat with the Soviets. McNamara in his first two years as Secretary of Defense sought options between suicide and surrender, according to Stewart Alsop, "as Parsifal sought the Grail." Out of office, he has ended ironically by foreclosing all such options. With an intensity that dims his memory as well as his understanding, he doubts that any nuclear response to nuclear attack can limit destruction.

After the missile crisis, McNamara often talked of Assured Destruction—and later Mutual Assured Destruction—as if they were serious operational policies. Neither was. While Secretary, he never abandoned the goal of using strategic forces against Soviet military forces or the goal of limiting harm to American civilians. Even as declaratory doctrine he never stated MAD in the unqualified and brutal Orwellian form of the aphorism "killing weapons is bad, killing people is good." When he talked about a capability for assured destruction of 20-25 percent of the Soviet population, he was thinking of deterring the Joint Chiefs of Staff from asking for higher budgets rather than the Soviets from attacking the U.S. It was his way, if not the best way, of winning a budget battle and putting a lower ceiling on the size of our strategic forces. He stressed that we would have the capability for destroying the Soviet population—and he expected that capacity to deter the Soviets; but if deterrence failed, we would use our strategic forces to destroy Soviet forces attacking the United States. Later, when he drifted toward regarding it as desirable for the Soviets to deter us, he was still talking about capabilities.

In short, the form of MAD doctrine he introduced can best be described by the acronym MADCAP rather than MAD.

McNamara said we would use a MAD *capability* for deterrence without seriously intending to assure the destruction of enemy noncombatants. Nor was he entirely serious about attacks on combatants. MADCAP did not lead to any persistent thought about how to improve the force to make it increasingly discriminating, and it discouraged thinking about the selection of various theater and other military targets suited to proportionate responses. It led to slowing or stopping various programs that would have increased our ability to discriminate between military and civilian targets. It made us less serious about the problems of nuclear targeting of combatants *or* noncombatants: it avoided some of the obloquy of *seriously* threatening to do the cheap and easy job of killing large "soft" concentrations of civilians without forcing thought about the harder job of carefully selecting and, if necessary, destroying military targets without killing bystanders; or about the hard but feasible and necessary job of keeping violence under control.

The bishops, their defenders, and the strategists on whom they rely all talk of the uncontrollability of nuclear weapons as a deplorable but unavoidable fact of life. However, they make a virtue of this supposed necessity. John Garvey, columnist for the Catholic *Commonweal,* knows that one may not threaten what one does not intend to do, and grants that "if your enemy knows that you will absolutely refuse to use a weapon, what you have is no longer a weapon and is therefore useless"; but he claims that "it would be naive to think that we are so fully in control of ourselves that in the event of an attack we would not say. 'What the hell,' and hit them with everything we've got." Which apparently would give the threat, however immoral, some use as a deterrent.

However, it would be naive or worse to suppose that we cannot impose controls over both initial and subsequent uses of nuclear weapons. "Permissive action links," which we place on all our weapons overseas and which microchips and other electronic advances are constantly improving, can make it essentially infeasible for military commanders to use nuclear weapons without release by a remote political authority. Moreover, if we really thought political authority were reckless, we could make this release mechanism as elaborate as we liked and even divide the releasing codes so that they would require the agreement of many parties. But the processes of consultation in the Alliance are now complex, and would affect not only the initial, but also subsequent releases. It is most unlikely that we would simply say "Whee!" and let everything go. In Europe the problem is quite the opposite. We should not and do not rely on the threat of losing control to deter either nuclear or conventional attack. But MAD and the fictions of uncontrollability it has propagated encourage us to rely on the threat of losing control as a substitute for dealing with the dangers of conventional conflicts. In short, they have led us to be less serious about conventional war as well.

The bishops' strategists, who believe that one can deter even if one is plainly committed never to use nuclear weapons, first, second, or ever, would maintain a capability but never use nuclear weapons at all. McNamara, when he changed from the doctrine of his first two years to talk of capabilities for mutual assured destruction, said he would maintain the capability to kill Russian civilians but would actually use nuclear weapons against certain military targets. That's rather different. Nonetheless it was a long step on the way to the present absurdities and evasions of the moral and prudential problems of discouraging a nuclear attack on the U.S. or one of its allies. Or a conventional attack.

Soviet Values and MAD Nuclear Threats to Deter Conventional Attack

Michael Walzer writes perceptively about the use of terror by guerrillas to provoke counterterror against innocents. But when it comes to nuclear weapons, he accepts the MAD stereotype about the use of threats of terror against innocents to deter attack. He doesn't question the technical determinism of the nuclear technologists that limiting harm to civilians on either side is impossible. He advances comfortably the familiar paradox about "the monstrous immorality that our policy contemplates" but thinks it inevitable. "The unavoidable truth is that all of these policies rest ultimately on immoral threats." Like Tucker, Walzer is unwilling to give up immoral threats because he thinks they are necessary for deterrence. Here he rests on the baseless judgment that the *only* thing that will deter Soviet aggression is the prospect that Russian bystanders will be killed.

To reject that view one need not assume that Soviet values are the same as our own; nor that the Soviets are simply monsters who don't care or even like to see civilians killed. We need only observe that the Soviets value military power and the means of domination at least as much and possibly more than the lives of Russian civilians. This is surely evidenced by a long history documented by careful scholars like Adam Ulam, Robert Conquest, Nikolai

Tolstoy, and many others, in which the Soviets have sacrificed civilian lives for the sake of Soviet power. Their collectivization program in the 1920's gained control over the peasants at the expense of slaughtering some 12-15 million of them. (Stalin told Churchill that the great bulk of 10 million kulaks had to be wiped out or transferred to Siberia.) The Soviet government sharply increased grain exports during the famine year of 1933, when 5 million Ukrainian peasants were dying. If Robert Conquest is right, the Great Purge of the late 1930's killed several million more Soviet citizens. If Nikolai Tolstoy is right, Stalin and the NKVD were responsible for more than half of the 20-30 million deaths suffered by the Soviets during World War II. Soviet refusal to abide by the Geneva Convention on Prisoners of War doomed many additional Soviet as well as German prisoners.

Whatever else one may say of these actions, they do not suggest that Soviet leaders value the life of Russian citizens above political and military power. If the West responded to Soviet military attack by destroying military targets, it would affect something on which Soviet leaders continue to lavish a huge part of their painfully scarce resources and which they appear to cherish quite as much as they do Russian citizens; and the prospects of such a Western response would be the best deterrent to their initiating war. Moreover, continued attacks during a war on elements of their military power and means of domination would appear to be the best way to bring the war to a rapid close. Prudence does not force us to rely for deterrence on even *unintended* damage done to civilians. Discrimination remains an important goal during the war—and an important capability to achieve in advance of the war. It helps deter the war or bring it to an end.

But Walzer believes that "counterpopulation deterrence" is basic. He also believes it is perfectly effective. It "rules out" (i.e., makes so unlikely as to be negligible) any nuclear war between the great powers; even though the Soviets know we believe that nuclear attacks on populations would be suicidal, our threat would be sure to deter them. And, typical of his time, he is also quite comfortable about the effectiveness of counterpopulation deterrence for forestalling a conventional invasion. His complacency here parallels that expressed in various British and American magisterial writings of the late 1960's and 1970's. He quotes with approval a passage from Bernard Brodie: "The spectacle of a large Soviet field army crashing across the line into Western Europe in the hope and expectation that nuclear weapons would not be used against it—thereby putting itself and the U.S.S.R. totally at risk while leaving the choice of weapons to us—would seem to be hardly worth a second thought. . . ." One may surmise that if Brodie were alive he would be having second thoughts. Many who wrote that way in the late 1960's and 1970's are less comfortable today, in particular about threatening mutual annihilation as a way of deterring a conventional attack on Western Europe.

* * * * *

McGeorge Bundy illustrates the change in the American establishment. He had chided Henry Kissinger for expressing public doubts on the credibility of American strategy for the protection of West Europe at Brussels in 1979. "American strategy for the protection of West Europe," he was satisfied, was "a classic case of doctrinal confusion and pragmatic success." (He inserted the two words "so far," suggesting he was not completely satisfied.) I cautioned at the time that it would be a great mistake to attribute the pragmatic success to the doctrinal confusion; and Bundy did not disagree. The protest movements in Europe were already visible, for one thing; for another, there were the Soviets, and they might not be confused just because we were. We cannot count on a Mutual Assured Confusion. In any case, Bundy, less confident now about MAD threats to deter conventional invasion, has joined Robert McNamara, George Kennan, and Gerard Smith in proposing that we exchange pledges with the Soviets that neither would be the first to use nuclear weapons. The four stress the No-First-Use pledge much more than any serious and extensive program to improve the size or quality of NATO conventional forces, so that NATO could depend less on nuclear threats to overcome Soviet advantages in the use of conventional force. These advantages have to do not only with the massive and increasing size and quality of the Soviet force, but with the Soviets' geographical position and their relatively improving access to air space and bases near critical areas. Japan and Korea as well as all our European allies are within immediate range of Soviet, but far from the center of American, conventional power. So is Persian Gulf oil on which they all have come to depend.

Indeed, it seems that Bundy and his three co-authors have not really abandoned an implicit threat of the first use of nuclear weapons to make up for our conventional disadvantage. For while the four may *mean* the Western pledge [of no-first-use], they rely on the Soviets not trusting us to live up to our pledge and so continuing to keep their ground forces dispersed and less effective for conventional attack and defense. In short, the policy they advocate resembles the pastoral letter in *explicitly* abandoning a nuclear threat, while implicitly continuing to rely on it. In their case, the threat is implicit in NATO's continued capability to use nuclear weapons first. If their policy led each side to believe the *other's* pledge, the Soviet Union would be more likely to concentrate its conventional force effectively — and safely since, on their recommendation, we would keep our pledge. On the other hand, if we trusted the Soviet pledge, we might concentrate our defenses at the likely points of attack. That would *not* be safe since NATO has no way of enforcing such a Soviet pledge. It seems that the four want neither side to believe the other's pledge. In sum, recommendations for exchanging unenforceable pledges about the first use of nuclear weapons in Europe do not reduce the doctrinal confusion that has been troubling NATO even on the subject of nuclear deterrence of conventional attack. They only alarm West European leaders who continue to rely excessively on nuclear weapons.

Many have observed that the four are rather perfunctory about a program to improve NATO conventional forces — in size, quality, method of deployment, or strategy — which would make it less necessary for European leaders to rely on nuclear weapons by making it more likely we could defeat by conventional means any of several plausible Soviet conventional attacks. They do talk of "maintaining and improving the specifically American conventional forces in Europe" but claim, in the face of much evidence of an unanticipated worsening in our ability to defend Europe's interests in more than one critical area near the Soviet periphery, that we tend to exaggerate Soviet relative conventional strength. And they say we underestimate "Soviet awareness of the enormous costs and risks of any form of aggression against NATO" — which is to rely covertly on the threat of first use of nuclear weapons that they overtly abjure.

* * * * *

Recently Bundy and McNamara have joined Cyrus Vance and Elmo Zumwalt in a letter to the Congressional Budget Committees calling for large cuts in the administration's FY '84-

FY '89 defense budget—with two-thirds of the dollars cut coming out of conventional programs. Like some drafts of the pastoral letter warning that an "upward spiral even in conventional arms may lead to war," and saying that "we do not in any way want to . . . [make] 'the world safe for conventional war,' which introduces its own horrors," their budget letter warns of the dangers of "spurring the arms race." What is more, the conventional arms cuts it recommends are squarely incompatible with reduced reliance on the early first use of nuclear weapons or indeed with any coherent view of potential critical conventional conflicts. It plans for only a short conventional war, cutting in half the program for increasing the number of days of stocks of "modern conventional munitions" in Europe. But it would cancel the C-5B program for rapid airlift and depend much more on the comparatively slow sealift that would be important in a long conventional war. It would focus the Navy largely on the defense of the sea lines of communication in the North Atlantic, yet drastically cut Navy programs important for defending these sea lines, such as those permitting long-range precise conventional attacks on the Soviet naval air bases from which Backfire bombers could menace both the sea lines and ships defending them.

I do not doubt the earnestness of the authors' desire for a more than nominal decrease in NATO's reliance on nuclear weapons. I can testify that Robert McNamara's interest goes back at least twenty-two years. I was his representative on the Acheson Committee which drafted the National Security Council decision formally to end the U.S. policy of massive retaliation in the spring of 1961. That decision called for raising the nuclear threshold by preparing a capability to defeat at its own level all but a very massive conventional attack; and the use of nuclear weapons only if our increased conventional force did not suffice. But as the stormy reaction to the McNamara doctrine of his first two years indicated, NATO's threats of first use showed its reluctance to spend the resources needed for an adequate conventional defense rather than any convincing willingness actually to use nuclear weapons quickly or at all. Moreover, though McNamara doubted the utility of battlefield nuclear weapons, to quiet the political storm he did not resist sending several thousand more tactical nuclear weapons to Europe, making a stockpile there of 7,000. And contrary to his recent memory, he increased our total stock of nuclear weapons until it reached its peak in his last year as Secretary. When six years after the Acheson Report the Europeans

587

did agree to "flexible response," it was a grudging compromise—agreeing on the need for improved conventional forces but insisting that the main defense would be nuclear. That tended to undercut the seriousness with which they or we attended to the problem of improving NATO's conventional ability to defend itself against conventional attack.

Carl Kaysen, McGeorge Bundy's former deputy as National Security Adviser, in his influential contribution to the 1968 Brookings study, *Agenda for the Nation*, contemplated a No-First-Use pledge, but also called for large cuts in defense including the halving of U.S. ground forces in Germany. Senator Mark Hatfield and Senator William Proxmire, eager to freeze nuclear weapons then as now, led the battle to cut conventional arms. All that may seem bizarre, but it is not. The wave of "study groups" that deplored "exaggerations" of the Soviet build-up and the supposed spiraling of U.S. strategic budgets that forced the Soviets unwillingly to follow our lead, continued to set national priorities toward more social spending. But not much social spending could be got out of strategic budgets. They had been spiraling not up but down at 8 percent a year. By the early 1970's, they were less than 1 percent of GNP, and by FY '76, less than one-half of 1 percent. The Soviet deployment of ICBM's, SLBM's, and heavy and medium bombers averaged twice as great as the "greater-than-expected" threat predicted by Defense Secretaries for ten years starting with Secretary McNamara. Now, once more with program cuts in mind, the Bundy *et al.* budget letter talks of "greater-than-expected" threats and, like the bishops, resurrects the old apparition of our spurring an arms race by doing too much.

From the beginning of the 1960's to the late 1970's, the U.S. and all its major allies, while prattling about a U.S.-driven arms race, halved defense budgets in percent of GNP, while the Soviets steadily spent more in real terms for conventional as well as nuclear forces. As a result, NATO found itself continuing to rely on the early and first use of nuclear weapons, while the "correlation of forces" was changing so as to make that less convincing than ever before.

If the anti-nuclear movement in West Europe has served any useful function at all, it has done so by making responsible West Europeans more aware of the recklessness of depending on apocalyptic nuclear threats to meet conventional attacks. And given Europe's economic problems, key Western leaders are forced to think not merely of multiplying brute numbers but also of exploiting the new intelligent technologies to increase the effectiveness of the resources used. Such an effort has been hampered up to now by a kind of Luddite and moralistic resistance to qualitative improvement and by a particular antipathy to technologies that improve the possibility of discrimination and choice.

* * * * *

Moralists who have chosen to emphasize the shallow paradoxes associated with deterrence by immoral threats against population have been at their worst when they have opposed any attempts to improve the capability to attack targets precisely and discriminately. While they have thought of themselves as aiming their opposition at the dangers of bringing on nuclear mass destruction, they have often stopped research and engineering on ways to destroy military targets without mass destruction; and they have done collateral damage to the development of precise, long-range conventional weapons. (Junior Congressmen like Thomas Downey and Edward Markey, who had their fun with talk of *Star Wars* in March, might have benefited from observing that Luke Skywalker used one accurately placed weapon to destroy the indiscriminately destructive Death Star. And with advanced terminal guidance we need not rely on "The Force.") They have tried to stop, and have slowed, the development of technologies which can free us from the loose and wishful paradoxes involved in efforts to save the peace with unstable threats to terrorize our own as well as adversary civilians.

The events leading to the destruction of German and Japanese cities in World War II offer parallels. British scientists, when the menace of Hitler overcame their natural distaste for arms research, formed a Committee for the Scientific Study of Air Defense which backed Watson Watts's development of radar for the defense of Britain. Their distaste was not overcome enough for them to support as energetically the Committee for the Scientific Study of Air Offense, whose work was quite desultory. The lag in developing radar for navigation and bombing, however, did not prevent the bombing of German targets. It only assured that the raids would destroy more German civilians. Some blame lies with the Royal Air Force's failure to improve accuracy in the period between the wars. Marshall Trenchard, relying on the special experience of strategic bombing in clear weather against undefended targets in Iraq, thought British accuracy in general excellent. In 1928 he argued, "What is illegitimate, as being contrary to the dictates of humanity, is the indiscriminate bombing of a city for the sole purpose of terrorizing the civilian population." Citing the draft code of rules for air war drawn up at the Hague in 1922-23, he held that air attacks were legitimate—"provided all reasonable care is taken to confine the scope of the bombing to the military objective. . . ." But he hardly took reasonable care to improve discriminateness *before* the war. (A minor fault, compared to that of religious strategists who testified to Congress *against* "targeting systems that minimize collateral damage to civilian life" and against any defense of U.S. civilians.) Trenchard's opposite numbers in the British Army and Navy had doubted that the state of accuracy in 1928 would permit either the effectiveness or the discrimination that Trenchard claimed. During World War II, when he found how poor its aim was, Trenchard advised that if Bomber Command missed its intended targets it would still kill Germans and so do good work.

Declaratory doctrine for the American defense of Europe started in the 1950's with the belief that strategic and tactical nuclear weapons could replace the conventional firepower which our NATO allies hesitated to supply against conventional invasion. It went through a phase in which many of the present advocates of MAD entertained exaggerated hopes for limiting the harm done by the large-scale use of tactical nuclear weapons on European battlefields; and for using massive active and civil defense, limiting to quite small amounts the damage done by a large raid on U.S. cities. When their hopes began to seem excessive, they switched to the view that the *threat* of unlimited mutual destruction was actually good, since it was nearly sure to deter even a conventional invasion. The last year or two have seen signs of a renewed serious interest in improving NATO's ability to meet a conventional invasion in Europe on its own terms. Manfred Woerner, the current Minister of Defense in the German Federal Republic, has set forth a program which is designed not only to discourage a Soviet conventional invasion, but to do it responsibly in a way that will also put to rest the growing West German anti-nuclear movement. He would exploit the advanced technologies that are coming to be available for that purpose.

Woerner's view stands in contrast to that of his predecessor, who held that even a conventional war in Europe would be "the end of Europe," and that it was essential that tactical nuclear weapons be used quickly but only as a link to the "intercontinental exchange" — which would be "the end of the world." But anyone who relies on such threats to deter a conventional attack is likely to threaten up to the last minute and then, when it would have become clear that the Soviets did not believe that NATO leaders would consciously bring on the end of Europe and then the end of the world, rush to reassure the Soviets that they did not really mean to execute the "threat." Such a policy, Herman Kahn accurately labeled "preemptive surrender." It differs from the policy advocated by West Germany's party of the Greens in the anti-nuclear movement who would make their accommodation with the Soviets now, in time of peace, safely in advance of a threatened Soviet attack. Pierre Hassner has characterized the difference between the leaders of the anti-nuclear movement and some leading figures in the West European establishment who rely on suicidal threats: it is the difference between "preventive surrender" and "preemptive surrender."

V

Deterring Nuclear Attack on an Ally

Bundy, McNamara, Kennan, and Smith have lost their faith in suicidal threats as a way of deterring a conventional invasion. They believe in the necessity and adequacy of such threats to deter nuclear attacks. However, a hope that an adversary can be safely deterred by our threat to blow him up along with ourselves, is unfounded not only for a conventional attack but also for a *nuclear* attack on the ally.

Consider a strategically placed ally like Norway with an American nuclear guarantee and no nuclear weapons of its own. How would a capability to destroy Soviet civilians, along with American civilians and possibly the civilization of Europe itself, discourage Soviet use of nuclear weapons against military targets in the course of an attack aimed at seizing the sparsely populated but strategic northernmost counties of Norway? No one — no Norwegian, no American leader, and no Soviet leader — would seriously expect us to respond to such an attack by consciously initiating the killing of 100 million or so innocent Soviet civilians and a corresponding number of Americans and/or West Europeans. That is one reason why some believers in

591

MAD are explicitly *for* threats and *against* their execution. But a capability which plainly will never be used to initiate a chain of events we believe would lead to the end of civilization will terrify an adversary no more than a capability that would destroy half, or a tenth, or a millionth the number of civilians, or no civilians at all. The only way weapons can inspire concern is by the likelihood that they will be used. The residual fear that the West might deliberately blow up the world tends to terrify some in our own elites much more than the Soviets who chatter less on this subject.

The Incoherence of "Deterrence Only" Even for Deterring Nuclear Attack on Oneself

Dogmas of "Minimum Deterrence" and "Deterrence Only" had their origins in the late 1950's in the writings of General Pierre Gallois. Gallois believed that nuclear weapons spelled the end of alliance: no nuclear guarantee to a non-nuclear ally was credible since no nation would commit suicide for another. His version of Minimum Deterrence formed the center of his justification for the spread of nuclear weapons to any nation, even very small ones that wanted protection against nuclear attack or coercion. Initial American variants of the Minimum-Deterrence doctrine in 1958 cited some of Gallois's principal arguments and the calculations he had designed in order to prove the necessity for targeting cities rather than opposing military forces; and some 1958 American writings on Minimum Deterrence recommended distributing Polaris submarines to NATO allies to replace the American guarantee. However, the incoherence of the Deterrence Only view is thorough and applies to deterring an attack on oneself. If it is true that a nation will not commit suicide for another, neither can it commit suicide to assure its own survival. Suicidal threats are *in general* not a reliable means of dissuasion.

Yet the total separation of threat from any possibility of execution has been common in establishments abroad as well as here, even among those who would maintain the Alliance. A former associate director of that pillar of the European establishment, the International Institute of Strategic Studies (IISS), talked in much the way Father Hehir does. Father Hehir holds that nuclear weapons exist "to be not used; their purpose is to threaten, not to strike." Ian Smart, then of IISS, has said that "nuclear weapons are exclusively destined to deter" and suggested that only certain misguided American hawks view them "as reasonable and effective" for fighting. An instrument that destiny or purpose plainly made unreasonable and ineffective for actual use, and thus sure to remain unused, could hardly deter. It would make war more likely, not less.

William O'Brien's 1981 book, *The Conduct of Just and Limited War,* while a painstakingly honest and informed inquiry into the circumstances in which war is justified and into its discriminate and proportionate conduct in a wide range of historical conflicts, is less incisive on MAD. He gives a little credence to the possibility that at least a one-sided abandonment of the threat against innocents might be destabilizing, and, though he is aware of the possibilities, he appears to underestimate the actual progress in technologies that gives us a choice between destroying military targets and destroying innocents. However, he is right on the mark in his more recent writings answering the Deterrence Only version of the pastoral letter proposed by Father Hehir and the Jesuit Father Francis Winters.

O'Brien is blunt about the insanity of deception labeling itself deception, as does the doctrine of Deterrence Only. Father Winters has an enthusiastic explication of the pastoral letter as opting "with notable casuistic ingenuity for possession of the strategic arsenal along with renunciation of the intention to employ it." O'Brien responds that, "given the centrality of credibility to deterrence . . . this proposition is insane. What is needed is not casuistic ingenuity, but a serious commitment to face the dilemmas of nuclear deterrence without recourse to escapist diversions."

As for Father Hehir, he is aware of but troubled by the fact that some nuclear weapons are less destructive than some conventional ones. He has argued on the basis of "psychological criteria" that we may continue to threaten to use nuclear weapons but should ban their actual use because he wants to solidify in our minds the dangers of crossing the gap between conventional and nuclear weapons. He wants to set up a psychological barrier against *our* ever using them. Unfortunately, like the lay strategists who are his model, he is less concerned to set up a psychological barrier against the use of nuclear weapons by our *adversaries.* Assuring them that we would never use nuclear weapons, even in response to a nuclear attack, cancels the deterrent and, for them, opens up a psychological expressway.

One can see why "casuistry," which once meant dealing with

cases of conscience and the resolution of questions of right or wrong in conduct, acquired a bad name and came to refer to the trivial and false application of moral principles to make things seem like their opposite. The upholders of the bishops' doctrine of "Use, Never" (i.e., No Use—First-Second-Or Ever) seem unaware that an adversary might be concerned not only about the magnitude of the harm we threaten but about the likelihood that we will inflict it.

However, it is a familiar fact of everyday life that we consider implicitly in our behavior not only the size of the assorted catastrophes we might conceivably face when we get up each morning but also their likelihood. Blizzards in August might find us peculiarly unequipped to survive them. So also sunstroke in December. Neither bothers us much, nor leads us to wear furs in summer and carry parasols in winter. Even when we face adversaries and not merely environmental dangers, we have a way of arraying threats according to the probability that they will be carried out and not only in terms of the damage they would do if they were. When a threatener can execute a terrible threat to us with little harm to himself, we worry more than when he would suffer at least as much as we would. Moreover, when a threatener, who expects to destroy himself and his allies along with the aggressor, says that he has no intention whatsoever and, in fact, would regard it as immoral to execute his threat, this can only be reassuring to a potential aggressor. It is an invitation rather than a deterrent. Somehow it does not occur to those who hope to deter by a suicidal threat (which they loudly proclaim they will never execute) that they may be doing the opposite of deterring. Their policy is—to use that dread catchword—"destabilizing."

Soviet leaders who were not deterred by a threat they knew would never be executed would not, as Cardinal Krol suggests, have to be insane. It seems more nearly insane, as O'Brien says, to hold that in all circumstances, even during a stalled conventional invasion when all alternatives looked risky to them, the Soviets would be deterred "beyond question" from using nuclear weapons by our self-confessed suicidal bluff. Nonetheless, the doctrine of "Use, Never" advanced by the bishops merely makes more explicit the operational meaning of secular strategies of Deterrence Only. The Stanford physicist, Sidney Drell, recently has repeated the standard jumble about deterrence and fighting: instead of observing that our *threat* to fight back will dissuade an opponent only if he thinks we are able and if necessary willing to fight back, Drell says deterring and fighting are incompatible goals.

*****

Deterrence only focuses on deterring Western responses rather than Soviet attacks. It assumes that it is really the West, and especially the United States, in its misunderstanding of the Soviets, that menaces the nuclear peace and not the Soviets. This is an assumption widely held, even by those who oppose the disarmers. Michael Howard of Oxford tells us that the Soviets are entirely satisfied with the present division of Europe and that only Western extremists are not. He grants that the Soviets would revise the rest of the world, but doesn't notice that in that process they might effectively alter the division of power within West Europe too. It would be hard for the Soviet Union to avoid altering the division of power in Europe, even if unintentionally, if it seized some future opportunity to satisfy its long expressed interest in expanding toward the Persian Gulf and the Eastern Mediterranean. (England is said to have acquired its empire in a fit of absentmindedness.) Moreover, from the Soviet point of view, the destruction of the Western alliance that would result would surely be a bonus in defense of Soviet Western borders. George Kennan draws rather more satisfaction than is warranted from Soviet paranoid defensiveness. Paranoids can be dangerous.

But Michael Howard isn't terribly worried about the Soviets beginning a war. He worries about Americans. Though he has been subject to attack by E. P. Thompson and the nuclear disarmers, he sometimes sounds a little like them. He says: "Whether I could encounter the same phenomenon in the Soviet Union, I do not know. But wars begin in the minds of men, and in many American minds the flames of war seem already to have taken a very firm hold." And: "When I hear some of my American friends speak of that country [the Soviet Union], when I note how their eyes glaze over, their voices drop an octave, and they grind out the words '*the Soviets*' in tones of gravelly hatred, I become really frightened; far more frightened than I am by the nuclear arsenals themselves or the various proposals for their use." I know some of Howard's American friends (indeed have counted myself as one), but none resembling that description. If such glazed-eyed monsters controlled the U.S. arsenal, instead of planning proportionate Western responses that might credibly discourage Soviet attack, the West might focus its attention entirely on stopping us and let the credibility of U.S. guarantees erode.

Unfortunately, the reactions to the President's speech of March 23 on protecting civilians showed that the view of some Americans, indeed of some former Cabinet officers firmly attached to MAD doctrine, resembles that of Michael Howard. These Americans, like their British counterparts, may deplore the "oversimple" view of Soviet leaders which they attribute to American "hawks." But when seized by MAD dogmas their view of U.S. leaders is more outrageously simple. They suppose American leaders to be so wantonly unconcerned about the unprecedented catastrophe of nuclear war that they are very likely to start one in any grave crisis. Anyone professing to believe that finds it even easier to believe that an American President would casually unleash nuclear war if he thought that American civil society had some substantial protection. But it is absurd to think that American *or Soviet* leaders are straining at the nuclear leash.

* * * * *

Former Defense Secretary Harold Brown answered the President with a variant of the fantasy that American hawks are likely to unleash nuclear war if they think the U.S. has a fair chance of coming out gravely but not totally ruined. The bishops cite him in support of their view that there is "an overwhelming probability that a nuclear exchange would have no limits." While in office, Brown was torn between, on the one hand, the view forced upon him by evidence that Soviet arms had been going up while ours went down and, on the other hand, the view that *both* superpowers are engaged in a spiraling build-up incapable of yielding either side the ability to fight, to coerce, or even to gain some political advantage. Thus "the Soviets have as great an interest and should have as great an interest in strategic arms limitations as we do." And he oscillated between the MAD dogma that all either side needs is to be able to destroy the other as a "functioning modern society" — an implicit pact for mutual suicide — and the recognition embodied in Presidential Directive 59 that the Soviets have made no such pact and shown no desire to make any possible Soviet attack an act of suicide. Like Hamlet (and McNamara) he is "but MAD north-northwest; when the wind is southerly, he knows a hawk from a handsaw." But now the political winds blow more from the north and Brown's American leaders are amazingly susceptible to clever briefers:

> Deterrence must leave no doubt that an all-out nuclear
> war would destroy the nation — and the leadership — that
> launched it. Realistically we must contemplate deploy-
> ments by both superpowers, investing huge amounts in
> such defensive systems. If a clever military briefer, in a
> time of grave crisis, with such systems in place, can per-
> suade the political decision-makers that the defensive
> systems, operating together with other strategic forces,
> had a reasonable chance to function well enough to re-
> sult in even a severely damaged "victor," the scene will
> have been set for the ultimate disaster.

One might suppose that leaders on either side might be given pause
if they thought that *they* would be completely destroyed even if
the nation were not. But evidently the American leaders Brown
contemplates wouldn't mind that and would be easily swayed
by a military briefer who told them that the nation would have a
reasonable chance of coming out only "severely damaged."

The United States could have launched a nuclear attack on
the Soviet Union during any of several crises that came up while
we had nuclear weapons and they did not. For example, we had
50 nuclear weapons and they had none in 1948 at the time of
the Berlin crisis. It would not have taken a very clever military
briefer to convince our leadership that the United States would
not be destroyed by a nuclear attack in 1948. Yet since McNamara
introduced the notion that it was very important for the U.S. that
the Soviets be able to threaten the U.S. with annihilation of its
cities, the absurdities implicit in MAD have become gospel even
with intelligent men like Harold Brown.

The United States never seriously considered an attack on the
Soviets when it had a nuclear monopoly; nor for many years after,
while Soviet nuclear forces were extremely vulnerable. The idea
that it would launch nuclear aggression now is a fantasy worthy
only of the conspiracy theorists in the disarmament movement.
Nor should we take seriously the idea that the Soviets tremble in
fear that the United States might launch a nuclear attack simply
because it had deployed some defense of innocent bystanders.

Many analyses in the 1960's related the use of our strategic
forces to the objective of limiting harm done to ourselves and our
allies in case deterrence should fail; and they related deterring an

adversary to the ability to harm him *if* we responded. McNamara's Annual Posture Statements after the missile crisis, for example, tended to treat these two aims as independent. However, the separation misconstrues the problem of deterring. In a war, when all alternatives may be extremely risky to an adversary, we may not convince him that the alternative of nuclear attack is riskier than the others if we have persuaded him also that it can be done safely because we won't retaliate for fear of the unlimited harm we would bring on ourselves. We only complete the absurdity and undermining of deterrence when we *say* that we have no intention to fight, that is, to use nuclear weapons if deterrence fails. Unfortunately, the principle of deterrence and the principle of "Use, Never" mutually annihilate each other.

VI

Declaring — or telling oneself — that one does not really mean to use nuclear weapons if deterrence fails is one way of stilling uneasiness about threatening to kill innocents in order to deter. Another standard way of softening guilt is to say that the West should continue to raise such a threat even implicitly only if it is making serious progress toward the total elimination of nuclear weapons. That, however, does not lie solely within the West's power. It depends on others who have or may acquire nuclear weapons, and in particular it depends on the disposition of the deeply suspicious, hostile leadership of the Soviet Union.

For a brief time in the immediate aftermath of Hiroshima, some Western leaders talked fervently about world government and the need to sacrifice national sovereignties to assure world peace. British Prime Minister Clement Attlee invoked "an act of faith" by the United States, the United Kingdom, and other nations, and "a new valuation of what are called national interests." Secretary of War Henry L. Stimson "spoke continuously about a way to use nuclear energy for other things 'than killing people' " and of "the changed relation of man to his universe." It is easy to understand and sympathize with their initial emotional reaction to the enormous destruction released at Hiroshima and to feel their disappointment as Soviet behavior made evident that such hopes were utopian. But thirty-eight years later, the utopian hopes expressed by Jonathan Schell and others are more obviously groundless. Since then, Soviet behavior has made clear many times that Soviet versions of utopia differ from our own.

The Soviets see the lasting independence of Western democracies side by side with their own system as a permanent danger to its maintenance, not to say its expansion toward an international utopia. Meanwhile, there is little evidence that some plausible arrangement would lead them to surrender so powerful an instrument of coercion or defense. That, after all, was indicated in their rejection of the Baruch-Acheson-Lilienthal plan for international control of atomic energy. Stalin exhibited none of the anguish sincerely felt by Western leaders and none of their momentary hopes for a world authority governing Communist and non-Communist nations side by side. The contrast of his private view with that of Western leadership is illustrated by the accounts of such privileged and reliable witnesses as Milovan Djilas: "He spoke of the A-bomb. 'That is a powerful thing, power-ful!' His expression was full of admiration. . . ."

Nor have Soviet leaders since Stalin shown any lesser awareness of the value of nuclear weapons as an implicit or explicit means of intimidation in a hostile world they do not dominate. Their value is only enhanced by the contrasting Western scruples on the same subject. If Western political as well as religious leaders take Western possession of nuclear weapons as justified only if there is progress toward agreement with the Russians to eliminate them altogether, they place in Soviet hands the decision as to whether the West will continue to maintain a nuclear deterrent.

Not all differences are negotiable. Pretending that they are suggests a willingness to disarm unilaterally — either because the Soviets prevent agreement or because they agree only to a disarmament which would be purely nominal for them but real for the West. The Greens in West Germany look forward to the total elimination of nuclear weapons and their immediate withdrawal from Eastern and Western Europe. They are not noted for their realism. However, they reject Reagan's zero option for intermediate nuclear forces in Europe as "unrealistic," even though it would seem to be a substantial step on the way to their own goal. Petra Kelly and Manon Maren-Griesbach, two of their principal leaders, explain that the zero option is "unrealistic" because the Russians would never agree to it. It is therefore "not even an honest step toward arms reduction." But the inconsistency of the Greens and their willingness to see the West accommodate to an unwavering Soviet aim to increase Soviet advantage does not differ substantially from many in the West who complain that the American government has not been able to convince the *Soviets* that we are sincere.

Paul Ramsey has understood very well what was involved in Western tendencies to take agreement with adversaries as an absolute essential. He questions the "omnicompetence of negotiation" and observes about some statements in *Pacem in Terris* that there can be hope in negotiations only if these proceed "from inner conviction" that, if such statements mean that "the way to conduct negotiations is not to permit them to fail," then for any single nation to adopt that way of negotiating would mean "its premature surrender. . . . It takes two to negotiate in any such fashion."

* * * * *

The view of the present administration on this subject is, at best, mixed and sometimes lacks conviction. The President has said "it takes two to tango." But when *The New York Times* editorialist, who apparently thinks the impulse for social dancing is universal, said "So Tango!," and when the American Catholic bishops proposed negotiating rather than responding to the Soviet build-up, the administration tended mainly to justify its programs as the best way to get agreements. Implicitly, the administration, then, seems to see no escape from the holocaust except by agreeing with the Soviets. But this particular apocalyptic view also has no basis in fact.

We should recognize that utopian hopes for total nuclear disarmament cannot excuse a Western failure to defend its independence soberly without using reckless threats. Unfortunately, our elites now link the phrase "arms control" not only to millennial dreams of early complete nuclear disarmament, but to the strategy of using threats to annihilate cities as a way of deterring attack; and to a perverse myth of the "arms race" that suggests that nuclear war is imminent because our nuclear arms have been spiraling exponentially and will continue to do so unless we limit our objectives to the destruction of a fixed small number of vulnerable population centers. (No one has ever suggested that the only way to avoid an exponential race in conventional arms is to train our fire on villages rather than enemy tanks. But when it comes to nuclear arms our elites will believe almost anything.) That is not the "arms control" Donald Brennan had in mind. "Arms control," as he and the Princeton physicist, Freeman Dyson, have understood it, should aim at the more traditional and more sensible goal of restraining the bombardment of civilians. But the phrase is now loaded with wishful and mistaken prejudices. It suggests that without arms agreements our spending on defense inevitably will rise exponentially and uncontrollably; and that with arms agreements Soviet arms efforts will diminish. Experience for nearly two decades after the Cuban missile crisis illustrates the opposite.

A serious effort to negotiate agreements with the Soviets might enable us to achieve our objectives at lower levels of armaments than might otherwise be possible. (Improved active defenses, as J. Robert Oppenheimer observed, could facilitate such bilateral agreements since they would make us safer from cheating or assaults by third countries.) Being serious about arms agreements, however, is not the same as being desperate. Even without agreements the West is quite able to deter war and defend its independence against a formidable and persistently hostile adversary committed, as the Soviet Union has been, to changing the "correlation of forces" in its favor. The contrary view is deeply pessimistic and ultimately irresponsible, leading easily to treaties and "understandings" which only worsen the situation of the West.

For a serious and indeed sincere pursuit of arms negotiation by the West calls for a sober assessment of how any arrangements contemplated in an agreement are likely to affect the West's long-term objectives of security and independence, and its intermediate objective of redressing the balance which worsened during the period of détente. These are not merely technical matters. The actual results of arms negotiations have, in the past, contrasted sharply with our expectations and desires. The negotiations of the last two decades started with Western expectations that the agreements achieved would reduce arms spending on both sides without any change in the balance. We assumed that the Soviets, like ourselves, had, as a principal objective, the desire to reduce the percentage of their resources devoted to arms spending and that they would choose "arms control" rather than arms competition. The record plainly shows that Western assumptions were wishful. The Soviets pursued arms agreements as a method of limiting Western spending—which did decline as a proportion of GNP by nearly half in the period after the missile crisis—while they themselves steadily increased their spending and did succeed in changing the balance. Now the West has the problem of catching up and that is especially hard to negotiate.

* * * * *

Serious negotiations today must recognize the limits to what they can accomplish. We and the Soviets share an interest in avoiding mutual suicide, an interest which each of us will pursue whether or not we reach genuine agreement in various understandings and formal treaties. But the Soviets also have interests in expanding their influence and control and, in the process, destabilizing the West, if necessary by the use of external force rather than simply by manipulating internal dissension. Arms agreements might temper, but are unlikely to eliminate, this reality. In particular, there seems scant basis to hope for major economies in our security effort through negotiated limits or reductions.

Experience suggests that when the Soviets agree to close off one path of effort, they redirect their resources to other projects posing differing but no lesser dangers. On the other hand, many of the ostensible goals of arms agreements are best achieved through measures which we can and should implement on our own. Our current efforts — which a freeze would stop — to design and deploy nuclear weapons which are more accident-proof and more secure against theft or unauthorized use, are a good example. Measures to improve the safety, security, and invulnerability of nuclear weapons can be implemented by both sides individually because they make sense for each side independently of formal treaties or elaborate verification measures. These need not mean a net increase in the numbers or destructiveness of nuclear weapons in our stockpile. The United States has already greatly reduced both the megatonnage and the numbers of its nuclear weapons. It recently removed 1,000 weapons from Europe and has said that if, in accordance with NATO's decision in 1979, it installs 572 intermediate-range nuclear missiles, it will withdraw an equal number of warheads. If we increase precision further, we can drastically further reduce the number and destructiveness of our nuclear weapons. Increased precision can also improve the effectiveness of conventional weapons so that they may increasingly replace nuclear brute force. And it would improve our ability to avoid the unintended bombing of innocents with nuclear or conventional warheads. It would enlarge rather than foreclose our freedom to choose.

But many strategists in our foreign-policy establishment prefer to foreclose choice. The orthodox view, expressed by editors of our magazines dealing with foreign affairs, liberal Senators, scientists, and many former officials, holds that any use of nuclear weapons by us will almost surely end in a disaster leaving almost everybody dead or worse than dead; yet that we should have no alternative other than to threaten the bombing of cities; and that we should therefore make clear to our adversaries and allies that we will never fight a nuclear war. Anyone who holds that as the true faith will want to believe that he has no other choice. If he cannot say, like Flip Wilson, "The Devil made me do it," he can introduce the *deus ex machina* of technology: Nuclear Technology makes me do it. He is likely to be outraged by any heretic who dares suggest we might have choices.

The grand inquisitors on the Senate Foreign Relations Committee had Kenneth Adelman on the rack recently during the hearings on his appointment as director of the Arms Control and Disarmament Agency. They probed to find some trace of a doubt in him on the question as to whether we should try to be able to limit nuclear destruction. Dostoevsky would have been fascinated. His Grand Inquisitor, a venerable Jesuit who had had Christ seized on the streets of Seville, argued with the savior that his mistake was not to recognize that men cannot bear the burden of free choice. That's a point on which many in our establishment have impaled themselves.

ENDNOTES - Wohlstetter - Bishops, Statesmen, and Other Strategists

1. In the final version of the article, "80 one-megaton" was printed as "100 one-megaton." Albert Wohlstetter wrote a letter to the journal's editor to correct this error. See Wohlstetter, "Letter to Norman Podhoretz, editor of *Commentary*," June 16, 1983, Albert and Roberta Wohlstetter Papers, Writings, Box 180, Folder 13. — *Zarate*

2. Wohlstetter had intended "after Hiroshima" to be added after the word "immediately." See *ibid*. — *Zarate*

Connecting the Elements of the Strategy:
Excerpt from *Discriminate Deterrence* **(1988)**

From *Discriminate Deterrence,* final report of the Commission on Integrated Long Term Strategy, Washington, DC:U.S. Government Printing Office, January 1988,
pp. 63-69, available from *www.albertwohlstetter.com/
writings/DiscriminateDeterrence.*

The Enduring Aims of U.S. Policy

We live in a world whose nations are increasingly connected
by their economies, cultures, and politics — sometimes explosively
connected as in the repeated vast migrations since World War II
of refugees escaping political, religious, and racial persecution. It
is a world in which military as well as economic power will be
more and more widely distributed and in which the United States
must continue to expect some nations to be deeply hostile to its
purposes.

The United States does not seek to expand its territory at the
expense of the Soviet Union or any other country. Nor do any of
our allies present a danger of an invasion of the Soviet Union or the
territories it dominates. The Soviets, nonetheless, insist that we,
our allies and other countries, the weak as well as the powerful,
do threaten attack. Such Soviet suspicions or assertions have been
inherent in their system of rule: they need to posit a hostile world
to establish the legitimacy of their regime. We would, needless to
say, welcome a basic change in their antagonistic stance.

However, even if *perestroika* and *glasnost* signal an intention
to make that change, it will not be easy to accomplish. Moscow's
suspicion and hostility are rooted in 70 years of Soviet and 400
years of Tsarist history. Relaxing their hold on the countries they
dominate on their borders can threaten their control of dissident
nationalities within their borders. We should not deceive ourselves. The Western democracies cannot do much to advance the
process simply by persuading the Soviets that we are not about
to attack them, or by trying to shed any capability for offense —
and thus for counterattack. Such efforts would merely reflect
misunderstandings of the internal role played by external threats
in Soviet rule; and might encourage aggression. The Soviets feel
threatened by the autonomy of the free countries on their border.

The United States has critical interests in the continuing
autonomy of some allies very distant from us — in Europe and

604

the Mediterranean, in the Middle East and Southwest Asia, in East Asia and the Pacific, and in the Western Hemisphere. We use bases, ports and air space in helping these allies defend themselves and one another. In some cases, where the danger to them from an adversary close by is especially great, it has been a durable element of U.S. strategy to deploy our forces forward. We do this, however, at the invitation of allies who are sovereign and independent of us and on conditions that they name. They can always ask us to leave. In some cases they have; and unlike the Soviets, we have always complied.

The fact that we lead sovereign allies who can differ from us in their interests in various circumstances and places has direct implications for defense; it means that even where there are gathering but ambiguous signs of danger to our common interests, getting a cohesive allied response and bringing it to bear in time to block the danger may be difficult. A dictator, or an involuntary coalition dominated by a dictatorship, has less trouble in preparing to launch military operations. And the Soviets are not, and will not be, the only danger to our interests.

In the changing environment of the next 20 years, the U.S. and its allies, formal and informal, will need to improve their ability to bring force to bear effectively, with discrimination and in time to thwart any of a wide range of plausible aggressions against their major common interests—and in that way to deter such aggressions.

We need to bring a longer view to the necessary day-to-day decisions on national security. The next two decades are likely to exhibit sharp discontinuities as well as gradual changes with effects that are cumulatively revolutionary: major new military powers, new technology, new sources of conflict and opportunities for cooperation. To cope with these changes, we will need versatile and adaptive forces.

An Integrated Strategy

Because our problems in the real world are connected and because budgets compel trade-offs, we need to fit together strategies for a wide range of conflicts: from the most confined, lowest intensity and highest probability to the most widespread, apocalyptic and least likely. We want the worse conflicts to be less likely, but that holds only if our weakness at some higher level—or the lack of a higher level response that democratic leaders would be willing to use—does not invite such raising of the ante. For genuine stability, we need to assure our adversaries that military aggression at any level of violence against our important interest will be opposed by military force.

More violent wars grow out of less violent ones, and locally confined aggression (e.g., a Soviet invasion of the Persian Gulf) could drastically alter the correlation of forces. And one cannot completely separate "internal" and "external" conflicts. The shadow of Soviet intervention could affect the outcome of an internal succession crisis in Iran for example. (In the past the Soviets have used a puppet "Free Azerbaijan" to cloak their preparations for intervention in Iran and Eastern Turkey, which they appear to regard as strategically linked). Even terrorism can have a large effect on our ability to meet greater dangers by destabilizing vulnerable allies, dividing allies from each other, and dividing public opinion at home.

Policy statements on deterring and on fighting aggression should fit together. We cannot dissuade an attacker if he believes we are not willing as well as able to fight back. Our will is called into question by frequent statements about "mutual deterrence" that imply that we want the Soviets to be able to deter the United States unless the United States has been attacked. Such statements undermine the essential pledge that we will use conventional, and if they fail, nuclear weapons in response to a Soviet attack directed solely at an ally. Similarly, the Soviet leadership might be misled by statements, heard in Europe, that even winning a conventional war would be "unacceptable." If such statements mean that fighting with nuclear weapons would do less harm to civilians than precisely delivered conventional weapons, or that such conventional weapons would cause "more harm to civilians than World War II," they are plainly wrong. If they mean that the West would be unwilling to use either non-nuclear or nuclear weapons, then they suggest we would not respond at all and so erode our ability to deter an attack. The issue is about how effectively to deter a non-nuclear or a nuclear attack. We and our allies would rather deter than defeat an aggression, but a bluff is less effective and more dangerous in a crisis than the ability and will to use conventional and, if necessary, nuclear weapons with at least a rough discrimination that preserves the values we are defending.

Offense and defense (both active and passive) complement each other at any level of conflict. Just as our offensive capabilities can discourage an adversary from concentrating to penetrate defenses, so active defense and passive defenses (such as concealment and mobility) are mutually reinforcing.

Decisions on military systems are interconnected and ought not to be dealt with piecemeal. The connections must be reflected in arms negotiations, in force planning and in the definition of military "requirements" during the acquisition process.

The Need to Consider a Wider Range of More Plausible, Important Contingencies

Alliance policy and weapons modernization...have focused largely on the two extreme contingencies of a massive Warsaw Pact conventional attack and an unrestrained Soviet nuclear attack aimed at widespread military targets, doing mortal damage. The first contingency diverts allied attention from obligations underlying the basic premise of the Alliance — that an attack on one possibly vulnerable ally is an attack on all — and it ignores the Soviet interest in inducing other allies to opt out. The second contingency assumes the Soviets would have little concern about inviting their own self-destruction, since it would leave us no incentive to exercise discrimination and restraint.

However, Soviet military planners have shown an awareness that if the Politburo uses military force, it has a strong incentive to do so selectively and keep the force under political control. They do not want their nuclear attack to get in the way of their invading forces or destroy what is being taken over. And above all, they do not want to risk the destruction of the Soviet Union. They recognize as revolutionary for the nature of war the ongoing revolution in microelectronics which makes possible the strategic use of non-nuclear weapons. Their 40 years of investment in protecting their national command system, as well as their careful attention to the wartime uses of space and other means of command and control, show they are serious about directing force for political ends and keeping it under control. If we take the extreme contingencies as the primary basis for planning, we will move less rapidly toward a more versatile, discriminating and controlled capability.

It will always be possible to slip mindlessly toward such an apocalypse, so we will always need to deter the extreme contingencies. But it does not take much nuclear force to destroy a civil society. We need to devote our predominant effort to a wide range of more plausible, important contingencies.

Changes in the Security Environment

Our central challenge since World War II has been to find ways, in formal and informal alliances with other sovereign states, to defeat and therefore deter aggression against our major interests at points much closer to our adversaries than to us. "Military balances," i.e., matching numbers of NATO and Warsaw Pact tanks, guns, anti-tank weapons, etc. (even adjusted for qualitative differences in technology) fail to reveal the problem. The issue is not simply one of distance, but of timely political access en route to and in a threatened area, and of getting cohesive, preparatory responses by sovereign allies in answer to ambiguous signs of gathering danger.

The Atlantic Alliance has a problem of cohesion. In dealing with countries like Nicaragua or Libya, it is perhaps not surprising that the allies differ in how they conceive their interests. But even on NATO's flanks and in the Persian Gulf, where the vital interests of our European allies in blocking a Soviet takeover are more direct and massive than ours, the problem has been worsening. In recent base negotiations, Spain and Portugal have shown little concern for their role in reinforcing Turkey or allied forces in the Gulf. And some NATO countries on the Northern Flank, with small military forces of their own, have opposed measures that would help timely reinforcement for themselves; they justify this opposition on the farfetched grounds that the Soviets need reassurance that they will not be the victims of an unprovoked attack. The increasing number of European advocates of "Non-Offensive Defense" would carry reassurance further by eschewing all "offensive" weapons. That would not prevent enemy attack, but it would prevent counterattacking.

While our timely access has deteriorated sharply since the 1950s, the Soviets have used their internal lines of communication to improve greatly their ability to bring conventional force to bear quickly at points on their periphery and have systematically improved their access to air space and bases near their periphery. As a result, in some vital theaters such as the Persian Gulf, their ability to bring force to bear has improved dramatically while ours has declined in absolute terms. In the next 20 years and in other theaters of conflict, increasingly well equipped smaller powers as well as new major military powers are likely to give us still stronger incentives to develop a more versatile and discriminate force.

We have developed a variety of precise weapons, both long and short range, and have taken important steps to improve the robustness and effectiveness of our command, control, communications and intelligence as well as the training of our forces. Cumulative advances in microelectronics have already had a revolutionary impact on the possibility of increasing the effectiveness of attacks on military targets while confining effects largely to these targets. The advances have enormously improved the possibilities of large scale battle management and the maintenance of political control. In the next decade or two, they will do so even more. Most importantly, these cumulative changes have made a single, or a few, nonnuclear weapons effective for many missions previously requiring thousands of nonnuclear weapons, or nuclear ones.

As stated elsewhere in this report, we would depend heavily on space systems for the control and direction of our conventional forces needed to defeat a Soviet invasion, and the Soviets would use their own satellites as an essential support for their invasion. Each side would have strong reasons to defend its own space system and to degrade the other side's.

The dynamism of our private sector gives us an inherent advantage in realizing the benefits offered by the new technologies. Nevertheless, we and our allies have often lagged in actually fielding the capabilities needed to meet the increasingly formidable dangers presented by the growing strength of the Soviets and other potential antagonists.

Wars on the Soviet Periphery and in the Third World

We and the Soviets will have very large incentives to exploit the greater effectiveness and discrimination of conventional weapons afforded by the new information technologies and to confine destruction so as to give the other side a stake in keeping destruction within bounds. If nuclear weapons were used, both sides would have even larger incentives to rely on technologies of control, since losing control then would be most disastrous. Both sides have devoted growing efforts to ensure the survivability of their command and control under wartime conditions.

The equipment, training, uses of intelligence, and methods of operation we have developed mainly for contingencies involving massive worldwide attacks by the Soviet Union do not prepare us very well for conflicts in the Third World. Such conflicts are likely

609

to feature terrorism, sabotage, and other "low intensity" violence. Assisting allies to respond to such violence will put a premium on the use of some of the same information technologies we find increasingly relevant for selective operations in higher intensity conflicts. The need to use force for political purposes and to discriminate between civilian and legitimate targets is even more evident here. In particular, we will need optical and electronic intelligence, communications and control, and precise delivery of weapons so as to minimize damage to noncombatants. We will need advanced technologies for training local forces. These will be important both for obtaining local political support and support in the United States and elsewhere in the West.

The Northern and Southern Flanks of NATO are more weakly defended than the Center. Both are of critical importance for the Center's defense, but both suffer from political problems which inhibit reinforcement in a timely manner. Defense of the Northern Flank depends critically on rapid reinforcement from the U.S. and the rest of NATO; yet increased restrictions on U.S. and NATO activities in Norway limit our ability to bring force to bear quickly in defense of the region. In the south, Turkey is of key importance both in the defense of U.S. and other naval forces in the Eastern Mediterranean and defense of our interests in the Persian Gulf. Turkey's critical importance should be recognized by increasing security assistance from the U.S. and from other members of NATO as well as countries such as Japan that have a vital interest in the areas Turkey would help to defend.

In the Persian Gulf itself, the great distances and political difficulties involved in obtaining timely access must be overcome to mount a credible defense of the region. Improvements in technology, and a greater allied willingness to share the political risks of getting such access, would greatly improve our ability to deter attacks.

Both South Korea and Japan will be increasingly able to defend themselves against a conventional invasion. The U.S. presence in both countries works to discourage possible dangers, such as Soviet (or Chinese) intervention or use of nuclear weapons, and should be continued, not least because it is also of great importance in increasing our capability to deal in a timely way with threats elsewhere in the Western Pacific.

It has long been the policy of the Atlantic Alliance that if non-nuclear force proves inadequate, we must be prepared to use nuclear force to stop a conventional invasion. But this force should be effective and discriminate—kept under control rather than a suicidal bluff. We need in any case the ability to deter plausible nuclear attacks on U.S. and allied forces. This should include a large role in defending common interests outside national boundaries and outside Alliance boundaries where, as in the Persian Gulf, allied critical interests clearly coincide with our own. A larger nuclear role in the defense of other European allies, which has been suggested for the British and French, will require, as in our own case, an effective and discriminate nuclear force capable of use to defeat a Soviet invasion into allied territory. The French and British now have options to move in that direction.

The Coherent Use of Resources for Security

We have lagged in fielding weapons systems needed to cope with the increasingly capable forces of the Soviet Union and lesser adversaries of the Third World. As the Packard Commission has stressed, this lag has to do with cumbersome and unstable acquisition and R&D funding procedures and the lack of adequate and early testing. To overcome this lag, we should turn to faster prototyping and testing of systems that would make our forces more versatile and discriminate.

Equally important, however, will be clearly defined "require-ments" that are related to a coherent national strategy. "Require-ments" guided by a long-term strategy are critical to getting the most out of a given budget.

The increasingly widespread latent dangers with which we and our allies must cope do not justify the belief that we can safely hold our defense budget level, much less reduce it. However, if tighter budgets impose an increase in risks, we should, for the near term, accept a greater risk of the unlikely extreme attacks, in order to bring about a reduced risk of the more probable conflicts, both now and in the future. Instead of giving priority to buying various types of large "platforms," we should seek continued improvement in the sensors and command, control and intelligence systems which can multiply the effectiveness of our ships and aircraft. And we must provide the resources needed to maintain the training, morale, and excellence in leadership of the men and women in the armed forces.

Arms Agreements and the Continuing Problem of Bringing Discriminate and Timely Force to Bear Against Aggression

Carefully designed and enforceable arms agreements can help reduce the risk of war by diminishing military threats for a range of plausible contingencies while preserving, or facilitating, our capability to keep the application of force discriminate and effective. Recent proposals by the Soviets and some in the West to stop the testing of missiles, nuclear warheads, anti-satellite systems and active defenses have been based on the premise that this would slow the qualitative arms race that is assumed to drive a quantitative arms race. However, such restraints frequently would have the opposite effect to that intended; they would make the job of getting a credible deterrent harder. As explained elsewhere in this report, a well-designed agreement on self-defense zones in space could make it easier to protect the space-borne sensors, and command, control and communications systems. An agreement that would drastically reduce the Soviet advantage in non-nuclear force has been proposed by leaders in both American Parties and by many prominent Europeans. Its purpose would be to make more equal the ability of NATO and the Warsaw Pact to bring timely, effective force to bear at critical danger points. It would thus address the basic East-West asymmetries due to geography and the greater Soviet conventional effort.

The strategy recommended in this report should guide arms negotiations as well as national and Alliance decisions on defense. Such a strategy of discriminate deterrence seems in any case more capable of building a community of interests with adversaries over the long run than reckless threats to annihilate their populations. Our arms control policy must be connected coherently to a viable, long-term Alliance strategy.

RPM, or Revolutions by the Minute (1992)

Albert Wohlstetter

A previously unpublished address to the American Enterprise Institute for Public Policy Research, Washington, DC, June 10, 1992, revised June 29, 1992, available from the Albert and Roberta Wohlstetter Papers, Speeches, Box 138, Folder 21. Courtesy of the Wohlstetter Estate.

"Revolutions per Minute," of course, exaggerates. After years of battering by headline and sound bite, it only *seems* we need tachometers to measure ongoing rates of revolutionary change. Nonetheless, the continuing technical changes, as well as their political, economic and military consequences, have already been genuinely revolutionary. Not media hype. They change things by many orders of magnitude.

One technical change didn't need hype—the one that gave the Cold War just ending its other name: The Atomic Age. Nuclear fission and fusion completed the possibilities of releasing energy from the atom. Together they multiplied the destructive energy that a single weapon can release one million-fold and the area it could obliterate indiscriminately about ten thousand-fold. Fission and fusion announced themselves suddenly and unmistakably: Hiroshima. Nagasaki. Bikini. Eniwetok. The wartime annihilation of a whole city or the sinking, in what was just a test, of an entire coral island was hard to miss. A glimpse of the apocalypse.

Yet the less sudden continuing changes that make up the Information Revolution dwarf in significance these two spectacular leaps in nuclear technology. They transform military security, politics within and among nations, the costs and efficiency of market transactions and economic growth. The technical changes are larger, and their effects more ramified, more closely interconnected and much more important than the changes worked by fission and fusion.

I

The advances in microelectronics and optics that *underlie* the Information Revolution have been happening quietly over a long period. They happen at an exponential rate small in any given year compared to the big leaps in nuclear energy. But they've been accumulating to much more.

The number of transistors on a chip has increased by a factor of 100 every ten years. In 1989, chips the size of a child's fingernail contained over a million transistors, performed many tens of millions of instructions per second, and had reduced costs per operation a million-fold in the preceding thirty years. Such superscalar chips are being used to design new chips and so accelerate this exponential rate of growth. In a decade, Intel expects a chip with a billion transistors. All this speeds the acquiring, processing and transmission of information.

One nice thing about the Information Revolution is that something *good* – the spread of knowledge, which has no limits – is increasing at an exponential rate. That contrasts with the typical doomsdays announced, one after another, by natural scientists, the Apocalypse Of The Month: Silent Spring, the Population Bomb, the Exhaustion of Fossil Fuels, the Coming Ice Age, Nuclear Winter, Global Warming, and others. Several doomsayers have gained celebrity by announcing in quick succession Nuclear Winter, the Coming Ice Age, and Global Warming – without embarrassment, without troubling their primetime hosts, and without damage to their celebrity status or their academic careers.

In such predictions of global disaster, only something *bad* increases exponentially. The good, countering factors run against a fixed limit – or increase only arithmetically – or at a lower exponential rate.

A characteristic problem for policy choice raised by current doomsday prophecies is that the predicted catastrophe may be distant in time but is always vague and highly uncertain. The actions urged are immediate, costly, risky – sometimes desperate.

The granddaddy of all apocalyptic prophecies, of course, was The Inevitability of Nuclear War. The argument ran that a global holocaust was inevitable unless politics within and among nations changed drastically and immediately: The arms race would multiply nuclear weapons exponentially, and the probability of war in any given year (unconsciously assumed to be fixed or rising) would cumulate steadily until the holocaust was nearly certain.

The argument had gaping logical holes. Yet it was made by some splendid physicists, Russian as well as Western. And by at least one great – or once great – mathematical logician, Bertrand Russell.

The fathers of the Nuclear Revolution wanted the awful prospect of a nuclear holocaust to shock political rulers, including Stalin, into an end to secrecy and sovereignty. The stark choice was *One World* – an open world – *Or None*. They believed that civilian applications of nuclear energy would make that world one of plenty; that they would revolutionize industry and transport and that world politics would be transformed. But the release of energy from the nucleus meant only a revolution in warfare, not a revolution in transport and industry. Nor in politics.

Exaggerating the civilian benefits made Stalin less willing to give up national civilian programs. Political openness is simply incompatible with a Communist dictatorship. The huge destructive potential of the atom only prompted an increase in secrecy – the building of some 200 secret Soviet cities.

II

For a democracy, the ability to destroy a huge area indiscriminately is usable only in desperate circumstances. And the more indiscriminate the destruction, the less likely it is to be used. This is especially so if one is responding to an attack not on oneself but on an ally, and destruction is likely to be reciprocal. Academic babble about suicide pacts couldn't change that. It *did* slow the application of information technology to increase precision and to reduce the yield and indiscriminateness of nuclear weapons. But in any case, the precision revolution had its most important application to *non*nuclear force. Desert Storm demonstrated this brilliantly, with missiles that destroyed the contents of a military structure while leaving its walls standing and nearby buildings untouched. And even more by the rapid destruction of artillery, tanks and other heavy combat equipment on the battlefield – until we stopped.

Desert Storm exploited only *some* of the advances in the precise application of nonnuclear military force that had been made since the late 1960s. Because we had been preoccupied mainly with monitoring agreements on strategic arms and with the contingencies of an all-out strategic nuclear attack on the continental United States and a potential massive conventional invasion through the center of Europe that we would feel compelled quickly to turn nuclear, we were less adequately prepared to use developments in information technology needed to forestall or defeat less massive incursions in less obviously central theaters of war. We had devoted much less thought and effort to buying systems for delivering—at any range—nonnuclear explosives against small fixed or moving military targets; and to acquiring information on the exact location and vulnerabilities of small military targets; and to communicating this information in the theater. We had, for example, spent tens of billions of dollars on reconnaissance satellites capable of intermittent observation and detection of the changes that take place slowly, over a period of years, in the throw weight of intercontinental missiles deep in the Soviet Union—but very little on small, inexpensive, unmanned airplanes that could provide continuous or frequent observation of SCUD missile launchers moving in a theater of operations such as the Persian Gulf.

Yet, research and development in the early 1970s could have made such weapons and reconnaissance systems widely available. We developed them, but frequently other countries acquired them. The Israelis and the Egyptians had more of these than we did. The Egyptians had *stealthy* unmanned vehicles.

It was not just a matter of having systems that could deliver nonnuclear weapons to a target. To benefit fully from miss distances of a few feet, targets need to be located even more accurately, and we have to know what small part of a target is critical for its function. Also, we have to know how direct immediate damage to the target is related to delayed and indirect system effects on other military targets and on the civilian systems we want to avoid harming. Politically useable force needs clear-cut military aims, and clearer political aims than those of the Gulf War Coalition. Above all, in a period of revolutionary change, we need to rethink not only the means but the ends of military force.

Still, we can get one relevant measure of the change over the last 50 years in our ability to use nonnuclear force precisely if we compare the F-117A Stealth bomber attacks in 1991 with the British Bombing Offensive against Germany in 1941. The British found they had missed their targets so completely that they would have to abandon precision attacks and resort to huge incendiary raids against entire cities. The F-117A attacked and hit targets in

Baghdad at night that were more heavily defended and at greater range than the targets in the 1941 Offensive. That comparison suggests that the cumulative information revolution has had a greater effect on our ability to destroy a military target that we aim at than the fission and fusion revolutions combined. It has shrunk the area of uncertainty as to where a bomb would hit by a factor of a hundred million. This is four orders of magnitude more effective than the ten thousand-fold increase in the area destroyed by nuclear brute force. Nuclear weapons, like the huge bomber raids that destroyed Dresden by blast and fire, make up for incompetence in aiming at a target like a missile factory or a military communications building by filling the huge area of aiming error with destruction. In the process, they are likely to destroy a great deal that is not aimed at.

For a democracy, however, the ability to apply military force selectively—and to hit only what one is aiming at and avoid hitting anything else—has an even larger political and strategic importance than an increase merely in destructive power. We can then preserve what we should want to preserve: Civilians that do us no harm, irreplaceable cultural monuments, and friendly forces. If not, another information development—instant satellite transmission to home TV screens showing the outcomes of attack—would make it essential in order to maintain allied and domestic support.

III

Not only arms, but arms control have been affected by the Information Revolution. In the aftermath of Desert Storm, for example, attempts to find and destroy Iraqi nuclear facilities have displayed the vacuity of relying exclusively on satellite photography to monitor agreements limiting weapons of mass destruction. It offers strong hints of how ground inspection, if it were supported by the wide dispersal of mobile shirt-pocket-size transmitters using communication satellites, might improve matters. Important given the imminent spread of such weapons and the means to deliver them. David Kay, leader of the UN team, was surrounded for four days by Republican Guards intent on keeping him from leaving Iraq with key documents on a nuclear facility. He simply faxed them to the U.S. by satellite. And he had only Radio Shack-level equipment.

In the future, small, mobile, more advanced computers and communications equipment spread widely in the population will play a key role in economic growth. They will also make it safer for potential whistle-blowers, not only official inspectors. And they will help frustrate the reversal of popular moves towards independence.

Western leaders have tried to keep the Soviet Union together, in part so as to have someone to sign arms agreements with. Since they failed, they've been trying to make Russia a close equivalent. But it was the *disintegration* of the Soviet Empire, including the Soviet Union — not arms control — that reduced the arms in the center of Europe and the danger of invasion which had preoccupied us.

Secretary Baker has said that for Russia to eliminate nuclear missiles — even those missiles aimed at us — would "undermine the whole concept of deterrence," which is mysterious. We don't say that Germany or Japan or Ukraine needs some missiles to deter us. Some former Soviet republics feel more nervous than Mr. Baker about Russian missiles as a menace to their independence. They were ready to transfer their nuclear weapons to Russia, but said they had no way of being sure that Russia was actually destroying them. Neither do we. And since the General Staff and the KGB are alive and well and in charge of these weapons, it's not clear that Yeltsin has.

We could have said to the non-Russian republics, whose claim on these weapons is as valid as Russia's, that they had a point. Since the actual destruction of weapons transferred will in any case take years (the General Staff is more eager to get the weapons on their territory than they are to destroy them), we should have encouraged arrangements for all the non-Russian nuclear republics to share in monitoring on the ground the dismantling and storage of weapons. Personal satellite communications in the hands of those interested in enforcing the agreement could then assure a timely warning never feasible up to now.

The example has general relevance for future arms control. With the end of the Cold War, the U.S. has reduced the hair-trigger alertness of its strategic forces. As former adversaries indicate their willingness to enter into more open, cooperative arms arrangements, we can exploit the new technologies to make sure their forces are in a much lower state of readiness, to get warning if they increase readiness, and to have available a range of offsetting readying moves of our own starting from any new level.

IV

These effects of the Information Revolution on arms and arms agreements reinforce and are reinforced by parallel changes in worldwide market transactions and growth, and in politics within and among nations. I've dealt with these last two subjects and their connection at some length in "The Fax Shall Make You Free," a talk that I gave in Prague two years ago.

Here I can only make a few summary statements.

The Information Revolution is the most powerful engine driving innovation and economic growth, creating world markets, and reducing the costs and uncertainties of innumerable widely separated, individual, voluntary transactions. These innovations have been decentralizing. They have dispersed rather than concentrated the ability to acquire, process and transmit information.

The new technology fits well the view of economics typified by Friedrich Hayek, which sees economic activities as adjusting themselves by responses to signals sent by market clearing prices — without the need or possibility of a central plan. By improving the operation of dispersed markets, the new technologies improve the operation of the system as a whole.

Moving from dictatorship and full socialism to democracy and free markets was bound to be painful. It's never happened. Disasters are likely. But moving towards one and not the other may be even harder. The irrationalities of socialist planning led to its breakdown even with the most ruthless compulsion to replace economic incentives. Getting it to work *without* compulsion would be less possible.

On the other hand, the tempting notion — suggested by the experience of Pinochet in Chile — that free markets might be introduced more easily by dictators than by a simultaneous move toward democracy is quite doubtful. And Pinochet didn't start from a full socialist economy.

The dictators want to catch up with the dynamic Western economies today. And to attract Western investment. They can't do that without dispersing to their subjects fax machines, modems, copiers, mobile telephones, and a good deal else. That will make it extremely difficult to prevent dissidents from talking to each other and to the outside world — very hard on any dictatorship.

China is trying to contain its market experiments in coastal enclaves. But these enclaves have been the greatest source of dissent. And, if the experiment is to succeed for China as a whole, decentralized communications — and their use by dissidents — will have to spread.

There is nothing, of course, inevitable about these developments. But it seems a good bet that, as Friedrich Hayek said, the intrinsic connection between free markets and political freedom will assert itself. And the new decentralizing technologies essential to the modern dynamic growth dictators want will help make it happen.

"May you live in a revolutionary time" is an old Chinese curse. So it may turn out for the old men of Tiananmen. But not for the dissidents.

Commentators stunned by the succession of revolutions in Eastern Europe, by the breakdown of the economies of the Communist countries, by the upsurge of nationalism in the Soviet Union, and by the outbreak of war in the Persian Gulf rather than in the center of Europe — where proper contingencies were supposed to happen — have tended to prefix all their comments on these matters by the phrase "Nobody could have predicted that...." That suggests that they have been no wronger than anybody else.

Not so. On each of these subjects, a minority of distinguished scholars persistently differed from the consensus. All such predictions are wagers. But their bets were based on a better informed and better reasoned analysis of the forces at work than the wagers of the majority.

The apocalyptic prophecies are wagers too. Poor bets so far, but there's no *guarantee* that we'll avoid all global catastrophes. The increase in world travel, for instance, raises the risks of a pandemic. Some deadly virus might mutate more rapidly than our ability to devise counter-therapies. The species that survives we may see as a lower order than mankind. This possibility is plausible enough for us to continue to devote resources to biogenetic research, to resist opposition to testing therapies on animals, and to reserve some skepticism about vague proposals about biodiversity that might cripple such research. Some species we may *want* to endanger.

There is a lovely, well-known passage in the *Pensées* of Blaise Pascal, the seventeenth century probability theorist and philosopher. It's about the condition of man — his evident fragility

620

and vulnerability by comparison to some other species — killed by a vapor, a drop of water. "Man," he wrote, "is only a reed. The weakest in nature." But, he added, "a thinking reed."

As we leave the apocalyptic age, a homely paraphrase might run: Man, like all other species in nature, faces daunting odds. But man is the species that can use information, reasoning, and insight to improve the odds.

VI. LIMITING AND MANAGING NEW RISKS

Commentary: *Strategy as a Profession in the Future Security Environment*

Andrew W. Marshall

Revised and updated version of Marshall's essay, "Strategy as a Profession for Future Generations," in Marshall, J. J. Martin and Henry S. Rowen, eds., *On Not Confusing Ourselves: Essays on National Security Strategy in Honor of Albert and Roberta Wohlstetter*, Boulder, CO: Westview Press, 1991, pp. 302-311.

The future is always full of uncertainties. A common error is to underestimate the scale and multiplicity of the uncertainties. This is a general failing that Nassim Taleb in his book, *The Black Swan*, explores in detail.[1] Here we are concerned with the national security area. In this case, as elsewhere, some aspects of the future are more predictable than others, and good assessments and strategies take whatever advantage they can of this. Demographic trends, relative rates of economic growth are some examples of relatively more predictable aspects of the future. Also cultural beliefs in different societies are more stable than other aspects of the future.

But big changes are also common, indeed major shocks can occur, and tend to be under-represented in forecasts of the future not only for the reasons that psychologists tell us about, but in the national security area because of the pressures of political correctness. Some topics, some future scenarios, may tend to be avoided, almost as taboo for a variety of reasons.

We need a strategy, or strategies, that both takes account of our best assessment of the competition we are involved in, now and in the future, and in some way takes account of the uncertainties of the future situation. As I will address below, Albert Wohlstetter was especially adept in his strategic thinking, particularly on this score. And Roberta Wohlstetter in her book on Pearl Harbor stresses the inevitable uncertainty of the future. We will never know, ahead of time, the future. I have found it useful to think in terms of the following model: there are the players, all with their individual goals, resources, distinctive culture, and strategies; and there is the context, which none of the players controls, for example, technology, climate, etc. There are long-term trends in many of these variables, and enduring asymmetries between the players. A good strategy would have to accommodate in some way all of this, reflect the trends that are changing the situation, as well as exploit some asymmetry that provides the basis for advantages he has in achieving his goals. Strategies can involve coalitions, and obviously they must address adversaries. And, in some way, they must aim to limit the risks that the uncertainties pose.

Richard Rumelt in his forthcoming book has an excellent characterization of strategies as solutions to solve complex problems. One of the virtues of Rumelt's discussion is that it provides real clarity about how the word *strategy* should be used. In practice, the word strategy tends to be used in too many ways. In particular I would note that in the national security area, which is the main focus here, there is a constant tendency to think of military strategy as related principally to the application of resources in a possible future war and the general guidance for more detailed planning for specific contingencies. The result is that there is relatively little discussion of strategies for the peacetime management of our military organizations and for the allocation of resources over time so as to develop more efficient, effective, competitive military forces with appropriate doctrines and concepts of operations. Most statements of national security strategy tend to be just long lists of desirable goals with little to say about how these goals might be achieved. Good examples of fully developed national security strategies are thus very few. There is, then, a special problem in the national security area.

Given the existence of nuclear weapons, the highest priority objective for the United States has been deterrence of large-scale war. In this we have been largely successful. Therefore, the strategic management problem in our national security establishment was for a long time the peacetime competition to preserve and indeed enhance in the future our ability to deter the Soviet Union from actions adverse to our interests. Now this definition of our priority objective may need serious amendment as we move into a different world. The discernible aspects of this world are: the rise of Asia and decline of Europe, a long, extended struggle with Islamic extremists, wider proliferation of weapons, including nuclear weapons, and continued rapid scientific and technological changes.

With new problems, new thinking will be required. It is not that the uncertainty is higher. There were lots of uncertainties in the late 1940s and the 1950s, indeed throughout the Cold War.

But there are new players, new options, and the natures of the competitions are different. We will need to be as serious about strategy as we were in the early stages of the Cold War. Finding the right people and organizing the right sorts of teams will be important.

It is clear that some people among us seem more readily able to address issues of strategy, in particular the strategic management of our national security efforts. They have a willingness and a self-confidence to address the larger issues than do others. They appear to bring a very different perspective to the discussion of what our strategy ought to be. How do they get this way? What sort of training is useful? This is what I want to address in the next two sections.

What Environments Produce Strategists?

This is a question that deserves extensive study. The best I can do is to draw upon my experience in and observations of the environment at the RAND Corporation in the 1950s and early 1960s and my later experience in government in the period 1972 to the present. One disadvantage of focusing on RAND as a producer of strategists is that it clearly biases the discussion toward an analysis of the development of people whose role has been "advising," in the sense that Herb Goldhamer used in his book, *The Adviser.*[2] There are other routes to becoming a strategist, including those who reach high positions in the military services or enter government service from other career lines such as the law or investment banking. But the case of RAND is perhaps of special interest because it did provide in the 1950s and early 1960s an environment that produced a number of people who are now acknowledged as major strategic thinkers.

The RAND Experience

There was something special about the RAND environment from the late 1940s through most of the 1960s. For one thing, especially in the late 1940s and the 1950s, there was a sense of being on the leading edge, of dealing with the centrally important problems. The invention of nuclear weapons and several other technology developments at the end of World War II produced a situation that was quite new, one in which the issue of what our strategy should be was extremely important. Another aspect of this situation, given the large increase in destructive power nuclear weapons introduced, was that there were no experts. Two small weapons had been used at the very end of World War II; what larger numbers of weapons and more powerful weapons might do to change the nature of war was unclear. Nobel prizewinners were no better than graduate students in thinking about the relevant issues, and at meetings and working groups at RAND in the early days there was no hierarchy. This was an ideal situation for younger people (the average age of the professional staff at RAND in 1950 was about twenty-eight), who were immediately treated as equals and valued for what they could contribute to the discussions. This is a rare situation, certainly not characteristic of academia or normal organizations, and it led to the rapid development of individuals who were willing to address the broadest issues of national security. There was also a sense of having a preferred position with respect to access to information on the new developments taking place in weaponry, in particular in the design of nuclear weapons, their delivery systems, and other relevant technology.

Two other things favored the development of strategic thinking and innovation at RAND, and the willingness of the people there to address the highest level national strategy issues. One was the freedom RAND had to select the problems and the issues on which it worked. This is very different from the environment in contract studies organizations, especially now. The other was the presence of several remarkable men who set the intellectual tone and style of much of the broader strategies analysis that began in the early 1950s. Two I would name are Charles Hitch and John Williams, the heads respectively of the Economics and the Mathematics Divisions. Apart from their own intellectual contributions, their cultivation of full-ranging discussion, their intellectual fairness, and their interest in the development of younger people and of new methods of analysis all favored the fullest examination of all issues of U.S. national security.

One of the interesting things that happened at RAND was the success of the economists in assuming a leading role in the direction of a number of important studies and, more generally, in shaping the way in which RAND addressed national security issues. Initially the economists were brought into what had been largely a technological organization to deal with what was called the military worth issue. It had become clear to the technical people that they needed some assistance in thinking about the objectives that military weapon systems were to achieve. There was also some interest in the economics of defense, especially as it dealt with issues of mobilization, and in the targeting of an opponent's industrial capacity and assessing damage to industrial societies from strategic bombing. The economists soon played a much larger and more central role in managing and directing a number of the successful studies. Why was this?

Herman Kahn and I used to discuss this puzzle. We had a number of hypotheses. For one thing the economics of the situation, broadly conceived, were important. What things cost, the level of resources that nations are able to devote to defense over an extended period — these all shape one's views as to the kinds of weapon systems and forces that are desirable and feasible. But another advantage the economists had was that they knew from their own experience that experts could be wrong. Indeed, they also knew that much discussion of economic problems is foolish and that many widely-held views, even among responsible people, are faulty. The experience of engineers and physicists is different. In those fields there are real experts who are much more likely to be right than are others. Economists, therefore, were more intellectually comfortable in the situation that existed with respect to nuclear warfare, in which there were no experts.

One of the people in the economics department who was the first to lead and manage a large RAND study was Albert Wohlstetter. Beginning in the early 1950s, he examined a set of issues connected with the basing of long-range bombers. I want to note what seems to me one of the major innovations or inventions Albert made in the conduct of that study. In previous large RAND studies, the practice had been to lay out a number of alternative systems or programs at the very beginning of the study. The study itself focused on evaluating which of the alternative systems was the most cost-effective.

Albert's approach was different. He started with a few alternatives to the existing plan or program, but as the study went on he evolved improved alternatives. He was also less rigid than had been reflected in the earlier practice in setting down the criteria, the objective functions, the measures of effectiveness at the beginning of the study, and then simply sticking with them. His evolutionary approach developed additional criteria and tests of performance as more understanding of the problems and the issues emerged. And a wider range of situations within which the alternative possible solutions could be tested grew as the study went on. This was, in my judgment, a crucial invention for doing these kinds of studies, because one would learn much more about the nature of the issues and the problems, how one ought to look at them, and what criteria were relevant as one went further along in the studies. Also, this way of conducting the analysis had the advantage of inventing additional and better alternative solutions to examine as one went along. Albert's study was in many ways emblematic of the kind of good strategic analysis I wrote about at the beginning of this essay: it accepted certain structural elements of the situations, and then sought measures to both limit and mitigate effects of the uncertainty about the future.[3]

Another aspect of the situation at RAND that was exceptionally favorable to strategic thinking and innovation during the early period was the practice of inviting first-rate people to come and spend the summer. This created an environment in which the important thing was to try to tap into the very best talent in the whole country. The objective was not to do the best that RAND could do with its existing staff, but in a sense to do an analysis that was the best that the country as a whole could accomplish. By its very nature, any organization is limited in the amount and variety of talent, backgrounds, and insights that it can include among its staff. This attitude of searching for the very best people and drawing on the best talent is a key to excellence in broad thinking about any problem or issue. Unfortunately, most organizations do not operate this way.

Another way in which Albert was especially good was in reaching outside Rand to get the best technical advice. In the mid-1950s the experts, at Rand and a DoD advisory group on physical vulnerability, believed that no structures could be built to withstand blast overpressures exceeding something like 25 psi. Albert recruited Paul Weidlinger, an innovative structural engineer, to design hardened structures for protecting aircraft and missiles to withstand overpressures far beyond this limit. Herman Kahn was also involved because of his knowledge of the physics of nuclear weapons effects. This led, after a long argument and tests, to a major shift in views of what was possible.

The RAND of the 1950s and early 1960s was a remarkable place, both for the talent it recruited and for its atmosphere and intellectual dynamic. It was also remarkable for its boldness in addressing broader questions of strategy. It is, therefore, not surprising that some interesting and influential people developed there.

The next experience that is perhaps relevant comes from my time in government. Beginning in the middle 1970s, I was involved in attempts to initiate strategic planning activities in the Department of Defense including some strategic planning experiments. In particular, James Roche, then a U.S. Navy Commander, and I wrote several papers during 1975-1976 to promote strategic thinking in the Defense Department. We also sponsored contractor research on some aspects of strategic planning. This experience led me to believe that, while systems analysis had been a liberating force during its early development, by the middle 1970s it had become a constraint on thinking strategically. People who were systems analysts found it difficult to address the sorts of questions that we felt needed to be considered in strategic planning. People with a business background or a combination of business school and military service seemed to be among the best at taking up and addressing the questions we wanted dealt with.

We saw it as a vaccination problem: some backgrounds promoted strategic thinking and others seemed to inoculate people against it. Why is that? To some extent, the systems analysts had by that time developed routine approaches to analysis and perhaps had ceased paying sufficient attention to the complex consequences of acquiring the systems they dealt with. James Schlesinger commented to me a number of years ago that systems analysis proceeds by trivializing the measurement of effectiveness while perfecting the analysis and estimate of costs. Programmatic actions, the acquisition of particular weapon systems, the adoption of a new concept of operations, and the setting of new objectives for military forces have complex consequences, including their effects upon the beliefs, actions, and resource allocation patterns of potential opponents. Most of these consequences are not usually considered in the standard kinds of analysis. One result is that the top leaders of the Department of Defense often get remarkably little assistance from their staffs when truly strategic decisions are addressed. This is because the focus of the work of the staffs, the criteria they use, and their measures of effectiveness are too narrow to account for the considerations that top-level decisionmakers in fact want to consider, are concerned with, and take into account as best they can.

Some decisions have larger and different consequences than others. For example, a decision to pursue or create a major strategic defense capability is different from a choice among several alternative programs for the next generation of fighter aircraft. The former involves going into a new business for the U.S. military (although it is a business we once were in), the latter the continuation of an existing business. Different issues are involved, different forms of analysis seem needed, but existing analysis methods tend to treat the two types of decisions the same way. Part of the problem may be that much if not all of the existing analysis methodology was developed to assist in procurement or operational planning decisions. Other methods of analysis are necessary when the questions are more like: What businesses should I be in? What are my competitive advantages? One advantage people from the business world or business schools may have is that they are used to addressing these kinds of questions, though often with analysis methods that are less systematic.

What Backgrounds and Experiences Are Conducive to Strategic Thinking?

There is no specific set of disciplines that must be mastered to be a strategist. People who think strategically come from a number of different backgrounds. Among those whom I have met, and feel that I know personally, the best academic backgrounds seem to be economics, business school, applied technology (especially for those who have been in the business world), and in some cases political science. But what seems to be central is a cast of mind that is questioning, eclectic, able to address the broadest kinds of issues and goals, and able to formulate appropriate ways of achieving these goals. A high tolerance for the uncertainty that necessarily accompanies any effort to think forward five, ten, or twenty years is required. For many people, some period of intense involvement in an important, large-scale project or enterprise has proved to be crucial.

World War II was such an experience for a number of people and, indeed, there may be a generational factor at work: living in interesting times may contribute to being a good strategist. People who were involved—even if only in staff positions or on the peripheries—in some major decisionmaking body connected with that war had a special quality about them. Experiences in

World War II clearly had a significant impact on a number of the people who were at RAND during the 1950s. Because they contained many people with World War II experience the Truman and Eisenhower administrations had a character to them that favored strategic thinking. This characteristic of administrations has gradually eroded since the late 1950s.

The changes that we now see in the security environment of the United States are forcing another major effort of rethinking our situation, our goals, and our strategies. It might, therefore, be a period in which a new generation of strategic thinkers will emerge as a result of the critical experiences they will go through in the next decade.

Turning to the question of what kind of academic study or professional training might be useful, I would start with economics and business school training, especially business schools that have strong programs in business policy and strategy. My recommendation about economics is, however, a guarded one. Since the 1940s and 1950s, economics training has become too mathematical, too focused on the acquisition of particular analytic tools that are not, in fact, of much use in the national security area. Something like the first courses in graduate school may be enough. They are important, however, because people who do not have a sense of macroeconomics and the fundamental tradeoffs that societies have to make, find it difficult to think clearly about the long-term implications of devoting large, possibly excessive, percentages of gross national product (GNP) to military uses.

In the early 1980s, when the first initiatives were taken within the Defense Department to encourage application of a set of ideas that later were labeled as competitive strategies, I had a discussion with the chief of one of the military services. His reaction to the idea of designing some military programs so as to impose increased costs upon the Soviets was negative, or at least cautious. He had two arguments against focusing on increasing Soviet costs or expenditures.

The first was that the Soviets would simply spend the extra money, there being no reasons for them not to do so; the second was that our own budgets fluctuate so much that it was unwise to stimulate a competition which we ourselves might not sustain. The second of these arguments has real merit to it. The first shows an unawareness of the long-term consequences for the Soviets of high levels of military expenditures or of possible tradeoffs between individual programs the Soviets might be compelled to make, since resources always are limited.

Another virtue of economics training, or for that matter business school training, is that a modest amount of mathematics is acquired, as is some sense of the importance of technology and an ability to interact more effectively with technologists and hard scientists. This was one of the advantages the economists had over the political scientists at RAND in the early 1950s: quantitative analysis was something the economists were used to, and their interest in or ability to discuss and understand what the technologists were up to was somewhat better than that of the political scientists.

Demography is another area that deserves much more attention than it has had in the past in the development of strategy. The relationship of demography to political and military behavior is likely to be an area of increased importance and attention. Demography is often brought into discussions of strategy and broad national policy, but only in the most obvious and limited ways. William McNeill a few years ago wrote a small volume addressing some of the broader relationships of demography to political behavior.[4] As in other of his works, he provides a number of hypotheses and sketches out areas that deserve considerably more attention.

Additional fields of interest are cultural anthropology, ethnology, and some areas of psychology. In some ways a new understanding of man is emerging, based on study of the evolution of man and human society and on new analyses of the biology of man, in particular the functioning of the brain. How men process information, make decisions, and behave are central issues on which much new knowledge exists and more will be available in the future.

But above all, if I had a suggestion to make, it would be that people study, in any case at least read, history of all kinds: military history, of course, but also economic and technological history. The history or analysis of past wars is a major antidote to the narrow focus of many existing methods of analysis of defense issues. Most discussion of strategy and defense programs is, if anything, too focused on technology and weaponry and not enough on the other factors that often dominate actual warfare. Also, if one considers the extended competition between states such as Rome and Carthage, the issue of why the Romans won in the end may shed interesting light on the key variables that need to be considered in our conceptions of strategy.

Another factor of great importance is to understand the differences in the ways in which other nations are likely to perceive situations and react to them. Specialized studies of the strategic cultures of Russia, China, India, Japan, Iran, and the European nations and many others are of great use. Some of this can be gained by reading the history of these nations, especially the development of their military and other national security organizations. Other aspects relate to the particular cultural characteristics of these societies.

The Future of Strategy

We are at a major turning point in history. Uncertainty about what the future competitive environment will be like is especially pronounced. There are at least three major issues that our defense or national security strategy must deal with. There is the problem of radical Islam, which both poses an immediate threat and has the potential to be a long-running problem. Any serious strategy dealing with this problem will have to have a substantial nonmilitary component. A second issue is the potential emergence of a strong hostile China. A major problem of strategy here is setting and articulating in some definitive way the goals for the U.S., or a picture of what, ideally, we would like to see Asia as a region look like in 20 or 30 years. The third major strategic issue, I believe, is the likely proliferation of WMD (particularly nuclear weapons) and long-range strike systems. We can of course try to prevent proliferation, but any realistic strategy must take account of the possibility that these efforts will fail and that the future world will have many more nuclear powers, some of whom would employ weapons in ways very different from how we have tended to focus on.

Of course, a defense or national security strategy for the long term must deal with all of these problems. It must attempt to shape the future security environment where possible, and develop hedges against the emergence of particular threats or problems. There is also pronounced uncertainty about the character of future warfare: new kinds of weapons systems are being developed, which in turn will require the development of new doctrines, new concepts of operations, and new kinds of military organizations to exploit fully the new technologies. What our strategy should be for the more complex competition that is emerging will require consideration of many aspects of the changing security environment and changing technology. We will need to know much more than we now do about the emerging regional powers, as well as about the likely major actors, their strategic orientation, their strengths, and their weaknesses.

It is hoped that new centers of strategic thought and innovation will arise and a new generation of strategists and military innovators will develop to deal with these problems.

ENDNOTES - Marshall

1. Nassim Nicholas Taleb, *The Black Swan: The Impact of the Highly Improbable*, New York: Random House, 2007.

2. Herbert Goldhamer, *The Advisers*, New York, NY: Elsevier, 1978.

3. "Theory and Opposed-Systems Design" (1968), Wohlstetter's essay on the theory and design of competitive systems in an earlier part of the present volume, reflects this approach.

4. William H. McNeill, *Population and Politics Since 1750*, Charlottesville, VA: University Press of Virginia, 1990.

End of the Cold War? End of History and All War?
Excerpt from an Outline for a Memoir (1989)

Albert Wohlstetter

Excerpted from Albert and Roberta Wohlstetter, *Proposal to the Ford Foundation*, June 30, 1989, revised July 10, 1989, pp. 15-17, private papers of Joan Wohlstetter. Courtesy of the Wohlstetter Estate.

The democracies appear to need imminent threats in order to induce them to prepare for latent long-term dangers. However, *Protecting U.S. Power to Strike Back in the 1950s and 1960s* (R-290), "The Delicate Balance [of Terror]," "The Objectives of U.S. Military Power" [RM-2373], "No Highway to High Purpose" and other [of my] writings on the second-strike theory of deterrence took pains to make clear that they were directed not at the immediate likelihood of a Soviet nuclear attack—due to Sputnik or a supposed "missile gap" or a "window of vulnerability" or the like. None of these writings held that the Soviets were straining at the leash to launch a nuclear attack and that an adequate second-strike capability was the only thing that held them back.

Even though R-290 had shown that Strategic Air Command (SAC) was very vulnerable in the mid-1950s, it said that its authors did not believe that an attack was imminent: that would depend on the Soviet alternatives to such an attack and the comparative risks. Unanticipated obstacles in the course of a Soviet conventional invasion in Eurasia, for example, might make the risks of a disastrous defeat so large that we would want the risks to the Soviets in a nuclear attack to be even larger.

In the mid 1950s, it was disturbing that the risks of such an attack to the Soviets were smaller than was generally understood. But rumors about SAC that appeared in the press at the time of the Gaither report were considerably less modulated. Even so matter-of-fact a reporter as Stewart Alsop said, "The American government has recently been presented with just about the grimmest warning in its history." And other reporters suggested that they were talking of a present danger of imminent attack.

"The Delicate Balance" and "No Highway to High Purpose," in contrast, talked about "a new image of ourselves in a world of *persistent* danger" and that the problem was more "like staying thin after 30." The serious danger, in any case, was never that of an unrestrained Soviet version of a massive SIOP [Single Integrated Operational Plan] — the RISOP [Red Integrated Strategic Offensive/Operational Plan] — which preoccupies military planners.

Today the danger of a sudden massive all-out nuclear attack by the Soviet Union, or of a global conventional war focused on a Soviet invasion of the center of Europe which would quickly become an all-out nuclear war — never very large — has been receding even further. Moreover, the ideals of liberal democracy and free markets nearly everywhere seem to be gaining at the expense of the Utopian dreams of communism.

Does this mean there are no latent long-term dangers demanding prudence? Georgy Arbatov has suggested that we are deprived now of any adversary and need to focus only on problems of the environment and of economic development. We would all welcome that. However, the political and economic futures of the heavily armed communist states and of the increasingly lethally armed Third World countries are, to say the least, rather cloudy.

Even if, implausibly, the Second and Third Worlds change rapidly to the market economies of the First World, nice though this would be, we are likely to discover once again that, contrary to Cobden and the Manchester School, trade and investment — good things though they are — are not all that pacifying. Trading partners have found a good many reasons to go to war.

We haven't seen the end of fanaticism, mortal national and racial rivalries, and expansionist ambitions. It is conceivable that all the variously sized lions and lambs will lie down together, that there will be the kind of universal moral revolution that many hoped for at the end of World War II when they thought it, in any case, the only alternative to nuclear destruction. But, as Jacob Viner wrote at the time, "It is a long, long time between moral revolutions." We should not count on it. . . .

638

The Fax Shall Make You Free (1990)

Albert Wohlstetter

A previously unpublished speech delivered to T*he Peaceful Road to Democracy*, a meeting of the leaders of the independent democratic movements from the republics of the Soviet Union and the countries of East/Central Europe, Prague, Czechoslovakia, July 1990.

"Ye shall know the truth and the truth shall make you free." Dissidents in communist empires have given this ancient promise a new secular meaning. "Living in truth," to use Vaclav Havel's phrase, has been hazardous in societies whose Ministries of Truth spread variations of Big Brother's slogans — Freedom is Slavery. War is Peace. Ignorance is Strength. But the dissidents have used the explosive growth in western information technology to end the isolation which had made resistance seem hopeless. Information technology has moved in a direction opposite to that feared by Orwell in his mercilessly honest dystopia, *1984*. It has surprised even the bureaucracies of the information giants like IBM and AT&T, with their past emphasis on massive impersonally shared mainframe computers and centralized, hierarchical communications networks.

Personal computers. Laptops. Modems. Fax machines. Copiers. Satellites. Flexible "packet" networks enabling individuals to skip the bottleneck of central control to talk with each other. These have dispersed rather than concentrated information. They've been decentralizing. In the West, they are now the most powerful engine driving innovation and economic growth, creating world markets and reducing the costs and uncertainties of innumerable widely separated voluntary transactions. In the East, the same technologies have helped dissidents escape Big Brother's clutches. Even the Anarchist Party in the Soviet Union uses word processors. The Center for Democracy in the U.S.S.R., as one of its early acts, sent laptops and modems to put dissidents in touch with each other and with the world outside. Its conveners have good reason to use this conference for distributing copiers and fax machines to the leaders of the movements towards independence and democracy.

It is the dissidents who have spread the unsparing truth at great peril. They've made increasingly visible the contrast between free, individual, political and economic choice and prosperity in the West, and the political and economic disasters of state ownership and central planning, and the resulting brittleness of communist power. Western media and Western leaders aren't nearly as clear as they might be that it's the dissidents who deserve our principal thanks. Not the communist leaders who tolerated the telling of the truth only when they could not suppress it, and when they glimpsed the catastrophe involved in continuing on the course they had been following.

European and American leaders have helped. But, to understate the matter, they've been rather less brave than the dissidents. Western pressure at Helsinki in 1975 was critical for opening channels of communication. Even more, the democracies, by spreading information through such agencies as Radio Free Europe (RFE), Radio Liberty and the BBC, have played an essential role in the process of opening the closed socialist societies and ending the isolation of their subjects. RFE has been a forum for dissidents talking to each other. Mr. Havel has said it was RFE that made Charter 77 and his own name known to Czechs and Slovaks. For the hard journey from communism to free individual political and economic choice, RFE and Radio Liberty should continue to provide a vital forum. To see how important this can be, one need only look at China today, whose dissidents have had to make themselves heard and known without nearly as much help from Western governments. "Tell the Truth" was their most elementary demand in Tiananmen Square. The Chinese old guard can't survive that truth. So far its spread has had to rely on satellite images sent by CNN and the ingenuity of students talking with each other through modems and fax machines in Cambridge, Palo Alto, Hong Kong, and Beijing. The truth that surfaced in Tiananmen Square hasn't—yet—had its ultimate effect in China. But it helped end the isolation and fortify hope in Central and Eastern Europe. Tiananmen Square was reflected a few months later in the satellite images of Czech students in Wenceslas Square who wore headbands with Chinese characters about their Goddess of Liberty.

Gorbachev deserves some credit. However, he is not the Man of the Decade; still less, as Robert McNamara suggests with characteristic excess, Man of the Half-Century. Solzhenitsyn, Sakharov, Bukovsky, Hayrikyan, Djilas, Walesa, Havel, Fang Li Zhi, and many others are much more plausible candidates for that title. Gorbachev sensed that the Soviet Empire was coming apart, and, more than his communist predecessors, he should get credit for letting some of his subjects tell the truth more freely. But the Western media and many Western leaders have gone overboard about him. They sometimes seem only a little less vaguely enthusiastic than the coed who greeted him at Stanford University, gushing "Gorby, Gorby, he's a real stud." Even the Iron Lady seems to have succumbed to the smile of the man Gromyko described as having Iron Teeth. Vaclav Havel notes that Mrs. Thatcher was "enchanted with the charm of Mr. Gorbachev" and that the entire civilized world is "fascinated by the fact that Mr. G. drinks whiskey and plays golf—thanks to which mankind is not utterly bereft of all hope of survival."

We can't thank Gorby for telling the truth unsparingly himself. He doesn't. On Lithuania, he squirts ink like a cuttlefish, leaving Congressmen, who asked recently whether he could throw a little light on the matter of Baltic independence, swimming in nearly total darkness. In September 1989, after more than five years of Glasnost, Gorbachev was still saying with a straight face that the U.S.S.R. had swallowed Lithuania in 1940 *legitimately*. (After the Red Army's tanks rolled in to help explain things, Stalin's experts on democratic voting counted 99.19% of voters as favoring a government that *asked* to be swallowed up.)

A reasonable man, Gorbachev has said that all he wants is to negotiate, not to coerce. (While Red Amy tanks and armored personnel carriers rumble through the streets of Vilnius in the middle of the night.) All he asks is that the Lithuanians—and the Estonians, and the Latvians, and the Azeris, and the Ukrainians, *et al.*—recognize the Rule of Law that binds *everyone* in the Soviet Union including himself. But he uses the word "law" like Humpty Dumpty in *Through the Looking Glass,* who took the view that when *he* used a word it meant exactly what he chose it to mean, no more, no less. "The question," Humpty Dumpty explained to Alice, "is, who is to be master, that's all." Gorbachev rushed through new laws defining rules for secession and vastly increasing emergency presidential power to replace governments opting for secession. After the Lithuanians had declared their independence. These laws set so many traps that they can make independence under Soviet law unreachable.

The United States, the Council of Europe, and many independent bodies have held that the Soviet occupation of the Baltic Republics in 1940 created no legal basis for Soviet rights against the countries invaded. Oddly enough, in December 1989, Gorbachev and his advisor, Alexander Yakovlev, in official statements, agreed. Three months after and three months before saying the opposite. Late news has him swinging again. Stay tuned.

Gorbachev's oscillations on Lithuania and other nationalities suggest that he is divided. He *may* mean it when he says, as he has several times, that he wants to see the Soviet Union make a transition to a loose federation like that of the British Commonwealth. The purpose of the Commonwealth has been "to give expression to a continuing sense of affinity and to foster cooperation with states presently or formerly owing allegiance to the British Crown." It has included several dozen sovereign nations, each with its own foreign and economic policies, some of which—like India and Pakistan—have gone to war with each other. It has been described as the least structured of any of the major international organizations. Its secretariat wasn't established until some thirty-five years after its inception.

It's conceivable that Gorbachev intends his federation, like the Commonwealth, merely to serve as a framework for a peaceful process of nearly total decolonization. However, he continues also to say the opposite—that he has no intention of allowing the republics to separate. He has stirred up old ethnic antagonisms between Georgian Christians and Muslim Meshketians, Armenians and Azeris, Uzbeks and Khirgizians, and he has tried to mobilize Great Russian minorities against majorities in Lithuania, Latvia and Estonia. Gorbachev's Ministry of Truth is working on the theory that Ignorance is Strength. Though voters in a democratic election endorsed Sajudis overwhelmingly and the party that supported Gorbachev got only four out of 141 seats in the Lithuanian Supreme Soviet, he has denounced the Sajudis as coup d'etatists, sneaks and adventurers. He's tried to divide and to continue to rule nationalities that want to be free. He has not had much success in mobilizing Great Russians. Present leaders of the Russian Federal Republic would like independence themselves and are much more friendly to the idea of independence for the other republics.

Captive nations in the Soviet empire are not likely to bet the farm on Gorbachev's desire for peaceful decolonization. Neither should Western governments. They should encourage him in that desire in the way the U.S. encouraged its closest ally, Great Britain. For peaceful movements towards independence in the Soviet Republics—more than anything else, including arms agreements—can redraw the political map of all Eurasia.

The moves towards democracy in the center of Europe reduced the threat to Western interests there. The moves in the Soviet Republics can reduce the threats to Western interests not only in the center of Europe but also in the Persian Gulf and Indian Ocean area.

Gorbachev's economic gyrations have been just as extreme. His party job, before he assumed the chairmanship over five years ago, gave him a glimpse of the grim economic disorder shrouded by the statistics of the central planners. But his actions since have swung from an attempt to strengthen and accelerate the central plan by moral exhortation—a kind of Stakhanovism without the compensations Stakhanov drew from vodka—to announcements of moves towards decentralized markets that show little understanding of what makes markets work. Each of his improvisations has aimed at incompatible ends: Market-clearing prices that change to balance supply and demand vs. prices fixed or regulated by planners: Securing the benefits of venture capital while maintaining the state's monopoly of most productive assets and of the right to employ the human capital needed to operate them. His defense of socialism doesn't differ much from that of his archrival, Ligachev, who recently called for "planned markets." Gorbachev's programs ignore the results of several decades of experiments with Reform or Market Socialism.

The idea of a Market Socialism, which Gorbachev clings to even while his advisors increasingly tell him to forget it, has inspired attempts to reform for over thirty years. On the results of these many experiments, Janos Kornai—a splendid economist who, as a young staff member at the Hungarian Academy of Sciences in the summer of 1956, made his first proposal for reforming Hungarian socialism—tells the unsparing truth. Under the Market Socialism which guided the reform process in Hungary and several other socialist countries, he says, the idea was that state-owned firms should remain in state ownership, but

> should be made to act *as if* they were part of a market
> . . . I wish to use strong words here, without any adorn-
> ment: the basic idea of market socialism simply fizzled
> out. Yugoslavia, Hungary, China, the Soviet Union, and
> Poland bear witness to its fiasco. The time has come to
> look this fact in the face and abandon the principle of
> market socialism. . . .

Moving from the disasters of state ownership and central planning to free markets and institutions of individual ownership that encourage risk taking and growth is a hard job. It will take decisive, mutually reinforcing actions on several closely connected matters: among other things on monetary and fiscal reform, making currencies convertible for foreign trade, freeing prices and wages while assuring a safety net—a floor to income but no ceiling. Above all, it will call for shifts from state-owned enterprises to private ownership and institutions which define property rights coupling rewards and responsibilities. That is much harder than confiscating property and moving from capitalism to bureaucratic central control. The joke that socialism is the hardest path from capitalism to capitalism is a bitter truth.

A reformed robber is not one species of robber. Reform Socialism, unluckily, *is* a form of socialism. A reformed robber, having given up a life of crime, isn't a robber at all. But Reform Socialism— "Market Socialism"—haplessly tries to save socialist state ownership rather than to face the need to abandon it. Kornai and many other economists who lived through these experiments have a lot to say, not only to Gorbachev, but to the many Western economists who have mismeasured and overestimated socialist performance and so have led to Western leaders being astonished by events. They could have something to say also about some dramatic economic policies in the West, which have been less ruinous than those in the East, only because the choices have been narrower and their defects have not been writ as large.

In the 1920s and 30s "Market Socialists," including the Polish Keynesian Oskar Lange and the President of the American Economic Association, Fred Taylor, debated the Austrian free market economists Hayek and Mises. The market socialists held that managers of state-owned enterprises and their superiors who managed whole industries, and *their* superiors, the bureaucrats in the Central Planning Bureaus, *could* act as if they were capitalists. They would choose prices, inputs and outputs so as to maximize expected profits without actually getting the rewards or suffering the risk of failure and personal losses that, for private entrepreneurs, vary greatly with skill and luck. They would receive only the theoretically chaste rewards of socialist bureaucrats. But such socialist imitation markets don't provide the essential motivation to managers or to labor to act efficiently and innovatively. They provide very large incentives for lying about the numbers—not least about the sensitive numbers relevant to the actual distribution

644

of rewards under socialism. And they don't provide the context for the natural selection — out of a multiplicity of chancy competing inventions and innovations — of those surviving inventions and innovations that drive economic evolution. Central planning in a complex economy requires an enormous amount of accurate information in the hands of the planners about the uncertain supply and demand at various prices of millions of dispersed individual commodities and services. Not even the most massive number-crunching supercomputers of the future can solve the problems of central planning. Hayek, Mises, and others understood its infeasibility. It's no wonder that Western measurements of Soviet economic performance have been so far off the mark. The numbers aren't there to be crunched. And the critical problem, neglected by Taylor and Lange, of command economies has to do with motivation, rewards, and personal responsibilities.

The critical deficiency of socialist state property, Janos Kornai observes, consists in "the impersonalization of ownership: state property belongs to everyone and to no one." Vaclav Havel says that in a command economy "the company allegedly belongs to everyone, but in reality it belongs to no one." This common sense observation goes back in time long before Hayek to Aristotle's critique of Plato's egalitarian Utopia where all property was to be owned in common. Aristotle noted as one of many drawbacks to common ownership that "the greater the number of owners, the less respect for the property. People are more careful of their own possessions." The Russian economist, Vassily Selyunin, observes that "because the state's property belongs to everyone and therefore to no one, it is considered perfectly normal to make off with the company dump truck to take the family to the countryside." Many other economists in the Soviet Union and Eastern Europe use other examples, but almost the same words. Oddly enough, Gorbachev has used *almost* the same words about state property belonging to no one but thinks that's just an *attitude* that needs changing, not the institution.

A remarkable number of able Western economists have agreed that the Hayek-Mises arguments had "no force," and that Lange had won the debate about a command economy's ability to work very well. And that the actual Socialist economies were catching up with the West and might even, as Khrushchev said, bury us. From 1963 to 1973 the Soviet Union and China were generally supposed to be growing much faster than the 22 advanced economies of the Organization for Economic Cooperation and

645

Development. China, during this period that included the chaos of the Cultural Revolution, was supposed to be growing at 10% a year. A World Bank study in 1979 estimated the annual rate of growth in Romania at nearly 10% for the 25 year period ending in 1975. The 1989 *Handbook of Economic Statistics,* published by the CIA, shows East Germany's per capita income as 87.5% of West Germany's in 1988. The estimate for 1985 in the 1990 *Statistical Abstract of the United States* shows it as slightly *more* than that of West Germany's. One wonders why traffic between the two Germany's has moved West rather than East. As recently as 1988, a Brookings study expressed the establishment view that "Soviet leaders have good reason to be proud of Soviet economic growth" and claimed that Soviet income distribution is "far more equal than...in the U.S." Why in the world do Soviet citizens or their leaders want any sort of economic restructuring?

As for the real ability of the Politburos to make command economies work or to meld dissident nationalities into one happy homogeneous Socialist Man, Western establishments – except for a few steady clear-eyed men – seem to have been looking the other way.

Realpolitikers in the West tend to have a very tenuous grasp on reality. Those that place their bets today on a Socialist dictator's ability to suppress the movements for democracy and independence aren't realists. Not really. They're quixotic. Cynical dreamers. Fifteen years ago, the State Department Counselor advised the Poles to give up their romantic notions about independence and face reality. Sooner or later, they were going to be part of the Soviet Union, and it was better not to wait before seeking a more "organic" relationship with it. That was shortly before Lech Walesa and Solidarity exploded on the scene.

Today it should be obvious. Realpolitikers selling friends or principles are not likely to get hard currency in exchange. Gorbachev is short on both political and economic hard cash. Advocates of large Western loans to save "perestroika" or Gorbachev would be well advised to face up to the reality that Gorbachev has given "perestroika" no coherent sense. Nor has *he* faced up to the reality that socialism can be abandoned but not reformed. Except of course in the sense of "the Reformed Robber."

The information revolution raises credibility problems also for western governments. It affects their attempts to shroud warnings to dictators in a decent ambiguity just as it offers instant, visible refutations of the dictators' descriptions of events. The images of Soviet leaders vowing that they would not use force in Lithuania and of NATO leaders pretending that they believed them and cautioning them to *continue* not to use force shared television screens with images of invaded hospitals in Vilnius with blood on the walls. Western political leaders and Western media talked as if the actual Soviet use of coercion and bloody use of force were only a possibility while it was actually happening. And they continue to talk as if the actual were only hypothetical long after the Soviet government has admitted that it had used force to suppress peaceful demonstrations — as it did in the case of their use of airborne troops and poison gas in Tbilisi, Georgia. When supposed political realists in the West talk of the actual past and present as if they were merely possible, they exorcise reality. They are not realists. They do not inspire confidence about their ability to discern the forces at work that will bound future options realistically. And they encourage Communist leaders not to take warnings seriously, to continue on precisely the course they have publicly urged Communist leaders not to follow.

A Socialist ruler wanting both dynamic economic growth and to hold colonies captive faces a dilemma today. The ongoing revolution in microelectronics and in optics has brought us high-speed, high density sensors, and data processing and communications, increased the number of features of a chip by a factor of 100 every ten years so that, in the 1989 state of the art, chips the size of a child's little fingernail contained over a million gates and performed many tens of millions of instructions per second, and have reduced the cost per operation a million-fold in the last thirty years. This revolution has had patent importance for world trade and economic growth. It also has had consequences for political change. And the two are not separable.

It's plain that Gorbachev's economic crisis worsens his nationalities problem, and vice versa. Aside from this obvious unfavorable interaction, the two problems are related, but not in the way visually assumed. Neither these colonies nor the huge size of the Soviet Union are needed to achieve a rapidly growing per capita GDP. Rapid growers like Taiwan, not to say Singapore and Hong Kong, are smaller than the nine million square mile extent of the Soviet Union, and have many fewer than 280 million people. The star economic performance of the small islands of Japan shows that the natural resources of various republics aren't essential either. The key to rapid economic growth has to do with human capital and the institutions of ownership that encourage people to take large personal risks for big prizes, to compete and to innovate in world markets. An attempt by Russia to hold on to a colony by force imposes an economic burden on both. It insures an instability that discourages foreign investment.

Perhaps most important, isolating and suppressing dissidents are incompatible with using the decentralizing information technologies which power domestic economic growth. And which prospective foreign investors now insist on if they are to do business in the Soviet Union. A vivid example of this key dilemma is the recent failure of Gorbachev to persuade American businessmen during his stop in San Francisco that the Soviet economy offers investment opportunities as good as those available elsewhere. John Sculley, Chairman of Apple Computers, Inc., told reporters,

> Without telephones and fax machines, we can't do business . . . Right now there are a lot safer investments that all of us could make. Many of the people who had been thinking last fall of investing in the Soviet Union are now looking to Hungary, Poland, and Czechoslovakia.

In short, if Communist leaders want domestic economic growth and expanded foreign investment, they will have to accept a vast expansion and spread to millions and even tens of millions of individuals of the decentralizing technologies that put dissidents in touch with each other and the outside world and make it impossible for Big Brother to keep them from learning and telling the truth. Gorbachev wants fax machines, personal computers, modems and the lot. Prospective foreign investors will insist upon it.

But the fax can make you free.

The Bitter End: The Case for Re-Intervention in Iraq (1991)

Albert Wohlstetter and Fred S. Hoffman

From *The New Republic*, Vol. 204, No. 17, April 29, 1991, pp. 20-24. Courtesy of the Wohlstetter Estate and Fred S. Hoffman.

The United States and other members of the coalition, having intervened so massively in Iraq, have an obvious moral obligation to see to it that ethnic and religious minorities and the Shiite majority there have some protection against the deadly revenge of the Baath government. State Department and White House spokesmen, in a hopeless attempt to cover the obvious, have been emitting a dense fog of statements justifying first the vacillation and then the reversal of policy on using force to prevent the Republican Guards from training their helicopter gunships, artillery, and other heavy equipment on innocent Iraqis.

They continue to blur easily documented truths: that the president and the U.N. announced aims beyond the retaking of Kuwait, that the U.N. specifically authorized the use of force to implement *all* of its resolutions on Iraq, and that near the very outset of the war, the president plainly said the fighting wouldn't end when we got Saddam out of Kuwait—it would go on until Iraq's cooperation on all of the resolutions was assured. Members of the administration seem unaware that the disastrous direction in policy since the rout of the Iraqi army greatly reduces any chance that we can bring about substantial improvements in the protection of our interests and those of our partners in the region.

A key illusion held by the administration is that the war now being waged in Iraq is an "internal affair" that does not affect our interests or the interests of stability in the region. Yet the chronic disorder and factions in the Near East and Persian Gulf have their roots precisely in the internal violence of regimes there: their use of terror to suppress advocates of conciliation and all reports of violations in the letter or spirit of agreements, the absence of any internal check on the ambition of leaders, and the widespread use of schoolchildren and women as targets and shields. It is naive to suppose that the many arms control arrangements, border adjustments, and sanctions we have in mind can be sustained and would operate effectively without substantial changes in many "internal affairs."

649

Last week's U.N. Resolution 687 on the cease-fire in the Gulf, to take one example, "decides" that "Iraq shall unconditionally undertake not to use, develop, construct or acquire ... all chemical and biological weapons and all stocks of agents; and all related subsystems and components and all research, development, support, and manufacturing facilities" useful for acquiring components and subsystems of such weapons. For this even to appear to be a serious undertaking would require a permanent and continuous intervention in the internal affairs of an Iraqi government far more extensive than a one-time U.N. supervision of an election arranged by a provisional government. Enforcing such an undertaking by a totalitarian dictatorship is essentially infeasible. Arms control in this area, if feasible, can only occur in a society in which the government can't stop individuals from telling the outside world what's happening.

U.N. Resolution 688, to take another example, condemns Iraq's handling of the rebels and was approved 10-3 by the Security Council including the U.S. representative. It should finally put to rest the U.S. claim that we can't stop the mass killings in Iraq because they are an "internal affair." U.N. 688, over Iraq's protest, states that the mass killings are not an internal matter: they threaten "international peace and security."

The president had remarkably thoughtful aides but deserves the principal credit for the skill with which Desert Storm was prepared and pursued. He deserves this not least for explicitly recognizing, in the course of the muddled debate that followed the invasion, what most of his critics never seemed to grasp: that we had more than one reason and more than one aim in responding forcefully, and that these reasons were mutually reinforcing. It seems incredible that he should now forget what he achieved in leading the U.N. Security Council to authorize the use of force—"all necessary means"—for aims beyond getting Iraq out of Kuwait; and that he should now let the dogma that encouraged Iraq's invasions of Iran and Kuwait—that we need an Iraqi dictator to balance Iran and Syria—cloud everything that he accomplished and wants to achieve.

The president himself intended Desert Storm to serve some longer-term and broader aims beyond the operation's immediate goal—embodied in U.N. Resolution 660—of getting Iraq out of Kuwait. Six days before the U.N.'s January 15 deadline for Saddam to accept all its resolutions, the president said, "I am more determined than ever that the United Nations' resolutions, including 678, be implemented fully." U.N. 678 authorized continuing force after Iraq left Kuwait, i.e., "to use all necessary means to uphold and implement Security Council resolution 660 (1990) and *all subsequent* relevant resolutions and to restore international peace and security in the area" (our italics).

Thirty-seven hours into Operation Desert Storm and the liberation of Kuwait, the president said the liberation of Kuwait "would not end the fighting." We would then seek compliance with all the U.N. resolutions. The fighting "isn't going to end short of the total fulfillment of our objectives." General Norman Schwarzkopf, in his now famous strategy briefing during the last hours of the operation, said:

> ... There's a lot more purpose of this war than just get the Iraqis out of Kuwait [sic]. The purpose of this war was to enforce the resolutions of the United Nations. There are some twelve different resolutions of the United Nations, not all of which have been accepted by Iraq to date. . . .

Moreover, at the outset of Desert Storm, the general reflected the president's view that we would make some sacrifice in overcoming Iraq's powerful military machine because we wanted to "minimize any harm done to innocent civilians." While the president was saying that at a news conference in Washington, the general was saying the same thing in his briefing in Riyadh: "We are doing absolutely everything we possibly can in this campaign to avoid injuring or hurting or destroying innocent people."

The president's decision was right, but also prudent. The myth that we must destroy a country in order to save it paralyzes policy. In Desert Storm, we concentrated, with imperfect but widespread success, on highly accurate, discriminating weapons against military targets, exploiting a cumulative revolution in information technology. Saddam's arsenal, in contrast, was primarily rooted in weapons of mass destruction. We wanted to destroy the Iraqi army as an organized force. Saddam wanted us to destroy Iraqi innocents. He used them as shields at strategic installations because he believed our destroying innocents would cost us essential domestic and coalition support. Killing Iraqi innocents doesn't bother him. He's been doing it himself for years. For us to kill them would blur a defining difference, which we should never lose sight of, between us and him, and his likes.

The revolution in technology made it feasible in Desert Storm to be discriminate. A strong focus on isolating and destroying Saddam's army in and near Kuwait fit well with reducing our killing of Iraqi civilians. With Desert Storm over, we can still discriminate. Using air power selectively now to stop the Republican Guards from killing Iraqi civilians fits very well with our longer-term aim for a stable balance of power in the region.

The president said he wanted to "leave it to the Iraqi military and the Iraqi people" to take care of Saddam. He failed to make the distinction between the Republican Guards (which acts as praetorian guard for Saddam and his Baath thugs) and the regular army (at which the Guard pointed its guns to enforce the army's role as cannon fodder). Yet it is the rebels in the regular army joining forces with the Iraqi resistance who might help bring about some necessary political change in Iraq.

Only a very murky, fantasy realpolitik suggests that the brutal Baath dictatorship, and only it or its murderous Republican Guards, can keep Iraq together as a peaceful "balance" to the power of fundamentalist Iran or Syria. No regional balance will be stable without the West's involvement. Any Baath regime would be not only a potential aggressor but also a continuing major opponent of any Western intervention on behalf of the weaker powers. The same vague delusionary realpolitik about a Baath Iraq seems to be the source of the embarrassing indecisiveness of the last two weeks. The president's instincts to stop the slaughter by Baath thugs would better serve his desire for a stable peace in the area.

In any case, we can't avoid intervening. The president already broadcast worldwide his invitation to the Iraqi dissidents: "[T]he Iraqi military and the Iraqi people [should] take matters into their own hands to force Saddam Hussein the dictator to step aside." We were intervening massively in Iraq's "internal affairs" when we destroyed much of an Iraqi army, whose main function since Iraq gained independence in 1932 has been the repression of Iraqi civilians. And we intervened massively in Iraq's internal affairs when we targeted so large a proportion of our air sorties against Iraqi industry.

The intent of coalition leaders was to avoid killing civilians, and, on the whole, they conducted the campaign with unprecedented care. Some normally quite accurate weapons inevitably went astray. Some targets were mislocated. The choice by the strategic intelligence and target selection bureaucracy of some industrial targets such as electric power, which affects sewage and water distribution for Iraqi civilians, was questionable. And the repeated strategic bombing of second-and third-order industrial targets in Iraqi cities, in contrast to the use of air power to isolate and destroy Iraqi ground divisions in the Kuwaiti theater of operations, disrupted essential human services as well as political control. If we want medical aid and food restored for civilians, and if we want those civilians to survive assaults and eventually achieve some measure of self-rule and freedom from a tyranny that has been lethal to the outside world as well as to Iraqis, they'll need some help. We'll have to force the Baath government to refrain from its normal practice of slaughtering civilians.

At the end of February, if we had continued the fighting to achieve all our objectives as the president had said we would on January 18, it would not have taken much force. Not with the Iraqi air defense network destroyed. It would have meant continuing for only a few days the rapid destruction of artillery, tanks, and warplanes, continuing a rout that many called an unfairly riskless and inhumane "turkey shoot." They called it that before they understood that these "turkeys" were deadly and intended to slaughter defenseless civilians. Those who now blame the United States for deaths of Republican Guards, civilians the Guards murder, and civilians we tried not to kill are themselves indiscriminate. If the coalition continues fighting, it could have clear-cut aims to complete the rapid rout of a defeated regular military force. Very different from guerrillas under dense jungle canopies. Or a Lebanese terrorist driving a truck loaded with explosives against a U.S. Embassy standing as a permanent target. The Vietnam and Lebanon "quagmires" that those who opposed Desert Storm conjured up near its start, to assure us, by analogy, that Desert Storm would take years and pile up tens of thousands of casualties, turned out to exist mainly in their heads. The analogies should look even more irrelevant after Desert Storm. Desert Storm went more rapidly than even the coalition expected, in part because they underestimated the latent resentment and rebelliousness of the ordinary Iraqi soldier and his readiness to surrender, defect, or turn on his Baath and Republican Guard tormentors.

In the administration's search for another military or Baath party dictator it continues to overestimate the amount of force required to even the odds for the resistance. Even now it will not take a great deal of force. Nothing like restarting a ground war. Nor anything like the full-scale air campaign. The coalition has

653

been flying combat air patrols unopposed over north and south Iraq. AWACS surveillance aircraft can detect and identify any Iraqi fighters or helicopter gunships in violation of the truce and can guide patrolling aircraft to intercept them. With tanker aircraft over Iraq to refuel tactical reconnaissance as well as combat planes, we can spot and use precision weapons to destroy on the ground Iraqi warplanes and artillery used in violation of the truce. We can airdrop communications equipment that enables the resistance to coordinate their actions and to stay in touch with the outside world. And we can surely deliver medical supplies, food, and other humanitarian aid directly to civilians in territory held by the resistance and to resistance fighters whom the Baath government is starving out.

The last is the most obviously urgent and also the most risky of the above measures. It involves exposing big, vulnerable air cargo planes and their crews flying low and slow over the delivery areas to the large numbers of shoulder-fired missiles and machine guns in the hands of infantry. Yet in a belated reversal of policy, the U.S. government announced that it will fly C-130 cargo planes from Turkish air bases to make air drops of humanitarian aid to the Kurdish resistance. We have warned the Iraqi government not to interfere, and the Pentagon has declared that we will fly combat air patrols with jet fighters as cover for the C-130s. There is a substantial chance that some of the very large number of Iraqi infantrymen who have hand-held and shoulder-fired weapons will use them to bring down a cargo plane and its crew. This amounts to a reversal by the president of his statement that he will not risk the precious life of even one American soldier in the current civil war.

But if we can undertake this risky mission to bring aid to those who have been subjected to mass killing and maiming, why can't we undertake less risky missions in order to reduce drastically the gunships, the artillery, and the like that are doing the maiming? The U.N. coalition has more than enough means to even or reverse the present odds. But serious signals of our intentions have to be clearly made through the clouded media of the press and TV. Signals of our intent have been far too mixed ever to make clear that we really did want Saddam to stop slaughtering Iraqi citizens and to let them pick their leaders. The signals have baffled the press. And maybe Saddam. Saddam simply ignored warnings not to use helicopter gunships. If Iraqi Kurds, Shiites, and ordinary soldiers misunderstood our intention when we said "the Iraqi military and the Iraqi people should take matters into their own hands," it would be absurd now to make the issue trivial, like deconstructivist literary *explication de texte*. We have an obligation to make such momentous signals clear.

If we are unwilling now to use a minimal amount of force out of the vast air power that still gives us air supremacy in Iraq, how likely are we to use force in the future when we will have neither the power in place, nor as heartrending a cause, nor as urgent an obligation, nor as unified a coalition and domestic support? In the days after victory, public support for continuing the fight to oust Saddam was high. As the genocide grew, Arab members of the coalition—for example, Kuwait and Egypt—were urging "all necessary means" to stop the annihilation by the Republican Guards. While we held back, France and Turkey took the lead in pressing for U.N. condemnation of the Iraqi government's war on the Iraqi people. And British Prime Minister John Major, urged by Mrs. Thatcher, preceded us in announcing plans to send humanitarian aid directly to the resistance. The U.S. government, which led the way into Desert Storm, cannot plausibly attribute its delayed response to its coalition partners.

On the whole, it might be better for government spokesmen to replace the embarrassing noise they have substituted for explanation with total silence. But better still, the administration should think through the implications of our current actions for the longer run in the Gulf and in the Near East. And cast a cold eye on the uncritical assumption underlying its indecision: the view of our diplomats, persisting since the fall of the Shah, that an Iraqi dictatorship would be a lesser evil and the only real alternative to fundamentalist fanatics or the "Lebanonization" of Iraq.

Lebanon is not a convincing analogy. Much of the factional strife there is the heritage of French attempts to preserve the dominance of the Maronites, as demographic trends increased the numbers of Muslims, especially poor Shiite Muslims, and as the Palestinians, excluded from political participation by almost all Arab states as well as by Israel, multiplied in camps like Shatila. What serious parallel is there in Lebanon to Iraq, where a few members of the Sunni Arab minority, making up perhaps one-fifth of the population, preside over a Shiite majority that is mainly in the south, where it competes very little with the Kurds in the northern province of Mosul who form a minority about as large as that of the Sunni Arabs? The Shiites in the south and the Kurds in the north oppose their Baath oppressors. The Kurdish opposition

655

has indicated that it is seeking greater cultural autonomy in a federal structure in Iraq. President Ozal of Turkey has accepted the idea of cultural autonomy in a federal Iraq and is increasing the cultural autonomy of Kurds in Turkey. The Shiite Arabs in the south during the Iraq-Iran war did not respond to Khomeini's appeal to join forces with the Iranian Shiites any more than Arabs in [Iran's] Khuzistan answered Saddam's call to join Shiite Arabs in southern Iraq.

Why is it against the interests of the West for Iraqis to vote on such a loose federal structure? What magic does our own Arabist establishment see in an Iraq unified and dominated by a dictatorship of a few members of the Sunni Arab minority? Yet in many background briefings anonymous officials have been telling reporters that "all-out military efforts to assist anti-Hussein forces may not serve our long-term interests." They may "make Iran dominant in the Gulf." We need the present dictatorship for the balance of power. Of course, Saddam himself is a bit hard to swallow. So the talk is of a Republican Guard general or a Baath Party without Saddam. It's doubtful that we know how to arrange that. Trying to do so would be not only meddling in the internal affairs of Iraq, but micromanaging the selection of personnel in the party or the army.

This bipartisan view of the importance of a Baath Iraq for regional stability has long held sway. In April 1980 Zbigniew Brzezinski, President Carter's national security adviser, on PBS's "MacNeil/Lehrer News Hour," responded to many broad Iraqi hints that they could take care of our Iranian problem, and sent two nominally separate but deliberately and ominously juxtaposed messages: "We see no fundamental incompatibility of interests between the U.S. and Iraq," and "I make two separate propositions: one that we do not wish to continue the anomalous state of U.S.-Iraqi relations, though . . . the road towards improvement is a long one. Secondly, the Iranians themselves ought to consider the potential consequences for Iran of Iran's continued isolation." Four months later, Baath Iraq invaded Iran. That did not bring about a stable balance of power.

When the Iraq-Iran war ended in 1988, many Western Arabists, including our own diplomats and some key figures in the Reagan and Bush State Departments, held that Baath Iraq, weakened by that war, had shifted permanently toward moderation, cooperation with neighbors like Kuwait, the building of its civilian economy, and avoidance of foreign adventures. It's no wonder they were surprised in August 1990. Their continuing preference in the current civil war for the Baath party over the present opposition may be preparing future shocks.

There is no reason to believe that preserving the Baath dictatorship or a military substitute is the only way or the best way or any way at all to keep Iraq whole. And there is plenty of reason to believe that if the Baath government does survive and is in charge of Iraq and its oil revenues, Baath Iraq will not remain weak. It will use its oil reserves to revive its strength and its menace to the neighborhood. Supporting a Baath tyranny strong enough to avoid "Lebanonization" but too weak to threaten the stability of the region would be like trying to walk a tightrope in a hurricane — in the wrong direction.

Even if we don't help the resistance, the Baath government might lose control in one place or another. Then the chance of dismemberment by the outside parties who have supported various opposition groups while we stood idly by is greater. But if we take a forthright stance against outside parties dismembering Iraq and in favor of letting the Iraqis vote on their own future, including their own future leaders, the threat of Lebanonization is likely to be quite small.

Neither the United States nor the U.N. has made a change of government in Iraq an explicit "formal war aim." Secretary Baker is right about that. However, both the United States and the U.N. have made formal demands on Iraq that cannot be fulfilled unless there is an Iraqi government whose agreement to comply is credible. If the formal demands are serious, they entail such a change. The president understands that. Time and again he's made clear that he can't conceive of negotiating in the future with the present Iraqi government. He's said that Saddam's "credibility is zero, zilch, zed."

"Leaving it to the Iraqis" does not mean staying neutral in the uneven military struggle between a Baath tyranny armed with jet fighters, helicopter gunships, tanks, and artillery and the spontaneous, poorly equipped, diverse but widespread opposition. Nor does it mean that the only alternative to staying neutral or siding with the Baath dictators is for us to pick the leaders who will rule Iraq—as the British, after World War I, picked Faisal, after his expulsion by the French from Syria, to rule in Iraq. It should mean letting Iraqi citizens have a chance to pick their leaders. No one should expect a Jeffersonian democracy to emerge full-blown from the present chaos, like Aphrodite from the sea. But even a government selected by a random process would be better than Baath rule.

Political elites in the West, especially those who opposed the U.N. coalition's use of force against Saddam, have talked much about the need for immediate elections in Kuwait. They seem more eager to intervene in the internal affairs of the least repressive country in the Gulf—the victim of a catastrophic invasion—than in Iraq, its perpetrator. It's more urgent to improve the political process in Iraq—to give Iraqi citizens access to information and some opportunity for making informed political choices. Is it likely that Arabs and Muslims, of all peoples in the world, are unable to judge their own self-interest and move toward self-rule? Turkey shows that, contrary to the received wisdom of many Western Arabists, Islam is not incompatible with democratic rule. The disaster visited on Iraqi subjects by the Baath dictatorship, and the avowal of democracy by the resistance groups, are the right occasion for testing the myth about the incapacity of "the Arab street" to make informed choices.

It was essential that the Desert Storm campaign have a clear-cut political and territorial objective that could be accomplished rapidly and decisively. Nonetheless, we have always had other goals, and if we are to bring about useful long-run change toward a moderately stable order in the Gulf and in the Near East, we have to be ready to use discriminate force, and to use some force now, in the service of other clear-cut limited aims. We can slow somewhat the pace with which we bring our airmen home without stopping it; or we could send in some replacements. In any case, no matter how fast our planned withdrawal, the onset of disease and famine produced by the devastation of Iraq's infrastructure and by the prolonged internal fighting is taking place before the eyes of our forces in the region. We and the coalition will still have a massive amount of force in the area, a selection of which can be used for clear, limited ends that are political as well as humanitarian.

What the U.N. coalition needs most is a little clarity about its essential aims beyond U.N. 660's demand on Iraq to get out of Kuwait. Many are embodied in the dozen or so U.N. Security Council resolutions that directed the coalition and empowered it. They include holding the present Iraqi government to account for the enormous harm it has done to other nations. The public accounting of the harm done can be as important as the compensation. And the latest U.N. resolution, U.N. 688, calls for a detailed report to the Council of the harm done by the Iraqi government to its own people. Just airing the atrocities against innocents, whom the Baath government has used both as targets and shields for its military power, will be clarifying generally in the Middle East, where, for example, a member of the coalition, Syria, and all factions of the PLO have used innocents as both targets and shields. That has been a chronic, continuing source of regional instability. But holding the present Baath dictatorship to account for the harm it has done against innocents is incompatible with trying to preserve it or standing by while it suppresses all opposition.

Paramount among the conditions for getting Iraq to fulfill the demands made in these resolutions is ensuring that individuals in Iraq can freely communicate with each other and with the outside world. Such freedom of information is essential not only for Iraqis to choose leaders whose promises will be credible, but also for the viability of any arms agreements to control manufacturing activities that can quickly be converted to the manufacture of weapons of mass destruction. It is an essential — and not yet adequately understood — prerequisite for the improved order the president seeks in the region.

If we are clear enough about our purposes, we can use military force discriminately in ways that will avoid both chaos and the restoration of Baath totalitarian control. The United States and other members of the U.N. coalition should announce their support for U.N.-supervised democratic elections in a unified Iraq after a period in which the U.N. member nations have made available to Iraqi citizens an accounting of the atrocities of the Baath regime. The allies should also clearly state that they oppose the Baath government's use of helicopter gunships, jet fighters, artillery, rockets, and tanks to suppress opposition, and regard the use of such force as a violation of the current truce; and that they will use air power selectively to compel the present government to live up to the conditions of the truce and to stop the slaughter of innocents.

Members of the coalition should use photo reconnaissance and surveillance by other sensors and other means to verify, document, and publicize any aspects of the war the Iraqi government is waging against its people, such as the reported use of chemicals. And the coalition should air-drop communications equipment to the Iraqi resistance to aid in this process and to help them coordinate their actions.

The allies should also consider inserting some special forces to aid in their use of air power by bringing equipment useful in identifying and locating Republican Guard units and their heavy equipment, and in calling in and directing any use by the coalition of precision weapons against such units, and to help organize and direct the resistance to the Baath government's reimposing its control. In any such use of special forces, Arab members of the coalition should play a most prominent role.

While the present battle goes on between the resistance forces and the Baath government, and as the United States brings soldiers home, the coalition should not hurry to withdraw all its forces from the substantial part of southern Iraq that it currently occupies, nor formally conclude the occupation. Air power based nearby and air patrols over Iraq—"Eyes in the Sky" and the air power to pursue infractions of U.N. demands selectively—are the last things we ought to take out.

It would be a terrible irony if our historic military success were to end in an equally historic political and human disaster.

What the West Must Do in Bosnia:
An Open Letter to President Clinton (1993)

Albert Wohlstetter and Margaret Thatcher

From *Wall Street Journal*, opinion section, September 2, 1993, p. A12.

In Bosnia, the situation goes from bad to worse. The people there are in despair about their future. They are victims of brutal aggression. But they are also the victims of the failure of the democracies to act.

Instead of opposing the acquisition of territory by force, the United Nations and the democracies have dispatched humanitarian assistance to Bosnia. But welcome as it is, this will not stop the massacres or halt the ethnic cleansing. Humanitarian aid will not protect the besieged children of Bosnia from being herded into Muslim ghettos or orphaned or maimed or slaughtered.

These could have been our children.

If we do not act, immediately and decisively, history will record that in the last decade of this century the democracies failed to heed its most unforgiving lesson: that unopposed aggression will be enlarged and repeated, that a failure of will by the democracies will strengthen and encourage those who gain territory and rule by force.

1. *Humanitarian Aid and Future Ethnic Cleansing.*

In Bosnia the democracies have used the need to deliver humanitarian aid both to excuse their own inaction and to keep the recognized multiethnic state of Bosnia outgunned and therefore itself unable to protect its civilian centers from slaughter by a dictator bent on making a Greater Serbia. Western governments now vying publicly to save several hundred maimed Bosnian children will not escape the responsibility they assumed for the slaughter of hundreds of thousands of other children and their parents, when they refused to let an independent Bosnia defend itself.

Recently, the U.N. and EC [European Community] mediators, with U.S. support, threatened to withdraw humanitarian aid in order to coerce the Bosnian government into accepting violent changes in its borders and a partition into ethnically pure states, with Bosnia a set of widely dispersed, unarmed Muslim ghettos.

But the U.N., the EC and the U.S. have continually condemned such changes and that partition as totally unacceptable. Such a partition, they've said, is unstable: It will mean still more killing, broken families, and the expulsion of millions at a time when Europe is closing its doors to refugees. If the fall of Sarajevo is a preface to a partition creating unarmed Muslim ghettos, it will be a preface also to further disasters, ethnic cleansing and instability — in Sarajevo itself and other Bosnian "safe havens" protected only by the U.N., in the rest of the Balkans, and beyond.

Bosnia, unlike Somalia, was no civil war. Like Kuwait, it was a case of clear-cut aggression against a member of the U.N. — a member whose independence the U.S., Europe and the international community have recognized for at least 16 months.

When the Baath dictatorship seized all of Kuwait in August 1990, it tried to erase Kuwaiti identity using rape, torture, the seizure of Kuwaiti passports and the forging of a new identity of Kuwait as a province of Iraq. A coalition of several NATO powers and some non-NATO countries joined the U.S. in demanding and then, in January 1991, compelling Iraq's withdrawal by using first air power throughout Iraq and then ground forces in Kuwait and southern Iraq. The coalition was exercising the right of individual and collective self-defense of each of its members and of Kuwait. It aimed at more than mitigating Kuwait's suffering. The U.N. endorsed the coalition's aim to get Iraq out of Kuwait, and the aims beyond Kuwait to reduce Iraq's power to terrorize its neighbors. But the U.N. exercised no authority over the coalition.

In the same way, the U.S. should now lead a coalition of Western governments that exercises the right of each to individual and collective self-defense. The U.N. Charter does not confer that right; it acknowledges it to be "inherent." Nor is that right conditioned on the secretary-general's approval.

The West's air-to-air fighters overflying Bosnia needed no further preparations to shoot down the command helicopters and helicopter gunships that the Serbs, in yet another blatant violation of their promises, used to drive the Bosnian army from their defenses of Sarajevo on Mounts Igman and Bjelasnica. The West could have done this without elaborate plans to coordinate air strikes against ground targets without endangering U.N. forces on the ground, and without the permission of the secretary-general, Europe's Council of Ministers, the 16 NATO ambassadors and a variety of U.N. commanders — procedures that appear designed to make the fall of Sarajevo a fait accompli. A disaster not only for the Bosnians, but for the relevance of the U.N., Europe, NATO—and the U.S.

Western governments should act now substantially to reduce Serbia's immediate and future power of aggression and ultimately to put the Bosnians in a position where they won't have to rely indefinitely on the protection of the international community.

With this limited political aim, Western air power would play a much larger role, and U.S. and other Western ground forces a much smaller and more transient role, than in U.N.-directed options that look toward an indefinite future of protecting on the ground helpless Muslim ghettos and besieged corridors of supply to them. The ghettos and the corridors to them would be subject to continuing artillery, armor and sniper attacks so long as the source of these attacks in Serbia is left intact.

Air power directed against the present and future potential sources of such attack can be used selectively and discriminately. The no-fly zone could be enforced and defenses suppressed over Serbia as well as Bosnia. And a very high percentage of the military aircraft on the large airfields in Serbia could be destroyed, with minimal danger to Serbian civilians or to UNPROFOR (U.N. Protective Force) troops.

The U.N. alternatives mean a future of ethnic cleansing and endless military protection by the international community.

2. *Bosnia Is Not History.*

What the West says and does now in Bosnia will affect the future in Bosnia itself; in the rest of the Balkans; and in other newly independent countries that, having gained their freedom when a communist dictatorship fell apart, now find that freedom threatened by former rulers who would, like Milosevic, use the pretext of protecting minorities to retake strategic facilities and territory that their pan-national military has never been reconciled to giving up.

Even now, after 16 months of a perverse Western policy piously condemning the pan-Serbian aggressors while doing nothing to stop the massacres, the West can use military force substantially and discriminately to reduce the power of the poorly motivated and ill-disciplined Serbian Army in Bosnia and its source of support in Serbia itself. And the West can help arm the larger, highly motivated Bosnian Army that still maintains a precarious control of the towns containing most of Bosnia's industry, including its weapons industry. In this way the West can improve the odds for the survival of a free multiethnic Bosnia.

On the other hand, if Western mediators and UNPROFOR confine unarmed Bosnian Muslims to small, purified remnants of Bosnia, the public will watch with horror as these ghettos disappear before its eyes on television while Serbs violate this ceasefire — as they have all the others for 23 months in Croatia and Bosnia. A spectacular display, at the same time, of the unshakably naive faith in Serbian promises that underlies Western cynicism. Realpolitik revealed as fantasy in real time.

Even if, like Kuwait in August 1990, all Bosnia (and not just Sarajevo) were seized, it would be essential for the democracies to make clear, as they did in the case of Kuwait, that violent border changes and ethnic cleansing will not stand, whether by Serbia in Croatia and Bosnia, or by Croatia in Bosnia.

If the West does not make that clear, it will have nothing persuasive to say to the Croats and the Serbs who have already renewed the conflict Serbia started two years ago when it used the Yugoslavian Army to seize territory in Croatia and then turned to invading Bosnia. Nor will the West be able to stop Serbian ethnic cleansing of Albanians in Kosovo and of Hungarians in Vojvodina. In Macedonia (unrecognized by either the U.S. or Europe because the Greeks object), where the U.S. and Sweden have deployed ground forces with no clear purpose, Western policy seems even murkier than for the other former Yugoslavian republics. There the West will have nothing coherent to say to resolve potential conflicts among Greeks, Serbs, Albanians, Bulgarians, Turks, and frustrated Macedonian nationalists who may topple the moderate Grigorov. Finally, the West will have nothing to say to discourage the now serious threat presented by pan-nationalists in the former Soviet Union and elsewhere.

3. *The Role of Force and of Empty Threats.*
    Empty threats have a perverse effect.
    Against a dictator who will yield only to superior force the West can threaten most ferociously in the hope that threats alone will be enough to stop aggression — that its threats and endless preparations will "send a message." But if the West doesn't use force at all or if it uses it symbolically rather than substantially to reduce Milosevic's power, or if it uses force to coerce Bosnian capitulation, "the message" received will only bring American and Western resolve into contempt.

Signatories:

Margaret Thatcher, Former Prime Minister of the U.K.
George Shultz, Former Secretary of State
Prince Sadruddin Aga Khan, Former U.N. High Commissioner
    for Refugees
Frank Carlucci, Former Secretary of Defense
Francois Heisbourg, Former Senior Adviser to President
    Mitterrand
Jeane J. Kirkpatrick, Former U.S. Ambassador to the U.N.
Zbigniew Brzezinski, Former National Security Adviser to the
    President
William Clark, Former National Security Adviser to the
    President
Paul H. Nitze, Former Chief Adviser on Arms Control
Max Kampelman, Former Head of the U.S. Negotiating Team on
    Nuclear and Space Talks with the Soviet Union
Walther Leisler Kiep, Chairman, Atlantik Bruecke (Bonn)
Natan Sharansky, Former Soviet prisoner of conscience
George Soros, Creator of the Open Society Fund, supporting
    opposition in Belgrade
Murat Karayallin, Mayor of Ankara
Elie Wiesel, Nobel Laureate
Czeslaw Milosz, Nobel Laureate
Joseph Brodsky, Nobel Laureate
Susan Sontag, Writer
Sir Karl Popper, Philosopher
Albert Wohlstetter, Winner, Presidential Medal of Freedom

Morton I. Abramowitz, Pres., Carnegie Endowment for
    International Peace
Fouad Ajami, Johns Hopkins University
Mark Almond, Fellow of Oriel College, Oxford University
Muhyi Al-Khateeb, Member of Iraqi National Congress
    (London)
Abdulrahman Al-Rashed, Editor in Chief, *Al Majalla* (London)
Ivo Banac, Professor of Modern History, Yale University
Daniel Bell, Professor Emeritus, Harvard University
Ishik K. Camoglu, Political Commentator, *Turkish Times*

Laith Kubba, Member, Iraqi Natl. Congress (London)

Beate Lindemann, Executive Vice Chairman, Atlantik-Bruecke (Bonn)

Gerhard Lowenthal, Journalist, ZDF-TV, Germany

J.J. Martin, Senior Counselor, Presidential Commission on Integrated Long-Term Strategy

Stjepan G. Mestrovic, Professor of Sociology, Texas A&M University

Joshua Muravchik, Resident Scholar, American Enterprise Institute

Uwe Nerlich, Director of Research, *Stiftung Wissenschaft und Politik* (Germany)

Emma Nicholson, M.P., Chairman of Iraqi Humanitarian Relief Committee

John O'Sullivan, Editor, *National Review*

Martin Peretz, Editor-in-Chief and Chairman, *The New Republic*

Richard N. Perle, Former Assistant Secretary of Defense for International Security Policy

Boris Petrovchich, Chairman, American Committee to Support Democratic Croatia

Norman Podhoretz, Editor, *Commentary*

Srdja Popovic, Founder of *Vrema*, opposition weekly in Belgrade

Reha Poroy, Vice Chairman, the Social and Political Studies Foundation, Ankara

Igor Primorac, Professor, Hebrew University, Jerusalem

Nasser Rabbat, Assistant Professor, M.I.T.

Paul A. Rahe, University of Tulsa Law School

Ghassan N. Rassan, Scientist, American Geophysical Union

Andras Riedlmayer, Harvard University

Peter W. Rodman, Senior Editor, *National Review*

Eugene V. Rostow, Former Director, U.S. Arms Control and Disarmament Agency

Nicholas Rostow, Former Special Assistant to the President for National Security Affairs

Henry S. Rowen, Former Assistant Secretary of Defense for International Security Affairs

Stefan Schwarz, Member, German Bundestag

Christian Schwarz-Schilling, Member, German Bundestag

Namik K. Senturk, Former Governor of Istanbul

Ismail Seysal, Former Ambassador of Turkey

Albert Shanker, President, American Federation of Teachers

Henry Siegman, Executive Director, American Jewish Congress

Robert H. Silk, Coalition for Intervention Against Genocide
Michael H. Spreng, Chief Editor, *Bild am Sonntag* (Hamburg)
Hans Sterken, Chairman of Foreign Affairs Committee, German
     Bundestag
Norman Stone, Professor of Modern History, Oxford University
Andrew Sullivan, Editor, *The New Republic*
Seyfi Tashan, Director of Foreign Policy Institute, Hacettepe
     University (Ankara)
Bassam Tibi, Professor of International Relations, University of
     Gottingen
Abdurrachman Wachid, Head of Nahdutal Ulama, Indonesia
Helga Walter, National Strategy Information Center
Max M. Warburg, Partner, M.M. Warburg & Co. (Hamburg)
Leon Wieseltier, Literary Editor, *The New Republic*
Roberta Wohlstetter, Winner, Presidential Medal of Freedom
Otto Wolff von Amerongen, Chairman, German East-West Trade
     Committee (Cologne)
Paul Wolfowitz, Former Undersecretary of Defense for Policy
Aydin Yalcin, Editor, *New Forum* (Ankara)
Memduh Yasa, Chairman, the Political and Social Studies
     Foundation (Istanbul)
Mesut Yilmaz, Leader, Motherland Party (Turkey)
Rex J. Zedalis, University of Tulsa Law School

Boris Yeltsin as Abraham Lincoln? (1995)

Albert Wohlstetter

A draft essay posthumously published in Stjepan G. Meštrović, ed., *The Conceit of Innocence: Losing the Conscience of the West in the War against Bosnia,* College Station, TX: Texas A&M University Press, 1997, pp. 200-207. Courtesy of the Wohlstetter Estate.

Andrei Kozyrev, Russia's foreign minister, has been defending the bombing of Chechen civilians to suppress the independence that the Chechens declared in 1991. He compares Yeltsin's war to Lincoln's Civil War against the secessionist South. And Michael McCurry, then about to debut as the new White House spokesman, offered some smooth support for Yeltsin's and Kozyrev's "new democracy . . . in the former Soviet Union," saying "in *our* long history as a democracy . . . we dealt with a secessionist movement in an armed conflict called the Civil War." He added later that while "we don't like innocent civilians losing their lives . . . Chechnya is by international recognition part of Russia."

So was Yeltsin's Russia by international recognition part of Gorbachev's Soviet Union in 1991, when Soviet soldiers killed innocent civilians in Vilnius seeking independence for Lithuania, shot at citizens in Baku to head off independence for Azerbaijan, and fired into a peaceful demonstration in Tbilisi to stop Georgian independence. Yeltsin in 1991 was president of the Russian republic and was *for Russia seceding.* He denounced the use of the Soviet army against Soviet citizens in the Baltics as a violation of the Soviet constitution—just as now civilian leaders of the movement toward democracy in Russia and some of Russia's highest-ranking generals are denouncing the repeated bombing of innocent Chechens as unconstitutional, barbarous and a political disaster.

In a January 1990 editorial, George Will observed that "[t]he contrast between Lithuania's arguments now and South Carolina's then [in 1860] is striking, beginning with the fact that Carolinians wanted secession to preserve slavery, whereas Lithuanians want secession to escape it." He wrote "The best the Soviet Union can hope for is the choice between imploding and exploding." If Gorbachev didn't choose, Will suggested, the Soviet Union "would suffer both fates—implosion and explosion—

669

simultaneously." The same might be said for Russia and Yeltsin today. Unfortunately, Western policies, by encouraging both internal repression and external expansion, make both fates more likely.

Secretary of State Warren Christopher's immediate reaction to the bombing and shelling of Chechen civilians was to express "sympathy" for Yeltsin—the bombardier. He had only "done what he had to do to prevent [Chechnya] from breaking away." He was as "restrained as [he] could be." *In 1995, as in 1991, West European and U.S. leaders are blindly resolved to preserve the integrity of states whose subjects have to be bombed into subjection.* Western leaders expressing pious concerns about the killing of Chechen innocents resisting Russian domination cannot escape all responsibility for it if they insist on Russia's unconditional right to keep the Chechens in subjection.

So, while Bill Clinton and Warren Christopher are saying it's an "internal affair" for Russia, Russian democrats and some top Russian generals are saying that, in the days of instant global television, no slaughter of innocent civilians is an internal affair.

The situation in Chechnya, a place that Boris Yeltsin vows to cleanse of "gangsters"—using the word broadly enough to apply to any Chechen who resists—is an affair that is neither local nor confined to Russia. Its ramifications extend far beyond Chechnya, to other Russian republics and to now-independent former Soviet republics (FSRs) where Yeltsin and Kozyrev have been using the latest incarnation of the KGB, as well as Russian troops acting as "peacekeepers," to stir up ethnic conflicts that drive civilians on all sides from their homes and leave Russian troops in place, frequently on former Soviet military bases. Yeltsin's assaults on Chechnya and the FSRs, moreover, are closely related to Milosevic's cleansing of non-Serbs from former Yugoslav republics and from Kosovo, an internal part of Serbia seized in 1913, to which two U.S. administrations have inconsistently issued a guarantee against Serbian attack.

Milosevic was the only European head of state who sent a letter of congratulations to the plotters of the August 1991 coup in the Soviet Union. Yeltsin, who was at the top of the plotters' hit list, denounced Milosevic's barbarism; in April 1992 Yeltsin joined the U.S. in voting for UN sanctions against Serbia for its seizure of land and "forcible expulsions" designed to "change the ethnic composition of the population" of Bosnia and its "continued expulsion of non-Serb civilians" from Croatia. There was no doubt about the source of the genocidal aggression. But the steady retreat of Western mediators from even a show of enforcing the sanctions against Serbia that prohibit Serbia's continued reinforcement and resupply of its proxies in Bosnia and Croatia, taught Yeltsin and Kozyrev they could answer Russian critics of their Western bias against asserting Russian interests in East Europe and the FSRs by adopting the critics' own program of Great Russian expansion — and still could be "Western." Until late in the assault on Chechnya, U.S. and other Western leaders have largely ignored fears of Russia expressed by the newly independent states and some Russian republics. And Western "mediation" has helped Milosevic create a Greater Serbia.

Russia soon became the most overt supplier of the tools of war that Serbia was sending to its proxies in Bosnia and Croatia. By the summer of 1994 Yeltsin and Kozyrev had announced that Russia had no international borders other than those of the former Soviet Union; and they have made clear that Russia's sphere of interest extends to its "near abroad" and beyond that—even to Bosnia and Croatia, which have never been in Moscow's sphere of interest. Milosevic's Greater Serbia had become the model for the Greater Russia of Yeltsin and Kozyrev.

In fact, the assault on Chechnya resembles in detail Milosevic's 1991 assault on Croatia: for example, his use of fifth columns and paramilitary and military forces from Serbia (initially in disguise and then used openly to "separate" the combatants); the bombing into rubble of hospitals and other buildings in Croatian towns like Vukovar; brazenly silly claims that it was the victims who were bombing and shelling their own women and children and their own slender means of defense; the offer of cease-fires as a means of disarming the victims; and, above all, the use of terror to drive out the population of strategic towns. All to be repeated in Bosnia.

For some time now, Russia, as a member of the Contact Group, has surpassed the Europeans in openly supporting a confederation of Serbia with its proxies. The confederation would make sure that a heavily-armed Serbia will continue after the Contact Group "peace" to send soldiers and war materials to complete the creation of a contiguous Greater Serbia at the expense of Bosnia and Croatia, which the Contact Group persists in trying to deprive of arms.

Western governments supported Gorbachev against Yeltsin in the years leading up to the August coup, just as they now back

Yeltsin against any alternative. But they are mistaken now, just as they were then, to support an individual rather than a path of evolution towards democracy, free markets and conformity to international norms banning the seizure of territory by force and genocidal attacks on civilians. Western policy makes it more likely that Russia will keep moving in the wrong direction.

The expansion of Russian control and influence in its near and not-so-near abroad has dire implications for the future of democracy and free markets in Russia, as well as in the FSRs, and for the future of Russia as a trustworthy "partner" for peace and for arms control agreements. In fact, the "new democracy . . . in the former Soviet Union" referred to by McCurry — unlike that of Lincoln — has yet to come into being. Russia has a long way to travel to reach a democratic government with the checks and balances of a parliament, presidency and judiciary under the rule of law. Yeltsin has himself said that "Russia comprehends democracy poorly.... In our history, it has been all or nothing. Either revolutionary anarchy or a ruthless regime."

It's most unlikely that Yeltsin's repeated bombardments interlaced with pledges to stop bombing civilians in Grozny and surrounding villages indicate that he is not in charge — that General Pavel Grachev, the defense minister, has repeatedly surprised Yeltsin by disobeying the orders to stop. Yeltsin can hardly have been repeatedly surprised in Chechnya, as some pundits suggest; the attacks appeared in Russian media as well as on CNN International. In Yeltsin's October 1993 confrontation with the parliament, it was Yeltsin who ordered Grachev to bring tanks into Moscow to use against parliament. And it was a reluctant Grachev whom Yeltsin describes as hostage to the "deeply democratic slogan" that "the army is outside politics."[1]

Yeltsin made his narrow escape in that confrontation with the Supreme Soviet by, he says, "formally ... violating the constitution, going the route of anti-democratic measures and dispersing the parliament, all for the sake of establishing democracy and the rule of law in the country, while the parliament was defending the constitution in order to overthrow the lawfully elected president." Yeltsin applies his doubts about parliaments much more widely than to the Supreme Soviet, the congress conceived by Gorbachev. He doesn't think much of the "bandits, fascists and criminals" who make up the Supreme Soviet. He says, with heavy sarcasm, that, bad as it is, it is no "freak in the wonderful family of parliaments of the world." His doubts extend to the U.S. Congress:

The word *congressman, deputy,* or *senator* in various languages is not surrounded by such a glowing halo. We have only to recall Mark Twain to realize that this elected body has long been associated in the minds of Western people with corruption, official sloth, and an inflated and empty self-importance . . . constantly beset with scandals and exposés.

But Yelstin is no humorist.

His low opinion of the present Russian parliament—on which the West relies for ratifying extensions of the Anti-Ballistic Missile (ABM) Treaty, the Strategic Arms Reduction Talks (START) Treaty, etc.—exceed his contempt for the parliament that ratified the original treaties. *Yeltsin says that the latter — Congress's dedicated arms controllers will be interested to learn—was only "feigning advocacy for disarmament [and] peace throughout the world. The present one is "not even pretending to pass itself off as peaceloving, as its predecessor in the era of Communist stagnation had done."* None of this qualifies Russia as a believable NATO "partner for peace." Nor as a trustworthy signatory of new treaties on strategic arms and strategic defense. Nor as a credibly impartial member of a group working out a "just and lasting peace" in the Balkans.

In the Balkans, the American, British, French, German and Russian leaders of the five-nation Contact Group have been trying to compel the acceptance of their continually changing "take it or leave it" "peace" plan. Jimmy Carter, after three and a half years of Serbian ethnic cleansing, has made a breakthrough, we are told, and the State Department has joined him in pressing Bosnians and Croats to accept. Meanwhile, the Krajina Serbs in Croatia continue to punctuate Carter's "cease-fire" with cross-border attacks violating Bosnian and Croatian sovereignty, and have just stated that their next step will be to unite with the Serbs in Bosnia and, as a step after that, with Serbia itself.

That just happens to be the Contact Group's deliberately obscure "peace plan." It would create a contiguous Greater Serbia. And that, as any fine-grained analysis of the thoroughly mixed demography shows, means "cleansing" the area of non-Serbs, severing Croatia, and breaking Bosnia into a half dozen islands under Serbian siege with no defendable connection with each other or with the outside world of trade and investment they need to survive. It would mean increased forced migrations and civil disorder in a Europe whose imperial past has left its populations irrevocably impure. The overreaching of Eurocrats, who confidently expected to "solve" the Balkan problem quickly, has already revived old antagonisms among the members of the new "united" Europe and has bitterly divided the Atlantic Alliance.

Ideas for a NATO expanded to the east by the inclusion of Russia as a "Partner for Peace" as well as the East European and former Soviet republics appear mutually incompatible rather than merely Utopian. It is a resurgent, expansive Russia from whom these FSRs and former members of the Warsaw Pact need protection.

The last five years of European and American policy for southeast and east central Europe and for the Former Soviet Republics have resulted in both implosion and explosion — neither peace nor containment. *It is time for a basic reassessment of policy for the world emerging from the fall of the Communist dictatorships.*

The new Congress is taking as part of its first order of business hearings for a "Peace Powers Act of 1995" to replace the War Powers Resolution. It will cast a critical eye on the wild growth of "peacekeeping" where there is no peace to keep. What most urgently needs consideration, based on Balkan recent history, is the assurance that no American forces will be used in peacekeeping operations inconsistent with the UN Charter and the Convention Against Genocide: that they will not be used to consolidate a country's hold on territory seized by violence; that they will not facilitate the cleansing from that territory of any ethnic group; and that American forces will be able to achieve a clearly defined political objective and to defend themselves without fear of veto by any country supporting the aggressor. Congress should also consider imposing constraints on the billions of dollars now used, directly or by way of international organizations such as the International Monetary Fund or the World Bank, to support "peacekeeping" operations by other countries which do not meet the above criteria.

In hearings on a "Bosnia and Herzegovina Self-Defense Act," Congress will review the increasingly zany political arguments advanced by the Mitterrand and Major governments for continuing an arms embargo that never validly applied to Bosnia since it violates the inherent rights of Bosnia, a recognized, independent member of the UN, to receive arms for its self-defense. The Clinton administration, at its outset, strongly opposed the embargo, but characteristically reversed itself under European pressure, just when European policies in the Balkans and the embargo itself had become admitted failures. The administration now is making an all-out effort to silence doubts and to muster the Pentagon and the intelligence community in support of the failed policy.

Besides rigorously examining the old bad arguments for starving the victims of means of self-defense, the new Congress should outflank the administration by going to the heart of the problem: the persistent failure of Europe and the UN bureaucracy, since May 1992, even to try enforcing the valid ban on Serbia's reinforcement and resupply of its proxies in Bosnia and Croatia. Russia has been in the lead of Britain and France in an effort to legalize Serbia's reinforcement and resupply of its proxies, even though that puts U.S. and other NATO airmen as well as UN peacekeepers at risk and would make even riskier a complex and dangerous operation of withdrawing them.

That operation in particular would bring out an essential connection between the changes these two pieces of legislation should make. For a dangerous operation engaging so many American foot soldiers and airmen, it would be essential for U.S. commanders to be in control of the campaign and to be able to decide (without UN second-guessing) on when, where and how to suppress enemy capabilities to disrupt the operation and inflict serious harm on our own and allied forces.

ENDNOTES - Wohlstetter - Boris Yeltsen as Abraham Lincoln?

1. As Yeltsin writes: "Grachev raised his hand and addressed me, slowly squeezing out the words: 'Boris Nikolayevich, are you giving me sanction to use tanks in Moscow?' I looked at him in silence. . . . 'I'll send you a written order'." See Boris Yeltsin, *The Struggle for Russia,* trans. Catherin A. Fitzpatrick, New York: Times Books, 1994, p. 278.

ABOUT THE EDITORS AND CONTRIBUTORS

Robert Zarate is a Research Fellow at the Nonproliferation Policy Education Center in Washington, DC. He previously worked as a policy analyst of controls on encryption and other dual-use goods at Steptoe & Johnson LLP. Mr. Zarate has published essays and articles on national security, technology, politics, law, and business in *The Weekly Standard*, *National Review Online*, *Wired News*, and other publications. Most recently, he contributed an essay, "The NPT, IAEA Safeguards and Peaceful Nuclear Energy: An 'Inalienable Right,' But Precisely to What?" to *Falling Behind: International Scrutiny of the Peaceful Atom* (2008), a volume edited by Henry Sokolski. Mr. Zarate earned his undergraduate and graduate degrees from the University of Chicago.

Henry Sokolski is the Executive Director of the Nonproliferation Policy Education Center (NPEC), a Washington-based nonprofit founded in 1994 to promote a better understanding of strategic weapons proliferation issues. He currently teaches courses on nuclear issues at the Institute of World Politics in Washington. He recently served on the Congressional Commission on the Prevention of Weapons of Mass Destruction Proliferation and Terrorism to which he was appointed in 2008. Prior to that, he served on the Commission to Assess the Organization of the Federal Government to Combat the Proliferation of Weapons of Mass Destruction, chaired by former Director of Central Intelligence John Deutch; and on the CIA's Senior Advisory Board. From 1989 to 1993, Mr. Sokolski worked in the Pentagon as Deputy for Nonproliferation Policy and received a medal for distinguished service. Earlier, he worked in the Department of Defense for the Director of Net Assessment on weapons proliferation issues, and in the U.S. Senate as an aide on nuclear energy matters and military affairs. Mr. Sokolski has authored and edited several volumes on military and foreign, affairs including *Best of Intentions: America's Campaign Against Strategic Weapons Proliferation* (2001). He attended the University of Southern California and Pomona College, and received his graduate education at the University of Chicago.

Alain C. Enthoven is the Marriner S. Eccles Professor of Public and Private Management, Emeritus, at Stanford University, and a core faculty member at Stanford's Center for Health Policy and Center for Primary Care and Outcomes Research (CHP/ PCOR). During the Kennedy and Johnson administrations, Dr. Enthoven served as Deputy Assistant Secretary of Defense for Systems Analysis from 1961 to 1965, and as Assistant Secretary of Defense for Systems Analysis from 1965 to 1969. He received the President's Award for Distinguished Federal Civilian Service from President John F. Kennedy in 1963. Dr. Enthoven describes his work and methodological approach within the Pentagon's Office of Systems Analysis in *How Much is Enough? Shaping the Defense Program, 1961-1969*, a book which he co-authored with K. Wayne Smith in 1971, and a new edition of which was published by the RAND Corporation in 2005. Dr. Enthoven was a RAND Corporation economist between 1956 and 1960. He received his B.A. from Stanford University in 1952, an M.Phil. from the Oxford University in 1954, and a Ph.D. from MIT in 1956. He is a member of the Institute of Medicine, a fellow of the American Academy of Arts and Sciences, and a former Rhodes Scholar.

Stephen J. Lukasik is a Distinguished Senior Research Fellow at the Center for International Strategy, Technology, and Policy, at Georgia Institute of Technology. Dr. Lukasik, as a member of the Department of Defense's Advanced Research Projects Agency (ARPA, now DARPA) in the early 1960s, was responsible for research in support of nuclear test ban negotiations. From 1967 to 1974, he served as the Deputy Director, and later as the Director, of ARPA, and was awarded the Defense Department's Distinguished Service Medal in 1973. He also served as Chief Scientist of the Federal Communications Commission from 1979 to 1982. Dr. Lukasik subsequently served as a consultant with SAIC for about 14 years, a Visiting Fellow at Stanford University's Center for International Security and Cooperation (CISAC) and a Visiting Professor of International Affairs at the Sam Nunn School of International Affairs at Georgia Tech. He received a B.S. in physics from Rensselaer Polytechnic Institute and the Ph.D. in physics from the Massachusetts Institute of Technology.

Andrew W. Marshall is the founder of the Office of Net Assessment in the Office of the Secretary of Defense, and has served as its director since 1973. He worked as an economist at the RAND Corporation from the late 1940s until the early 1970s. Mr. Marshall earned his graduate degree in economics from the University of Chicago.

Richard Perle is Resident Fellow at the American Enterprise Institute for Public Policy Research in Washington, DC. Previously he served as Chairman of the Defense Policy Board from 2001 to 2003; as Assistant Secretary of Defense for International Security Policy from 1981 to 1987; and as a member of the U.S. Senate staff, working for Senator Henry "Scoop" Jackson (D-WA) from 1969 to 1980. Mr. Perle writes frequently for the op-ed pages of *The New York Times, Washington Post, Wall Street Journal, The Daily Telegraph* (London), *Jerusalem Post*, and other publications. He is the co-author of *An End to Evil* (2003), and author of *Hard Line* (1992), a political novel. Mr. Perle earned his B.A. in International Politics from University of Southern California in 1964, and his M.A in Politics from Princeton University in 1967.

Henry S. Rowen is a senior fellow at the Hoover Institution, a professor of public policy and management emeritus at Stanford University's Graduate School of Business, and a member of Stanford University's Asia/Pacific Research Center. He was Assistant Secretary of Defense for International Security Affairs in the U.S. Department of Defense from 1989 to 1991, and earlier from 1961 to 1965. He was also Chairman of the National Intelligence Council from 1981 to 1983. He served as president of the RAND Corporation from 1967 to 1972, and was assistant director, U.S. Bureau of the Budget, from 1965 to 1966. Mr. Rowen served on the Secretary of Defense's Policy Advisory Board from 2001 to 2004. From 2004 to 2005, he served on the Presidential Commission on the Intelligence of the United States Regarding Weapons of Mass Destruction. He earned a Bachelor's degree in industrial management from the Massachusetts Institute of Technology in 1949, and a Master's in economics from Oxford University in 1955.

www.ingramcontent.com/pod-product-compliance
Lightning Source LLC
Chambersburg PA
CBHW050835300326
41935CB00043B/1749